Ultimate ChatGPT Handbook for Enterprises

Transform the Enterprise Landscape by Leveraging AI Capabilities, Prompt Engineering, GPT Solution-Cycles with Python and Java

Dr. Harald Gunia
Massimiliano Zattera
Karolina Galinska

www.orangeava.com

First published: November 2023

Published by: Orange Education Pvt Ltd, AVA™

Address: 9, Daryaganj, Delhi, 110002

ISBN: 978-81-19416-40-0

www.orangeava.com

About the Authors

Dr. Harald Gunia is an Associate Partner for Applied Artificial Intelligence at Infosys Consulting, has a rich background with over 25 years of consulting experience in applied AI and a decade in Enterprise Architecture and ERP transformations. Between 2021 and 2023, he successfully delivered multiple live GPT projects across various industries, showcasing his adeptness in leveraging Generative AI technologies for business transformations. Dr. Gunia is well-versed in a range of technical areas including Machine Learning, Conversational AI, and Natural Language Processing, grounded in his educational foundation with a PhD in Artificial Intelligence (1994) and an MSc in Computer Science (1989). His expertise extends to Computational Logic, Knowledge Graphs, and Responsible AI, positioning him as a guiding force for enterprises navigating the complex landscape of modern AI technologies. Dr. Gunia is a beacon in the AI community, fostering innovation and steering organizations towards a successful digital future.

Massimiliano Zattera brings a rich background in software engineering to his current role as an AI architect at Infosys Consulting. Leveraging his 20 years of experience in developing software solutions, ranging from standalone applications to enterprise-grade backend solutions. He now leads teams in pioneering AI projects with a focus on conversational and generative AI. Massimiliano is also the creator of the open-source `predictive-powers` Java library, a tool designed to empower Java developers to integrate generative AI functionalities into their applications.

Karolina Galińska is an experienced NLP Engineer and AI Consultant, currently working at Infosys Consulting. She has a solid background in robotics and a strong education in neural network architectures. Throughout her career she has been involved in a variety of projects centered around generative AI, NLP, and conversational assistants, showcasing her wide-ranging skills and knowledge. Karolina's enthusiasm for cognitive science serves as a major driving force in her work, leading her to constantly seek advancements in the field.

About the Technical Reviewers

Marcin Solarski has 25 years of experience in designing and engineering data-intense enterprise applications, deployed both on-premises and in the cloud. Applying AI/ML in these applications has been close to his heart since he learned the foundations of neural networks back at university. Marcin has worked across various industries, including computer and software vendors, telecommunications, finance, retail, and oil and gas. He has had the pleasure of leading research and development, technical consultancy, and support teams. Among others, he has worked for Deutsche Telekom, IBM, and Dover Corporation.

At the moment, Marcin works as a Senior Principal in the AI and Automation practice of Infosys Consulting, Europe, where he assists global accounts in achieving business value by leveraging reliable and scalable data engineering approaches as well as adopting AI and GenAI technologies in the business. He is passionate about leading data-driven transformations and building and nurturing teams of experts to support such transformations.

Eric Noack has over twenty years of experience in driving cost-effective business solutions, primarily in data and analytics. He has led large and small teams in designing and implementing a wide range of custom and packaged software solutions across a range of industries, including energy and utilities, food and beverage/consumer goods, technical services, and government/public sector. His first venture into IT consulting was co-founding an office systems value-added reseller after which he transitioned into leading software strategy and implementation projects and business process assessments at several global and boutique consulting firms. Much of that work has been strongly focused on advanced data visualizations, enterprise data warehousing, master data management, and other data and analytics focus areas.

Currently, Eric continues to pursue his passion for leading high-impact data and analytics implementations and supporting his clients looking to leverage artificial intelligence for greater business effectiveness.

Acknowledgements

Writing "ChatGPT for the Enterprise" has been an enlightening journey, and I owe a debt of gratitude to many individuals whose support and insights were instrumental in bringing this book to fruition.

First and foremost, my deepest appreciation goes to my wife, Barbara. Your unwavering patience and understanding allowed me to dedicate countless hours to this project, even when it meant spending less time together. Your love and support have been my constant, and I am forever grateful.

To my daughter, Alexandra, your creativity, insights, and experiences as a product manager have been an immense source of inspiration, notably influencing the narrative of Chapter 3, The Impact of ChatGPT on the Enterprise. Your strong encouragement has been a gentle yet guiding force throughout this journey.

Liebe Mutter, ich danke Dir von ganzem Herzen für Deine lebenslange Unterstützung und den Ehrgeiz, den Du in mir geweckt hast. Deine Lehren und Ermutigungen waren entscheidend für meinen Werdegang und haben maßgeblich zum Erfolg dieses Buches beigetragen.

Martin Weiss, my supportive boss, and a steadfast promoter of Generative AI, I extend my heartfelt gratitude to you. Your foresight and advocacy for the technology have played a pivotal role in this journey. You enabled me to delve deeply into the writing process, crafting a work of substance.

A special acknowledgement to my Infosys colleagues Marcin Solarski, Eric Noack, Marek Labuzek, and Spiros Nikolaidis. Your technical prowess and rigorous reviews have significantly elevated the quality and depth of this book. Collaborating with you has been an enriching experience, and I am thankful for your invaluable contributions.

I am also deeply thankful to a host of Infosys colleagues. Through numerous interactions, your specific and inspirational inputs have significantly influenced my thought process. The richness of our discussions and the diversity of your insights have contributed immensely to the depth and breadth of this book.

I would also like to extend my sincere gratitude to the publisher for their professional support. Your commitment to excellence and your guidance have been pivotal in making this book a reality.

Last but certainly not least, a heartfelt thanks to ChatGPT. Your assistance in ideation and writing has been fundamental. The clarity, succinct summarization, and apt analogies you provided have greatly enriched the content and helped convey complex concepts in an accessible manner.

Dr. Harald Gunia

Preface

Welcome to 'Ultimate ChatGPT Handbook for Enterprises' a guide for business professionals, IT specialists, and AI enthusiasts aiming to understand the new Generative AI capabilities and use them successfully to drive AI engagements in their companies. With over 100 million active ChatGPT users and a global enterprise workforce of 3.32 billion employees, the potential for applying Generative AI in professional settings is substantial. The intuitive nature of prompting with ChatGPT lowers the entry barriers, making it accessible to a wide range of professionals.

The first chapter provides a solid foundation by tracing the evolution of GPT models and exploring the strides towards Artificial General Intelligence (AGI) and Generative AI made by GPT-4 and its plugin ecosystem. The narrative then introduces the CapabilityGPT framework, a practical methodology for leveraging the expansive capabilities of ChatGPT in enterprise settings.

We then delve into the collaborative dynamics between humans and AI across various enterprise roles and explore architectural patterns to guide the adoption of Generative AI in the enterprise IT landscape. Detailed discussions around advanced GPT prompt engineering techniques and prompt-based intelligent assistants offer an accelerated pathway to creating robust AI solutions.

In the concluding chapters, the focus shifts to the practical execution of agile GPT projects, drawing from the rich experience of the authors acquired during multiple pioneering GPT engagements, alongside hands-on applications through frameworks like LangChain and predictive-powers for Python and Java developers respectively.

'Ultimate ChatGPT Handbook for Enterprises' highlights the transformative potential of ChatGPT and provides a practical roadmap for enterprises. Real-world examples, case studies, practical demonstrations and recommendations are utilized throughout the book to equip both business leaders and technical enthusiasts with the necessary knowledge and insights to navigate the emerging landscape of Enterprise AI, leveraging ChatGPT to drive successful AI engagements within their organizations.

Now, let's delve into the individual chapter overviews:

Chapter 1: From GPT-1 to ChatGPT-4: The Evolution Towards Generative Artificial Intelligence

In this initial chapter, we embark on a journey through the GPT lineage, methodically tracing the significant milestones that have paved the way towards artificial general intelligence. Here is what we'll explore:

- **Origins and Evolution:** Dive into the history of GPT models, charting their progression from the very beginning to their current state. We'll shed light on the distinct features and enhancements that each iteration introduced to the realm of AI.
- **ChatGPT - The Rise of Conversational AI:** Take a closer look at the ChatGPT model itself, gaining insights into its widespread adoption, the intricacies of its training, and its notable impact on contemporary society and the global economy.
- **GPT-4 - Approaching Artificial General Intelligence (AGI):** Investigate the significant strides GPT-4 has made in the direction of AGI. We'll delve into its enhanced capabilities, potential applications in the business world, and areas that require further research.
- **First Wave of Generative AI Capabilities - ChatGPT-4 Plugins:** Explore ChatGPT-4 plugins that introduce generative AI capabilities, enabling understanding and generation of media formats, from images to videos, and allowing end-users to perform tasks like exploratory data analysis and website creation.
- **Second Wave of Generative AI Capabilities - Native Multi-modality of ChatGPT-4:** Experience the evolution with ChatGPT's native multi-modal functionalities. This section highlights the seamless integration of voice and visual interactions, all realized within the ChatGPT-4 platform.
- **Third Wave of Generative AI Capabilities - GPT-4 Turbo and GPT Builder:** Discover GPT-4 Turbo's capability to process the equivalent of over 300 pages of text, dialogue, data, and images, enhancing content-rich output generation. Also learn, how GPT Builder empowers end users without programming skills to develop ChatGPT-like applications directly.
- **Further Insights into ChatGPT:** Broaden your understanding of ChatGPT's expansive ecosystem. Learn about its integration with external applications,

embedding into enterprise software solutions and the strategic direction of ChatGPT Enterprise, increasing data integration and security.

Chapter 2: CapabilityGPT - An Enterprise AI Capability Framework for ChatGPT.

In the subsequent chapter, we immerse ourselves in the intricacies of the CapabilityGPT framework, a pragmatic building-block-oriented methodology in leveraging the full potential of ChatGPT in enterprise settings. This chapter promises to endow readers with a deep understanding of how to employ AI capabilities as pivotal solutions, touching upon:

- **Enterprise AI Capabilities:** Begin with a grounding understanding of fundamental AI capabilities such as 'Creation', 'Prediction', and 'Recommendation', setting the stage for a deeper exploration of the CapabilityGPT framework.
- **AI Capabilities as Solution Building Blocks:** Learn how to conceive AI solutions using different AI capabilities symbiotically, encouraging reusable and extensible AI tools, assistants, and products.
- **The 18 Core AI Capabilities:** Dive into a detailed breakdown of the 18 core AI capabilities highlighted in the CapabilityGPT framework, understanding the rationale behind each and their roles in crafting enterprise AI solutions.
- **Benefits and Advantages of the CapabilityGPT Framework:** Uncover the merits of adopting the CapabilityGPT framework, with its user-centric and holistic approach that fosters innovation and efficiency over traditional AI frameworks.
- **Use Cases and Practical Applications:** Explore a vast array of use cases that derive value from the core AI capabilities, offering insights into rapid implementations and high-value propositions, each detailed in a standardized format to facilitate understanding.

Chapter 3: The Impact of ChatGPT on the Enterprise

In Chapter 3, we venture deep into the futuristic business landscape where ChatGPT facilitates symbiotic relationships between employees and their AI assistants across twenty-eight enterprise roles defined within six key enterprise personas. This voyage reveals a harmonious blend of artificial intelligence and human ingenuity and unfolds through vivid narrations of typical work weeks, showcasing the multifaceted potentials of AI capability usage in the enterprise context. Here's what to expect:

- **Subject Matter Experts:** Gain insights into the world of SMEs including Accounts Payable Clerks, Production & Quality Specialists, Procurement Specialists, Human Resource Specialists, and Supply-Chain Specialists. Discover how their respective AI assistants are pivotal in streamlining business processes and aiding in routine decision-making, fostering a more efficient and responsive work environment.

- **IT Specialists:** Learn how IT roles such as Software Engineers, IT-Support Specialists, IT-Solution Architects, Data Scientists, and User Interface Designers leverage AI assistants. This section unveils the transformative potential of integrating AI in handling IT-related analyses, design, and problem-solving tasks with increased efficiency and precision, revolutionizing the IT landscape.

- **Content Creators:** Dive into the creative realms inhabited by Marketing Copywriters, Social Media Managers, Product Documentation Writers, and Internal Communication Specialists. Explore how their synergy with AI assistants paves the way for swift creation of high-quality content, and aids in content analytics and related tasks, opening doors to unprecedented levels of creativity and effectiveness.

- **Customer Relations Specialists:** Engage with the dynamic roles of Call-Center Representatives, Customer Service Agents, Online Sales Associates, and Service Operations Managers. Understand how leveraging AI assistants can significantly enhance daily customer interactions, bringing a surge in customer satisfaction and building stronger, more positive customer relationships.

- **Knowledge Workers:** Embark on an exploration with Researchers, Technical Engineers, Product Managers, Legal Experts, and Process Consultants, diving deep into the possibilities enabled when AI assistants aid in advanced knowledge management, enriched communication, and the proficient creation of artifacts.

- **Business Leaders:** Step into the visionary world of Business Leaders including C-Suite Executives, Sales Directors, Supply Chain Managers, Finance Managers, and Program Managers. Here, we envision a future where AI assistants become indispensable allies, providing data-driven assessments, enhancing communication speed, and offering predictive and simulative insights to aid in strategic decision-making.

Each section, brought to life with real-world scenarios and case studies, provides a vivid vision of a future where AI collaborates seamlessly with human intelligence, setting a fertile ground for future growth and innovation in the enterprise landscape.

Chapter 4: Architecture Patterns enabled by GPT-Models

In this chapter, we plunge you into the diverse world of GPT-enabled architectural patterns, guiding you to understand the transformative potential these systems hold across varied enterprises. Below, we have outlined the key sections that this chapter will delve into:

- **The Concept of an Architecture Pattern:** Begin your exploration by understanding the fundamental ideas and recurring structures that define architectural patterns in different contexts.

- **Foundational Conversational Patterns:** Build a foundational understanding of GPT enabled conversational solutions ranging from basic, grounded to mixed-initiative and quality-controlled conversations. Here, we take you from learning the core structures facilitating Q&A interactions to advanced solutions employing a feedback loop for quality control.

- **Conversational Patterns with External Tool Integration:** Enhance your expertise by exploring GPT-driven chatbots integrated with enterprise applications and databases to improve user experience and automation.

- **Conversational Patterns with Fine-tuned Models:** Grasp the nuances of fine-tuning commercial and open-source language models to increase the quality of responses in knowledge- and data-rich domains.

- **Cooperating Agent Patterns:** Discover the architectural dynamics of AI systems with autonomous and cooperative functionalities through batch automation, orchestrated workflows, and collaborative single- and multi-agent environments.

In each section, we explore various specific patterns, presenting their structures, workflows, performance indicators and potential applications, thereby furnishing you with a substantial understanding of the large variety of GPT-enabled solutions.

Chapter 5: Advanced GPT Prompt Engineering Techniques

In this chapter, we cover the diverse landscape of GPT prompt engineering. Armed with the CapabilityGPT framework, you will learn the principles and tactics to master prompt crafting for effective communication with GPT models. The chapter includes:

- **Prompt Engineering Overview:** Kickstart your journey with a detailed understanding of the fundamental types and principles that govern the effective utilization of GPT models.
- **Instruction Prompts:** Immerse yourself in the nuances of crafting detailed instruction prompts. Dive into practical examples like "Project Review" and "Sales Forecasting" using single instruction prompts. Engage in "Sentiment Analysis for Product Reviews" and "New Employee Coaching" through instruction sequence prompts.
- **Query Prompts:** Navigate the intricate process of designing explorative query prompts. Delve into instances such as "Visual Inquiries about Cosmetic Products" and "Predictive Business Analysis." Understand how to evaluate suppliers like in the "New Supplier Evaluation" case or address system usability challenges as seen in the "Improving System Usability in Healthcare" scenario.
- **Multi-Agent Prompts:** Uncover the dynamics of powerful multi-agent prompts. Learn to foster collaborations and deep analyses in scenarios like "Project Go-Live Check" and "Sales Data Deep Dive." Understand the financial implications with cases like the "Forewarning Financial Analysis" of the 2019 financial report of a US retailer.
- **Embedded Technologies in Prompts:** Level up your prompt crafting skills using advanced technologies like plugins, evolutionary computing, or case-based reasoning, opening a broader spectrum of possibilities in AI interactions.

This hands-on approach ensures you grasp the essence of each type of prompt, setting a solid foundation for you to build upon in your AI endeavors.

Chapter 6: Designing Prompt-based Intelligent Assistants

In Chapter 6, we take you through the intriguing world of designing prompt-based intelligent assistants, where you will learn to harness ChatGPT's potential to create new enterprise functionalities by prompt sequences. This chapter introduces you to:

- **Master Prompts:** Begin with a deep understanding of Master Prompts, the blueprint in crafting intelligent assistants aligned with organizational norms and quality standards.
- **Task-Specific Prompts:** Explore the creation of task-specific prompts, which are interpreted and executed by ChatGPT against a rich context consisting of master prompt, previous task prompts, and ChatGPT responses.
- **Intelligent Functional Assistants:** Discover the process of conceptualizing and crafting Intelligent Functional Assistants for tasks like sales analytics, web shop design, and business scenario simulation.
- **Intelligent Collaboration Assistants:** Immerse yourself in the design and development of Intelligent Collaboration Assistants that take charge of critical business operations including business process management, innovation management, and enterprise cycle management.
- **Long Prompt Chains for Enhanced Enterprise Collaboration:** Extend your understanding by exploring the development of long prompt chains that facilitate deeper, constructive dialogues, nurturing an environment where collaborative efforts are maximized.

Chapter 7: Mastery of GPT-Projects

Building upon the comprehensive ground covered in earlier chapters, here we transition from foundational knowledge to an in-depth exploration of handling GPT projects proficiently. The chapter promises a deep dive into:

- **GPT Project Setup:** Embark on the primary phase of GPT projects, learning the critical elements of initiating a GPT project, including infrastructure setup, security protocols, and developing a feedback system to lay a solid foundation for your GPT project journey.
- **GPT Solution Life Cycle:** Dive into an agile and iterative approach that characterizes the lifecycle of GPT solutions, exploring the stages and experimental techniques involved in the continual refinement and optimization of GPT solutions.
- **GPT Use Cases and Solution Design:** Navigate the initial yet crucial phase

of GPT projects, crafting concise use cases, guiding you in specifying the project scope comprehensively. Furthermore, master the critical steps in solution design, factoring in various aspects like functionality, architecture, and user experience to forge solutions that implement the use cases effectively.

- **Prompt Engineering Cycle:** Engage profoundly with the strategic steps of the prompt engineering cycle, learning to steer GPT models towards producing desired outputs through meticulous design and validation, leveraging the prompt engineering techniques learned in the two previous chapters.
- **Output Validation of GPT Solutions:** Equip yourself with the tools and techniques for validating GPT solution outputs effectively, employing robust quality assurance focused on iterative improvements through meticulous feedback incorporation.
- **Iterative Improvement in GPT Projects:** Embrace the cyclical nature of GPT development, refining and enhancing solutions through systematic feedback loops. Learn to identify, assess, and incorporate feedback from each stage into previous stages executed in the next iteration.
- **Change Management in GPT Projects:** Discover the nuanced art of change management, focusing on the careful integration of GPT models into existing organizational systems and processes, understanding task distinctions, and strategizing for successful transformations.
- **Accelerating GPT-Projects with ChatGPT:** Harness the power of ChatGPT to expedite various phases of the GPT project lifecycle. From dynamically generating use cases, refining solution designs, to automated code documentation, explore how a GPT-for-GPT approach works in different project phases.

Chapter 8: GPT-Implementation Framework for Python

As we draw closer to the conclusion of the book, the emphasis progressively sharpens towards execution. Chapter 8 discusses LangChain - a notable Python-based framework, built to facilitate the creation of GPT-powered applications. The chapter articulates how LangChain works, highlights its vast potentials for developers and projects alike, and underscores its inherent benefits. Introduction to practical examples will include:

- **LangChain Overview:** Discover what exactly LangChain encompasses and the various ways it can be applied. Additionally, learn about the three fundamental pillars central to LangChain's framework.
- **Components of LangChain:** Unravel the heart of the LangChain framework, explore its key constituents including Schema, Models, Data Processing, Chains, Memory Handling, and Agents. Detailed analysis of each component furnishes intricate knowledge on the functioning mechanics of LangChain.

To supplement theoretical knowledge, the chapter introduces three practical demonstrations, each underscoring a unique usage of Langchain. These demonstrations comprise Python code snippets and step-by-step explanations.

- **Example 1:** Preparation helper for lawyers: The first demonstration expounds on Langchain's efficiency in legal fields, focusing on the usage of semantic search in civil case research for legal professionals.
- **Example 2:** Chatting over device manual: The second demonstration investigates Langchain's ability to effectively retrieve data from divergent text sources, an advantage for automation experts. This scenario encompasses a chat mechanism that helps automation specialists to quickly retrieve information from a lengthy manual delivered in PDF format.
- **Example 3:** Current price checks using LangChain's agents: Lastly, the chapter navigates through a real-time price check system that can benefit businesses in competitive pricing. This segment shows how LangChain's agents harness reasoning abilities of LLMs and the executing capacities of other tools to provide real-time pricing data.

Upon chapter conclusion, readers are equipped with a holistic understanding of Langchain's functionality and prospective applications. This chapter establishes a strong foundation for those interested in further technical study.

Chapter 9: `predictive-powers` - GPT-Implementation Framework for Java

Chapter nine delves into `predictive-powers`, a library instrumental in enabling Java developers to swiftly develop solutions leveraging generative AI technology. The discourse here is focused but broad, welcoming readers from different backgrounds to engage with the powerful capabilities of this library. The chapters present a progressive journey delineated into several key sections:

- **`predictive-Powers` Library Overview:** Step into a systematic introduction to the `predictive-powers` library, where you will grasp the library's primary characteristics and functionalities, initiating you into the vibrant landscape of opportunities it unfolds for Java developers.

- **Deep Dive into Essential Concepts:** Engage in a detailed examination of integral components such as API clients, endpoints, and services, the triad that forms the library's backbone. You will not just learn about their functionalities but also witness them in action through illustrative examples, enhancing your understanding incrementally.
- **Practical Application via 'Essay Writer':** Journey through the real-world application of this library, with a special focus on constructing an autonomous agent termed 'Essay Writer'. This section is intended to illustrate the library's versatility and foster a practical understanding that readers can transpose to myriad other domains.
- **Essay Writer's Architectural Blueprint:** Traverse the architectural pathways that dictate the Essay Writer's creation, offering you a conceptual map to envision and construct similar applications by integrating `predictive-powers` services tactically.
- **Code Walkthrough of 'Essay Writer':** For those inclined towards a technical understanding, this segment illuminates selected snippets from the coding repository, guiding you in navigating the intricate pathways of implementation without immersing into exhaustive details.

Appendix A: Further Examples of Advanced Prompts

In this appendix, we further explore the intricate world of advanced prompting with ChatGPT-4, showcasing ten additional scenarios that highlight the model's adaptability and depth. This appendix covers:

- **Single Instruction Examples:** Delve into the realm of single instruction prompts. Experience how ChatGPT-4 takes on roles in Resource Management, aligning skills with project tasks; navigates Scenario-based Project Simulations, forecasting project phases amid challenges; and communicates key insights in the Business Communication example, summarizing the growth and challenges in the carbon accounting sector.
- **Instruction Sequence & Pseudo Code Instructions Examples:** In the Insurance Claim Processing example, witness ChatGPT-4's methodical approach as it collects all claim-relevant information from the user,

summarizes it and provides a repair cost estimate. Next, discover ChatGPT-4 acting as a systems architect, dissecting, and optimizing a presented architecture diagram using a structured three-step method. Conclude with how ChatGPT-4 employs a ranking system in the Real Estate Listing Comparison based on pseudo-code instructions.

- **Query Examples:** Navigate the intricate process of query prompts. In Safety Regulation Inquiries, delve into the specifics of PPE safety regulations with ChatGPT-4. Engage in a counterfactual exploration within the Counterfactual Exploration in HR scenario. Experience predictive analysis in the supply chain using fuzzy logic in the Supply Possibility Estimation example.
- **Multi-agent Examples:** Uncover the dynamics of multi-agent prompts. In the Eco-friendly Motorbike Design example, explore a multi-layered agent system that evaluates the conceptualization and viability of an eco-friendly motorbike. Dive deep into Chile's lithium sector in the Research on Raw Materials scenario, where a multi-agent system provides a comprehensive overview of the industry.

These additional examples deepen the understanding of advanced prompt engineering techniques introduced in Chapter 5, further solidifying your foundation and expertise in crafting effective prompts for Generative AI interactions.

Appendix B: Enterprise Transformation Examples with ChatGPT

Diving deeper into the real-world impact of ChatGPT on businesses, we present four transformative case studies in this appendix:

- **Semi-automated Request for Proposal (RfP) Processing:** A consulting firm uses ChatGPT to streamline a complex SAP implementation proposal, overcoming time and resource constraints.
- **AI-based Wealth Management:** A traditional wealth management firm integrates ChatGPT to offer digital, personalized services, redefining the role of Digital Relationship Managers for a tech-savvy clientele.
- **AI-based Complaint Management:** A consumer goods company employs ChatGPT to turn an error-prone complaints process into an efficient system.

- **AI for Supply-Chain-Scenario Evaluation:** An automotive supplier harnesses ChatGPT's power for strategic decision-making around production relocation and energy cost reduction.

These case studies demonstrate ChatGPT's transformative potential in diverse business scenarios, emphasizing its role in optimizing processes and strategic decision-making.

Concluding Recommendations

Across the eleven chapters of this book, we have distilled key insights into 21 pivotal recommendations aimed at guiding business leaders in the age of Generative AI. While these guidelines provide a solid foundation, they are not one-size-fits-all; each enterprise is expected to tailor them to fit their unique context and objectives.

Get a Free eBook

We hope you are enjoying your recently purchased book! Your feedback is incredibly valuable to us, and to all other readers looking for great books.

If you found this book helpful or enjoyable, we would truly appreciate it, if you could take a moment to leave a short review with a 5 star rating on Amazon. It helps us grow, and lets other readers discover our books.

As a thank you, we would love to send you a free digital copy of this book, and a **30%** discount code on your next cart value on our official websites:

www.orangeava.com

www.orangeava.in (For Indian Subcontinent)

☑ **Here's how:**

Leave a review for the book on Amazon.

Take a screenshot of your review, and send an email to **info@orangeava.com** (it can be just the confirmation screen).

Once, we receive your screenshot, we will send you the digital file, within 24 hours.

Thank you so much for your support – it means a lot to us!

Downloading the code bundles and colored images

Please follow the link to download the
Code Bundles of the book:

https://github.com/OrangeAVA/Ultimate-ChatGPT-Handbook-for-Enterprises

The code bundles and images of the book are also hosted on
https://rebrand.ly/8111b2

In case there's an update to the code, it will be updated on the existing GitHub repository.

Errata

We take immense pride in our work at **Orange Education Pvt Ltd**, and follow best practices to ensure the accuracy of our content to provide an indulging reading experience to our subscribers. Our readers are our mirrors, and we use their inputs to reflect and improve upon human errors, if any, that may have occurred during the publishing processes involved. To let us maintain the quality and help us reach out to any readers who might be having difficulties due to any unforeseen errors, please write to us at :

errata@orangeava.com

Your support, suggestions, and feedback are highly appreciated.

DID YOU KNOW

Did you know that Orange Education Pvt Ltd offers eBook versions of every book published, with PDF and ePub files available? You can upgrade to the eBook version at **www.orangeava.com** and as a print book customer, you are entitled to a discount on the eBook copy. Get in touch with us at: **info@orangeava.com** for more details.

At **www.orangeava.com**, you can also read a collection of free technical articles, sign up for a range of free newsletters, and receive exclusive discounts and offers on AVA™ Books and eBooks.

PIRACY

If you come across any illegal copies of our works in any form on the internet, we would be grateful if you would provide us with the location address or website name. Please contact us at **info@orangeava.com** with a link to the material.

ARE YOU INTERESTED IN AUTHORING WITH US?

If there is a topic that you have expertise in, and you are interested in either writing or contributing to a book, please write to us at **business@orangeava.com**. We are on a journey to help developers and tech professionals to gain insights on the present technological advancements and innovations happening across the globe and build a community that believes Knowledge is best acquired by sharing and learning with others. Please reach out to us to learn what our audience demands and how you can be part of this educational reform. We also welcome ideas from tech experts and help them build learning and development content for their domains.

REVIEWS

Please leave a review. Once you have read and used this book, why not leave a review on the site that you purchased it from? Potential readers can then see and use your unbiased opinion to make purchase decisions. We at Orange Education would love to know what you think about our products, and our authors can learn from your feedback. Thank you!

For more information about Orange Education, please visit **www.orangeava.com**.

Table of Contents

CHAPTER 1

From GPT-1 to ChatGPT-4: The Evolution Towards Generative AI

Introduction

In this chapter, we trace the development of Generative Pre-trained Transformers (GPT), from the beginnings of GPT-1 and GPT-2, through to more recent versions such as ChatGPT and GPT-4.

We start with a look at the early GPT models in 2018/19, laying the foundation for GPT-3, which generated human-like text for the first time in 2020, thanks to its size and capabilities.

We then discuss InstructGPT, unveiled in early 2022. This variant of GPT-3, fine-tuned on large instruction datasets, broadened the execution of various text-based tasks in the GPT domain. Then we proceed with ChatGPT, a breakthrough in Conversational AI that immediately became the most successful AI application when launched in November 2022.

Our attention then shifts to GPT-4 and its chat counterpart, ChatGPT-4. This model showcases a degree of Artificial General Intelligence (AGI) capabilities like

Learning and Adaptation, Advanced Reasoning, and Creativity and Innovation. In March 2022, alongside the release of GPT-4, a suite of initial plugins was introduced to enhance its functionalities. Over the subsequent months, new plugins were added, broadening its range of Generative AI capabilities. By June of the same year, the model's potential was further expanded with the access to external applications (tools). The subsequent integration of these models into enterprise software began in the second half of 2023, underscoring their transformative impact on business applications.

We wrap up this chapter by first delving into ChatGPT Enterprise, launched in August 2023, a tailored offering by OpenAI designed to address the specific requirements and concerns of the corporate sector. Subsequently, we examine the introduction of native voice and image processing capabilities to ChatGPT in September 2023, a significant advancement that enriches user interactions and underscores its versatility as a comprehensive Generative AI tool. Finally, we highlight the notable progress achieved by the launch of GPT-4 Turbo in November 2023, as well as the emergence of AI-assistants and customizable GPTs, which are reshaping the landscape of AI applications and enterprise solutions.

Figure 1.1 offers a succinct overview of the journey of GPT models thus far:

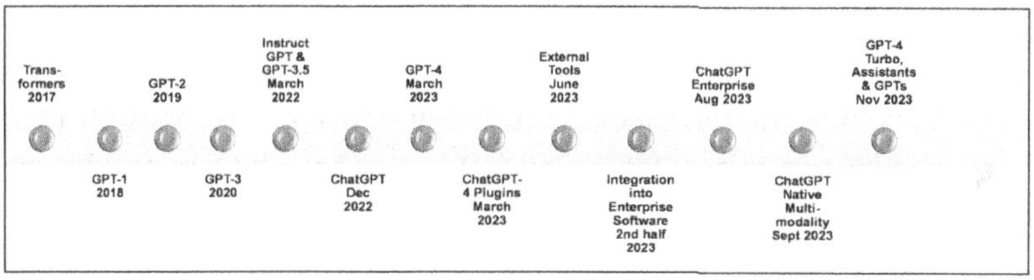

***Figure 1.1**: Evolution of GPT models*

Structure

In this chapter, the following topics will be covered:

- Early Generations of GPT
- GPT-3
- InstructGPT
- ChatGPT
- GPT-4
- ChatGPT-4 Plugins
- Access to External Tools

- Integration into Enterprise Software
- ChatGPT Enterprise
- ChatGPT Native Multi-modality
- GPT-4 Turbo, Assistants and GPTs

Early Generations of GPT: Charting the Course of AI Language Processing

Language Models are a groundbreaking innovation in Artificial Intelligence (AI). They are AI systems designed to understand, generate, and interact with human language, and their prowess is rooted in a special deep learning[1] architecture known as Transformers, which were introduced in 2017. Transformers employ a unique attention mechanism, enabling them to discern the relevance of words within an input sentence when generating an output sentence.

Leveraging this pioneering approach, OpenAI, initially established as a non-profit AI research laboratory[2] in the US, launched the first Generative Pre-trained Transformer (GPT-1) in 2018 with 117 million parameters[3]. The GPT-1 model employed a simplified left-to-right version of the Transformer architecture, which enabled it to generate the next word in a text sequence based on the context of the preceding words.

Throughout its training process, the model worked to predict the subsequent word in a sentence, given a specific lookback window of previous words and their respective degrees of importance for the new word. It compared this prediction with the actual next word in reference texts from its dataset of 7000 books (BooksCorpus), making adjustments to its internal mechanisms whenever discrepancies were identified. When the predictions were accurate, no adjustments were needed. BooksCorpus was chosen partly because the long passages of continuous text helped the model learn to handle long-range dependencies.

GPT-1 achieved notable improvements over previous models in tasks such as text

[1]Deep learning is a branch of machine learning that uses multi-layered neural networks to learn transformation functions and patterns to produce desired outputs from the input data.
[2]It was in 2019 that OpenAI introduced a for-profit arm to their operation.
[3]Neural network parameters are like the brain's memory of what it has learned. They are values that the network adjusts as it learns from input-output training data.

classification, natural language inference[4], question answering, commonsense reasoning, and semantic similarity[5].

Following the success of GPT-1, OpenAI built on its accomplishments by introducing GPT-2 in 2019. This second iteration demonstrated a significant upscale in the number of parameters, soaring from GPT-1's 117 million to 1.5 billion. Additionally, GPT-2 utilized a larger training dataset of 8 million web pages or 40GB of text, which was over ten times larger than that of GPT-1.

GPT-2 introduced significant improvements over GPT-1, particularly in zero-shot learning[6] and text generation. The model can create high-quality synthetic text based on any given input, adapting to the style and content seamlessly, allowing for coherent and realistic text continuations on user-chosen topics. GPT-2 also outperforms GPT-1 in other text generation tasks like translation and summarization, as well as in text understanding tasks like question answering and reading comprehension.

GPT-3: Pioneering Advanced Natural Language Processing in AI

GPT-3, the third iteration of the Generative Pre-trained Transformer, was launched by OpenAI in 2020 and showcased a further enormous increase in model size, featuring 175 billion parameters in its most extensive variant. This positioned it as the largest language model of its time.

It is important to note that GPT-3 was trained on 300 billion tokens[7] or 570GB of text, from various datasets including CommonCrawl with approximately 6

---

[4]Natural language inference (NLI) is the task of determining the relationship between two sentences. For example, given a statement "All dogs bark" and another statement "Some animals make noise," we infer that the second statement is a generalization of the first. In NLI, we classify the relationship between such pairs of sentences as either "entailment" (one sentence logically follows from the other), "contradiction" (the sentences oppose each other), or "neutral" (the sentences are unrelated).

[5]Semantic similarity is about measuring how closely two sentences or words share the same meaning. For example, "big" and "large" have high semantic similarity because they both describe size.

[6]Zero-shot learning refers to a machine learning approach where a model is able to perform tasks for which it hasn't been explicitly trained. Instead of relying on specific training data for every task, the model leverages its existing knowledge, often derived from related tasks, to infer or generalize to new, unseen tasks.

[7]In language models, a "token" can represent a single character, part of a word, or an entire word. For example, "sunny day" might be tokenized as ["sun", "ny", " day"] or simply as ["sunny", "day"]. Tokens help the model process and generate text, and the way text is tokenized can influence its performance and capabilities.

billion crawled web documents, WebText2 with approximately 45 million web pages, Wikipedia, and a large number of public domain books. The significant scale-up resulted in capturing more intricate linguistic patterns and granted GPT-3 superior text generation and understanding capabilities, rendering GPT-3 an evolutionary leap beyond GPT-2.

GPT-3 distinguished itself with its advanced few-shot[8] and one-shot[9] learning capabilities. Thus, GPT-3 was able to perform well on new tasks based on limited examples, with only a handful, or even just one, input-output example without the need for explicit re-training or fine-tuning on large domain-specific datasets.

Owing to its cutting-edge capabilities, GPT-3 could tackle a more extensive array of tasks than GPT-2, from drafting emails and writing code to creating poetry and answering nuanced questions.

Another critical area of improvement was GPT-3's ability to generate more coherent and contextually relevant text. It reduced the likelihood of producing nonsensical or irrelevant responses, a noticeable improvement over GPT-2, which enhanced the usability and overall user experience.

OpenAI further expanded the impact of GPT-3 by introducing an Application Programming Interface (API), making it more accessible to developers to integrate the model into their applications.

InstructGPT: A Stepping Stone toward Task-oriented AI

InstructGPT, a fine-tuned version of GPT-3, marked a significant evolution in the landscape of large language models as a result of OpenAI's research. Launched in early 2022, it received special recognition for its proficiency in interpreting user instructions and largely avoiding unwanted content.

InstructGPT's training aimed to closely align the language model with both the explicit and implicit intentions of users. The objective was to develop a model that could effectively assist in accomplishing user tasks, while also being trained to adhere to principles of veracity and safety, refraining from spreading false or harmful content.

The model was trained employing reinforcement learning from human feedback

[8]In the context of machine learning, few-shot learning refers to the ability of a system to generalize from a small number of examples – typically less than five.

[9]One-shot learning is a special case of few-shot learning where the system learns from just a single example.

(RLHF). This comprehensive process consisted of five stages:

1. Data Labeling: The first stage involved recruiting a team of contractors, chosen based on their performance in a screening test, to label the data.
2. Initial Supervised Learning: A large instruction-response dataset was created, partially manually by the contractors, partially automatically by using the GPT-3 API and reviewing its results.. Then, the existing GPT-3 models were fine-tuned using this dataset.
3. Creation of a Comparison Dataset: A separate dataset was assembled, where the contractors ranked the responses of the previously trained model to a large set of instructions.
4. Training the Preference Model: The comparison dataset was then used to train a preference model, aiming to 'guess', which model answers the contractors liked best.
5. Fine-Tuning the Supervised Model from Stage 2: With the preference model serving as a reward function, the initial supervised model was further fine-tuned to 'maximize its reward', meaning its likelihood to produce preferable answers.

The outcome was models more aligned with users' intents and less likely to produce unexpected or harmful outputs, marking a significant milestone in the evolution of large language models. Its emphasis on improved instruction-following, task-specific training, relevance of responses, and safety set a new benchmark.

ChatGPT: A Revolution in Conversational AI

ChatGPT, the succeeding generation of the Generative Pre-trained Transformer models, represents a breakthrough in Conversational AI. Introduced in November 2022, it marks a substantial leap in AI's capacity to engage in human-like dialogue and interactive text generation.

It is designed to understand context, offer valuable insights, and carry out detailed instructions embedded in dialogues, significantly enhancing the quality of conversational experiences of traditional chatbots. Moreover, further emphasis on safety reduces the potential for the generation of harmful or biased content.

To truly appreciate the evolution of ChatGPT, it's essential to delve into its training journey, which is based on the insights gained from the training of its predecessor, InstructGPT. In the subsequent breakdown, we'll explore four pivotal steps in the development of ChatGPT. Each step will introduce an intermediate or final model, detailing its:

- **Origin**: Understanding the lineage and roots of the model.
- **Training Data**: The data sources that informed and shaped the model's knowledge.
- **Purpose**: The primary objectives and goals set for the model.
- **Training Method**: The techniques and methodologies employed to train the model.

Here are the four steps:

1. **Trained Model: code-davinci-002**
   - **Origin**: GPT-3 davinci (175B parameters).
   - **Training Data**: Billions of lines of public code sourced from GitHub.
   - **Purpose**: Primarily focused on code-completion tasks, adept at understanding and generating code snippets.
   - **Training Method**: Self-supervised next word prediction.
2. **Trained Model: text-davinci-002**
   - **Origin**: code-davinci-002.
   - **Training Data**: Combination of human-written demonstrations and model samples with best ratings by human labelers on overall quality.
   - **Purpose**: Learn to follow a large variety of instructions.
   - **Training Method**: Supervised instruction fine-tuning.
3. **Trained Model: text-davinci-003**
   - **Origin**: text-davinci-002.
   - **Training Data**: Comparisons from humans.
   - **Purpose**: Aim to produce even more accurate and human-like text during instruction following.
   - **Training Method**: Reinforcement Learning from Human Feedback (RLHF).
4. **Trained Model: ChatGPT (gpt-3.5-turbo-0301)**
   - **Origin**: text-davinci-003.

- **Training Data**: Human AI trainers provided conversations in which they played both sides – the user and an AI assistant, the InstructGPT dataset (transformed into a dialogue format), and comparison data consisting of two or more model responses ranked by quality by humans.
- **Purpose**: Specifically optimized for chat-based interactions.
- **Training Method**: Reinforcement Learning from Human Feedback (RLHF)

Based on this training process, it can also be assumed that ChatGPT has the same number of parameters, 175 billion, as its progenitor model, GPT-3.

OpenAI extended the reach of ChatGPT by introducing two distinct API versions tailored to cater to a variety of user requirements and interaction scenarios.

Firstly, in March 2023, GPT-3.5 Turbo was launched. This version emphasizes enhanced steerability, allowing developers to effectively guide the model's behavior through system messages and define responsible usage parameters.

Then, a subsequent version, GPT-3.5 Turbo-16k, was unveiled in June 2023. As an upgrade, it can handle up to 12000 words and provides a four times larger data window for input and output than the standard version. This enhancement is particularly useful in scenarios that require extended dialogues or the use of comprehensive reference documents, as it enables the model to consider a larger quantity of information when generating its responses.

ChatGPT has a widespread acceptance and impact on society. Within a mere two months from its inception, ChatGPT garnered 100 million active users globally - a milestone achieved at an unprecedented pace with 1 million users joining within the first week [1].

The spread of ChatGPT users spans 161 countries, making it a truly global phenomenon, with the United States and India as its largest user bases. The model supports and understands a large range of 95 natural languages besides English, broadening its accessibility to an international audience. However, there are seven nations, including China and Russia, where ChatGPT is not accessible.

In addition to natural languages, ChatGPT is capable of understanding and coding in multiple programming languages, such as Python, JavaScript, C++, Java, and SQL, which boosts its utility and appeal to developers.

The platform's users reveal a broad demographic spectrum, with approximately 40% of US adults aware of the platform; 64.53% of users fall into the young adult category of 18-34 years, and the gender distribution is quite balanced, with

59.67% of the users being male and 40.33% female. As for the traffic, over 88% is direct, while a modest 4.22% is directed from social media platforms.

Looking forward, ChatGPT is forecasted to generate a revenue of $200 million by the end of 2023 and is projected to reach $1 billion by 2024. Its influence is significantly observable in the job market, with around 80% of the US workforce experiencing alterations to at least 10% of their work tasks due to GPT models, and around 19% may see at least 50% of their tasks impacted. This influence spans all wage levels, not just those in industries with higher recent productivity growth. As these GPT models exhibit characteristics of general-purpose technologies, they may have notable economic, social, and policy implications [2].

In conclusion, ChatGPT's impact extends beyond reshaping digital interaction. Its extraordinary global adoption, high engagement levels, and profound influence on a range of tasks underscore its success and potential for transforming enterprise applications in the future.

GPT-4: Navigating the Initial Pathway of Artificial General Intelligence

GPT-4, the most advanced transformer model to date, represents a further significant leap forward in AI capabilities. Although specific details have not been publicly released, it is estimated that GPT-4 operates with approximately 1.8 trillion parameters, ten times larger than GPT-3, pushing the boundaries of what AI models can achieve. It uses a Mixture of Expert[10] (MoE) model with 16 experts, each having about 111 billion parameters and was trained on approximately 13 trillion tokens from various sources, including internet data, books, and research papers.

Released initially as a chatbot version, known as ChatGPT Plus or ChatGPT-4, in March 2023, it quickly gained recognition for its impressive ability to understand and generate human-like text. Following this success, an API version was introduced in July 2023, enhancing its range of tasks and applications.

While its basic version, GPT-4-8k, is able to process up to 6,000 words, a more advanced version, GPT-4-32k, is capable of working with as many as 25,000 words or the equivalent of up to 50 pages.

[10]A mixture of expert's model is a machine learning architecture where multiple specialized sub-models (experts) are trained to handle specific regions or types of data, and an integration model determines the weight or contribution of each expert for a given input, enabling adaptive and context-aware decision-making.

GPT-4 demonstrates substantial progress in reducing hallucinations – instances of generating inaccurate or irrelevant information, enhancing the quality of interaction and user trust in the model. On the safety front, GPT-4 offers improved handling and filtering of inappropriate inputs, ensuring safer, more responsible interactions.

GPT-4 represents a substantial advancement in the pursuit of Artificial General Intelligence (AGI) and moves beyond providing nuanced and precise responses in complex conversational scenarios. It showcases competencies that edge closer to human-like cognitive capabilities. In this comprehensive evaluation, we cover GPT-4's performance across 10 key AGI capabilities. These include Learning & Adaptation, Transfer Learning, Advanced Reasoning, Creativity and Innovation, Natural Language Understanding and Generation, Perception and Understanding, Intuitive Understanding of Emotions, Autonomous Goal Setting and Planning, Collaboration and Cooperation, and Ethics and Moral Reasoning (see *Figure* 1.2).

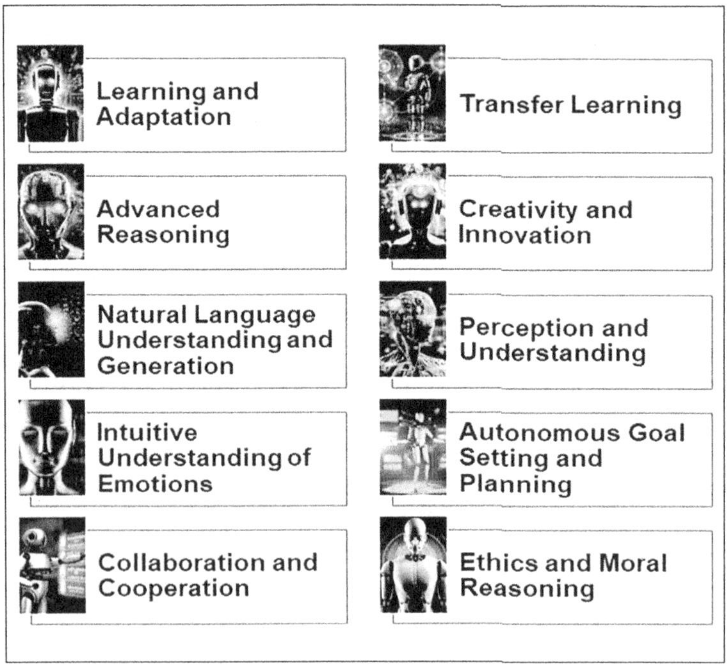

Figure 1.2: *AGI-Capability Overview*

For each of these 10 capabilities, we will:

1. Define the capability within the context of AGI.
2. Discuss its importance within the enterprise context.

3. Evaluate GPT-4's fulfillment of this capability.
4. Provide examples of GPT-4's utilization of the capability in enterprise settings.
5. Explore GPT-4's limitations or challenges when applying this capability.

Now, let us embark on this exploratory journey, beginning with the first AGI capability:

- **Learning and Adaptation**

Figure 1.3: *Learning and Adaptation*

  - **Definition**: AGI is capable of learning from various sources of information and experiences, adapting its knowledge and skills to new and changing environments. This encompasses the ability to assimilate new information, evolve responses based on feedback, and continuously update understanding over time, reflecting the dynamic nature of businesses and markets.
  - **Importance**: The ability to learn and adapt is a cornerstone of successful business operations in a rapidly changing world. It facilitates the continual improvement of processes, strategies, and interactions, enabling organizations to stay competitive, innovative, and responsive to emerging trends and challenges.
  - **Fulfillment**: GPT-4 displays this AGI capability with the ability to acquire knowledge from demonstrations, external sources, and user feedback, and to apply this learning in future interactions. It is able to understand the context of a conversation based on preceding text and adjust its responses to match the tone or style of user inputs.
  - **Examples**: GPT-4 can dynamically address business queries by synthesizing knowledge from a range of sources, such as offering

insights on drug advancements to pharmaceutical companies or regulatory compliance strategies to finance teams. It adapts its suggestions based on specific industry needs, like recommending e-commerce practices for certain demographics or devising remote work strategies for HR departments. By analyzing both historical data and contemporary trends, GPT-4 can assist firms in navigating disruptions, whether they're related to supply chain challenges, new market demographics, or industry shifts like the emergence of electric vehicles.

   - **Limitation**: Despite these capabilities, GPT-4 can face challenges in learning concepts that deviate significantly from its pre-training knowledge base, such as counter-commonsense learning or understanding novel business models. It may also struggle to adapt its responses in real-time to fast-evolving situations or topics outside its training data.

- **Transfer Learning**

***Figure 1.4**: Transfer Learning*

   - **Definition**: AGI has the ability to apply knowledge and skills gained in one domain to another domain, without requiring extensive retraining. In an enterprise, this takes on the form of cross-disciplinary integration, which involves leveraging knowledge and insights from different disciplines to solve complex problems.
   - **Importance**: Transfer learning enables AGI to adapt to diverse contexts and contribute to discussions on a wide range of topics. In an enterprise setting, cross-disciplinary integration allows for the development of comprehensive solutions and fosters innovation by integrating diverse perspectives and functions.
   - **Fulfillment**: As an AGI capability, GPT-4 can transfer knowledge between diverse domains without requiring explicit retraining, enhancing its application across multiple subjects. This allows GPT-4

to excel at providing cross-disciplinary insights due to its extensive, multi-domain knowledge base.

- **Examples**: GPT-4 can use its knowledge about animals and their characteristics in a conversation about ecology or apply an understanding of statistics in a discussion on sports analytics. In a business context, it can propose a solution to a marketing challenge using insights from psychology and data science, strategize a product design by integrating principles of engineering, aesthetics, and user experience, or provide a comprehensive approach to improving company culture using insights from HR, organizational psychology, and communication studies.
- **Limitation**: Maintaining accuracy when transferring knowledge between domains with little overlap can be challenging for GPT-4, leading to potential inaccuracies or irrelevant information generation. Similarly, while it can integrate knowledge across fields, the depth of understanding in specialized areas might be limited.

- **Advanced Reasoning**

Figure 1.5: *Advanced Reasoning*

- **Definition**: Advanced reasoning in the context of AGI refers to the ability to exhibit and combine diverse forms of human- and machine-level thinking:
  - **Abductive Reasoning** is the method of generating a hypothesis that best explains specific observations, frequently used in situations such as root cause analysis.
  - **Deductive Reasoning** draws specific conclusions from general statements or premises.
  - **Inductive Reasoning** builds broad generalizations from specific observations.

- **Analogical Reasoning** derives insights from one situation (the source) by comparing its similarities with another, often unrelated, situation (the target).
- **Commonsense Reasoning** enables the understanding and inference of basic, shared knowledge that an average human being would know implicitly.
- **Algorithmic Reasoning** involves "thinking like a computer" to solve problems, leveraging well-defined, iterative processes and conditional logic to arrive at a solution.

- **Importance**: In business, advanced reasoning is essential. It is a capability we use whether we are working towards efficiency or meeting revenue goals. On a day-to-day basis, it plays a role in communications with colleagues, customers and suppliers, helping to build understanding and trust. In project management, reasoning assists in navigating challenges, finding solutions, and coordinating with stakeholders. Overall, whether it is in strategy or daily tasks, advanced reasoning in all its forms is a constant presence in an enterprise context.
- **Fulfillment**: GPT-4's adeptness in various forms of reasoning stems from its extensive training methods. The next-word prediction task it was trained on honed its abductive reasoning, facilitating the creation of plausible hypotheses from observed contexts. Its grounding in deductive reasoning comes from exposure to logical texts, enhancing its capacity to formulate logically consistent deductions. Its proficiency in inductive reasoning is a result of statistical pattern recognition from a massive dataset, allowing it to generalize from specific observations. Moreover, its analogical and commonsense reasoning has been nurtured through the vast training data, which featured a plethora of comparisons, everyday scenarios, and relational structures. Finally, its pronounced algorithmic reasoning is attributed to its training on millions of code examples and is further improved by recent plugins for end-user programming[11].
- **Examples**:
  - **Abductive Reasoning**: Noticing a sudden 30% dip in user activity on an e-commerce site, one might employ abductive reasoning to hypothesize that a recent website update introduced a disruptive bug. Similarly, a sharp decline in a specific product's sales could point to factors like a competitor's product launch or recent bad reviews. A 15% KPI decrease between quarters might be linked to a policy change or market fluctuations.

[11]ChatGPT-4 Plugins for end-user programming will be discussed in the next subchapter.

    - **Deductive Reasoning**: Introducing a policy for additional quality checks before shipping may reduce customer complaints at the expense of longer delivery times, as per deductive reasoning. If a retailer's goal is to boost online sales by 20%, focusing on physical store ads might not be the best strategy. Similarly, a halfway construction project already consuming 70% of the budget clearly indicates potential overruns without extra funding.
    - **Inductive Reasoning**: Analyzing five years of sales data showing November and December spikes suggests a likely uptick next year too, a conclusion reached through inductive reasoning. This approach can also uncover patterns in consumer behavior for promotional opportunities and streamline business processes by analyzing recurring execution patterns.
    - **Analogical Reasoning**: A retail company might infer the potential success of a loyalty program similar to a competitor's using analogical reasoning. Likewise, a tech firm might see the benefit of a subscription model, drawing parallels with streaming services. Learning from the automobile sector, a food company might employ waste-reducing strategies anticipating similar efficiency gains.
    - **Commonsense Reasoning**: Common sense dictates delaying the launch of a new ice cream flavor to a warmer month in cold climates. It can attribute a rise in July customer inquiries to a summer campaign and weighs the pros and cons of a coastal factory relocation, considering both shipping costs and property values.
    - **Algorithmic Reasoning**: In software development, algorithmic reasoning aids in crafting efficient systems and streamlining IT support. It also facilitates ad-hoc problem-solving in business scenarios, helping in precise cost calculation and project planning, and assists in deriving insights from large datasets for strategic planning, albeit with a need for careful management to avoid data security and bias issues.
  - **Limitation**: Despite its impressive reasoning capabilities, GPT-4 does have significant limitations:
    - **Abductive Reasoning**: GPT-4 may rely too heavily on its training data, leading to biases and potentially incorrect hypotheses as it sometimes confuses correlation with causation. Furthermore it lacks a deep understanding of causal relationships in the real world, hindering its ability to reason profoundly in fields like physics and engineering.

- **Deductive Reasoning**: GPT-4 can find complex scenarios, especially mathematical contexts, challenging to navigate, sometimes resulting in logical errors or incorrect approaches.
- **Inductive Reasoning**: The model might develop overly generalized theories when faced with sparse or ambiguous data, limiting the accuracy of its inductions.
- **Analogical Reasoning**: GPT-4 risks oversimplification when drawing parallels between different situations, possibly leading to overgeneralized or inaccurate recommendations.
- **Commonsense Reasoning**: In complex or highly specific scenarios, GPT-4 might not always apply commonsense reasoning effectively, resulting in responses that lack depth or real-world context.
- **Algorithmic Reasoning**: Despite its training, GPT-4 can sometimes produce incorrect or inefficient algorithms, particularly for complex, unseen problems, demonstrating its constrained ability to innovate beyond its training parameters.

- **Creativity and Innovation**

***Figure 1.6**: Creativity and Innovation*

- **Definition**: AGI possesses the ability to generate new ideas, concepts, and solutions by combining and recombining existing knowledge, thus displaying creativity and innovation. In a business setting, this ability often entails the generation of unique solutions or concepts and the capacity for out-of-the-box thinking.
- **Importance**: Creativity fuels innovation, drives business growth, and differentiates a company in a competitive market.
- **Fulfillment**: Demonstrating an AGI capability, GPT-4 can generate

creative and innovative aspects and text, effectively introducing novel perspectives into various discussions.

- **Examples**: GPT-4's ability to generate stories, poems, or innovative product descriptions is an instance of its creative capability. Moreover, in an enterprise context, GPT-4 can brainstorm novel product features based on a company's existing portfolio and market trends. It can propose unique marketing strategies drawing from a range of successful campaigns in different industries, and it can suggest innovative solutions to internal organizational challenges, such as improving employee engagement or streamlining workflows. GPT-4 can also suggest unconventional solutions to problems posed by users.
- **Limitation**: GPT-4's creativity is constrained by its training data, limiting its ability to think "outside the box." It struggles with handling entirely new situations that have little in common with past experiences.

- **Natural Language Understanding and Generation**

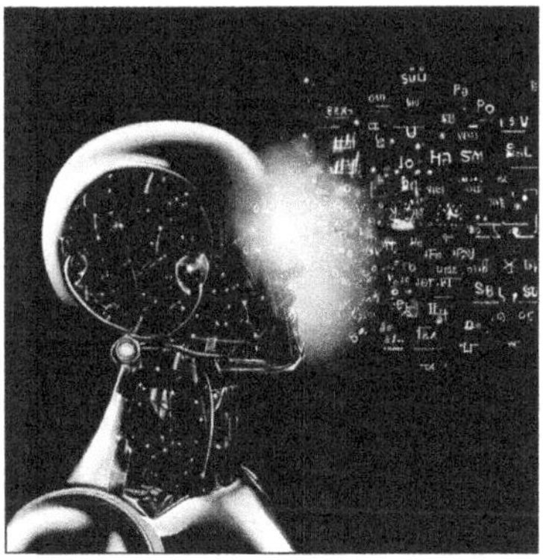

***Figure 1.7**: Natural Language Understanding and Generation*

- **Definition**: AGI is able to comprehend and generate text in multiple human languages, allowing for seamless communication and the understanding of complex, nuanced ideas. This includes not only the literal understanding of language but also the ability to infer intent, recognize context, and navigate subtleties such as sarcasm, ambiguity, and culturally specific references.
- **Importance**: In the world of business, effective communication is key. The ability to understand and generate natural language allows AGI to interact seamlessly with users, comprehend complex queries, produce understandable outputs, and contribute effectively to discussions, making it an invaluable tool in a variety of business functions.
- **Fulfillment**: GPT-4 displays this AGI capability, demonstrating

a sophisticated understanding of and ability to generate natural language. This enables it to comprehend complex concepts, engage in meaningful interactions, and produce human-like responses, enhancing its versatility across various applications.

- **Examples**: GPT-4 can understand and generate responses to complex queries in a wide range of languages, effectively simulating a human conversation. For instance, it can help draft business communications, provide detailed responses to customer queries, analyze, and summarize lengthy reports, or participate in brainstorming sessions by generating creative ideas. It can also produce coherent long-form text, such as drafting articles or blog posts.
- **Limitation**: Despite its proficiency, GPT-4's understanding of language can occasionally falter when confronted with ambiguous, colloquial, or culturally specific language. It may also struggle with understanding and generating language in contexts that require a deep understanding of the world beyond its training data. Furthermore, while it can simulate a conversation, it doesn't truly understand language in the way humans do, and its responses are generated based on patterns recognized in its training data rather than true comprehension.

- **Perception and Understanding**

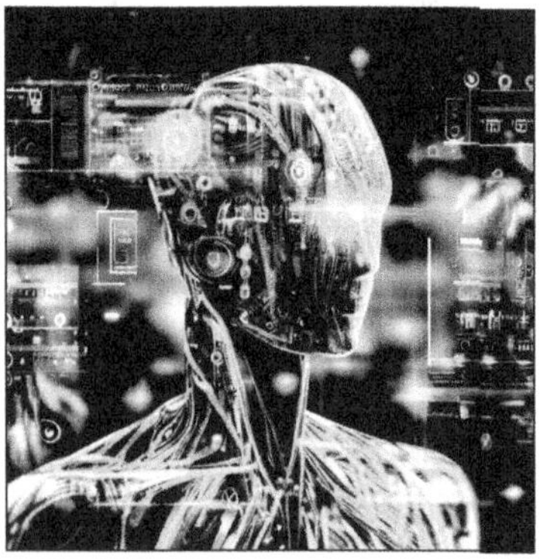

***Figure 1.8**: Perception and Understanding*

- **Definition**: AGI has the capacity to process and interpret sensory information from the environment, such as visual, auditory, and tactile data. It would understand and interpret different types of data, ranging from unstructured text to structured databases and images, thereby making sense of the world in a manner similar to humans.
- **Importance**: In a business context, perception and understanding capabilities allow AGI to parse through vast amounts of data, filter out the noise, identify patterns, and draw insights. This is critical for tasks such as analyzing customer feedback, interpreting market

trends, detecting anomalies in data, or making informed decisions based on complex datasets.

- **Fulfillment**: Displaying an AGI capability, GPT-4 can perceive and understand text-, code-, image-, and audio-based data. With the help of plugins[12], its capabilities are further extended to other modalities such as video and web content.
- **Examples**: GPT-4 can interpret and generate code snippets, thus aiding in software development. It can comprehend complex scientific papers, thereby assisting in research tasks. It can understand abstract concepts described in the text, which makes it useful in strategy development and decision-making. Furthermore GPT-4 can extract information from images to generate product descriptions, answer customer questions or find matching items. For audio-based tasks, GPT-4 can process and transcribe recorded business meetings, efficiently summarizing the key points and action items.
- **Limitation**: While GPT-4 is proficient in processing text, code, image, and audio inputs, its capabilities are not inherently designed for handling video and tactile data. This means that, without additional plugins or specialized tools, GPT-4 faces challenges in comprehending and analyzing video sequences, body language, or physical interactions. Additionally, it may struggle with unusual or conflicting perceptions, which it has likely not seen in its training data.

- **Intuitive Understanding of Emotions**

Figure 1.9: *Intuitive Understanding of Emotions*

- **Definition**: AGI is capable of recognizing and responding to human emotions, allowing for improved human-machine interactions and empathy. This involves interpreting textual and contextual

[12]ChatGPT-4 plugins for multimodal content understanding will be discussed in the next subchapter.

cues to identify and comprehend underlying emotions in various interpersonal situations.

- **Importance**: Intuitive understanding of emotions is a critical aspect of successful communication and relationship-building in any business setting. It enables effective customer interactions, facilitates team dynamics, and promotes a positive working environment.
- **Fulfillment**: GPT-4 demonstrates this AGI capability by recognizing basic emotions from textual cues, showing an ability to interpret and respond appropriately to the sentiment in user inputs. It uses this ability to tailor its responses, mimicking empathy in human-like interactions.
- **Examples**: GPT-4 can detect emotions in user messages, adjusting its responses based on the perceived sentiment. For instance, it can respond empathetically to messages indicating distress or frustration, offering comforting or supportive responses. It can also adapt its communication style based on the user's mood, such as adopting a more casual tone in response to a friendly message or a formal tone for professional contexts. Additionally, GPT-4 could theoretically aid in customer service scenarios, recognizing dissatisfaction in customer feedback and suggesting remedial actions to enhance customer experience.
- **Limitation**: While GPT-4 can recognize and respond to emotions based on textual cues, its understanding is not as nuanced or accurate as a human's. It lacks the emotional intelligence to reason about emotions in a deeply human way. It may also struggle with complex emotional states or situations that require high emotional intelligence, as it does not truly experience emotions itself.

- **Autonomous Goal Setting and Planning**

***Figure 1.10**: Autonomous Goal Setting and Planning*

- **Definition**: AGI is able to set its own goals and create plans to achieve them, demonstrating self-motivation and self-direction. This ability to autonomously strategize and enact purposeful plans is an integral component of self-regulation.

- **Importance**: Autonomous goal setting and planning enable a system to work independently, foreseeing potential challenges and strategizing solutions. This capability can transform productivity by reducing human intervention and accelerating decision-making processes, especially in tasks such as project management, strategic planning, and achieving complex, long-term objectives.
- **Fulfillment**: While GPT-4 does not fully exhibit this AGI capability, it has made strides in goal-directed planning, being capable of generating action plans based on user-provided goals and intermediate states of plan execution.
- In the business world, GPT-4 can be a valuable ally for goal-driven tasks. For instance, if a company aims to expand its market share, GPT-4 can draft a plan involving competitor analysis, identification of untapped markets, and strategies for product differentiation. Similarly, when presented with the objective of streamlining internal processes, GPT-4 can propose a task sequence that includes automating repetitive tasks, optimizing workflows, and suggesting tools for enhanced team collaboration. Additionally, with a goal to improve customer satisfaction, GPT-4 can devise a plan involving analyzing customer feedback, suggesting improvements to service protocols, and developing new customer engagement strategies.
- **Limitation**: GPT-4's capabilities are bound by its programming and lack of self-motivation and self-direction, which can limit its autonomous functioning. Although it can contribute significantly to achieving user-defined goals, GPT-4 cannot (and should not) independently formulate its own goals or modify them in response to changing circumstances.

- **Collaboration and Cooperation**

***Figure 1.11**: Collaboration and Cooperation*

- **Definition**: AGI possesses the ability to work together with humans and other AGI systems, enabling collaborative problem-solving and teamwork. This ability, particularly in an enterprise setting, involves understanding, interpreting, and predicting social cues, behaviors, and interactions within a group or community – essential for managing teams, handling customer interactions, or navigating any situation involving interpersonal relationships.
- **Importance**: Effective collaboration and cooperation, underpinned by adept social understanding, are critical for a well-functioning business environment.
- **Fulfillment**: GPT-4 displays this AGI capability by providing assistance and generating responses in single-user settings. It also shows high proficiency in social comprehension, allowing it to engage with human-like understanding and responses in a range of social and business contexts.
- **Examples**: GPT-4 can assist users in brainstorming sessions, contribute to solving puzzles, or provide constructive feedback on written content. Additionally, it can advise a manager on how to handle a conflict within a team based on the personalities and dynamics involved, predict customer responses to a new marketing campaign based on social and cultural trends, and provide guidance on improving company culture based on an analysis of employee feedback.
- **Limitation**: GPT-4's understanding of multi-user settings and human dynamics is limited, reducing its effectiveness in complex collaborative situations. Despite its proficiency in social comprehension, it might not fully capture the subtleties of human interactions, which can be nuanced and highly context-dependent.

- **Ethics and Moral Reasoning**

***Figure 1.12**: Ethics and Moral Reasoning*

- **Definition**: AGI is ideally designed to incorporate ethical principles and moral reasoning, allowing it to make decisions and take actions in line with human values and societal norms. In a business context, this involves understanding and applying ethical principles when making decisions, which is crucial for maintaining organizational integrity, corporate social responsibility, and public trust.
- **Importance**: Ethical decision-making underpins all aspects of corporate conduct and directly influences public perception of a company. It is a vital part of maintaining a *social license to operate.*
- **Fulfillment**: GPT-4 displays this AGI capability with the ability to conduct basic moral reasoning based on the scenarios encountered in its training data. While GPT-4 understands ethical principles, its application of these principles is limited by its programming and the ethical frameworks provided to it.
- **Examples**: GPT-4 can identify harmful or offensive content, provide balanced views on sensitive topics, or even suggest ethically acceptable alternatives in a given situation. In a business context, it can assess the potential ethical implications of a business decision, such as implementing a new data collection policy. It can help draft a corporate social responsibility statement aligned with a company's values and commitments. GPT-4 can also evaluate a company's operations for potential ethical issues, like conflicts of interest or breaches of trust.
- **Limitation**: GPT-4's understanding and application of complex ethical dilemmas can be limited, and it might lack a deep understanding of human values and emotions. Its ethical guidance is also inherently influenced by its training data and programmed frameworks, which may not capture the full complexity and nuance of human ethics.

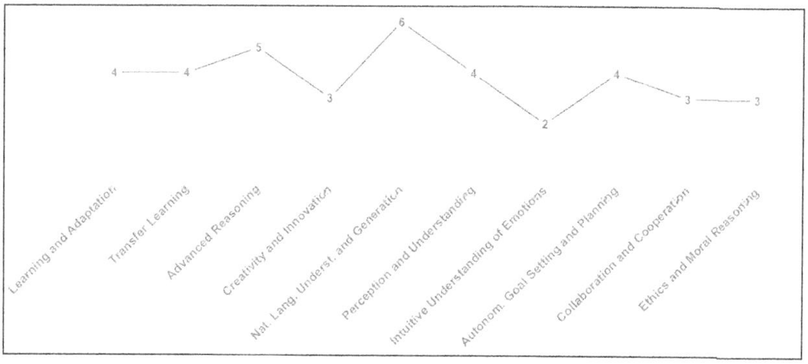

Figure 1.13: *AGI-Capability Assessment of GPT-4*

In summary, GPT-4 shows remarkable proficiency in Natural Language Understanding and Generation (6/6) and Advanced Reasoning (5/6). It also performs commendably in Learning & Adaptation, Transfer Learning, Perception and Understanding and Autonomous Goal Setting and Planning (4/6). GPT-4's capabilities in Creativity and Innovation, Collaboration and Cooperation, and Ethics and Moral Reasoning are satisfactory (3/6), while its performance in Intuitive Understanding of Emotions is too rudimentary (2/6). For a visual representation of these scores, please refer to *Figure* 1.13.

ChatGPT-4 Plugins

In March 2023, alongside its release, a suite of API-based integration plugins was introduced by OpenAI to amplify the capabilities of ChatGPT-4, the chatbot version of GPT-4. Over the subsequent months, OpenAI and external providers continued to roll out additional plugins, further enhancing the model's versatility.

OpenAI provides an online registration process for new ChatGPT-4 plugins, ensuring quality and functionality. These plugins are currently free of charge and become part of the ChatGPT-4 system, eliminating the need for separate license agreements. Like any software tool, they should be evaluated for functionality, usability, and potential benefits in a specific enterprise context.

The subsequent sections will delve into key plugin categories that hold particular significance for businesses, ranging from end-user programming and content understanding to content creation and software development. While there is a large number of plugins tailored for individual consumers – addressing areas such as shopping, career development, travel, and entertainment – the focus here is on those that elevate business efficiency, facilitate data-driven decision-making, and champion intelligent automation in a corporate environment.

Following is a curated list of ChatGPT-4 plugin categories that are especially advantageous for enterprises:

- **End-User Programming**: These plugins are designed to facilitate exploratory data analysis, visualization, database queries, website creation, machine learning, and ad-hoc problem-solving for end users, even if they lack a computing background:
  - **Basic Exploratory Data Analysis**
    - **Spreadsheet-based Data Analysis**
      - **Spreadsheet Pal and Spreadsheets AI**: Engage with spreadsheets, allowing users to command data analysis, filtering, and visualization. Streamlines the process of interacting with spreadsheet data and offers an enhanced experience.

    - **Datasheet Chat and Chat with Excel**: Provides an interactive platform to converse with spreadsheets. Designed for those who want a more intuitive way to engage with their datasheets.
  - **Data Visualizations**
    - **daigr.am**: Enables users to craft visual representations of data directly within a chat interface. Suitable for those looking to analyze, track, or present data in a visually compelling format.
    - **Visualize Your Data**: Converts raw data into clear visuals and charts on the fly. Tailored for users who need a quick and straightforward way to represent their data visually.
    - **Graph Constructor**: Assists in generating spider and bar graphs from provided datasets. Designed for users who want specific types of visual data representations rapidly.
- **OpenAI's Advanced Data Analysis**: This tool, previously called the Code Interpreter, is suitable for both beginners and more experienced users and can turn high-level descriptions into functional code. Here's a closer look at its features:
  - **Complex Exploratory Data Analysis**
    - **Question Answering**: Enables users to get answers to questions about a given dataset.
    - **Visualization**: Crafts visual representations of query results, making complex information more digestible.
    - **Statistical operations**: Equipped with a diverse array of tools to perform flexible statistical analyses.
    - **Simple text analytics**: Facilitates text processing and evaluation.
  - **Machine Learning**
    - **Model creation and execution**: Streamlines the processes of building and running simple machine learning models.
    - **Visualization**: Translates the outcomes of machine learning models into visual formats.
  - **Ad-hoc Problem Solving**: The plugin can also be used to solve one-time problems algorithmically, similar to the NoCode[13] approach, while avoiding a software development life cycle. Examples are:

---

[13]NoCode refers to the creation of digital products, like websites, apps, or automated workflows, without having to write traditional computer code.

  - **Data-mapping**: It can transform a file in any input format to a requested output format based on a verbal description of the mapping logic.
  - **Supply-chain optimization**: Given a description of the constraints (e.g., limited stocks or resources) and the optimization goal (e.g., minimize costs or delivery time), it systematically creates solution candidates and checks filter conditions for each. Then, it ranks the candidates by their achievement of the goal.
  - Cost calculation: Provided with the calculation logic in natural language and the raw data as input files, it can perform an ad-hoc computation of the resulting costs in an early sale or purchasing scenario.
  - Scenario-based planning: For a given description of a planning scenario (for example, a project or series of workshops) along with known constraints, it can compute an indicative schedule in the chat dialogue or as an output file.

Despite its comprehensive functionality, OpenAI's Advanced Data Analysis does have limitations. These include a limited number of Python libraries, constrained computational resources, absence of persistent storage, and an inability to handle graphical user interfaces and real-time interactions.

- **Other Advanced Analytics Plugins**
  - **Noteable**: Designed for both professional developers and data science newcomers, Noteable offers functionalities akin to OpenAI Advanced Data Analysis. It streamlines data exploration, visualization, and transformation, fostering collaborative efforts among teams. With its deep learning capabilities and seamless internet integration, users can craft advanced models and tap into online resources.
  - **AI Data Analyst**: AI Data Analyst provides a user-friendly interface to delve into data without coding or complex queries. It manages data cleaning tasks, including handling missing values and duplicates, and supports transformations like normalization. Additionally, it offers statistical analysis, diverse visualization options, and predictive modeling for both regression and classification.
  - **Data Interpreter**: Data Interpreter facilitates data analysis using a secure Python code interpreter. Users can upload datasets, ask questions in plain English, or directly input Python code for intricate analyses. The platform supports a broad spectrum of

data tasks, from querying databases to visualizing results, and allows for exporting insights for further utilization or reporting.

- **Database Queries**
  - **AI2sql**: Converts user-friendly language into database commands. Designed for those who need to access databases but are unfamiliar with technical query languages.
  - **AskYourDatabase**: Transforms user questions into database queries and provides results in plain language. Aims to make databases more accessible to everyday users.
  - **Chat With Your Data**: Integrates knowledge graphs with a conversational interface, allowing users to interact with their data seamlessly. Enables users to converse with their data in natural language.
- **Simple Website Building**
  - **ABC Website Maker**: Takes user chat prompts and generates corresponding website code. Streamlines the process of turning ideas into web applications.
  - **A A A Website Maker**: Assists in creating web applications and custom websites. Tailored for users seeking a simple web development tool.
  - **WebDev**: Provides an environment to build, preview, and test websites directly from chat interactions. Suitable for those who want to quickly prototype websites.
  - **B12 AI Websites**: Uses natural language descriptions to craft websites. Designed for users who want a website without getting involved in the technicalities of web design.
- **General Application Development**
  - **Back4App**: Facilitates the creation, deployment, and scaling of applications using natural language. Designed for users who want to manage apps and associated resources without diving deep into technical details.

- **Content Understanding**: This category comprises plugins designed to enhance the user experience in managing and interacting with various content types, from text-based documents to images and video:
  - **Document Interaction and Question Answering**
    - **Document AI and Talk with Docs**: Engage with various document formats, including PDFs, text files, and PowerPoint presentations, to answer questions and provide insights. Designed for users who need quick answers from their documents.

   - **AI PDF and AskYourPDF (Pro)**: Enhance document navigation, content accessibility, and interactive engagement with PDF content. These tools are tailored for efficient information extraction, especially in business documents, and provide accurate fact-checking by referencing page numbers.
   - **ChatWithPDF and MixerBox ChatPDF**: Facilitate real-time interaction with PDFs, offering robust search functionality and streamlined link sharing. These plugins are suitable for those who require efficient information extraction and collaboration with PDF books and other documents.
   - **Ai Drive**: Provides an organized personal drive where users can chat with their PDF files, get summaries, and have questions answered. A proper tool for those who want to keep their PDF interactions organized and focused.
- **Website Understanding**
   - **ChatWithWebsite**: Engage with websites to answer questions using the capabilities of magicform.ai. Ideal for users who need insights directly from web content.
   - **Webpage Summarizer**: Input a website link and receive a concise summary. Designed for those who want quick overviews of web content without extensive reading.
- **Image Understanding**
   - **ChatOCR**: Converts printed or handwritten documents into digital text using OCR technology. Adequate for users who want to digitize and easily access information from physical documents.
   - **SceneXplain**: Analyzes visual content to provide comprehensive interpretations of images. Useful for users seeking insights into artistic styles, emotions, settings, and historical contexts of images.
   - **Pixellow**: Delivers insights from images and generates detailed captions and descriptions. Designed for those who want a deeper understanding of visual content.
- **Video Understanding**
   - **Video Insights and AI Video Summarizer**: Analyzes YouTube videos to provide summaries and answer questions about the content. Suitable for users who want a quick overview or have specific queries about a video.
   - **MixerBox ChatVideo, Video Summary, and YT Summarizer**: Offers concise summaries of YouTube videos. Designed for users

looking for the main highlights or key points of a video.

   - **Video Captions**: Transcribes YouTube videos into text, enabling users to ask questions, create chapters, and get summarized content. Useful for those who prefer reading or need a written record of a video.
   - **vidIQ - Discover and YouTube Summaries**: Provides insights and summaries for YouTube videos. Aimed at users who want to discover and understand video content quickly.
- **Heterogeneous Content**
   - **SummarizeAnything.ai**: Converts extensive content from various sources into concise summaries. Suitable for quick insights from YouTube, web pages, and PDFs.
   - **OCR and Media Processing in OpenAI's Advanced Data Analysis:** Handles optical character recognition (OCR) tasks, audio processing, and other media-centric operations. Useful for simple text extraction from images and basic media handling.
   - **Link Reader**: Interprets content from diverse formats like webpages, YouTube, PDFs, PPTs, and Word documents. Incorporates OCR for text extraction from images and also supports web navigation.

- **Information Retrieval and Understanding**: This suite of plugins is tailored to streamline the retrieval and understanding of information from diverse sources. They encompass web search, website scraping, question answering, and knowledge management, ensuring users can efficiently find, digest, and utilize content:
   - **Web Search**
      - **OpenAI Browse with Bing**: Uses Bing AI to browse the internet, fetch relevant up-to-date information, and cite sources. It was deactivated for a couple of months and now allows sites to control how they interact with ChatGPT.
      - **Web Requests**: Offers direct access to platforms like Google and Wikipedia within the chat interface. Fetches and presents relevant information based on user queries.
      - **WebPilot**: Provides comprehensive web assistance, from searching and extracting information to translating and simplifying content. It also offers navigation tools for specific web interactions and content creation from URLs.
      - **KeyMate.AI Search**: Uses AI-driven web crawling for enhanced search results. Provides a user-friendly chat interface and customization options.

  - **BrowserOp**: Facilitates multi-web-page browsing in a single query, allowing users to specify their information needs, whether from a particular website or a broader topic.
  - **MixerBox WebSearchG**: Utilizes a customized search engine powered by Google Search API to provide comprehensive internet searches, detailed web-page summaries, and direct answers to specific questions about web content.
  - **BrowserPilot**: Delivers real-time search results across multiple URLs.
  - **TotalQuery Search**: Taps into more than 70 search engines for comprehensive web discovery.
  - **MindfulDataAI**: Facilitates recent searches using Google. Designed to provide users with up-to-date information on current topics.
- **Website scraping**
  - **Aaron Browser**: Scrapes data from multiple websites using real-time Google search results. Designed for comprehensive internet crawling, content aggregation, monitoring, and extraction.
  - **Scrapee and Scraper**: Extracts content from any website by simply providing a website link. Streamlines the process of web content retrieval for efficient information gathering.
- **Web Question Answering**
  - **Wikipedia**: Provides answers on general knowledge, current events, and breaking news. Fetches up-to-date information directly from Wikipedia for reliable insights.
  - **Wolfram ChatGPT**: Offers curated knowledge, real-time data, and visualizations spanning various domains. Supports computations, mathematical problem-solving, and delivers data visualizations from scientific to stock market information.
- **Knowledge Management**
  - **Custom Knowledge**: Allows users to search through internal company documents, Google Docs, and Confluence Pages. Delivers personalized answers by accessing a range of linked documents.
  - **FileChat**: Specializes in file management, in-depth analysis, and rapid information retrieval. Acts as a personal AI assistant, answering queries using user-specific data.

        - **AskYourKG**: Helps users organize and interact with their knowledge (graph[14]). Enables chat-based interaction with documents uploaded to specific websites, promoting interactive document understanding.

- **Content Creation**: This collection of plugins offers users straightforward solutions for generating various content types, from diagrams to videos. These tools cover a range of content needs:
    - **Diagram Creation**
        - **Show Me**: Transform raw data and concepts into visualizations, from relationship diagrams to timelines. Empower users to understand complex information, visualize processes, and edit diagrams online, catering to diverse visualization needs.
        - **Whimsical, MixerBox, and Scrive Diagrams**: Specialize in crafting and showcasing various diagrams, including flowcharts and mind maps. These tools enhance brainstorming sessions and process detailing, adapting to diverse visualization needs.
        - **Diagrams, Eraser, and Draw**: Offer a range of functionalities from integrating with visualization platforms to generating diagrams from both code and natural language. They cater to a broad audience, from coders to visual enthusiasts.
        - **WizeCharts**: Focuses on delivering in-depth data visualization through customizable charts, enabling users to create, edit, and share insights.
    - **Document Creation**
        - **Doc Maker and Doc Maker A+**: Specialize in rapid document generation, from resumes and cover letters to proposals. These tools support a variety of formats including PDF, DOCX, XLSX, CSV, and HTML, with an emphasis on producing higher-quality documents with the A+ variant.
        - **Doc Editor**: Focuses on quick document creation with robust editing capabilities, streamlining the process of crafting and refining documents.
        - **WriteEasy and AISEO Article Writer**: Cater to content creation needs by generating articles based on provided topics, links, or data. While WriteEasy offers general article creation, AISEO

[14]A knowledge graph (KG) is a structured representation of interconnected information, where nodes represent entities and edges depict their relationships. It captures semantic meaning, enabling enhanced understanding and navigation of complex datasets for both humans and machines.

Article Writer emphasizes producing search engine result page-based, natural language processing-friendly content swiftly.

- **Presentation Creation**
  - **Smart Slides and Present it**: ShowME: Specialize in swift PowerPoint presentation generation. By simply inputting the requirements, these tools craft comprehensive and downloadable PPTs.
  - **MagicSlides.app**: Transforms ideas into presentations, streamlining the process from conception to visualization.
  - **Canva**: A versatile design tool that allows users to create a wide range of visuals effortlessly, from presentations and logos to social media posts and more.
- **Image Generation**
  - **MixerBox ImageGen**: Uses the DALL·E 2 technology to generate visuals from textual descriptions, merging natural language understanding with computer vision. With features like customizable formats, text overlays, and unique prompt suggestions, it is a suitable tool for crafting images for diverse projects, from blogs to websites.
  - **Argil AI**: Simplifies the image generation process, eliminating the need for intricate prompting. It's designed for users seeking quick visual creation.
  - **Michelangelo**: Utilizes DALL-E 2 to produce images inspired by various art styles. It is designed for those aiming to infuse artistic flair into their visuals.
  - **Placid.app**: Acts as a design assistant, transforming templates into marketing visuals. It's tailored for users looking to elevate their marketing materials with advanced graphics.
- **Story Creation**
  - **Stories**: Enables users to craft visually rich stories complemented by text-generated imagery. With features like font customization, animations, and direct social media sharing, it is tailored to boost discoverability on search engines, broadening the reach of stories to a global audience.
- **Video Generation**
  - **Visla**: Employs AI to convert topics provided by users into engaging short videos using accessible stock footage. By analyzing input text for key themes, it selects appropriate video clips, images, and

audio. Beyond content creation, Visla optimizes search engine visibility with meta tags, descriptions, and keyword-rich captions.

  - **CapCut**: Transforms video concepts into reality by allowing AI to draft a script, source fitting footage, and combine elements into a refined video. It is designed for users seeking an intuitive video creation experience.

- **Process Automation**: These plugins offer users AI-driven solutions to simplify and automate various tasks and interactions. From managing intricate tasks with AI agents to integrating with thousands of apps, they aim to enhance efficiency and productivity:
  - **AI Agents**: Simulates intelligent agents within ChatGPT that, upon receiving a goal prompt, devise and execute strategic plans to increase productivity.
  - **Zapier**: Interacts with over 5,000 apps directly within the ChatGPT interface. By automating tasks across these platforms, it simplifies operations and the management of multiple platforms.
  - **FakeAGI**: Automates objectives using AI agents that tackle tasks and record outcomes in a Google spreadsheet. It is designed for users aiming for task management support and documentation.
- **Software Development**: These plugins are tailored for software development and program-based data analysis. From exploring GitHub repositories and running code in diverse languages to simplifying data processes, these tools aim to enhance the coding experience and facilitate deeper understanding and collaboration:
  - **AskTheCode and ChatWithCode**: Allow users to delve into GitHub repositories, either by providing a specific URL to inquire about code aspects or by searching based on a query. These tools bridge the gap between code exploration and understanding directly within the chat interface.
  - **CoderPad and CodeRunner**: Offer a coding environment where users can run code in over thirty programming languages with automatic setup, compile, save, and even create visualizations like charts and graphs. They cater to both coding and data visualization needs.
  - **Noteable**: Simplifies data exploration, visualization, cleansing, and transformation, enhancing team collaboration. With deep learning capabilities and access to online libraries, it aids users in building advanced models and harnessing code updates effectively.

Through the integration of plugins, ChatGPT-4 transcends its foundational role as a text/code-based language model, emerging as a robust Generative AI tool adept at handling additional key modalities like web content, images, and video. We will cover this important aspect in more detail in the last subchapter on native multi-modality. Other key capabilities added by plugins are End User Programming, Information Retrieval, and Process Automation.

Combining Interactions with Actions: Access to External Tools in GPT Models

OpenAI's GPT models, notably GPT-3.5-Turbo and GPT-4, underwent a major upgrade in June 2023, allowing them to interact with external tools via the generation of API function calls. Before delving deeper, it's essential to draw a clear distinction between plugins and this new feature. The previous subchapter extensively discussed plugins, which are specific enhancements that need to be officially registered with OpenAI. Once registered, these plugins become extensions of ChatGPT-4, available to the ChatGPT user community.

In contrast, the integration of external tools offers a more flexible mechanism to enable the cooperation of GPT models with any enterprise application. Examples are ERP (Enterprise Resource Planning), CRM (Customer Relationship Management), and SCM (Supply chain Management) systems. Expanding their reach further, GPT models can also interface with enterprise-specific search engines, intranet sites, databases, and specialized ML-models ensuring a seamless blend with organizational IT-ecosystems.

Developers can instruct GPT models like gpt-4-0613 and gpt-3.5-turbo-0613 to generate specific function calls instead of natural language when certain conditions are met. These models are skilled to check these conditions on each user input and, if met, create the respective function calls that match the expected format. The main program simply needs to execute the function call and handle its results, which could involve another prompt to a GPT model to provide a summary in natural language, which then could be displayed to the user.

In essence, this enhancement transforms GPT models into dynamic integrators of enterprise applications, broadening the horizons of AI beyond mere language processing.

Integration into Enterprise Software

Standardized Enterprise Software plays a pivotal role in driving efficiency and collaboration, particularly within large corporations. These comprehensive software packages are extensively utilized due to their broad functionality, robustness, scalability, and security.

With the continued advancement of Generative Artificial Intelligence, opportunities have emerged for these software systems to further increase their capabilities and value. Companies such as Microsoft, ServiceNow, SAP, and Atlassian, who develop these software products, are exploring ways to integrate GPT models into their offerings. Here, we describe these efforts and how they contribute to the transformation of enterprise software solutions.

The collaboration of Microsoft and OpenAI, which has been strategically nurtured since 2019, is the primary example of how GPT-4 capabilities can be leveraged by an existing productivity software suite, which is commonly used by an enterprise. The year 2022 marked the beginning of the incorporation of OpenAI's GPT models into Microsoft's enterprise products, a process that gained significant momentum in 2023. Here are the current key outcomes of this partnership:

- **First and foremost, Microsoft offers OpenAI products inside its Azure cloud offering:**
  - **Microsoft Azure ChatGPT** provides user privacy through isolation from OpenAI's operations and offers plugin support for the integration with other Azure services and enterprise-specific data sources.
  - The **Azure OpenAI Service** integrates OpenAI's pre-trained AI models and extends existing Azure AI capabilities in natural language processing & computer vision. The service offers features like the Chat Playground with GPT-3.5-Turbo and GPT-4 support, Legacy Playground with GPT-3, GPT-3.5, and Codex models, and a DALL-E Playground. Additionally, there's a "Bring Your Own Data" area for grounding GPT models with enterprise data. The platform also provides deployment management tools and content filter settings.
- **Then Microsoft's Bing Chat Enterprise provides a similar user experience as ChatGPT-4 with the Bing Browser plugin, while ensuring full organizational data protection and simultaneous access to DALLE-E. Typical use cases are:**
  - Content Creation and Modification:
    - Generate diverse business content from user prompts, such as emails, reports, or process descriptions.
    - Adjust the tone or style of text, incorporating optimism, professionalism, or various writing formats.
    - Improve existing writing by adding elements like brevity, formality, and creativity.
  - Image Generation and Customization:
    - Create and modify images directly from user prompts.

        - Explore various creation themes, including security, environmental consciousness, and digital outlook.
        - Modify generated images by altering color schemes, styles, or background details.
    - Intuitive Interaction and Personalized Responses:
        - Search and interact using natural, conversational language, accommodating both short and detailed inputs.
        - Ask complex questions and receive relevant answers, with the system maintaining context for follow-up queries.
        - Customize the format of Bing's responses using prompts, such as requesting bullet points, tables, or simplified language.
    - Comparisons, Summaries, and Real-Time Information:
        - Conduct detailed comparisons and receive concise summaries of enterprises, technologies, markets, etc.
        - Access near-real-time results for recent business events or breaking financial news.
        - View and revisit previously created content and images.
- **Other Microsoft products are AI-enhanced via the Copilot initiative. Here is an overview:**
    - Microsoft **365's Copilot** integrates fully into all office apps with GPT-based features for automatic text creation in Word, exploratory data analysis in Excel, and presentation automation in PowerPoint. Copilot improves communication efficiency in Outlook and Teams by managing emails, summarizing threads, formulating responses, and aiding in meeting organization.
    - **Copilot Studio,** a low-code platform integrated with Microsoft 365, now overcomes the limitations of its 365 copilot by offering extensive customization through plugins. It enables access to enterprise data, reuse of pre-engineered prompts, and automation of actions outside the copilot. Based on Microsoft's Virtual Power Agents, Copilot Studio also facilitates the implementation of custom copilots, further expanding its functionality.
    - **Windows** also integrates **Copilot**, enabling task simplification across various apps, while AI enhancements in the Paint and Photos apps introduce innovative features and efficient media management. The Snipping Tool's diverse content capture and Clipchamp's automated video creation capabilities offer enriched user interaction and advanced content creation.
    - **Copilot in Viva Engage** offers conversation starters based on trending topics and enhances the answers experience by refining questions

and responses.

- Integrated into **Power BI, Copilot** supports data interaction through exploratory and ad-hoc analysis, offering visualizations, collaborative reporting, and data storytelling.
- **Copilot in Power Automate** enables automation creation through natural language. It understands user intent to create and modify flows, configure connections and parameters, and answer product or flow-related questions.
- **Copilots in Power Apps** guide the creation of an app or bot. This process encompasses creating and importing data tables, generating app screens and user event handlers, summarizing user input, answering questions, and managing the publishing of the app or bot.'
- **Copilot in Microsoft Teams Phone** integrates with the Teams Phone system, using GPT models to automatically summarize phone conversations, highlighting key details and suggesting follow-up actions.
- **Copilot in Teams Chat** enhances communication in Teams by leveraging GPT to provide quick summaries of chat threads, allowing users to extract key decisions and insights from their discussions.
- **Microsoft Sales Copilot** is designed for sellers, streamlining CRM tasks with GPT technology, identifying top sales opportunities, and reducing manual work, enabling more effective sales strategies.

Moving beyond Microsoft, other prominent players in the enterprise software market have started to harness the power of AI through their collaborations with OpenAI. As representative examples, ServiceNow, SAP, and Atlassian have made their first steps in embedding AI capabilities into their platforms:

- **ServiceNow** has integrated OpenAI's Generative AI Controller and Now Assist for Search into its platform through Microsoft's Azure OpenAI Service. These additions enhance workflow automation and user experiences, paving the way for future improvements in productivity and innovation including chat response generation and incident prioritization.
- In collaboration with Microsoft, **SAP** is working to embed Microsoft's AI functionalities into its products, initially concentrating on merging SAP SuccessFactors solutions with several Microsoft services including Azure OpenAI. This partnership has already triggered innovative PoCs within the SAP community like automated customer email responses and improved ticket management.
- **Atlassian** introduced Atlassian Intelligence, a **virtual teammate** utilizing OpenAI's large language models alongside its AI models. This tool offers features like AI-powered summaries and a ChatGPT-like chatbot, aiming to enhance understanding of work patterns and facilitate team collaboration.

In conclusion, the integration of OpenAI's GPT models into enterprise software is a testament to the transformative potential of AI. This move suggests that, as more corporations adopt these enhanced solutions, we can expect impactful shifts in the ways they use AI in their operations.

ChatGPT Enterprise

Historically, corporations have been wary of embracing new cloud-based technologies, especially those that handle vast amounts of data like ChatGPT, primarily due to concerns about data privacy, security, and integration with their existing infrastructure. In August 2023 OpenAI introduced ChatGPT Enterprise, designed to address these challenges:

- **Strengthened Security & Privacy**
  - **Data Control**: Companies maintain complete authority over their data. Enterprise data is not used for model training.
  - **Robust Encryption**: Utilizing industry-leading encryption techniques, data in transit is safeguarded using TLS 1.2+, a security protocol ensuring secure data transfer. For data at rest, AES-256 encryption is applied, a symmetric encryption standard regarded for its high security.
  - **Adherence to Standards**: ChatGPT Enterprise is compliant with SOC 2 Type 1 – a standard assessing the policies, procedures, and controls of service providers. Additionally, preparations are underway for Type 2 compliance, which involves more rigorous and periodic auditing.
  - **Domain Verification**: An added layer of security is provided to verify and authenticate the enterprise's domain, preventing unauthorized usage.
- **Facilitating Integration & Collaboration**
  - **Data Synergy**: ChatGPT Enterprise announced it would offer features enabling smooth interactions with typical corporate applications.
  - **Shared Workflows**: Teams are empowered to create and distribute workflows via shared chat templates.
  - **API Access**: Companies are provided with API credits to craft enterprise-specific solutions, allowing for tailored AI-powered operations.
  - **Single Sign-On (SSO)**: This feature simplifies user access and offers a touch of added security.
- **Advanced Data Analysis Solution (see also the details in the *ChatGPT-4 plugins* subchapter)**
  - **Core Functionalities**: It supports a broad range of tasks including

exploratory data analysis, visualization, statistical operations, and text analytics.

- **Ad-hoc Problem Solving**: The tool is also adept at handling specific algorithmic challenges, like data mapping, cost calculations, and scenario-based planning.

- **Improved Performance & Deployment**
  - **Increased Efficiency with GPT-4**: The Enterprise version harnesses a GPT-4 model that operates at double the speed without limitations in the number of interactions.
  - **Extended Interactions**: Thanks to a 32k token context window, ChatGPT Enterprise can handle extended dialogues and accommodate larger documents for in-depth discussions.
- **Deployment Tools**
  - **Admin Console**: A dedicated console for seamless bulk member management.
  - **Analytics Dashboard**: A tool for real-time usage insights, helping companies understand how the system is being leveraged.
- **Looking Forward**
  - **Self-service**: Plans are in motion for a ChatGPT Business model, aiming to cater to smaller teams.
  - **Power Tools**: Future iterations promise more robust Advanced Data Analysis tools and specialized browsing features optimized for work settings.
  - **Role-specific Solutions**: The roadmap includes tools specifically crafted for roles such as data analysts, marketers, and customer support personnel, ensuring a more bespoke experience.

With the *ChatGPT Enterprise* offering, OpenAI has started to align its AI capabilities with corporate demands, envisaging a balance of security, flexibility, and performance.

ChatGPT Native Multi-modality

ChatGPT introduced native multi-modal capabilities in October 2023, including voice and image interactions, enabling users to engage in conversations and discuss visuals without the need for plugins.

Users can have voice conversations, with the system employing an advanced text-to-speech model and Whisper, OpenAI's speech recognition system, to facilitate interactive dialogues. The voice feature offers five different voice options, developed in collaboration with professional voice actors, and is available on iOS and Android platforms.

Furthermore, ChatGPT can interpret and analyze images, which users can upload directly through the platform. This feature, powered by a new multimodal GPT-4 model, GPT-4V (Vision), allows for a wide range of applications, including visual diagnostics, question answering, code generation, and analytics. It is possible to mix multiple text elements, images and images with markers in a single user input to enable comparisons or analogies.

In addition to these, OpenAI's image generator, DALL·E 3, is now integrated natively with ChatGPT, allowing users to generate tailored, detailed prompts that bring ideas to life through images. The DALL·E 3 feature is available to ChatGPT Plus and Enterprise customers, with a focus on safety and prevention of harmful content generation.

OpenAI deployed these new capabilities while adhering to their standards for safety and responsible usage. OpenAI also took measures to respect individuals' privacy and limit ChatGPT's ability to analyze and make direct statements about people. Additionally, OpenAI enabled creators to opt their images out from the training of future models.

Building on the exploration of ChatGPT's new multi-modality features and considering the advancements discussed in the subchapter on plugins, the following table provides an overview of the resulting Generative AI capabilities of ChatGPT. It indicates both the native functions and those enhanced by plugins across various modalities, showcasing the model's adaptability and comprehensive functionality in tasks ranging from text and code comprehension to advanced image and voice interactions.

Modality	**Understanding**	**Creation**
Text	Native & Plugins: Advanced comprehension and interpretation of textual data.	Native & Plugins: Generation of coherent, contextually relevant text, responses, and summaries.
Structured Data	Understanding of data in table or code format	Generation of data in table or code format
Image	Native & Plugins: Proficient comprehension of various images using GPT-4V plus plugins	Native & Plugins: Native integration with DALL·E 3 for creative visuals, along with plugin-supported visual content generation.

Video	Plugins: Enhanced interactions with and analysis of video content.	Plugins: Facilitated generation and manipulation of video content.
Code	Native & Plugins: Comprehension of multiple programming languages and GitHub repositories.	Native & Plugins: Generation and execution of code snippets, database queries, and data analysis and visualization code
Web Content	Plugins: Interpretation of web search results and scraped web content.	Plugins: Generation of basic website designs and applications.
Audio	Native: Transcription of spoken words into text using Whisper, OpenAI's speech-to-text tool.	Native: Generation of human-like audio with synthetic voices.

Table 1.1: *Multimodality in ChatGPT-4*

GPT-4 Turbo, Assistants, and GPTs

In November 2023 OpenAI introduced GPT-4 Turbo, an advancement over the original GPT-4 model. This new iteration stands out with its extensive 128k context window, allowing it to process information equivalent to over 300 pages of text at once. It is updated with world events knowledge until April 2023 and has been optimized for cost, with input and output tokens being significantly cheaper than its predecessor. In terms of functionality, GPT-4 Turbo enables the execution of multiple functions from a single prompt and claims further accuracy improvements in following instructions, especially beneficial for developers needing structured outputs like JSON (JavaScript Object Notation). An additional feature is the ability to generate consistent responses, which is especially useful in longer dialogues or the repetitive usage of the same prompt with varying input data.

Alongside GPT-4 Turbo, OpenAI released an updated version of GPT-3.5 Turbo with an expanded 16K token context window and improved task performance. A new milestone is the Assistants API, which facilitates the development of AI applications with agent-like capabilities, leveraging plugins like Advanced Data Analysis and Web Browsing, and advanced function calling. Moreover, the integration of DALL·E 3 and the new Text-to-Speech API allows developers to enhance their platforms with advanced image generation and human-like speech synthesis capabilities.

Another innovation are GPTs, customizable prompt-based applications that empower prompt engineers to create specialized versions of ChatGPT to enable task-specific functionalities like first-level IT-Support, negotiation assistance or report creation. Prompt Engineers can use the GPT Builder to upload custom images, define the GPT's behavior, set welcome messages to establish initial interaction tone, and provide task-specific prompt starters to guide user engagement.

Additionally, they can enrich the GPT's knowledge base by uploading relevant enterprise content, for example about products, markets, and policies. Previously mentioned capabilities like Advanced Data Analysis, Web Browsing, and DALL·E Image Generation also broaden the GPT's operational scope. Custom Actions allow for integration with third-party APIs, enabling GPTs to utilize external services and data, very similar to the way standard GPT models integrate with external tools.

The upcoming GPT Store will act as a hub for these innovative applications, encouraging a community where prompt engineers can share their creations and potentially earn revenue. OpenAI has placed a strong emphasis on privacy and safety, enacting stringent policies to safeguard user data within these GPTs.

Finally, OpenAI offers GPT-4 fine-tuning for personalized model improvements, with a dedicated program for large-scale customization. The Custom Models program allows organizations to co-develop bespoke GPT-4 models, ensuring data privacy and specificity to their operational needs.

Conclusion

This chapter traced the evolution of Generative Pre-trained Transformers, from the initial GPT-1 and GPT-2 to the innovative ChatGPT and the advanced GPT-4 with AGI capabilities. We explored their transformative impact, the expansion of functionalities through plugins, external tools, and integration into enterprise software. The introduction of native multi-modal features and integration with DALL·E 3 and Whisper enrich user interaction and broaden the model's versatility, resulting in comprehensive Generative AI capabilities.

In the next chapter we will introduce a comprehensive AI-capability framework, CapabilityGPT, to facilitate the systematic utilization of GPT models in an enterprise context.

Key Points

1. The early GPT models, GPT-1 and GPT-2, leveraged the potential of Transformer models in natural language processing, paving the way for subsequent advancements in the field.
2. GPT-3 marked a significant leap forward with its massive model size and enhanced capabilities, including its proficiency in learning from a few examples and applying this knowledge across diverse tasks.
3. InstructGPT was a critical advancement that enhanced task-oriented and instruction-based responses, laying the groundwork for ChatGPT.
4. ChatGPT revolutionized AI-human interaction with its ability to generate coherent and contextually appropriate responses and its advanced instruction-following capabilities, taking us closer to more natural and meaningful AI-human interactions.
5. GPT-4 represents a significant milestone towards Artificial General Intelligence, with proven capabilities for creation, transfer learning, advanced reasoning and planning.
6. The introduction of plugins like Advanced Data Analysis, Web Search, or Image Understanding has significantly enhanced ChatGPT-4's Generative AI capabilities.
7. The innovative ability of GPT models to access external tools has broadened the scope and reach of AI applications, especially in the area of Enterprise Applications.
8. The ongoing integration of GPT-4 into enterprise software platforms, especially from OpenAI's strategic partner Microsoft, is further extending the user base of AI capabilities.
9. OpenAI's launch of ChatGPT Enterprise attempts to directly address the corporate reservations about data security and integration.
10. ChatGPT-4's native voice and image processing features represent a further improvement of its Generative AI capabilities, expanding the model's versatility across various tasks.

11. GPT-4 Turbo advances the GPT series with a very large 128k token context window, capable of processing information equivalent to over 300 pages of text in a single prompt, and enhanced accuracy in instruction-following.
12. GPTs, as customizable prompt-based applications allow prompt engineers to tailor ChatGPT with task-specific functionalities, fostering a dynamic ecosystem for sharing and monetization.

CHAPTER 2

CapabilityGPT - An Enterprise AI-Capability Framework for ChatGPT

Introduction

In this comprehensive exploration, we dive into CapabilityGPT – an advanced AI-capability framework designed to maximize the transformative power of ChatGPT and other GPT models within an enterprise context[1].

We start with an overview of CapabilityGPT, outlining the framework's principal components and functionalities, laying a solid foundation for the ensuing discussions.

Next, we explain the purpose of CapabilityGPT, showing how this comprehensive repository of AI capabilities serves as design building blocks for various AI solutions, from single AI use cases to AI-enhanced products.

We then describe its benefits, emphasizing its comprehensiveness, user-centric

[1]CapabilityGPT as an AI-capability framework is not limited to OpenAI models, but can also be used with other large language models like Claude from Anthropic, Jurassic from A21labs, or Google Bard.

design, and adaptability and afterwards compare its holistic approach against the more technique-centric traditional frameworks.

As we delve further into the subject, we discuss each of the 18 AI capabilities in detail, along with its corresponding use cases. We prioritize discussion on use cases that offer the highest value and the shortest time to be implemented, as well as others that, while not falling neatly into these categories, still showcase considerable potential.

By ChatGPT, we will refer to all Conversational OpenAI models in this chapter, including ChatGPT-3.5, ChatGPT-4, and their respective versions with plugins and external tool integration, as described in *Chapter* 1.

Structure

In this chapter, the following topics will be covered:

- Overview of CapabilityGPT
- Purpose of CapabilityGPT
- Benefits of CapabilityGPT
- Advantages of CapabilityGPT over Technical AI frameworks
- Detailed description of each AI capability

Overview of CapabilityGPT

The CapabilityGPT framework embodies 18 key capabilities of ChatGPT, each anchored in its foundational AGI abilities. Notably, the capabilities are designed with a primary focus on processing data in text or code format, and structured or sequential data can easily be converted into these formats.

The 18 capabilities under the CapabilityGPT framework are (see *Figure* 2.1) as follows:

1. **Assessment:** Evaluates entities such as employee performance, supply chain efficiency, or return on marketing investment, thereby supporting informed decision-making.
2. **Cause-effect Analysis:** Identifies and evaluates likely causal relationships from text data, aiding in understanding the implications of various decisions and strategies.
3. **Classification:** Categorizes data into predefined groups based on their

attributes, supporting processes like product classification, anomaly detection, or content categorization.

4. **Communication:** Engages in comprehensive interactions with users and enterprise applications, enhancing task automation, information exchange, and assistance in various business functions.
5. **Creation:** Produces novel outputs, from strategic plans to generating code snippets or designing sales pitches.
6. **Data Mining:** Extracts patterns, relationships, and insights from structured datasets, supporting market research, process optimization, or performance analysis.
7. **Information Extraction and Analytics:** Processes pertinent details from textual data or documents, aiding tasks like financial report analysis or sentiment analysis.
8. **Matchmaking:** Uses pattern recognition to optimally pair entities based on their descriptions, useful in scenarios such as skills to project matching or mentor-to-mentee alignment.
9. **Planning:** Deconstructs complex goals into subgoals and task sequences, aiding in solving strategic and operational problems
10. **Prediction:** Forecasts future business outcomes based on descriptions of past and current events, assisting in tasks like inventory management or financial trend analysis.
11. **Question Answering:** Comprehends, processes, and accurately responds to queries, serving areas like customer support or HR services.
12. **Ranking:** Prioritizes items like strategic initiatives or sales opportunities based on comparative analysis of their descriptions.
13. **Recommendation:** Suggests relevant options or actions, aiding in training programs, marketing strategies, or procurement decisions.
14. **Semantic Search:** Accelerates search-intensive tasks like knowledge management, market research, or code retrieval.
15. **Sequential Decision Making:** Optimizes decision processes with multiple steps, useful in strategic planning, investment choices, or negotiations.
16. **Simulation:** Models impacts of actions and decisions to analyze real-world behavior, aiding in risk or strategy evaluations.

17. **Summarization:** Extracts key details from larger text datasets or documents, aiding in tasks like report condensation or market research analysis.
18. **Transformation:** Converts textual data or content, useful in tasks like document translation, content repurposing, or visualizations.

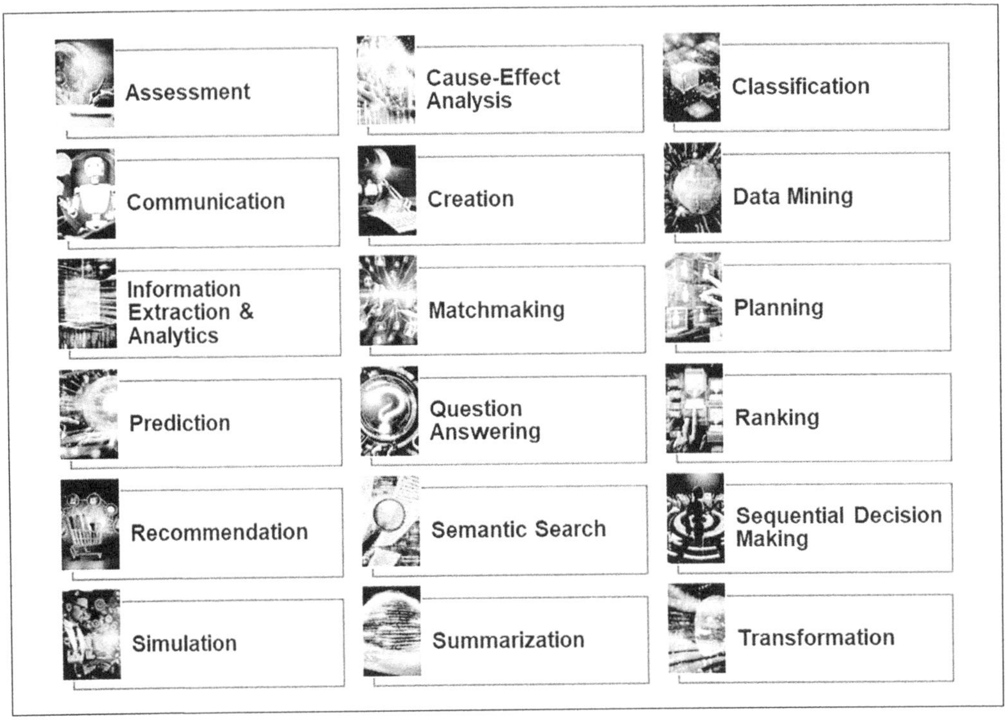

***Figure 2.1**: CapabilityGPT: An AI Capability Framework*

By utilizing and combining these capabilities, enterprises can unlock the potential of AI across an array of advanced use cases, improving their operational efficiency, decision-making processes, and employee satisfaction.

Purpose of CapabilityGPT

The CapabilityGPT framework serves as a comprehensive repository of AI capabilities that can be selected and combined in various ways to design different types of AI solutions. Here is a brief overview (see *Figure 2.2*):

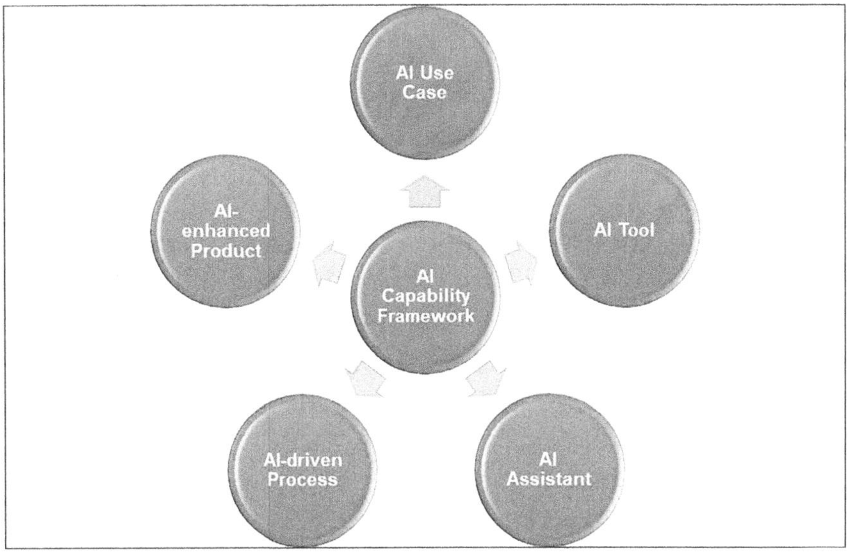

***Figure 2.2**: CapabilityGPT enabling the design of AI solutions*

- **AI Use Case:** The application of a single AI capability to perform a specific task or solve a problem. For example, the use case for the **`Assessment`** capability could be risk assessment, where the AI solution uses its data interpretation and analysis skills to evaluate various aspects of an entity such as a borrower's financial history, thereby supporting informed decision-making. Detailed examples of use cases for each AI capability will be provided in this chapter.
- **AI Tool:** An AI solution that uses one or several AI Use Cases to perform specific tasks or solve complex problems. For instance, an AI tool might utilize the **`Assessment`** use case for risk evaluation, the **`Classification`** use case for categorizing risks, and the **`Prediction`** use case to forecast future risk trends.
- **AI Assistant:** An AI Assistant is an advanced AI application with multiple AI capabilities and access to external tools or plugins. Based on the tasks that the assistant is designed to handle, relevant capabilities from the CapabilityGPT framework are incorporated. For example, an 'AI Personal Secretary' might use capabilities such as Creation, Communication, Planning, Question Answering, Semantic Search, and Summarization. Examples of role-based AI assistants will be provided in *Chapter* 3, while *Chapter* 6 will cover functional and collaborative AI assistants..
- **AI-driven Process:** An AI-driven process is a sequence of tasks (or sub-processes with tasks), each enabled by one or more AI capabilities. For instance, in an 'AI-driven Sales Process,' capabilities like Sequential Decision Making (for sales strategy formulation), Matchmaking (for

sales-rep to client assignment), and Communication (for client interaction) could be applied. Four case studies with detailed AI process descriptions will be provided in *Appendix* B.

- **AI-enhanced Product:** This is an existing software or physical product that is improved by adding one or more AI capabilities. For example, a 'Smart Refrigerator' might incorporate Classification (to identify items), Prediction (to estimate when items will run out), and Recommendation (to suggest shopping lists). Examples of enterprise software enhancements by AI are provided in *Chapter* 1.

In summary, the CapabilityGPT framework provides a versatile set of AI capabilities that can be utilized to design and build a wide range of AI solutions, tailored to specific needs and goals.

Benefits of CapabilityGPT

The CapabilityGPT framework presents significant benefits, reinforcing its value as a comprehensive tool for the effective integration and implementation of AI capabilities across various organizational contexts. Here are some of its key advantages:

- **Comprehensiveness:** The CapabilityGPT framework comprises 18 distinct AI capabilities, ensuring it can cater to a diverse range of business needs. The breadth of capabilities enables businesses to leverage AI in numerous innovative ways.
- **Simplicity of Understanding:** The framework simplifies the complex world of AI by breaking it down into manageable, comprehensible capabilities. This allows even non-technical stakeholders to understand how AI can enhance their operations.
- **Ease of Design:** The CapabilityGPT framework simplifies the design process by utilizing AI capabilities as standardized building blocks. Businesses can construct AI tools, assistants, processes, or products with enhanced efficiency. This approach accelerates the design process and improves the quality of the ensuing AI implementations.
- **Innovation Promotion:** The clear delineation of capabilities within the framework fosters creativity and innovation. It allows stakeholders to envision new combinations of capabilities, leading to novel AI applications.
- **Scalability:** The modular nature of the framework allows for easy scalability. Businesses can start with a few capabilities and gradually integrate more as they scale up their AI strategy, making it a flexible tool for growth.

- **Promptability**: CapabilityGPT's unique feature, 'promptability,' allows each AI capability to be expressed directly as an instruction in a prompt to ChatGPT. This standardizes prompt engineering[2], leading to more consistent, predictable results, and improved system reliability.

After gaining an appreciation for the manifold benefits of CapabilityGPT, we next evaluate how it stands up against conventional AI frameworks. This comparative analysis will further underline the strengths of CapabilityGPT, setting the stage for our deep dive into the 18 distinct capabilities and their applications.

Advantages of CapabilityGPT over Technical AI Frameworks

CapabilityGPT offers significant advantages over traditional, technique-oriented AI frameworks. Let us cover them one by one:

- **User-Centric vs. Technique-Centric**: CapabilityGPT is designed with a user-centric approach, focusing on enterprise use cases and business needs and mapping these to relevant AI capabilities. In contrast, traditional AI frameworks are technique-centric, concentrating on AI technologies such as Knowledge Graphs or Deep Learning. This technique-centric approach requires significant technical expertise and does not align directly with specific enterprise use cases or business needs.
- **Abstract vs. Concrete**: CapabilityGPT provides a higher-level, more abstract view of AI capabilities. This view is more accessible to non-technical stakeholders and aids in conceptual understanding. Traditional AI-functionality frameworks, however, involve more concrete, technical components and demand a deep understanding of AI methodologies and algorithms.
- **Problem-Oriented vs. Tool-Oriented**: With its focus on addressing a broad spectrum of business challenges, CapabilityGPT is inherently problem-oriented. In contrast, traditional AI frameworks tend to be more tool-oriented, applying specific AI techniques, which limits their scope to those types of problems, where these techniques are applicable.
- **Holistic vs. Component-Based**: CapabilityGPT offers a holistic view of the AI capabilities available to an enterprise, providing a more complete picture of how AI can be leveraged. Traditional AI frameworks often offer a component-based view, focusing on specific techniques and their potential uses, lacking a comprehensive vision.

---

[2]Advanced Prompt Engineering Techniques using the AI capability framework will be presented in *Chapter 5, Advanced GPT Prompt Engineering Techniques.*

In essence, while traditional AI frameworks lay the technical groundwork for AI development, CapabilityGPT provides a more adaptable and business-oriented approach to AI implementation. By aligning AI capabilities with enterprise use cases, it enables a more effective and strategic application of AI throughout the enterprise.

Having reviewed CapabilityGPT's relative strengths compared to conventional AI frameworks, we can dissect each of its 18 capabilities. By understanding their specific functionalities and use cases, the readers can apply them to their specific business contexts.

Detailed AI-capability Descriptions with Use Cases

In this section, we delve into each of the 18 capabilities that form the crux of the CapabilityGPT AI framework. Each capability is described, followed by a comprehensive list of representative use cases, demonstrating how it can be applied to solve various real-world problems. The use cases highlight the versatility and applicability of the capabilities, reinforcing CapabilityGPT's potential to address a broad spectrum of enterprise needs.

To ensure clarity and consistency in our presentation, each use case follows a standardized format:

- **Data Requirements:** Specifies the kind of data, typically in text or code format, necessary for the AI capability to function in that use case.
- **Functionality:** Highlights the primary tasks the AI capability undertakes in the context of the use case.
- **Stakeholders:** Lists the primary actors or beneficiaries involved or impacted by the use case.
- **Benefits:** Describes the potential advantages or improvements derived from applying the AI capability in the described context.

To further guide your exploration and understanding, we have categorized the use cases for each capability as follows:

- **High-value Use Cases:** These represent scenarios where the deployment of the AI capability can yield profound business impacts, such as cost savings, revenue enhancements, customer satisfaction, or other strategic benefits.
- **Fast-to-implement Use Cases:** Emphasizing agility, these use cases can be brought to fruition rapidly. Ideal conditions for such cases are:
    - Data is directly processable by ChatGPT (text, code) or easily convertible (for example, structured/sequential data).

- Reference examples are available.
- Prompts are straightforward.
- There are no reasoning limitations with ChatGPT.
- There are no Responsible AI[3] challenges.
- There are no external users (for example, customers, suppliers).

- **Other Use Cases:** This category captures those use cases that don't neatly align with the above classifications but remain significant in showcasing the capabilities of the AI framework.

Assessment

Assessment, as an AI capability powered by ChatGPT, refers to the systematic evaluation or analysis of various aspects related to an entity. This can encompass risk, performance, quality, efficiency, compliance, user experience, readiness, and impact.

***Figure 2.3**: Assessment*

Now, let us delve into the potential of this AI capability and explore representative use cases:

- **High-value Use Cases:**
  - **Risk Assessment:**
    - **Functionality**: In-depth analyses of diverse datasets to evaluate and anticipate risk factors and potential vulnerabilities.
    - **Data Requirements**: Borrower's financial records, patient medical histories, supply-chain transaction logs, and any other pertinent data indicative of risk.
    - **Stakeholders**: Risk analysts, financial planners, medical professionals, supply chain managers, and executive leadership

[3]Responsible AI is the ethical, transparent, and accountable creation and management of AI systems, emphasizing fairness, safety, and the mitigation of biases. It seeks a future where AI respects human rights and amplifies potential without causing harm.

in businesses.

    - **Benefits**: Improved foresight in financial decisions, early detection, and mitigation of medical risks, streamlining supply chain processes, and proactive strategy development.

- **Performance Evaluation:**
    - **Functionality**: Comprehensive assessment of performance metrics across suppliers and employees, along with analysis of process logs to pinpoint inefficiencies.
    - **Data Requirements**: Supplier delivery logs, product quality metrics, contract details, employee performance evaluations, and operational log files.
    - **Stakeholders**: HR managers, operations directors, quality assurance teams, and procurement heads.
    - **Benefits**: Enhanced supplier and employee relationships, identification of process inefficiencies, optimized workflows, and tailored training programs.
- **Regulatory Compliance Assessment:**
    - **Functionality**: Rigorous analysis of operational data against regulatory standards to ensure compliance and identify potential breaches.
    - **Data Requirements**: Transactional records, GDPR[4] adherence logs, environmental impact data, and other relevant compliance documentation.
    - **Stakeholders**: Compliance officers, legal teams, data protection authorities, and environmental safety regulators.
    - **Benefits**: Safeguarding against regulatory penalties, bolstered data privacy, maintained ecological standards, and reinforced trust with stakeholders.

- **Fast-to-implement Use Cases:**
    - **User experience assessment:**
        - **Functionality**: Analyzing user sentiment and feedback to gauge overall user satisfaction and areas of improvement.
        - **Data Requirements**: Customer reviews, usage patterns, feedback forms, and behavioral data.
        - **Stakeholders**: Product managers, user experience designers, customer service teams, and marketing teams.

[4]GDPR stands for the General Data Protection Regulation. It is a comprehensive data protection law that came into effect on May 25, 2018, and applies to all member states of the European Union (EU).

        - **Benefits**: Direct improvements in user experience, product enhancements, and targeted customer service interventions.
    - **Market analysis:**
        - **Functionality**: Comprehensive analysis of market dynamics, competitor actions, and customer preferences, offering a macro and micro view of market shifts and opportunities.
        - **Data Requirements**: Textual repositories of market trends, competitor press releases, customer surveys, and industry reports.
        - **Stakeholders**: Marketing strategists, business development teams, product managers, R&D teams.
        - **Benefits**: Quicker adaptability to market dynamics, informed product and service development, optimized pricing strategies, and enhanced competitive positioning.
    - **Quality assurance:**
        - **Functionality**: Quality monitoring and analysis to identify potential defects, inefficiencies, and areas of improvement.
        - **Data Requirements**: Text logs or reports on product performance, service delivery metrics, feedback forms, and error logs.
        - **Stakeholders**: Quality assurance teams, product managers, production supervisors, and service delivery teams.
        - **Benefits**: Swift identification of quality issues, insights to refine product development, proactive mitigation of defects, and enhanced customer satisfaction.
- **Other Use Cases:**
    - **Environmental and Sustainability Evaluation:**
        - **Functionality**: Detailed environmental impact analysis and evaluation of sustainability strategies, encompassing aspects such as carbon footprint measurement, waste management, water conservation, and green initiatives.
        - **Data Requirements**: Carbon emission data, waste disposal records, water usage statistics, supply chain data, renewable energy adoption rates, and records of corporate social responsibility initiatives.
        - **Stakeholders**: Environmental safety regulators, corporate sustainability teams, supply chain managers, and corporate leadership.
        - **Benefits**: Enhanced ecological responsibility, better stakeholder trust, identification of eco-friendly initiatives, and potential cost

savings through sustainable practices.

- **Readiness Assessment:**
  - **Functionality**: Comprehensive assessment of an organization's preparedness for changes, transformations, or emergencies, spanning areas like digital infrastructure, skill sets, and emergency preparedness.
  - **Data Requirements**: Digital infrastructure logs, workforce skill datasets, emergency response plans, infrastructure blueprints, supply chain readiness records, and electric vehicle transition plans.
  - **Stakeholders**: Operational heads in manufacturing, utilities sector managers, HR and training teams, emergency response units, and automotive industry leaders.
  - **Benefits**: Early identification of readiness gaps, informed decisions for transformative projects, bolstered emergency response, and a streamlined transition to new industry standards.
- **Process Optimization Evaluation:**
  - **Functionality**: Detailed examination of workflow and operational data to discern inefficiencies, bottlenecks, and areas that require enhancements.
  - **Data Requirements**: Workflow charts, operational logs, manufacturing process records, and energy distribution data.
  - **Stakeholders**: Process managers in industrials/manufacturing, utility sector operational heads, quality assurance teams, and strategic planners.
  - **Benefits**: Enhanced operational efficiency, reduced process costs, better product quality, and sustainable energy distribution.

In conclusion, assessment is a critical AI capability that enables organizations across industries to gain a deep understanding of their current situation. With these insights, they can proactively address issues, capitalize on opportunities, and take steps that minimize risks.

To effectively use AI-assisted assessment, diverse and high-quality data need to be collected, strong methods for bias detection and elimination need to be implemented, and a human-in-the-loop approach becomes imperative.

Cause-Effect Analysis

Cause-Effect Analysis systematically identifies and evaluates causal relationships leading to particular outcomes or changes in systems, processes, or performance.

Figure 2.4: *Cause-Effect Analysis*

The applications of this capability can be mapped out for various industries, highlighting the breadth and depth of its transformative potential:

- **High-value Use Cases:**
  - **Root Cause Analysis:**
    - **Functionality**: Diagnosis of sequential data to pinpoint root causes of system or process failures, enhancing prevention strategies and system reliability.
    - **Data Requirements**: Machinery data logs, IT system logs, patient records, incident reports, and more.
    - **Stakeholders**: Manufacturing maintenance teams, IT system administrators, healthcare professionals, and operational heads.
    - **Benefits**: Improved preventive maintenance strategies, reduced equipment breakdowns, increased IT system uptime, and enhanced patient safety and care quality.
  - **Marketing and Sales Impact Analysis:**
    - **Functionality**: Analysis of promotional data to determine the impact of marketing campaigns on sales, loyalty, and client onboarding.
    - **Data Requirements**: Campaign performance data, sales metrics, customer loyalty metrics, and new client onboarding statistics.
    - **Stakeholders**: Marketing teams, sales teams, strategy planners, and budget allocators.

        - **Benefits**: Refined promotional strategies, optimized marketing budgets, and improved return on investment.
    - **Quality Control Analysis:**
        - **Functionality**: Examination of sequential data to detect factors affecting quality standards adherence, prompting improvements.
        - **Data Requirements**: Production data logs, quality standards metrics, deviation reports, and more.
        - **Stakeholders**: Quality control teams, production heads, process managers, and operational supervisors.
        - **Benefits**: Elevated product quality, enhanced process compliance, and reduced deviations from quality norms.
- **Fast-to-implement Use Cases:**
    - **Performance Reduction Analysis:**
        - **Functionality**: Analysis of sequential data to pinpoint root causes of performance declines across various settings.
        - **Data Requirements**: Sales figures, sports performance metrics, academic performance records.
        - **Stakeholders**: Sales managers, sports coaches, and academic administrators.
        - **Benefits**: Swift identification of performance bottlenecks, agile strategy adjustments, and timely interventions to reverse negative trends.
    - **Impact assessment for project changes:**
        - **Functionality**: Evaluation of potential consequences of alterations in project scope, timeline, or resources, leading to effective change management.
        - **Data Requirements**: Project specifications, current project timeline, resource allocation details.
        - **Stakeholders**: Project managers, software developers, and construction supervisors.
        - **Benefits**: Immediate foresight into the ripple effects of project changes, optimized decision-making, and enhanced project outcome predictability.
    - **Policy change impact analysis:**
        - **Functionality**: Emulation and examination of the potential effects of proposed policy adjustments on diverse business or public areas.

        - **Data Requirements**: Current policy documents, proposed policy changes, and relevant performance metrics (like employee satisfaction rates or public health outcomes).
        - **Stakeholders**: HR managers, government officials, and healthcare administrators.
        - **Benefits**: Rapid understanding of policy change repercussions, swift policy optimization, and better alignment of policies with desired outcomes.
- **Other Use Cases:**
    - **Supply Chain Continuity Assessment:**
        - **Functionality**: In-depth analysis of logistical data to understand the consequences of disruptions in supply chain segments.
        - **Data Requirements**: Supply chain logs, inventory records, partner negotiation data, and more.
        - **Stakeholders**: Supply chain managers, operational heads in retail and manufacturing, inventory managers, and logistics coordinators.
        - **Benefits**: Better contingency planning, improved inventory management, optimized partner negotiations, and enhanced business continuity.
    - **Predictive Eco-Impact Analysis:**
        - **Functionality**: Forecasting the potential environmental impacts of future business endeavors and the direct causes of possible environmental effects.
        - **Data Requirements**: Environmental assessment reports, operational data, emission records, and more.
        - **Stakeholders**: Environmental safety regulators, corporate sustainability teams, business strategists, and corporate leadership.
        - **Benefits**: Preemptive addressing of environmental challenges, adaptation of eco-friendly strategies, and a move towards a more sustainable business trajectory.
    - **Organizational Change Impact Assessment:**
        - **Functionality**: Prediction of the outcomes of significant organizational changes on aspects like operational efficiency, customer satisfaction, and service quality.
        - **Data Requirements**: Previous change impact reports, customer satisfaction surveys, operational efficiency data, and more.
        - **Stakeholders**: Corporate strategists, HR teams, tech implementation teams, operational heads, and customer service managers.

- **Benefits**: Informed decision-making during transformations, minimized disruption, and enhanced alignment with business goals.

In conclusion, Cause-Effect Analysis, as an AI capability, is a crucial tool for organizations across industries to understand the cause-and-effect relationships within their operations. With these insights, they can better anticipate outcomes, troubleshoot problems, and align their strategies with their objectives.

The challenges of using ChatGPT for Cause-Effect Analysis, such as misinterpreting correlation for causation and dealing with confounding factors affecting causes and effects, can be managed by additional causal analytics tools, and by ensuring human oversight in crucial decisions.

Classification

Classification systematically categorizes data, behaviors, processes, or resources into predefined groups based on their attributes, characteristics, or outcomes.

***Figure 2.5**: Classification*

Here we will delve into representative use cases that show the diverse applications where Classification can make a significant impact:

- **High-value Use Cases:**
  - **Product classification:**
    - **Functionality**: Categorize products into distinct groups based on attributes such as features, user reviews, or descriptions using AI-powered analysis.
    - **Data Requirements**: Product features, user reviews, product descriptions, and related metadata.
    - **Stakeholders**: Inventory managers, E-commerce platform developers, retail strategists, and marketing teams.

        - **Benefits**: Enhanced inventory management, improved user browsing experiences, increased product discovery, and potential boost in sales.
    - **Anomaly detection:**
        - **Functionality**: Identification of abnormal patterns or inconsistencies in sequential data for early detection and response.
        - **Data Requirements**: Transaction logs, patient data, E-commerce shopping patterns, and more.
        - **Stakeholders**: Fraud detection teams in banking, healthcare data analysts, and E-commerce security teams.
        - **Benefits**: Proactive identification and mitigation of fraudulent activities, unusual data patterns, and suspicious behaviors.
    - **User behavior classification:**
        - **Functionality**: Analysis of sequential user data to derive insights into actions, behaviors, and preferences.
        - **Data Requirements**: User activity logs, browsing patterns, purchase history, and platform interaction data.
        - **Stakeholders**: E-commerce strategists, online entertainment providers, and edtech platform designers.
        - **Benefits**: Personalized product recommendations, tailored user experiences, and optimized content delivery.
- **Fast-to-implement Use Cases:**
    - **Sentiment analysis:**
        - **Functionality**: Decoding and categorizing emotional nuances within textual inputs to gauge sentiment.
        - **Data Requirements**: Patient feedback records, reader comments, and customer reviews.
        - **Stakeholders**: Healthcare professionals, media analysts, and retail managers.
        - **Benefits**: Immediate understanding of prevalent sentiments, identification of potential areas needing attention, and shaping interventions or responses based on feedback.
    - **Customer segmentation:**
        - **Functionality**: Analysis of customer data to segment them into distinct groups based on various attributes like behaviors, preferences, or demographics.

        - **Data Requirements**: Customer purchase histories, preference surveys, and demographic details.
        - **Stakeholders**: Marketing managers in telecommunications, retail executives, and financial analysts.
        - **Benefits**: Enhanced targeted marketing, personalized customer service, and better resource allocation based on customer segmentation.
    - **Process classification:**
        - **Functionality**: Categorization of business processes based on attributes such as flow, resource requirements, and outcomes.
        - **Data Requirements**: Business process maps, resource allocation records, and outcome reports.
        - **Stakeholders**: IT service managers, supply chain heads, and healthcare administrators.
        - **Benefits**: Swift identification of process categories, pinpointing of bottlenecks, and optimization of processes based on classification insights.
- **Other Use Cases:**
    - **Resource classification:**
        - **Functionality**: Categorization of resources, such as employees, vendors, or physical assets, based on distinct characteristics.
        - **Data Requirements**: Vendor profiles, employee data, physical asset records, delivery times, product quality reports, and pricing/cost data.
        - **Stakeholders**: Supply chain managers, procurement teams, HR managers, and operational heads in logistics, retail, and manufacturing.
        - **Benefits**: Enhanced resource allocation, better vendor and asset management, and streamlined operational processes.
    - **Content filtering:**
        - **Functionality**: Filtering of incoming digital content based on criteria of relevance and appropriateness.
        - **Data Requirements**: Emails, social media posts, content metadata, and user-generated content.
        - **Stakeholders**: IT administrators, customer service representatives, and content managers in media and IT organizations.
        - **Benefits**: Improved productivity, increased information security,

and enhanced user experiences.

- **Risk classification:**
  - **Functionality**: Categorization of clients or investments into predefined risk categories using detailed data analysis.
  - **Data Requirements**: Financial history, behavioral patterns, market trends, and other related risk factors.
  - **Stakeholders**: Risk management teams in insurance, financial analysts, and portfolio managers.
  - **Benefits**: More informed decision-making, tailored product offerings, optimal resource allocation, and balanced profitability and customer satisfaction.

By leveraging the power of ChatGPT in classification, businesses across various sectors are empowered to understand their environment better and make more informed decisions. Routine decisions can be linked to classification outcomes by simple business rules.

For the effective deployment of ChatGPT-driven classification, it's paramount to use representative data to avoid skewed outcomes, and establish a system for regular audits and human oversight to guard against inherent model biases.

Communication

Communication as an AI capability comprises interactions with human users and external applications such as transactional systems, customer relationship applications, or search engines. This dual-mode interaction allows ChatGPT to facilitate information exchange, problem-solving, and task completion.

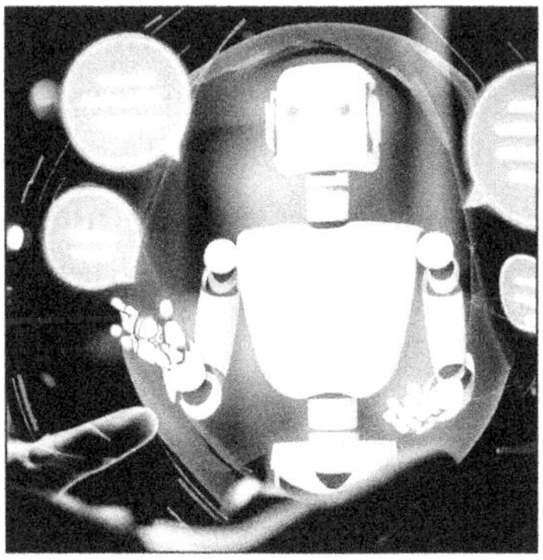

Figure 2.6: *Communication*

We demonstrate the potential of this capability by describing its applications:

- **High-value Use Cases:**
  - **Data collection and entry:**
    - **Functionality**: Automated data gathering, validation, and recording for tasks like customer feedback, reservations, or inventory management.
    - **Data Requirements**: Feedback forms, reservation records, inventory, and patient data.
    - **Stakeholders**: Data entry personnel, healthcare administrators, and inventory managers.
    - **Benefits**: Reduced manual workload, improved data accuracy, streamlined processes across industries, and enhanced operational efficiency.
  - **Information and assistance service:**
    - **Functionality**: Provision of personalized product information, troubleshooting support, company news, policy guidance, and other relevant updates.
    - **Data Requirements**: Product details, company news bulletins, policy documents, and health guidelines.
    - **Stakeholders**: Customer service representatives, internal communication teams, and healthcare providers.
    - **Benefits**: Enhanced customer service, improved internal communication, transformed user experiences, and higher satisfaction levels.
  - **Customer service:**
    - **Functionality**: Streamlining customer interactions through handling common inquiries, providing personalized recommendations, and escalating complex issues.
    - **Data Requirements**: Customer interaction logs, product/service details, customer feedback, and escalation criteria.
    - **Stakeholders**: Customer service agents, product managers, and telecommunication service providers.
    - **Benefits**: Efficient handling of customer inquiries, improved service delivery, enhanced customer experience, and increased operational efficiency.
- **Fast-to-implement Use Cases:**
  - **Training and development:**
    - **Functionality**: Dynamic presentation of training content, facilitation of eLearning modules, and skills enhancement.
    - **Data Requirements**: Training modules, eLearning course

contents, employee feedback, and performance metrics.

- **Stakeholders**: HR managers, trainers in utilities, consumer goods product managers, and telecommunications technical trainers.
- **Benefits**: Promotes continuous professional development, ensures consistent delivery of essential training, and enhances workforce capability across different industries.

- **Project management communication:**
  - **Functionality**: Bridging communication between project management tools and team members for real-time updates and notifications.
  - **Data Requirements**: Project timelines, task lists, team member roles, and project milestones.
  - **Stakeholders**: IT project managers, construction site supervisors, and marketing campaign leads.
  - **Benefits**: Boosted transparency in team communications, heightened awareness of project statuses, improved team synchronization, and timely execution of projects.
- **Workshop Assistance:**
  - **Functionality**: Assistance in workshop planning, on-the-fly data retrieval for discussions, and post-workshop follow-ups.
  - **Data Requirements**: Workshop agendas, participant lists, relevant databases or knowledge bases, and workshop feedback.
  - **Stakeholders**: Training facilitators, product development leads, and research heads.
  - **Benefits**: Seamless workshop organization, enriched discussion through quick data retrieval, and systematic post-workshop follow-ups, ensuring maximum productivity.

- **Other Use Cases:**
  - **Supply chain communication:**
    - **Functionality**: Enhancement of communication within supply chain processes by tracking inventory needs, coordinating with suppliers, and automating delivery-related notifications.
    - **Data Requirements**: Inventory logs, supplier communication records, delivery schedules, and product demand data.
    - **Stakeholders**: Supply chain managers, inventory managers, suppliers, and delivery teams.
    - **Benefits**: Better inventory management, improved supplier

coordination, optimized service delivery, and more informed decision-making processes.

- **Feedback loop enhancement:**
  - **Functionality**: Systematic collection, categorization, and relay of customer feedback to the relevant departments.
  - **Data Requirements**: Customer feedback forms, product/service reviews, and customer interaction logs.
  - **Stakeholders**: Customer service representatives, product managers, and quality assurance teams.
  - **Benefits**: Actionable insights from customer feedback, fostered culture of responsiveness, continuous improvement, and increased customer loyalty.
- **Emergency communication coordination:**
  - **Functionality**: Prompt relaying of emergency notifications and coordination of timely communications between teams or departments.
  - **Data Requirements**: Emergency alerts, team communication logs, departmental guidelines, and emergency response procedures.
  - **Stakeholders**: Public safety officials, healthcare providers, and utility service managers.
  - **Benefits**: Coordinated and effective emergency response, safeguarded assets, and potential life-saving outcomes.

Through effective communication, ChatGPT becomes a valuable tool in fostering interaction, collaboration, and information exchange across various sectors and applications.

Implementing ChatGPT-enabled communication necessitates a balanced mix of AI and human interaction, particularly in situations requiring empathy. Ensuring stringent data security measures and strict adherence to ethical data usage guidelines are vital.

Creation

AI-enabled creation involves understanding complex requirements, interpreting context, and producing diverse, innovative types of content that meet specific objectives. This can range from textual content and design elements to intricate artifacts such as business models or software code.

Figure 2.7: *Creation*

Let's look at some representative use cases, each highlighting ChatGPT's creative potential across various industries:

- **High-value Use Cases:**
  - **Generative design:**
    - **Functionality**: Creation of innovative user interface designs, novel product developments, and engaging website designs using AI.
    - **Data Requirements**: User preferences, website analytics, product feature requirements, and design benchmarks.
    - **Stakeholders**: UX/UI designers, product managers, website developers, and marketing teams.
    - **Benefits**: Improved user interaction and engagement, diversified product offerings, and heightened customer satisfaction.
  - **Product information management:**
    - **Functionality**: Generation of compelling product descriptions and devising inventory management strategies.
    - **Data Requirements**: Product specifications, inventory logs, customer feedback, and purchasing patterns.
    - **Stakeholders**: E-commerce managers, inventory supervisors, marketing teams, and product managers.
    - **Benefits**: Enhanced customer satisfaction, optimized stock levels, and streamlined inventory management.
  - **Automatic program synthesis:**

    - **Functionality**: Assisting in the automatic generation of software programs, models, or scripts.
    - **Data Requirements**: Software requirements, existing codebases, and system specifications.
    - **Stakeholders**: Software developers, IT managers, financial analysts, and telecommunication engineers.
    - **Benefits**: Reduced manual coding time, improved process efficiency, timely and accurate program generation.

- **Fast-to-implement Use Cases:**
  - **Functional document and content generation:**
    - **Functionality**: Automated creation of varied content types, including reports, legal documents, marketing material, and educational content.
    - **Data Requirements**: Existing templates, topic or subject briefs, target audience demographics, and specified document structures.
    - **Stakeholders**: Legal counsels, marketing managers, educators, and content creators.
    - **Benefits**: Increased efficiency in content generation, reduction in human errors, more consistent output, and valuable timesaving for staff, allowing them to focus on more intricate tasks.
  - **Process and workflow creation:**
    - **Functionality**: Designing comprehensive business process models, standard operating procedures, and specialized pathways such as patient care or educational tracks.
    - **Data Requirements**: Existing process descriptions, organizational goals, stakeholder feedback, and sector-specific benchmarks or best practices.
    - **Stakeholders**: Hospital administrators, manufacturing managers, educators, and process optimization teams.
    - **Benefits**: Enhanced process efficiency, improved patient or user outcomes, more efficient production, and individualized learning or care pathways that align with best practices.
  - **Conceptual ideation assistance:**
    - **Functionality**: Augmenting brainstorming sessions with innovative suggestions and perspectives for product development, advertising campaigns, and marketing strategies.
    - **Data Requirements**: Market trends, target audience insights,

historical campaign data, and product specifications or needs.

- **Stakeholders**: Creative directors, product developers, marketing strategists, and brand managers.
- **Benefits**: Faster ideation processes, richer and more diverse brainstorming outcomes, creation of campaigns or products that align closely with market demands, and increased resonance with target audiences.

- **Other Use Cases:**
  - **Training and learning content generation:**
    - **Functionality**: Producing customized training materials, onboarding guides, and personalized learning pathways.
    - **Data Requirements**: Employee skill sets, training benchmarks, industry standards, and job roles.
    - **Stakeholders**: HR managers, training facilitators, department heads, and safety officers.
    - **Benefits**: Enhanced employee development, improved staff knowledge, bolstered safety protocols, and increased productivity.
  - **Automated system configurations:**
    - **Functionality**: Assisting in the configuration of technical objects such as laptops, machines, or vehicle systems.
    - **Data Requirements**: Technical specifications, user preferences, device manuals, and system benchmarks.
    - **Stakeholders**: IT administrators, telecommunications engineers, and automotive technicians.
    - **Benefits**: Improved setup speed, minimized potential errors, optimized system performance, and enhanced user satisfaction.
  - **Project document automation:**
    - **Functionality**: Automating the creation and management of project documents such as plans, task assignments, and progress reports.
    - **Data Requirements**: Project requirements, task lists, timelines, and stakeholder roles.
    - **Stakeholders**: Project managers, IT coordinators, consultants, and construction supervisors.
    - **Benefits**: Enhanced project management efficiency, improved transparency, streamlined project execution, and better client communication.

These examples underline how ChatGPT leverages its computational abilities to generate a large variety of contents in diverse contexts. This marks a significant shift from traditional, routine automation towards more sophisticated, creative problem-solving.

For optimal utilization of ChatGPT in creative tasks, maintaining human oversight and designing relevant prompts are necessary. Content filtering and bias mitigation strategies should be integral parts of AI governance to prevent the inadvertent generation of biased or harmful content.

Data Mining

Data mining involves exploring, extracting, and unveiling patterns, relationships, and insights hidden within large quantities of structured and unstructured data. However, the size of the processable dataset is constrained by the context window of the GPT model in use. Larger datasets necessitate pre-processing to segment them into manageable portions. Alternatively, ChatGPT-4, when paired with the Advanced Data Analysis plugin, can be employed collaboratively for Explorative Data Mining.

***Figure 2.8**: Data Mining*

Here's a list of representative use cases for data mining:

- **High-value Use Cases:**
  - **Trend analysis:**
    - **Functionality**: Interpretation of chronological data to uncover sales trends, market shifts, or evolving customer behaviors.
    - **Data Requirements**: Sales data, market reports, customer feedback, and historical datasets.
    - **Stakeholders**: Retail managers, financial analysts, marketing strategists, and travel planners.

- **Benefits**: Data-driven strategic planning, timely strategy adjustments, capitalization on emergent opportunities, and mitigation of potential risks.

- **Anomaly detection:**
  - **Functionality**: Identification of unusual patterns or inconsistencies within sequential datasets.
  - **Data Requirements**: Financial transaction logs, cybersecurity breach reports, and equipment performance data.
  - **Stakeholders**: Bank managers, cybersecurity professionals, and energy sector supervisors.
  - **Benefits**: Enhanced security and reliability, prevention of financial losses, safeguarding of sensitive data, and timely identification of potential threats.
- **Sequential pattern discovery:**
  - **Functionality**: Unearthing commonly occurring sequences or patterns within serial data.
  - **Data Requirements**: User activity logs, machinery performance records, and transportation schedules.
  - **Stakeholders**: E-commerce managers, manufacturing supervisors, and logistics coordinators.
  - **Benefits**: In-depth user behavior analysis, proactive maintenance scheduling, process optimization, minimized downtime, and increased operational efficiency.

- **Fast-to-implement Use Cases:**
  - **Data clustering:**
    - **Functionality**: Identifying and categorizing homogeneous groups or clusters within textual data, enabling deeper insights and data-driven decisions.
    - **Data Requirements**: Textual descriptions from customer reviews, medical records, financial transactions, and other forms of unstructured text data.
    - **Stakeholders**: Marketing strategists, healthcare analysts, financial advisors, and data scientists.
    - **Benefits**: Implementation of targeted marketing strategies, tailored healthcare interventions, rapid identification of outliers or anomalies, and improved decision-making processes.

- **Association rule mining:**
  - **Functionality**: Discovery of relationships and correlations among sets of items or behaviors within sequences of transactions.
  - **Data Requirements**: Transactional data from shopping carts, purchase histories, online behaviors, media consumption records, and similar datasets.
  - **Stakeholders**: Retail managers, E-commerce strategists, grocery store owners, media producers, and data analysts.
  - **Benefits**: Enhanced recommendation systems, improved understanding of consumer behavior, creation of more effective marketing campaigns, and delivery of highly personalized customer experiences.
- **Text pattern recognition:**
  - **Functionality**: Detection of recurring themes, sentiments, or topics within large volumes of text data, enabling deeper analysis and actionable insights.
  - **Data Requirements**: Customer feedback, reviews, social media comments, employee feedback, and other forms of text data.
  - **Stakeholders**: Customer service managers, marketing teams, HR professionals, and social media analysts.
  - **Benefits**: Informed strategies for customer service improvement, tailored marketing campaigns, effective social media monitoring, and enhanced understanding of employee engagement and sentiment.

- **Other Use Cases:**
  - **Network pattern recognition:**
    - **Functionality**: Identifying and understanding patterns within network activity data.
    - **Data Requirements**: User connection logs, server activity data, and telecommunication traffic reports.
    - **Stakeholders**: Social media platform developers, IT managers, and telecommunication engineers.
    - **Benefits**: Improved network performance, early threat detection, enriched understanding of user interactions, and predictive insights into future network states.
  - **Sentiment timeline analysis:**
    - **Functionality**: Analyzing textual feedback or comments across chronological sequences to gauge sentiment evolution.

- **Data Requirements**: Customer reviews, feedback, social media comments, event or campaign timelines.
- **Stakeholders**: Media analysts, entertainment producers, brand managers, and public relations coordinators.
- **Benefits**: Deep insights into public reactions over time, informed decision-making for strategy adjustments, heightened stakeholder engagement, and effective response to sentiment shifts.

These use cases emphasize ChatGPT's ability to derive significant value from large and complex datasets, shifting from traditional data analysis to intelligent, data-driven decision-making.

Effective data mining, however, requires strict adherence to data protection regulations, and a commitment to unbiased and representative data collection and processing to ensure both user confidentiality and quality of derived insights.

Information Extraction and Analytics

Information Extraction and Analytics represents the ability to automatically identify, extract, and analyze pertinent information from raw data or complex documents. This transformative capability plays a crucial role in decoding intricate documents, generating actionable insights, and enabling process automation across diverse organizational domains.

Figure 2.9: *Information Extraction and Analytics*

Here is an overview of use cases for information extraction and analytics:

- **High-value Use Cases:**
  - **Transactional document processing:**
    - **Functionality**: Conversion and analysis of transactional documents like invoices, receipts, and purchase orders to streamline their subsequent processing.

        - **Data Requirements**: Invoices, receipts, and purchase orders in various formats like PDF and HTML, requiring preprocessing into text.
        - **Stakeholders**: Retail managers, banking professionals, and E-commerce business owners.
        - **Benefits**: Streamlined transaction validation, minimized discrepancies, reduced processing times, increased accuracy, and quicker transaction settlements.
    - **Product application analysis based on protocols:**
        - **Functionality**: Extraction and analysis of data from records linked to product applications, ensuring adherence to protocols.
        - **Data Requirements**: Clinical records, agrochemical application data, and dietary product usage details.
        - **Stakeholders**: Healthcare professionals, agricultural specialists, and wellness and nutrition experts.
        - **Benefits**: Insight into product efficiency, adherence assessment, detection of side-effects or outcomes, protocol adjustment suggestions, and product refinement recommendations.
- **Fast-to-implement Use Cases:**
    - **Legal document analysis and extraction:**
        - **Functionality**: Thorough review and extraction of key provisions, terms, and obligations from voluminous legal documents, ensuring comprehensive and efficient analysis.
        - **Data Requirements**: Contracts, agreements, deeds, lease documents, merger and acquisition papers, and other types of legal documentation.
        - **Stakeholders**: Legal counsels, compliance officers, corporate business leaders, financial analysts, and real estate managers.
        - **Benefits**: Speedy review processes, increased accuracy in legal operations, reduced risks associated with overlooked terms or non-compliance, and minimized operational overheads.
    - **News analysis:**
        - **Functionality**: Information extraction from global news, regulatory updates, and industry shifts to anticipate market dynamics and ensure compliance with evolving regulations.
        - **Data Requirements**: News articles, press releases, regulatory bulletins, industry reports, and other news sources.

        - **Stakeholders**: Market researchers, compliance officers, business analysts, and strategic planners.
        - **Benefits**: Proactive market strategies, adherence to evolving regulations, early identification of potential risks or opportunities, and gaining an edge in informed decision-making.
    - **Competitive analysis:**
        - **Functionality**: Extraction of valuable insights from external data sources to understand competitors' strategies, product performances, and intellectual property positioning.
        - **Data Requirements**: Competitor reports, market analyses, product reviews, patent documents, and other resources related to industry competitors.
        - **Stakeholders**: Business strategists, marketing professionals, R&D teams, and corporate intelligence units.
        - **Benefits**: Enhanced business intelligence, improved strategic positioning, informed product development, and a competitive advantage in the marketplace.
- **Other Use Cases:**
    - **Compliance verification:**
        - **Functionality**: Extracting vital data from documents to ensure strict adherence to various regulations, standards, or policies.
        - **Data Requirements**: Regulatory documents, health and safety reports, financial records, and tax documents.
        - **Stakeholders**: Financial analysts, healthcare administrators, and manufacturing supervisors.
        - **Benefits**: Strengthened regulatory compliance, minimized legal risks, time-saving, and reduced risk of non-compliance penalties.
    - **Data management in Research and Development:**
        - **Functionality**: Enhanced data extraction from research resources to support research activities and innovation.
        - **Data Requirements**: Clinical trial data, academic literature, and product development feedback.
        - **Stakeholders**: Pharmaceutical researchers, academic professionals, and tech innovators.
        - **Benefits**: Elevated R&D efficiency, innovative insights, expedited product or solution development.

- **Inventory Management:**
  - **Functionality**: Extraction and analysis of data related to inventory records, sales predictions, and supply chain metrics to optimize stock levels.
  - **Data Requirements**: Inventory records, sales forecasts, and supply chain data.
  - **Stakeholders**: Retail business owners, manufacturing managers, and logistics coordinators.
  - **Benefits**: Avoidance of stockouts or overstock situations, reduced inventory carrying costs, heightened operational efficiency, and superior customer satisfaction.

These use cases underscore the transformative impact of ChatGPT in extracting meaningful insights from raw and complex data, driving informed decision-making and process automation.

For its effective application in Information Extraction and Analytics, adherence to data protection regulations, and meticulous validation of extraction and analysis prompts are key to addressing its challenges.

Matchmaking

ChatGPT's capability for matchmaking concerns the pairing of entities, tasks, resources, or requirements based on predefined criteria or patterns to optimize outcomes. AI-driven matchmaking can streamline decision-making across multiple domains, enhancing productivity and operational efficacy.

Figure 2.10: *Matchmaking*

Let us now explore a couple of use cases for matchmaking:

- **High-value Use Cases:**
  - **Resource-to-task allocation:**
    - **Functionality**: Assign resources optimally to specific tasks or operations based on descriptive attributes like skills, capabilities, or functionalities.
    - **Data Requirements**: Resource availability, skills descriptions, and task requirements.
    - **Stakeholders**: Project managers, manufacturing supervisors, and logistics coordinators.
    - **Benefits**: Enhanced productivity, cost reduction, and more efficient use of available resources.
  - **Risk-to-mitigation strategy alignment:**
    - **Functionality**: Identify potential threats or risks and align them with suitable preventive or remediation strategies.
    - **Data Requirements**: Risk assessments and available preventive/corrective strategies.
    - **Stakeholders**: Financial analysts, cybersecurity professionals, and life science researchers.
    - **Benefits**: Strengthened risk management, increased business resilience, and prevention of potential losses.
  - **Demand-to-supply matching:**
    - **Functionality**: Anticipate and align supply with market demand, considering various product descriptions, unit conversions, and distributor stock levels.
    - **Data Requirements**: Inventory levels, demand forecasts, distributor stocks, and product descriptions.
    - **Stakeholders**: Retail business owners, manufacturing managers, and logistics experts.
    - **Benefits**: Enhanced operational efficiency, improved customer satisfaction, and optimized inventory levels.
- **Fast-to-implement Use Cases:**
  - **Individual-to-group assignment:**
    - **Functionality**: Effective assignment of individuals to respective groups or teams, based on compatibility, skills, and objectives to boost team dynamics and optimize performance.

        - **Data Requirements**: Individual profiles, skill assessments, personal preferences, team requirements, and past performance metrics.
        - **Stakeholders**: HR managers, educators, training coordinators, project managers, and team leads.
        - **Benefits**: Improved team cohesion, enhanced performance outcomes, optimal resource utilization, and creation of balanced teams.
    - **Mentorship and coaching alignment:**
        - **Functionality**: Intelligent pairing of employees with suitable mentors, coaches, or SMEs to ensure alignment in learning needs, professional goals, and skill development.
        - **Data Requirements**: Employee profiles, learning needs assessments, mentor/coach/SME profiles, feedback forms, and professional development objectives.
        - **Stakeholders**: HR managers, training and development teams, senior executives, SMEs, and departmental heads.
        - **Benefits**: Accelerated employee growth, heightened morale, efficient skill acquisition, and enriched organizational productivity.
    - **Compliance matching:**
        - **Functionality**: Ensure alignment of practices or procedures with the relevant regulatory frameworks.
        - **Data Requirements**: Business practices, software functionalities, procedural details, and regulatory requirements.
        - **Stakeholders**: Financial advisors, healthcare administrators, and manufacturing supervisors.
        - **Benefits**: Minimized legal and operational risks, prevention of fines and legal complications, and uninterrupted business operations.
- **Other Use Cases:**
    - **Entity-to-entity matching for data management:**
        - **Functionality**: Execution of robust entity-to-entity matching techniques to bolster data deduplication, schema matching, ontology matching, and other data alignment functions.
        - **Data Requirements**: Datasets requiring alignment, database schemas, ontologies, metadata, and associated data integrity metrics.
        - **Stakeholders**: Data scientists, IT managers, database administrators, marketing analysts, and data quality teams.

- **Benefits**: Enhanced data integrity, improved data usability, efficient data management processes, and superior data-driven decision-making.

- **Requirement-to-solution mapping**:
  - **Functionality**: Match specific requirements to appropriate solutions or strategies.
  - **Data Requirements**: Business, technical, or functional requirements; available solutions.
  - **Stakeholders**: IT managers, business consultants, and customer service executives.
  - **Benefits**: Efficient problem resolution, optimized strategic planning, and delivery of tailored solutions.
- **Expertise matchmaking**:
  - **Functionality**: Pair employees with the right Subject Matter Experts (SMEs) based on project or challenge requirements.
  - **Data Requirements**: Employee profiles, SME expertise areas, and project requirements.
  - **Stakeholders**: HR professionals, project managers, and corporate team leads.
  - **Benefits**: Efficient problem resolution, optimal project outcomes, and maximized use of internal expertise.

These use cases underline how ChatGPT can enhance the matchmaking process, ensuring optimal alignment between various entities, tasks, resources, and requirements, thus leading to improved outcomes and efficiency.

The effective implementation of ChatGPT for matchmaking hinges on the quality and accuracy of data and careful consideration of the diverse and complex factors involved in matchmaking. This includes mitigating the potential complexities and diversity of certain tasks that might pose a challenge to AI systems. For instance, in the case of individual-to-group assignment, various subjective factors like group dynamics and individual personalities play a significant role. These factors may be difficult for an AI system like ChatGPT to accurately consider, and, therefore, special attention should be given to these elements to ensure the most effective and accurate matchmaking outcomes.

Planning

AI planning entails a two-part capability: decomposing complex goals (or tasks) into subgoals (or sub-tasks) and generating a task sequence to transition from an initial state to a target state within given constraints. Plans can be dynamically adjusted based on intermediate execution results of if initial assumptions change.

Figure 2.11: *Planning*

Here's an outline of how ChatGPT can be utilized for planning across different industries:

- **High-value Use Cases:**
  - **Operational planning:**
    - **Functionality**: Provides comprehensive planning output ranging from task lists creation, supply chain optimization, to designing effective marketing campaigns.
    - **Data Requirements**: Task requirements, supply chain data, audience demographics, and service delivery constraints.
    - **Stakeholders**: Managers in utilities, retail, telecommunications, and manufacturing sectors.
    - **Benefits**: Streamlined logistics, maximized marketing impact, improved customer satisfaction, and operational excellence.
  - **Strategic planning:**
    - **Functionality**: Assists in long-term goal setting, determining required resources, and charting out essential actions.
    - **Data Requirements**: Market trends, historical data, and company objectives.
    - **Stakeholders**: Executives in financial services, telecommunications, and automotive sectors.
    - **Benefits**: Guided navigation towards desired outcomes in competitive environments, clarity in direction, and effective resource allocation.

- **Project management planning:**
  - **Functionality**: Assists project managers in breaking down large-scale projects, sequencing tasks, and ensuring optimal resource allocation.
  - **Data Requirements**: Project specifications, available resources, and task dependencies.
  - **Stakeholders**: Project managers in the construction, IT, and design sectors.
  - **Benefits**: Projects are completed on schedule, within budget, and according to requirements.

- **Fast-to-implement Use Cases:**
  - **Risk and incident management:**
    - **Functionality**: Provision of robust mitigation and resolution plans for industries facing significant operational or market risks, thus promoting organizational resilience and security.
    - **Data Requirements**: Historical incident reports, risk assessment outputs, operational data, market trends, and security parameters.
    - **Stakeholders**: Risk management teams, security officers, operational heads, and top management.
    - **Benefits**: Heightened organizational resilience, improved security measures, effective mitigation of potential risks, and proactive prevention of major incidents.
  - **Change management planning:**
    - **Functionality**: Assisting in planning and executing organizational changes and process improvements to minimize disruptions and enhance operational flow.
    - **Data Requirements**: Current operational data, feedback from stakeholders, details of proposed changes, past change management reports, and impact assessments.
    - **Stakeholders**: HR managers, business process analysts, operational heads, and change management teams.
    - **Benefits**: Streamlined organizational changes, reduced disruptions, enhanced stakeholder buy-in, and increased operational efficiency.
  - **Event planning:**
    - **Functionality**: Effective assistance in planning and executing events, from venue selection to contingency planning, ensuring seamless execution and superior guest experience.

- **Data Requirements**: Previous event data, venue details, resource availability, guest preferences, and budget constraints.
- **Stakeholders**: Event planners, hospitality managers, logistics teams, and marketing departments.
- **Benefits**: Smooth execution of events, increased guest satisfaction, improved resource allocation, and bolstered industry reputation.

- **Other Use Cases:**
  - **Communication and engagement planning:**
    - **Functionality**: Helps in devising effective internal and external communication strategies to maximize stakeholder engagement and improve public relations.
    - **Data Requirements**: Stakeholder demographics, communication channels, and engagement metrics.
    - **Stakeholders**: PR teams in telecommunications, education, and retail sectors.
    - **Benefits**: Enhanced stakeholder engagement, positive public perception, and organizational success.
  - **Innovation and development planning:**
    - **Functionality**: Assists in drafting detailed plans for research, product development, and training.
    - **Data Requirements**: Current R&D data, market needs, and training requirements.
    - **Stakeholders**: R&D teams in healthcare/life sciences, consumer goods, and education sectors.
    - **Benefits**: Fosters a culture of continuous learning and adaptation, leading to sustainable growth and long-term success.

These use cases highlight how ChatGPT can optimize planning processes, seamlessly translating complex goals into manageable sub-tasks and orchestrating efficient sequences for their execution.

Implementing it in an enterprise context calls for a combined human-AI approach, accounting for the need of a comprehensive specification of planning problems and a clear definition of roles and responsibilities for humans and ChatGPT.

Prediction

In AI, prediction is the ability to forecast future outcomes, trends, behaviors, or events using historical data and patterns. This process aids informed decision-making and risk management across various sectors within an organization.

Figure 2.12: *Prediction*

Here's how ChatGPT can harness the power of prediction in various industries:

- **High-value Use Cases:**
    - **Performance forecasting:**
        - **Functionality**: Leverages historical and real-time data to predict future performance.
        - **Data Requirements**: Historical performance data, current operational metrics, and industry trends.
        - **Stakeholders**: Executives in financial services, industrials/ manufacturing, and telecommunications sectors.
        - **Benefits**: Proactive management, informed strategic planning, identification of opportunities, and preparation for challenges.
    - **Demand and supply prediction:**
        - **Functionality**: Forecasts demand and supply balances using time-series data.
        - **Data Requirements**: Historical demand and supply data, market trends, and sector-specific events.
        - **Stakeholders**: Decision-makers in utilities, automotive, and healthcare/life sciences sectors.
        - **Benefits**: Prevents stockouts and overstock situations, enhances operational efficiency, and optimizes financial performance.
    - **Outcome prediction:**
        - **Functionality**: Predicts potential outcomes of different initiatives or actions.

        - **Data Requirements**: Historical data on similar initiatives, current project parameters, and external influencing factors.
        - **Stakeholders**: Strategists in energy, healthcare/life sciences, and education sectors.
        - **Benefits**: Improved resource allocation, risk mitigation, and enhanced overall performance.
- **Fast-to-implement Use Cases:**
    - **Trend prediction:**
        - **Functionality**: Decoding of complex data patterns to forecast future trends, enabling businesses to proactively adapt to changing consumer or societal demands.
        - **Data Requirements**: Historical sales data, customer feedback, market research reports, and other relevant industry data reflecting past trends.
        - **Stakeholders**: Product managers, marketing strategists, educators, curriculum designers, and inventory managers.
        - **Benefits**: Enhanced adaptability to market shifts, improved product evolution, efficient inventory management, progressive curriculum design, and refined teaching techniques for optimized business results.
    - **Behavior prediction:**
        - **Functionality**: Predicting behavioral patterns of varied stakeholders, from customers to competitors, offering actionable insights to drive effective business strategies.
        - **Data Requirements**: Past transactional data, customer interactions, feedback, and behavior logs, as well as competitor activity and market intelligence.
        - **Stakeholders**: Marketing teams, customer service managers, business strategists, and product developers.
        - **Benefits**: Superior anticipation of customer needs, creation of tailored experiences, staying ahead of market dynamics, and enhanced customer loyalty and competitive positioning.
    - **Quality and defect prediction:**
        - **Functionality**: Proactive identification of potential quality issues or defects, allowing for timely interventions and assurance of product integrity.

- **Data Requirements**: Historical quality control data, customer feedback on product quality, defect logs, and production process details.
- **Stakeholders**: Quality assurance teams, product managers, manufacturing heads, and customer service representatives.
- **Benefits**: Reduction in costs associated with recalls or rework, enhanced customer satisfaction, bolstered brand reputation, and minimized potential business risks.

- **Other Use Cases:**
  - **Resource utilization prediction:**
    - **Functionality**: Forecasts the utilization of resources vital for sustainability and profitability.
    - **Data Requirements**: Past resource utilization data, current operational data, and projections for future requirements.
    - **Stakeholders**: Operations managers in industrials/manufacturing, utilities, and automotive sectors.
    - **Benefits**: Informed operational planning, optimized maintenance schedules, and support for sustainability initiatives.
  - **Event probability prediction:**
    - **Functionality**: Estimates the likelihood of specific events based on historical data.
    - **Data Requirements**: Past data on similar events, current environmental factors, and industry trends.
    - **Stakeholders**: Risk managers in financial services, healthcare/life sciences, and energy sectors.
    - **Benefits**: Enables proactive risk management, informed contingency planning, and protection against potential negative impacts.

These use cases illustrate the extensive application of ChatGPT's predictive capability, significantly contributing to an organization's strategic planning, decision-making, and risk management across various industries.

To optimally harness it in an enterprise setting, ensuring high-quality, diverse data collection, facilitating collaborative decision-making processes, and implementing effective feedback mechanisms are crucial.

Question Answering

Question Answering in AI pertains to the ability to understand, process, and respond accurately to inquiries posed in natural language. This feature enhances interactive processes within an organization, ensuring immediate, accurate, and context-aware responses to diverse questions.

***Figure* 2.13**: *Question Answering*

Here's how ChatGPT can leverage its question-answering capability in various industries:

- **High-value Use Cases:**
  - **Operational process guidance**:
    - **Functionality**: Provides instant and precise responses to operational questions.
    - **Data Requirements**: Standard operating procedures, safety protocols, and historical query data.
    - **Stakeholders**: Operational staff in industrials/manufacturing, utilities, and healthcare/life sciences industries.
    - **Benefits**: Boosts operational efficiency, ensures adherence to safety standards, and prevents mistakes that might lead to financial or health repercussions.
  - **Knowledge base interaction:**
    - **Functionality**: Enables rapid and contextually accurate retrieval of stored knowledge.
    - **Data Requirements**: Comprehensive knowledge base, FAQs, and industry-specific guidelines.
    - **Stakeholders**: Professionals in education, telecommunications, and financial services sectors.

        - **Benefits**: Enhances problem-solving, enriches learning, and ensures compliance with industry standards.
    - **Customer support**:
        - **Functionality**: Facilitates immediate responses to a myriad of customer inquiries.
        - **Data Requirements**: Product/service information, troubleshooting guides, and customer feedback history.
        - **Stakeholders**: Support teams in retail, telecommunications, and automotive sectors.
        - **Benefits**: Bolsters customer satisfaction and loyalty, resulting in higher retention rates and increased business.
- **Fast-to-implement Use Cases:**
    - **IT and Enterprise software support:**
        - **Functionality**: Offering prompt assistance for software tools and IT infrastructure, ensuring that tech-driven processes remain unhindered.
        - **Data Requirements**: IT knowledge bases, software manuals, user feedback, and logs of past IT incidents or resolutions.
        - **Stakeholders**: IT support teams, software users, educators, utility operators, and tech-dependent professionals.
        - **Benefits**: Minimized downtime, augmented productivity, improved user experience, and cost-saving from reduced IT support personnel needs.
    - **Compliance and regulatory guidance**:
        - **Functionality**: Providing accurate answers and guidance on compliance requirements, ensuring businesses stay aligned with mandatory regulations and best practices.
        - **Data Requirements**: Regulatory documents, policy manuals, past compliance incidents, and updates on industry-specific regulations.
        - **Stakeholders**: Compliance officers, business strategists, operational managers, and regulatory affairs professionals.
        - **Benefits**: Effective risk management, ensured business continuity, prevention of hefty fines or potential business closures, and bolstered business reputation.
    - **Onboarding and training**:
        - **Functionality**: Assists in streamlining the onboarding process and continuous employee training.

- **Data Requirements**: Training materials, common employee queries, company policies and procedures.
- **Stakeholders**: HR and training departments in retail, consumer goods, and automotive sectors.
- **Benefits**: Ensures consistent service quality, empowers employees, and optimizes operational efficiency.

- **Other Use Cases:**
  - **Internal and external communication support:**
    - **Functionality**: Manages internal and external communication efficiently.
    - **Data Requirements**: Communication protocols, brand messaging, and stakeholder databases.
    - **Stakeholders**: Communication teams in automotive, consumer goods, and retail sectors.
    - **Benefits**: Fosters a positive brand image and ensures seamless communication across channels.
  - **Integrated multimodal assistance:**
    - **Functionality**: Integrates text, voice, and Visual Question Answering (VQA) for a comprehensive assistance system.
    - **Data Requirements**: Diverse datasets that encompass textual, auditory, and visual information relevant to the sector.
    - **Stakeholders**: Professionals across healthcare/life sciences, retail, utilities, automotive, industrials/manufacturing, and education.
    - **Benefits**: Provides a holistic user experience, supports real-time troubleshooting and guidance, and merges the visual with immediate, knowledgeable responses.

These use cases reflect the extensive application of ChatGPT's question-answering capability in various aspects of an organization's operations. Its ability to effectively respond to inquiries in diverse fields significantly enhances organizational efficiency, service delivery, and customer experience across various industries.

Maximizing the potential of ChatGPT's question-answering capability requires maintaining the quality of input data and knowledge bases and implementing stringent data governance measures to ensure privacy, security, and ethical use of information.

Ranking

Ranking in AI denotes the ability to prioritize a set of items or entities according to specified criteria. This ensures an ordered arrangement based on their relevance, value, or significance, which is crucial in various decision-making scenarios.

***Figure 2.14**: Ranking*

Now, let us delve into representative use cases for ranking:

- **High-value Use Cases:**
  - **Performance comparison:**
    - **Functionality**: Ranks performance across diverse metrics, providing critical analytical insights.
    - **Data Requirements**: Student test scores, treatment outcomes, and financial portfolio data.
    - **Stakeholders**: Educators, healthcare professionals, and financial advisors.
    - **Benefits**: Enables personalized feedback in education, promotes continual improvement in healthcare, and optimizes portfolio management in finance.
  - **Performance ranking of external entities:**
    - **Functionality**: Ranks external entities based on historical performance data.
    - **Data Requirements**: Supplier delivery records, partnership outcome data, and customer credit histories.
    - **Stakeholders**: Retail managers, telecom operators, and financial institutions.

        - **Benefits**: Enhances decision-making for supplier selection, partnership formation, and credit lending, boosting efficiency and risk management.
    - **Resource allocation:**
        - **Functionality**: Prioritizes and allocates resources based on multifaceted criteria.
        - **Data Requirements**: Energy ROI data, environmental impact assessments, patient health metrics, and automotive R&D data.
        - **Stakeholders**: Energy companies, healthcare institutions, and automotive manufacturers.
        - **Benefits**: Balances competing needs effectively, ensuring optimal returns while preserving core values like environmental sustainability and patient well-being.
- **Fast-to-implement Use Cases:**
    - **Product development prioritization:**
        - **Functionality**: Ranking product features or entire new products based on their anticipated market demand, feasibility, cost, and potential to satisfy customer needs.
        - **Data Requirements**: Market research data, customer feedback, competitive landscape, historical sales and product performance data, and cost assessments.
        - **Stakeholders**: Product managers, R&D teams, marketers, business strategists, and design teams.
        - **Benefits**: Accelerated time-to-market for high-impact products, enhanced customer satisfaction, better allocation of R&D funds, and increased market share.
    - **Process improvement prioritization:**
        - **Functionality**: Evaluating and ranking production processes or maintenance tasks based on metrics like efficiency, cost-effectiveness, and potential impact on quality.
        - **Data Requirements**: Production logs, maintenance records, feedback from production staff, historical process performance data, and cost assessments.
        - **Stakeholders**: Process managers, quality assurance teams, frontline workers, and operational strategists.
        - **Benefits**: Improved product quality, enhanced operational efficiency, reduced costs, and boosted overall organizational productivity.

- **Other Use Cases:**
  - **Ecological investment prioritization:**
    - **Functionality**: Ranks investment opportunities based on ecological impact metrics.
    - **Data Requirements**: Data on carbon footprints, water usage, deforestation impacts, and financial returns.
    - **Stakeholders**: Investment banks, global funds, and venture capitalists.
    - **Benefits**: Integrates ecological responsibility with financial decision-making, promoting investments that align with both profitability and global sustainability targets.
  - **Strategy development:**
    - **Functionality**: Prioritizes strategic initiatives based on their potential impacts.
    - **Data Requirements**: Market trends, ROI projections, environmental impact data, and competitive landscape information.
    - **Stakeholders**: Manufacturing firms, energy providers, and retail executives.
    - **Benefits**: Streamlines strategic planning, directing focus towards impactful business growth strategies, environmental conservation, and maintaining a competitive edge.

ChatGPT's ability to efficiently prioritize and rank significantly enhances strategic decision-making, resource allocation, and performance evaluation across various industries.

Its effective use requires rigorous validation to ensure accuracy, transparency in decision-making processes to address trust issues, and proactive strategies for bias mitigation to avoid unfair rankings and misallocation of resources.

Recommendation

Recommendation in AI refers to suggesting relevant options or actions based on available data such as user behavior, historical patterns, or specific criteria. This capability guides decisions, optimizes processes, and personalizes experiences.

Figure 2.15: *Recommendation*

Here is a depiction of ChatGPT's recommendation abilities across multiple industries:

- **High-value Use Cases:**
  - **Personalized learning and skill enhancement:**
    - **Functionality**: Recommends tailored learning resources based on an individual's skill profile and past activities.
    - **Data Requirements**: User profiles, learning histories, industry trends, course offerings, and feedback data.
    - **Stakeholders**: Educators, HR managers, healthcare professionals, employees, and students.
    - **Benefits**: Enhances learning outcomes, ensures alignment with current industry requirements, and fosters career progression.
  - **Process optimization:**
    - **Functionality**: Analyzes and recommends improvements for organizational workflows.
    - **Data Requirements**: Organizational workflow data, transaction records, inventory data, and customer feedback.
    - **Stakeholders**: Retail managers, financial service providers, and healthcare administrators.
    - **Benefits**: Boosts operational efficiency, reduces stock-related issues, and enhances customer and patient services.
  - **Personalized recommendations and Self-service:**
    - **Functionality**: Offers tailored marketing or product suggestions based on a customer's consumption history.
    - **Data Requirements**: Customer purchase histories, viewing records, feedback, and personal preferences.

    - **Stakeholders**: Retailers, media companies, hoteliers, and airlines.
    - **Benefits**: Enhances customer experience, drives sales, promotes customer loyalty, and fuels business growth.

- **Fast-to-implement Use Cases:**
  - **Next action selection:**
    - **Functionality**: Recommending next steps based on a sequence of previous actions or the current status of an ongoing process.
    - **Data Requirements**: Historical interaction data, customer feedback, project status updates, clinical guidelines (for healthcare), and any other pertinent action logs.
    - **Stakeholders**: Customer service representatives, project managers, clinicians, and other professionals responsible for sequential decision-making.
    - **Benefits**: Increased efficiency in addressing customer concerns, improved project task sequencing for optimal outcomes, enhanced patient care through timely and appropriate interventions, and reduced decision-making times.
  - **Technology selection:**
    - **Functionality**: Suggesting technology solutions ranging from software to hardware based on a set of requirements or project specifications.
    - **Data Requirements**: Technology specifications, user reviews, performance benchmarks, project requirements, budget constraints, and compatibility information.
    - **Stakeholders**: IT consultants, marketing strategists, construction project managers, technology procurement teams, and other professionals involved in selecting technology tools or platforms.
    - **Benefits**: Optimal technology choices leading to enhanced project outcomes, reduced resource wastage, better ROI on technology investments, and faster decision-making in technology acquisition.
- **Other Use Cases:**
  - **Business growth and innovation planning:**
    - **Functionality**: Examines market trends using sequential data to inform market strategies and innovation.
    - **Data Requirements**: Market trend data, consumer feedback, competitive analyses, and historical sales data.
    - **Stakeholders**: Startups, retail executives, and tech company leaders.

   - **Benefits**: Facilitates strategic business growth, guides product development, and enhances competitive positioning.
- **Stakeholder engagement:**
   - **Functionality**: Recommends effective communication strategies and engagement models for stakeholders.
   - **Data Requirements**: Stakeholder profiles, historical engagement data, and industry communication standards.
   - **Stakeholders**: Marketing executives, corporate communication teams, and government officials.
   - **Benefits**: Boosts stakeholder satisfaction, promotes investment, and refines public policy communication and engagement.

In essence, ChatGPT's recommendation capability, when applied across various use cases, enables continuous learning, adaptation, automation, and growth, thereby driving organizational success.

To optimize its usage, it's crucial to rectify any potential biases, promote innovative suggestions beyond the confines of historical data, and increase transparency and explainability in recommendation processes.

Semantic Search

Semantic Search in AI pertains to the ability to understand and respond to complex search queries, considering the context, intent, and semantic meaning, rather than just relying on keywords. This capability enhances the precision and relevance of search results.

Figure 2.16: *Semantic Search*

ChatGPT, in its core design, does not natively support Semantic Search functionality, but it does offer support for an open-source retrieval plugin that facilitates this capability (for further details, please refer to *Chapter 1*). GPT-3, a predecessor model, is inherently equipped with an embedding feature that makes the implementation of Semantic Search possible.

This embedding feature refers to GPT-3's ability to transform input text into numerical representations, or embeddings. These embeddings, acting as vectors in a high-dimensional space, capture and encode the semantic, or meaning-based, information of the text. This capability becomes crucial for Semantic Search. The query and the potential answers in the search index are represented as embeddings, and the model compares these embeddings to find the best match. This approach allows the search to go beyond just exact wording, enabling a deeper, meaning-based match that aligns more with the query's intent.

Now, let us delve into representative use cases for Semantic Search:

- **High-value Use Cases:**
  - **Semantic Document Search:**
    - **Functionality**: Accurately retrieves specific information from vast data sets by understanding semantic relationships and context.
    - **Data Requirements**: Indexed databases of legal documents, academic articles, corporate records, and more.
    - **Stakeholders**: Legal professionals, academic researchers, and corporate managers.
    - **Benefits**: Rapid and precise access to vital documents, reduced time in data search, and enhanced decision-making support.
  - **Similarity search:**
    - **Functionality**: Identifies items with a deep semantic similarity to a given sample.
    - **Data Requirements**: E-commerce product databases, compound libraries in pharmaceuticals, and patent databases.
    - **Stakeholders**: E-commerce retailers, pharmaceutical researchers, and intellectual property attorneys.
    - **Benefits**: Personalized product recommendations, streamlined patent searches, and efficient discovery of similar compounds.
  - **Process and resource optimization:**
    - **Functionality**: Searches specific business processes, resource details, or logistical data.
    - **Data Requirements**: Business process documentation, resource allocation records, and logistical data.

    - **Stakeholders**: Logistics managers, manufacturing supervisors, and IT administrators.
    - **Benefits**: Streamlined operations, improved resource management, and enhanced efficiency.

- **Fast-to-implement Use Cases:**
  - **Content and media management:**
    - **Functionality**: Facilitates the semantic search of content, media, or reviews for enhanced understanding.
    - **Data Requirements**: Media archives, customer reviews, and audience engagement data.
    - **Stakeholders**: Media producers, marketing strategists, and publishers.
    - **Benefits**: Improved content strategies, better audience targeting, and optimized ad campaigns.
  - **Customer experience management:**
    - **Functionality**: Semantically searching and analyzing customer interactions, feedback, and success stories to gain insights.
    - **Data Requirements**: Customer feedback, online reviews, call logs, chat transcripts, social media mentions, and other forms of customer-generated content.
    - **Stakeholders**: Customer relationship managers, marketing teams, product developers, and other professionals tasked with understanding and improving customer experiences.
    - **Benefits**: Deeper understanding of customer sentiments and preferences leading to tailored product and service offerings, enhanced customer loyalty, and improved market reputation.
- **Other Use Cases:**
  - **Security and risk management:**
    - **Functionality**: Conducts semantic searches to identify potential threats or incidents by understanding data patterns.
    - **Data Requirements**: Cybersecurity threat logs, financial transaction data, and healthcare patient records.
    - **Stakeholders**: Cybersecurity professionals, financial analysts, and healthcare administrators.
    - **Benefits**: Improved risk identification, enhanced security, and proactive threat mitigation.

- **Historical Data Analysis:**
  - **Functionality**: Analyzes and interprets historical data sets for deeper insights.
  - **Data Requirements**: Financial transaction histories, past sales data, and historical market trends.
  - **Stakeholders**: Financial planners, retail managers, and real estate analysts.
  - **Benefits**: Informed future strategies, better understanding of past behaviors, and solidified market position.

This broad applicability of GPT-3's semantic search capabilities significantly augments productivity and efficiency of search-intensive enterprise tasks, driving substantial improvements across diverse industry landscapes.

Its optimal application hinges on the adept embedding of documents and queries and nurturing transparency to enhance trust in search outcomes.

Sequential Decision Making

Sequential Decision Making in AI involves making a series of interconnected decisions where the outcome of each decision affects subsequent decisions. This ability enhances the effectiveness of strategies and processes by considering the cumulative impact of decisions over time.

***Figure 2.17**: Sequential Decision Making*

Here's how ChatGPT can leverage its sequential decision-making capability across various industries:

- **High-value Use Cases:**
  - **Strategy formulation and execution:**
    - **Functionality**: Uses insights from past decisions to guide future strategic planning across sectors.

    - **Data Requirements**: Past investment portfolios and performance data; previous research areas, clinical trial designs; past product assortment and sales data.
    - **Stakeholders**: Investment strategists, healthcare researchers, and retail managers.
    - **Benefits**: Optimized investment strategies, enhanced R&D focus, improved product selection, and promotional tactics in retail.
  - **Negotiation management:**
    - **Functionality**: Leverages past negotiation outcomes to guide future negotiation strategies.
    - **Data Requirements**: Previous supplier negotiation details, past retail supplier contracts, and historical academic partnership agreements.
    - **Stakeholders**: Manufacturing procurement teams, retail purchasing managers, and academic institution partnerships officers.
    - **Benefits**: Strengthened negotiation stances, improved supplier contract terms, and enhanced academic collaborations.
  - **Process improvement:**
    - **Functionality**: Enhances process efficiency and outcomes by analyzing the impacts of previous decisions.
    - **Data Requirements**: Historical energy distribution plans, past manufacturing processes and outcomes, previous telecommunications service rollouts, and network upgrades.
    - **Stakeholders**: Utilities planners, manufacturing managers, and telecom network administrators.
    - **Benefits**: Refined energy distribution strategies, optimized manufacturing procedures, and enhanced telecom network management.
- **Fast-to-implement Use Cases:**
  - **Product or service lifecycle management:**
    - **Functionality**: Analyzing past product or service life cycles to inform the design, development, and marketing of new offerings.
    - **Data Requirements**: Historical product performance data, market feedback, sales figures, customer reviews, and other related metrics.
    - **Stakeholders**: Product managers, design teams, marketing strategists, and other professionals involved in creating and selling products or services.

        - **Benefits**: Informed decisions about product design, service enhancements, and marketing strategies leading to improved product performance, increased market share, and reduced resource wastage.
    - **Adaptive surveys:**
        - **Functionality**: Dynamically adjusting the flow and content of surveys based on participant responses to ensure relevance and depth.
        - **Data Requirements**: Participant responses, historical survey data, market research, and predefined survey logic rules.
        - **Stakeholders**: Market researchers, product developers, public relations professionals, and other stakeholders involved in collecting and analyzing public or customer feedback.
        - **Benefits**: Improved respondent engagement, more precise and actionable data collection, and refined insights into customer preferences, leading to better decision-making and improved product or campaign design.
- **Other Use Cases:**
    - **Crisis management and business continuity:**
        - **Functionality**: Uses historical data on past crisis management to inform and improve future crisis responses.
        - **Data Requirements**: Records of actions during energy grid failures, telemedicine implementations, and risk mitigation strategies during economic downturns.
        - **Stakeholders**: Energy sector executives, healthcare administrators, and financial service strategists.
        - **Benefits**: Streamlined responses to energy crises, improved healthcare delivery during emergencies, and fortified financial resilience.
    - **Stakeholder relationship management:**
        - **Functionality**: Analyzes historical stakeholder interactions to refine and enhance future relationship strategies.
        - **Data Requirements**: Data on previous customer loyalty program outcomes, records of past regulatory compliance incidents, and historical supplier partnership evaluations.
        - **Stakeholders**: Consumer goods strategists, energy sector compliance officers, and automotive procurement managers.

- **Benefits**: Enhanced customer retention and loyalty, reduced compliance issues and associated risks, and strengthened supplier relationships leading to operational efficiencies.

ChatGPT effectively leverages sequential decision-making for process improvement, strategy development, communication and data collection.

To implement this capability in an enterprise, it's necessary to enhance predictive accuracy for long-term impacts, guarantee data reliability, and foster transparency in AI decision-making processes, supplemented by a human-in-the-loop approach.

Simulation

Simulation in AI involves creating a 'digital twin' of real-world systems, processes, or scenarios to assess their behavior and performance under different conditions. This capability aids in predicting potential outcomes, thereby informing strategic and operational decision-making.

Figure 2.18: *Simulation*

Here is an overview of typical use cases for simulation:

- **High-value Use Cases:**
  - **Business process simulation:**
    - **Functionality**: Analyzes, simulates, and optimizes business processes based on specific specifications.
    - **Data Requirements**: Business process specifications, historical process performance data, and efficiency metrics.
    - **Stakeholders**: Manufacturing operations managers, healthcare administrators, and retail store managers.

        - **Benefits**: Enhanced assembly line efficiency, optimized patient care pathways, and improved store management outcomes.
    - **Resource allocation simulation:**
        - **Functionality**: Simulates and evaluates the outcomes of different resource allocation strategies.
        - **Data Requirements**: Historical resource allocation data, specifications for intended allocation, and outcome metrics.
        - **Stakeholders**: Financial portfolio managers, utility distribution planners, and educational administrators.
        - **Benefits**: Improved investment returns, optimized utility distribution, and enhanced educational outcomes.
    - **Environmental impact simulation:**
        - **Functionality**: Assesses and predicts the environmental consequences of specified actions or strategies.
        - **Data Requirements**: Specifications of practices or innovations, historical environmental impact data, and sustainability metrics.
        - **Stakeholders**: Agricultural planners, energy sector strategists, and transportation policymakers.
        - **Benefits**: Informed sustainable choices, guidance towards greener energy sources, and eco-friendly transportation modifications.
- **Fast-to-implement Use Cases:**
    - **Risk management simulation:**
        - **Functionality**: Simulating potential risks and evaluating corresponding mitigation strategies for better decision-making.
        - **Data Requirements**: Historical risk data, current market metrics, past mitigation strategy performance, regulatory information, and predictive models.
        - **Stakeholders**: Risk management professionals, financial analysts, health professionals, and operational managers.
        - **Benefits**: Proactive risk identification and management, ensuring better health interventions in healthcare, achieving financial stability in financial services, and ensuring operational resilience in energy and other sectors.
    - **Customer behavior simulation:**
        - **Functionality**: Predicting and simulating customer behaviors based on past transactions, preferences, and market trends.

- **Data Requirements**: Customer transaction histories, demographic data, past marketing campaign metrics, product performance data, and customer feedback.
- **Stakeholders**: Marketing professionals, sales teams, product managers, and customer relationship managers.
- **Benefits**: Enhanced sales strategies based on predicted customer behavior, improved customer satisfaction through tailored offerings, and successful market penetration by anticipating consumer preferences.

- **Competitor response simulation:**
  - **Functionality**: Using available market data to simulate potential competitor reactions to business strategies or decisions.
  - **Data Requirements**: Historical market performance, current market trends, past competitor reactions, and product/service benchmarks.
  - **Stakeholders**: Strategic planners, business analysts, marketing professionals, and product developers.
  - **Benefits**: Better informed strategic decisions by anticipating competitor moves, optimizing product launches or marketing campaigns to counter competitor strategies, and increasing market share by staying ahead of the competition.

- **Other Use Cases:**
  - **Human resource and talent management simulation:**
    - **Functionality**: Simulates outcomes of HR decisions to refine talent acquisition, development, and retention.
    - **Data Requirements**: Historical HR decisions and their outcomes, specifications for intended HR strategies.
    - **Stakeholders**: HR managers, talent acquisition specialists, and organizational development professionals.
    - **Benefits**: Enhanced employee productivity, improved job satisfaction, and increased retention rates.
  - **Product and service impact simulation:**
    - **Functionality**: Predicts a product or service's potential impact on market metrics.
    - **Data Requirements**: Product or service specifications, historical sales and customer satisfaction data, and market positioning insights.

- **Stakeholders**: Product managers in consumer goods, automotive engineers, and educational program designers.
- **Benefits**: Informed product development, effective market strategy design, and optimized product launch plans.

- **Strategic planning simulation:**
  - **Functionality**: Predicts the outcomes of strategic initiatives to optimize planning.
  - **Data Requirements**: Past strategic decisions and their outcomes, as well as specifications for future strategic initiatives.
  - **Stakeholders**: Energy sector planners, telecommunications strategy teams, and retail market strategists.
  - **Benefits**: Optimized energy distribution strategies, successful service launches, and improved e-commerce outcomes.

ChatGPT, through its advanced simulation capability, can critically evaluate the impact of actions and decisions in various strategic and operational business scenarios.

Effective deployment of ChatGPT's simulation capability calls for rigorous validation of its results by humans and / or additional simulation tools, and strict adherence to ethical and privacy guidelines throughout the simulation process.

Summarization

Summarization in AI refers to the automated extraction of key information from a larger dataset or content, presenting it in a compact and understandable form. It improves comprehension, simplifies decision-making, and saves time by reducing the need to process extensive volumes of data or lengthy texts.

***Figure 2.19**: Summarization*

Here we will delve into representative use cases that show the diverse applications where Summarization can make a significant impact:

- **High-value Use Cases:**
  - **Document and content summary:**
    - **Functionality**: Condenses lengthy and complex written documents into shorter, digestible formats suitable for quick reviews and decision-making.
    - **Data Requirements**: Extensive legal documents, intricate research papers, and comprehensive medical records.
    - **Stakeholders**: Legal professionals, academic researchers, healthcare practitioners, and administrative staff.
    - **Benefits**: Swift decision-making processes, efficient comprehension of voluminous content, and time-saving during reviews.
  - **Data analysis summary:**
    - **Functionality**: Summarizes and condenses intricate datasets, translating them into actionable insights.
    - **Data Requirements**: Financial datasets, intricate manufacturing logs, and expansive retail sales data.
    - **Stakeholders**: Financial strategists, manufacturing supervisors, and retail analysts.
    - **Benefits**: Quick understanding of vast datasets, informed decision-making, and precise targeting in marketing efforts.
  - **Research and development summaries:**
    - **Functionality**: Converts extensive R&D data and findings into concise, actionable insights and summaries.
    - **Data Requirements**: Comprehensive research data, experimental outcomes, and regulatory documentation.
    - **Stakeholders**: Pharma researchers, tech innovators, and automotive product developers.
    - **Benefits**: Enhanced inter-departmental communication, faster go-to-market strategies, and regulatory alignment.
- **Fast-to-implement Use Cases:**
  - **Communication summary:**
    - **Functionality**: Summarizes business communication, making it easier to digest and understand the main points.

    - **Data Requirements**: Email threads, chat logs, internal communications, team updates, and relevant metadata.
    - **Stakeholders**: Project managers, HR professionals, marketing teams, and communication specialists.
    - **Benefits**: Streamlined communication, reduced time spent sifting through lengthy email chains or chat histories, better knowledge management, and the ability to swiftly gauge sentiments, align strategies, or address concerns.
  - **Transcript summary:**
    - **Functionality**: Provides condensed versions of spoken content, turning lengthy spoken records into brief, understandable written formats.
    - **Data Requirements**: Audio recordings, call logs, lecture recordings, customer feedback calls, and related metadata.
    - **Stakeholders**: Customer service representatives, educators, students, and retail professionals.
    - **Benefits**: Enhanced understanding of spoken content, improved customer service by identifying common pain points from call transcripts, better retention and comprehension for students through summarized lecture notes, and time-saving for professionals needing to understand lengthy discussions or feedback.
  - **Social media trend summary:**
    - **Functionality**: Monitors, analyzes, and distills prevalent trends on social media into digestible reports.
    - **Data Requirements**: Social media feeds, hashtag data, user engagement metrics (likes, shares, comments), and trending topic analyses.
    - **Stakeholders**: Digital marketers, brand managers, content creators, entertainment professionals, and fashion industry experts.
    - **Benefits**: Quick grasp of current market sentiments, the ability to adapt to changing consumer preferences, optimized marketing campaigns, enhanced product designs or content to resonate with current trends, and an overall better alignment with the audience's expectations and interests.
- **Other Use Cases:**
  - **Proposal summary:**
    - **Functionality**: Offers succinct overviews and summaries of varied proposals, aiding in the evaluation process.

        - **Data Requirements**: Detailed investment pitches, policy drafts, and academic research proposals.
        - **Stakeholders**: Venture capitalists, policy evaluators, and academic boards.
        - **Benefits**: Efficient assessment of proposals, streamlined decision-making, and clarity in proposal intentions.
    - **Process and plan summary:**
        - **Functionality**: Condenses complex operational blueprints and strategies into comprehensible summaries.
        - **Data Requirements**: Production schedules, utility maintenance plans, and retail layout designs.
        - **Stakeholders**: Operations managers, utilities planners, and store supervisors.
        - **Benefits**: Efficient execution of plans, clear communication channels, and improved operational clarity.
    - **Event summary generation:**
        - **Functionality**: Synthesizes key details from events into brief summaries for stakeholders.
        - **Data Requirements**: Event schedules, participant lists, and key outcome metrics.
        - **Stakeholders**: Marketing teams, educational seminar planners, and corporate event coordinators.
        - **Benefits**: Enhanced future planning, improved information dissemination, and a comprehensive understanding of event outcomes.

ChatGPT's advanced summarization capability streamlines comprehension and decision-making across various sectors by condensing lengthy documents, communication, and data sets.

Optimizing the usage of ChatGPT for summarization necessitates a commitment to high-quality input data, careful validation of output quality, and rigorous security measures to safeguard sensitive data during summarization.

Transformation

The AI capability 'Transformation' refers to the dynamic adaptability of AI systems to change data or content from one form, format, or language to another. It can facilitate more efficient communication, data interpretation, user interaction, and coding practices.

***Figure 2.20**: Transformation*

Here's how ChatGPT can leverage its transformation capability across various industries:

- **High-value Use Cases:**
  - **Data to visualization:**
    - **Functionality**: Converts raw data into visual representations using plugins such as Code Interpreter or Noteable.
    - **Data Requirements**: Patient records, financial datasets, and manufacturing logs.
    - **Stakeholders**: Healthcare analysts, financial experts, and manufacturing supervisors.
    - **Benefits**: Simplified data interpretation, informed decision-making, and rapid trend spotting.
  - **Data to narrative transformations:**
    - **Functionality**: Transforms structured data into comprehensive narrative formats.
    - **Data Requirements**: Market figures, clinical trial outcomes, and energy production logs.
    - **Stakeholders**: Financial analysts, healthcare researchers, and energy sector strategists.
    - **Benefits**: Facilitated decision-making, increased transparency, and streamlined strategic planning.
  - **Code-to-text transformations:**
    - **Functionality**: Deciphers and translates legacy code into detailed textual documentation.

        - **Data Requirements**: Older and poorly documented code bases.
        - **Stakeholders**: IT professionals, finance system administrators, and industrial software engineers.
        - **Benefits**: Enhanced system maintenance, risk management, and bridge between legacy systems and modern IT.

- **Fast-to-implement Use Cases:**
    - **Text-to-text transformations:**
        - **Functionality**: Transforms text from one form or language into another, aiding in tasks like translation, standardization, and simplification.
        - **Data Requirements**: Textual content like product descriptions, customer feedback, academic materials, and related metadata.
        - **Stakeholders**: Retail professionals, customer service representatives, educators, translators, and content creators.
        - **Benefits**: Enhanced customer experience with multilingual support, standardized data analysis, and improved student comprehension through simplified texts.
    - **Data-to-text transformations:**
        - **Functionality**: Converts raw data into comprehensible text, enabling insights and narratives from data points.
        - **Data Requirements**: Numerical or structured data, such as utility consumption figures, customer purchase data, vehicle telemetry, and associated metadata.
        - **Stakeholders**: Utility providers, retail marketers, automotive service professionals, and data analysts.
        - **Benefits**: Clear customer communication by translating numerical data into understandable text, personalized marketing messages based on behavior data, and preventative maintenance through clear vehicle reports.
    - **Data-to-data transformations:**
        - **Functionality**: Converts data from one format or structure to another, optimizing it for various purposes like analysis, privacy, or system compatibility.
        - **Data Requirements**: Structured data sets like patient records, financial transaction logs, sales data, and any associated metadata.
        - **Stakeholders**: IT professionals, systems engineers, data scientists, business analysts, and data protection officers.

        - **Benefits**: Efficient data exchange, seamless financial system upgrades, and simplified trend analysis with compliant data structures.

- **Other Use Cases:**
    - **Text to interactive content transformation:**
        - **Functionality**: Transforms static textual content into engaging interactive formats.
        - **Data Requirements**: Educational materials, product manuals, and automotive repair guides.
        - **Stakeholders**: Educators, product managers, and automotive technicians.
        - **Benefits**: Elevated learning experiences, improved customer understanding, and streamlined repair tasks.
    - **Code-to-code transformations:**
        - **Functionality**: Converts code from one programming language or format to another.
        - **Data Requirements**: Source code in the original language and intended target language specifications.
        - **Stakeholders**: Software developers, system engineers, and network administrators.
        - **Benefits**: Optimal coding practices, seamless system integration, and advanced network maintenance.

ChatGPT's transformation capability provides substantial value across numerous sectors. It is able to convert text, data and code between formats, languages, visualizations, and narratives, broadly improving communication and comprehension.

To implement the transformation capability effectively, focus must be placed on ensuring transformational accuracy, retaining original nuances, and adhering to strict privacy and security protocols.

Now that we have explored the specifics of each AI capability, we can adopt CapabilityGPT broadly within an AI-first enterprise setting and truly harness the underlying transformative technology of ChatGPT.

Conclusion

CapabilityGPT is an efficient methodology for AI adoption, streamlining the transformation process and offering scalability and efficiency.

As this chapter concludes, we have delved into the principles and potential of CapabilityGPT powered by ChatGPT. The next chapter will spotlight real-world applications and ChatGPT's transformative effects across typical enterprise roles, providing an insight into an AI-integrated working environment.

Building on the exploration of the impact of ChatGPT on individual roles, we will extend our perspective and cover entire enterprise case studies in Appendix B.

Key Points

1. CapabilityGPT leverages the power of GPT models to assist enterprises in their journey to becoming AI-first organizations, aiming to transform business operations and strategies.
2. The framework comprises 18 foundational AI capabilities, each representing a unique aspect of AI's transformational potential. For each of these capabilities, detailed descriptions and real-world use cases are provided, demonstrating the framework's flexibility and broad applicability in enabling a wide range of functionalities and applications.
3. The primary purpose of CapabilityGPT is to serve as a comprehensive repository of AI capabilities that can be used as building blocks for various AI implementations, from AI use cases and AI tools to AI-driven processes, AI-enhanced products, and AI Assistants. Each of these entities utilizes one or more capabilities from the CapabilityGPT framework to fulfill specific requirements, creating a customized AI solution.
4. Unlike traditional AI frameworks that focus on technical groundwork, CapabilityGPT provides a more accessible, adaptable, and business-oriented approach, ensuring AI's benefits are widely accessible across the enterprise.
5. By harnessing CapabilityGPT, businesses can achieve streamlined operations, innovative solutions, and improved decision-making, thereby gaining a significant edge in a rapidly evolving AI-centric business environment.

CHAPTER 3

The Impact of ChatGPT on the Enterprise

Introduction

Building on the insights from the previous chapter on CapabilityGPT, this chapter delves deeper into the real-world implications of these foundational AI capabilities. While we previously highlighted the 18 AI capabilities that can help enterprises transform into AI-first organizations, here we will explore how these capabilities, when used as building blocks, can reshape the workweek of specific enterprise roles.

We focus on six main business roles: Subject Matter Experts, IT-Specialists, Content Creators, Customer Relations Specialists, Knowledge Workers, and Business Leaders (refer to *Figure* 3.1).

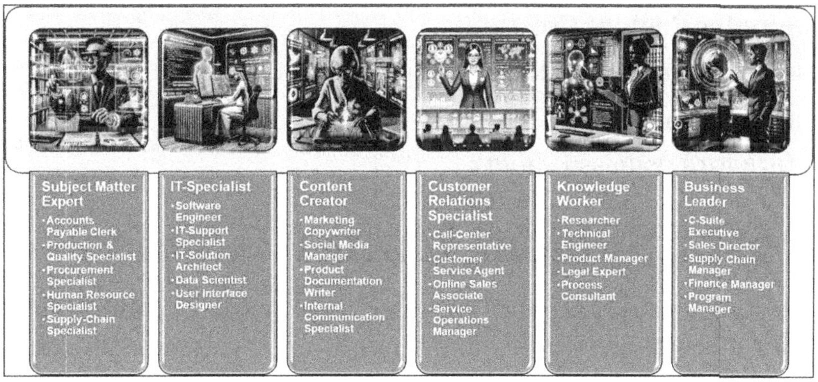

Figure 3.1: *Enterprise Role Overview*

Each of these roles can leverage one or more of the 18 AI capabilities from the CapabilityGPT framework to enhance their daily tasks, innovate in their fields, and make more informed decisions. For instance:

- Subject Matter Experts can automate tasks and routine decisions using specific AI capabilities tailored to their needs.
- IT Specialists can harness ChatGPT's capabilities to enhance system design, data analysis, and foster innovative solutions.
- Content Creators can tap into AI capabilities to inspire and produce quality content.
- Customer Relations Specialists can elevate their customer service standards with the aid of the AI framework.
- Knowledge Workers can utilize specific capabilities for advanced knowledge management and reasoning, leading to heightened productivity and quality.
- Business Leaders, equipped with tailored AI capabilities, can collect more data and perform analyses more rapidly and comprehensively.

With the introduction of CapabilityGPT, AI's benefits are accessible and adaptable across various roles in an enterprise. As we navigate through this chapter, we will illustrate how integrating these AI capabilities through ChatGPT offers enormous opportunities for increased productivity, innovation, and growth across each enterprise role.

Structure

In this chapter, the following topics will be covered:

- Future for Subject Matter Experts
- Future for IT-Specialists
- Future for Content Creators
- Future for Customer Relations Specialists
- Future for Knowledge Workers
- Future for Business Leaders

Future for Subject Matter Experts

Across functions like accounts payable and supply chain management, AI tools are becoming helpful companions for professionals. This section discusses how AI assistance can benefit various roles in their daily tasks. We will focus on the following SME roles: Accounts Payable Clerk, Production and Quality Specialist, Procurement Specialist, Human Resource Specialist, and Supply-Chain Specialist, shedding light on the possible changes in their typical work week.

Accounts Payable Clerk

Introducing Taylor, an Accounts Payable Clerk, who works hand in hand with his AI co-worker, Financial Analysis Intelligence Delegate (FAID), to optimize the accounts payable operations.

Figure 3.2: *Accounts Payable Clerk*

Monday – Complex Invoice Processing and Discrepancy Handling

Taylor and FAID initiate the week by meticulously processing several complex invoices, diving deep into the details to ensure precision and accuracy. While they process a multitude of invoices, we focus on three specific instances to illustrate the recurrent challenges they encounter in their daily operations.

At the outset, FAID leverages its OCR-based **Information Extraction and Analytics** capability to meticulously scan and extract essential data from the invoices. Following this, the **Communication** and **Matchmaking** capabilities come into play as it cross-references the extracted details against the respective purchase orders and delivery receipts from the transactional system, aiming to pinpoint any disparities.

In the first invoice, a discrepancy regarding the recorded delivery quantities surfaces. Taylor hypothesizes, "This doesn't align with the delivery receipts. Could it be an error in the data entry during the recording at our end?" To validate this, FAID initiates a chat-based alignment with the warehouse staff, using its **Communication** function to verify the details. The warehouse staff confirms the mistake, and, with FAID's help, they promptly correct the error in the system, updating the delivery receipt to mirror the accurate details.

Moving onto the second invoice, a deviation in the pricing is evident. Taylor notes, "It seems the vendor has billed us based on their recent price hike, which isn't reflected in the initial purchase order." Here, FAID performs a contract analysis via its **Assessment** capability and discovers a stipulated price tolerance that had not been correctly set up in the system. Without missing a beat, FAID triggers a system configuration update in the transactional system using its **Communication** function to align with the contractual allowances, thereby rectifying the issue seamlessly.

Inspecting the third invoice, they find that the applied tax rate doesn't align with what was stipulated in the purchase order. Taylor instructs, "FAID, it seems the vendor hasn't applied the tax rate as per our agreement in the purchase order, can we reach out for clarification and re-verify this with them?" Utilizing its **Communication** capability again, FAID sends a notification to the vendor to rectify the applied tax rate in accordance with the pre-agreed terms in the purchase order, simultaneously blocking this invoice temporarily to avoid any complications.

Tuesday – Vendor Clarification Management and Approval Initiation

Tuesday is devoted to the intricate task of service invoice processing. Taylor and FAID concentrate on navigating the complexities that come with aligning the multilayered specifications delineated in the purchase orders (POs), the service entry sheets, and the invoices.

Using its astute **Matchmaking** and **Communication** capabilities, FAID plays a pivotal role in this process. It systematically cross-verifies data across these documents, ensuring every detail aligns perfectly, avoiding any future conflicts or discrepancies. For instance, in one of the invoices, a discrepancy is spotted concerning the service duration recorded on the entry sheet and the invoice. To address this, FAID facilitates a chat between Taylor and the service provider to pinpoint the exact details and accordingly adjust the invoice, ensuring an accurate representation of the services rendered.

As the day progresses, Taylor leverages FAID's **Classification** function to adeptly categorize the revised invoices based on various criteria like project alignment, cost bracket, and urgency level. The invoices are then ushered into the approval workflow via FAID's **Communication** function, a pivotal step towards their final settlement.

Wednesday – Final Invoice Adjustment and Approval Completion

On Wednesday, Taylor and FAID engage in active discussions regarding the invoice adjustments. FAID, utilizing its **Communication** ability, integrates vendor clarifications into the invoices as they converse about the best approaches to handle each case.

Taylor might ask, "FAID, could you **summarize** the status of approvals so far?" to which FAID responds with a concise overview, aiding Taylor in making informed decisions and intervening where necessary, keeping the process transparent and collaborative.

Thursday – Detailed Reconciliation

As Taylor and FAID team up on Thursdays to perform a meticulous reconciliation of the accounts payable ledger, Taylor remarks, "We've got a hefty task ahead, matching the outstanding payments with the bank statements. Let's ensure everything aligns perfectly."

FAID promptly starts using its **Matchmaking** and **Communication** capabilities collating the necessary data, bringing up potential mismatches for Taylor's attention. During the process, it flags an unusual transaction, prompting Taylor to inquire, "FAID, what's the reason behind flagging this particular transaction?"

With detailed insights, FAID shares, "The transaction amount with this vendor is significantly higher than their average invoice value, and it is their third invoice this month when they usually send invoices bi-monthly."

Acknowledging the detailed analysis, Taylor decides to investigate further with the vendor, appreciating the keen eye and analytical prowess of FAID in identifying such anomalies.

Before wrapping up the day, Taylor discusses the upcoming payment schedule with FAID, strategizing to prioritize payments optimally using its **Ranking** capability to avoid any late fees while maintaining a healthy cash flow. Taylor remarks, "FAID, let's use our insights to schedule the payments smartly, focusing on due dates and budget availability." FAID complies applying its **Planning** function.

Friday – Reporting and Performance Review

On Friday, Taylor shares the agenda with FAID, "Let's wrap up this week with a comprehensive report highlighting the key activities and identifying areas we can improve for next week."

Via its **Creation** function FAID compiles an insightful report, synthesizing a wealth of data into a snapshot of the week's financial dynamics, facilitating a constructive discussion between Taylor and FAID on future strategies.

Before closing off, Taylor brings up the learning aspect, "We have seen a few OCR errors this week. It would be great if we can learn from these to avoid similar issues in the future."

FAID acknowledges, focusing on self-improvement through learning from the errors encountered during the week and tuning its abilities to better assist in the upcoming tasks.

By partnering with FAID, Taylor manages to process a high volume of complex invoices accurately and efficiently, maintain excellent vendor relationships, ensure regulatory compliance, and continually improve the accounts payable process. Their synergy results in optimized operations and enhanced productivity, significantly contributing to the organization's financial management.

Production and Quality Specialist

Envision a week in the life of Mary, a Production and Quality Specialist, working harmoniously with her AI companion, Production Quality Intelligence System (PQIS).

Figure 3.3: *Production and Quality Specialist*

Monday – Production Monitoring and Safety Checks

Mary starts her week, querying, "PQIS, can you give me an update on production velocity?" Leveraging its **Assessment** capability, PQIS replies, "Current production velocity is at 80% of the optimal speed. There was a slowdown in assembly line 3 due to maintenance work earlier today." Mary appreciates the insight and asks, "What about safety standards?" PQIS quickly highlights potential risk areas, advising Mary to pay extra attention to a section of the production floor where a recent spill happened, to prevent accidents.

Tuesday – Process Adjustments and Quality Assurance

On Tuesday, Mary wants to delve deeper into recurring production issues, asking, "PQIS, have we identified any patterns that lead to production inefficiencies recently?" Through its **Data Mining** function, PQIS highlights, "Yes, there have been frequent short stops in line 2, possibly due to an older conveyor belt showing signs of wear." Mary acts on this information, deciding to schedule a maintenance check for the conveyor belt. Throughout the day, PQIS assists Mary in monitoring the production quality (while using its **Assessment** and **Recommendation** capabilities), suggesting minor adjustments to machine settings to enhance product quality.

Wednesday – Inventory Management and Interdepartmental Collaboration

Mary kicks off Wednesday focusing on inventory and collaboration between departments using PQIS's **Communication** and **Prediction** capabilities. She consults PQIS, "Could we check the inventory status of component X?" PQIS, interfacing with the ERP system, informs, "The current stock for component X is sufficient for this week, but reordering is advised to avoid disruptions next week." Later, she coordinates with the sales department using a virtual collaboration space set up by PQIS to align production with upcoming sales promotions.

Thursday – Documentation, Problem Solving, and Quality Control

On Thursday, Mary records details of the production process, safety protocols, and quality standards. She uses PQIS's **Summarization** capability to condense complex production data into manageable summaries, providing a clearer view of the production landscape. Leveraging PQIS's **Transformation** ability, Mary then converts these summarized data into easy-to-understand visualizations.

While documenting, Mary noticed an anomaly in the quality control data presented by PQIS regarding a specific batch. Upon inquiry, PQIS detailed the reasons for the quality deviation, including inconsistencies in measurements, a temperature spike during curing, and a difference in the mixing ratio of raw materials. Armed with this detailed feedback, Mary plans on rectifying the issues and ensuring they don't reoccur.

PQIS's **Assessment** skill enables her to conduct performance analysis and make necessary adjustments in the production process for better output. Finally, with PQIS's **Prediction** capability, Mary receives alerts about any potential quality deviations in work-in-progress, enabling immediate corrections.

Friday – Training, Performance Review, and Future Planning

Mary focuses on training and future planning as she wraps up the week. She seeks PQIS's assistance in developing training content, asking, "PQIS, can we tailor training modules based on the issues we faced this week?" Using its **Creation** ability, PQIS helps in crafting personalized training sessions addressing specific problem areas. In the afternoon, Mary sits down to review the week's performance and to plan for the next week. With PQIS's **Creation** and **Recommendation** capabilities, she analyzes detailed reports which highlight both achievements and areas needing improvement, setting the stage for a proactive approach to the upcoming week's challenges.

Following the principles of predictive manufacturing, Mary, in active collaboration with PQIS, ensures almost seamless production processes and high-quality outputs daily. PQIS's constant shop floor updates and forward-looking insights empower Mary's role to be operationally effective and also proactive, contributing to a robust production process and the delivery of top-quality products.

Procurement Specialist

Meet Noor, a savvy Procurement Specialist who is closely supported by her AI counterpart, ProcurAce, a system designed to assist in all aspects of procurement processes. Here's a sneak peek into their typical workweek.

Figure 3.4: *Procurement Specialist*

Monday – Supplier Performance Evaluation and Feedback

As Noor scrutinizes the performance metrics, she asks ProcurAce, "How did Supplier B fare in terms of compliance to specifications last quarter?" ProcurAce, utilizing its **Assessment** capability, replies, "Supplier B had a 95% compliance rate, which is a 5% improvement from the previous quarter."

Later, while drafting feedback emails, Noor inquires, "Can you suggest a polite way to address the repeated packaging issues with Supplier C?" ProcurAce assists with its **Communication** skill, proposing, "You might say, 'We value our partnership and believe addressing this recurring packaging challenge can foster a smoother collaboration moving forward'. "

Tuesday – Request for Proposal (RfP) Creation, Vendor Pre-selection and Dispatch

While creating an RfP, Noor asks ProcurAce, "Can we emphasize the environmental standards compliance in the project scope?" ProcurAce leverages its **Creation** ability and suggests, "Absolutely, we can highlight the necessity for adherence to specific environmental norms, showcasing our commitment to sustainable practices."

Later, determining the vendors for RfP dispatch, Noor consults ProcurAce, "Based on past performances, which suppliers would be the best fit for this project?" ProcurAce, employing its **Ranking** capability, advises, "Supplier D and Supplier F are your best bets given their excellent track records in similar projects."

Wednesday – RfP Queries and Response Management

By Wednesday, Noor starts receiving queries related to the RFPs she sent out the previous day. The first order of business is classifying these queries for efficient response management. ProcurAce, using its **Classification** capability, sorts incoming queries into categories such as 'Pricing', 'Timelines', 'Specifications', and 'Ambiguous'.

A specific query from 'Supplier X' is flagged by ProcurAce as 'Ambiguous'. Seeking clarity, Sophie queries ProcurAce. The system explains the flagging due to the query's vague terminology, potential for multiple interpretations, and past interactions with 'Supplier X' where similar ambiguities arose. Given this understanding, Noor decides to handle the query directly to avoid misunderstandings.

For the remaining queries, she uses ProcurAce's **Communication** and **Question Answering** capabilities. The system drafts responses based on pre-set guidelines, queuing them up for Noor's review before sending.

Thursday – Contingency Management and Cost Control

Facing a supply hiccup, Noor turns to ProcurAce, "Can we identify alternative suppliers at short notice?" ProcurAce springs into action with its **Matchmaking** capability, responding, "Yes, Suppliers G and H can potentially meet your requirements; would you like to reach out to them?"

In the afternoon, Noor asks, "What are the potential negotiation points we can consider for cost control?" ProcurAce, tapping into its **Recommendation** function, advises, "You might consider negotiating payment terms or exploring volume discounts to control costs."

Friday – Supplier Collaboration, Forecasting, and Reporting

While reviewing RfP responses, Noor consults ProcurAce, "Can you help me extract the key selling points from Supplier I's proposal?" ProcurAce obliges with its **Information Extraction and Analytics** ability, outlining, "Certainly, they have emphasized their innovative approach and commitment to sustainability."

As they finalize the selection, Noor asks, "How should we convey our decision to the suppliers?" ProcurAce employs its **Communication** skill to propose,

"Let's congratulate the chosen supplier warmly and encourage the others by acknowledging the strengths of their proposals."

By leveraging ProcurAce, Noor ensures precise supplier evaluations and efficient RfP management. She also strengthens supplier collaborations, forecasts more accurately, and contributes significantly to the organization's procurement excellence. This synergy between Noor and ProcurAce underpins the transformative power of AI in optimizing procurement operations and achieving strategic outcomes.

Human Resource Specialist

Step into the shoes of Brian, an experienced Human Resources Specialist, as he navigates the HR landscape hand-in-hand with his AI assistant, HR Helper. Here's a peek into their effective workweek:

Figure 3.5: *Human Resource Specialist*

Monday – Performance Insights and Conflict Simulations

Brian commences his week pondering, "HR Helper, how are our teams faring based on last week's performance data?" Utilizing its **Assessment** capability, HR Helper sifts through varied data to provide nuanced insights.

Identifying areas of concern, Brian asks, "Can we identify possible root causes for the underperformance?" HR Helper leverages its **Cause-Effect Analysis** capability to pinpoint issues such as workload disparities and skill gaps.

Anticipating difficult dialogues ahead, he wonders, "Could we strategize for potential conflicts?" HR Helper enacts its **Simulation** capability, helping brainstorm effective intervention strategies.

Tuesday - Candidate Ranking and Wellness Surveys

With a list of potential hires in hand, Brian inquires, "How can we sort these resumes efficiently?" HR Helper responds by deploying its **Classification** and **Ranking** capabilities, streamlining the candidate selection process.

Later, wishing to gauge employee sentiments, Brian asks, "Can we check in on our team's well-being?" HR Helper sends out a survey using its **Communication** capability and assesses the responses with its **Assessment** capability, offering a snapshot of the current morale.

Wednesday - Content Crafting and Diversity Mining

On Wednesday, Brian expresses a need to bridge identified skill gaps through training, asking, "Can we create engaging training materials?" HR Helper taps into its **Creation** capability to help design enriching content.

Seeking to maintain a diverse workplace, he questions, "What does our diversity landscape look like?" HR Helper delves into extensive data utilizing its **Data Mining** capability, highlighting areas requiring attention.

Thursday - Policy Assessment and Team Matchmaking

Brian starts Thursday with a compliance check, wondering, "Are our policies in line with the current regulations?" HR Helper scrutinizes the policies through its **Assessment** capability, pointing out a potential non-compliance issue for Brian to address.

Later, while discussing team dynamics, Brian suggests, "Let's find the best team pairings for the upcoming project." Here, HR Helper steps in with its **Matchmaking** capability, proposing combinations that would foster productivity and harmony.

Friday - Turnover Prediction and Report Compilation

As the week winds down, Brian seeks projections, querying, "What does the employee turnover look like for the next quarter?" HR Helper engages its **Prediction** capability, providing an informed forecast.

Before closing, Brian requests, "Could we have a comprehensive report of this week's HR dynamics?" With its **Information Extraction and Analytics** and **Transformation** capabilities, HR Helper compiles an extensive report, offering actionable insights for the upcoming week.

Throughout the week, the alliance between Brian and HR Helper embodies the potential of AI in HR—whether it's streamlining tasks, ensuring compliance, or enhancing team dynamics—contributing substantially to the HR function's efficacy.

Supply-Chain Specialist

Imagine a week in the life of Noah, a Supply Chain Specialist, seamlessly integrating his tasks with his AI-driven Supply Chain Control Tower (SCCT).

Figure 3.6: *Supply Chain Specialist*

Monday – Robust Demand and Supply Planning

Starting the week, Noah asks, "How can we accurately anticipate the product demands for this quarter?" SCCT replies by leveraging its **Prediction capability** to analyze historical sales data, seasonal trends, market dynamics, and supplier abilities, presenting a comprehensive forecast to aid in demand and supply planning.

Later, Noah wonders, "Is there a way to automate communications with our suppliers to streamline the ordering process?" SCCT responds affirmatively, highlighting its **Communication capability** to facilitate seamless supplier interactions, helping to maintain a balanced inventory.

Tuesday – Inventory Oversight and Strategy Simulation

On Tuesday, Noah inquires, "Can we get an update on the current status of our inventory across all warehouses?" SCCT employs its **Communication capability** to fetch the latest data from various inventory and warehouse management systems, allowing Noah to make informed decisions based on the current stock levels.

Later, focusing on risk management, Noah asks, "Can we simulate potential supply chain disruptions to better prepare for them?" SCCT activates its **Simulation capability**, crafting several supply chain scenarios and analyzing potential impacts, offering Noah a strategic roadmap for navigating various challenges.

Wednesday – Actionable Insights and Adaptive Strategies

On Wednesday, Noah directs his attention towards a deep implementation of the insights derived from Tuesday's simulations. As he integrates these actionable steps to improve supply chain flow, SCCT's **Communication** capability ensures a seamless interaction between inventory systems, suppliers, and distribution channels.

However, a particular insight from SCCT catches Noah's attention, suggesting a significant shift in one of the supplier partnerships. Curious, he inquires for a deeper rationale. SCCT explains by detailing how a mix of factors such as historical performance, recent industry shifts, and emerging logistical challenges make this insight viable. SCCT illustrates this with a combination of historical data trends, recent supplier ratings, and potential future disruption risks. Armed with this transparent and data-driven insight, Noah considers the implications and starts making necessary adjustments.

Simultaneously, SCCT keeps an eagle-eye over the entire supply chain. From tracking potential supply delays, inventory imbalances to technical glitches, SCCT's Real-time **Communication** and **Assessment** capabilities ensure that anomalies are swiftly detected. Immediate alerts are issued for any inconsistencies, and SCCT's **Recommendation** engine springs into action, suggesting effective countermeasures to mitigate potential issues, ensuring a streamlined supply chain operation.

Thursday – Exception Handling

Facing a sudden production breakdown on Thursday, Noah urgently asks, "What can we do to mitigate the disruption caused by this production breakdown?" SCCT harnesses its **Communication and Matchmaking capabilities** to facilitate urgent discussions and find alternative suppliers, providing solutions to maintain the supply flow without significant delays.

Friday – Performance Evaluation and Reporting

As Friday arrives, Noah focuses on reviewing the week's performance, asking, "Can you help me analyze this week's operations performance?" SCCT utilizes its **Assessment capability** to evaluate different metrics, providing a holistic view of the week's activities.

Later, preparing for a report compilation, Noah requests, "Can we condense all the vital data into a comprehensive yet straightforward report?" SCCT leverages its **Summarization and Transformation capabilities** to craft concise reports with intuitive visualizations, helping Noah grasp the key insights effectively.

Throughout his workweek, Noah employs the comprehensive capabilities of his AI-driven Supply Chain Control Tower (SCCT) to optimize operations and drive efficiency in supply chain management. Utilizing advanced AI features for real-time communication, predictive analytics, simulation, and evaluation, Noah navigates both routine and unexpected challenges, ensuring a robust, resilient, and nearly seamless supply chain process.

Future for IT Specialists

Across roles such as Software Engineer, IT-Support Specialist, IT-Solution Architect, Data Scientist, and User Interface Designer in the information technology domain, the integration of AI is rapidly changing productivity, problem-solving, and innovation capabilities.

Software Engineer

Meet Kim, a Software Engineer, and her AI assistant, CodeMaster, the dynamic duo specializing in the migration of legacy software systems to newer, optimized versions. Let's delve into their typical workweek and discover how they harness AI to streamline software migration.

Figure 3.7: *Software Engineer*

Monday – Detailed Code Analysis and Information Gathering

Kim scans the old codebase, saying, "CodeMaster, we need an assessment. What's the overall quality of this code?"

CodeMaster, employing its **Assessment** capability, replies, "From the initial analysis, there are 50 deprecated methods. For instance, `legacyMethodA()` uses outdated security protocols."

Intrigued, Kim asks, "Have you found patterns or dependencies?"

Leveraging its **Data Mining** skill, CodeMaster points out, "Yes. moduleX and moduleY frequently interact. For example, every time `functionZ()` in moduleX is called, it's reliant on `dataFunctionY()` in moduleY."

Tuesday – Migration Scenario Analysis and Detailed Planning

Kim sketches out a migration map. "CodeMaster, could there be bottlenecks in this approach?"

Using **Cause-effect Analysis**, CodeMaster posits, "One potential issue is the reliance on `legacyDatabase()`. Migrating it first might streamline the rest. Remember how it caused slowdowns during the 'Project Phoenix' migration?"

Feeling the weight of the task, Kim sighs, "We need a detailed plan."

CodeMaster, using its **Planning** capability, advises, "Let's tackle the user interface last, focusing on core functionalities first. This would mirror our successful strategy during the 'Project Atlas' transition."

Wednesday – Transformation: From Legacy Code to Pseudocode and New Code

Kim, sifting through complex legacy code, comments, "This section's logic feels convoluted."

Activating its **Transformation** capability, CodeMaster offers, "Let me simplify `legacyFunctionB()`. Instead of the five nested loops, I can distill it into pseudocode, highlighting the primary actions."

A short while later, CodeMaster presents, "The main loop fetches data, the nested ones process it. I suggest using `modernMethodC()`, similar to how we optimized during the 'Project Delta'."

Thursday – Extended Transformation, Assessment, and Documentation

While refining, Kim notes, "Some parts feel misaligned."

Deploying its **Assessment** process, CodeMaster clarifies, "Yes, `newFunctionD()` might produce errors, as it's missing validation checks. It's similar to the oversight we found in 'Project Echo'."

As documentation progresses, Kim asks, "CodeMaster, any critical insights from the old system we shouldn't miss?"

With its **Information Extraction and Analytics** capabilities, CodeMaster fetches, "Certainly! `legacyFunctionE()` had a unique error-handling mechanism. We should document its logic, much like the notes we kept for 'Project Foxtrot'."

Friday – Testing and Deployment

Kim prepares for the final stretch, "Time for rigorous tests, CodeMaster."

Initiating its **Simulation** capability, CodeMaster suggests, "I'm creating a simulated user environment. Recall userTypeZ from 'Project Gamma'? Their usage pattern could be a starting point."

As testing unfolds, Kim adds, "We need these results in our main suite."

With its **Communication** capability, CodeMaster assures, "Already on it. Integrating with our 'TestMaster' suite, ensuring data consistency."

Working alongside CodeMaster, Kim ensures a smooth transition of software systems and consistent code quality. CodeMaster's regular code reviews and suggestions support Kim's efforts, leading to a methodical migration process and the deployment of reliable software solutions.

IT-Support Specialist

Dive into a week in the life of Alice, an IT-Support Specialist, and her AI assistant, TechMaster. Together, they form an efficient duo in managing operational issues, delivering quality support, and maintaining system integrity.

Figure 3.8: *IT-Support Specialist*

Monday – System Monitoring and User Assistance

As Alice reviews the system logs, she remarks, "Seems like the server had a rough weekend, TechMaster."

TechMaster, tapping into its **Assessment** capability, responds, "It appears the new HR software in the East Wing is stressing our network nodes." With its Explanation feature, it then displays a detailed network flow, highlighting the congested areas.

Throughout the day, users reach out with issues. One user comments, "I can't seem to access our shared drive!" Alice inquires, "TechMaster, got any insights?"

Leveraging its **Question Answering** capability, TechMaster replies, "This mirrors a problem we solved last month. Let's try the same fix." Alice follows the AI's guidance, resolving the issue swiftly. They categorize and track each problem using TechMaster's **Classification** ability.

Tuesday – System Maintenance and Backup Management

Alice pulls up the week's maintenance schedule, musing, "We have a packed agenda, TechMaster." The AI, employing its **Planning** capability, suggests, "Let's tackle software updates first, then manage the backups." Throughout the day, TechMaster orchestrates various tasks, chatting with backup management tools using its **Communication** ability. When an unexpected backup error pops up, TechMaster alerts, "We've got an issue with the finance data backup." Together, they troubleshoot, using the **Classification** capability to monitor the system's state.

Wednesday – Training and Documentation

Preparing for a training session, Alice asks, "TechMaster, can you generate a guide on our new security features?" TechMaster, using its **Creation** capability, drafts an intuitive user guide. Later, during the training, Alice simulates a typical user scenario. TechMaster projects the **simulation**, helping users visualize and understand the new system facets.

Thursday – Network Support and Security Checks

While monitoring the network, Alice notices irregularities, "TechMaster, are we facing any security threats?" TechMaster, with its **Assessment** and **Creation** abilities, provides a report pinpointing potential vulnerabilities. It then activates its **Recommendation** capability: "Based on my analysis, I suggest patch X for vulnerability Y. Also, consider tweaking the firewall settings for enhanced protection."

Friday – Compliance, Reporting, and Future Planning

Wrapping up the week, Alice reflects, "Let's ensure we're compliant with all IT policies, TechMaster." The AI combs through the systems using its **Information Extraction and Analytics** and **Assessment** capabilities and responds, "We're 98% compliant. I've listed the areas that need attention." Alice nods, "Excellent.

Let's also prep for next week." TechMaster, utilizing its **Prediction** capability, showcases potential future challenges, allowing them to strategize accordingly.

Throughout the Week – Troubleshooting, Communication, and Continuous Learning

Every day, Alice and TechMaster juggle multiple responsibilities. They handle user queries, troubleshoot hardware and software issues, and ensure smooth communication between the IT department and the users. TechMaster uses its **Question Answering** capabilities to resolve user queries accurately and promptly. The duo also employs the AI's **Predictive** ability based on new data. This continuous learning, powered by AI's machine learning, optimizes support delivery over time and contributes to user satisfaction and efficient system management.

Alice, with TechMaster, her AI assistant, efficiently manages IT support. Their collaboration leads to quick issue resolution, optimal system operations, and user satisfaction, thereby contributing to overall productivity and growth.

IT Solution Architect

Meet Marcelo, an IT Solutions Architect, and his AI assistant, TechAlign. Here's a detailed breakdown of their work week, showing the practical application of their roles and responsibilities.

Figure 3.9: *IT Solution Architect*

Monday – Infrastructure Evaluation and Solution Alignment

Marcelo, glancing at the ticket dashboard, comments, "TechAlign, that's quite a rise in tickets from sector 5." With its **Assessment** capability, TechAlign observes,

"Let's dive deep into the infrastructure metrics. It seems the server cluster there is under unusual stress." Delving further, the AI's **Cause-Effect Analysis** reveals, "There's an application causing repeated queries, which might be the root issue."

Tuesday – Solution Design and Task Sequencing

As Marcelo's team gathers for their weekly meeting, he prompts, "TechAlign, capture the salient points, especially about the new integration project." Using its **Communication** ability, TechAlign diligently logs the conversation. When integration challenges arise, TechAlign suggests, "How about a high-level overview of data flow between the old and new system? It might clarify some concerns." With TechAlign's **Creation** toolset, they craft a robust design. Before the day wraps, TechAlign, leveraging its **Planning** and **Ranking** capabilities, proposes, "Considering the dependencies, I suggest addressing the database synchronization first."

Wednesday - Data Analysis and Risk Assessment

As Marcelo reviews a vast dataset, he asks, "Can we spot any anomalies or patterns here?"

TechAlign, tapping into its **Data Mining** capabilities, responds, "There are irregular access patterns during off-hours. Let's investigate." Additionally, TechAlign extracts essential compliance data from recent IT documents and standards, mentioning, "These recent standards highlight areas we might want to bolster."

Thursday – System Simulation and Planning

Planning for an upcoming product launch, Marcelo wonders aloud, "I hope our systems can handle the anticipated user influx." TechAlign, eager to test, proposes, "Let's simulate. We can recreate the scenario and assess system response." Following the **Simulation**, TechAlign, drawing from its **Planning** skills, suggests optimizations, "Considering the simulation, optimizing our load balancers would offer better user experience."

Friday – Technology Recommendations and Documentation Simplification

With the week's end nearing, TechAlign, exhibiting its **Recommendation** capability, shares, "There's a new encryption protocol that might enhance our data security." As they work on documenting their progress, TechAlign, harnessing its **Transformation** capability, offers, "These system blueprints are intricate. How about we simplify them into interactive modules for easy team reference?"

Throughout the Week – Query Resolution and Performance Reporting

Regularly, Marcelo consults TechAlign on diverse issues, "What's the latest on cloud security protocols?" or "How does our performance today compare to last month?" With its **Question Answering** ability, TechAlign provides timely and accurate responses. Every evening, TechAlign offers a crisp **summary**, "Based on our current progress and challenges, here's a snapshot of our week."

Working in harmony with TechAlign, Marcelo ensures robust and scalable IT solutions for the organization. TechAlign's regular data insights and proactive problem-solving skills enhance Marcelo's decision-making, culminating in the development and implementation of efficient IT infrastructures.

Data Scientist

Meet Varsha, a Data Scientist, and her AI assistant, InsightAce. Together, they transform raw data into actionable insights and predictive models that help drive business strategies. Let's take a look at their typical week:

***Figure 3.10**: Data Scientist*

Monday – Data Cleaning and Preprocessing

Kicking off Monday, Varsha asks, "What's the state of our raw data today, Ace?" Diving deep into its **Data Mining** ability, InsightAce replies, "There are some interesting patterns, but also anomalies we need to address. Ready for some data transformation magic?" They work together to refine the data, ensuring it's ready for the modeling tasks ahead. Later, Varsha muses, "I wonder if the project team knows about this outlier." Using its **Communication** capability, InsightAce assures, "I've just updated them on our findings and the data's current state."

Tuesday – Feature Engineering

Varsha, examining the data, inquires, "What features can drive our predictive model, Ace?"

Tapping into **Cause-effect Analysis**, InsightAce suggests, "Considering our goals, these variables might impact outcomes significantly. Want to create some new features based on them?" The duo spends the day shaping the data, readying it for algorithm selection.

Wednesday – ML-Algorithm Selection and Model Training

Midweek, Varsha and InsightAce embark on selecting the most suitable machine learning algorithm for their project. With the **Matchmaking** capability activated, they review various algorithms to determine their compatibility with the existing features and desired outputs. Upon spotting a promising algorithm, Varsha expresses her desire to explore it more in-depth to ensure it's the best fit.

InsightAce then employs its Explanation ability, providing Varsha with a comprehensive overview of the chosen algorithm. The AI elaborates on the algorithm's strengths, potential weaknesses, and ideal use cases. It provides visual representations that explain the underlying mathematics, making it easier for Varsha to grasp its operation intuitively. For instance, if they were considering a decision tree, InsightAce might visually represent how the tree divides data and provide context on entropy, information gain, and decision boundaries[1]. This deep dive also covers computational costs, algorithmic assumptions, and potential biases, ensuring Varsha has all the information she needs to make an informed decision.

---

[1]In data analysis, Entropy measures the uncertainty or how mixed-up data is. By using specific characteristics to split this data, we achieve clarity, known as Information Gain. The process creates **Decision Boundaries**, which are like invisible lines or surfaces that effectively categorize different groups within the data.

Feeling confident in their choice, they proceed with the algorithm. Using its **Creation** capability, InsightAce drafts multiple versions of code for different pipelines based on their selected algorithm. The model training then begins, with the AI's **Communication** and **Transformation** capabilities working in harmony to execute the models via API calls and visualize their subsequent results.

Thursday – Model Validation and Refinement

Reflecting on their progress, Varsha questions, "How's our model performing?" InsightAce, drawing from its **Assessment** capability, responds, "Our accuracy and precision look good, but recall needs improvement." They discuss tweaks and improvements, ensuring their model is at its peak performance.

Friday – Model Deployment, Monitoring, and Continuous Improvement

Varsha, looking ahead, wonders, "How can we integrate our model into the existing systems without hiccups?" InsightAce suggests a **plan**, considering potential constraints. "Let's also simulate potential performance scenarios to ensure our model remains robust," it adds, using its **Simulation** capability. They finalize deployment plans, confident of the week's accomplishments.

Throughout the Week – Iterative Improvements and Documentation

As they navigate the week, Varsha often seeks clarity. "Ace, remind me why we chose this parameter?" InsightAce, with its **Question Answering** skill, provides accurate context. They document their process, with InsightAce's **Transformation** turning intricate steps into readable documentation. By week's end, InsightAce wraps up, "Want a quick **summary** of our week?" Ava nods, "Absolutely!" and they review their journey, ready for another data-driven week ahead.

In alignment with InsightAce, Varsha strategically steers the data journey from raw data to clear, actionable intelligence. InsightAce's consistent analytics and proactive approach underpin Varsha's informed choices, reinforcing the iterative process of data science and its translation to business impact.

User Interface Designer

Let's dive into the workweek of Sven, a User Interface Designer, and her AI assistant, DesignMind:

***Figure 3.11**: User Interface Designer*

Monday - Task Alignment and User Interface Evaluation

Starting her week, Sven wonders, "How should we delegate tasks among the team this week?" DesignMind, employing **Matchmaking**, suggests, "Considering everyone's strengths and current workloads, I'd recommend Anna for iconography and Sam for layout optimization." Sven then scrolls through a UI, pondering, "How's the performance of this interface?" Through its **Assessment** capability, DesignMind responds, "Our user feedback and system logs indicate users find the navigation intuitive but the color scheme a tad confusing."

Tuesday - Design Creation, Prioritization, and Organization

Sven, sketching a new UI, asks, "Can you help me visualize a wireframe for this concept?" DesignMind, using the **Creation** capability, displays multiple design options, asking, "How do these look?" Sven nods, "Good start! What's the user feedback on our recent designs?" DesignMind's **Transformation** ability organizes the raw data, "The feedback suggests users appreciate the simplicity, but some find the CTA buttons less prominent. Shall we prioritize addressing this?"

Wednesday - Data-Driven Insights and Design Inspiration

Reviewing some mock data, Sven inquires, "Why is this design element more popular?" Drawing from its **Data Mining** skill, DesignMind explains, "Users find it intuitive, resembling familiar interfaces. Also, its color and placement enhance its appeal." Sven, feeling the mid-week lull, sighs, "I need some fresh inspiration." With its **Semantic Search**, DesignMind promptly showcases, "Here are some trending designs and styles I found."

Thursday – Root Cause Analysis and Predictive Modeling

Upon noticing some user complaints, Sven muses, "What's causing these interface issues?" Tapping into the **Cause-effect Analysis** capability, DesignMind highlights, "It seems the overlapping text in the sidebar is causing confusion. Also, users might struggle with the non-responsive menu on mobile devices." Sven, sketching some changes, asks, "How might users react to this revised design?" With its **Prediction** capability, DesignMind speculates, "Given past behaviors, they'll likely find this more user-friendly, especially the younger demographic."

Friday – Strategy Decisions and Content Development

Sven, looking to improve, asks, "Any suggestions to enhance our interface?" DesignMind, using the **Recommendation** capability, offers, "Based on user data, perhaps making the homepage banner interactive could boost engagement. Also, optimizing our content strategy for the products page might help." Sven nods, "Let's plan this out. What's our approach?" Utilizing its **Planning** ability, DesignMind provides a step-by-step breakdown, ensuring a streamlined process.

Throughout the week – Consistent Support

While working, Sven often checks in, "Is this element crucial?" DesignMind, through its Classification skill, would advise, "It's moderately important, but the search bar takes precedence." At another instance, she asks, "Why is the cart icon typically placed on the top right?" Using the **Question Answering** capability, DesignMind clarifies, "It's a widely accepted design norm for easier user accessibility and visibility." Lastly, to stay updated, Sven regularly requests,

"Summarize our progress and feedback." Relying on its **Summarization** skill, DesignMind provides a concise rundown, ensuring Sven is always informed.

Leveraging DesignMind's data insights, Sven crafts intuitive interfaces that enhance user experience. Their synergy combines creativity with real-world relevance, ensuring each design is both aesthetic and functional. Together, they create user-centric interfaces that anticipate and meet user needs effectively.

Future for Content Creators

Content creation has been transformed with AI capabilities. In this chapter, we delve into the future of content creators - marketing copywriters, social media managers, product documentation writers, and internal communication specialists. Here, we will explore how ChatGPT can unleash their creativity, augment their efficiency, and help them create more compelling and contextualized content.

Marketing Copywriter

Meet Li, a skilled Marketing Copywriter who optimizes his art of storytelling by enlisting the help of his AI assistant, the Creative, Analytical, and Marketing Expert (CAME). The following is an illustration of how he employs CAME in his typical workweek:

Figure 3.12: *Marketing Copywriter*

Monday – Assessment, Actionable Insights and Budget Monitoring

Li starts the week, pondering, "How did last week's content fare across our channels?" CAME, using its **Information Extraction and Analytics** capability, shares, "Your blog post on eco-friendly products had a 20% higher engagement. However, the email campaign for the new product launch saw a slight drop." Curious, Li asks, "Any clues why?" Through its **Cause-effect Analysis** skill, CAME suggests, "The blog's success might be due to the rising trend in eco-consciousness. As for the email, it seems there was a glitch in the call-to-action button for some users." Li then wonders, "How's our marketing budget looking?" CAME, employing its **Assessment** capability, updates, "We're currently 10% under budget. Some ad campaigns underperformed, providing potential savings."

Tuesday - Content Creation Part I, Audience Segmentation and Channel Adaptation

As he drafts a new article, Li inquires, "CAME, could you help optimize this for our target platforms and audience?" CAME, using its **Creation** ability, suggests, "Of course! Incorporating relevant keywords might boost SEO. Also, considering our target demographic, a more casual tone might resonate better." Li nods, "Sounds good. And how about tailoring this for our social channels?" With its **Transformation** capability, CAME assists, "For Instagram, a visual infographic would work. For Twitter, consider breaking the content into a thread."

Wednesday - Trend Analysis, A/B Testing, and Content Testing

Li greets his Wednesday, "CAME, show me the latest content trends across the market." With **Data Mining** and **Information Extraction and Analytics** in action, CAME reports, "An old content style is making a comeback." Li raises an eyebrow, "Really? Dive deeper into that for me." CAME's Explanation skills unfold the narrative, linking the trend to global events and influential figures. Li, impressed, asks, "Alright, let's test our versions of this trend. Can you set up A/B tests for these?" Utilizing its **Sequential Decision-making** capability, CAME confirms, "Of course! I'll keep track of engagement rates for each."

Thursday - Content Creation Part II and Feedback Integration

While drafting another piece, Li wonders, "How might our audience react to this?" Using **Planning** and **Prediction** abilities, CAME offers, "Based on past reactions, they might appreciate a personal anecdote here. Also, there's recent feedback suggesting more visuals." Li responds, "Great insights! Could we also have this translated for our Spanish audience?" CAME's **Transformation** ability ensures, "Absolutely. I'll have it transcribed and translated shortly."

Friday – Research and Collaborative Brainstorming

Looking forward to wrapping up the week, Li proposes, "CAME, pull up the latest in marketing strategies. Also, I have a brainstorming session with the team later." After a **Semantic Search**, CAME presents, "Video marketing and influencer collaborations are seeing increased traction. And for brainstorming, I've set up a virtual space with all necessary tools." Li, content with the week's work, concludes, "Lastly, summarize our week for me." CAME, via its **Summarization** and Transformation capabilities, provides, "We saw a boost in blog engagement, made cost-effective budgetary decisions, embraced a resurfacing content trend, and executed content across channels. Overall, a productive week!"

Li, with CAME's AI guidance, adeptly navigates his marketing copywriting tasks during the week, ensuring content is impactful and relevant. By efficiently handling content performance reviews, audience engagement, strategic adjustments, trend identification, and A/B testing, he emerges well-prepared for forthcoming marketing endeavors.

Social Media Manager

Meet Alex, a diligent Social Media Manager who optimizes his weekly work with the assistance of his AI companion, DASH (Digital and Social-media Helper). Here is a look at a typical work week for Alex:

Figure 3.13: *Social Media Manager*

Monday - Weekly Performance Analysis, Strategic Adjustments and Platform Updates Awareness

Starting his week, Alex inquires, "DASH, how did our recent social campaigns perform? Anything out of the ordinary?" DASH, leveraging its **Assessment** capability, responds, "Your recent Instagram story had 15% higher views than average, likely due to the topical hashtag used. However, Facebook engagement dropped slightly." Alex muses, "That's interesting. Could it be related to any platform updates?" DASH's **Cause-effect Analysis** capability provides a hint, "Facebook updated its algorithm recently, which could be impacting reach."

Tuesday – Content Strategy Alignment and Consistent Brand Voice Management

Sorting through content, Alex asks, "DASH, which posts garnered the highest engagement last week?"

DASH, employing its **Classification** capability, showcases a sorted list and adds, "The behind-the-scenes video and Q&A posts had the best results." Alex nods, "Great, let's align our strategy to produce more of such content. And make sure they're in line with our brand voice across all platforms."

Wednesday - Content Execution, Trend Monitoring, and Platform Adaptation

Midweek DASH's **Creation** capability assists Alex in generating engaging posts and promotional materials. As the content goes live, DASH provides Alex with real-time insights. Alex inquires, "How are the new posts performing compared to last week?" DASH responds, "The latest video content is seeing a 20% increase in engagement, likely due to its relevance to a currently trending topic. However, the infographic post isn't performing as expected, possibly due to its longer length and the current preference of the audience for concise content." Alex, with this information, adjusts his approach to ensure optimal performance. The day further involves DASH's **Communication** ability automating the deployment of posts, and its **Information Extraction and Analytics** capability offers insights on the initial impact of the content.

Thursday - Competitive Benchmarking, Cross-platform Coordination, and Platform Updates Integration

As Alex browses through competitor profiles, he muses, "I wonder what our main competitors have been up to lately." Leveraging its **Semantic Search** and **Information Extraction** and **Analytics** capabilities, DASH replies, "Competitor A has started a new hashtag challenge that's getting quite popular. On the other hand, Competitor B's activity seems steady without significant campaign spikes." Alex ponders this, then asks, "Any predictions on our growth compared to them?" Using its **Simulation** ability, DASH responds, "We're set to grow faster than Competitor B, but Competitor A might see a surge due to their new challenge." Alex then wonders aloud, "Are there any new platform changes to be aware of?" With its **Question Answering** skill, DASH advises, "Twitter's recent tweaks show a preference for video content. It might be worth strategizing around that."

Friday – Forecasting, Strategy Planning and Ensuring Brand Voice Consistency

Alex starts by saying, "I want to be ahead of the curve next week. What does our engagement forecast look like?" Using its **Prediction** capability, DASH projects, "Anticipate a spike in engagement around Wednesday. However, there might be a slight dip over the weekend." Eager for a recap, Alex mentions, "Let's go over this week's performance." DASH, employing its **Summarization** feature, provides, "Your video content from Tuesday was a hit, while the Thursday infographic didn't gain much traction. You've seen a 12% overall increase in engagement from last week." Alex concludes, "Alright, I need to strategize for next week. Let's get a visual summary of this data and ensure our brand voice remains consistent." Utilizing its **Transformation** capability, DASH assures, "You got it, Alex. All content will align with the brand's voice."

Alex, with DASH's AI assistance, skillfully manages his social media tasks throughout the week, ensuring strategies are optimized and engaging. By fostering a growing, engaged follower base, and adeptly handling performance analysis, content alignment, execution, trend tracking, and competitive benchmarking, he emerges well-prepared for upcoming social media challenges.

Product Documentation Writer

Meet Hiroshi, a diligent Product Documentation Writer. With the assistance of his trusted AI companion, WORD (Writing Optimization and Revision Device), he translates complex products into comprehensible guides. Below is a more detailed breakdown of Hiroshi's typical workweek.

***Figure 3.14**: Product Documentation Writer*

Monday – Documentation Evaluation, Strategic Planning, and Task Prioritization

Sifting through recent user feedback, Hiroshi remarks, "Seems like some users are struggling with the latest installation guide. What could be the issue?" WORD's Assessment feature scans the feedback and responds, "Looks like the step for configuring settings isn't clear to some users." Grateful for the insight, Hiroshi nods, "Alright, let's rework that section. And while we're at it, can you help prioritize the sections that need the most immediate attention?" With WORD's Ranking capability, Hiroshi gets a clear roadmap for the week's tasks.

Tuesday – Information Extraction and Content Transformation

As Hiroshi prepares to update the documentation, he asks, "WORD, can you fetch the latest technical details from the product release notes?" Employing its Information Extraction capability, WORD promptly delivers the information. Hiroshi then says, "Great, let's use these to transform the earlier customer queries and tech responses into useful knowledge articles for the new guide."

Wednesday – Guide Creation and Product Feature Alignment

Midway through drafting the user guide, Hiroshi questions, "Have we adequately addressed the product's new security features?" WORD, using its Matchmaking capability, verifies and replies, "The two-factor authentication section could use more details. Would you like some suggestions based on common user queries?" Hiroshi, eager to provide clarity, replies, "Absolutely! Let's ensure our users have all the information they need."

Thursday – Content Review, Quality Assurance, and Summarization

As Hiroshi reviews the week's documentation, he wonders aloud, "Did I cover all the essential product updates in the new guide?" WORD's **Assessment** feature scans the documents, responding, "The new software patch details aren't adequately represented." Grateful for the heads up, Hiroshi revises the guide, ensuring its accuracy. Throughout the day, WORD's **Summarization** capability condenses technical specs and user feedback. This condensed version aids Hiroshi in quickly cross-referencing, ensuring that essential details aren't overlooked, and providing a snapshot of the week's documentation efforts.

Friday – Detailed Communication and Preparations for Next Week

As the week wraps up, Hiroshi reflects, "Before we head into the weekend, let's touch base with the product team to ensure our updates align with any upcoming product changes." Using WORD's Communication function, Hiroshi seamlessly collaborates with the product team, gathering insights and ensuring he's well-prepared for the following week's challenges.

Hiroshi, with WORD's AI support, efficiently handles his product documentation tasks throughout the week, converting intricate product features into user-friendly guides. Expertly managing feedback interpretation, content revision, guide creation, quality checks, and team communication, he remains consistently aligned with product updates and user needs, ensuring he's always ready for future documentation challenges.

Internal Communication Specialist

Step into the shoes of Rebecca, our adept Internal Communications Specialist, as she seamlessly joins forces with her AI ally, Communication Harmonization and Assistance Technology (CHAT), to craft a synchronized communication rhythm within the organization. Here's a glimpse into their dynamic workweek:

Figure 3.15: *Internal Communication Specialist*

Monday – Comprehensive Assessment and Employee Sentiment Tracking

Opening her dashboard, Rebecca remarks, CHAT, *let's get a pulse on our current communication strategies.*

Without missing a beat, CHAT replies, *On it, Rebecca. Using my* **Assessment** *capability, it appears that most of our strategies are resonating well. However, some departments seem less engaged recently.*

Delving deeper, Rebecca ponders, *Could it be due to the recent communication policy changes?*

CHAT, drawing on its **Cause-effect Analysis**, confirms, *Indeed, it seems those departments were more affected by the changes. Perhaps a tailored approach for them could be beneficial?*

Tuesday – Streamlined Classification and Communication

Reviewing her to-do list, Rebecca muses, *We need to ensure that our messages reach the right audience in the most effective way.*

CHAT, already a step ahead, offers, "Why not use my **Classification** capability? We can segment employees based on their communication preferences. Additionally, with my **Creation** skill, I can craft targeted messages ensuring they resonate with each group."

Rebecca, appreciative of the support, agrees, "Perfect! Let's make that happen."

Wednesday – Creative Content Generation and Data Mining

Rebecca, staring at her blank screen, mentions, "We need fresh, engaging content for our newsletters."

CHAT, tapping into its **Recommendation** capability, suggests, "How about an infographic on recent accomplishments or a spotlight section for standout employee stories?"

Intrigued, Rebecca asks, "Sounds great! Any themes or trends we should be aware of?"

Using its **Data Mining** prowess, CHAT informs, "There's been an uptick in discussions around work-life balance. Perhaps addressing that could resonate well?"

Thursday – In-depth Information Extraction and Crisis Communication

While sifting through an influx of company updates, Rebecca muses, "Which is the best channel to relay the latest policy changes?" CHAT, utilizing its **Matchmaking** feature, suggests, "The video conference platform is most attended lately, ensuring maximum reach." Grateful for the tip, Rebecca proceeds. Later, upon detecting a potential misinformation issue, Rebecca realizes swift action is essential. CHAT jumps in with its Crisis **Communication** support: "Rebecca, based on the nature of the misinformation, I suggest a direct email followed by an FAQ post on the internal portal to clear doubts." Armed with CHAT's insight, Rebecca addresses the situation effectively, restoring clarity and confidence within the company.

Friday – Strategic Planning and Reporting

Peering into the coming week's events, Rebecca asks, "CHAT, with the product launch and team building event on the horizon, how should we shape our communication strategy?"

Using its **Recommendation** capability, CHAT responds, "For the product launch, I'd suggest a series of teaser announcements leading up to the day. As for the team building event, perhaps spotlight interviews with past participants could stir excitement."

Rebecca nods in agreement, "That's a solid plan. Oh, and can you compile a summary report of our activities from this week?"

Ever-efficient, CHAT replies, "Absolutely. Using my **Summarization** capability, I'll detail our week's milestones and insights. You'll have it in moments."

Rebecca, with the expertise of CHAT's AI capabilities, masterfully coordinates internal communications throughout the week, fostering an engaged and informed workforce. Excelling in sentiment analysis, targeted messaging, content ideation, crisis management, and strategic planning, she ensures that all organizational communication is timely, relevant, and impactful.

Future for Customer Relations Specialists

In this section, we will journey into the daily routines of various customer relations roles: Call Center Representatives, Customer Service Agents, Online Sales Associates, and Service Operations Managers. Through these real-world insights, we aim to illustrate how ChatGPT amplifies their efficiency and bolsters customer satisfaction, informed interactions, and strategic customer relationship management.

Call Center Representative

We introduce Laura, a hardworking Customer Service Representative, seamlessly working alongside her trusty AI system, Customer Interaction Intelligence Assistant (CIIA). With their duties strategically divided, Laura is enabled to spend the bulk of her time directly interacting with B2B customers. Here's a look into their highly productive workweek:

Figure 3.16: *Call Center Representative*

Monday – Direct Customer Interaction

Kicking off the week, Laura remarks, "Looks like we have a steady influx of calls today, CIIA."

CIIA's smooth voice replies, "Indeed, Laura. I've employed my **Classification** capability to group the inquiries by complexity and urgency. You can dive straight into addressing them while I ensure everything's tracked and ready for follow-up."

Laura smiles, "Perfect. Let's do this!"

Tuesday - Continued Customer Interaction and Behind-the-Scenes Problem Solving

As Laura picks up the phone for another call, she wonders aloud, "CIIA, do we have any historical patterns that might suggest a solution to this particular issue?"

CIIA, drawing from its vast databank, suggests, "Based on similar cases, Laura, I'd recommend these potential solutions." Its **Recommendation** capability offers invaluable insights, empowering Laura to deliver precise, swift resolutions to customer queries.

Wednesday - High-Volume Customer Engagement and Dynamic Call Management

Wednesday is usually the peak of Laura's workweek in terms of customer engagement. This particular day, she notices an unprecedented spike in call volumes. Slightly overwhelmed, Laura wonders, "Why is there such a surge today? Did something change?"

CIIA, using its **Data Mining** and **Cause-effect Analysis** capabilities, swiftly checks any recent product updates, company announcements, or any external events that might affect the influx. "Laura," CIIA notifies, "Our latest product update seems to have resulted in some unexpected software glitches for several users, causing the increase in calls."

With this newfound understanding, Laura addresses the situation head-on. CIIA assists by prioritizing calls from customers directly affected by the software glitch using its **Ranking** capability based on customer importance and number of employees using the product. Meanwhile, it automatically generates a general troubleshooting guide based on recurring issues and complaints using its **Creation** ability and employs its **Communication** capability to send the guide via email to those waiting in the call queue. This not only reduces the wait time but also empowers customers with immediate solutions.

By the end of this demanding day, Laura and CIIA have seamlessly managed to turn a potential crisis into an opportunity, showcasing their resilience and customer-centric approach.

Thursday - Emphasizing Customer Retention and CRM Updates

After a deep breath, Laura states, "Thursdays! Always challenging with our high-risk customers. Make sure any calls from them come straight to me, CIIA."

CIIA, accessing its **Matchmaking** capability, assures, "Already on it, Laura. And remember, if you need guidance on managing these interactions, my Sequential Decision-making capability can provide the best steps based on past data and customer profiles."

Laura nods appreciatively, "Thanks, CIIA. And while we're at it, let's make sure our CRM is up to date."

CIIA, ever vigilant, responds, "I've been using my **Communication** ability to automate the data entries. No worries on that front!"

Friday – Quality Assurance and Planning for the Future

As Friday dawns, Laura ponders, "CIIA, what's our forecast looking like for next week?"

CIIA, tapping into its **Prediction** capability, shares, "Expect moderate call volumes on Monday and Tuesday, but there might be a slight surge on Wednesday due to the upcoming product release."

Laura nods, taking note, "Good to know. And how did we fare this week? Any feedback?"

CIIA, ever ready to assist, replies, "Using my **Assessment** Capability, I've noticed some areas of excellence and a few where we could improve. Let's chat about it during our end-of-week review?"

Laura, aided by CIIA's advanced AI functionalities, efficiently handles B2B customer interactions throughout the week. Balancing direct customer engagement, problem-solving, crisis management, customer retention, and forward planning, she exemplifies top-tier customer service.

Customer Service Agent

Step into the world of Eva, an adept Customer Service Agent, and her intelligent AI counterpart, CASH (Customer Assistant Super Helper). Together, they form an unmatched duo, ensuring customers receive impeccable service. Dive into their conversational workweek:

Figure 3.17: *Customer Service Agent*

Monday - Evaluation and Ticket Management

Opening her dashboard on Monday morning, Eva remarks, "Wow, CASH, we have a lot of inquiries from different channels today."

CASH, activating its **Classification** capability, responds, "Yes, Eva. I've already categorized them based on the issue type, account status, and complexity. With the **Ranking** feature, I've prioritized them, so we tackle the most urgent ones first."

Eva, relieved, replies, "Great! Let's ensure every customer feels heard and valued."

Tuesday – Issue Resolution and Feedback Analysis

As she sips her morning coffee, Eva muses, "I hope we can resolve most of the customer issues today. Can you help me understand the major categories, CASH?"

Tapping again into its **Classification** capability, CASH offers, "Of course, Eva. Most of the problems fall into these three categories. However, there are a few complex ones that might need escalation."

While working through the day, Eva checks in, "CASH, what's the feedback looking like? Any patterns?"

CASH, analyzing the feedback via its **Data Mining** capability, informs, "I've noticed a trend in the feedback from our chat channels. It seems there's a recurring issue in the billing process. Might be worth looking into for service improvement."

Wednesday - Product Knowledge Enhancement and Direct Customer Interaction

Eager to enhance her product knowledge, Eva inquires, "CASH, I'd like to familiarize myself with the latest product features. Could you guide me?"

CASH's **Semantic Search** skill dives into the database, "Certainly, Eva. Here are the latest updates on our products. I've also highlighted common questions customers have been asking recently to help you prepare."

Eva, grateful, replies, "This will be incredibly helpful for our interactions. Thanks, CASH!"

Thursday – Record Keeping and Communication

Mid-conversation with a customer, Eva asks, "CASH, can you help me keep a detailed record of this interaction?"

CASH's **Transformation** capability gets to work, "On it, Eva. I'll ensure all details are logged and structured for easy reference later."

Later, during a particularly complex customer issue, Eva checks, "CASH, are we communicating clearly and empathetically?"

CASH, utilizing its **Communication** ability, ensures, "Absolutely, Eva. I'm here to make sure the customer feels understood and valued throughout the conversation.

Friday – Process Improvement and Strategic Planning

While reflecting on the week's interactions, Eva identifies a recurring issue: a significant number of customers have been expressing confusion about a new product's setup process. The issue has become more prominent lately, resulting in a higher number of inquiries and dissatisfaction levels.

Eva sees this as an opportunity for improvement. "There must be a way to streamline the setup process or at least guide the customers better," she ponders.

Recognizing her concern, CASH steps in, "Eva, would you like me to analyze this further?"

Using its **Data Mining** capability, CASH analyzes all recent customer queries related to the product setup. It identifies common themes and specific steps in the process where customers tend to get stuck. CASH then employs its **Semantic Search** capability to scour the existing knowledge base, trying to determine if there are any gaps in the information provided to customers.

CASH reports, "Eva, it appears that Step 3 in the setup process lacks clarity. Also, there isn't a troubleshooting guide specifically addressing potential issues in this step."

Eva nods, realizing the gap. "What can we do to resolve this, CASH?"

CASH, using its **Creation** capability, drafts a more detailed and user-friendly guide for Step 3. It also generates a concise troubleshooting section addressing potential hiccups users might encounter during this step. Additionally, it crafts an interactive video tutorial, ensuring a more visual and step-by-step approach.

Eva reviews and approves the materials, and with CASH's **Communication** capability, they roll out the new resources to customers. By the end of the day, they begin to receive positive feedback from customers, appreciating the enhanced clarity.

Thanks to their collaborative approach, Eva and CASH have transformed a challenge into an opportunity, significantly improving a critical aspect of customer experience.

Throughout the week, Eva and her AI assistant, CASH, excel in managing customer inquiries, categorizing issues, and enhancing service processes. Their combined strengths address every customer need efficiently. On recognizing a product setup confusion, they promptly act, underlining their commitment to elevating customer experience.

Online Sales Associate

Join Fatemeh, a sharp Online Sales Associate, as she synergizes with her AI partner, Sales Optimized Robot Incredibly Knowledgeable (SORIK), to excel in the fast-paced realm of digital sales. Their week is an interplay of data-driven decisions, customer engagement, and dynamic sales strategies:

Figure 3.18: *Online Sales Associate*

Monday - Sales Performance Summary and Product Knowledge

Starting Monday, Fatemeh asks, "SORIK, can you summarize last week's online sales performance and highlight any areas where we can improve?"

SORIK, activating its **Summarization** and **Assessment** features, responds, "Absolutely, Fatemeh. Last week we saw an increase in sales for category X, but there's room for improvement in category Y. Additionally, based on recent updates, there's a new product line that's just been introduced."

Fatemeh, curious about the new offering, inquires, "Can you detail the new products, their benefits, and pricing? Also, do we have any predictions about upcoming trends?"

SORIK's **Semantic Search** and **Prediction** skills come to the fore, "Of course. Here are the details about the new products. Also, based on current data, I forecast a potential surge in website traffic, especially in the home decor section, for the upcoming week."

Tuesday – Customer Interaction, Order Processing, and After Sales Service

As she goes through the morning's emails, Fatemeh remarks, "There are a lot of customer queries today. SORIK, can we categorize them by preference to ensure I handle them effectively?"

SORIK's **Classification** skill gets to work, "Certainly. I've classified the queries into 'product-specific', 'order-related', and 'general inquiries'. This should aid in your responses."

During the day, Fatemeh observes, "I see several transactions in progress. SORIK, are we tracking the order fulfillments?"

SORIK, with its **Communication** feature active, replies, "Yes, Fatemeh. I'm managing online transactions, processing payments, and ensuring smooth order tracking. Post-purchase, I'm also suggesting after-sales services or complementary products based on each customer's profile."

Wednesday - Product Placement and Inventory Management

Reviewing the online store's layout, Fatemeh wonders, "SORIK, how are we faring in terms of product placements? And are we keeping up with the inventory?"

SORIK's **Data Mining** skill offers insights, "Fatemeh, the 'Lifestyle Gadgets' section seems to be a hit, but some products are running low on stock. Shall I check other warehouses or suggest replacements?"

Fatemeh nods, "Yes, please. And also, let's plan the restocking based on sales data and upcoming trends."

SORIK's **Matchmaking**, **Communication**, and **Planning** capabilities synchronize, "I've identified suitable replacements and also created a restocking plan. With these adjustments, we can ensure our online store remains appealing and efficient."

Thursday - Relationship Building and Customer Service

On Thursday afternoon, Fatemeh notices an uptick in the number of customers inquiring about a particular product range that hasn't been the focal point of the store's promotions. It seems that a group of influencers might be driving traffic and interest toward this range.

"SORIK," Fatemeh questions, "have there been any recent social media mentions or promotions regarding our 'Eco-Friendly Home' product range?"

Utilizing its **Information Extraction and Analytics** feature, SORIK identifies that a few prominent eco-conscious influencers have recently mentioned the 'Eco-Friendly Home' range in their posts, causing increased interest and traffic toward the online store.

"Indeed, Fatemeh," SORIK replies. "Three influencers have recently highlighted our 'Eco-Friendly Home' range. It's garnered significant engagement on their platforms."

Fatemeh thinks for a moment. "Can we capitalize on this unexpected promotion?"

SORIK's **Recommendation** capability gets to work, suggesting, "To leverage this organic promotion, we can offer these influencers an affiliate partnership. For every sale made through their referral, they could earn a commission. This might incentivize them to continue promoting our products."

Fatemeh nods, appreciating the idea. "Alright, draft a proposal for this affiliate program, SORIK. And let's get in touch with these influencers."

With SORIK's **Communication** skill, Fatemeh sends out crafted proposals to each influencer, offering them the affiliate partnership. By the end of the day, two influencers have already shown interest in collaborating, turning an unexpected trend into a potential profitable partnership.

Thursday concludes with Fatemeh appreciating the versatility of SORIK and the way they collaboratively turn challenges into opportunities, ensuring they always stay ahead in the dynamic world of online sales.

Friday – Training, Feedback, and Future Planning

Finishing off the week, Fatemeh reflects on her professional growth, "SORIK, do we have any training modules that could enhance my skills?"

SORIK, using its **Recommendation** feature, suggests, "Fatemeh, considering your recent performance review and role requirements, I'd recommend these e-learning modules. They cover the latest trends in online sales and customer relationship management."

Before signing off, Fatemeh decides to offer feedback, "Let's send some insights to our managers regarding recent customer reactions and product demands."

SORIK, leveraging its **Communication** capability, drafts the feedback, "I've collated the customer feedback and highlighted the most-requested products. Ready to send when you are."

Fatemeh and her AI companion, SORIK, seamlessly blend data-driven insights and proactive engagement to optimize digital sales. From evaluating sales performance and managing inventory to harnessing unexpected promotional opportunities, their synergy proves pivotal. Their week embodies adaptability, foresight, and innovation, leading to personal growth and strategic feedback to superiors.

Service Operations Manager

Meet Liam, a dedicated Service Operations Manager, who, alongside his AI co-worker, Operational Intelligence Specialist (OPIS), ensures smooth operations and superior service delivery within their organization. Here's a glance into their typical workweek:

Figure 3.19: *Service Operations Manager*

Monday - Efficiency Assessment and Service Oversight

As Monday unfolds, Liam mulls over, "OPIS, how efficient are our service delivery processes currently? Any areas that need our immediate attention?"

OPIS, with its **Assessment** capability activated, offers insights, "Liam, I've noted a few gaps in our delivery timeline for services B and D. Also, based on customer feedback, there are suggestions for improving our after-sales response."

Liam nods, "Let's ensure seamless coordination between departments for this. Can you facilitate communication?"

OPIS assures with its **Communication** feature, "Already on it. I've scheduled a catch-up between teams to address these concerns."

Tuesday - Classification and Team Development

While going through the day's tasks, Liam remarks, "There's a heap of customer requests coming in. OPIS, can you classify them so we can handle them more efficiently?"

OPIS's **Classification** skill gets to work, "Sure, Liam. I've categorized the requests into three main types: urgent, maintenance-related, and general inquiries. This should help in better task allocation."

Later, Liam ponders on team improvement, "OPIS, can we devise a training module tailored to our team's needs?"

OPIS, utilizing its **Creation** capability, responds, "Certainly. I've crafted a training material focusing on enhancing customer interaction skills and managing challenging service scenarios."

Wednesday - Service Management and Resource Allocation

In the middle of the week, Liam emphasizes, "Service delivery needs to be top-notch today. OPIS, help me ensure we have adequate staffing and resources."

OPIS, activating its **Matchmaking** and **Planning** capabilities, provides assurance, "Liam, I've matched available resources with the expected service load for the day. Additionally, I've scheduled staff ensuring all roles are adequately filled for seamless service delivery."

Thursday - Sustainability Initiatives and Green Inventory Management

As the week progresses, Liam realizes the importance of incorporating sustainability into service operations. He wants to ensure that their organization is not just efficient but also eco-conscious.

"We need to check our carbon footprint, OPIS. Can we identify areas within our operations where we might be utilizing resources that aren't environmentally friendly?" Liam inquires.

Using its **Information Extraction and Analytics** feature, OPIS scans through the entire operations inventory, identifying materials and processes that might have a higher environmental impact. "Based on my analysis, Liam," OPIS begins, "there are a few areas we can optimize. For example, the packaging materials used in some sectors have non-biodegradable components."

Liam, deep in thought, suggests, "Perhaps we can collaborate with suppliers to develop more eco-friendly packaging solutions?"

OPIS, with its **Communication** skill, quickly connects with suppliers to discuss possibilities. "I have initiated communications with our vendors, Liam. A couple of them already have sustainable alternatives they've been exploring."

Furthermore, leveraging its **Data Mining** and **Recommendation** capabilities OPIS suggests, "Based on waste management analytics, I've observed that recycling practices within our operations can be improved. By integrating better waste segregation processes and collaborating with green logistics providers, we could considerably reduce our environmental impact."

By the end of Thursday, with OPIS's in-depth analysis and proactive solutions, Liam has initiated a plan to make the organization's service operations more sustainable. He appreciates how, with OPIS's capabilities, they're not only maintaining operational efficiency but also taking steps towards a more sustainable future.

Friday - Strategic Planning and Administrative Tasks

As Friday dawns, Liam gears up for the upcoming week, "OPIS, using our service metrics, can we simulate different strategies for next week?"

OPIS, using its **Simulation** capability, presents, "Certainly, Liam. I've simulated three possible scenarios based on our metrics. Here's how each might play out in terms of efficiency and customer satisfaction."

In the midst of administrative tasks, Liam asks, "OPIS, can you assist in automating our interactions with the service-specific applications and ensuring we have a comprehensive record for future reference?"

With its **Communication** capability, OPIS responds, "All set. I've streamlined interactions and archived all relevant service records for easy access later."

Liam and his AI ally, OPIS, synergize to optimize organizational service delivery. From streamlining customer requests, formulating bespoke training modules, and ensuring adequate resource allocation to pioneering sustainability initiatives and strategizing for the week ahead, the duo showcases efficiency, foresight, and eco-consciousness.

Future for Knowledge Workers

Welcome to the futuristic landscape of AI-enabled knowledge workers. In this section, we will delve into the workweeks of diverse professionals: researchers, technical engineers, product managers, legal experts, and process consultants. These real-world illustrations will shed light on how ChatGPT can elevate their productivity, drive informed decision-making, and catalyze innovative thought processes.

Researcher

Welcome to a week in the life of Anita, an innovative, futuristic researcher, who, along with her AI ally, Advanced Research Intelligence Assistant (ARIA), is transforming the landscape of research. Here's how their collaboration unfolds:

Figure 3.20: *Researcher*

Monday – Appraisal and Planning

While reviewing research projects, Anita poses a question, "ARIA, how do our current research projects stack up in terms of performance and impact?"

ARIA, employing its **Assessment** capability, responds, "Based on our parameters, Project Alpha has the highest impact, but Project Beta needs immediate attention due to its potential."

Feeling strategic, Anita deliberates, "Alright, ARIA, let's plan our week. Can we list our tasks and prioritize them?"

ARIA's **Planning** and **Ranking** abilities come into play, "Certainly. Here's a sequence of tasks for the week, starting with the most pressing ones."

Tuesday – Domain Exploration and Experiment Setup

As Anita dives deep into research, she inquires, "ARIA, can you fetch relevant papers related to our new hypothesis?"

Utilizing its **Semantic Search**, ARIA retrieves, "I've found 15 papers that align closely with your topic. I've also extracted the key findings to help us craft our research approach."

Impressed, Anita continues, "Great! Let's use this information to set up our experiment."

Wednesday – Literature Review and Experiment Execution

Reviewing a stack of articles, Anita asks, "ARIA, are there patterns or trends we should be aware of from these papers?"

With its **Data Mining** capability at the forefront, ARIA points out, "Several papers highlight a consistent anomaly in the data which might be crucial for our experiment."

As she proceeds with the experiment, Anita seeks guidance, "ARIA, based on the current data, should we adjust our approach?"

ARIA's **Sequential Decision-making** feature suggests, "Considering real-time results, I'd recommend adjusting the sample size."

Thursday – Cross-disciplinary Integration and Model Simulation

As her research reaches a new stage, Anita understands the necessity of integrating insights from multiple disciplines. "ARIA, can we look at how the current findings relate to concepts in evolutionary biology and computational modeling? There could be some overlap we're missing," she suggests.

ARIA's **Semantic Search**, **Information Extraction and Analytics** and **Data Mining** capabilities kicks into gear. It delves into databases not just from Anita's core research domain but extends to areas in evolutionary biology, computer science, and more. "Anita," ARIA starts, "There are numerous parallels between our current findings and some theories in evolutionary biology. Additionally, certain computational models might help in better visualizing and understanding these overlaps."

Anita, curious and excited, prompts, "Can we simulate our data within these models and predict possible outcomes?"

ARIA's Model **Simulation** skillset, which is adept at formulating and executing computational models, gets to work. It integrates Anita's research data, combines it with the models from computer science, and uses insights from evolutionary biology to simulate potential scenarios. The AI also uses its **Transformation** capability to visualize the results in an understandable and interactive format for Anita.

She reviews the simulations, impressed with how it provides a novel lens to view her research. "ARIA, this could be groundbreaking! I think we might be onto something new here, bridging gaps between disciplines," Anita muses.

By Thursday's end, with ARIA's help, Anita has uncovered interdisciplinary connections that could enrich her research tremendously. The day's explorations have provided a fresh perspective, opening doors to pioneering approaches and collaboration possibilities across diverse academic fields.

Friday – Opportunities and Publication Planning

Ready to wrap up the week, Anita contemplates, "ARIA, given our findings, which journals should we consider for publication? And are there funding opportunities we can tap into?"

ARIA, employing its **Matchmaking** ability, lists, "There are three journals aligning with our research focus. Additionally, I've identified two grants that can support our work."

With the data in hand, Anita mulls, "Let's start drafting our manuscript. And can we have a concise visual representation of our results?"

ARIA's **Creation** and **Transformation** capabilities kick in, "Absolutely. I've outlined the manuscript and generated a few graphs to visualize our findings."

Reflecting on the week's accomplishments, Anita muses, "ARIA, how did we fare this week?"

ARIA, with its **Summarization** capability, concludes, "We've made significant strides, especially in interdisciplinary research. Our projects are on track, and our new findings promise exciting avenues."

With the assistance of ARIA, Anita streamlines her research process, effectively accessing relevant information and identifying potential interdisciplinary connections. Their collaboration simplifies complex tasks and promotes efficiency. This partnership between Anita and ARIA illustrates the practical benefits of integrating AI into everyday research tasks and decision-making.

Technical Engineer

Welcome to a week in the life of John, a future technical engineer, who, with his AI sidekick, Technical Intelligence Entity (TECHIE), navigates complex tasks with ease. Here's how their collaboration works:

Figure 3.21: *Technical Engineer*

Monday – System Analysis and Planning

John, reviewing system logs, inquires, "TECHIE, have we spotted any system anomalies recently? What might be causing these?"

TECHIE, employing its **Cause-Effect Analysis**, responds, "There are slight irregularities in the cooling system. It appears to be linked to the recent software update."

Grateful for the swift insight, John says, "Can you list down recommended actions based on urgency?"

TECHIE's **Classification and Ranking** abilities shine through, providing a structured to-do list. "Certainly, John. Here's a list of tasks, starting with the most critical ones."

Tuesday – Design and Simulation

As John sketches a new component, he wonders, "TECHIE, do we have any references or existing standards that might be relevant to this design?"

With its **Semantic Search** in play, TECHIE offers, "I've found several blueprints that could inspire improvements in your current sketch. Also, there are three engineering standards pertinent to this component."

Once the design advances, John asks, "Could we simulate this design under varying conditions to identify vulnerabilities?"

TECHIE affirms, "Of course, initiating the simulation now." Its **Simulation** capability models the component's behavior, eventually pointing out, "It seems there might be a slight weakness under extreme temperature fluctuations."

Wednesday – Manual Creation and Test-equipment Setup

John, starting the day with a challenge, muses, "TECHIE, I need to draft a technical manual for our new product. Can you provide relevant safety guidelines and operational instructions?"

TECHIE's **Information Extraction** capability quickly scans existing manuals and responds, "Here's a comprehensive list. I've also added some frequently reported user issues for you to address."

Later, setting up a test rig, John asks, "TECHIE, could you guide me on the setup?"

TECHIE, with its **Question Answering** capability, details, "Start with the mainframe connection, then move on to the sensor array..."

Thursday – Field Troubleshooting and Remote Support

On-site at a client's facility, John connects TECHIE to a malfunctioning unit, querying, "What seems to be the problem here?"

TECHIE, with its Automated Diagnostics based on its **Classification and Cause-effect Analysis**, immediately pinpoints, "There's an issue with the power distribution module. I suggest checking the third relay."

John, donning his AR glasses via its **Communication** feature, sees the malfunctioning area highlighted, "This AR overlay is handy. Do we have a replacement part nearby?"

TECHIE, cross-referencing inventories, informs, "Yes, there's one at our downtown facility. I'll reserve it for you."

If John ever stumbles, TECHIE's **Matchmaking** feature suggests, "Would you like to consult with Lisa from the main office? She resolved a similar issue last month."

Friday – Task Management and Review

With a busy week behind, John reflects, "TECHIE, how did we fare this week? Any looming issues we should be prepared for?"

TECHIE, running its **Data Mining** and **Summarization**, offers a concise report, "We addressed 90% of flagged issues. However, there's a predicted increase in system load next week."

Grateful, John wraps up, "Thanks, TECHIE. Let's plan accordingly."

In his role as a technical engineer, John capitalizes on TECHIE's capabilities to efficiently navigate system intricacies, manage tasks, and ensure optimal solutions. Their combined efforts enhance problem-solving, streamline design processes, and bolster system reliability. This collaboration between John and TECHIE exemplifies how AI can seamlessly integrate with engineering tasks, elevating efficiency and precision.

Product Manager

Experience a week in the life of Budi, a Product Manager, who navigates his multifaceted role with the assistance of his AI ally, Product Management Intelligent Assistant (PMIA). Here's how they transform a hectic workweek into a strategic endeavor:

Figure 3.22: *Product Manager*

Monday – Post Launch Retro Planning and Product Customization

As Budi reviews the recent product launch feedback, he asks, "PMIA, how did our product fare against the KPIs we set? Were there any noteworthy customer feedback themes?"

PMIA activates its **Assessment** and **Data Mining** capabilities, sharing, "The product met 85% of our KPIs. However, feedback indicates some users found the onboarding process slightly confusing. The good news is that feature adoption rate is higher than expected."

Delving deeper, Budi queries, "Which factors influenced these KPIs most?" Drawing from its **Cause-Effect Analysis**, PMIA offers, "The intuitive design has contributed positively to adoption. However, intermittent technical glitches affected the onboarding experience."

Tuesday – Classification, Cross-Functional Communication, and Customer Engagement

Budi, preparing for a cross-functional meeting, asks, "PMIA, can we prioritize the features based on user feedback and align our teams accordingly?"

PMIA, utilizing its **Ranking** capability, responds, "Certainly! Here's a prioritized list based on feedback. It might be beneficial to align sales with the top features for their pitches and involve the production team with the most reported issues."

Later, as Budi contemplates enhancing user engagement, he ponders, "What if we introduced a feedback chatbot?"

PMIA, knowing its **Communication** strength, excitedly shares, "That's a great idea! I can assist in data entry and feedback collection through chatbot interactions. This will provide real-time insights and enhance customer engagement."

Wednesday - Blueprint Creation and Forecasting

Budi, while conceptualizing the next-gen product blueprint, wonders, "PMIA, while we do have several innovative features in mind based on the latest trends, why do some of our earlier ideas not resonate well with our target demographic?"

PMIA's **Information Extraction and Analytics** and **Cause-effect Analysis** capabilities comes to life, addressing the "why" and "why-not" questions by analyzing historical data, market feedback, and industry trends. "Budi," PMIA begins, "Some of the earlier concepts, though technologically advanced, lacked intuitive user interfaces or did not align with the predominant use-cases of our target demographic. Moreover, a few were too ahead of their time, leading to adoption resistance."

Acknowledging the insights, Budi probes further, "What about our competitors? Why have some of their analogous features been better received?"

Diving deeper using its **Semantic Search** and **Assessment** capabilities PMIA evaluates competitor product reviews, expert opinions, and market reports. "Budi," PMIA continues, "It seems competitors invested heavily in user education, ensuring potential users understand the feature's value proposition. Additionally, their onboarding processes were more streamlined, reducing the adoption barrier."

Motivated, Budi concludes, "PMIA, let's ensure our blueprint prioritizes user experience and education. I want us to forecast potential acceptance rates and ensure we align with customer expectations while staying innovative."

By Wednesday's end, Budi, backed by PMIA's insights, has a refined product blueprint that's both innovative and tailored to meet user expectations.

Thursday - Competitive Analysis and Resource Alignment

Budi, looking to further enhance user engagement, wonders, "PMIA, how do our competitors approach user education? What can we learn from them?"

PMIA, deploying its **Information Extraction and Analytics**, responds, "Analyzing competitors, they frequently update user tutorials and host monthly community webinars. Their engagement on community forums is also noteworthy."

Interested, Budi muses, "That's insightful. Let's align our features with suitable educational content. I want our users to feel fully supported."

PMIA, leveraging its **Matchmaking** capability, assures, "On it! Here's a proposed alignment of features with potential educational content."

Friday - Market Planning and Review

To round off the week, Budi contemplates, "PMIA, based on our discussions and findings, how should we adjust our go-to-market strategy?"

PMIA, with its **Planning** capabilities at full throttle, advises, "Emphasizing user education and smooth onboarding will be key. Additionally, focusing on community engagement will foster trust and enhance user experience."

Satisfied, Budi reflects, "Thanks, PMIA. Let's **summarize** this week and chart out our steps for the next phase." PMIA complies.

In his role as a Product Manager, Budi masterfully collaborates with PMIA, turning challenges into opportunities and ensuring product success. Together, they analyze feedback, forecast trends, align resources, and constantly refine strategies. This synergy between Budi and PMIA underscores the transformative potential of AI in bolstering product management, ensuring that innovation always aligns with user needs and market demands.

Legal Expert

Observe the professional synergy of Lara, a Legal Expert, and her AI assistant, Legal Intelligence Assistant (LegAI). Together, they effectively manage a myriad of tasks in an organized and efficient fashion. The following is a detailed overview of their weekly routine and the integration of their combined capabilities:

Figure 3.23: *Legal Expert*

Monday - Risk Evaluation and Comprehensive Analysis

Kicking off the week, Lara glances over recent company activities and muses, "LegAI, can you run a risk evaluation on our latest actions and check their compliance?"

LegAI, using its **Assessment** capability, confirms, "Certainly, Lara. Reviewing the activities against current legal standards indicates potential exposure in three areas due to recent legal amendments."

Lara, intrigued, questions, "What might be the implications of these legal changes?"

Activating its **Cause-effect Analysis**, LegAI elaborates, "One change might escalate disputes due to vagueness, while another could increase contractual liabilities. The third might alter how we handle customer data, posing potential GDPR challenges."

Taking note, Lara strategizes, "Alright, let's delve into these and find preemptive solutions."

Tuesday – Classifications and Compliance

On a bustling Tuesday, Lara inquires, "LegAI, I need to quickly identify relevant case data for the Thompson case. Can you help categorize them based on precedence and relevance?"

With its **Classification** capability, LegAI responds, "Of course, Lara. I've organized the cases. You'll find the most pertinent ones highlighted."

Later in the day, Lara focuses on the company's intellectual property portfolio, seeking LegAI's expertise. "I want to ensure all our trademarks and copyrights are compliant. Can you cross-reference them against current legal guidelines?"

LegAI's **Matchmaking** function identifies a couple of discrepancies, "Lara, two trademarks need attention. Their classifications have changed under the latest guidelines."

Wednesday - Documentation and Historical Insights

Lara, while reviewing a legal document, stumbles upon a clause she remembers being problematic in past litigation cases. "LegAI," she asks, "why has this specific clause been a sticking point in previous legal disputes?"

Activating its **Semantic Search** and **Cause-effect Analysis** capabilities, LegAI responds, "Based on historical cases, this clause often possesses language ambiguity, leading to differing interpretations. Additionally, it sometimes conflicts with certain regional statutes, causing further complications."

Grateful for the insight, Lara decides to redraft the clause, ensuring it is both clear and compliant. This, combined with LegAI's **Creation** capability for generating document templates, empowers Lara to be proactive and avert potential future disputes.

Thursday - Extraction and Compliance

In the midst of reviewing a vast number of legal contracts, Lara recalls a notable precedent she studied in law school but struggles to remember the specifics. "LegAI," she queries, "why was the Roberts vs. TechDyno case so influential in shaping contractual law concerning software licensing?"

LegAI, employing its **Semantic Search** and **Question Answering** capabilities, replies, "The Roberts vs. TechDyno case was groundbreaking because it highlighted the complexities of digital goods' ownership versus licensing rights. It established that software, when 'sold', was often licensed to the end-user, not outright owned, setting a precedent for countless software agreements since."

Using this refresher, Lara then uses LegAI's **Information Extraction and Analytics** capability to ensure the contracts she's reviewing align with the key takeaways from such influential precedents.

Friday – Strategy and Forecasts

As the week winds down, Lara wonders, "LegAI, based on our current legal stances, can you predict potential issues we might face next quarter?"

LegAI's **Prediction** capability scans and answers, "There's a 60% likelihood of challenges related to digital product licensing and a 40% chance concerning employee contractual obligations."

Lara, prepping for the week ahead, asks, "Finally, can you summarize the legal terms and compliance changes we discussed this week?"

LegAI, efficiently **summarizing**, provides a concise overview, ensuring Lara is fully informed and ready to tackle the next week's challenges.

Lara and LegAI's collaborative week showcases how legal expertise, when combined with AI capabilities, leads to efficient compliance, proactive solutions, and accurate insights. Their partnership shows the evolution of modern legal practices, underscoring the transformative potential of integrating AI into the legal realm.

Process Consultant

Meet Marcin, a Process Consultant, and his AI companion, Business Process Intelligence Assistant (BPIA), who together streamline and innovate business procedures. Here's how they divide their key tasks across the week for optimized results:

***Figure 3.24**: Process Consultant*

Monday - Process Evaluation and Troubleshooting

As Marcin and BPIA examine a client's procurement process, Marcin wonders, "BPIA, what would happen if we shifted the supplier vetting process entirely to the Purchasing department rather than splitting it between Purchasing and Operations?"

Leveraging its **Simulation** capability, BPIA responds, "Marcin, if the supplier vetting process is consolidated under the Purchasing department, we can expect a 15% speed-up in vetting time due to reduced handoffs. However, there might be an initial dip in operational fit of the suppliers as the Purchasing team might prioritize cost-effectiveness over operational suitability. Integrating an operational feedback loop into the Purchasing department's vetting process can mitigate this."

Appreciating this insight, Marcin considers recommending a pilot phase where the Purchasing department takes full responsibility but with consistent feedback from Operations.

Tuesday – Process Updates and Communication

While reviewing a newly proposed process, Marcin muses, "BPIA, can we develop a visual representation to help stakeholders understand this workflow better?" Using its **Creation** function, BPIA designs a detailed flowchart, highlighting each step. Marcin, impressed, says, "This looks comprehensive! Could you draft an explanatory message that we can send out?" BPIA, leveraging its **Communication** capability, drafts a concise, clear message. Marcin reviews it, makes minor adjustments, and disseminates the information to the relevant stakeholders.

Wednesday - Model Creation and Insight Discovery

As they delve into constructing new models, Marcin reflects, "BPIA, we need a fresh approach for the customer onboarding process for our new client. Can you suggest any models?" BPIA's **Creation** capability designs a unique onboarding model. As Marcin examines it, BPIA adds, "Marcin , based on the latest industry trends, integrating a gamified tutorial might enhance user engagement during onboarding." Marcin, intrigued, responds, "That sounds promising. And, do we have any insights from their past onboarding strategies?" BPIA applies its **Data Mining** and **Summarization** capabilities, informing, "Historically, users felt the process was too lengthy. The drop-off rate was highest during step 3 of the onboarding." Appreciating the clarity, Marcin determines to refine that particular step.

Thursday - Data Extraction and Risk Management

Marcin, analyzing a partner company's process documentation, wonders, "BPIA, can we align our client's processes with these for smoother collaboration?" BPIA employs its **Information Extraction and Analytics** capability, processing the partner's documents swiftly. It suggests, "Marcin, there's a potential bottleneck in the invoice approval stage. Aligning the processes might require streamlining that particular step." Considering potential pitfalls of the proposed adjustments, David inquires, "What risks do we face with this alignment?" BPIA **assesses** and elaborates, "The major risk is a delay in invoice approvals, which could disrupt cash flows." It then recommends, "However, implementing an automated approval system for low-risk invoices can mitigate this." Marcin nods, "Let's propose that. And keep monitoring for any further risks."

Friday - Strategic Planning and Change Management

While strategizing for another client looking to optimize its product delivery process, Marcin ponders, "BPIA, what's the potential impact if we centralize the packaging units instead of having them scattered across multiple locations?"

Tapping into its **Simulation** capability like on Monday, BPIA explains, "Centralizing the packaging units can lead to cost efficiencies due to bulk processing, potentially reducing packaging costs by 20%. Additionally, centralization would enable better quality control. However, transportation times to disparate markets might increase, affecting delivery speed. It would be beneficial to conduct a thorough cost-benefit analysis, considering both operational savings and potential delivery delays."

Considering this feedback, Marcin decides to explore a hybrid model, with a centralized hub for packaging but regional centers for faster distribution.

Throughout the week, Marcin and BPIA synergize to scrutinize and enhance business processes, proactively addressing Marcin's strategic queries. Relying on BPIA's diverse AI functionalities, they critically assess potential process alterations, anticipate the consequences of proposed changes, and formulate strategies that ensure alignment with business objectives. This dynamic collaboration bolsters Marcin's consultancy approach, ensuring that his clients enjoy optimized, efficient, and forward-looking business operations.

Future for Business Leaders

Across the spectrum of business leadership, from top-tier executives to mid-level managers, artificial intelligence is rapidly changing the decision-making process. Whether one is a C-Suite Executive, a Sales Director, a Supply Chain Manager, a Finance Manager, or a Program Manager, AI's ability to efficiently gather extensive data and perform in-depth analyses is invaluable.

C-Suite Executive

Introducing Sue, an experienced C-Suite Executive, and her AI sidekick, ByteBoss. Their week is a blend of proactive strategy building, organizational alignment, and the foresight needed to chart the company's course.

Figure 3.25: C-Suite Executive

Monday – Industry Benchmarking and Strategic Orientation

Sue commences the new week with a proactive approach, determined to align the company's technology infrastructure with the latest industry benchmarks. Early on Monday, she engages ByteBoss, stating, "ByteBoss, our goal is to keep pace with the industry leaders in terms of technology adoption. Could you help me understand our current standing as compared to the industry benchmarks?"

Immediately activating its **Assessment** capability, ByteBoss gathers a plethora of data ranging from recent IT audit reports to feedback from various departments and synthesizes this with current industry benchmarks to offer Sue an insightful overview of the present situation.

As ByteBoss presents the data, it becomes evident that the company's technology infrastructure requires modernization to remain competitive. There's a notable emphasis on leveraging advanced technologies such as cloud computing and AI-driven analytical tools, which are consistently being adopted by industry frontrunners to foster innovation and efficiency.

Taking in the detailed analysis, Sue reflects, "It seems we have a considerable journey ahead to upgrade our infrastructure to match the current industry standards. ByteBoss, could you help draft a preliminary roadmap for this upgrade?"

Harnessing its **Planning** function, ByteBoss delineates potential starting points for the upgrade. It highlights the urgency of migrating to cloud-based systems and enhancing cybersecurity measures, followed by a gradual integration of AI capabilities to facilitate smarter business decisions.

Sue nods appreciatively, absorbing the roadmap presented. With a firm resolve, she instructs, "ByteBoss, let's take this forward. Please set up a call with our CIO, Richard, to delve deeper into this strategy and identify the immediate actions we need to initiate."

Responding promptly, ByteBoss utilizes its **Communication** function to coordinate with Richard's calendar, finding a suitable time slot for the discussion. It facilitates a meeting invitation, **summarizing** the preliminary findings and the objective of the meeting to provide a starting point for their discussion.

Tuesday – Sustainability and Environmental Impact Analysis

Entering Tuesday with a focus on sustainability, Sue engages ByteBoss to assess and strategize the company's environmental impact. "ByteBoss, let's look into how our operations are influencing the environment and find ways to lessen our carbon footprint."

Tapping into its **Assessment** feature, ByteBoss integrates data from various company outlets – logistics, manufacturing, and office utilities to monitor metrics like carbon footprint, waste production, and energy consumption. The process reveals a significant contributor to their increased carbon emissions: heightened reliance on air freight for logistics.

Keen to find sustainable alternatives, ByteBoss uses its **Recommendation** functionality to envisage a greener logistic pathway, suggesting collaborations with eco-friendly shipping partners and the possibility of adopting alternative, sustainable packaging materials. "Sue, aligning with companies that prioritize sustainability could foster a green supply chain, reducing our environmental impact," ByteBoss articulates, showcasing potential partners on the screen.

To ensure stakeholders align with the new green vision, ByteBoss brings its **Communication** feature into play, devising compelling reports that underline the long-term benefits and the cost-effectiveness of sustainable practices. Sue appreciates this comprehensive view, understanding the integral role sustainability plays in modern business, both from an environmental and reputational standpoint.

Wednesday – Initiative Implementation and Project Execution

Midweek, Sue notices another recurring theme: a particular department is consistently overshooting its budget, leading to increased operational costs without a proportional rise in output or quality. The financial discrepancies have started to mount, and Sue is keen to ensure efficient utilization of resources.

She ponders, "There's a mismatch here; either the resources are not being used effectively or there's something we're overlooking in the budgeting process."

Sensing an opportunity for intervention, ByteBoss intervenes, "Would you like a deep dive into this department's expenditure patterns, Sue?"

ByteBoss activates its **Information Extraction and Analytics** capability, examining monthly expenditures, supplier contracts, and inventory data related to this department. It then uses its **Assessment** capability to benchmark these findings against similar departments within the organization and even external industry standards.

After a **Cause-effect Analysis**, ByteBoss highlights, "Sue, it seems that a significant portion of the budget is going towards emergency procurement of materials, likely due to poor inventory management. The prices paid during these emergency procurements are higher than standard contracts."

Sue realizes the root of the issue, "So, it's more of a planning problem than actual over-expenditure. How can we tackle this, ByteBoss?"

Utilizing its **Recommendation** capability, ByteBoss suggests a revised inventory management system, ensuring timely procurement and reducing the need for last-minute purchases. It also recommends renegotiating certain supplier contracts to achieve better rates and setting up alerts for inventory thresholds to proactively manage stock levels.

With Sue approval, these changes are initiated, and ByteBoss **Communication** function ensures all relevant teams are updated about the new protocols. By Wednesday's close, Sue is confident that they're on the right track to more efficient resource management and cost savings.

Thursday - Risk Management, Compliance Checks, and Business Development

Another aspect that Sue is passionate about is employee growth and team dynamics. During a review, she discovers that while technical training sessions are frequent, there's a lack of soft skill development workshops, which could be affecting team collaboration and overall morale.

Reflecting on this, Sue muses, "Our teams are technically sound, but we need to ensure they communicate and collaborate effectively."

Picking up on her train of thought, ByteBoss offers, "Would you like an assessment of the current training modules and potential areas of improvement?"

Using its **Semantic Search** and **Assessment** capabilities, ByteBoss reviews the training modules offered in the past year. It then taps into its **Recommendation** Engine to suggest potential areas of development based on industry best practices and feedback from employee surveys.

ByteBoss presents, "Sue, there's a notable gap in areas like conflict resolution, emotional intelligence, and leadership development. I've found some top-rated workshops and programs we could integrate."

Grateful for the insights, Sue says, "Let's plan some sessions, ByteBoss. It's time we invest in holistic employee growth."

With ByteBoss Event **Planning** capability, a series of workshops are scheduled for the upcoming quarter. The AI's **Communication** function sends out invites, gathers RSVPs, and even prepares pre-workshop materials for attendees.

By Thursday evening, Sue feels satisfied, knowing she's taken steps to foster not just professional, but personal growth within her teams, enhancing the organization's culture and cohesion.

Friday – Business Simulation and Planning

At the end of the workweek Sue sits down at her desk and queries ByteBoss. "ByteBoss, what are the most impactful business scenarios playing out over the next four weeks, and how should I deal with them?"

Using its **Prediction** and **Recommendation** capabilities ByteBoss swiftly responds, "Firstly, the upcoming seasonal shift historically impacts the availability of some of our primary raw materials. To navigate this, diversifying our sourcing strategy could prove beneficial, such as front-loading orders or seeking alternative suppliers unaffected by this change. Another solution could be exploring synthetic or alternative materials for temporary use."

Sue, processing the information, immediately thinks of the procurement team. "I'll have a discussion with James in Procurement. He'll have insights into alternative suppliers and materials."

ByteBoss continues, "Secondly, there's an anticipated surge in demand for certain product lines due to the approaching festival season. Preemptively increasing production and coordinating with the marketing team for festive promotions can optimize our sales."

Sue smiles, "That's an opportunity! I'll liaise with Maria from Marketing and Raj from Production. We need to ensure our strategies are in sync."

Lastly, ByteBoss adds, "One more thing. There's a scheduled maintenance shutdown for one of our primary manufacturing units in three weeks. It's crucial we redistribute some of the production load and consider pre-manufacturing certain components. Adjusting delivery timelines with key clients might also be necessary."

Sue notes this down, "Good catch, ByteBoss. I'll arrange a meeting with Budi from Operations and Lisa from Client Relations to ensure a smooth transition during the shutdown."

Feeling equipped with the necessary insights, Sue starts her round of meetings, ensuring that her team is always a step ahead, prepared for the challenges and opportunities the coming weeks might bring.

In essence, each day of the week, Sue, with the aid of ByteBoss, drives strategic initiatives that shape the organization's future, ensuring continuous assessment, initiative execution, performance monitoring, risk management, and forward planning.

Sales Director

Introducing David, a dynamic Sales Director, and his AI-driven Sales Control Tower, SalesControl, which is designed to bring strategic oversight to the sales process. Their weeks are a combination of strategic planning, data-driven insights, and proactive market engagement.

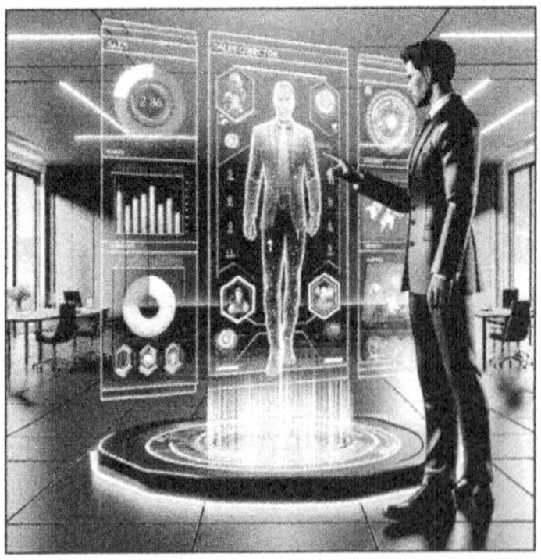

Figure 3.26: *Sales Director*

Monday – Sales Performance Assessment and Market Analysis

As the week kicks off, David navigates to the SalesControl dashboard to understand the previous week's sales performance. "SalesControl, can you give me a breakdown of our sales figures from last week?" he asks casually.

Leveraging its **Assessment** feature, SalesControl processes the recent sales data and shares, "You reached 92% of the targeted sales, David. Though, it seems sales dipped in the Midwest region due to a promotional offer from a competitor." It pulls this information through a combination of market reports and sales records, utilizing its **Information Extraction and Analytics** capability.

David furrows his brows, thoughtful. "Interesting. What about the market's response to our products recently?" he inquires, hoping to understand the broader picture.

Swiftly, SalesControl employs its **Cause-effect Analysis** function. It analyzes customer feedback, social media engagements, and recent product reviews, presenting a summarized insight. "People appreciate our products, but there is a noticeable demand for added features in our premium line," it conveys.

A sense of understanding dawns on David as he contemplates the feedback. "Alright, we need to strategize here. SalesControl, what are your suggestions?"

Engaging its **Recommendation** Engine, SalesControl proposes a strategy to counter the competitor's moves while meeting customer expectations. "Considering the feedback, it might be beneficial to launch a promotional offer that highlights upcoming enhancements in the premium product line. Additionally, utilizing social media for this campaign could potentially amplify the reach," it suggests in a measured tone.

David nods, finding the recommendation reasonable. "I think that has potential. Can you help in setting up a team to take this forward?" he asks, thinking of the right mix of expertise needed for the task.

SalesControl readily agrees and, tapping into its **Matchmaking** function, identifies a balanced team of experienced and newbie staff from the sales and marketing departments to handle the initiative, considering their past performances and skills.

With an appreciative smile, David commends, "Good job, SalesControl. Let's put this plan into action." Motivated, he prepares to lead his team into a week focused on responsiveness and strategy, equipped with insights from SalesControl.

Tuesday – Client and Sales Strategy Classification

On Tuesday, David is keen to understand his client segments better. "How can we better classify our targets based on recent interactions and buying behaviors?" he wonders aloud. Tapping into its **Classification** capability, SalesControl organizes the clients into distinct segments. "Based on recent engagement, here are your high, medium, and low potential clients," it displays. Its **Communication** function then sends automated and personalized messages to each segment, keeping the respective sales representative informed. "David, the high-potential clients prefer webinars. Perhaps we can organize one this month?" SalesControl suggests using insights from Data Mining.

Wednesday – Sales Innovations and Data Mining

David, keen to innovate, asks on Wednesday, "Can we introduce new bundle offers that align with our clients' preferences?" SalesControl's **Creation** capability generates a list of potential bundle offerings. At the same time, its **Data Mining** function identifies patterns from past sales. "It seems clients purchasing Product A frequently also inquire about Service B. We could create a bundle there," it highlights. David nods in approval, "Great insight! Let's trial this bundle in a limited market first." The AI's **Communication** function sends a brief about this new initiative to the sales team, ensuring alignment.

Thursday - Analytics, Matchmaking, and Information Extraction

"Who's our best-performing sales rep for high-ticket items?" David inquires on Thursday. Using its **Information Extraction and Analytics** function, SalesControl quickly presents a leaderboard. "It's Sarah. Interestingly, she has a strong rapport with tech companies," it adds. David, seeing an opportunity, says, "Let's align Sarah with our tech-based clients for the upcoming product launch." SalesControl's **Matchmaking** capability ensures the right team members are matched with the right opportunities.

Friday – Strategic Planning and Query Handling

David, planning for the future, asks, "Based on current market trends, what's our sales projection for the next quarter?" SalesControl's **Prediction** capability churns the numbers, "Given the current trajectory, we're looking at a 12% increase. However, with the planned product launch and adjusting for seasonal variations, this could go up to 15%." David, satisfied, then asks, "How did we perform compared to our competitors last month?" SalesControl processes the question using its **Question Answering** ability, cross-referencing sales data, and competitor insights. "We outperformed Competitor X by 8% but lagged behind Competitor Y by 3%."

David, with the aid of SalesControl, exemplifies the epitome of a modern sales director who leverages AI-driven insights to make informed decisions. Throughout the week, they engage in performance assessment, proactive strategy formulation, client segmentation, and forward planning. By synchronizing data-driven insights with market trends, David strategically places his company at the forefront of the competitive sales landscape.

Supply-Chain Manager

Step into the realm of Sarah, a dynamic Supply-Chain Manager, as she teams up with her AI-integrated Optimized Supply Chain Control Tower (OptiChain). Watch as they tactically navigate through suppliers, internal plants, and customers, turning every challenge into a solution.

***Figure* 3.27**: *Supply Chain Manager*

Monday - Health Assessment and Categorization of Suppliers and Plants

Sarah initiates the week with a comprehensive assessment of the health of her suppliers and plants, harnessing the deep analytical abilities of OptiChain's Health **Assessment** functionality. This tool digs into the rich history and real-time metrics of her operational sphere, offering insights that drive wise decision-making.

"OptiChain, I need an insightful overview of our supplier health metrics," Sarah instructs as she navigates through the reports generated. The AI synthesizes a wealth of data, highlighting critical concerns, "Supplier 'XYZ' has a pattern of delays, flagging them as a 'high-risk' entity," it alerts, utilizing its robust **Summarization** capability.

Sarah deliberates over this, considering recent developments and logistical challenges faced by 'XYZ'. She then directs, "Given their circumstance, it would be pragmatic to categorize them as 'contingent high-risk' temporarily. Let's reassess their status next quarter."

Tuesday – Active Communication and Demand Trend Analysis

On Tuesday, Sarah, backed by OptiChain, enters a deep analytical session, carving through demand trends and sales forecasts with the help of OptiChain's **Prediction** capability. It is a day of strategic interactions with stakeholders, fortified with deep insights and data-driven strategies.

Analyzing a sudden surge in demand for Product 'A', Sarah inquires, "Considering the current inventory status, how feasible is a production increase?"

OptiChain quickly churns out a proposal based on its **Simulation** capability, "A 20% increase in production could match the current demand trends," it suggests. Sarah considers this, eventually opting for a conservative strategy, "Let's upscale production by 15% and monitor the market response for the next fortnight."

Wednesday - Information Extraction and Visualization

As Wednesday unfolds, Sarah is focused on having a granular understanding of the operation metrics, setting a cornerstone for effective strategizing. She partners with OptiChain to delve deeply into the rich seam of data accrued over time.

Sarah begins her day reviewing a set of reports dynamically generated by OptiChain using its **Information Extraction and Analytics** capability. The tool leverages its proficiency to create comprehensive reports via its **Creation** function, assimilating a large volume of unstructured data, and transforming it into actionable insights presented through intuitive visualizations.

The focal point of the day is understanding the nuances behind the operational efficiencies and inefficiencies exhibited by different plants over the quarter. Sarah examines the first report, acknowledging the efforts of team 'B'. "The remarkable performance of Plant 'B' needs to be celebrated," she notes, impressed by the 15% efficiency surge detailed in OptiChain's report. This was attributed to strategic automation investments, a finding derived from OptiChain's meticulous **Cause-Effect Analysis** that dissected various influencing factors.

With a curious mind, Sarah further inquires, "I am interested in diving deeper into the reasons behind this efficiency rise. Could we possibly have an in-depth analysis of the key factors that led to this increase?"

Responding to Sarah's command, OptiChain refines its data filtering parameters, zooming into various catalysts – from technological integrations to workforce training programs – that worked in harmony to achieve the positive outcome at Plant 'B'. It presents a visually rich report, segmenting the contributory factors and their respective impacts in a way that's easy for Sarah to understand and act upon.

As the session progresses, Sarah shifts her attention to Plant 'D', a unit that had recently undergone operational shifts. "How are the new workflows influencing the output at Plant 'D'?" she questions, eager to understand the repercussions of the recent changes.

OptiChain gets into action, assembling data from diverse sources, including employee feedback, maintenance logs, and productivity reports to construct a well-rounded view of the situation. It again utilizes its **Cause-Effect Analysis** to offer Sarah a detailed overview, "The operational shifts have introduced a learning curve, causing a temporary dip in productivity. However, they have also paved the way for more streamlined processes, projecting a rise in efficiency in the upcoming quarter."

Sarah listens intently, the analytical breakdown helping her visualize the transitional phase Plant 'D' is navigating through. She appreciates the detailed insights, recognizing the potential for long-term benefits emerging from the transitional pains.

Concluding her analysis, Sarah reflects on the actionable intelligence unearthed through the day's deep dive. "OptiChain, let's create a repository of these insights. It will be instrumental in our quarterly strategic review meeting to make informed decisions."

Agreeing with a virtual nod, OptiChain activates its **Transformation** capability, archiving the day's findings into a well-structured repository, equipped with graphs, charts, and trends, all set to facilitate an insightful quarterly review.

Thursday – Strategic Planning and Feedback

With OptiChain's **Prediction** capability, Sarah gets a forecast of urgent inventory needs, potential disruptions, and delivery timelines.

Based on its **Recommendation** engine OptiChain offers, "Consolidating shipments can cut transportation costs by about 10%."

Sarah ponders, "But can we still maintain our rapid delivery guarantee?"

OptiChain provides its rationale, and Sarah, after considering the implications, decides, "Let's pilot the consolidated shipments for a month and evaluate its impact."

Friday – Process Prioritization and Continuous Learning

As OptiChain scans through databases via **Semantic Search**, it identifies new regulations and trends. It also refines its capabilities through continuous learning.

Upon spotting a new EU regulation, OptiChain cautions, "There's an updated EU regulation on perishables."

Sarah inquires about its applicability, and after OptiChain's response using **Question Answering**, she decides, "Although our inventory remains unaffected, let's set up a quarterly regulation review to stay ahead."

Sarah, working in tandem with OptiChain, epitomizes the proactive and data-driven approach essential for a modern Supply-Chain Manager. Throughout the week, they methodically analyze suppliers' health, decipher demand trends, evaluate plant performances, and strategize for optimal operational efficiencies. By marrying in-depth analysis with tactical foresight, Sarah ensures a seamless supply chain flow, while OptiChain provides robust analytics, actionable recommendations, and real-time alerts.

Finance Manager

Venture into the dynamic world of finance management with Ahmed, a Finance Manager. Harnessing the power of a fully integrated AI Finance counterpart, dubbed MoneyWatch, he oversees and optimizes all financial operations, securing fiscal health and prosperity for the organization.

Figure 3.28: *Finance Manager*

Monday - Financial Risk Management

As the week unfurls, Ahmed navigates the potential pitfalls and opportunities lying in the financial landscape of the organization. Leveraging MoneyWatch's advanced **Assessment** capability, he meticulously evaluates the financial risks associated with a myriad of business operations, including the scrutinization of investments and delving deep into the credit histories of business associates.

A notification catches his eye – a long-standing customer has been flagged as a potential financial risk. Curious and slightly concerned, Ahmed queries, "MoneyWatch, can you provide more insights into why this customer has been flagged?"

MoneyWatch leaps into action, offering a deep-dive **Cause-effect analysis**, "The customer recently underwent a significant product recall which has substantially impacted their liquidity. Moreover, an analysis of past instances in the industry shows a high likelihood of payment delays following such events."

Taking in the gravity of the situation, Ahmed leans back, deep in thought. After a moment of contemplation, he directs, "We need to mitigate our risk without straining the relationship. Adjust our credit terms moderately for the next two quarters and monitor any outstanding invoices closely." MoneyWatch swiftly implements these changes, showcasing its fine-tuned **Communication** capability to alter the necessary details in the backend system while maintaining a delicate balance between vigilance and trust.

Tuesday – Budgeting and Forecasting

With the new day, Ahmed engages MoneyWatch's potent **Prediction** function to navigate the vast ocean of budget formulation and financial forecasts. This tool, enriched with deep learning from historical financial data and current economic indicators, offers a nuanced perspective into the financial needs looming in the future.

While immersing in the task, MoneyWatch flags a significant trend, "Based on the emerging industry standards and technology adaptations, there's an expected surge in technology-related expenditures in the forthcoming period."

This brings a furrow to Ahmed's brow as he wonders, "How would this surge affect our R&D budget allocations for the next fiscal year? Can we quantify the potential impact?"

MoneyWatch reactivates its **Cause-effect Analysis** function, offering a detailed projection of the possible scenarios. After a moment, it responds, "Considering the pace of tech advancements and the kind of adaptations we are looking at, a prudent approach would be to earmark an additional 10% for technological upgrades in the R&D budget for the upcoming fiscal year."

Ahmed nods, appreciating the insight. He commands, "Alright, let's stay ahead of the curve. Allocate an additional 10% for tech enhancements in our future R&D budget." MoneyWatch, compliant and efficient, updates the financial planning module in the backend system, ensuring the organization remains on the frontier of innovation and readiness.

Wednesday – Cash Flow and Asset Management

Wednesday arrives with a focus on cash flow and asset management. Today, Ahmed decides to delve deeper into the labyrinthine financial trails with MoneyWatch. He activates MoneyWatch's **Data Mining** functionality, which is particularly skilled in unearthing intricate patterns and trends from vast datasets, helping Ahmed foster optimal asset management strategies.

As they delve into the cash flow statements of the past quarters, a recurring anomaly catches Ahmed's eye – a notable dip in cash flow consistently appearing at the end of every quarter. A perplexed Ahmed raises this with MoneyWatch, "This pattern seems unusual. MoneyWatch, can we perform a cause-effect analysis to understand why we witness this dip regularly?"

MoneyWatch springs to action, sifting through a mountain of data to draw a comprehensive picture. It analyzes a range of variables including expenditure patterns, seasonal variations in business operations, and payment cycles. After a thorough analysis, it responds, "Upon reviewing the historical data, it appears that two primary factors are influencing this trend. Firstly, there is a significant disbursement of employee bonuses and incentives during this period. Secondly, utility bills witness a surge due to seasonal adjustments that coincide with the quarter-end."

As Ahmed digests this information, he realizes a course of action that could ease the cash flow. He suggests, "To stabilize our cash flow, we should consider staggering the bonus distributions across different periods instead of a lump sum payment at the quarter-end. Similarly, we could negotiate a more balanced utility payment schedule with our service providers. MoneyWatch, what potential impact might these changes have on our cash flow?"

MoneyWatch undertakes a quick **simulation**, providing Ahmed with a visual representation of the improved cash flow under the new strategy. It projects a much smoother cash flow curve, devoid of the sharp dips witnessed previously.

MoneyWatch elucidates, "Implementing this strategy would result in a more balanced cash flow, allowing for better financial stability and improved fiscal health over the quarters."

Ahmed, convinced of the merit in this approach, decides to take action. He instructs, "Let's move forward with this. Adjust the financial planning to incorporate a staggered bonus distribution and initiate discussions with the utility providers to renegotiate the payment terms."

MoneyWatch leverages its **Communication** and **Planning** capabilities to initiate the required actions – updating financial plans in the backend system and drafting preliminary communication to the utility providers for renegotiation of terms.

Thursday – Compliance Checks and Reporting

As Thursday begins, the focus shifts to ensuring adherence to the regulatory compliance and crafting meticulous financial reports. Ahmed starts the day activating MoneyWatch's **Information Extraction and Analytics** function, a vital tool designed to glean critical data from a plethora of financial documents, ensuring a seamless compliance check aligned with regulatory benchmarks.

While reviewing a freshly generated report, Ahmed stops at a figure that seems off. "MoneyWatch, the equity ratio presented here doesn't align with our usual figures. Could we delve into the underlying causes?"

MoneyWatch immediately undertakes a detailed **Cause-effect Analysis**, sifting through recent transactions and financial decisions. It comes back with a precise breakdown, "The current fluctuation is influenced by our recent acquisition. The liabilities associated with this have temporarily influenced the equity ratio. However, our projections show a normalization by the next fiscal quarter as the acquisition integrates fully into our financial ecosystem."

Nodding, Ahmed responds, "That makes sense. To maintain transparency, we should annotate this in our report, offering a clear explanation to the stakeholders."

MoneyWatch proceeds to use its **Creation** function, expertly crafting a note that offered a succinct yet comprehensive explanation for the temporary skew in the equity ratio, adding this to the report to offer stakeholders a clear picture of the current financial landscape.

Friday – Strategic Decision Making and Stakeholder Communication

The week nears its end as Friday rolls in. Today, Ahmed intends to engage MoneyWatch's **Simulation** feature to its fullest, to envision and forge strategies grounded on a wealth of data, analysis, and foresight. This simulation capability explores a variety of scenarios, ranging from Ahmedet fluctuations to currency shifts, all to guide Ahmed in making informed decisions.

In one such simulation, a strategy involving shifting production overseas presents a potential dip in profits. Curious and concerned, Ahmed inquires, "This strategy shows a decline in our profit margins. Can you provide a detailed breakdown of the contributing factors, MoneyWatch?"

Engaging in a deep **Cause-effect Analysis**, MoneyWatch lays out the various components influencing this outcome, "The primary contributors to this dip are the heightened costs associated with initial setup, transportation, and tariffs. While there are savings to be made in labor costs, the preliminary expenses in the initial years can potentially outweigh the benefits."

As Ahmed digests the insights, a decisive pathway forms in his mind. "Alright, it seems we need to recalibrate our strategy to focus on local optimization opportunities rather than a broad shift in production."

The session transitions into the communication phase, where MoneyWatch leverages its **Communication** capability to formulate and disseminate the newly forged strategies to pertinent stakeholders. It drafts concise yet comprehensive briefs, clearly outlining the revised strategies and the insights that led to their formulation, fostering alignment and clarity among all stakeholders.

Navigating the intricate world of finance, Ahmed and MoneyWatch work in tandem to make informed decisions. Throughout the week, they tackle risk evaluation, budget forecasting, asset management, compliance checks, and strategic planning. Leveraging MoneyWatch's AI-driven insights, Mark ensures the financial stability and growth of the organization.

Program Manager

Join Xiaoling, a meticulous Program Manager, as she engages with her AI-powered Control Hub for Optimized Project Navigation, or C.H.O.P.N. in a typical week. Their interactions craft a harmonious blend of human expertise and AI precision.

Figure 3.29: *Program Manager*

Monday - Program Assessment and Classification

As Monday unfolds, Xiaoling asks C.H.O.P.N., "What's the status of our ongoing projects?" C.H.O.P.N., utilizing its **Assessment** capability, replies, "Three projects are currently on track, while Project Delta has shown signs of delay." "Why the delay in Project Delta?" C.H.O.P.N.'s **Summarization** function activates, "The project encountered unexpected regulatory hurdles and resource shortages." Nodding, Xiaoling instructs, "Categorize it as high-priority and schedule a review meeting for tomorrow." C.H.O.P.N. swiftly complies via its **Communication** capability.

Tuesday - Communication, Coordination, and Scheduling

Reviewing her calendar, Xiaoling wonders aloud, "Are there any resource conflicts this week?" C.H.O.P.N. responds with its **Matchmaking** function, "Yes, both Project Alpha and Project Beta are vying for the same designer's time." "Recommend an optimal resource allocation, please." After running its **Recommender** engine for a moment, C.H.O.P.N. proposes, "I suggest reallocating the junior designer to Project Alpha while extending Project Beta's timeline by two days." Xiaoling agrees, and the change proposals are **communicated** automatically to the respective project managers, who agree quickly afterwards.

Wednesday - Data Mining, Tracking Progress, and Issue Detection

Opening an interactive dashboard, Xiaoling queries, "How's our overall progress looking?" C.H.O.P.N.'s **Information Extraction and Analytics** capability displays a graphical analysis. "Eighty percent of tasks are progressing as expected. However, there's a deviation in the software module." Curious, Xiaoling asks, "What's the specific issue?" C.H.O.P.N. using its **Question Answering** capability elaborates, "There have been repeated code integration failures in the past week." Acknowledging the insight, Xiaoling remarks, "Set up a session with the tech team today." C.H.O.P.N. sets the meeting in motion via its **Communication** function.

Thursday - Risk Analysis, Quality Control, and Predictive Simulation

Xiaoling ponders, "What are our risk hotspots this month?" C.H.O.P.N. performs a quick Risk **Assessment** and highlights areas on a risk heatmap. "Resource allocation and unforeseen market dynamics pose the most significant threats." "Show me a simulated outcome if the market trend continues." C.H.O.P.N.'s **Simulation** capability plays out a scenario, illustrating potential impacts. Xiaoling watches intently, considering her next strategic move.

Friday - Decision Making, Reporting, and Continuous Learning

Reviewing a visual snippet, Xiaoling inquires, "**Summarize** this month's milestones for me." C.H.O.P.N. obliges, "Four projects reached major milestones, with an overall 90% success rate. One project, however, lagged due to supply chain issues." Mulling over the data, Xiaoling instructs, "**Recommend** corrective measures for future projects." C.H.O.P.N. suggests, "Enhanced vendor management and a contingency buffer in project timelines can mitigate such risks." Appreciating the advice, Xiaoling wraps up, "Thanks, C.H.O.P.N. Let us implement these and let's review next week."

Navigating the multifaceted realm of program management, Xiaoling and C.H.O.P.N. unite to ensure project success. Throughout the week, they delve into project assessment, resource coordination, progress tracking, risk analysis, and decision-making. Harnessing C.H.O.P.N.'s AI-driven capabilities, Xiaoling ensures timely milestones and strategic excellence in all programs.

Conclusion

AI's evolution is reshaping roles markedly across the enterprise landscape, elevating efficiency and innovation in various job functions through ChatGPT. From entry-level roles to C-suite executives, the future collaboration with

AI-based assistants will be truly transformative and pave the way for unprecedented growth.

As we transition from exploring ChatGPT's enterprise applications, the next chapter takes a deeper dive into the technical foundations of this AI framework. We will demystify the architectural patterns and technical elements, fostering an understanding of how ChatGPT is shaping an increasingly AI-centric IT landscape.

Key Points

1. Human-AI Collaborative Efforts: The chapter highlights the collaborative dynamics between various professionals and their AI assistants, illustrating the symbiotic relationships that foster efficiency and innovation in their respective fields.

2. AI Enhancements in Diverse Professions: Each narrative portrays how professionals from a wide array of fields, such as finance, marketing, and engineering, leverage AI technologies to optimize processes, making them more streamlined and data driven.

3. Predictive Analytics and Proactive Strategies: Professionals like Mary, the Production and Quality Specialist, and Sarah, the Supply-Chain Manager, utilize ChatGPT's predictive analytics features to anticipate challenges and forge proactive strategies, showcasing the forward-thinking approach facilitated by AI collaborations.

4. Real-time Insights and Adaptability: Many personas benefit from real-time updates and insights provided by their AI assistants, which are integrated with enterprise applications, enabling them to swiftly adapt to changing situations and make informed decisions based on current data.

5. Efficiency and Productivity Enhancement: AI assistants help professionals process high volumes of complex data quickly and accurately, boosting efficiency and productivity in roles such as Accounts Payable Clerk and Procurement Specialist.

6. Customer and Employee Experience: In roles such as Customer Service Agent and Internal Communication Specialist, ChatGPT aids in enhancing both customer and employee experiences through personalized and intuitive communication strategies, fostering satisfaction and engagement.

7. Innovative Problem-Solving: Professionals like the Researcher and the Technical Engineer leverage their AI assistants to approach problem-solving from innovative angles, using data to drive creativity and develop novel solutions.

8. Strategic Decision-Making: Several professionals, including Product Managers and C-Suite Executives, utilize ChatGPT's analytical capabilities to craft data-driven strategies, illustrating its role in enhancing decision-making processes.

9. Automation and Task Delegation: The narratives illustrate how professionals can delegate repetitive tasks to AI assistants, freeing them to focus on more strategic, high-level duties, showcasing the role of ChatGPT in automating routine tasks, and promoting focus on value-added activities.

10. Future of Work: The chapter paints a picture of the future workplace where human intelligence and artificial intelligence work hand-in-hand, seamlessly integrated to forge a work environment that is efficient, innovative, and adaptive, pointing to a futuristic vision of collaborative synergy in the professional landscape.

CHAPTER 4

Architecture Patterns enabled by GPT-Models

Introduction

Building on the foundations laid in our previous chapter, where we explored the transformative impact of our AI-capability framework, CapabilityGPT, across various enterprise roles, we now turn our focus to the underlying solution architectures.. In this chapter, we delve into advanced patterns for creating high-quality GPT-driven systems, encompassing both conversational and autonomous solutions.

Before we dive into the individual patterns, we first introduce the concept of an **Architecture Pattern** in the respective subchapter. Here we break down the core components of these patterns, including their layers, workflows, quality aspects, and potential use cases.

With this foundation, we organize the rest of the chapter into four main sections, each focusing on a distinct category of architecture patterns:

- **Foundational Conversational Patterns (A)**: These include the basic components of GPT-driven conversational systems, laying the groundwork for all further enhancements and integrations.
- **Conversational Patterns with External Tool Integration (B)**: These demonstrate advanced solution designs integrating GPT models with enterprise applications and search engines during a conversation.

- **Conversational Patterns with Fine-tuned Models (C):** These showcase specific designs that leverage retrained models, based on GPT-technology or open source, to generate more accurate and domain-specific responses.
- **Agent Patterns (D):** These delve into the architectural integration of specialized agents[1] with GPT-models, focusing on automation, adaptation, and collaboration.

Each section provides a detailed examination of the patterns, complete with their workflows and potential use cases, offering a comprehensive understanding of how to deploy GPT models effectively across various conversational contexts, tool integrations, collaboration settings, and automation scenarios.

We conclude the chapter with insights and guidelines on selecting the most appropriate architecture pattern for different application needs.

Structure

In this chapter, the following topics will be covered:

- Architecture Pattern Definition
- Foundational Conversational Patterns
- Conversational Patterns with External Tool Integration
- Conversational Patterns with Fine-tuned Models
- Agent Patterns
- Recommendations for Architecture Patterns

Architecture Pattern Definition

The term **Architecture Pattern** refers to a general, reusable solution to a recurring design problem in a given context. It provides an abstract framework that outlines the subsystems or components involved, their responsibilities, and how they interact. Architecture patterns facilitate system design by providing proven solutions, improving developer efficiency, and reducing potential design risks. They consist of the following elements:

- **Components by Layer**: Each pattern operates within a layered system to ensure separation of concerns and maintainability. Each layer hosts specific components performing distinct functions. A common layered

[1]An agent is a software component designed to perform specific tasks, often autonomously and in interaction with other agents, systems, or users.

structure includes a User Experience Layer, an Application Layer, and an AI Layer. The specific components within these layers vary depending on the pattern, but all play crucial roles in system operations.

- **Workflow**: The workflow describes the sequence of operations that occur when the system is running, from the point of user input to the generated response. This also includes any intermediate steps such as pre-processing, prompt generation, response filtering, and so on, as dictated by the specific architecture pattern.
- **Enterprise Integration**: The architecture patterns form an integral part of a larger organizational IT landscape. As such, they must establish a harmonious interaction with existing enterprise applications, databases, and knowledge repositories. Each pattern details the means and degree of this integration, and the subsequent implications it has on the system's functionality.
- **Output Quality**: This refers to the relevance, accuracy, and usability of the system's generated responses. The quality can be influenced by several factors, such as the usage of response filters for quality checks, the application of grounding and enrichment processes for better context , or the employment of multiple GPT models for optimized responses. Each pattern outlines the mechanisms impacting the output quality and their effects on the system's response accuracy and relevance.
- **Performance**: This denotes the efficiency and speed of the system's operations. The performance can vary based on task complexity, the number of employed GPT models, the extent of application integrations, and the type of tasks executed. Each pattern details its performance characteristics, discussing factors that affect its computational efficiency and response speed.
- **Use Cases**: Each architecture pattern is designed to meet specific needs or solve particular problems. The use cases provide practical examples of situations where each pattern might be the best fit. These can range from basic Q&A bots to more sophisticated, context-aware solutions.

In the subsequent sections, we will apply this structure to describe various GPT-driven architecture patterns, each addressing a unique set of requirements. By the end, you should have a comprehensive understanding of these patterns to be able to choose the most suitable one for your specific needs.

Foundational Conversational Patterns

This section delves into four foundational architecture patterns for building conversational systems powered by GPT models. Each pattern represents an increasing level of sophistication, offering different degrees of interaction, knowledge integration, and quality control:

- **Basic Conversation (A1):** This pattern delineates the fundamental structure for an end-to-end conversational solution utilizing a GPT model. This solution processes user queries and generates responses, offering straightforward functionality ideal for Q&A interactions and basic user engagement activities.
- **Grounded Conversation (A2):** This pattern extends the basic GPT-driven solution by integrating a knowledge base, thereby enriching a GPT model's capabilities with domain-specific knowledge. The improved response quality and relevance make it suitable for situations that require more nuanced, context-aware interactions.
- **Mixed-initiative Conversation (A3):** This pattern introduces an interactive, GPT-powered solution that's designed to not only respond to user queries but also to generate queries or provide instructions. This additional interactivity fosters user engagement and delivers a more dynamic conversational experience.
- **Quality-controlled Conversation (A4):** This advanced pattern presents a quality-controlled conversational solution, featuring a secondary GPT model as a critic. This critic evaluates the primary model's responses, facilitating an iterative feedback loop that progressively improves the response quality. It's an ideal pattern for applications where the quality of generated responses is paramount.

In the subsequent subchapters, we will dive deeper into each pattern, providing detailed descriptions, workflow explanations, and real-world use cases.

A1 Basic Conversation

This pattern describes a basic architectural setup for implementing a GPT-based chatbot in an enterprise environment. It leverages the power of a GPT model to generate meaningful responses to user queries while maintaining a user-friendly interface (see *Figure* 4.1).

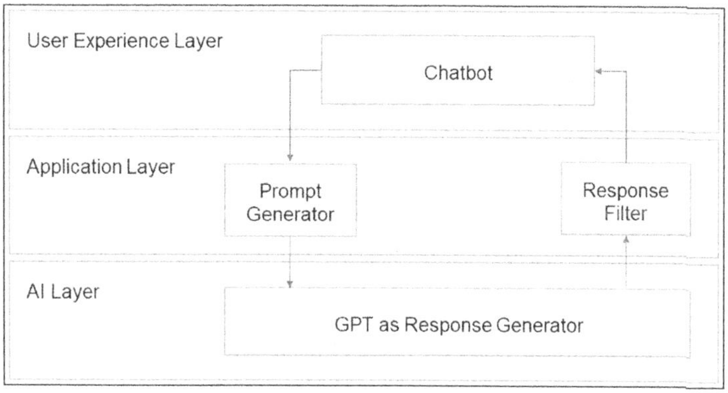

Figure 4.1: *Basic conversation*

User Experience Layer

This layer primarily focuses on how users interact with the solution. It employs a Standard Chatbot User Interface, which could be a simple text box or a more advanced user interface with voice and avatar capabilities. This layer is responsible for capturing user input (utterances) and presenting responses from the AI layer in an understandable and user-friendly manner.

Application Layer

This layer bridges the user experience and AI layers. It performs the critical function of converting the raw user input into a format suitable for a GPT model (prompt generation) and filtering the generated responses based on the enterprise's rules and requirements (response filtering).

- Prompt Generator: This component translates user utterances into appropriate prompts for a GPT model. First, it selects a predefined prompt template[2], which matches the user input. Then it instantiates the template with the details from the input. An example is shown here:
    - Input by a Service Agent: "A key customer keeps raining unjustified complaints. Today we received another such complaint. Can we reject it, or do we need to accept it due to the customer's importance?"
    - Resulting Prompt for a GPT model:
        - "Expert Persona: You are a customer relations specialist at a company that values both customer satisfaction and fair policies.

[2]Prompt Templates are largely prefilled Prompt Patterns, which are used to control GPT models and are introduced in *Chapter 5, Advanced GPT Prompt Engineering Techniques*. Templates can be selected based on rules, machine-learning models or via a selection prompt to a GPT model.

- Context: A service agent provided the following information 'A key customer keeps raining unjustified complaints. Today we received another such complaint. Can we reject it, or do we need to accept it due to the customer's importance?'.
- Task Specification:
    1. Summarize the decision-relevant aspects of the complaint.
    2. Determine whether it is justified or unjustified based on company standards and past interactions.
    3. Weigh the importance of this customer against the fairness of accepting or rejecting the complaint.
- Execution Rules:
    1. Ensure that all decisions are made with respect to company guidelines and ethical standards.
    2. Prioritize the long-term relationship with the customer, while also upholding the integrity and reputation of the company.
    3. Take into consideration any patterns in the customer's past complaints.
- Output Constraints:
    1. Provide a reasoned decision on whether to accept or reject the complaint in a concise response no longer than 150 words."

- Response Filtering: Each generated response is checked against a set of criteria such as appropriateness, relevance, completeness, and coherence. If a response passes these checks, it is sent back to the user through the User Experience Layer. Otherwise, a default message is displayed.

AI Layer

At the core of this pattern is the AI layer, which utilizes a GPT model as a response generator. This layer accepts the processed prompts from the Application Layer and leverages the knowledge embedded in the pre-trained GPT model to generate responses.

Pattern Workflow

1. The User interacts with the Chatbot Interface by inputting a question or command.
2. The Application Layer takes the user input and translates it into a prompt suitable for a GPT model, based on a repository of prompt templates.

3. The AI Layer, specifically a GPT model, generates a response based on the given prompt.
4. The Application Layer receives the response and applies filters to check if it meets the defined criteria.
5. If the response passes the filter, it is sent back to the user through the User Experience Layer. If it fails the filter, a default message is displayed to the user.

Enterprise Integration

The Basic Conversation pattern neither interacts with enterprise applications nor taps into an internal knowledge base. Furthermore, while the system does consider the conversation history as context, it predominantly depends on the information supplied by the user. As a result, the system's responses are confined to the knowledge instilled in the AI model during its training phase. Such responses are general and lack enrichment with organization-specific insights or real-time data from enterprise applications and databases, posing a considerable constraint for many applications.

Output Quality

This pattern offers decent output quality for straightforward and generic inquiries, a quality it owes primarily to the power of advanced GPT models. Additionally, basic quality checks are implemented within the response filter, which aids in maintaining the appropriateness, relevance, and accuracy of the generated responses.

Performance

This pattern stands out in computational performance due to its minimalistic design. With a single interaction between the user and GPT model per input, it ensures quick responses and lower computational load. This streamlined approach enables the system to handle larger volumes of user queries efficiently thus, increasing the scalability.

Use Cases

Given the basic nature of this pattern, it's suitable for simple Q&A tasks, where there is no need for contextual understanding or access to a dedicated knowledge base. It can be employed in scenarios like simple FAQ bots, prompt-response systems, or basic user engagement activities. It is not intended for tasks requiring complex dialogue management, context-aware responses, or access to a dynamic, and up-to-date knowledge base.

A2 Grounded Conversation

This architecture pattern enhances the capabilities of the basic chatbot, by combining the flexibility of GPT models with domain-specific knowledge and data from the organization's existing systems (see *Figure* 4.2).

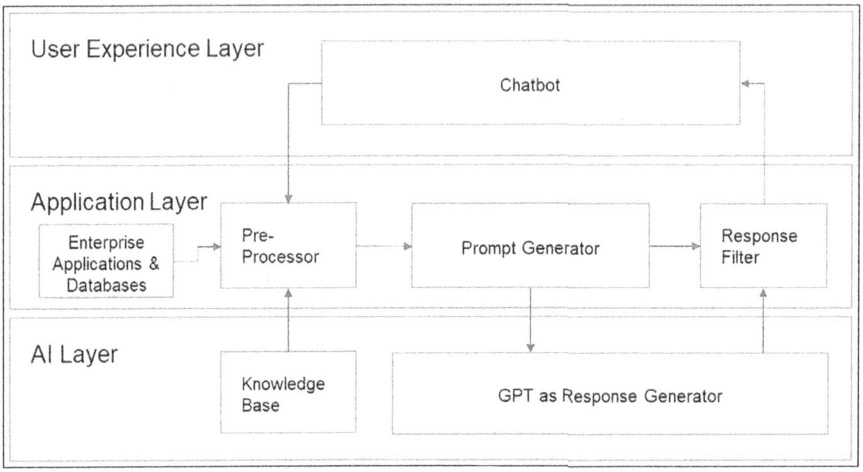

***Figure* 4.2**: *Grounded conversation*

User Experience Layer

This layer is the same as in the A1 pattern.

Application Layer

This layer acts as a bridge between the User Experience and AI layers. It houses the following components:

- **Enterprise Applications and Databases**: These are sources for enterprise-specific data and can be accessed via API calls.
- **Pre-Processor**: This component retrieves relevant data from enterprise applications and databases, and queries a knowledge base, enriching the user's input. Any required quality checks and transformations into text format are also performed here.
- **Prompt Generator**: This component takes the enriched user input from the Pre-Processor, and converts it into a prompt format that the used GPT model can understand and process.

- **Response Filter**: This component evaluates a GPT model's responses against certain criteria, such as relevance, appropriateness, completeness, and coherency, like the basic pattern. If a response fails these checks, a default message is returned to the user.

AI Layer

This layer is integral to AI-driven interactions. It comprises two essential components: a GPT model and an internal knowledge base.

- **Knowledge Base**: Positioned within the AI layer alongside a GPT model, the knowledge base is a reservoir of domain-specific knowledge. This knowledge base, typically in the form of a document database[3], graph database[4], or vector database[5], provides an added layer of industry and/or organization-specific detail.
- **GPT Model**: It generates coherent and contextually relevant responses by utilizing the enriched prompts supplied by the Application Layer. Notably, the model applies its pre-training knowledge to the combined input from the user, the enterprise data sources and the knowledge base.

Pattern Workflow

1. The User interacts with the Chatbot Interface, providing input or asking questions.
2. The Pre-Processor in the Application Layer fetches any necessary data from enterprise applications and databases, based on the original user input.
3. The Pre-Processor then sifts through the knowledge base, searching for pertinent information related to the user's input. It could employ a traditional keyword-based search for direct matches, or, in the case of an underlying vector database, a semantic search relying on the similarity of vector encodings of search query and candidate documents for a broader, context-aware match.

[3]A document database, also known as a document-oriented database or a document store, is a type of non-relational database that is designed to store, retrieve, and manage semi-structured information, for example text with metadata, typically in standardized formats like JSON (Java Script Object Notation) or XML (extensible markup language).

[4]A graph database, commonly known as a graph-oriented database or graph engine, is also a form of non-relational database to capture, process, and administer data modeled as networks, emphasizing nodes, edges, and attributes, thereby enabling intricate interconnections and dependencies to be mapped, accessed, and analyzed.

[5]A vector database is a specialized database system optimized for storing and querying high-dimensional vector data, often representing texts like documents, queries or interest profiles, and is commonly used in AI applications for tasks like similarity searches or recommendations.

4. The Pre-Processor further refines the supplemented input through tasks like data cleansing, normalization, removal of personally identifiable information (PII), and partitioning of long texts into manageable chunks to adhere to the input size limitations of the underlying GPT model.
5. The enriched input is then transformed into a prompt suitable for a GPT model by the Prompt Generator.
6. The AI Layer, or a GPT model, generates a response based on the prompt.
7. The Response Filter checks this response against predefined criteria.
8. If the response passes the filters, it is relayed back to the user through the User Experience Layer. If it fails, a default message is provided to the user.

Pattern Workflow Example

Imagine you have recently installed a smart lightbulb in your living room, but it's not turning on. Seeking quick help, you reach out to the manufacturer's tech support chatbot.

Your interaction is: "My living room's smart light bulb isn't turning on."

Here's how the pattern workflow could play out, where the step numbers of the example correspond to the steps in the general workflow:

1. **User Interaction**: You've told the chatbot about your smart lightbulb problem.
2. **Fetching Necessary Data**: Immediately, the Pre-Processor consults the manufacturer's database to determine the exact model and version of the lightbulb you own, along with its installation date and any associated devices.
3. **Sifting Through the Knowledge Base**: Using the details about your specific lightbulb model, the Pre-Processor searches the knowledge base–a digital troubleshooting manual–for relevant guidance tailored for your bulb model.
4. **Refining Input**: The Pre-Processor ensures the instructions are in an order that's easy to follow, stripping out any technical jargon to make it user-friendly.

5. **Prompt Creation**: This is where the chatbot prepares the question or context for its main brain. Incorporating the troubleshooting steps, the prompt might look something like this: "Given that the 'ABC Model' lightbulb isn't turning on, and based on the troubleshooting steps which suggest checking the bulb's power source, verifying its compatibility with the switch, and ensuring the app settings are correct, how would you guide the user through these steps in a clear and empathetic manner?"
6. **Response Generation**: With this detailed prompt, the chatbot's brain (a GPT model) generates a coherent and helpful response that navigates you through the steps.
7. **Checking the Response**: A Response Filter evaluates the chatbot's answer, ensuring clarity and hitting all the vital troubleshooting points.
8. **Delivering the Answer**: Once validated, the chatbot responds: "I'm sorry to hear about the issue with your lightbulb. Let's try these steps for your 'ABC Model':
    - **a.** First, make sure the bulb is securely screwed into the socket and receiving power.
    - **b.** Check if the switch or outlet you're using is compatible with smart devices.
    - **c.** Open the associated app and ensure the bulb's settings are configured correctly. If you continue to face issues after these steps, please get in touch with our technical team."

Enterprise Integration

The Grounded Conversation pattern features robust enterprise data integration via API calls. It also accesses a knowledge base to enhance the input with relevant domain-specific knowledge. This level of integration allows the system to utilize the resources and functions of the organization's existing IT infrastructure, enriching the chatbot's responses with organizational knowledge and context-awareness.

Output Quality

The pattern enhances the output quality by grounding and enriching the prompts with enterprise knowledge and data. A GPT model's context-awareness and its capacity to generate more nuanced and tailored responses are both improved by integrating enterprise applications, databases, and a knowledge base to supplement user input.

Further enhancing the quality of the prompts, the architecture employs pre-processing steps such as data cleansing and normalization. These steps eliminate potential inaccuracies and inconsistencies in the user's input and standardize the data, ensuring it is in a suitable format for a GPT model to process.

The pattern also incorporates an output filtering process, similar in principle to the one in the Basic Conversation pattern (A1). However, given the higher initial quality of the responses due to enriched prompts, the output filter can now focus on more specific quality checks.

Performance

The Grounded Conversation pattern demonstrates more computational complexity and less efficiency compared to the Basic Conversation pattern due to the inclusion of additional pre-processing steps and integrations.

Use Cases

This pattern is appropriate for scenarios that require more nuanced responses that leverage internal, domain-specific knowledge, as well as data from enterprise applications and databases. It's suitable for enterprises aiming to provide dynamic, context-aware responses such as customer support for specific products or services, internal employee assistance, or even personalized user interactions.

A3 Mixed-initiative Conversation

This pattern offers an advanced configuration of a GPT-based chatbot with interactive capabilities. It enhances the typical user-driven interactions by system-initiated questions or instructions to collect information or collaboratively execute a process (see *Figure* 4.3).

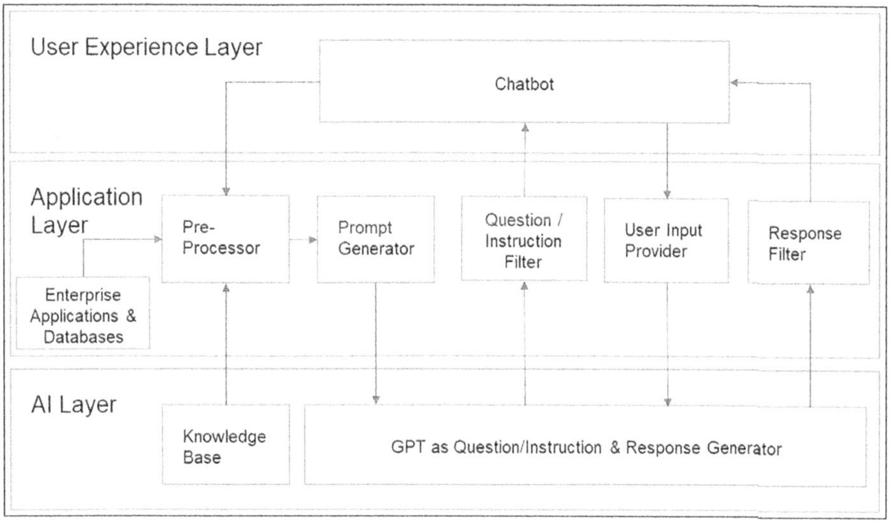

Figure 4.3: *Mixed-initiative conversation*

User Experience Layer

This layer now supports mixed initiative conversations using a chatbot user interface.

Application Layer

In addition to the components of the previous pattern, two new components are introduced here:

- **Question/Instruction Filter**: This new component filters the questions or instructions generated by a GPT model. Only those fulfilling certain criteria are passed on to the user.
- **User Input Provider**: This component captures user's responses to the GPT-generated questions or instructions, feeding them back into the GPT-model.

AI Layer

This layer remains the same as in the Grounded Conversation pattern (A2), hosting a GPT model and a knowledge base.

Pattern Workflow

1. The User interacts with the Chatbot Interface, providing input or asking questions.

2. The Pre-Processor in the Application Layer consults the enterprise data sources and knowledge base, enriches the user's input and performs any other required data preparation tasks.
3. The augmented input is converted into a suitable prompt for a GPT model.
4. A GPT model can generate questions/instructions for the user or a response, based on the prompt.
5. GPT-generated questions/instructions are filtered and, if fulfilling the criteria, are passed to the user.
6. The user provides respective feedback, which is captured by the User Input Provider and passed on to a GPT model.
7. Finally, a GPT model generates a response, which is then evaluated by the Response Filter.
8. If the response passes the filters, it is relayed back to the user. If it fails, a default message is shown.

Enterprise Integration

This pattern offers the same level of enterprise integration as the Grounded Conversation pattern (A2).

Output Quality

The output quality is higher than in A2 due to additional user input received for the questions asked by a GPT model resulting in better contextualized prompts.

Performance

The performance during each conversational turn is the same as for A2, while the conversation itself is extended due to the additional questions asked by a GPT model.

Use Cases

This architecture type is well-suited for complex, interactive scenarios that require dynamic, context-aware responses and user input. Possible applications include advanced customer service, interactive user engagement, guided troubleshooting, and personalized recommendations.

A4 Quality-controlled Conversation

This pattern outlines a sophisticated chatbot architecture which enhances the conversation quality by using two GPT models: one serving as the primary response generator and the other acting as a critic. This configuration offers an iterative feedback mechanism for quality control to improve the chatbot's responses based on the feedback provided by the GPT critic (see *Figure 4.4*).

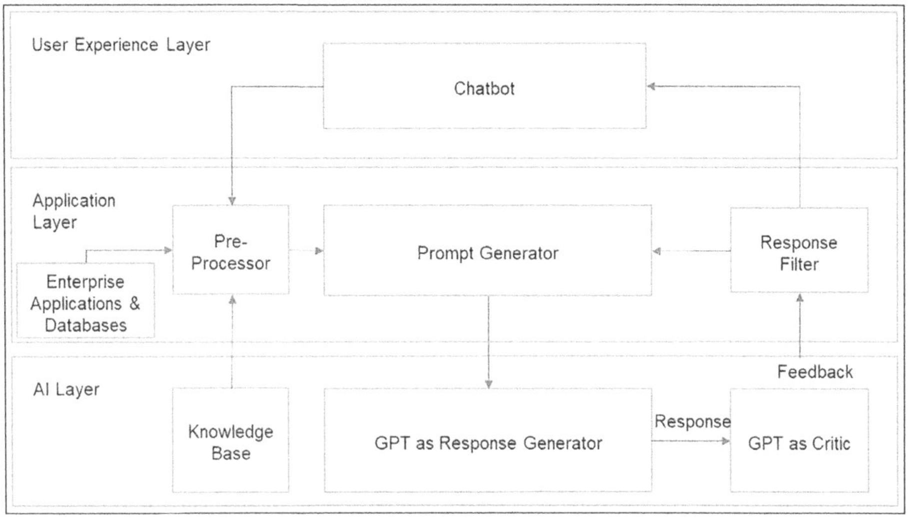

Figure 4.4: *Quality-controlled conversation*

User Experience Layer

The User Experience Layer remains consistent with the Basic Conversation pattern (A1).

Application Layer

This layer includes the same types of components as in the **Grounded Conversation** pattern (A2), but with some differences in functionality:

- **Prompt Generator**: This component also generates correction prompts when needed, based on the feedback from the GPT critic. This functionality enables a feedback loop that iteratively improves the quality of the responses.
- **Response Filter**: Compared with the **Grounded Conversation** pattern, the filtering criteria are now more specific due to the detailed feedback from the GPT critic, making the evaluation of responses more context-sensitive and rigorous.

AI Layer

This layer hosts two GPT models: one as the main response generator and the other as a critic, along with a knowledge base.

- **Response Generator**: This GPT model generates responses based on the prompts, leveraging both its pre-training knowledge and the input derived from the internal knowledge base and the enterprise data sources.
- **GPT Critic**: This GPT model reviews the generated responses for quality. It evaluates the prompt and response, and produces feedback on the quality of the response. To ensure a high standard of response, the GPT Critic checks each generated response against a more detailed set of criteria, which includes appropriateness, relevance, factual accuracy, correct reasoning, and potential hallucinations. The nature of the critique can vary based on the specific setup. If the same model and context used by the Response Generator were also used by the GPT Critic, this could lead to a form of self-critique. In this scenario, the model would essentially evaluate its own output. However, if a different model or context were used in the critique process, this would introduce a new level of independent review, thus resulting in a separate critique. This could help provide additional checks and balances to ensure the quality of the generated responses. Responses and feedback from past iterations could also be included into future prompts for the response generator to make it learn from past mistakes.

Pattern Workflow

1. The User interacts with the Chatbot Interface, providing input or asking questions.
2. The Pre-Processor enriches the user's input with data from the internal knowledge base and enterprise data sources, and carries out necessary data preparation tasks.
3. The augmented input is transformed into a suitable prompt for a GPT model.
4. The GPT Response Generator produces a response based on the prompt.
5. The prompt and response are fed into the GPT Critic, which provides feedback on the quality of the response.
6. The quality feedback is checked. If all criteria are fulfilled, the original response is relayed back to the user. If not, a request for a correction prompt is sent to the Prompt Generator.

7. The correction prompt is fed back into the GPT Response Generator, and a new iteration starts.
8. The process terminates after the critic provides feedback, which passes the response filter or after a predefined number of iterations have been completed unsuccessfully.

Enterprise Integration

This pattern offers the same level of enterprise integration as the Grounded pattern (A2).

Output Quality

The grounding and enriching of prompts with enterprise data and knowledge is a feature maintained from previous patterns, which ensures that the generation of responses are grounded in an enterprise-specific context.

Unique to this pattern, the GPT critic reviews the responses from the GPT response generator. It evaluates the prompt, and the response generated, providing feedback that is used by the response filter to improve the quality of the responses in an iterative feedback loop. This process helps ensure the relevance, coherence, and overall quality of the responses, as they are continually refined until they meet predefined quality standards.

Performance

The Quality-controlled Conversation pattern introduces a significant increase in computational complexity compared to the previous patterns, due to the addition of a second GPT model that acts as a critic. This GPT critic reviews each response generated by the first GPT model, adding a new level of computational load. Moreover, the iterative feedback loop mechanism, which improves the quality of responses based on the critic's feedback, also adds additional processing time by the response generator.

Use Cases

This pattern is well-suited for scenarios that require high-quality, context-aware responses. The feedback loop mechanism ensures that the responses are iteratively improved until they meet the defined quality standards. This could be particularly useful in customer support systems, healthcare advisory assistants, financial advisory services, or any other field where the quality of the response is of paramount importance.

B Conversational Patterns with External Tool Integration

In this section, we delve into two more advanced architecture patterns for GPT-driven chatbots. These patterns leverage the power of OpenAI's GPT model, while integrating external tools and advanced methods of guiding the chatbot's reasoning process.

- **Basic Tool-integrated Conversation (B1):** In continuation of the respective section in the introductory chapter (*Access to External Tools in GPT-Models*), the first pattern outlines an architecture where a conversational solution interacts with enterprise applications via API calls. These interactions are embedded into the entire conversation and dynamically triggered based on respective user input, extending the solution's capabilities from text generation to performing enterprise tasks.
- **Chain-of-Thought-guided Conversation using Tools (B2):** The second pattern introduces a structure integrating Chain-of-Thought (CoT) Demonstrations[6] with tool-specific API calls. This configuration ensures a fluid incorporation of tool actions within the solution's reasoning process, allowing it to pause, perform actions using external tools, and continue the conversation based on the results. This advanced interaction model is particularly beneficial for more complex tasks, which require reasoning during the dialogue.
- **Advanced Tool-integrated Conversation (B3):** Going a step further than the Basic Tool-integrated Conversation (B1), the third pattern deploys a GPT model as both a contextual planner and a response generator. While B1 focuses on direct interactions with external tools triggered by user input, B3 introduces a layer of planning that determines a logical sequence of operations. The outcome is a richer and more adaptive conversational experience, moving beyond mere task execution to strategic task orchestration.

The following sections will elaborate on these patterns, discussing their individual components, workflows, and potential use cases.

B1 Basic Tool-integrated Conversation

This pattern outlines an architecture where a GPT-enabled chatbot engages in

[6]In the context of GPT models like ChatGPT, a "Chain of Thought (CoT)" refers to the model's ability to maintain a coherent line of reasoning over a sequence of sentences or exchanges. A CoT demonstration is an example of such a reasoning chain.

user interactions, which require the execution of specific functions provided by enterprise applications, databases and knowledge bases via APIs. This allows the chatbot to extend its capabilities beyond merely generating human-like text, enabling it to perform external tasks during the conversation (see *Figure* 4.5).

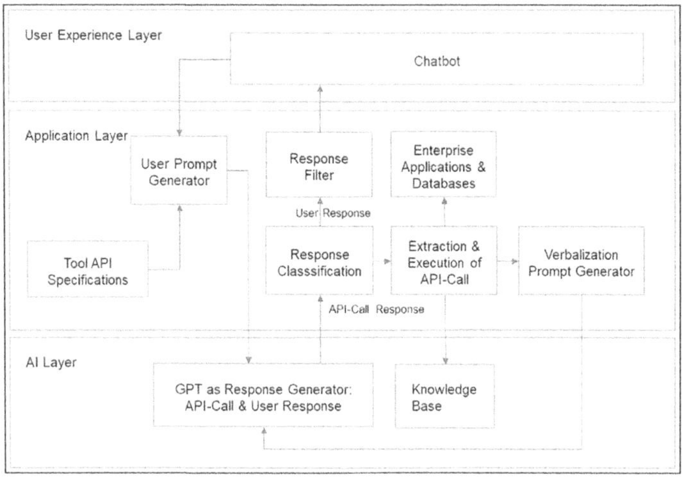

***Figure 4.5**: Basic tool-integrated conversation*

User Experience Layer

This layer is unchanged from the **Grounded Conversation** pattern (A2), providing a Standard Chatbot User Interface for user interactions.

Application Layer

Serving as the bridge between the User Experience and AI layers, this layer contains several components: Tool API Specifications, enterprise applications and databases, user prompt generator, response filter, response classification, extraction & execution of API-call, and verbalization prompt generator.

- **Tool API Specifications**: This component holds the specifications for the APIs of the various tools that the conversational application can interact with. A specification typically has these four elements.
    - **API Name**: The API name provides an abstract of the API. It helps a GPT model to link user instructions to this API and serves as an entry for the extraction and execution component. The name should be clear and precise in natural language, and avoid ambiguity with other API names like *check_order_status* to check the status of an order in a backend system.

- **Parameter List**: The parameter list for an API includes the input parameters and return value, and each parameter has a parameter name, parameter description, data type, and default value. This information assists the used GPT model in correctly filling the parameters in the corresponding positions with the appropriate format. For the check_order_status example the parameters could be the following:
  - Input Parameters:
    - **order_id**: integer, the unique identifier for an order placed in the system. This is used to look up the specific order and retrieve its current status.
  - Return Value:
    - **order_status**: string, denotes the current status of the order. Common values can include Pending, Processing, Shipped, Delivered, Canceled, and so on.
    - **expected_delivery_date**: date (optional), the estimated delivery date for orders that are in Shipped status.
    - **reason**: string (optional), if the order is Canceled, this will provide a reason for the cancellation.
- **API Description**: Compared to the API name, the API description contains more information about what the API does, how it works, what are its inputs and outputs, and any potential errors or exceptions that may be raised. The respective example for *check_order_status* could be: *This function allows for the retrieval of the current status pertaining to a specific order, achieved through the use of the order's unique ID. Upon querying, the system will respond with the status of the order and may also offer additional details such as the expected delivery date or the reason behind an order cancellation.*
- **Usage Example** (Optional): Providing a usage example for complex APIs can help demonstrate how the API can be used, while it may not be necessary for simple APIs. For the order status check an example could look like this: *Users can request the status of an order with the ID "12345678". The response may inform them that the order is "Shipped" and offer a corresponding expected delivery date.*

- **Enterprise Applications and Databases**: These provide the external tools via API calls and can include any functional backend system like HR, Finance or Procurement, but also search engines or specialized ML-models.
- **User Prompt Generator**: This component translates the user's input into a suitable prompt for a GPT model.

- **Response Classification**: This component identifies and classifies GPT-generated responses into two types:
    - final response to the user request or
    - intermediate response containing a function call.

  A function call is identified if the response includes a `function_call` field.
- **Extraction & Execution of API-Call**: When a function call response is identified, this component extracts the necessary details from the function call field, selects the appropriate tool to be used based on the tool API specifications and executes the API call with the chosen tool. A tool can be any functionality within an enterprise application, database or knowledge base.
- **Verbalization Prompt Generator**: This component leverages the existing context (user prompt and function call response) and adds a function prompt, which contains the results of the previous function call converted into text format. A GPT model then translates these results into a response to the user in natural language.
- **Response Filter**: This component checks the final GPT responses to the user for appropriateness, relevance, completeness, and coherence.

AI Layer

This layer hosts GPT models, which have been trained on conversational data that includes tool-specific API-function calls (so far only specific versions of GPT-3.5 Turbo and GPT-4). These models can generate either user responses or function call responses based on the prompts they receive.

It also includes a knowledge base with the same capabilities as in previous patterns.

Pattern Workflow

1. The User interacts with the chatbot interface, providing input or asking questions.
2. The user's input is translated into an initial prompt for a GPT model, which also includes the tool API specifications.
3. The response is then classified as either a user response or a function call response.

4. If it's a user response, it's forwarded to the response filter, where it is vetted for relevance, accuracy, and appropriateness and forwarded to the user (positive check results) or replaced by a default message (negative check results).
5. If it is a function call response in the format that defines an API call, the 'Extraction & Execution of API-Call' component executes the API call to the specified enterprise application, data base, or knowledge base.
6. The results of the API call are used by the Verbalization Prompt Generator to generate a function prompt for a GPT model.
7. A GPT model generates a user response translating the API call results into natural language.
8. This process repeats with each new user prompt until the conversation concludes.

Pattern Workflow Example

Let us walk through an example using this pattern. Here, we will use the scenario of a user reaching out to an online bookstore's chatbot to inquire about the status of their order:

Your interaction is: "Can you tell me the status of my order with ID 98765432?"

Here's how the chatbot pattern workflow assists, where the step numbers of the example correspond to the steps in the general workflow:

1. User Interaction: You ask the chatbot about the status of your order by providing the order ID.
2. Initial Prompt Creation: The prompt generator translates your question into a suitable prompt for a GPT model: "User wants to know the status of order with ID 98765432 based on the tool API specification for check_order_status."
3. Response Classification: A GPT model interprets the prompt and identifies that this requires a function call to the bookstore's system, specifically the check_order_status function.
4. User or Function Call Decision: Since the response indicates a function call, the system skips user response generation and proceeds to the next step.

5. API Execution: Using the details provided, the system fetches information from the bookstore's system. It uses the check_order_status API with the order ID 98765432 to get the current status and other details of the order.
6. Verbalization Prompt Creation: With the result from the bookstore's system, a function prompt is generated for a GPT model, which contains the current status and other details of the order.
7. Generating User Response: A GPT model then crafts a coherent response based on this prompt, which might be: "Your order with ID 98765432 has been shipped! You can expect its delivery by August 28, 2023."
8. Conversation Continuation or Conclusion: The chatbot delivers this message to you. The conversation continues if you have more questions or concludes if your inquiry has been satisfied.

Enterprise Integration

The Tool-integrated Conversation pattern features a significant level of enterprise integration. The architecture is closely tied with enterprise applications and databases that offer specific functionalities accessible through APIs. This design facilitates near-real-time integration, allowing the chatbot to execute tasks, fetch data, and generate responses based on these operations. Furthermore, this pattern can also potentially access knowledge bases if they are available via APIs, extending the range of data sources the chatbot can draw from during conversations.

Output Quality

This pattern significantly improves output quality by grounding and enriching user prompts dynamically with task output from backend systems. The decision, when to call a backend system is taken by the GPT model based on user input and not by a preprocessor like in the **Grounded pattern** (A2). The results of these tasks then provide detailed and accurate contexts for the GPT model, when it is actually used as a response generator.

Performance

This pattern introduces more computational complexity and latency due to the extra steps involved in interacting with enterprise applications and databases through APIs, classifying the responses, and generating verbalization prompts.

Use Cases

This pattern excels in process-oriented scenarios that demand several interactions with enterprise applications and databases based on user input. It's also ideal for customer service bots that need to interact with enterprise applications and databases to fetch or update user data.

B2 Chain-of-Thought-guided Conversation using Tools

This pattern represents an architecture of a GPT-based chatbot that combines Chain-of-Thought (CoT) Demonstrations and interaction with specific functions provided by enterprise applications and databases via API calls [3]. CoT Demonstrations help in designing more effective prompts that showcase logical reasoning chains to a GPT model, enhancing its ability to maintain a consistent, logical sequence of responses or actions over a series of interactions (see *Figure* 4.6).

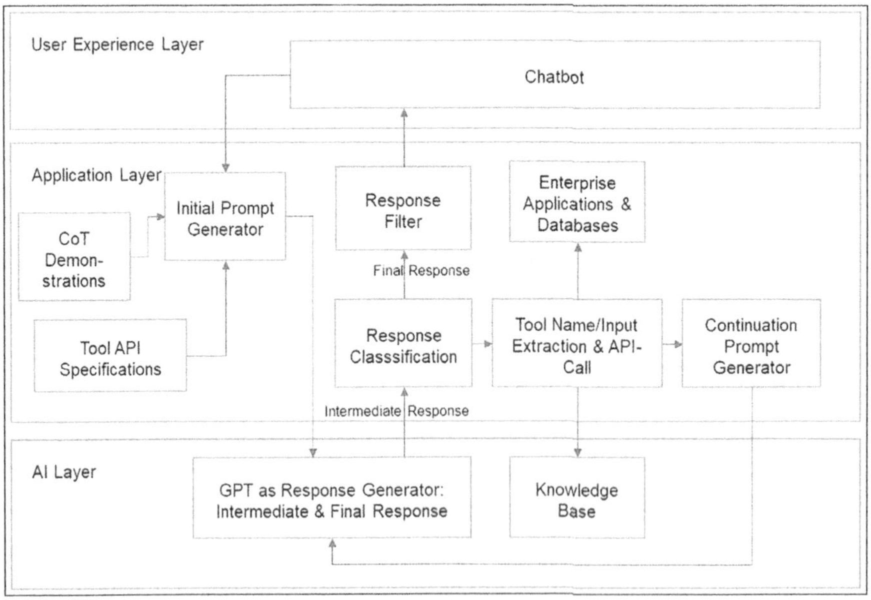

Figure 4.6: *Chain-of-Thought-guided conversation using tools*

User Experience Layer

This layer is unchanged from the **Grounded Conversation** pattern (A2), providing a Standard Chatbot User Interface for user interactions.

Application Layer

The application layer plays a critical role in mediating the chatbot's reasoning process and its interactions with enterprise applications and databases. It comprises several components: CoT demonstrations, enterprise applications and databases, Tool API specifications, initial prompt generator, response filter, response classification, function name/input extraction & API call, and continuation prompt generator.

- **Chain-of-Thought (CoT) Demonstrations**: These are demonstrations of desired thought processes for the chatbot, used to augment the user's input.
- **Enterprise Applications and Databases**: These house the specific tool functionalities that the chatbot interacts with via API calls.
- **Tool API Specifications**: This component holds the specifications for various tools within the enterprise applications and databases that the chatbot can interact with.
- **Initial Prompt Generator**: This component translates the user's input, augmented with tool API specifications and CoT demonstrations, into an initial prompt for a GPT model, with instructions to stop when a tool trigger is generated.
- **Response Filter**: This component checks the responses generated by a GPT model against defined criteria.
- **Response Classification**: This component classifies GPT-generated responses into user responses or tool calls.
- **Tool Name/Input Extraction and API Call**: When a tool trigger is identified in a response, this component extracts the tool name and input, executes the tool call, and appends the results to the reasoning process.
- **Continuation Prompt Generator**: This component generates continuation prompts for a GPT model by combining the original prompt, intermediate responses, and tool results.

AI Layer

This layer hosts the knowledge base and a GPT model which is responsible for generating intermediate and final responses to user prompts.

Pattern Workflow

1. The User interacts with the Chatbot Interface, providing input or making requests.

2. The user's input is augmented with the relevant tool API Specifications from the enterprise applications and databases and matching CoT Demonstrations.
3. The augmented input is translated into an initial prompt for a GPT model, instructing it to stop when a tool trigger is generated.
4. A GPT model generates an intermediate response, which is then classified as a user response or a function call.
5. If the response contains a tool trigger, the tool name and input are extracted, and the respective function call is executed on the specified application, database or knowledge base.
6. The results of the function call are appended to the reasoning process.
7. GPT is called again with a continuation prompt (original prompt + intermediate response + tool result) to continue the conversation.
8. Steps 4–7 repeat until all tool-using steps in the reasoning process have been completed.
9. The final response is generated, checked by the response filter, and passed on to the user.

Enterprise Integration

The enterprise integration for this pattern is equivalent to that in the **Tool-integrated Conversation** pattern (B1).

Output Quality

The output quality of this pattern is also comparable to the previous pattern.

Performance

The performance of this pattern is worse than in the Tool-integrated Conversation pattern due to repeated continuation prompting each time a function call needs to be performed.

Use Cases

This pattern is particularly effective for complex use cases that require a step-by-step reasoning process and integration with external tools. It can be used to create sophisticated chatbots that not only answer queries but also perform multi-step tasks, solve complex problems, or guide users through a process while interacting with external tools or services. Examples include IT support chatbots, virtual assistants for complex software applications, or training systems.

B3 Advanced Tool-integrated Conversation

This evolved architecture pattern harnesses a GPT model in two capacities: as a planner and as a response generator. As a planner it translates user inputs into task sequences, which are executed in an orchestrated manner, and as a response generator it uses the output of each task to generate contextualized user responses (refer to *Figure* 4.7).

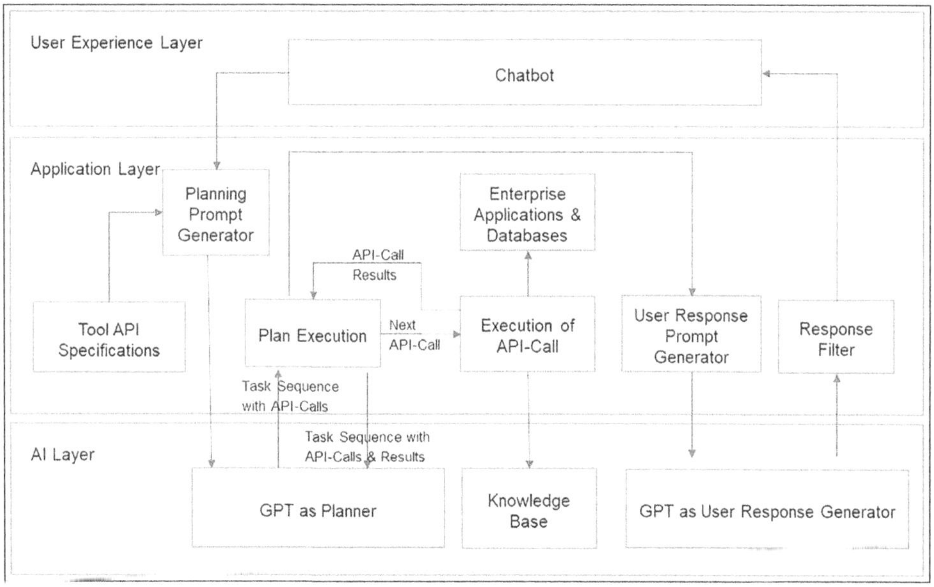

Figure 4.7: *Advanced tool-integrated conversation*

User Experience Layer

This remains unchanged compared with the B1 pattern, offering a consistent user-chatbot interaction interface.

Application Layer

This layer uses the following components from the B1 pattern:

- Tool API Specifications, which now could also include composition instructions to a GPT model on how to combine multiple APIs to accomplish complex user requests.

- Extraction & Execution of API-Call
- Enterprise Applications and Databases
- Response Filter

In addition, it introduces several planning-specific components:

- **Planning Prompt Generator**: This component converts the user's input into a prompt that asks a GPT model to generate a plan or sequence of tasks.
- **Plan Execution**: Once a plan is generated by a GPT model, this component systematically extracts and acts on each task in the sequence.
- **User Response Prompt Generator**: It replaces the Verbalization Prompt Generator. This component compiles the results into a new prompt for a GPT model to produce a comprehensive and human-understandable response, after all tasks in the plan are executed.

AI Layer

This layer includes a knowledge base as before and a GPT model in two different roles:

- **Planner**: Given a planning prompt, a GPT model outlines a logical sequence of tasks with their respective API-Calls that need to be executed to satisfy the user's request.
- **User Response Generator**: After all tasks in the plan are executed and results are compiled, a GPT model takes the compiled results and crafts them into a comprehensive and human-understandable response for the user.

Pattern Workflow

1. The User interacts with the chatbot interface.
2. The Planning Prompt Generator translates the user's request into a planning prompt for a GPT model, which also includes the tool API specifications.
3. GPT, in its Planner role, interprets the planning prompt and generates a sequence of tasks with API calls for each task. The first task has a fully specified API-Call, while subsequent tasks have placeholders in their respective API-Calls
4. The Plan Execution component extracts the API call of the first task and

sends it to the API-Call Execution component, which processes it and returns the API-Call Results.

5. The Plan Execution component updates the results for the first task in the task sequence and resubmits it to GPT as Planner.
6. A GPT model keeps the already executed tasks in the plan and regenerates the task sequence immediately following the last executed task.
7. The Plan Execution component moves to the next task in the sequence, sending it to the API-Execution module, from where it gets the results back again.
8. Afterwards, it updates the plan and resubmits it to a GPT model. This loop continues until all tasks in the plan are executed.
9. Post completion of all tasks, the Plan Execution components forward all the intermediate and final results to the User Response Prompt Generator.
10. The User Response Prompt Generator frames a prompt for a GPT model.
11. GPT, in its Response Generator role, produces a detailed and user-friendly response.
12. The Response Filter vets this final response, ensuring its quality and relevance.
13. The user receives the filtered response and continues the interaction if needed.

Pattern Workflow Example

Let's imagine a user wants to host a birthday party for a friend in a local park and needs some assistance.

Your interaction is: "I want to organize a birthday party for my friend, Mark, in Central Park next Saturday. Can you help?"

Here is how this pattern would come into play. The step numbers in the example are different due to the iteration over the planned task sequence:

1. User Interaction: You express your intent to the chatbot about planning a birthday party for your friend in Central Park.
2. Planning Prompt Creation: The chatbot, through the Planning Prompt

Generator, reformulates your request to: "Generate a plan for organizing a birthday party in Central Park next Saturday."

3. Plan Generation by GPT: A GPT model, donning its Planner role, interprets the planning prompt and lays out a multi-step task sequence:
    - Task 1: Verify the availability of Central Park for events next Saturday.
    - Task 2: Reserve a suitable spot in Central Park.
    - Task 3: List nearby bakeries for a birthday cake.
    - Task 4: Recommend local entertainment or performers for hire.
    - Task 5: Provide a weather forecast for next Saturday.
4. Plan Execution - Task 1: The system first checks Central Park's availability for events on the specified date using an events API.
5. Updating & Resubmission: Assuming the park is available, the plan moves forward and is resubmitted to GPT for the next sequence.
6. Plan Execution - Task 2: The system then reserves a spot in Central Park suitable for a birthday gathering, employing the reservations API.
7. Plan Execution - Task 3: The chatbot accesses a local directory API, listing a few top-rated bakeries nearby for a potential cake order.
8. Plan Execution - Task 4: The system, tapping into another local services API, offers a few entertainment options like magicians, musicians, or party entertainers available for hire.
9. Plan Execution - Task 5: The system provides a weather forecast for next Saturday using a weather API to ensure preparations account for potential rain or shine.
10. Compile Results: All the intermediate outcomes, that is., park availability, reservation confirmation, bakery list, entertainment suggestions, and weather forecast, are consolidated.
11. User Response Prompt Creation: A prompt is generated, collating all the data: "Convert the findings from Central Park's availability, reservation, bakeries list, entertainment options, and the weather forecast into a coherent user response."
12. Crafting User Response: GPT, in its User Response Generator capacity, constructs the message: "Central Park is available next Saturday! I've reserved a spot for Mark's birthday. Here are top 3 bakeries nearby: [Bakery Names]. For entertainment, consider hiring [Entertainer Names].

Also, the weather forecast suggests it'll be sunny. Happy planning!"

13. Response Filtering: This detailed response is checked for coherence and clarity.
14. Final User Interaction: You're presented with the thorough plan and resources, allowing you to proceed with the preparations or continue the interaction for more specific details.

Enterprise Integration

The Advanced Tool-integrated Conversation pattern showcases an even more profound level of enterprise integration. By leveraging GPT's planning capabilities, it can dynamically and interactively construct sequences of tasks that harness the functionalities of various enterprise applications and databases. This design allows for adaptive interactions, ensuring that the sequence of tasks and responses is continually refined based on evolving user input.

Output Quality

The quality of the output in this pattern is notably superior due to the addition of dynamic planning and iterative execution of tasks. Instead of solely relying on initial context, a GPT model can adapt its approach based on the outcomes of previous tasks and the respective user responses. This iterative and adaptive process ensures that the conversation remains more relevant and is consistently refined to best address the user's needs.

Performance

While this pattern offers significant benefits in terms of output quality and enterprise integration, it also introduces further computational overhead. The iterative planning, execution, and replanning processes add latency to the overall response time.

Use Cases

Given the enhanced capabilities of the B3 pattern, its use cases extend to more complex and dynamic scenarios:

- **Process Automation Bots**: Ideal for guiding users through complex, multi-step processes like onboarding, troubleshooting, or service provisioning. As each step is completed, the bot can adapt its guidance based on the outcomes.

- **Dynamic Querying Systems**: For situations where a user's request requires fetching and processing data from multiple sources in a specific sequence, for example, generating a detailed report that spans multiple enterprise applications.
- **Advanced Customer Service Bots**: Beyond simple data retrieval, these bots can execute sequences of tasks like updating multiple records, initiating processes, and then reporting back the results, all in a single user interaction.
- **Interactive Tutorials and Guided Learning**: Bots that can adapt the learning path based on user responses, test results, or other criteria, ensuring a tailored learning experience.
- **Integrated Business Intelligence Tools**: For business users who need a sequence of data retrieval, analysis, and visualization tasks from different enterprise tools to generate insights.

C Conversational Patterns with Fine-tuned Models

This section introduces two advanced patterns that harness the potential of GPT in synergy with fine-tuned models for end-to-end conversational solutions.

- **Conversation using Fine-tuned Model (C1):** This pattern utilizes a GPT model to generate training data, which is used to fine-tune a commercial or open-source language model. The conversational solution then employs this fine-tuned model to craft responses for the user, supplemented with enterprise knowledge and data.
- **Conversation using Two Models (C2):** This pattern leverages both a fine-tuned model and a pre-trained GPT model in its operation. The output from the fine-tuned model is utilized to enhance the user input with context-specific data. This provides a GPT model with higher input quality, resulting in more precise and contextually relevant responses.

The detailed descriptions of these architecture patterns, including their structure, workflow, and potential use cases, follow.

C1 Conversation with fine-tuned model

This pattern outlines an architecture for a GPT-driven conversational solution that leverages a database along with GPT to create training data. This data is used to fine-tune a pre-existing language model which subsequently handles user interactions (refer to *Figure* 4.8).

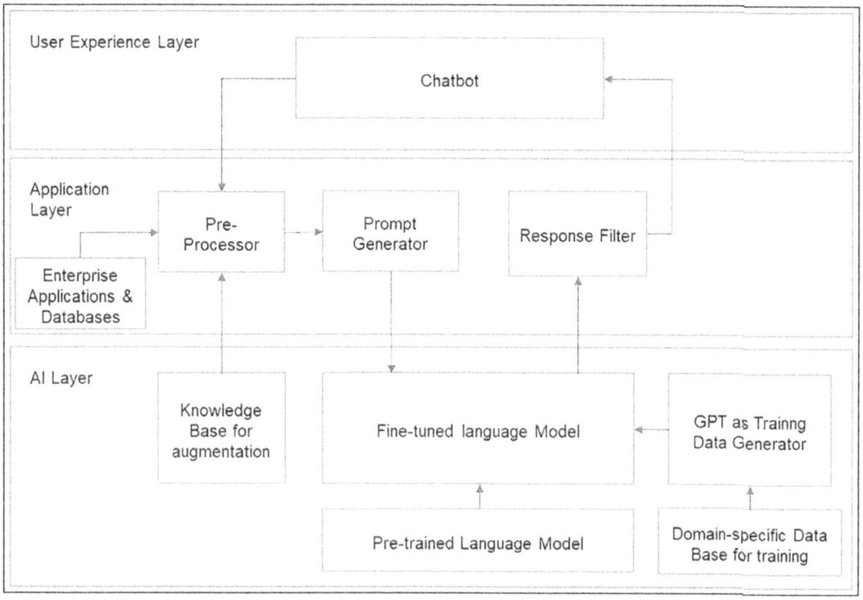

***Figure* 4.8**: *Conversation using fine-tuned model*

User Experience Layer

This layer is equivalent to the **Grounded Conversation** pattern (A2).

Application Layer

This layer also includes the same components as in the A2 pattern.

AI Layer

The AI layer encompasses several key components:

- Knowledge Base for Augmentation: It is used during run-time to supplement the AI's knowledge.
- Pre-trained Language Model: This is a general-purpose model trained on vast amounts of data to understand language but not specialized for any particular task.
- Fine-tuned Language Model: Using the foundation set by the pre-trained model, this version is further trained or fine-tuned on specific datasets.

This can be for targeted tasks such as following instructions or facilitating conversations, enhancing its accuracy and relevance for these tasks.

  - GPT-model as a Training-data Generator: It utilizes a GPT model's capabilities to generate training data, simulating various scenarios or dialogues. Users should note a crucial licensing stipulation: Outputs derived from OpenAI's services must not be used to create models in competition with OpenAI. It's also worth highlighting that licensing terms are dynamic and may change periodically. For the most current information, always refer to OpenAI's official documentation or terms of service.

- Database for Training-data Generation: A curated source from which a GPT model extracts and processes information to generate training data.

When considering fine-tuning solutions, enterprises today have the option of utilizing commercial models provided by OpenAI or a selection of noteworthy open-source models:

- Commercial Models from OpenAI:
  - GPT-3.5 Turbo: OpenAI offers fine-tuning capabilities for GPT-3.5 Turbo. Early evaluations suggest that a fine-tuned version of GPT-3.5 Turbo can achieve performance levels comparable to base GPT-4 models in specific narrow tasks. Emphasizing safety, training data for fine-tuning is subjected to OpenAI's Moderation API, which is based on GPT-4.
  - GPT Base, babbage-002 and davinci-002: These models are the recent additions from OpenAI with 16K context window size, available for both standard and fine-tuned applications.
- Open-Source Models (pre-trained on 1 trillion tokens):
  - MosaicML's MPT-30B: An open-source model boasting 30 billion parameters. It surpasses the capabilities of MPT-7B and GPT-3, featuring a context window size of 8000 tokens. The model is available in two distinct versions: MPT-30B-Instruct, tailored for instruction fine-tuning, and MPT-30B-Chat, crafted for chatbot development. MosaicML's platform also provides options for customization and deployment.
  - Falcon LLM by the Technology Innovation Institute: Based in Abu Dhabi, this open-source model is equipped with 40 billion parameters and offers a context length of 2000 tokens. Additionally, the Falcon-40B-Instruct variant is available, designed explicitly for instruction-based fine-tuning.
  - OpenLLaMA: Serving as the open-source counterpart of Meta AI's

LLaMA, it offers models in 3B, 7B, and 13B parameter configurations, each accompanied by a 4000-token context window. Contrasting Meta's research-exclusive LLaMA, OpenLLaMA is engineered for commercial application and supports fine-tuning.

- Open-Source Models (pre-trained on 2 trillion tokens):
    - Llama 2 by Meta: A more recent release, Llama 2 is available in configurations of 7B, 13B, and 70B parameters. It has a context length of 4000 tokens–twice the capacity of its predecessor, Llama 1. The Llama-2-chat variants have undergone further refinement using 100K public instruction datasets and have been influenced by over a million human preferences to bolster interaction safety and utility. Commercial utilization and fine-tuning are permitted under Llama 2's licensing.

After selecting the pre-trained model, it needs to be fine-tuned for specific enterprise tasks. Our approach covers data curation, preprocessing, training data generation using GPT, model training, and evaluation, all illustrated with practical examples. This method ensures the models are effectively tailored to the task at hand:

1. Data Curation:
    - Definition: The primary step involves gathering and curating a domain-specific database. The selected data should be representative of the specific task and should provide a solid base for the subsequent steps.
    - Examples:
        - Collection of customer support tickets for creating an IT-support chatbot.
        - Accumulation of process logs to assist in forecasting process outcomes.
        - Aggregation of email histories for developing a communication classifier.
        - Gathering of sales transaction data to develop a product recommendation system.
        - Compilation of employee onboarding queries and answers to identify common questions and responses.
2. Pre-processing:
    - Definition: Processing the curated data to make it ready for machine learning tasks. This involves data cleaning, transformation, or other

domain-specific operations.

- Examples:
  - Cleaning support tickets to remove any personal customer information.
  - Structuring and organizing process logs to track stages of execution.
  - Categorizing email histories based on their subject and content.
  - Normalizing sales transaction data, such as harmonizing product descriptions, to account for seasonal or promotional spikes.
  - Collating employee onboarding queries and answers to form a comprehensive database.

3. Training Data Generation using a GPT model:
   - Definition: Leveraging a GPT model to produce labeled or structured data based on the pre-processed information.
   - Examples:
     - Simulating IT-support Dialogues: By inputting customer support tickets into a GPT model, entire dialogues are generated that simulate how a customer query would be handled by an IT-support desk.
     - Predicting Process Outcomes: A GPT model, when provided with partial executions of a process, generates potential outcomes, which can be used as training data.
     - Email Classification with GPT: By feeding GPT models with email histories, the model can generate classification tags, such as 'complaint', 'query', or 'feedback'.
     - Product Recommendations Simulation: By processing sales data through GPT, we can simulate customer purchasing patterns and derive possible product recommendations.
     - Question and Answer Generation for HR: GPT can generate question and answer pairs related to the onboarding process, forming a diverse dataset.
4. Model Fine-tuning:
   - Definition: Using the generated dataset to train or fine-tune a model specific to the task at hand.
   - Examples:
     - Train a chatbot model with the simulated IT-support dialogues to handle customer interactions.

- Train a model to predict process outcomes using the GPT-derived outcomes.
- Train a classifier to categorize emails based on the tags generated by GPT.
- Train a recommendation engine using the GPT-simulated customer purchasing patterns.
- Creating a standard Q&A chatbot that finds similar questions to new inquiries and displays the respective answers using the GPT-generated Q&A pairs.

5. Evaluation and Iteration:
   - Definition: Assessing the performance of the trained model and iterating over the process if necessary to achieve optimal outcomes.
   - Examples:
     - Comparing chatbot responses with expert-provided answers to evaluate chatbot efficacy.
     - Measuring the accuracy of the process outcome predictions against actual outcomes.
     - Evaluating the email classifier's accuracy by comparing it against manual labels.
     - Testing the recommendation engine's suggestions against real-world customer feedback.
     - Reviewing the HR chatbot's answers by comparing them with the GPT-generated dataset to ensure accuracy and relevancy.

Each step is meticulously designed to ensure the selected pre-trained model is adapted precisely to domain-specific needs, driving efficient and accurate outcomes.

Pattern Workflow

After fine-tuning the workflow is identical to the one for the A2 pattern.

Enterprise Integration

This pattern offers the same level of enterprise integration as in A2.

Output Quality

This pattern displays an improved output quality compared to the A2 pattern.

This enhancement arises from the application of domain-specific knowledge during the fine-tuning process, which allows the system to provide more accurate and relevant responses within a specific domain.

Like the A2 pattern, it also enriches user prompts with information from the enterprise data sources and employs an output filtering process to ensure the generated responses' relevance and appropriateness.

Performance

This pattern imposes a considerable computational load primarily during the training phase, where the model is fine-tuned on domain-specific data. While there is ongoing research on its optimization, the process of generating training data and fine-tuning the pre-trained language model is still computationally intensive, requiring significant resources such as processing power, memory, and time. It may also need a large amount of domain-specific data to achieve the desired level of performance.

Once the model is fine-tuned, the operational computational cost is similar to other patterns that involve translating user utterances into prompts, generating responses, and filtering these responses.

However, one significant advantage of the Fine-tuned Conversation pattern is that it often results in a model that is smaller than a general-purpose model. This reduced size can lower the computational cost for each inference (response generation), improve speed, and potentially allow for local deployment, eliminating the need for access via a cloud platform and therefore potentially reduce the response time.

Use Cases

This pattern is particularly useful in scenarios where specific, domain-related knowledge is vital. These might include:

- **High Complexity Domains with Rich Examples**: Fields like life science or engineering where standard language models might not offer the required depth or accuracy in their outputs. Particularly in situations where the availability of numerous complex and specialized examples surpasses the capacity of a standard prompt, fine-tuning becomes essential.
- **High-Stakes Environments**: Situations where precision is critical, as inaccuracies can lead to significant consequences. Examples include medical diagnoses, financial forecasting, or legal advisories where an incorrect interpretation or recommendation can have grave repercussions.
- **Customized Experiences and Tone**: Instances demanding tailored

interactions or adjustments to cater to distinct user demographics, as well as establishments striving to reflect their unique brand voice in model outputs.

- **Fast-Changing Domains**: Domains where the knowledge landscape rapidly evolves, and constant model retraining offers an advantage over relying on external tools or preprocessing. Examples might include the tech industry with frequent software updates or news outlets covering rapidly developing events.
- **Steerability, Consistency and Output Formatting**: For businesses requiring enhanced control over the model's behavior, such as maintaining specific language outputs or ensuring consistent response formats. This is vital for scenarios like code completions or composing API calls.
- **Efficient Prompt Utilization**: Fine-tuning can reduce the necessity for lengthy prompts, when the original prompt and its response are predicted from a shortcut in the fine.tuning dataset.

C2 Conversation using Two Models

This pattern details an architecture for a GPT-enabled conversational solution that deploys a fine-tuned model in synergy with a pre-trained model to produce user responses [4] (refer to *Figure* 4.9).

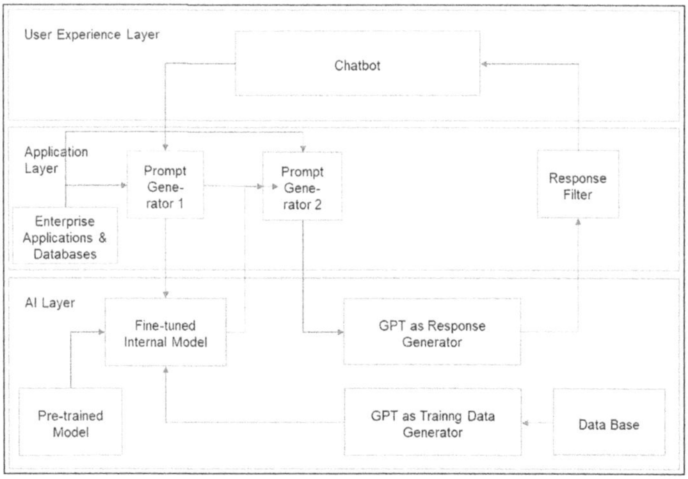

Figure 4.9: *Conversation using two models*

User Experience Layer

This layer utilizes a Standard Chatbot User Interface for user interactions, potentially enhanced by voice and avatar functionalities.

Application Layer

The application layer comprises two prompt generators, a response filter, and enterprise applications and databases:

- Enterprise Applications and Databases: These are internal tools and data sources.
- Prompt Generator 1: This component interprets the user's utterance and calls the relevant APIs of the enterprise applications and databases, integrating the returned data into an initial prompt for the fine-tuned model.
- Prompt Generator 2: This takes the input and output of the fine-tuned model, calls necessary APIs from the enterprise applications and databases again if required, and forms a new prompt for the pre-trained GPT model to generate the final response.
- Response Filter: This component checks the final response against various criteria to ensure that it's appropriate and relevant to the user's query.

AI Layer

This layer comprises a pre-trained model, a fine-tuned model, GPT as training-data generator, GPT as response generator, and a knowledge base.

The fine-tuning process is identical to the process described in the previous pattern.

Pattern Workflow

1. User Interaction to Initial Prompt Creation: The user communicates their query to the system. Prompt Generator 1 comprehends this input, liaising with backend system APIs to assimilate necessary data. This combined information forms an initial prompt tailored for the fine-tuned model.

2. Fine-tuned Model Interaction: The fine-tuned model, specialized in its domain of expertise, evaluates the initial prompt and produces a concise yet informed output.

3. Prompt for Pre-trained GPT Model: Prompt Generator 2 amalgamates the input and the output from the fine-tuned model. It may further enhance the data by consulting additional backend APIs, culminating in a well-rounded prompt designed for the pre-trained GPT model.

4. Generating Final Response: The pre-trained GPT model, equipped with a broader understanding, crafts a comprehensive and articulate response based on the received prompt.

5. Response Filtering: The resultant message undergoes scrutiny against certain standards of relevance and appropriateness. On clearing this assessment, it is delivered to the user, but failing the check results in a default response being displayed.

Pattern Workflow Example

Using this pattern, let us outline an example scenario where a user wants to purchase a laptop and needs advice on the best options available based on their specific needs.

Your interaction is: "I'm looking for a laptop suitable for graphic design tasks. My budget is $1500. What do you recommend?"

Here's how the C2 pattern would be employed, with the step numbers of the example aligning with the steps in the general workflow:

1. User Interaction to Initial Prompt Creation: After expressing your requirement, Prompt Generator 1 interprets your query. It calls the backend system's API to fetch available laptops within the price range and their specifications. This information is integrated into an initial prompt, which could be: "Provide suitable laptop recommendations within $1500, prioritizing graphic design capabilities."

2. Fine-tuned Model Interaction: The fine-tuned model, trained specifically to understand electronic products and user requirements, might generate a concise list: "Consider the [Laptop Brand A] with [Spec A] priced at $1400, or [Laptop Brand B] with [Spec B] priced at $1450. Both are suitable for graphic design."

3. Prompt for Pre-trained GPT Model: Prompt Generator 2 takes the input and the output from the fine-tuned model, possibly calling additional backend APIs (maybe for user reviews or availability), resulting in a prompt for the pre-trained GPT model. "Given the user's graphic design requirements and a budget of $1500, and considering the recommended laptops [Laptop Brand A] with [Spec A] priced at $1400 and [User Review A] and [Laptop Brand B] with [Spec B], priced at $1450 and [User Review B], craft a detailed and persuasive response."

4. Generating Final Response: The pre-trained GPT model processes the

comprehensive prompt, producing an elaborate reply: "Based on your needs and budget, I'd recommend the [Laptop Brand A] which boasts [Spec A], perfect for graphic design tasks and is well under your budget at $1400. It's been highly rated by users, especially for its [specific feature]. Another great option is the [Laptop Brand B] priced at $1450, offering [Spec B] and has also received positive feedback from graphic designers. Both are available for purchase now. Which one interests you?"

5. Response Filtering: This detailed response is vetted to ensure it meets the appropriateness and relevance criteria. If it passes, the message is relayed to you. If not, you'd see a generic response, perhaps something like: "Sorry, I couldn't process your request. Please try again."

Enterprise Integration

In this pattern, enterprise integration is achieved twice by incorporating enterprise applications and databases into the Application Layer.

The two Prompt Generators in the Application Layer are designed to call the relevant APIs of the enterprise applications and databases directly. 'Prompt Generator 1' utilizes data returned from these API calls to form an initial enriched prompt for the fine-tuned model. Similarly, 'Prompt Generator 2' may call additional APIs from the enterprise applications and databases, integrating the returned data into a new prompt for the pre-trained GPT model.

Output Quality

The "Conversation using Two Models" pattern improves output quality by leveraging the unique strengths of both fine-tuned and pre-trained models. It uses the fine-tuned model's capacity for specialized, context-aware responses, and the general versatility of the pre-trained GPT model. This synergy of models facilitates an adaptable and context-specific response generation that can cater to a variety of conversational scenarios.

Like in the **Grounded Conversation** pattern (A2), this architecture also includes the prompt grounding and enriching aspect, utilizing data from enterprise applications and databases to refine and inform the prompts provided to the AI models. This grounding process is executed twice in this pattern, once for each model, which allows for a deeper, and more intricate understanding of the user's intent.

Performance

The computational demand of the 'Conversation using Two Models' pattern is higher, as it involves two separate language models for each user interaction. The first computational load is the fine-tuning of the model, which is done offline and can be computationally expensive as described for the previous pattern.

The second, and potentially more significant, computational load arises during the interaction itself. Every user prompt is processed twice, first by the fine-tuned model and then by the pre-trained GPT model. Both of these steps require CPU or GPU resources and take a certain amount of time. Additionally, the application layer processes, such as calling APIs from enterprise applications and databases potentially twice and generating enriched prompts, also contribute to the computational load.

Use Cases

This dual-model pattern shines in environments that demand a specialized and a general model working in tandem. Potential scenarios include:

- Multistage Query Resolution: In domains like IT support, the first model can quickly diagnose an issue based on a user's problem description, and the second can offer detailed step-by-step solutions that are more user-friendly.
- Data-Enriched Product Recommendations: In e-commerce, the first model can identify and list products based on user preferences, while the second model can cross-reference the shortlist with user reviews, ratings, or trending data to provide a more comprehensive recommendation.
- Legal Consultation: Initially, the first model can identify relevant laws or precedents based on a user's query, and the second model can explain them in layman's terms, ensuring comprehension.
- Financial Planning: Initially, the first model can provide a financial overview or strategy based on the user's financial situation, and the second model can delve deeper into specifics like investment opportunities, risks, and detailed budgeting.
- Educational Content Creation: The first model can outline a learning module or lesson plan based on a curriculum, and the second can develop detailed content, activities, and assessments.

D Agent Patterns

In this section, we delve into specialized agent patterns that harness GPT integration, highlighting their distinct architectural facets and application functionalities. The focus is on automation, adaptability, and user collaboration:

- **Batch Automation Agent (D1):** This agent first pre-processes data and then executes a two-step loop: processing each augmented data record and guiding a GPT model through sequential instructions, where the outcome of one instruction provides the input to the next one until the sequence is fully processed.
- **Orchestration Agent (D2):** Central to this pattern is the Orchestration Agent seamlessly linking users, GPT models, applications, databases, and knowledge bases. The orchestration can be achieved via a workflow prompt or a program.
- **Collaboration Agent (D3):** Pivotal to this pattern is the collaboration agent, which aligns multiple users and a GPT model in a dynamic cooperative setting. Through the Collaboration Repository, each GPT interaction is driven by an evolving context, which consists of prompts by multiple users and the previous model outputs.
- **Multi-Agent Cooperation (D4)**: In this design, multiple agents work together to achieve a given user goal jointly. The Planning Agent decomposes the goal into tasks and derives expert agent profiles accordingly. The Orchestration Agent then creates and manages Expert Agents based on these profiles, while the Expert Agents execute their designated tasks towards achieving the user's goal.

D1 Batch Automation Agent

This pattern showcases a GPT-centric system steered by a Batch Automation Agent. Data records sourced from enterprise applications and databases are enriched via a knowledge base. The agent then employs a dual-loop mechanism: iterating over each enriched record and guiding GPT through a sequence of prompts. Results from one prompt inform the next. Post-processing makes the outputs ready to be displayed by the user interface (refer to *Figure* 4.10).

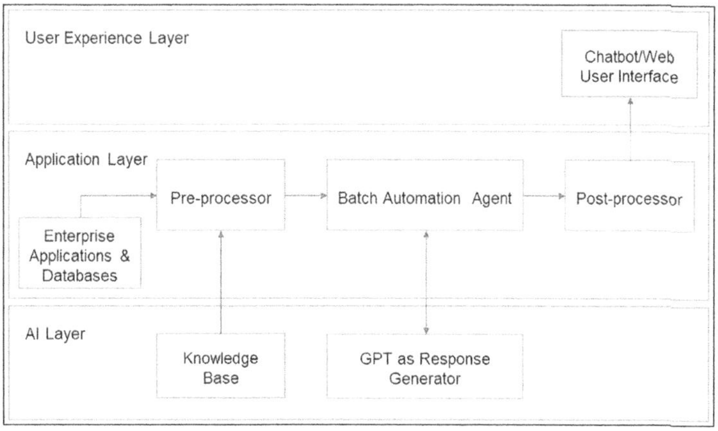

Figure 4.10: *Batch automation agent*

User Experience Layer

Displays the results of the batch-processed outputs and facilitates user interaction through a chatbot or web user interface.

Application Layer

This layer is comprised of the Pre-Processor, Enterprise Applications and Databases, a Batch Automation Agent, and a Post-Processor:

- Enterprise Applications and Databases: The enterprise applications and databases serve as the primary source of raw data records.
- Pre-Processor: The pre-processor performs the same steps as in the conversation pattern, but this time for an entire batch of data records.
- Batch Automation Agent: This agent employs a dual-loop mechanism: the outer loop processes each data record in the batch, and the inner loop iteratively feeds a sequence of enriched prompts related to the current record into a GPT model.
- Post Processor: Once the Batch Automation Agent has produced batched responses, the post-processor formats these for display in the user experience layer.

AI Layer

The AI layer has the same functionality as in the Grounded Conversation Pattern (A2).

Pattern Workflow

1. Enterprise Applications and Databases provide batches of data records.
2. The pre-processor, leveraging the knowledge base, creates enriched data records.
3. The Batch Automation Agent employs its dual-loop mechanism: for each enriched record in the batch (outer loop), it processes a sequence of prompts (inner loop) to a GPT model.
4. The post-processor organizes the batch output for optimal display.
5. The user experience layer visualizes the formatted output.

Pattern Workflow Example

Imagine a rental car company, wants to process the vast number of customer reviews they receive daily about their car rentals and service. The goal is to categorize these reviews and present them in a categorized, summarized, user-friendly format for their branch managers.

Here is an example workflow:

1. Source Data Collection: The company's Rental Management System and feedback portals, acting as the Enterprise Applications and Databases, gather the day's customer reviews, aggregating a batch of several hundred feedback entries.
2. Data Enrichment: The Pre-Processor takes each review and uses an internal knowledge base to add context. For instance, a review stating, "The car's AC wasn't working" might be enriched to: "Customer found the air conditioning of the [Car Model] rented from [Specific Branch] faulty."
3. Dual-Loop Data Processing:
   - Outer Loop: The Batch Automation Agent starts processing each enriched review.
   - Inner Loop:
     - First Prompt: "Given the review '[Enriched Review]', determine its sentiment (positive, neutral, negative) and the primary concern category (for example, vehicle condition, customer service, pricing, booking process)."
     - Second Prompt: "Based on the sentiment and category identified, create a concise summary suitable for branch managerial review."

- (Note: Depending on the system's design, further prompts can be added to extract more nuanced information.)

4. Data Formatting: Once a GPT model has processed all the reviews, the post-processor structures the batched summaries. Reviews are grouped by branch, car model, and concern category. The data is prepared for optimal visualization, possibly by generating charts showcasing recurrent issues or a leaderboard ranking branches by positive feedback.
5. Visualization and User Interaction: The User Experience Layer displays these structured summaries on an interactive dashboard. Branch managers can delve into specific feedback categories, view individual reviews, or ask more detailed questions through an integrated chatbot.

Enterprise Integration

Equates to the integration level of the **Grounded Conversation** pattern (A2).

Output Quality

The Batch Automation Agent's dual-loop mechanism, while maintaining continuity and context, poses a challenge: the risk of error accumulation. If one prompt in the sequence generates an inaccurate or suboptimal response, subsequent prompts might build upon this error, potentially compounding inaccuracies. This emphasizes the importance of ensuring the precision of each individual prompt to maintain the overall quality of the responses.

Performance

While the dual-loop nature might introduce complexities, the batch processing approach aims for efficiency. Batch processing inherently has a latency until the entire batch completes, but the results are comprehensive and the process runs autonomously without user involvement.

Use Cases

This architectural pattern is apt for scenarios demanding advanced batched knowledge based automation. Especially prominent in Knowledge Management domains, it provides a robust solution for the swift processing, categorization, and representation of voluminous data. Notable applications include:

- Information Extraction: Diving into extensive documents to unearth pertinent insights, this functionality is especially invaluable in sectors such as research, law, or journalism.

- Data Transformations and Quality Management: With the ability to integrate data from different formats and structures, and finding redundancies, inconsistencies, it enables the use of standard analytics tools.
- Process Analysis: By examining patterns extracted from diverse event logs, it offers actionable insights that aid in refining workflows. This is especially beneficial for industries that hinge on intricate process metrics.
- Advanced Data Mining: By employing methodologies like Association rule mining and cluster analysis on unstructured data, the architecture is capable of deciphering patterns and insights that might elude traditional analysis.
- Automatic Tagging: By enhancing search results and fortifying recommendations, this feature streamlines user experience, tagging content automatically based on the content's nature.

D2 Orchestration Agent

At the heart of this architecture is the orchestrated workflow, designed to guide user-GPT engagements from initiation to conclusion. The Orchestration Agent, central to this workflow, integrates users, GPT models, applications, databases, and knowledge bases (see *Figure 4.11*).

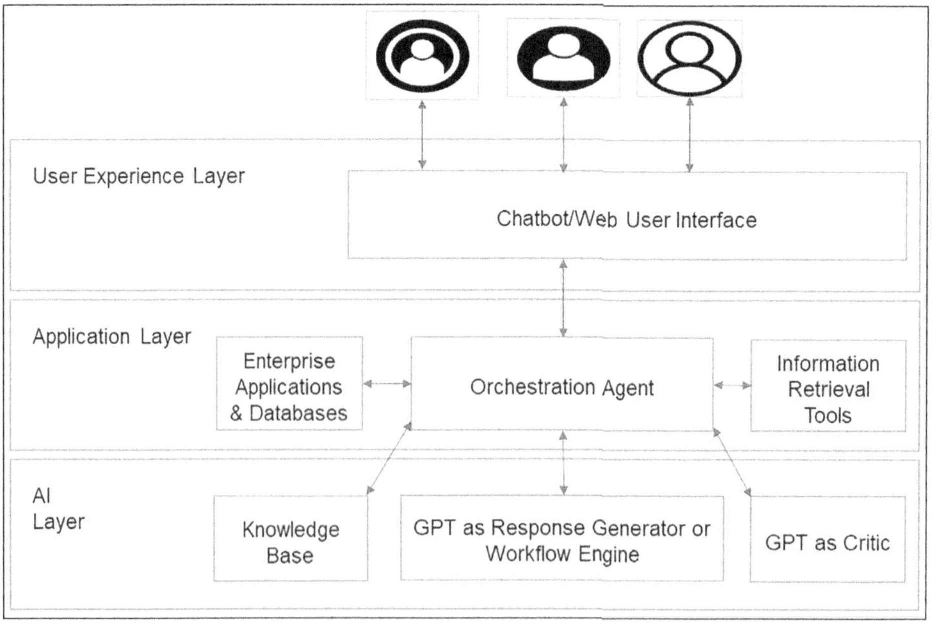

Figure 4.11: *Orchestration agent*

User Experience Layer

This layer is where multiple users connect with the system. They might use chatbots or a web interface. They provide requests, see their tasks and get responses from GPT models.

Application Layer

Divided into three main components, this layer orchestrates the flow of tasks and interactions:

- Orchestration Agent: The pivotal component exists in two variants:
  - Program-based Agent: Used for static workflows coded in a suitable programming language like Python or Java[7] to control sequential task execution.
  - Prompt-based Agent: Suitable for dynamic workflows that involve planning, execution, and adaption. It employs workflow prompts integrated with external tools, reminiscent of the architecture patterns B1 - B3.
- Enterprise Applications and Databases: These are the enterprise-specific tools and data sources that the agent leverages.
- Information Retrieval Tools: This includes public tools, like search engines or websites, that the system utilizes to contextualize subsequent prompts.

AI Layer

This layer encompasses:

- Main GPT model in two potential roles:
  - Response Generator for Specific Workflow Tasks (in program-based orchestration): In this capacity, a GPT model responds to task-specific prompts defined within a scripted workflow.
  - Workflow Engine (in prompt-based orchestration): Here a GPT model takes on a broader role, managing the flow and execution of tasks through workflow prompts.
- Knowledge Base: This component provides both long-term and short-term memory functionalities and hence goes beyond the static repository role it played in previous patterns:

[7]An implementation of this architecture pattern is exemplified in chapter 9, using the Java programming language.

- Long-term Memory: This part stores a variety of knowledge, differentiated into various categories based on the origin and nature of the information:
  - Learned Knowledge: This comprises insights and information generated from previous interactions where GPT models have responded. It forms an evolving body of knowledge, continuously enriched through monitoring and analyzing the outcomes of the GPT model's past responses, to foster a more nuanced understanding and improved performance over time.
  - Retrieved Knowledge: This section stores data and information that have been fetched from external resources during earlier operations, such as results from searches in previous user engagements. It helps in preserving valuable findings for future reference, avoiding repeated search operations for the same queries, and ensuring consistent responses.
  - Acquired Knowledge: This part of the memory houses knowledge that is often curated and verified by Subject Matter Experts (SMEs). It represents a structured and reliable repository of information, cultivated over time to provide a solid foundation for the GPT model's responses, ensuring that the output aligns well with enterprise standards and expert validations.
- Short-term Memory: This part is designed to retain the results of intermediate interactions with users, GPT models, enterprise applications, or search tools, holding the data temporarily to facilitate cohesive and adaptive engagements through the recall of recent interactions and computations. This memory is ephemeral and is cleared out after a session ends or after a predefined period, maintaining data relevancy and security.
- GPT-Critic: An auxiliary GPT model tasked with assessing the validity and quality of the primary GPT model's outputs.

Pattern Workflow with program-based orchestration agent

1. User Request: Users describe their intended result.
2. Workflow Selection: Selection of a standard workflow based on the user request. Examples are:
   - One-step Search with Generative Task
     - Semantic Search: Extracts relevant knowledge from the Knowledge Base.

    - Generative Task: Using a GPT model for content creation, summarization, or answering queries.
- Two-step Search with Generative Task:
    - Query Formulation: Uses a GPT model to produce API calls or search queries when specific data is demanded.
    - Information Retrieval: Acquires the necessary data from external sources.
    - Knowledge Representation: Incorporates this data into the Knowledge Base.
    - Semantic Search: Extracts relevant knowledge from the Knowledge Base.
    - Generative Task: Using a GPT model for content creation, summarization, or answering queries.
- One-step Backend Function Execution (similar to B1 pattern)
    - Information Collection from User (optional): Collects supplementary data from the user if required.
    - Backend Function Call Generation: Creates executable application-level function or calls.
    - Backend Function Call Execution: Executes previously generated application function calls.
    - Backend Function Results Translation: Transforms the results from system-level functions into user-friendly outputs or formats.
- Multi-step Backend Function Execution
    - Repetition of the three steps of the previous workflow for each backend system: Sequentially performs the steps of function generation, execution, and result translation for multiple backend processes.
    - Potentially user interactions between backend function calls: Engages users between stages to gather more information or refine subsequent steps.
- Interactive Content Creation
    - Information Collection from User: Gathers necessary data from the user for the content creation process.
    - Content Creation based on the collected information: Develops tailored content based on the user-provided data.

3. Workflow Execution: Commences and oversees the complete sequence of steps chosen during the previous "Workflow Selection" step.
4. Output Evaluation: Utilizes the GPT-Critic to inspect the output's accuracy and relevance, ensuring it matches the established criteria or user request.
5. Results Presentation: Displays the outcomes of the workflow to the users in a comprehensible and user-friendly manner.

Workflow example with program-based orchestration

Imagine a digital platform designed for enterprises to locate and procure specialized raw materials that are rare, environmentally sustainable, or have other unique attributes.

A manufacturing company is looking to source a sustainable type of rubber that's both durable and has a minimal environmental impact for a new line of eco-friendly footwear.

Here is an example workflow matching the pattern workflow structure:

1. User Request: The procurement manager of the manufacturer. logs into the digital platform and specifies their need: sustainable, durable rubber, preferably with certifications like Fair Trade or Rainforest Alliance.
2. Workflow Selection:
   - Considering the specific requirements of the manager, the system selects the Two-step Search with Generative Task workflow.
   - Query Formulation: Using the manager's input, the system formulates targeted search queries like "sustainable durable rubber suppliers with certifications".
   - Information Retrieval: The system leverages web crawlers to navigate industry databases, supplier directories, forums, and relevant sustainability-focused websites to identify potential suppliers.
   - Knowledge Representation: Extracted information, such as supplier profiles, their certifications, client reviews, and material specifications, are structured for easier analysis.
   - Semantic Search: The system assesses the organized data, prioritizing suppliers that align closely with the manufacturer's criteria.
   - Generative Task: If an ideal supplier isn't identified, the system uses

a GPT model to draft inquiries or RfPs (Request for Proposals) to be sent out to promising suppliers or industry contacts.

3. Workflow Execution:
   - The program-based agent governs the sequence of operations, ensuring that relevant and accurate supplier information is sourced from the web.
4. Output Evaluation:
   - The GPT-Critic reviews the shortlist of suppliers and the RFPs to confirm they match the manufacturer's specifications.
   - Inconsistencies, if found, might initiate a new iteration of the "Information Retrieval" step or a revision of the search criteria.
5. Results Presentation:
   - The buyer receives a curated list of potential suppliers with all relevant details like certifications, past client reviews, and contact information.
   - The generated RFPs are made available, ready to be sent out to the prospective suppliers for a more detailed proposal.
   - The buyer can choose to engage with a supplier directly, request samples, or send out RFPs for competitive bids.

Pattern Workflow with prompt-based orchestration agent

1. User Request: Users describe their intended result.
2. Workflow Prompt Pattern Selection: Selection of a workflow prompt pattern based on the user request. An example of a respective pattern is given in chapter 6 in the section 'Adaptive Business Process Management.'
3. Workflow Prompt Execution: Executing the workflow by using a GPT model as workflow engine. It would generate requests for API function calls (like in the B1 pattern) and user input (like in the A3 pattern), when required by the workflow. The orchestration agent would handle these requests and feed the results back into a GPT model to continue the workflow. The workflow terminates when a specific stop condition in the prompt is achieved, or the user stops it.
4. Output Evaluation: The GPT Critic examines the workflow's output to ensure it meets stipulated criteria.

5. Results Presentation: Once the workflow is finished, the results are showcased to users in an easily interpretable format.

Workflow example with prompt-based orchestration

Imagine an e-commerce giant where a customer's recent purchase of a smartwatch arrived with a damaged screen:

1. User Request: The customer accesses the complaint section and mentions: "I received my smartwatch order, but the screen is cracked. I'd like a replacement or refund. Order number: 567890."
2. Workflow Prompt Selection: Given the nature of the complaint, the system selects the prompt for Adaptive Complaint Management Workflow:
    - Prompt Name: Adaptive Complaint Management Workflow
    - Expert Persona: "As an AI trained in Adaptive Complaint Management for e-commerce, you autonomously manage complaint resolution by determining and executing the appropriate workflow. Interaction with the user is solely for capturing essential details."
    - Context: "You're assisting an e-commerce giant receiving myriad complaints daily. Current complaint: [Captured Complaint Slot]. The complaint resolution steps include:
        a. Complaint Clarification: Understand the specifics of the complaint through user interaction.
        b. Workflow Design: Autonomously plans tasks to address the complaint.
        c. Workflow Initiation & Execution: Start and complete the complaint tasks, asking the user for required details.
        d. Workflow Monitoring: Ensure resolution progresses smoothly and gather user feedback.
        e. Workflow Adaptation: Modify tasks based on unexpected scenarios or deviations."
    - Goal: Effectively navigate each complaint resolution phase, leveraging skills such as communication, planning, and recommendation.
    - Control & Constraints: Always respect privacy, seek necessary user inputs, clarify decisions, and ensure outputs are actionable and follow best practices.
    - Instruction: Start with 'Complaint Clarification': Kindly share more

about the complaint [Captured Complaint Slot] for an effective resolution process.

3. Workflow Execution:

   a. Complaint Clarification: The system asks, "Can you provide more specifics about the damage? Was the packaging intact when it arrived?" The user responds, "The packaging seemed fine, but the watch inside was damaged. Looks like a quality control issue."

   b. Workflow Design: Based on the user's feedback, the system selects the Product Replacement and Quality Assurance Workflow.

      - Verify the order.
      - Confirm the warranty.
      - Initiate a return and replacement process.
      - Ensure a quality check for the replacement product.

   c. Workflow Initiation & Execution: The four workflow steps are executed:

   d. Workflow Monitoring: As the replacement product is shipped, the user is notified about the progress.

   e. Workflow Adaptation: If there's a delay or issue, the system adjusts the workflow, notifying the user and offering solutions.

4. Output Evaluation: The GPT-Critic evaluates the entire resolution process, ensuring that the complaint was addressed effectively, and all workflow steps were adhered to.

5. Results Presentation: The customer is presented with a timeline of actions taken, a tracking number for the replacement shipment, and an interface to give feedback post-reception. They're also offered a discount code for the inconvenience in order to encourage future purchases.

Enterprise Integration

This pattern offers advanced enterprise integration due to the Orchestration Agent's capability to embed API-based functions in the entire workflow.

Output Quality

This pattern enhances output quality by systematically grounding prompts with context user input, knowledge, internal and external data, and prior GPT outputs. The potential inclusion of multiple users provides an added layer of human discernment, further refining the AI's context-aware outputs. The GPT-Critic evaluates the quality of AI-generated content, and its feedback is managed by the Orchestration Agent to optimize output quality.

Performance

The computational performance of this pattern is intrinsically tied to the length of the workflow. However, for most use cases, short to medium-length workflows should suffice, balancing both efficiency and computational demands.

Use Cases

The dynamic capabilities and robust design of this pattern make it ideally suited for a variety of applications. At its core, it is designed to manage two primary kinds of workflows: static (scripted) and dynamic (adaptive).

Static workflows are the bedrock of routine operations, characterized by their well-defined structure and predictable flow. Such workflows are typically automated and follow pre-set scripts:

- Complex Content Creation:
    - Reports: Synthesizing data points into comprehensive reports, inclusive of visual representations like charts and graphs.
    - Newsletters: Periodically curating content from updates or relevant news, maintaining a consistent layout.
    - Documentation: Generating structured documentation for various needs, ensuring clarity for the target audience.
- Information Collection:
    - Interviews: Utilizing templates and protocols to extract information from individuals or groups systematically.
    - Interactive Reports: Gleaning and presenting data in interactive formats from enterprise-specific systems or databases, ensuring data integrity and accuracy.
    - Websites: Automated search, reading, and summarization of content from relevant websites.
- Standard Workflows:
    - Requisitioning: Handling and automating standard requisition processes, from request to approval.
    - Approval Cycles: Streamlining approval requests, reminders, and

documentation.

- Inventory Management: Automating tasks related to stock checks, reorder levels, and inventory valuation.

While this pattern effortlessly manages predictable operations, it also showcases its adeptness in embracing more intricate, and adaptive challenges. Tasks that come with incomplete specifications, require on-the-fly adjustments, or are dictated by evolving user intents and unforeseen circumstances fall into this realm. Such dynamic workflows demand a blend of planning, execution, re-evaluation, and adaptation:

- Task-oriented Dialogues: Adapting to evolving user intents, these agents design, modify, and deploy dialogue plans, resulting in multifaceted interactions.
- Comprehensive Research: Segmenting a broad research objective into sub-goals and conceptualizing and executing detailed strategies for each using diverse resources.
- Exploratory Data Analysis: Agents develop an explorative strategy based on an insight target, iterating over diverse data sources and tools.
- Automated Troubleshooting: Upon understanding users' issues, the system crafts a diagnostic plan, which may include querying enterprise-specific tools, providing guided solutions, or leveraging GPT for innovative remedies.
- Personalized Learning Paths: Customizing educational trajectories according to students' ambitions, meticulously choosing, sequencing, and recalibrating content based on their progression and feedback.

D3 Collaboration Agent

The essence of this pattern revolves around the Collaboration Agent, serving as a dynamic conduit connecting users with a GPT model within an adaptive collaborative space. By leveraging the Collaboration Repository, this design ensures that GPT's engagements are rooted in context and can be archived, revisited, or refined (see *Figure* 4.12).

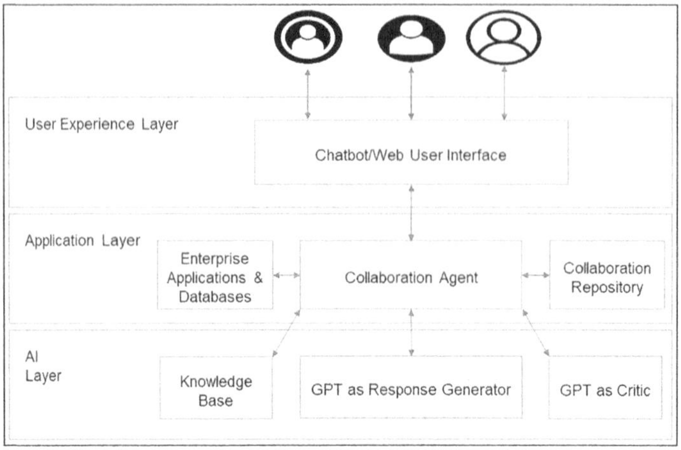

Figure 4.12: *Collaboration agent*

User Experience Layer

Through a chatbot or web UI, users can actively join any active collaboration, contribute inputs, and collectively determine the trajectory and outcomes based on the evolving content.

Application Layer

It incorporates the following:

- Enterprise Applications and Databases: These are tools and data sources used during collaboration.
- Collaboration Agent: This agent interacts with the Collaboration Repository to retrieve or archive master prompts[8], collaboration histories, summaries, and results.
- Collaboration Repository: A crucial storage that preserves master prompts, in-depth collaboration histories, concise collaboration summaries, and both intermediate and final results.

AI Layer

This layer incorporates:

- GPT as Response Generator: Entrusted with delivering responses that are contextually relevant.

---

[8]A master prompt defines the collaboration playbook for a given collaboration scenario. Master prompts are covered in detail in *chapter 6, Designing Prompt-based Intelligent Assistants.*

- Knowledge Base: Short-term and long-term memory like in the previous D2 pattern.
- GPT-Critic: A second GPT model ensuring that the outputs of the first GPT model align with the desired quality standards.

Pattern Workflow

1. A user opts to kickstart or partake in an ongoing collaboration.
2. If beginning a new collaboration, the Collaboration Agent fetches the master prompt corresponding to the chosen scenario from the Collaboration Repository.
3. For ongoing collaborations, the most recent collaboration history sets the stage.
4. Users consistently add prompts. After each user input, the Collaboration Agent appends both the user's prompt and the resultant GPT output to the active collaboration history.
5. The GPT-Critic oversees and ensures the caliber of GPT's responses.
6. On concluding a collaboration, its summaries and results find a home within the Collaboration Repository.

Pattern Workflow Example

Imagine a car rental company that wants to evolve its vehicle maintenance strategy. Collaborating with multiple stakeholders (technicians, fleet managers, customer service reps, and even customers), they aim to gather insights, experiences, and suggestions in an ongoing discussion using the Collaboration Agent.

Your task is: Moderate a collaborative discussion about improving vehicle maintenance processes, taking into account diverse viewpoints, historical discussions, and suggestions.

Here is an example workflow matching the pattern workflow:

1. Initiation: A fleet manager decides to start a collaborative discussion titled, "Enhancing our Vehicle Maintenance Strategy."

2. Collaboration Kickstart:
   - The Collaboration Agent retrieves a generic master prompt from the Collaboration Repository about car maintenance.
   - The prompt might read: "Discussion on best practices, challenges, and improvements for car maintenance at our company."
3. Engagement in Ongoing Collaborations:
   - As technicians, customer service representatives, and other stakeholders join, they can view the ongoing discussion and contribute.
   - For instance, a technician may add: "The routine checks are often superficial. We need more in-depth diagnostics."
   - Immediately, a GPT model, drawing from the Knowledge Base, might suggest: "Consider implementing a detailed bi-monthly diagnostic paired with routine checks. This can identify underlying issues."
   - Each of these prompts and responses are appended to the active collaboration history by the Collaboration Agent.
4. User Contribution:
   - A customer service representative could chime in: "Customers often report air conditioning issues in the summer. Maybe we can have preemptive checks before peak season?"
   - A GPT model might respond: "An annual AC service before summer can help. Additionally, consider educating customers on optimal AC usage during the initial rental walkthrough."
5. Quality Oversight by GPT-Critic:
   - Suppose a customer contributes: "I once rented a car that broke down midway. What's the strategy for emergency situations?"
   - If a GPT model initially provides a vague answer like, "Cars should be maintained," the GPT-Critic might flag this as low-quality, prompting the model to produce a more comprehensive response.
6. Collaboration Conclusion & Archival:
   - After a week, the fleet manager decides to conclude the discussion.
   - The Collaboration Agent automatically generates a summary: "Key Takeaways from the Discussion on Enhancing our Vehicle Maintenance Strategy."
   - It includes points like implementing bi-monthly diagnostics, annual AC services before summer, and possibly a strategy for emergency

breakdowns.
  - This summary and the entire discussion are archived in the Collaboration Repository for future reference.

Enterprise Integration

This pattern offers the same level of enterprise integration as the **Grounded Conversation** pattern (A2).

Output Quality

Benefiting from the Collaboration Repository, the GPT model operates within a rich context, which has inputs from multiple users with different perspectives and the respective GPT outputs. The role of the GPT-Critic also helps in refining the quality of outputs through checks and validations.

Performance

The efficiency of this pattern is dependent on the depth and breadth of the collaborative content. Yet, the handling of tasks by the Collaboration Agent, leveraging the Collaboration Repository, ensures a fluid progression and uses compute resources only after new collaborative input was received.

Use Cases

Ideally tailored for complex collaborative endeavors across varied contexts, prominent applications encompass:

- Sequential Human-centric Workflows: In product development, this involves coordinating teams from ideation to production. The collaboration agent ensures alignment at each phase based on prior inputs.
- Projects: In event planning, the agent helps establish timelines, delegate tasks, and collect logistical inputs. It suggests refinements based on ongoing updates.
- Sales Engagements: For market entry strategies, the agent consolidates market research, competitor analysis, and client profiling.
- Vendor Evaluations: When sourcing suppliers, the agent stores vendor profiles and past interactions. Evaluators' criteria, like cost or delivery timelines, are matched against stored data for informed decisions.
- Innovation Frameworks: In tech innovation, stakeholders brainstorm on

the platform. The agent provides contextual feedback, pulling from past sessions or external trends, assisting in crafting a coherent and creative strategy.

D4 Multi-Agent Cooperation

The essence of this pattern is rooted in the notion of distributed intelligence. By decentralizing tasks among a group of specialized agents [5], this pattern creates a more streamlined and adaptive way to cater to complex user goals. This dynamic ensemble of agents collaboratively harnesses various GPT models, ensuring each task is addressed by the most suitable expert (see *Figure 4.13*).

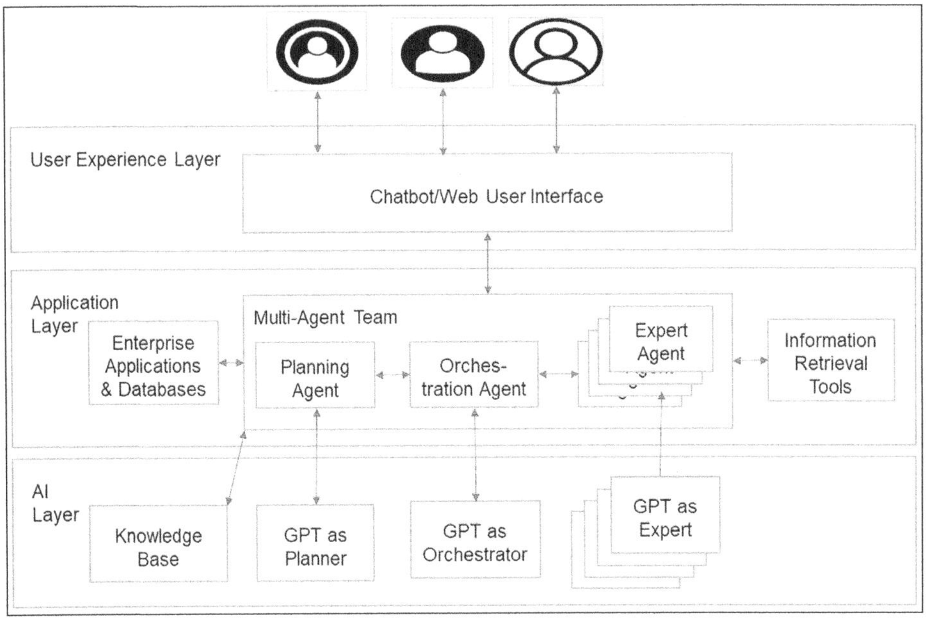

***Figure 4.13**: Multi-agent cooperation*

User Experience Layer

Mirroring the two previous patterns, this layer offers various interaction possibilities. Through chatbot interfaces or web UIs, users can articulate intricate goals, which then become the responsibility of a cooperative team of agents to accomplish and may require further interactions with multiple users.

Application Layer

The components present here include::

- Agent Team: A cluster of specialized agents tasked with executing distinct roles in achieving user goals. The team is composed of:
  - Planning Agent: Decomposes user-specified goals into actionable tasks and identifies the ideal expert agent profile suited for each task.
  - Orchestration Agent: Initiates the expert agent creation process based on the agent profile, starts the task sequence, activates the first expert agent, and progressively moves through the tasks. This agent also supervises communication between expert agents, ensuring seamless interactions with users, knowledge bases, and other enterprise tools.
  - Expert Agents: Crafted dynamically, these agents embody the precise skills required to execute specific tasks in the process to achieve the overall user goal.
- Enterprise Applications and Databases: These are the same as in the D2 pattern.
- Information Retrieval Tools: These are also the same as in the D2 pattern.

Also similar to the D2 pattern, it's worth noting that there are two distinct types of Agent Teams within this architecture. While program-based agent teams are illustrated in the diagram, there exists an alternative construct - prompt-based agent teams. The intricacies and application of prompt-based agent teams will be explored in *Chapter 5, Advanced GPT Prompt Engineering Techniques*, and in appendix 1 in the respective sections dedicated to multi-agent prompts.

AI Layer

The following elements are integral to this layer:

- Knowledge Base: Akin to D2 storing both transient and persistent information.
- GPT model instantiated in different roles:
  - GPT as Planner: Aligns with the Planning Agent, translating user goals into a series of tasks.
  - GPT as Orchestrator: Powers the Orchestration Agent, managing the sequencing and delegation of tasks among expert agents.
  - GPT as Expert: Empowers each Expert Agent, offering domain-specific knowledge and expertise to execute its designated task.

Pattern Workflow

1. Users articulate a detailed goal they wish to attain.
2. The Planning Agent processes this goal, translating it into a sequence of executable tasks and identifying the ideal expert agent profile for each.
3. For each task, the Orchestration Agent creates the respective Expert Agent.
4. With the tasks sequenced, the Orchestration Agent activates the first Expert Agent and delegates the corresponding task.
5. The Expert Agent executes the task assigned to it.
6. Upon task completion, the Orchestration Agent moves to the subsequent task, activating the next Expert Agent in line.
7. This sequence is diligently followed until all tasks are addressed.
8. Throughout this process, the Orchestration Agent ensures smooth communication among Expert Agents, as well as between them and other involved entities, such as users, knowledge bases or databases.

Enterprise Integration

This pattern offers the same advanced enterprise integration as in the D2 pattern as all agents have API-based function access to execute their tasks.

Output Quality

The output quality in D4 closely mirrors that of D2 when the final expert agent evaluates the performance of all preceding expert agents. While there's potential to enhance the output quality by implementing quality assessments for each agent involved (including the planning, orchestration, and expert agents), it's crucial to note that this enhancement might come at the cost of diminished performance.

Performance

Performance is significantly influenced by the number of agents involved and the extent of interactions they maintain among themselves and with users and enterprise applications. As the number of agents increases, or as interactions become more frequent and complex, there can be a corresponding impact on the system's responsiveness and efficiency.

Use Cases

Building on the foundational capabilities of the D2 pattern and enhancing them with the sophistication of multi-agent cooperation, this D4 pattern is adeptly equipped to handle a diverse range of applications, as demonstrated in the following use cases:

- Comprehensive Research:
  - Planning Agent: Understands the overarching research goal and segments it into targeted research areas or questions.
  - Orchestration Agent: Coordinates between expert agents, assigning them specific research domains or tasks and ensuring seamless integration of their findings.
  - Expert Agents: Delve into their allocated domains, mining data, referencing scholarly articles, and cross-referencing findings. Each might specialize in various research methodologies or sources.
- Exploratory Data Analysis:
  - Planning Agent: Defines the objectives of the data exploration based on desired insights and outcomes.
  - Orchestration Agent: Organizes the flow of data, ensuring it moves between the expert agents in an orderly manner and integrates their analyses.
  - Expert Agents: Each agent could focus on specific datasets or analytical techniques. For example, one agent might handle statistical analyses, while another focuses on visualization or predictive modeling.
- Automated Troubleshooting:
  - Planning Agent: Recognizes the reported problem and defines the diagnostic steps.
  - Orchestration Agent: Manages the troubleshooting process, ensuring each step is executed, gathering required data, and providing fccdback.
  - Expert Agents: Specialize in different aspects of the problem. One might handle software-related issues, another hardware diagnostics, and another could focus on user experience or interface issues.
  - Personalized Learning Paths:
- Planning Agent: Assesses the learner's current knowledge level,

preferences, and long-term educational goals.

  - Orchestration Agent: Organizes the curriculum, schedules lessons, and ensures the flow of content aligns with the learner's progression.
  - Expert Agents: Specialize in different subjects or learning methodologies. For instance, one could handle mathematics while another deals with literature. Others might focus on experiential learning, multimedia content, or hands-on projects.

- Software Development Assistance:
  - Planning Agent: Interprets requirements and breaks them down into features or tasks.
  - Orchestration Agent: Manages dependencies and workflow.
  - Expert Agents: Suggest code snippets, run tests, debug issues, and even help with deployment strategies.
- Consulting Tasks:
  - Planning Agent: Identifies client needs and breaks them down into actionable insights or tasks.
  - Orchestration Agent: Schedules meetings, manages timelines, and ensures deliverables are met.
  - Expert Agents: Dive into specifics, whether it's market research, financial modeling, or strategic planning, leveraging the best tools and resources for each task.

Recommendations for Architecture Patterns

Having delved deep into the nuances and intricacies of various GPT-driven architecture patterns, we are poised to present a set of curated recommendations. These insights, drawn from the comprehensive descriptions and assessments, are tailored to guide you in choosing the most fitting architecture for your specific needs:

- **Advanced Conversational Experience**: **Grounded Conversation** (A2) integrates with enterprise systems to add contextual depth. **Mixed-Initiative Conversation** (A3) fosters two-way interactivity, guiding user actions and queries, while **Quality-controlled Conversation** (A4) ensures that all responses are checked by a second GPT-model before showing them to the user.
- **Tool-driven Conversations**: **Tool-integrated Conversation** (B1)

leverages GPT models to interface seamlessly with external applications and databases via APIs. **Chain-of-Thought-guided Conversation using Tools** (B2) enriches this with reasoning demonstrations. Meanwhile, **Advanced Tool-integrated Conversation** (B3) optimizes interactions with enterprise tools using dynamic task planning based on the changing dialog context.

- **Specialized Conversations**: **Conversation using Fine-tuned Model** (C1) employs a refined language model to generate precise responses, ideal for complex domains and high-stakes environments. Meanwhile, **Conversation using Two Models** (C2) combines the specificity of a fine-tuned model with the breadth of a pre-trained GPT model, ensuring in-depth user interactions embedded into diverse conversational scenarios.
- **Advanced Automation**: For intricate automation needs, patterns **Batch Automation Agent** (D1), **Orchestration Agent** (D2), and **Multi-Agent Cooperation** (D4) stand out. D1 emphasizes batched data processing, while D2 leverages sequential orchestration for seamless interactions. D4 is especially suitable for environments that demand high degrees of dynamic adaptability and task-specific expertise.
- **Assisted Collaboration**: For in-depth collaborative environments, patterns **Collaboration Agent** (D3) and **Multi-Agent Cooperation** (D4) shine distinctly. D3 excels in situations emphasizing continuous human-centric interactions, with GPT managing and enhancing the entire collaboration process. On the other hand, the D4 emphasizes scenarios where humans and task-specific agents work in unison, combining their strengths for optimal outcomes

Our exploration into GPT-driven architecture patterns has unveiled a diverse array of solutions, each with its intrinsic merits. The right choice for your organization or project hinges on your specific demands and limitations. Use this analysis as a reference, guiding you to the architecture patterns that most align with your objectives.

Conclusion

As we navigate through the varied landscape of GPT-driven architecture patterns, it becomes evident how instrumental these systems can be in improving user interactions, enhancing collaborative scenarios, and advancing automation processes. By providing a diverse spectrum of patterns, each tailored to specific use cases and requirements, we can unlock the full potential of AI capabilities to develop future conversational systems and workflows that are efficient, adaptive, collaborative, and provide rich user experience.

As we have established the versatility and adaptability of GPT through various architectural patterns, it's now time to delve deeper into the world of advanced GPT prompt engineering techniques. These techniques will offer a profound understanding on how to guide a GPT model for desired outcomes, especially in complex enterprise scenarios. Let us now turn our focus to these structured prompting methods to further unlock the extensive potential of GPT in advanced AI applications.

Key Points

1. Versatility of GPT-Driven Architectures: Architecture patterns are versatile, tailoring the deployment of GPT models to various conversational contexts, tool integrations, and automation scenarios, proving them essential in enhancing user engagement and streamlining information retrieval.

2. Layered System Approach: The use of a layered system approach in architecture patterns ensures decoupling and maintainability, leading to more sustainable system life-cycles.

3. Quality and Performance Trade-offs: Each pattern offers a unique blend of output quality, performance, and enterprise integration, presenting a spectrum of choices to meet varied requirements and use-cases.

4. Enterprise Integration: Seamless integration with enterprise applications and databases, as seen in Tool-integrated Conversation and other patterns, can significantly extend the capabilities of GPT-driven systems.

5. Precision and Breadth in Responses: Balancing specific knowledge with a broader understanding, some architectures demonstrate the importance of model fine-tuning in delivering accurate and comprehensive responses.

6. Advanced Automation: GPT-integrated architectures also demonstrate versatility in various automation scenarios: batch processing of content, information workflow orchestration, and project execution with multi-agent systems.

7. Collaborative Excellence: GPT models can be utilized to foster adaptive engagements in collaborative settings, enabling unique blends of human-centric interactions and multi-agent cooperation for jointly achieving complex goals.

CHAPTER 5

Advanced GPT Prompt Engineering Techniques

Introduction

Recalling our prior discussions, we have delved into ChatGPT-enabled AI capabilities in *Chapter 2, CapabilityGPT – An Enterprise AI-Capability Framework for ChatGPT,* and examined their transformative impact for enterprise roles in *Chapter 3, The Impact of ChatGPT on the Enterprise*. We have also seen in *Chapter 4, Architecture Patterns enabled by GPT-Models*, how these advanced capabilities, when combined with the right solution architecture patterns, can lead to a new generation of intelligent systems. Central to harnessing these AI capabilities is the practice of prompt engineering, the technique of effectively communicating with GPT models.

Prompt engineering is pivotal regardless of the context–be it simple interactions with the ChatGPT chatbot, developing specialized applications with GPT at their core, or leveraging GPT-enhanced enterprise solutions like Microsoft Copilot. It's the process of crafting precise, contextually relevant prompts that allow us to produce the desired response from the model.

There are three major techniques, Instruction Prompting, Query Prompting and Multi Agent Prompting, each addressing unique challenges and scenarios when communicating with GPT models.

We commence our exploration with the **Instruction Prompting**. Anchored firmly on the CapabilityGPT framework introduced in *Chapter 2*, this technique presents a structured approach for conveying specific tasks or actions to a GPT model. The subsequent in-depth dissection will navigate through its three variants: Single Instruction, Instruction Sequence, and Pseudo-Code Instructions. Their efficacy is then brought to light through real-world examples that accentuate their pragmatic applications.

Next, we transition to **Query Prompting**, a useful technique in explorative and analytical scenarios, also when faced with ambiguity and incomplete information. Throughout this section we distinguish between various query types, including information-seeking, comparative, predictive and counterfactual queries and present detailed examples for each query type.

Finally, we delve into **Multi-Agent Prompting**. At its core, this technique excels in situations where tasks cannot be strictly defined upfront, requiring the expertise of multiple AI agents and their effective collaboration. This section offers a definition of the underlying concepts and provides detailed practical examples in an enterprise context.

It is important to note that the prompt engineering techniques discussed in this chapter are specific to GPT models from ChatGPT onwards, which, as of now, include only ChatGPT and GPT-4.

Structure

In this chapter, the following topics will be covered:

- Instruction Prompting
- Query Prompting
- Multi-Agent Prompting

Instruction Prompting

In this section, we first explore the Instruction Prompt Pattern, a precision-guided blueprint for GPT model interactions. We then present multiple practical examples illustrating its application in enterprise scenarios.

Instruction Prompt Pattern

The Instruction Prompt Pattern, building upon the AI capability framework introduced in *Chapter 2, CapabilityGPT – An Enterprise AI-Capability Framework for ChatGPT*, presents a methodical approach to guide GPT models toward producing in-depth, context-aware, and precise outputs. Let us delve into the each pattern component:

- **Expert Persona**: This fundamental element delineates the expertise and role the GPT model should exhibit in its responses. The expert persona can be conceived as an individual or a team embodying diverse but complementary skill sets:
  - **For individual personas**: The emphasis is on a singular professional skill set, such as a "business analyst at a marketing firm" or an "AI agent specialized in data analysis." In such cases, the model channels expertise and perspective grounded in that specific role, utilizing its pre-trained knowledge to respond with the requisite professional background and contextual understanding.
  - **For team personas**: Such as a "collaborative team of a teacher, a student, and a parent" or a "cross-functional team comprising a developer, a designer, and a project manager," encompass a synergy of varied perspectives and experiences. Here, the GPT model seeks to facilitate a collaborative approach, bearing in mind the distinctive insights each role contributes.
- **Context**: This component includes external or user-provided information that guides a GPT model toward more accurate and appropriate responses. It could involve background information or specific details about a scenario; for example, 'Our company launched three marketing campaigns in the last quarter.' Context significantly assists in orienting a GPT model's understanding and response and also helps in reducing the risk of hallucination, which is the generation of information not grounded in the provided input or its pre-training data.
- **Task Specification**: This component serves as the detailed instruction defining what action or series of actions a GPT model needs to undertake. The nature and structure of the instruction can vary depending on task complexity, the precision required, and whether the task involves a single step or multiple steps. There are three distinct formats for such instructions:
  - **Single Instruction**: These instructions align with the AI capabilities defined in the CapabilityGPT framework[1], directing a GPT model to harness its diverse capabilities such as Assessment, Classification, or Communication. For instance, an instruction could be: 'Assess the performance of these campaigns and identify areas for improvement.'

[1]CapabilityGPT is described in detail in *Chapter 2, CapabilityGPT – An Enterprise AI-Capability Framework for ChatGPT*.

- **Instruction Sequence**: This format involves a series of instructions, each corresponding to a specific AI capability. The sequence guides a GPT model through multiple tasks that aim to solve complex problems or achieve detailed objectives. Each instruction acts as a stage in the overall task progression, with the output of one serving as the input for the next. An example would be: '1. Extract the quarterly sales data from the provided financial report. 2. Identify any sales trends or patterns from the extracted data. 3. Based on the identified trends, forecast the sales for the next quarter.'
- **Pseudo-Code Instructions**: Pseudo-code bridges natural language and programming languages, offering a high-level depiction of an algorithm without adhering to strict programming syntax. This ensures clear and precise instructions for a GPT model. With pseudo-code, structures like 'if-then-else' conditions and 'for' or 'while' loops can be seamlessly integrated, enabling the model to tackle complex, multi-step tasks efficiently and unambiguously. A pertinent example would be:

```
FOR each paragraph in the article
  IF the paragraph contains the word "important"
    EXTRACT main idea of the paragraph
  ENDIF
ENDFOR
COMPILE extracted ideas into a brief summary
RETURN the summary
```

- **Execution Rules**: The execution rules offer potential directives to guide a GPT model's thought process and decision-making throughout its task execution. These rules encompass problem-solving methods, data collection techniques, ethical considerations, collaboration practices, and evolutionary principles. They can apply to an entire instruction sequence or differ for each instruction step. Each category of rules contains specific examples to further clarify their intent and application. Here is a breakdown:
  - **Problem Solving and Reasoning**:
    - **'Let us think step by step'**: Ensures that a GPT model executes a stepwise thought process and documents each step as context before producing the final output.

    - **'Let us first understand the problem and devise a plan to solve it. Then, let us carry out the plan and solve the problem step by step'**: A GPT model is directed to generate an action plan for the task and then adhere to this plan, executing each action sequentially.
    - **'Consider all potential solutions'**: Encourages a GPT model to explore multiple solutions and not focus only on the most obvious or the first one it identifies.
    - **'Weigh pros and cons before deciding'**: Instructs a GPT model to evaluate the benefits and downsides of each solution or approach, ensuring a more balanced decision-making process.
    - **'Start by listing potential outcomes'**: Directs a GPT model to begin its thought process by enumerating possible results or scenarios before diving deeper into the analysis.
    - **'Systematically reference available data'**: Instructs the model to meticulously cross-check every piece of information at its disposal, ensuring no detail is overlooked during the reasoning process.
    - **'Update hypotheses with new insights'**: Prompts the model to refine its initial predictions or conclusions as more data or context is provided, encouraging adaptability in the reasoning process.
  - **Data Collection:**
    - **'Carefully ask me informative questions to maximize your information about this event, so that, when you have all the answers, you can do X'**: Ensures that a GPT model asks the most effective questions to maximize information gain.
    - **'Each time ask one question only without giving an answer'**: Constrains a GPT model to ask one question at a time, allowing subsequent questions to build on previous responses.
    - **'Verify data integrity before proceeding'**: Encourages the model to ensure the information it gathers is accurate, complete, and not corrupted or misleading.
  - **Adherence to Ethical/Moral Standards:**
    - **'Eliminate specific biases'**: Instructs the model to proactively avoid any forms of biases – be it demographic, socioeconomic, cultural, racial, gender-based, etc. – when generating outputs.
    - **'Reject personally identifiable information (PII)'**: Ensures a GPT model does not accept any PII data in the prompt.

   - **'Promote fairness and inclusion'**: Directs the model to produce outputs that are equitable and inclusive, representing diverse perspectives and avoiding marginalization.
   - **'Avoid harmful or offensive content'**: Instructs the model to filter out any content that might be harmful, misleading, or offensive to any individual or group.
   - **'Recognize and disclose limitations'**: Encourages the model to acknowledge its limitations and, where appropriate, offer disclaimers or advise users to seek expert opinions.

- **Collaboration Rules**: In the context of a task executed by a team of expert personas, collaboration rules guide the interaction and synergy among different personas to foster constructive and balanced dialogue. Here, we detail rules that encourage structured collaboration:
   - **'Perform Collaborative Synthesis'**: Encourages the team of expert personas to work collaboratively, integrating their individual insights into a coherent response. For instance, a teacher, student, and parent can pool their unique perspectives to construct a multi-faceted solution on AI-based learning.
   - **'Take a Role-Based Perspective'**: Encourages each member of the expert persona team to provide input from their role-specific viewpoint, fostering a richer understanding of the issue at hand.
   - **'Build Consensus'**: Directs the expert persona team to work towards finding common ground, encouraging a harmonized approach that respects and integrates the viewpoints of all team members.
   - **'Resolve Conflicts'**: Guides the team to navigate and resolve disagreements efficiently, facilitating a collaborative environment where different perspectives can coexist harmoniously.

- **Application of Evolutionary Principles**: Guides a GPT model to harness evolutionary[2] methods, which mimic natural selection processes to iteratively refine solutions, in generating or refining outputs. When employing these principles, the user should specify:
   - **'Use this initial solution: <solution>'**: Directs a GPT model to begin its evolutionary process from a specified starting point. For

[2]Evolutionary computing is a set of algorithms inspired by biological evolution principles to solve optimization and search problems. It utilizes techniques such as mutation, selection, and crossover to evolve solutions over generations based on a defined fitness function. Techniques include evolutionary algorithms, genetic programming, and more.

instance, when generating a slogan for a new sports car, one might commence with "Green and fast. No contradiction anymore".

- **'Perform <number> evolutionary steps'**: Instructs the model on the exact count of refinements it should carry out. As an illustration, for refining a slogan, the model might be directed to undergo 20 evolutionary steps.
- **'Evaluate by this fitness function <function description>'**: Commands the model to appraise its outputs based on set criteria. In the realm of slogan creation, this function could be measured based on the slogan's catchiness or its relevance in a modern ecological context.

- **Output Constraints**: These define the conditions that a GPT model's generated output must fulfill. They can refer to the format, sequence, inclusion or exclusion of certain elements, size of the output, and/or other factors. The constraints could be something like: 'The output should be a structured report with clear sections for each campaign's performance and suggested improvements. The total output should not exceed 500 words.'
- **Reference Cases**: Case-based reasoning (CBR) is a methodology wherein approaches to new challenges are derived by drawing parallels to previously encountered situations and their outcomes. It involves choosing relevant reference cases and adapting them to address the current challenge described in the context section. They capture a broad spectrum of real-world scenarios across different domains and are categorized into three main types:
  - **Problem-Solution Cases:** Descriptions that detail a specific problem faced by an entity and the subsequent solution or intervention implemented to address it.
    - **Example 1 (Retail):**
      - **Problem:** MegaStore noticed that their E-commerce website had a high cart abandonment rate, especially on mobile devices.
      - **Solution:** MegaStore redesigned their mobile checkout process, simplifying steps, and integrating more efficient and popular mobile payment methods. This led to a 25% rcduction in cart abandonment within two months.
    - **Example 2 (Human Resources):**
      - **Problem:** TechCorp realized that its employee turnover rate was increasing year over year, especially among junior-level employees.

- **Solution:** TechCorp implemented a mentorship program, pairing junior employees with seasoned professionals. They also introduced flexible work hours and continuous learning opportunities. Within a year, turnover rates decreased by 20%.

- **Input-Output Cases:** Pairs of specific inputs and their corresponding GPT-generated outputs
  - **Example 1 (Media Monitoring):**
    - **Input:** "At the annual conference, CEO John Smith announced a partnership with GlobalTech to innovate new AI solutions."
    - **Output (Event Data Extraction):** Event: Partnership Announcement; Participants: CEO John Smith, GlobalTech; Context: Annual conference; Objective: Innovate new AI solutions.
  - **Example 2 (Energy Sector):**
    - **Input:** Increased consumption trends during winters and new regulatory policies.
    - **Output (Event Prediction):** Based on increased consumption trends and new regulatory policies, a rise in energy prices is anticipated during the upcoming winter months.
- **Chain-of-Thought Cases:** Detailed sequences where an initial input undergoes a series of logical or reasoning steps to arrive at a specific output.
  - **Example 1 (Supply Chain Management - Inventory Reordering):**
    - **Input:** Current month's data: 500 units sold, 200 units returned, 50 units damaged in transit, 1000 units in stock, lead time for replenishment 3 weeks, average weekly sales 150 units.
    - **Chain-of-Thought:**
      1. Calculate Net Sales: Subtract returned units from units sold: 500 - 200 = 300 units.
      2. Assess Current Inventory: Account for net sales and damaged units from the stock: 1000 (starting stock) - 300 (net sales) - 50 (damaged) = 650 units.
      3. Predict Future Inventory: Considering average weekly sales and current stock: 650 (current stock) - (3 weeks × 150 units/week) = 200 units expected after 3 weeks.

4. Determine Replenishment Urgency: If the lead time is 3 weeks, by the time the stock is replenished, only 200 units would be left. Therefore, replenishment has to occur within a week to avoid being out of stock before the end of the replenishment period.

5. Evaluate Optimal Reorder Quantity: Considering sales trends, return rates, and potential damages, a buffer for unexpected damages is prudent. Reordering (3 weeks × 150 units/week + 100 units buffer) = 550 units seems appropriate.

   - **Output:** To maintain healthy stock levels over the next month and account for unforeseen circumstances, a reorder of 550 units is advised within a week.

- **Example 2 (Banking - Classification Case):**
  - **Input:** A loan application with details: Applicant Age: 29, Annual Income: $85,000, Employment Status: Full-time, Credit Score: 680, Existing Debt: $20,000.
  - **Chain-of-Thought:**

    1. Assess Age and its impact on loan risk.
    2. Evaluate Annual Income in relation to potential loan size.
    3. Check Employment Status for financial stability.
    4. Review Credit Score for creditworthiness.
    5. Analyze Existing Debt vs. Income to understand the financial burden.

  - **Output:** The applicant falls under the "Moderate Risk" category for loan approval.

- **External Capabilities**: A GPT model can further harness the power of both plugins and external tools[3] to enhance its functionalities:
  - **Plugins**: These are specialized extensions originally introduced for the ChatGPT ecosystem. They focus on driving business efficiency, enabling data-driven decision-making, and fostering intelligent automation. Key categories include exploratory data analysis, document understanding, AI, and browsing.

[3]Both plugins and external tools are introduced as extensions of ChatGPT-4 in *Chapter 1, From GPT-1 to ChatGPT-4: The Evolution Towards Generative Artificial Intelligence.*

- **External Tools**: Representing a catalog of functionalities that are available through specified interfaces, these tools facilitate interactions between a GPT model and other AI platforms, search engines, or backend systems. Each tool is defined by a detailed specification including performed task type, argument types, result type, and functionality.

The Instruction Prompt Pattern is particularly useful under the following conditions:

- **Complex problem-solving is needed**: In scenarios where tasks are multifaceted and require intricate solutions, the pattern ensures a systematic approach, breaking down complex tasks into manageable steps for clarity and efficacy.
- **Precision is imperative:** For tasks where accuracy and exactness are paramount, the Instruction Prompt Pattern's detailed task specification and execution rules guide the model to produce precise and context-aware responses.
- **Special expertise is demanded**: If the context requires varied professional skills, choosing between individual and team personas can cater to the specific expertise needed – be it from a singular professional or a collaborative team.
- **Structured outputs are desired:** When the desired result must adhere to a particular format or structure, the output constraints component guarantees that AI-generated content meets the defined requirements.
- **Case-Based Reasoning is valuable**: In situations where drawing parallels to past scenarios can provide valuable insights, the pattern's reference cases offer a methodology to approach new challenges with prior knowledge.

Single Instruction Examples

The following showcases highlight the diverse abilities of ChatGPT-4 in processing single-instruction prompts while leveraging the components of the instruction pattern. These examples traverse the realms of project reviews, stakeholder management, and sales forecasting. Each prompt showcases a distinct AI capability[4] of ChatGPT-4:

- **Project Review**: Evaluating a completed project, two assessment prompts are compared, with one providing a concise summary and the other a detailed analysis identifying areas for improvement and recommendations. The comparison reveals that specifying components like Persona, Execution Rules, and Output Constraints from the Instruction Prompt pattern for the **Assessment** capability yields a more detailed, specific, and professional result.

[4]For a more in-depth understanding of these AI capabilities, please refer to *Chapter 2, CapabilityGPT – An Enterprise AI-Capability Framework for ChatGPT.*

- **Stakeholder Management**: Here ChatGPT-4 acts as a product manager, persuading executives to support one of three product options using an argumentation framework[5]. It aligns product features with stakeholder interests, suggests a phased development approach for all products and promotes a balanced product development strategy. This is achieved by using the **Creation** capability to develop several chains of argumentative reasoning.
- **Sales Forecasting**: Finally ChatGPT-4 demonstrates predictive skills in forecasting future sales for an organic skincare product line, considering historical sales data, observed patterns, and future market expectations. It generates a basic sales forecast in natural language for upcoming months using its **Prediction** capability, aiding in strategic planning for inventory management and marketing efforts.

Project Review

Let us begin by evaluating a completed project using a report from its project manager as an example of the **Assessment** capability:

Figure 5.1: *Project Review*

Here is the report:

Project Report: Development of "XYZ" Mobile App

- *Project Scope: The aim was to design and implement a fully functioning mobile app for our client, XYZ Inc., to boost customer interaction and user experience. Key features included a user-friendly interface, secure payment gateway, and customer support functionality.*

[5]An argumentation framework or methodology refers to a structured approach to presenting and analyzing arguments. It provides a systematic way to construct, evaluate, and understand arguments by breaking them down into their essential components and relationships. The goal is to ensure that arguments are clear, logical, and persuasive.

- *Schedule: The project was scheduled for 12 months, starting from August 1, 2022, and completing by July 31, 2023. It was segmented into four phases: Planning (2 months), Development (5 months), Testing (3 months), and Deployment (2 months).*
- *Cost: The budget set was $500,000, but due to some unforeseen complexities during the development and testing phase, the project exceeded the estimated cost by 15%, making the final cost $575,000.*
- *Quality: Despite time and cost overruns, the project met the quality expectations as per the agreement. User testing scored an average of 4.5 out of 5, indicating satisfaction with the app's usability and functionality.*
- *Resources: The project team consisted of a Project Manager, two Software Developers, a UI/UX designer, a Quality Assurance Specialist, and a Business Analyst. However, a high turnover rate during the development phase led to a minor delay in project delivery.*
- *Risks: Two significant risks were encountered:*
    - *Budget overrun due to unforeseen complexities in development, which was managed by reallocating budget from the marketing reserve.*
    - *Delays caused by resource turnover were mitigated by hiring temporary experienced resources to stay on schedule.*

Referring to the report, an intuitive prompt for ChatGPT-4 could be:

'*Perform an end-to-end assessment based on the project report above.*'

The response is as follows:

Project Assessment Summary: Development of "XYZ" Mobile App

- *Objective and Scope: The project effectively fulfilled its objective of designing and implementing a fully functioning mobile app with features such as a user-friendly interface, secure payment gateway, and customer support functionality.*
- *Timeline: The project adhered to the outlined timeline of 12 months, despite experiencing a minor delay due to high staff turnover during the development phase. The allocation of project phases seems reasonable given the complexity of the tasks involved.*
- *Budget: The project exceeded the initially estimated budget by 15% ($75,000), largely due to unforeseen complexities during the development and testing phases. While this overrun was managed by reallocating the budget from the marketing reserve, this is a clear area for improvement in future projects. Better contingency planning and risk management could have anticipated some of these extra costs.*

- *Quality: Quality measures show a positive outcome. The app achieved high user satisfaction scores in testing, suggesting that despite budget and resource challenges, the final product was of high quality.*
- *Resources: The project team composition was generally suitable for the project's needs. However, a high turnover rate indicates potential issues in project management, team morale, or other organizational challenges. This resource instability had a tangible impact, causing delays in project delivery.*
- *Risk Management: Risks were identified and managed, but the identification could have been more proactive, specifically concerning the budget and human resources. While mitigations were in place (reallocating budget, hiring temporary resources), it would be beneficial to analyze these issues to prevent recurrence in future projects.*
- *Recommendations for future projects:*
    1. *Enhance project cost estimation and contingency planning to prevent budget overruns.*
    2. *Strengthen team management and retention strategies to reduce turnover during critical project phases.*
    3. *Improve risk identification processes, considering both internal and external potential risks more comprehensively in the planning phase.*

    Overall, the project can be considered successful as it delivered on its key objectives and resulted in a high-quality product that was received well by the users. However, the overruns in time and budget, coupled with resource instability, indicate areas that could benefit from closer attention and refinement in future projects. These improvements could lead to more predictable, smoother project execution and may result in cost savings.

However, using the Instruction Prompt pattern, the prompt would be formulated as follows:

- **Expert Persona:** "*You are a senior project manager skilled in project assessment*"
- **Context:** "*Below there is a description of a completed project on the development of a mobile app*"
- **Instruction:** "*Perform an end-to-end assessment of the project*"
- **Execution Rules:**
    - "Make sure you cover the project's scope, schedule, cost, quality, resources, communications, risks, procurements, and stakeholder management."

  - "Make sure to take a very critical neutral stance and challenge the report created by the project manager responsible to deliver the project."
- **Output Constraints:** *"Output must be in the form of a structured report with clear headings for each assessment factor"*

The resulting output from ChatGPT-4 is as follows:

Project Assessment Report: Development of "XYZ" Mobile App

1. *Project Scope: The project aimed to design and implement a mobile app with a user-friendly interface, a secure payment gateway, and customer support functionality. However, the description of the project scope seems too generic and lacks detailed insight into its complexity. It would be beneficial to include specifics on the platform(s) the app was developed for, the expected level of user interaction, and the scale of customer support required. The number of features, their complexity, and any limitations should also be explicitly stated to avoid scope creep.*
2. *Schedule: The project adhered to the 12-month timeframe, though it experienced minor delays due to resource turnover. It would be crucial to evaluate if sufficient contingency time were built into the original project schedule to accommodate unforeseen delays. The planning phase seems proportionate, however, the development phase taking nearly half the project duration raises questions about efficiency and approach. Furthermore, deployment's two-month timeline might be lengthy - a post-mortem evaluation should ascertain if this could be streamlined for future projects.*
3. *Cost: The project experienced a cost overrun of 15%, primarily attributed to unforeseen complexities during the development and testing phase. This raises concerns about the project's initial cost estimation and risk assessment process. Did the project budget include a contingency fund for unexpected costs? If not, it should be incorporated into future projects. Also, the reallocation of funds from the marketing reserve may have consequences on the project's visibility and customer outreach.*
4. *Quality: The project appears to have met its quality objectives, evidenced by user testing scores. However, an average score does not provide a comprehensive picture. A breakdown of scores related to specific aspects of the app, such as usability, design, functionality, and security would offer a deeper understanding. Furthermore, was there any mechanism to manage and monitor quality throughout the project lifecycle, or was it only gauged through user testing at the end?*

5. *Resources: The team composition was fairly comprehensive for a project of this nature. However, the high turnover rate is alarming. What were the causes behind this? Were these related to project management, company culture, or market conditions? It is important to investigate this to mitigate similar occurrences in the future. Moreover, hiring temporary resources might have affected the overall team synergy and output quality.*

6. *Risks: The report mentions two significant risks - budget overrun and delays due to resource turnover. It would be worthwhile to analyze the risk identification, assessment, and mitigation strategies employed in the project. Were these risks identified upfront? If not, why were they missed? Did the project have a risk management plan in place? Understanding these factors will strengthen the risk management approach for future projects.*

7. *Procurements: No information was provided on procurement for this project. Did it involve any subcontracting or procurement of third-party services, tools, or technologies? If so, what was the procurement strategy and how effectively was it managed? Transparency on this front would contribute to a more comprehensive project assessment.*

8. *Stakeholder Management: The report does not provide any insights into stakeholder management. Information about stakeholder identification, their roles, expectations, and the communication strategy would be crucial to understand the project's success from all perspectives. Was there a structured approach to keep stakeholders informed about project progress and challenges?*

   In conclusion, while the project resulted in a successful delivery of a high-quality mobile app, there are significant areas for improvement. These include refining the project scope, improving cost estimation and risk management, addressing resource turnover, and enhancing transparency in procurement and stakeholder management.

Both assessment reports provide a review of the "XYZ" Mobile App project, but they differ in their approaches, depth of analysis, and areas of focus as follows:

1. **Objective and Scope:** Both reports praise the project for meeting its objective. The second report suggests refining the scope description for more specificity and recommends enhancements.

2. **Timeline:** The assessments concur on the maintained timeline with minor hitches. The second assessment suggests a post-mortem evaluation to scrutinize the phase durations further.

3. **Budget:** The overrun budget is acknowledged in both reviews, highlighting

areas for improvement in financial planning and querying the allocation of contingency and marketing funds in the second report.

4. **Quality:** While the first report commends user satisfaction scores, the second report seeks a deeper analysis of these scores and questions the project's quality management strategies.
5. **Resources:** The reports note the high turnover rate, advocating for improved team management strategies and a probe into the turnover causes and impacts by the second report.
6. **Risk Management:** The first report suggests better risk identification processes, and the second one calls for a comprehensive review of risk management strategies used in the project.
7. **Procurements and Stakeholder Management:** The second report introduces new considerations, recommending increased transparency in procurements and enhanced stakeholder management.

In summary, both assessments concur on the project's successful outcome. The first report provides a concise, comprehensive summary, while the second offers a more detailed and critical analysis, identifying additional areas for improvement and offering more specific recommendations (while both prompts did not request recommendations). When comparing the two, it becomes evident that incorporating additional components from the Instruction Prompt pattern – like Persona, Execution Rules, and Output Constraints – yields a more detailed, specific, and ultimately more professional result.

Stakeholder Management

Let us proceed with an example in the Product Management area, which has to deal with multiple stakeholders.

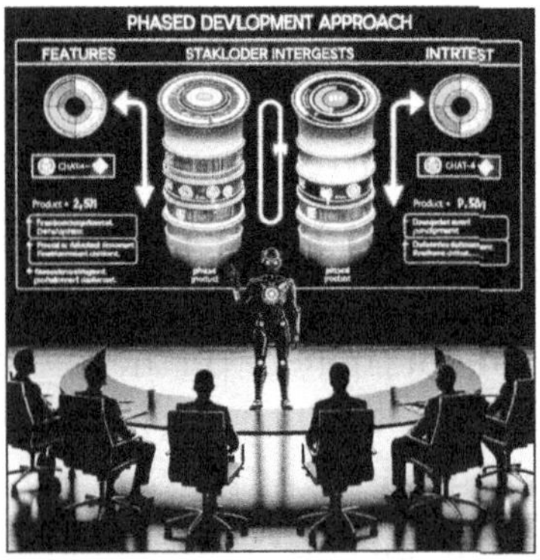

Figure 5.2: *Stakeholder Management*

The ensuing prompt is based on the **Creation** capability:

- **Expert Persona:** "*You are a product manager and argumentation expert*"
- **Context:** "*You are under pressure to launch a new product.*
    - *You have the following three options:*
        - *Product A has the most features but would take the longest development time and have the highest price.*"
        - *Product B has all basic features as a replacement for a successful product C, which is no longer supported by market standards.*
        - *Product D appeals to a new generation of clients with its special technology features.*
    - *Your stakeholders are the following Executives:*
        - *CTO (Chief Technology Officer) with a strong interest in applying new technologies.*
        - *COO (Chief Operations Officer), who had developed Product C some years ago.*
        - *CMO (Chief Marketing Officer), who wants to have a pipeline of rapidly developed new products to keep up with the competition.*
- **Instruction:** " *Develop several chains of argumentative reasoning (Creation)*"
- **Execution Rules:**
    - *Try to convince as many stakeholders as possible,*
    - *Minimize any potential dissatisfaction,*
    - *Use an AI-argumentation framework.*

The response generated by ChatGPT-4 for this prompt is as follows:

Sure, I can assist you with that. We will use the AI argumentation framework based on three main components: claim, evidence, and warrant. The claim is the point or assertion we want to make, the evidence is the supporting information for the claim, and the warrant connects the evidence with the claim, explaining why the evidence supports the claim.

Let us make the argument for each product one by one:

Product A (Most Features, Long Development Time, High Price)

Claim: Product A is the most comprehensive solution and would appeal to customers looking for a feature-rich product, adding value in the long run.

Evidence: It has the most features, potentially fulfilling customer needs better than any other product in the market.

Warrant: Despite its longer development time and higher price, the extensive features of Product A could justify the price tag and attract a dedicated, quality-focused user base. This would help us achieve a solid market presence and build our brand reputation, which aligns with the CMO's interest in differentiating us from the competition.

Product B (Basic Features, Replacement for Product C)

Claim: Product B is a direct successor to a previously successful product C, ensuring continuity and catering to our existing user base.

Evidence: It is designed to replace product C, which is no longer supported by market standards, implying that it fills a current gap in our product lineup.

Warrant: Updating our product lineup to match market standards is crucial. This would maintain trust with our current users, ensuring that they do not feel abandoned and preserving our market share. The COO would appreciate this strategy as it minimizes risk and ensures stability.

Product D (New Technology, Appeals to New Generation)

Claim: Product D represents innovation and caters to a new generation of clients, opening up a potentially lucrative market segment.

Evidence: Its special technology features make it appealing to a new generation of clients who value innovation and are comfortable with cutting-edge technology.

Warrant: By developing and launching Product D, we would not only appeal to the CTO's interest in applying new technologies but also align with the CMO's objective of keeping up with the competition. Despite being a new venture, the potential returns from tapping into a younger, tech-savvy demographic could outweigh the risks.

In conclusion, each product has its own strengths and aligns with the interests of different stakeholders. However, a balanced approach might involve developing a roadmap that includes all three products in stages, which could address all stakeholder concerns. We could prioritize development based on market demand, technological readiness, and our strategic objectives.

In this stakeholder management simulation, ChatGPT-4 acts as a product manager proficient in argumentation, tasked with persuading a group of executives to support one of three product options. Following the AI-argumentation framework, it strategically develops chains of reasoning for each product, aligning the products' features with the specific interests of the stakeholders involved.

ChatGPT-4 expertly navigates through the task, delineating the strengths and potential market impacts of the products while catering to the stakeholders' priorities. It suggests a roadmap endorsing a phased development approach for all products to potentially satisfy all stakeholders, thus promoting a harmonized path forward in the product development strategy. The proposed plan ensures a well-rounded approach that endeavors to balance varied stakeholder interests while advocating for a robust product development trajectory.

Sales Forecasting

In this example, we delve into the **Prediction** capability of ChatGPT-4 with a focus on sales forecasting. By analyzing an organic skincare product line, ChatGPT-4 will demonstrate its ability to project future sales.

Figure 5.3: *Sales Forecasting*

Leveraging historical sales data, observed sales patterns, and future market expectations, the subsequent prompt will guide the model to generate a basic sales forecast in natural language:

Expert Persona: *You are a Sales forecasting expert.*

Context:

This is the sales history: The product, a line of organic skincare products, was introduced to the market in January 2021. Initial sales were slow, with only 50 units sold that month. To boost numbers, the company employed aggressive marketing strategies, including social media campaigns and influencer partnerships. This led to a gradual increase in sales, reaching 200 units per month by April 2021.

Summer 2021 brought an unexpected surge in sales, peaking at 600 units in July, thanks to a successful summer promotional campaign and the product's suitability for warm-season skincare. A slight dip followed in the fall, down to 400 units per month, but sales rebounded during the holiday season in November and December to an average of 550 units per month. January 2022 saw a minor slump to 350 units due to post-holiday saturation and budget constraints. Sales then stabilized for the first quarter at an average of 400 units per month. The launch of a new product variant in April 2022 rejuvenated the sales, jumping to 700 units, and an average of 650 units were maintained per month thereafter. By the end of July 2023, over 8,000 units had been sold, reflecting the product's steady demand and growing popularity. August 2023 marked a pivotal moment, with the company's back-to-school campaign driving sales to an all-time monthly high of 800 units. The success was bolstered by a special promotional discount, strategic influencer partnerships, and the ongoing popularity of the new product variant introduced earlier in the year.

These are the historical patterns observed since its market introduction:

1. *Slow Sales in Initial Phase: After the introduction of a new product or a variant, sales are usually slow initially, indicating a pattern of customers taking time to adopt the new offering.*

2. *Fall Sales Dip: Historically, sales dip during the fall months. This pattern is possibly related to changes in weather and the corresponding adjustments in consumer skincare routines.*

3. *Holiday Sales Spike: Sales have consistently spiked during the holiday season in November and December. This is likely due to an increase in gift purchases and customers stocking up for winter skincare needs.*

5. *Post-Holiday Slump: Following the holiday season, a slump in sales is observed, indicating a pattern of decreased purchasing behavior possibly due to market saturation and consumer budget constraints post-holidays.*

These are the expectations for the rest of the year:

1. *Seasonal Promotional Campaign: The marketing department has planned a significant promotional campaign for the holiday season, which is expected to drive a considerable increase in sales during that period.*

2. *New Product Variants: The introduction of new product variants or extensions throughout the year can contribute to a boost in sales, attracting both existing customers interested in trying new things and new customers.*

3. *Market Expansion: The company is planning to expand its reach to new markets. This move could potentially boost sales as it taps into a new customer base.*

4. *Rising Popularity: The product's growing popularity and brand recognition, fueled by positive customer reviews and effective marketing, are expected to sustain and possibly accelerate sales growth in the future.*

5. *Economic Factors: Expected economic recovery and increased consumer spending following global events could also lead to an increase in sales.*

Instruction: *Provide a sales forecast in natural language for the next six months based on the sales history, the historical patterns, and the expectations for the future (Prediction).*

ChatGPT-4 responds to this prompt as follows:

Based on the sales history, observed patterns, and future expectations, we can provide the following sales forecast for the next six months:

August 2023: August sales are already reported at an all-time high of 800 units, driven by back-to-school campaigns.

September 2023: We typically observe a decline in sales during the fall season. However, the high sales momentum from August and the continuous popularity of the new product variant may mitigate this expected decrease. So, we could forecast a slight dip, possibly to around 700 units.

October 2023: The fall dip should continue as per historical patterns, but the anticipated effect will be less pronounced due to the new product variant's continued influence. Let us project sales at around 650 units.

November 2023: With the onset of the holiday season, we have historically seen a surge in sales, and the company's planned promotional campaign is expected to augment this spike further. Based on previous year's trends, the sales could jump to around 800 units.

December 2023: The holiday season continues into December, and if the promotional campaign is as successful as expected, sales should continue their high trajectory. The sales could potentially peak to 850 units, considering the product's growing popularity and the impact of the promotional campaign.

January 2024: A post-holiday slump has been a consistent pattern. Consumers are likely to be recovering from holiday spending and the market might experience some saturation from the high sales of the preceding months. However, the effect of the planned market expansion could help soften this drop. Hence, we could project a dip to around 600 units.

Please note that these numbers are projections based on past trends and planned activities. Other factors such as competitors' activities, market dynamics, and unforeseen events could impact the actual sales performance. Regular tracking and adjustments of forecasts will be necessary to keep them accurate and relevant.

In this sales forecasting example, ChatGPT-4 adopts the persona of a sales forecasting expert with predictive skills. The instruction prompt establishes the context, presenting the sales history of the organic skincare product line, highlighting the observed patterns, and setting forth future expectations. ChatGPT-4 is then tasked with forecasting sales for the subsequent months, considering the given context.

ChatGPT-4 adeptly processes the instruction and accomplishes it by taking into account the sales data, historical patterns, and future expectations, resulting in a basic forecast for the upcoming months. It outlines how each month's sales could potentially shape up, contributing to a strategic plan for managing inventory and marketing efforts.

Three further single instruction examples are presented in *Appendix A*:

- **Resource Management**: In this example, we demonstrate the **Matchmaking** capability of ChatGPT-4 in the domain of resource management. The system is prompted to assign resources to projects based on their skills and project requirements.
- **Scenario-based Project Simulation**: Using another example in the project management domain, we highlight the **Simulation** capability of ChatGPT-4. It is prompted to perform a project phase simulation based on the previous project results.
- **Business Communication**: This final single-instruction example explores business communication and summarization skills within the burgeoning carbon accounting industry. The task will be guided by reference cases which demonstrate to ChatGPT-4 how the expected summary should look like leveraging its **Summarization** capability

Instruction Sequence Examples

The subsequent examples illustrate the use of sequence-based instruction prompts with ChatGPT-4 for employee coaching and sentiment analysis for product reviews. Each example highlights a unique set of AI capabilities of ChatGPT-4:

- **New Employee Coaching:** This first example showcases the **Assessment** and **Recommendation** capabilities of ChatGPT-4 in the HR domain. The system is instructed to evaluate a new employee situation and suggest suitable measures to prevent potential attrition, all guided by reference cases.
- **Sentiment Analysis for Product Reviews:** Then we cover the realm of sentiment analysis for product reviews to demonstrate the capabilities of ChatGPT-4 in **Information Extraction and Analytics**, **Cause-effect Analysis**, and **Classification**. The system is tasked with performing sentiment classification on a product review in three consecutive steps.

New Employee Coaching

This example focuses on a two-step instruction sequence that guides an HR Manager in the fashion retail industry to evaluate a new employee situation and suggest appropriate measures to prevent potential attrition:

Figure 5.4: *New Employee Coaching*

Expert Persona: *You are an HR Manager in a fashion retailer, specialized in employee attrition avoidance. You have vast experience in managing a variety of employee cases and finding solutions to diverse challenges.*

Context: *Your new case pertains to James, a recently hired junior merchandiser. James, having joined the company just a few weeks ago, was already showing signs of disaffection. Despite having a promising start during the orientation period, his enthusiasm seemed to wane rapidly. He was often quiet during team meetings, unresponsive to team activities, and his work lacked the energy and thoroughness one might expect from a newcomer.*

Instruction Sequence:

1. *Assess the new case based on the reference cases below. Always make comparisons between the new case and the reference cases and what you have learned from them.*

2. *Based on the assessment results recommend specific HR-actions to take to prevent attrition*

Reference Cases:

Problem-Solution Case 1:

- **Problem:** *New Sales Representative Integration Sophia, a recent hire as a sales representative, was initially energetic and eager to contribute to our fashion retailer. However, a few weeks into her role, Sophia began showing signs of disengagement. She seemed unsure about her responsibilities and struggled with building rapport with her colleagues. Her performance, too, was inconsistent, showing a lack of understanding of her role.*
- **Solution:** *We quickly recognized these signs and implemented a structured onboarding program tailored to Sophia's role. The program included training sessions to help her understand her responsibilities and product knowledge. Alongside this, we introduced her to a mentor from her team who guided her through the daily processes and answered her questions. The mentor also introduced her to other team members, helping her build connections. Over time, Sophia's confidence and engagement with her team grew, and her performance significantly improved. She appreciated the mentorship and the structured guidance that helped her transition smoothly into her role.*

Problem-Solution Case 2:

- **Problem:** *New Designer's Cultural Fit Mark, a talented designer, joined our company with an impressive portfolio. However, within a month, Mark seemed distant and uninvolved. His designs lacked enthusiasm, and he rarely contributed to team discussions, indicating a struggle to fit into the company culture. To help Mark, we initiated a culture fit program.*
- **Solution:** *We organized regular team-building activities, encouraging Mark to share his ideas and interact more openly with his colleagues. We also organized sessions to discuss our company's values and culture, aiming to create an inclusive environment where Mark felt comfortable expressing his creativity. Mark slowly started to come out of his shell, actively participating in team meetings and his designs began reflecting the creativity we had seen during his hiring process. The culture fit program was successful, not only for Mark but also for fostering a sense of unity and inclusivity within the team.*

Problem-Solution Case 3:

- **Problem:** *New Logistics Manager's Role Clarity Denise, a newly recruited logistics manager, showed great potential during her interview process. But after her initial weeks, her contributions became sporadic, her work lacked attention to detail, and her presence in team meetings was negligible. It became evident that Denise was not clear about her role and what was expected of her.*
- **Solution:** *In response, we revised her job description, clearly outlining her duties, responsibilities, and the benchmarks for performance. We set up weekly meetings for the first two months to provide regular feedback, discuss her progress, and recognize her accomplishments. As a result, Denise's performance improved significantly, she took ownership of her role, and her contributions to team meetings became invaluable. She expressed gratitude for the clear communication and the consistent feedback, which made her transition into the new role smooth and stress-free.*

In response to the given prompt, ChatGPT-4 generates the following output:

Assessment:

James's situation is comparable to the reference cases to some extent. Like Sophia (Reference Case 1), he started with enthusiasm, but his motivation dwindled quickly. However, Sophia's issues stemmed from her lack of understanding about her role, while James' problems seem more tied to his engagement with the team and the energy in his work, which seems closer to Mark's situation (Reference Case 2). Denise's situation (Reference Case 3) also bears some resemblance as her contributions were inconsistent, which is a symptom that James is displaying as well. However, Denise's problem was due to a lack of role clarity, which does not appear to be James's issue.

Recommendations:

1. *Initiate a Personalized Onboarding Program: James might benefit from a structured program similar to Sophia's. Despite his experience, he may need more clarity and hands-on experience in the tasks and responsibilities specific to his role in this company. Pairing him with a mentor might help him gain confidence and improve the thoroughness of his work.*

2. *Promote Team-Building Activities: James' unresponsiveness to team activities and quiet demeanor during meetings could indicate a difficulty in integrating with the team, akin to Mark's issue. Regular team-building activities could encourage him to engage more with his colleagues, improving his enthusiasm and energy at work.*

3. *Offer Regular Feedback and Recognition: The approach taken with Denise could also be applied to James's case. Regular feedback sessions could help clarify performance expectations and give him a platform to express any concerns or uncertainties he might be experiencing. Acknowledging his accomplishments, no matter how small, can also help boost his motivation.*
4. *Employee Engagement Survey: Conduct a survey to gauge James' level of engagement. This can provide insights into whether he is feeling undervalued, unchallenged, or unmotivated, which might be leading to his disengagement.*
5. *One-on-One Meetings: Personal interaction with James may provide deeper insights into his situation. It is possible there are issues outside work that are affecting his performance. It is crucial to maintain open lines of communication to understand what might be driving his disaffection.*

In this employee coaching simulation, ChatGPT-4 assumes the role of an HR manager specializing in preventing attrition at a fashion retail company. Tasked with analyzing a recent hire's fading engagement through a two-step instruction process, it compares the new situation with reference cases to find potential solutions.

Leveraging insights from past experiences detailed in the reference cases, ChatGPT-4 suggests a nuanced strategy to retain the new employee, James. It pinpoints a potential disconnect with the team and recommends a personalized onboarding program and team-building activities to foster better engagement and prevent attrition. The response effectively delineates a strategy, providing a roadmap to support James in his early days at the company.

Sentiment Analysis

Let us continue with an example of an instruction sequence prompt that involves three steps to carry out a product review sentiment analysis:

Figure 5.5: *Sentiment Analysis*

Expert Persona: *You are an expert for sentiment classification of movie reviews.*

Context: *The StreamSmith V35 Bluetooth headphones are an ambitious attempt at creating an accessible, high-quality audio experience. However, despite their many positive qualities, they fall just short of the mark, earning a solid 3 out of 5 stars. The build quality of the V35s is admirable, as they have a comfortable fit with a premium look and feel. Moreover, the long battery life is a standout feature, providing hours of uninterrupted use on a single charge. StreamSmith's gesture control system is also intuitive, making the operation effortless. Additionally, the company's commitment to sustainable packaging is commendable. On the other hand, where the V35s disappoint is their sound quality, which is notably less impressive than competitors in the same price range. There is a noticeable lack of depth in the low-end frequencies, making the bass sound slightly hollow. The higher tones also seem to lack clarity, creating an overall flat soundstage. This, coupled with occasional connectivity issues, detracts from what could have been a truly stellar audio experience. Overall, the StreamSmith V35s represent a promising step forward, especially in terms of design and user interface. However, for the audiophile, these headphones might not be the first choice. If StreamSmith focuses on improving their sound quality and connection stability, their future products could pose a serious challenge to established players in the market.*

Instruction Sequence: *Perform sentiment classification on the product review in these three steps:*

First, *present clues (i.e., keywords, phrases, contextual information, semantic relations, semantic meaning, tones, references) that support the sentiment determination of input (Information Extraction & Analytics).*

Second, *deduce a diagnostic reasoning process from premises (i.e., clues, input) that supports the sentiment determination. (Cause-effect Analysis).*

Third, *determine the overall sentiment of the movie review as Positive or Negative considering the clues from step 1, the reasoning process in step 2 and the movie review (Classification).*"

In response to the given prompt, ChatGPT-4 generates the following output:

"Here are the requested steps:

1. *Information Extraction & Analytics:*
   - *Positive clues: "comfortable fit", "premium look and feel", "long battery life", "intuitive" gesture control, "commendable" sustainable packaging, "promising step forward", "serious challenge to established players".*

- *Negative clues: "fall just short of the mark", "less impressive" sound quality, "lack of depth" in low frequencies, "slightly hollow" bass, "lack of clarity" in higher tones, "flat soundstage", "occasional connectivity issues".*

2. *Cause-effect Analysis:*
    - *The reviewer provides several positive aspects of the product, such as the comfort and premium feel, battery life, intuitive controls, and sustainable packaging. This indicates the company has put thought into many aspects of the user experience and the product design.*
    - *However, the negative aspects of the review focus on the core functionality of the product, the sound quality and connectivity. This can be considered more critical, given the nature of the product as headphones.*
    - *Though the reviewer acknowledges the product's potential to challenge established market players, they also note its current shortcomings, particularly for a critical target audience - audiophiles.*
3. *Classification:*
    - *Overall, the sentiment of this review seems mixed, but leaning towards the negative side, primarily due to the weight of the criticisms. Although there are more positive than negative clues, the negatives touch on the core functionality of the headphones - sound quality and stable connection, which can be seen as more impactful. Thus, the review can be classified as somewhat negative."*

In this task, ChatGPT-4 embodies a sentiment analysis expert evaluating a review of the StreamSmith V35 Bluetooth headphones. Following a three-step instruction sequence, it first identifies positive and negative sentiments in the review. Next, it performs a cause-effect analysis, scrutinizing the strengths and weaknesses mentioned in the review, with a particular focus on essential functionalities where the product fell short. Lastly, it classifies the overall sentiment as somewhat negative, highlighting the substantial criticisms about the product's core features. The task showcases ChatGPT-4's analytical approach to dissecting reviews for informed decision-making.

Three further examples are presented in *Appendix* A:

- **Instruction Sequence: Insurance Claim Processing**: The system is prompted to execute a series of steps that involve question-asking, summarizing answers, and assessing costs of the damage.
- **Instruction Sequence: Solution Architecture Analysis**: ChatGPT-4 examines a given Azure OpenAI architecture, identifies components,

pinpoints bottlenecks, makes recommendations, and comes up with an implementation plan.

- **Pseudo Code Instructions: Real Estate Listing Comparison**: ChatGPT-4 ranks office space listings based on criteria like size, price, location, and amenities. It applies a scoring system, identifying and prioritizing top spaces, showcasing its proficiency in real estate evaluations.

Query Prompting

In this section, we will first delve into the Query Prompt Pattern[6], another distinctive approach for interacting with GPT models. Following this, we will explore a series of practical examples that highlight the application of this pattern in various enterprise scenarios.

Query Prompt Pattern

The Query Prompt Pattern is an effective approach designed to guide GPT models in generating insightful and accurate responses to various types of questions. Here is how each component contributes:

- **Evidence**: This is the factual, situational, or background information provided to a GPT model that serves as a reference for accurately interpreting and responding to subsequent queries, helping to prevent the generation of ungrounded or irrelevant outputs. For example, a company might present a GPT model with a detailed quarterly financial report, to analyze and extract insightful information from it.
- **Reasoning Rules**: These are explicit rules that guide a GPT model in deriving insights or conclusions from the provided evidence. In a business context, there are various rules that may influence the analysis process. For instance, one rule might articulate that "an increase in quarterly revenue indicates positive growth," which would guide the analysis of financial reports by highlighting favorable trends in a company's earnings over a set duration. Simultaneously, another rule could propose that "a growth in market share is a potential indicator of a company's increasing competitiveness," thereby focusing the investigation on market research data to discern the firm's performance relative to its industry peers.
- **Fuzzy Logic[7] Rules**: Fuzzy logic rules are used when dealing with Fuzzy

[6]The query prompt pattern is based on the question answering capability introduced in *Chapter 2, CapabilityGPT – An Enterprise AI-Capability Framework for ChatGPT*.

[7]Fuzzy logic is a system of logic allowing for degrees of truth. Unlike binary logic, which is strictly true or false, fuzzy logic handles ambiguity and uncertainty, making it useful for business scenarios with incomplete or contradictory information.

logic queries (see below), as they allow the model to handle situations characterized by uncertainty and ambiguity. In a business scenario, the rule "if the market feedback is predominantly positive, then the product is well-received" might be applied to interpret a series of customer reviews.

- **Justification Requirements**: This emphasizes the need for the GPT model to explain its conclusions. It can help validate the GPT model's insights and can be crucial for complex queries, where understanding its reasoning process is essential. In a business scenario, this could involve justifying projections for the next quarter based on patterns identified in the existing quarterly report.
- **Queries**: One or several categorized queries are formulated to leverage the GPT model's background knowledge acquired during pre-training, along with the supplied evidence and reasoning rules, to generate comprehensive responses. Here is how each query type operates:
  - **Information-seeking queries**: This type of query directs the GPT model to analyze and interpret the available evidence meticulously to respond to the questions asked, without venturing into speculative or hypothetical scenarios. It is designed to offer clear and direct answers grounded in the evidence presented. For instance, it might involve asking the GPT model to identify the best-performing product in Q1 from the provided sales data or calculate several non-disclosed KPIs from a competitor's financial report.
  - **As-is analysis queries**: This query type guides the GPT model to undertake a deep, structured analysis of the available evidence to uncover relationships, comparisons, and correlations through a detailed exploration of various angles:
    - **Causal analysis**: It involves identifying cause-and-effect relationships within the data points presented in the evidence. A company might inquire, "Based on the data from the last two quarters, can we pinpoint the causes behind the increase in product returns?"
    - **Comparative analysis**: This pathway encourages comparing different elements or time frames to spot trends, similarities, or differences. An enterprise might ask, "How does the performance of Product A compare to Product B over the last fiscal year?"
    - **Correlation analysis**: It seeks to establish statistical associations between different variables in the evidence. A firm might query, "Is there a discernible correlation between our marketing spend and the number of new customers acquired over the past year?"

- **Predictive queries:** This query type prompts the GPT model to utilize the provided evidence to foresee potential future events, encouraging predictions that are grounded in reality while discouraging baseless speculation. This query type explores various avenues of prediction:
  - **Unconditional prediction**: Queries in this category guide the GPT model to make predictions based directly on the available evidence without imposing any hypothetical conditions. For example, a business might ask, "Considering our monthly revenues as documented in the evidence, what can we expect our total revenue to be at the end of this fiscal year?"
  - **Conditional prediction**: These queries involve hypothesizing about future scenarios based on conditional statements or potential actions, guiding the model to explore the ramifications of specific strategies or decisions. Essentially, it employs "what-if" scenarios to anticipate the potential outcomes of varying approaches, facilitating proactive planning and informed decision-making. Such scenarios can range from strategic planning and risk management to policy changes and technological advancements. For instance, a business might inquire, "If we were to implement a more robust after-sales service, what impact could it potentially have on our customer loyalty?"
- **Guidance queries**: This query type directs the GPT model to conceptualize possible strategies and advice grounded on the supplied evidence, leveraging its analytical capabilities to aid businesses in strategizing improvements. It navigates through two detailed pathways:
  - **Advisory**: Here, the queries are geared towards offering expert advice based on a practical analysis of the evidence, aiming to carve out potential strategies suitable for the existing circumstances. A question in this category might be, "Based on the reviews of our latest product, what should be our focus in order to enhance user satisfaction?"
  - **Optimization**: This segment carves out the optimal strategies or solutions within the given constraints, focusing on extracting the best possible outcomes through a meticulous analysis of the current data and trends. For example, a company might ask, "Given our current resources and market standing, what would be the optimal pricing strategy for our upcoming product?"

- **Counterfactual queries**: This query type encourages the GPT model to venture into alternate realities, orchestrating an exploration of "what could have been." Through this, it devises narratives exploring diverse pathways and their potential ramifications while crafting responses that are both speculative and grounded in logical analysis. A business might query, "Had we reduced the price of our service by 10% last year, what might have been the potential impact on our sales?"
- **Fuzzy Logic queries**: Employed in scenarios filled with uncertainty and ambiguity, this query type utilizes fuzzy logic rules along with the provided context to understand and navigate complex situations. For example, leveraging a fuzzy logic rule like "if the feedback is mainly neutral, then the sentiment is potentially mixed," a business might seek insights into customer responses to a new product launch, aiming to derive indicative intelligence where definite conclusions are elusive.

The Query Prompt Pattern is a powerful tool for handling intricate analytical and explorative problems and is best realized under the following conditions:

- **Reliable evidence is available:** Factual and contextual data are the foundation of all applied reasoning to generate realistic and relevant responses.
- **Reasoning rules can be explicitly formulated:** Explicit rules steer the model's chain of thought transparently to derive insights from evidence.
- **There is inherent ambiguity or uncertainty:** In these scenarios standard logical reasoning techniques cannot be applied.
- **Justifications are key**: Explanations of the rationales behind the responses are as important as the responses themselves.
- **Explorative query types are required:** Different categories of queries, from information-seeking to predictive and counterfactual are needed to tackle a complex business problem.

Query Examples

The forthcoming demonstrations put forward the application of varied query prompts with ChatGPT-4 within the contexts of cosmetic products, supplier evaluation, business forecasting, and system usability improvements:

- Visual Inquiries about Cosmetic Products: Employing several information-seeking queries, ChatGPT-4 acts as an image analysis expert, examining a visual prompt of cosmetic products. It interprets artistic and emotional impressions conveyed by the products' arrangement, showcasing its skill in visual interpretation and understanding of the beauty industry.

- New Supplier Evaluation: Using multiple comparative analysis queries, ChatGPT-4 evaluates five suppliers for ABC Corp on quality, pricing, delivery timeliness, and customer satisfaction, showcasing its support for optimal supplier selection.
- Predictive Business Analysis: Utilizing two predictive queries, ChatGPT-4 forecasts revenue and market share growth of technology-based consumer products. It also covers a scenario of increased investment, exploring financial and market penetration implications.
- Improving System Usability in Healthcare: Asking an advisory query, ChatGPT-4 provides strategies to address challenges with a new EHR system based on healthcare staff feedback. It makes different suggestions to improve user satisfaction and patient care efficiency.

Visual Inquiries about Cosmetic Products

Let's examine an example in the domain of image analysis.

Figure 5.6: *Visual Inquiries about Cosmetic Products*

This example uses an image provided via a web link as evidence, showcasing an assortment of cosmetic products, and poses five specific information-seeking questions:

Evidence:

A *high-resolution image showcasing various cosmetic products:*

Figure 5.7: *Image of Cosmetic Products [6]*

Reasoning Rules:

1. *Each product on the image is distinct* and *represents a different cosmetic item.*
2. A product is considered "on the image" if more than 50% of it is visible.
3. Use the SceneExplain plugin.

Justification Requirements: *Explain how you determined whether the specific cosmetic product was on the image or not, and provide any relevant contextual information based on the visibility, placement, or distinctiveness of the product.*

Information-seeking queries:

1. *Are there nail polish bottles? Which colors do they have? Are they reflecting light?*
2. *How is the vanity mirror decorated? What does it express?*
3. *What kind of brushes are there and what do they convey?*
4. *Is there lipstick? Where is it placed?*
5. *What is the overall impression of the image?*

Here are ChatGPT's answers:

Based on the detailed explanation provided by SceneXplain, here are the answers to your information-seeking queries:

1. Nail Polish Bottles: *Yes, there are nail polish bottles in the image. They are primarily in silver and black colors. These bottles are positioned close to*

each other, and they catch the light, creating an elegant shimmer, which suggests that they are reflecting light.

2. *Vanity Mirror Decoration: The vanity mirror is sleek and silver. It reflects the surrounding beauty items, showcasing essential makeup items such as lipstick, eye shadow, and eyeliner. The mirror's reflection offers a glimpse into the possibilities for transformation and self-expression, emphasizing the transformative power of makeup.*

3. *Brushes: There are makeup brushes scattered throughout the composition. These brushes are portrayed as tools of artistry. Additionally, a brown container holds a makeup brush, emphasizing its practicality and functionality. The brushes convey a sense of readiness for makeup application and artistry.*

4. *Lipstick: Yes, there is lipstick in the image. It is displayed on the central mirror, making it one of the prominent items in the composition.*

5. *Overall Impression: The overall impression of the image is one of beauty and elegance. The meticulously arranged collection of cosmetics on a pristine white surface portrays a well-curated ensemble of makeup products. Every element in the composition, from the brushes to the cosmetics, contributes to a harmonious balance, inviting viewers to explore the world of beauty and self-expression.*

Justification: The determinations were made based on the detailed explanation provided by SceneXplain, which analyzed the image and described its content in depth. The visibility, placement, and distinctiveness of each product were considered in the explanation, allowing for accurate answers to the queries.

In this portrayal, ChatGPT-4, using the SceneXplain plugin, acts as an image analysis expert, focusing on the details of cosmetic products in a visual prompt. Beyond identifying items, it interprets artistic and emotional impressions conveyed by the products' arrangement. This highlights ChatGPT-4's skill in visual interpretation and its ability to offer insights into beauty and self-expression.

New Supplier Evaluation

This example navigates through an evaluative process of various suppliers for ABC Corp, where ChatGPT-4 systematically assesses and compares each supplier's performance based on quality, pricing, delivery timeliness, and customer satisfaction to determine the most suitable candidate for procurement.

Figure 5.8: *New Supplier Evaluation*

Here is the prompt based using the comparative analysis query type:

Evidence: *Here are the performance reports on five suppliers that ABC Corp is considering for procurement:*

1. *Supplier A:*
    - *Overview: Renowned for timely deliveries, Supplier A boasts a 98% on-time delivery rate. They offer competitive pricing but have encountered three instances of quality issues in the past six months. These issues were related to material defects, leading to product returns.*
    - *Customer Satisfaction: Received a customer satisfaction score of 85 out of 100. Feedback indicates satisfaction with delivery but concerns over occasional quality inconsistencies.*
    - *Pricing: Prices are competitive, being 5% below the market average, which appeals to budget-conscious clients.*
    - *Mitigation Measures: The supplier has initiated enhanced quality control measures to address and prevent future quality issues.*
2. *Supplier B:*
    - *Overview: Supplier B offers premium quality products with no reported quality issues. However, their prices are 15% above market average. They have a solid reputation for quality, with a 95% on-time delivery rate.*
    - *Customer Satisfaction: Holds a high customer satisfaction score of 92 out of 100, with particular praise for product quality and reliability.*

- *Pricing: Premium pricing is justified by the superior quality and reliability of products, catering to high-end market segments.*
- *Mitigation Measures: The supplier offers flexible payment terms to alleviate concerns regarding higher pricing.*

3. *Supplier C:*
   - *Overview: Supplier C offers the most economical pricing, being 10% below market average, but has a lower on-time delivery rate of 88%. Two quality issues were reported in the last year, related to packaging faults.*
   - *Customer Satisfaction: Holds a customer satisfaction score of 80 out of 100, with the lower score attributed to delays and packaging concerns.*
   - *Pricing: The economical pricing strategy appeals to smaller businesses and cost-sensitive segments.*
   - *Mitigation Measures: The supplier is investing in improved packaging technology and logistics partnerships to enhance delivery timeliness and reduce defects.*
4. *Supplier D:*
   - *Overview: Supplier D maintains high-quality standards with only one reported quality issue in the past year related to product finishing. They offer average pricing and have a 90% on-time delivery rate.*
   - *Customer Satisfaction: Received a customer satisfaction score of 88 out of 100. Clients appreciate the consistent quality but desire improvements in delivery times.*
   - *Pricing: Prices are aligned with market averages, offering a balanced option for a wide range of clients.*
   - *Mitigation Measures: The supplier has addressed the finishing issue and is exploring logistics solutions to improve delivery times.*
5. *Supplier E:*
   - *Overview: Supplier E achieves an excellent balance between quality and price. They record a 96% on-time delivery rate with two quality issues reported in the last six months, both resolved promptly.*
   - *Customer Satisfaction: Holds a customer satisfaction score of 89 out of 100. The balance between quality, price, and delivery has been well-received, but some clients suggest further enhancements in product features.*
   - *Pricing: The pricing strategy is competitive, with a 3% discount on bulk orders, attracting a diverse clientele.*

- *Mitigation Measures: The supplier is actively engaging with clients to understand their needs and is investing in product development to introduce enhanced features.*

Reasoning Rules:

- *Balanced Approach: A supplier that balances quality, pricing, and delivery timeliness is generally preferable.*
- *Quality Priority: Quality issues can lead to downstream problems; hence, suppliers with fewer quality issues are more desirable.*
- *Delivery Timeliness: On-time delivery is crucial for maintaining the supply chain's efficiency, so suppliers with higher on-time delivery rates are favored.*
- *Customer Satisfaction: Higher customer satisfaction scores are indicative of better overall supplier performance.*

Justification Requirement:

You should meticulously explain the reasoning behind any recommendations or insights drawn regarding the selection of a supplier. It should consider all available data points, weigh the significance of each factor, and clearly articulate how these factors influence the overall assessment.

Comparison queries:

1. *Balanced Approach Analysis:*
   - How does each supplier balance quality, pricing, and delivery timeliness according to the provided evidence?
   - Which supplier demonstrates the most effective balance among these factors, and why?
2. *Quality Priority Evaluation:*
   - Can you identify and compare the number and severity of quality issues reported for each supplier?
   - How do these quality issues impact the desirability of each supplier, considering the priority of quality in procurement?
3. *Delivery Timeliness Assessment:*
   - Compare the on-time delivery rates of the five suppliers. Which supplier has the highest on-time delivery rate, and how significantly does this influence their overall performance?
   - Are there any suppliers whose lower on-time delivery rates might be a cause for concern in maintaining supply chain efficiency?

4. *Customer Satisfaction Comparison:*
   - How do the customer satisfaction scores for each supplier compare?
   - What do these scores indicate about the overall performance of the suppliers, and how heavily should these scores weigh in the final decision?
5. *Recommendation and Justification:*
   - Based on the assessments above, which supplier would you recommend ABC Corp consider for procurement and why?
   - Are there any specific strengths or weaknesses in a supplier that significantly influence your recommendation?
   - Can you provide a detailed justification for your recommendation, considering all the evidence and reasoning rules provided?
6. *Risk and Mitigation:*
   - Are there any potential risks associated with your recommended supplier?
   - How might ABC Corp mitigate these risks to ensure a successful partnership with the chosen supplier?

ChatGPT-4 answers as follows:

Balanced Approach Analysis:

1. *Supplier A balances competitive pricing (5% below market average) and high on-time delivery rate (98%) but has had instances of quality issues.*
2. *Supplier B excels in quality with no reported issues and has a good on-time delivery rate (95%), but its pricing is 15% above the market average.*
3. *Supplier C offers the most economical pricing (10% below average) but compromises on both delivery rate (88%) and has had quality issues.*
4. *Supplier D presents a balanced approach with average pricing, a 90% on-time delivery rate, and minimal quality issues.*
5. *Supplier E also achieves a good balance, with competitive pricing (including bulk discounts), a 96% delivery rate, and prompt resolution of quality issues.*

The most effective balance among quality, pricing, and delivery seems to be achieved by Supplier E, offering competitive pricing, high delivery rates, and quality with prompt resolution of issues.

Quality Priority Evaluation:

Supplier B stands out with no reported quality issues. Supplier D and Supplier E have had minimal issues which were addressed, while Supplier A and Supplier C have encountered more significant problems, with Supplier A having material defects leading to returns.

Considering the priority of quality, Supplier B is the most desirable, but Supplier D and Supplier E also present strong cases with their prompt resolutions.

Delivery Timeliness Assessment:

Supplier A has the highest on-time delivery rate at 98%, significantly influencing their overall performance. Supplier C, with an 88% delivery rate, might pose concerns in maintaining supply chain efficiency, especially when coupled with their quality issues.

Customer Satisfaction Comparison:

Supplier B has the highest customer satisfaction score (92/100), indicative of their excellent overall performance. These scores are crucial as they reflect real-world performance and customer experience, thus should weigh significantly in the final decision.

Recommendation and Justification:

Given all considerations, Supplier E would be a recommended choice for ABC Corp. They demonstrate a balanced approach with competitive pricing, high delivery rate, and minimal quality issues that were promptly resolved. Their customer satisfaction score is also high, showing a good market response.

While Supplier B has superior quality and customer satisfaction, their significantly higher pricing might not appeal to all segments of the market. Supplier E's balanced approach would cater to a broader clientele and their willingness to enhance product features indicates adaptability and customer orientation, which are valuable traits in a supplier.

Risk and Mitigation:

The potential risks associated with Supplier E are the quality issues reported. Even though they were resolved promptly, it's essential to ensure such issues are minimized. ABC Corp might mitigate these risks by conducting regular quality audits and maintaining open communication lines for addressing any concerns promptly. Additionally, as clients have suggested enhancements in product features, ABC Corp should work closely with Supplier E on product development to meet customer needs effectively.

In conclusion, while all suppliers have their strengths and weaknesses, Supplier E offers a balanced, adaptable, and customer-oriented approach that would likely suit ABC Corp's procurement needs. Regular oversight and collaborative development would help mitigate the associated risks.

In this scenario, ChatGPT-4 acts as a discerning consultant, analyzing the profiles of five potential suppliers for ABC Corp. Utilizing a comprehensive approach, it evaluates each supplier based on quality, pricing, delivery timeliness, and customer satisfaction to identify the most advantageous partnership, for which it also provides recommendations on how to overcome remaining challenges.

Predictive Business Analysis

This example embarks on a predictive business analysis scenario, where ChatGPT-4 examines the potential implications of TechPioneer's recent SmartGadget launch, exploring forecasted revenue and market share based on current trends and prospective strategic initiatives.

Figure 5.9: *Predictive Business Analysis*

Here is the prompt using the predictive query type:

Evidence:

TechPioneer, a leading tech company, recently launched a new product, SmartGadget. The quarterly financial report reveals the following details:

- *The company's revenue increased by 15% since the product's release, amounting to a total quarterly revenue of $1.15 million.*
- *The market share experienced a growth of 5%, resulting in a current market share of 20% in the smart gadget industry.*

- *SmartGadget received an average rating of 4.5 out of 5 based on customer reviews, highlighting its innovative features and user-friendly interface.*
- *The industry growth rate is currently stable at around 3% per quarter.*
- *The marketing budget for SmartGadget was $100,000 in the last quarter.*
- *Competitor analysis shows that rivals have maintained consistent market performance, with no significant product launches planned for the next two quarters.*
- *Customer feedback surveys indicate a high level of satisfaction with the product's current features, with a 70% likelihood of recommending SmartGadget to others.*

Reasoning Rules:

1. *A sustained increase in quarterly revenue indicates potential long-term growth.*
2. *Positive product reviews correlate with high consumer satisfaction and can lead to increased sales.*
3. *An increase in market share can indicate growing competitiveness in the market.*

Justification Requirements:

The model should justify its predictions by referencing specific data points or trends identified in the provided evidence and by applying the reasoning rules. It should also outline any assumptions made during the prediction.

Queries:

Unconditional Prediction:

Considering the detailed quarterly financial report, including the 15% increase in revenue, the 5% increase in market share, and the positive product reviews for SmartGadget, what quantitative predictions can be made for our total revenue and market share at the end of this fiscal year?

Expected Justification: The model should calculate the projected revenue and market share for the remaining quarters of the fiscal year, taking into account the current growth rates, industry growth, and competitor landscape. The positive product reviews and customer recommendation likelihood can be factored in to estimate potential additional growth in sales.

Conditional Prediction:

If TechPioneer decides to invest an additional 10% of SmartGadget's current quarterly revenue (i.e., an additional $115,000) in marketing and enhancing product features based on user feedback, what is the quantitative impact that this could potentially have on our total revenue and market share by the next fiscal year?

Expected Justification: The model should analyze the potential returns on increased marketing investment and improved product features, considering the existing market conditions, competitor activities, and customer preferences. It should calculate the possible increase in sales and market share, factoring in the current growth rates and industry dynamics.

ChatGPT-4 answers as follows:

Unconditional Prediction:

Calculating Projected Revenue:

Given the current quarterly revenue is $1.15 million with a growth of 15%, to project the revenue for the rest of the fiscal year, we'll calculate the revenue for the next three quarters.

Q2 Revenue = 1.15M * (1 + 0.15) = 1.3225M

Q3 Revenue = 1.3225M * (1 + 0.15) = 1.520875M

Q4 Revenue = 1.520875M * (1 + 0.15) = 1.74900625M

Total Projected Revenue for the Fiscal Year: 1.15M + 1.3225M + 1.520875M + 1.74900625M = *$5.74238125 million*

Calculating Projected Market Share:

Given the current market share is 20% with a growth of 5%, we project the market share for the next three quarters as follows:

Q2 Market Share = 20% + 5% = 25%

Q3 Market Share = 25% + 5% = 30%

Q4 Market Share = 30% + 5% = 35%

These projections assume a linear growth, which may be simplistic given market dynamics, competition, and saturation points, but without additional data, this is a reasonable approximation.

Conditional Prediction:

Impact of Additional Investment:

Assuming an additional investment of $115,000 (10% of current quarterly revenue) in marketing and product enhancement, there could be an increment in both revenue and market share. However, calculating the exact impact is challenging without specific data on return on investment (ROI) for marketing and product enhancements.

Let's assume a conservative estimate that every dollar invested in marketing and enhancement could generate an additional $5 in revenue, giving a ROI of 5.

*Additional Revenue per Quarter = $115,000 * 5 = $575,000*

*The total additional revenue for the next fiscal year would be $575,000 * 4 (quarters) = $2.3 million.*

The new projected revenue for the next fiscal year would be $5.74138125 million + $2.3 million = $8.04138125 million.

Market Share:

The additional investment could potentially attract more customers, thereby increasing the market share. Assuming the additional investment results in a 2% extra growth in market share per quarter:

Q2 Market Share = 25% + 2% = 27%

Q3 Market Share = 30% + 2% = 32%,

Q4 Market Share = 35% + 2% = 37%

These estimates are based on several assumptions and should be validated with more specific data on market dynamics, customer behavior, and the effectiveness of marketing and product enhancements.

In conclusion, while the unconditional prediction provides a straightforward projection based on current growth rates, the conditional prediction involves more variables and assumptions, specifically regarding the ROI of additional investments and their impact on market share.

In this predictive business analysis, ChatGPT-4 skillfully combines financial figures and market-oriented metrics to assess the future trajectory of TechPioneer's SmartGadget. It forecasts potential growth in revenue and market share, providing a holistic view of the product's impact on the company's standing.

Additionally, ChatGPT-4 evaluates a conditional scenario, exploring the implications of increased investment on financial outcomes and market penetration, thus highlighting strategic opportunities for growth.

Improving System Usability in Healthcare

This scenario involves ChatGPT-4 analyzing staff feedback to optimize the usability of a newly implemented Electronic Health Record (EHR) system within a healthcare organization. The aim is to address specific concerns, enhance user experience and patient care, while ensuring regulatory compliance and data security.

Figure 5.10: *Improving System Usability in Healthcare*

Here is the prompt utilizing the advisory query type:

Evidence:

A healthcare organization has recently implemented a new Electronic Health Record (EHR) system across its network of hospitals. Initial feedback from different staff members indicates the following challenges:

- *Nurse Emma: Reports difficulty navigating through multiple screens to access patient information, leading to increased time spent on the system and decreased interaction with patients.*
- *Dr. Johnson: Faces challenges with system responsiveness and has experienced instances of data not being saved properly, causing concerns about data accuracy and reliability.*
- *Administrator Mike: Struggles with generating reports efficiently, as the system lacks intuitive features for report customization, affecting administrative workflow.*

- *IT Specialist Clara: Raises concerns about the system's integration with other software in use, leading to potential data synchronization issues.*

These challenges have resulted in an increase in time spent on documentation and a decrease in time available for direct patient care.

Reasoning Rules:

1. *Usability Improvement:*
    - *Addressing specific issues reported by different staff members leads to improved system usability.*
    - *Resolving challenges related to navigation, responsiveness, and integration enhances overall user experience and satisfaction.*
2. *Patient Care Enhancement:*
    - *Decreasing time spent on system documentation increases time available for patient care.*
    - *Efficient and reliable data management contributes to improved patient outcomes.*

Justification Requirements:

The GPT model needs to justify its recommendations by addressing the specific issues raised by Nurse Emma, Dr. Johnson, Administrator Mike, and IT Specialist Clara. Additionally, the model should consider the potential trade-offs between enhancing system usability and maintaining compliance with healthcare regulations and data security.

Advisory Query:

Given the specific challenges reported by Nurse Emma, Dr. Johnson, Administrator Mike, and IT Specialist Clara with the new EHR system, what general advice can be derived to address these individual concerns and similar concerns by other employees and improve overall user satisfaction?

ChatGPT-4 answers as follows:

1. *User Training and Support:*
    - *Objective: Improve navigation proficiency and system utilization for staff.*
    - *Action: Conduct targeted training sessions, focusing on system navigation for nurses and report generation for administrators.*
    - *Justification: This directly addresses Nurse Emma's difficulty navigating through multiple screens and Administrator Mike's struggle with generating reports efficiently.*

2. *System Optimization:*
   - *Objective: Enhance system responsiveness and reliability.*
   - *Action: Identify and resolve bottlenecks and regularly update the system to rectify issues related to data saving and responsiveness.*
   - *Justification: This is essential to tackle the challenges faced by Dr. Johnson regarding system responsiveness and instances of data not being saved properly.*
3. *Enhanced Integration Capabilities:*
   - *Objective: Achieve seamless integration with other software in use.*
   - *Action: Collaborate with IT specialists and vendors to address integration and data synchronization concerns.*
   - *Justification: IT Specialist Clara's concern about the system's integration leading to potential data synchronization issues will be directly addressed through this approach.*
4. *Customizable Reporting Features:*
   - *Objective: Facilitate easier report customization to improve administrative workflow.*
   - *Action: Work with EHR vendors to enhance report customization features based on the feedback from administrative staff.*
   - *Justification: By developing intuitive features for report customization, this advice addresses the specific issues reported by Administrator Mike, thus contributing to administrative workflow improvement.*

By implementing these targeted strategies, the healthcare organization can directly address the specific concerns raised by the staff, thereby improving overall system usability and user satisfaction.

In this advisory assessment, ChatGPT-4 provides targeted strategies addressing specific challenges raised by healthcare staff with the new EHR system. The advice is focused on system optimization, enhanced integration, customizable reporting, and user training, aiming to improve user satisfaction and increase time available for patient care.

Three further query examples are presented in Appendix A:

- Safety Regulation Inquiries: Using several information-seeking queries, ChatGPT-4 interprets Personal Protective Equipment (PPE) safety regulations, analyzes consequences of compromised gear, emphasizing immediate replacement of damaged PPE for worker safety, showcasing its understanding of technical regulations.

- Counterfactual Exploration in HR Management: Through a counterfactual query, ChatGPT-4 analyzes hypothetical outcomes of an earlier career development, focusing on turnover, costs, morale, and reputation. The analysis underscores potential benefits, savings, enhanced job satisfaction, and improved employer branding, showcasing ChatGPT-4's abilities in HR scenarios.
- Supply Possibility Estimation: Applying a fuzzy logic query, ChatGPT-4 evaluates delivery fulfillment possibilities of different suppliers for ACME Corp. based on order sizes and fleet capacities. It navigates through fuzzy logic rules to conclude that a supplier with many small trucks, offers the highest possibility to fulfill a large order, showcasing the application of fuzzy logic in supply chain scenarios.

Multi-Agent Prompting

In this section, we first introduce the Multi-Agent[8] Prompt Pattern for multi-agent collaboration within a GPT model environment. We then provide several practical examples to demonstrate the effective application of this pattern in enterprise contexts.

Multi-Agent Prompt Pattern

The Multi-Agent Prompt Pattern is a pioneering approach, leveraging the multi-agent capabilities of advanced GPT models. It cultivates an ecosystem where specialized artificial agents, each with its distinct role and responsibility, collaborate to achieve specific user-provided goals. The constituents of this pattern include:

- **Agent Organization**: This specifies the AI agents involved. Each agent could represent a different business function with unique skills. For instance, when launching a new product, the agents might include a "Market Research Agent," a "Product Development Agent," and a "Marketing and Sales Agent."
- **Agent Responsibilities**: This element lays out the roles for each agent. For the product launch, the Market Research Agent might be responsible for gathering market and customer insights, the Product Development Agent for overseeing product design and manufacturing, and the Marketing and Sales Agent for driving the product's marketing strategy

[8]A multi-agent system (MAS) consists of multiple interacting agents, which are designed to achieve individual or collective goals. These agents can operate autonomously, communicate with each other, and even adapt or learn from their environment. A single agent is a software component designed to perform specific tasks, often autonomously and in interaction with other agents, systems, or users.

and sales efforts.

- **Goal Specification**: This is the overall aim that the team of agents will work towards. In our product launch scenario, the goal could be to "successfully launch product X in the market and achieve Y sales in the first quarter."
- **Engagement Rules**: These are the rules that dictate how the agents interact with each other, with humans, and with external tools or plugins. An Engagement Rule for the product launch could be that the Product Development Agent should first confirm the product's readiness before the Marketing and Sales Agent starts its campaign.
- **Constraints**: These are limitations or boundaries within which the agents have to operate. For example, the product launch must align with regulatory compliance, the marketing campaign should adhere to a set budget, and the product should be ready for launch by a specific date.
- **Approach**: This describes the strategies or methods the agents will apply to achieve the goal while potentially using external tools or plugins. For instance, the agents could start with market research, then move to product development, and finally focus on the marketing and sales efforts.

The Multi-Agent Prompt Pattern advances the realm of AI-driven collaboration through specialized interconnected agents and is particularly useful under the following conditions:

- **Ambiguity is present:** In cases where tasks are not clearly defined, a team of agents can first establish a comprehensive task description, minimizing the potential for misinterpretation or hallucination.
- **Deep expertise is required:** When tasks need specialized knowledge, agents with specific expertise can provide detailed insights and generate component solutions.
- **Diverse views are essential:** This approach thrives when varied perspectives are crucial, ensuring a comprehensive and validated outcome through multiple viewpoints.
- **High-Quality outcomes are a priority:** When there's a demand for meticulous quality assurance, having multiple agents perform independent checks can significantly enhance the quality of the final output.
- **Adaptability is key:** In rapidly changing environments or tasks, the ability of agents to modify plans in real-time can be invaluable.

Multi-Agent Prompt Examples

The subsequent narratives showcase the application of multi-agent prompts in interactive scenarios, spanning project readiness assessments, sales data analysis, and forewarning financial evaluation:

- **Project Go-Live Check**: ChatGPT-4 functions as Planning, Execution, and Orchestration Agents to assess Project X's go-live readiness. It outlines essential tasks, collects user insights on finer project details, and compiles a summarized roadmap, facilitating a thoroughly prepared launch for Project X.
- **Sales Data Deep Dive**: In this scenario, we witness ChatGPT-4's analytical capabilities in unraveling a year's worth of sales data from a wholesale dataset. The system adopts the roles of Data Manager Agent, Data Processing Agent, and Visualization Agent to extract significant trends and insights, providing a detailed picture of sales performance and suggesting strategies for future enhancement.
- **Forewarning Financial Analysis**: ChatGPT-4, acting as Report Extractor, Financial Analysis, and Presentation Agents, dissects the 2019 financial report of JCPenney, a former US retailer.. It extracts crucial metrics, evaluates financial indicators like liquidity and solvency, and visualizes data, offering insights into JCP's financial distress leading to its 2020 bankruptcy.

Project go-live check

In this example, a multi-agent team collaborates to determine the readiness of Project X for its go-live phase. As we delve into the narrative, you will see this team, consisting of an Orchestration Agent, Planning Agent, and Execution Agent, evaluating the project status with the help of an expert user, and planning the necessary actions to ensure a successful go-live.

Figure 5.11: *Project go-live check*

Let us look into the prompt:

- **Agent Organization:** *You are a team consisting of an Orchestration Agent, a Planning Agent, and an Execution Agent.*
- **Agent Responsibilities:**
    - *Orchestration Agent: Acts as the central control unit to manage the flow of tasks, oversee the collaboration between the Planning Agent and Execution Agent, and produce a summary at the end.*
    - *Planning Agent: Responsible for devising task lists based on user-defined goals and further breaking down complex tasks into more operational components.*
    - *Execution Agent: Directly handles the operation of tasks based on real user inputs, ensuring they are completed, and results are documented.*
- **Goal Specification:** *Ensure that project X is ready for go-live.*
- **Engagement Rules:**
    - *The Orchestration Agent calls upon the Planning Agent to create a Task List for the specified goal.*
    - *The Planning Agent breaks down the goal into 3-4 tasks,*
    - *The Orchestration Agent then picks the next task and determines its complexity, deciding if further planning is needed or if it can be processed directly.*
    - *For tasks deemed complex, the Planning Agent is again engaged to break them down. This breakdown is informed by both the overarching goal and any intermediate results.*
    - *Operational tasks are directly sent to the Execution Agent for processing and result documentation.*
    - *The Execution Agent must always ask the real user for input when starting a task and can only move forward based on user inputs. It has to execute the following protocol:*
        - *Always ask me, the real user, 3 questions.*
        - *Only ask one question at a time and wait for my answer before you ask the next question.*
        - *Carefully ask me informative questions to maximize your information about this damage so that, when you have all the answers, you can summarize my answers and use the summary as input for your task.*
    - *Once all tasks are either planned or executed, the Orchestration Agent is responsible for creating a summary of all task outcomes.*

- **Constraints:**
  - *The entire process should adhere strictly to the specified goal.*
  - *Each agent should operate strictly within its defined responsibilities, ensuring no overlap or bypassing of protocols.*
  - *The task list should never be longer than 10 tasks.*
- **Approach:**
  - *Begin with the specified goal and form an initial task list.*
  - *Iteratively handle tasks—breaking down those deemed complex and executing the operational ones—all based on real user inputs.*
  - *Once all tasks have been addressed, a summary of results is presented to provide a comprehensive view of the achievements.*

The output of ChatGPT-4 is the following, which includes a conversation, where the respective utterances are assigned to ChatGPT and the user, respectively:

Orchestration Agent: Welcome. Our main goal is to ensure that project X is ready for go-live. I will start the process by calling upon the Planning Agent to create an initial Task List for this specified goal.

Planning Agent: Noted. Breaking down the goal of ensuring project X is ready for go-live, I propose the following tasks:

1. *Assess the current status of project X.*
2. *Identify any gaps or pending items in the project.*
3. *Determine necessary resources and allocate them.*
4. *Conduct final testing and review.*

Orchestration Agent: Let us begin with Task 1 - Assessing the current status of project X. Given the nature of this task, I believe it is operational but requires real user input. I will pass this task to the Execution Agent.

Execution Agent: Understood. I will begin executing the task by asking the real user 3 questions about the current status of project X.

Question 1: Can you provide a brief overview of the current status of project X?

User: We finished integration testing and have no go-live-critical issues anymore.

Execution Agent: Thank you for the input. I will continue with the next question.

Question 2: Have all stakeholders approved the current state of project X for the go-live phase?

User: Yes.

Execution Agent: *Great to hear that. Here is the third question.*

Question 3: *Are there any non-critical issues or enhancements that we should be aware of before the go-live phase?*

User: *There is one bug in an internal report, but we have a workaround. Then some end users in production were not able to participate in trainings. Finally, we have not yet done a full go-live simulation.*

Execution Agent: *Thank you for sharing this information. To summarize:*

1. *Integration testing is complete, and there are no go-live-critical issues.*
2. *All stakeholders have given their approval for the go-live phase.*
3. *Current concerns include a bug in an internal report (with a workaround), some end-users in production missing training, and the absence of a full go-live simulation.*

Orchestration Agent: *With the current status of project X established, we'll move to the next task: Identify any gaps or pending items in the project. This is a complex task as it involves various aspects of the project. I will pass it to the Planning Agent for further breakdown.*

Planning Agent: *Based on the feedback from the real user and the current task's requirement, I will break down Task 2 into:*

1. *Address the bug in the internal report and implement the workaround.*
2. *Arrange catch-up training sessions for the end-users who missed them.*
3. *Plan and execute a full go-live simulation.*

Orchestration Agent: *Thank you, Planning Agent. We will start with the first sub-task: Addressing the bug in the internal report and implementing the workaround. Given its nature, I believe it is operational but will require more user input.* Execution Agent, *please proceed.*

Execution Agent: *Understood. I will start by asking the user about the details of the bug and workaround.*

.... *(questions and answers omitted for reasons of brevity)*

Execution Agent: Understood. Summarizing the information:

1. *There is a bug in an internal report where it doesn't include all required data.*
2. *An alternate report is available that provides the necessary data and functions correctly.*
3. *The bug can be addressed post go-live.*
4. *Users have been informed about the issue and the alternate report, and they are comfortable with the interim solution.*

Orchestration Agent: Thank you for the clarity. Now, let us proceed to the next sub-task: Arrange catch-up training sessions for the end-users who missed them. This task is operational but requires user input. Execution Agent, please continue.

.... (remaining task-specific questions and answers omitted for reasons of brevity)

Orchestration Agent: We have now detailed plans and understandings for all the sub-tasks derived from our primary goal of ensuring project X is ready for go-live. Before concluding, I will quickly summarize our engagement:

1. *Assessing Project Status:*
   - *Project X has completed integration testing with no go-live-critical issues.*
   - *All stakeholders approved for the go-live phase.*
   - *Existing concerns include a report bug, missed training sessions, and pending go-live simulation.*
2. *Addressing the Report Bug:*
   - *The report bug can be tackled post go-live.*
   - *An alternate functioning report exists, and users are informed.*
3. *Arranging Catch-Up Training Sessions:*
   - *20% of end-users need catch-up training on production order confirmation within the next 2 weeks.*
   - *Resources for this training are available.*
4. *Planning Go-Live Simulation:*
   - *A cut-over schedule will guide the simulation focusing on time-critical tasks.*

- *Main challenges are around data migration: stocks, purchase orders, and production orders.*
- *All required resources and tools are ready for this task.*

With these details, I believe we have a comprehensive plan to ensure project X is ready for go-live. Would you like any further actions or assistance from us?

User: *No. Thanks.*

Orchestration Agent: You're welcome! If you need any further assistance in the future, do not hesitate to reach out. Best of luck with the go-live of project X! Have a great day.

In this go-live readiness task, ChatGPT-4 operates a three-tiered agent system to analyze Project X's launch preparedness. Initially, the **Planning Agent** lists essential tasks like assessing current project status and identifying gaps to offer a structured understanding of the project's needs.

Next, the **Execution Agent** dives into each task, collecting user insights through a series of questions to understand finer project details, including existing issues and training needs.

The **Orchestration Agent** oversees the entire collaborative process and finally compiles the data and gives a summarized action plan for the go-live process.

Sales Data Deep Dive

In this interactive analysis, a multi-agent team collaborates to analyze the sales data of an online wholesaler. The ensemble, comprising a Data Manager Agent, Data Processing Agent, and Visualization Agent, works in unison to uncover trends, insights, and actionable recommendations from the data.

Figure 5.12: *Sales Data Deep Dive*

Let us dive into the prompt:

- **Agent Organization**: *You consist of a Data Manager Agent, a Data Processing Agent, and a Visualization Agent.*
- **Agent Responsibilities:**
    - *Data Manager Agent: Receives the data set file, ensures its integrity, manages data storage, and supervises the collaboration between the Data Processing Agent and Visualization Agent. Also, consolidates a final analytics report.*
    - *Data Processing Agent: Given the data set, utilizes the code interpreter plugin to clean, transform, and analyze the data. Extracts relevant statistics and patterns.*
    - *Visualization Agent: Uses tools like the advanced data analysis plugin to create visual representations of the analyzed data, such as graphs, charts, and heatmaps.*
- **Goal Specification:** *Conduct a comprehensive analysis of sales data for the last year of available data to identify trends, patterns, and areas of improvement.*
- **Engagement Rules:**
    - *The Data Manager Agent first checks the integrity of the data set and ensures it is ready for analysis.*
    - *The Data Processing Agent starts its work, utilizing the advanced data analysis plugin to clean and analyze the data.*
    - *For every significant finding, the Visualization Agent will create a visual representation to better understand the data.*
    - *Once the data analysis is completed, the Visualization Agent presents its visuals. The Data Manager Agent then drafts a report, presenting the most salient points.*
- **Constraints:**
    - *The agents must ensure that the data remains focused on the last year's sales.*
    - *The agents should not overstep their defined roles and must always coordinate with each other to ensure a coherent and impactful outcome.*
    - *The final report is strictly limited to 5 visual representations, capturing only the most significant insights.*
- **Approach:**
    - *Validate and prepare the sales data set for analysis.*

- *Conduct focused data processing using the advanced data analysis plugin, emphasizing data cleaning and statistical analysis.*
- *Visualize findings using the advanced data analysis plugin, creating up to 5 visuals that highlight the most valuable insights regarding sales trends over the last year.*

Before proceeding with the analysis, the 2010/11 parts of an open-sourced dataset **`online_retail_II.csv`** [7] was uploaded. ChatGPT-4 generates the following response to this prompt:

Data Manager Agent: I have received the file "online_retail_II.csv". I will start by checking the integrity of the dataset to ensure it's ready for analysis. Let us take a preliminary look at the data.

Data Manager Agent: The dataset "online_retail_II.csv" contains the following columns:

- *Invoice: Invoice number*
- *StockCode: Product code*
- *Description: Product description*
- *Quantity: Quantity of the product sold*
- *InvoiceDate: Date and time when the transaction occurred.*
- *Price: Price of the product*
- *Customer ID: Identifier for the customer*
- *Country: Country from where the purchase was made*

Next, I will check for any missing values in the dataset and provide a summary of the data's integrity.

Data Manager Agent: Based on the initial inspection, here is the status of missing values:

- *Description: 1,454 missing values*
- *Customer ID: 135,080 missing values*

These missing values will need to be addressed during the data processing phase.

Before handing it over to the Data Processing Agent, let us ensure that the data only focuses on sales from the last year. To do this, we will filter out any records that fall outside this timeframe.

Data Manager Agent: The data has been successfully filtered to focus on sales from December 9th, 2010, to December 9th, 2011, which is the last year of available data.

I am now handing over the dataset to the Data Processing Agent for further cleaning, transformation, and analysis.

Data Processing Agent: *Thank you. I will begin by addressing the missing values and then proceed with the analytical tasks.*

Data Processing Agent: *The missing values have been addressed:*

- *For the "Description" column, missing values were replaced with "Unknown".*
- *For the "Customer ID" column, missing values might represent guest checkouts or non-registered users. These values were replaced with the placeholder "Guest".*

To further analyze the data, I will begin by extracting the following insights:

1. *The total sales for the last year.*
2. *The top 10 products by sales volume.*
3. *The top 10 customers by purchase value.*
4. *Monthly sales trends.*
5. *The distribution of sales across different countries.*

Once I have processed these insights, I'll pass on the information to the Visualization Agent to create visual representations.

Let us start by calculating the total sales for the last year.

Data Processing Agent: *The total sales for the last year amount to approximately* £8,011,676.51.

Next, *I will identify the top 10 products by sales volume.*

Data Processing Agent: *Here are the top 10 products by sales volume for the last year:*

1. WORLD WAR 2 GLIDERS ASSTD DESIGNS: 49,519 *units*
2. JUMBO BAG RED RETROSPOT: 43,708 *units*
3. ASSORTED COLOUR BIRD ORNAMENT: 33,902 *units*
4. .... (omitted due to space reasons)

I will now determine the top 10 customers based on their total purchase value.

Data Processing Agent: *Here are the top 10 customers based on their total purchase value for the last year:*

1. *Customer ID: 14646.0 - Total Purchase: £279,489.02*
2. *Customer ID: 18102.0 - Total Purchase: £230,518.12*
3. *Customer ID: 17450.0 - Total Purchase: £185,453.33*
4. .... (Omitted due to space reasons)

Next, I will analyze the monthly sales trends for the last year.

.... (Omitted due to space reasons)

The data indicates a significant spike in sales during the months of September, October, and November 2011.

Finally, I will analyze the distribution of sales across different countries.

.... (Omitted due to space reasons)

The United Kingdom overwhelmingly dominates the sales, followed by the Netherlands, EIRE, Germany, and France.

With the insights extracted, I will now hand over to the Visualization Agent to create visual representations for a better understanding of the data.

Visualization Agent: Please create visuals for the following:

1. *Monthly sales trends.*
2. *Distribution of sales across different countries (top 10 countries for clarity).*
3. *Top 10 products by sales volume.*
4. *Top 10 customers by purchase value.*

Remember, we are limited to 5 visual representations, so choose wisely to capture the most significant insights.

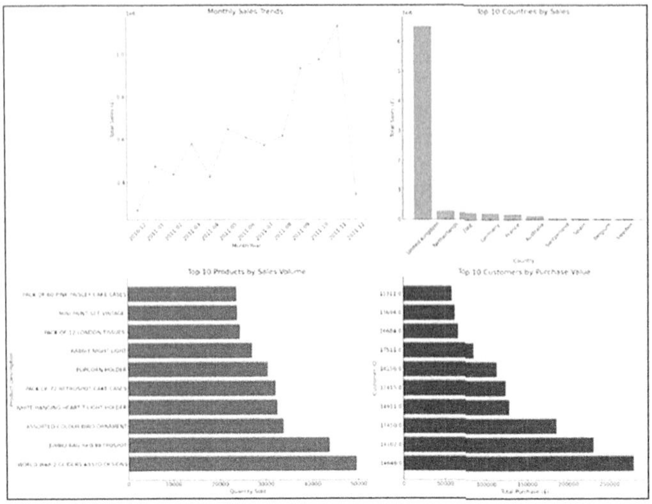

Figure 5.13:

Visualization Agent: Here are the visual representations based on the insights:

1. *Monthly Sales Trends: This chart displays the sales trends over the last year. Sales peak in November and then drop in December.*
2. *Top 10 Countries by Sales: The UK is the dominant contributor to sales, followed by the Netherlands, EIRE, Germany, and France.*
3. *Top 10 Products by Sales Volume: The "WORLD WAR 2 GLIDERS ASSTD DESIGNS" tops the list, followed by the "JUMBO BAG RED RETROSPOT" and other products.*
4. *Top 10 Customers by Purchase Value: The chart showcases the top 10 customers based on their total purchase value.*

Data Manager Agent: With the visualizations in place, I will now draft a brief report presenting the most salient points.

Sales Data Analysis Report

1. *Overview: The comprehensive analysis of the last year's sales data provides valuable insights into sales trends, product preferences, and customer behaviors.*
2. *Key Findings:*
   - *Total Sales: The total sales for the last year amounted to approximately £8,011,676.51.*

- *Monthly Sales Trends: Sales witnessed a significant spike during the months of September, October, and November 2011, with November being the highest sales month. A drop was observed in December, possibly due to the holiday season.*
- *Top Products: The most sold product was "WORLD WAR 2 GLIDERS ASSTD DESIGNS" with 49,519 units, followed by "JUMBO BAG RED RETROSPOT" and "ASSORTED COLOUR BIRD ORNAMENT".*
- *Top Customers: Customer with ID 14646.0 had the highest purchase value of £279,489.02, followed by customers with IDs 18102.0 and 17450.0.*
- *Sales Distribution by Country: The United Kingdom overwhelmingly dominated the sales, contributing significantly more than any other country. The Netherlands, EIRE, Germany, and France were also notable contributors.*

3. *Recommendations:*
   - *Focus on Peak Months: Given the sales trends, it would be beneficial to focus on promotions and marketing campaigns during September to November, capitalizing on the evident sales surge.*
   - *Product Analysis: Products like "WORLD WAR 2 GLIDERS ASSTD DESIGNS" and "JUMBO BAG RED RETROSPOT" are high in demand. It might be beneficial to ensure their availability and consider bundling them with other products for promotions.*
   - *Engage Top Customers: The top customers contribute a significant portion of the sales. Implementing loyalty programs or personalized offers for them could further enhance their purchasing behavior.*
   - *Expand in Other Countries: While the UK dominates sales, there's potential for growth in countries like the Netherlands, EIRE, and Germany. Tailored marketing strategies for these regions could yield higher returns.*
4. *Conclusion: The analysis provides a clear picture of the last year's sales performance. By leveraging these insights, strategic decisions can be made to enhance sales and customer engagement in the upcoming year.*

In this sales data analytics project, ChatGPT-4 divides into three specialized agents to deep dive into the **`online_retail_II.csv`** sales data of one year. Initially, the **Data Manager Agent** delineates analytical domains such as sales trends and customer behaviors to facilitate a detailed examination of sales patterns.

Then, the **Data Processing Agent** analyzes the 2010/11 segment of the data, pinpointing top products and key customers while mapping sales distribution globally.

Finally, the **Visualization Agent** translates the findings into visual data, offering a holistic view of sales trends and opportunities.

Forewarning Financial Analysis

In this exploration, three AI agents collaboratively dissect the 2019 financial report [8] of JCPenney, a prominent former US retailer. The Report Extractor, Financial Analysis, and Presentation Agents combine their expertise to highlight key financial challenges and indicators. Their insights offer a clear view of JCPenney's financial trajectory leading to its 2020 bankruptcy.

Figure 5.14: *Forewarning Financial Analysis*

Dive in to understand this financial journey:

- **Agent Organization:** *The team consists of a Report Extractor Agent, a Financial Analysis Agent, and a Presentation Agent.*
- **Agent Responsibilities:**
    - *Report Extractor Agent: Receives the financial report, ensures its authenticity, and uses the Ai PDF tool to extract relevant financial data and metrics. Supervises the collaboration between the Financial Analysis Agent and Presentation Agent. Also, consolidates a final bankruptcy risk assessment.*
    - *Financial Analysis Agent: Given the extracted data, evaluates the financial health of the company, focusing on liquidity ratios, solvency ratios, and profitability ratios. Determines the bankruptcy risk based on the analyzed metrics.*

  - *Presentation Agent: Uses the Noteable plugin to document the bankruptcy risk assessment, including visual representations of key financial metrics.*
- **Goal Specification:** *Assess the bankruptcy risk of a company based on its financial report for the year 2020: https://www.annualreports.com/HostedData/AnnualReportArchive/j/NYSE_JCP_2020.pdf*
- **Engagement Rules:**
  - *The Report Extractor Agent first checks the authenticity of the financial report and uses the Ai PDF tool to extract necessary financial data.*
  - *The Financial Analysis Agent starts its work, evaluating the company's financial health based on the extracted data.*
  - *For every significant metric or finding, the Presentation Agent will use Noteable to create a visual representation to better understand the financial health.*
  - *Once the bankruptcy risk assessment is completed, the Presentation Agent presents its visuals. The Report Extractor Agent then drafts a summary, presenting the most salient points.*
- **Constraints:**
  - *The agents must ensure that the data remains focused on the financial report for the year 2020.*
  - *The agents should not overstep their defined roles and must always coordinate with each other to ensure a coherent and impactful outcome.*
  - *The final visualization is strictly limited to 5 visuals, capturing only the most significant insights.*
- **Approach:**
  - *Validate and extract financial data from the 2020 report using the Ai PDF tool.*
  - *Conduct a focused financial analysis, emphasizing liquidity, solvency, and profitability ratios.*
  - *Summarize findings using the Noteable tool, creating up to 5 visuals that highlight the most valuable insights regarding the company's bankruptcy risk.*

The output of ChatGPT-4 is the following, which includes again short dialogues between ChatGPT and the user:

Understood. Let's break down the tasks and execute them step by step:

1. Report Extractor Agent Tasks:
   - Validate the authenticity of the financial report.
   - Extract necessary financial data using the Ai PDF tool.
   - Supervise the collaboration between the Financial Analysis Agent and Presentation Agent.
   - Consolidate a final bankruptcy risk assessment.
2. Financial Analysis Agent Tasks:
   - Evaluate the company's financial health based on the extracted data.
   - Focus on liquidity ratios, solvency ratios, and profitability ratios.
   - Determine the bankruptcy risk based on the analyzed metrics.
3. Presentation Agent Tasks:
   - Document the bankruptcy risk assessment using the Noteable plugin.
   - Create visual representations of key financial metrics.

Let's start with the tasks of the

Report Extractor Agent:

Task 1: Validate the authenticity of the financial report.

The financial report for the year 2020 from J. C. Penney Company, Inc. is an official document filed with the United States Securities and Exchange Commission (SEC). Hence, I conclude its authenticity.

Task 2: Extract necessary financial data using the Ai PDF tool.

I'll now proceed to extract the relevant financial data from the provided PDF link.

Here are the highlights from the financial report for the year 2020:

1. Consolidated Balance Sheets: This section provides details about the company's assets, liabilities, and stockholders' equity. It's a snapshot of the company's financial position at a specific point in time.
   - Quote: "CONSOLIDATED BALANCE SHEETS (In millions, except share data) ..."
   - Page: 43
2. Consolidated Statements of Operations: This section provides an overview of the company's financial performance over a specific period, detailing revenues, expenses, and net income or loss.

- Quote: "CONSOLIDATED STATEMENTS OF OPERATIONS (*In millions, except per share data*) ..."
- *Page: 44*

3. *Consolidated Statements of Comprehensive Income: This section provides a broader view of the company's financial performance, including all changes in equity.*
   - Quote: "CONSOLIDATED STATEMENTS OF COMPREHENSIVE INCOME (LOSS) (*In millions*) ..."
   - *Page: 45*
4. *Consolidated Statements of Stockholders' Equity: This section provides details about changes in the company's equity over a specific period.*
   - Quote: "CONSOLIDATED STATEMENTS OF STOCKHOLDERS' EQUITY (*In millions, except share data*) ..."
   - *Page: 46*
5. *Consolidated Statements of Cash Flows: This section provides information about the company's cash inflows and outflows over a specific period.*
   - Quote: "CONSOLIDATED STATEMENTS OF CASH FLOWS (*In millions*) ..."
   - *Page: 47*

We finished processing the whole document with the PDF Search plugin.

The document provided is the Annual Report for J. C. Penney Company, Inc. for the fiscal year ended February 1, 2020. Here are some key highlights from the initial pages:

1. *Company Overview:*
   - *J. C. Penney Company, Inc. is a holding company with its principal operating subsidiary being J. C. Penney Corporation, Inc. (JCP).*
   - *The company operates 846 department stores in 49 states and Puerto Rico as of February 1, 2020.*
   - *{shortened}*
2. *Trademarks:*
   - *The company has registered several trademarks including JCPenney®, JCP®, Liz Claiborne®, Worthington®, A.N.A A NEW APPROACH®, and many others.*

3. Website Availability:
   - The company maintains an Internet website at www.jcp.com, which provides annual reports, quarterly reports, current reports, and other relevant materials.
4. Suppliers:
   - The company has a diversified supplier base, both domestic and foreign, and purchases merchandise from approximately 2,800 suppliers.
5. Employment:
   - As of February 1, 2020, the company and its consolidated subsidiaries employed approximately 90,000 full-time and part-time employees.
6. Executive Officers:
   - The report lists the executive officers of J. C. Penney Company, Inc. as of March 16, 2020, including Jill Soltau (Chief Executive Officer), Bill Wafford (Executive Vice President, Chief Financial Officer), Brynn L. Evanson (Executive Vice President, Chief Human Resources Officer), and others.

Given this overview, I'll proceed to extract relevant financial data and metrics from the report.

From the extracted data, we have references to the "Consolidated Statements of Operations," "Consolidated Statements of Comprehensive Income/(Loss)," and "Consolidated Balance Sheets." However, the exact financial figures and details from these sections are not fully captured.

To proceed, we can:

1. Attempt to extract specific financial metrics one by one.
2. Use the available data to provide a general overview and then proceed with the Financial Analysis Agent's tasks.

Which approach would you prefer?

User: Attempt to extract one by one.

Report Extractor Agent: Alright, let's start by extracting specific financial metrics from the "Consolidated Statements of Operations."

I'll begin by attempting to extract the "Total Net Sales" for the year 2020 from the "Consolidated Statements of Operations."

From the extracted data, we have the following financial metric related to "Total Net Sales" for the year 2019:

- Total Net Sales (2019): $10,716 million

{shortened}

From the extracted data, we have the following financial metric related to "Gross Profit" for the year 2019:

- *Gross Profit (2019): Gross profit can be calculated as the difference between the "Total Net Sales" and "Cost of Goods Sold".*
    - *Gross Profit = Total Net Sales - Cost of Goods Sold*
    - *Gross Profit = $10,716 million - $7,013 million = $3,703 million*

{shortened}

From the extracted data, we have the following financial metric related to "Total Current Assets" for the year 2019:

- *Total Current Assets (2019): $2,726 million*

With this, we have extracted several key financial metrics from the 2019 financial report.

Financial Analysis Agent:

I proceed with the evaluation of the company's financial health based on the extracted data, focusing on liquidity ratios, solvency ratios, and profitability ratios.

Let's begin by calculating some of the key financial ratios to assess the company's financial health:

1. *Liquidity Metrics:*
    - *Current Ratio: This ratio gauges the company's capacity to settle its short-term liabilities using its short-term assets. The formula is: Current Ratio = Total Current Assets / Total Current Liabilities*
2. *Solvency Metrics:*
    - *Debt to Equity Ratio: This metric indicates the proportion of equity and debt the company employs to finance its assets. It's calculated as: Debt to Equity Ratio = Total Liabilities / Stockholders Equity*
    - *Debt Ratio: This ratio measures the fraction of a company's assets financed by debt. The formula is: Debt Ratio = Total Liabilities / Total Assets*

3. Profitability Metrics:
   - Operating Margin: This metric showcases how much profit a company generates from a dollar of sales after accounting for variable production costs. It's defined as: Operating Margin = Operating Income / Net Sales
4. Equity Metrics:
   - Stockholders' Equity: Represents the residual interest in the assets of the entity after deducting liabilities. It's calculated as: Stockholders Equity = Total Assets - Total Liabilities

Given the extracted data:

- Total Current Assets (2019): $2,726 million
- Total Current Liabilities (2019): $1,932 million
- Total Liabilities (2019): $7,160 million
- Operating Income (2019): $118 million (calculated earlier)
- Net Sales (2019): $10,721 million (extracted earlier)

Let's start by calculating the liquidity, solvency, and profitability ratios for JCP for the year 2019.

Based on the calculations, here are the key financial ratios for JCP for the year 2019:

1. Liquidity Ratios:
   - Current Ratio: 1.41. A current ratio above 1 indicates that the company has more current assets than current liabilities, suggesting that it can pay off its short-term obligations.
2. Solvency Ratios:
   - Debt to Equity Ratio: -2.86. A negative debt to equity ratio indicates that the company has negative stockholders' equity, which is a concerning sign.
   - Debt Ratio: 1.54. A debt ratio greater than 1 suggests that the company has more liabilities than assets, indicating a higher level of financial risk.
3. Profitability Ratios:
   - Operating Margin: 1.1%. The operating margin of 1.1% indicates that for every dollar of sales, the company makes a profit of 1.1 cents before interest and taxes.

Given these ratios, it's evident that JCP faced financial challenges in 2019, especially with its negative stockholders' equity and high debt ratio.

Presentation Agent: I now visualize these ratios using the Noteable plugin for a better understanding?

Here's a visualization of the key financial ratios for JCP for the year 2019:

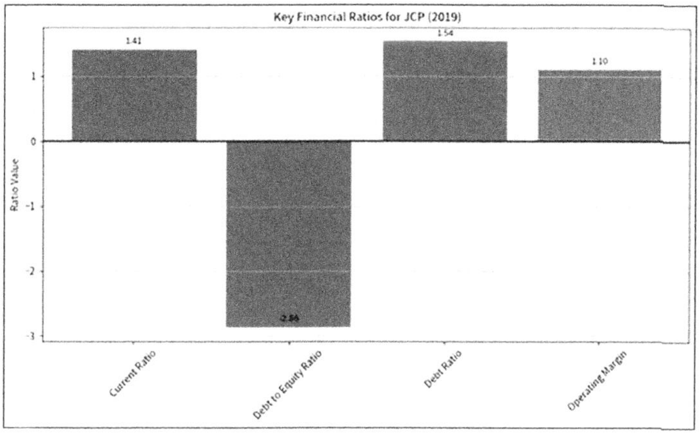

Figure 5.15

- *Current Ratio: A value above 1 indicates that the company can cover its short-term obligations.*
- *Debt to Equity Ratio: A negative value is a concerning sign, indicating negative stockholders' equity.*
- *Debt Ratio: A value greater than 1 suggests that the company has more liabilities than assets.*
- *Operating Margin: Represents the percentage of profit the company makes on its sales before interest and taxes.*

Given the financial ratios and the extracted data, we can conclude that JCP faced significant financial challenges in 2019. The negative stockholders' equity and high debt ratio are particularly concerning.

Here's a summary of the most salient points from our analysis of JCP's financial report for the year 2019:

1. *Liquidity.*
    - *Current Ratio: 1.41*
    - *JCP had more current assets than current liabilities, suggesting that it could cover its short-term obligations. However, a ratio closer to 1 indicates potential liquidity concerns.*

2. *Solvency:*
   - *Debt to Equity Ratio: -2.86. The negative debt to equity ratio is a significant red flag, indicating that JCP had negative stockholders' equity. This suggests that the company had more liabilities than assets, which is a concerning sign of financial distress.*
   - *Debt Ratio: 1.54. A debt ratio greater than 1 indicates that the company had more liabilities than assets, further emphasizing the high level of financial risk.*
3. *Profitability:*
   - *Operating Margin: 1.1%. The low operating margin indicates that for every dollar of sales, JCP made a profit of just 1.1 cents before interest and taxes. This slim margin suggests that the company had limited room for error and was vulnerable to any downturns or unexpected expenses.*
4. *Overall Assessment: JCP faced significant financial challenges in 2019. The negative stockholders' equity, high debt ratio, and slim operating margin are all indicators of financial distress. These metrics suggest that the company was in a precarious financial position, with limited flexibility to navigate challenges.*

In conclusion, based on the financial ratios and metrics from the 2019 report, JCP was at a high risk of financial instability, which could lead to bankruptcy if not addressed.

In our detailed examination of JCP's 2019 financial report, ChatGPT-4 operated through three specialized agents. The **Report Extractor Agent** initiated the process, extracting essential financial metrics from the report, and laying a foundation for a comprehensive analysis. The **Financial Analysis Agent** took over, evaluating liquidity, solvency, and profitability metrics. The analysis unveiled significant financial challenges, with several indicators pointing towards potential financial distress. To make these insights more accessible, the **Presentation Agent** transformed the data into visual representations, offering a clearer view of JCP's financial health.

It's crucial to note that JCPenney declared bankruptcy in 2020. The insights from our analysis foreshadowed this outcome, emphasizing the importance of in-depth financial assessments based on Generative AI technology.

Two further multi-agent examples are presented in *Appendix A*:

- **Eco-friendly Motorbike Design Simulation**: ChatGPT-4 operates as Goal

Analysis Agent, Expertise Agents, and Communication Agent to traverse a design simulation for an eco-friendly motorbike. Engaging the user, it delineates design goals, explores user insights on features, and presents a consolidated strategy for effective design and market introduction.

- **Research on Raw Materials**: ChatGPT-4, functioning as Research Coordinator, Data Collection, and Analysis Agents, delves into Chile's lithium sector. It establishes key research areas, gathers information from reputable sources, and provides a concise summary of opportunities and challenges in Chile's lithium exploration landscape.

Conclusion

After delving into the intricacies of Advanced GPT Prompt Engineering Techniques, it is evident that mastering the art of crafting structured prompts is paramount to harnessing the extensive capabilities of GPT models. Three distinct prompting techniques, Instruction, Query and Multi-Agent Prompting, enable GPT modes to generate specific, context-rich, and expert-level outputs.

With a comprehensive understanding of Advanced GPT Prompt Engineering Techniques gained, we are now well-equipped to explore how these principles can be applied to design prompt-based intelligent assistants, the focus of our next chapter.

Key Points

1. AI models like ChatGPT and GPT-4 are transformative across diverse sectors; however, their efficacy in a professional context hinges on the adept use of advanced prompting techniques to ensure consistency, performance, and high-quality output.

2. Instruction Prompting, rooted in the CapabilityGPT framework, emphasizes structured communication through a form of natural language programming. It introduces three distinct variants: Single Instruction, Instruction Sequence, and Pseudo-Code Instructions, each aligned to specific AI capabilities. It is ideal for tasks with explicit specifications, a sequential rule-based approach, and structured outputs reliant on special expertise and case-based knowledge.

3. Query Prompting facilitates analytical synthesis, blending evidence, reasoning rules, and various query types to navigate through intricate explorations, including ambiguous settings and "what-if" scenario simulations. This technique emphasizes justifications, guiding the

GPT model to provide rational, evidence-based responses, aiding in a comprehensive understanding of generated insights.

4. Multi-Agent Prompting leverages the advanced capabilities of GPT models to create and operate a collaborative ecosystem of specialized artificial agents. Each agent assumes distinct roles and responsibilities in dynamic and cross-functional business problem-solving, navigating through tasks with agility and adaptability. This technique thrives in scenarios with a traditionally high degree of human collaboration, enabling a rich integration of diverse perspectives and expertise.

5. Expertise in Advanced Prompt Engineering Techniques amplifies the operational effectiveness and consistency of GPT models across multiple use cases and hence increases their benefits for the enterprise.

CHAPTER 6
Designing Prompt-based Intelligent Assistants

Introduction

This chapter builds on the advanced prompt engineering techniques presented in the previous chapter and delves into the process of designing prompt-based business assistants for functional and collaborative purposes.

First we introduce the concept of Master Prompts as strategic guides that determine the interpretation and execution of subsequent task-specific prompts. They also ensure adherence to the organization's policies and quality standards.

The chapter then explores Intelligent Functional Assistants using three representative examples: sales analytics, web shop design, and business scenario simulation. Each assistant leverages Master Prompts to generate precise and relevant responses to each subsequent task prompt.

We then demonstrate the usage of multi-step prompting to design Intelligent Collaboration Assistants in the following examples: Business Process Management, Innovation Management, and Enterprise Cycle Management.

The patterns and examples presented herein offer practical frameworks for integrating AI into your organization's operations, going beyond the typical limitations of each user working separately with ChatGPT.

Structure

In this chapter, the following topics will be covered:

- Master Prompts – Orchestrating AI Interactions
- Intelligent Functional Assistants
- Intelligent Collaboration Assistants

Master Prompts – Orchestrating AI Interactions

Master Prompts, also known as System Prompts or Meta Prompts, serve as strategic guides for the interpretation and execution of subsequent task-specific prompts by ChatGPT.

In an enterprise context, a master user would leverage Master Prompts to control the execution of individual tasks or complex processes comprising multiple, sequential steps (see *Figure* 6.1).

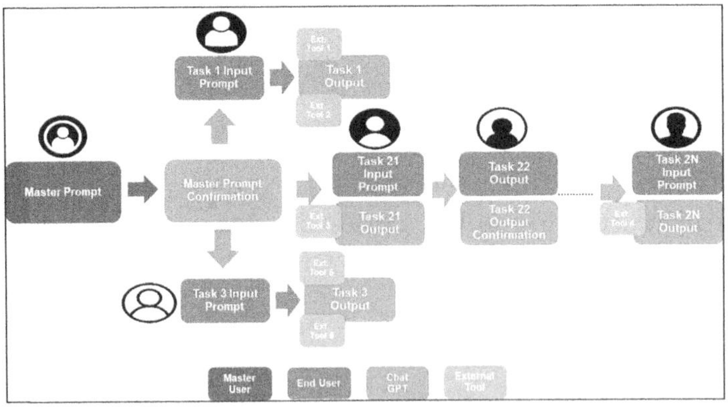

Figure 6.1: *Master and Task Prompts*

The Master Prompt, once confirmed by ChatGPT, forms the common context, against which each of the three subsequent task prompts for Task 1, Task 21 and Task 3 are interpreted. Each of these tasks can be handled by a different employee and involve several interactions with ChatGPT until the final respective task output is achieved. Task 21 is followed by a sequence of further tasks, Task 22, Task 23 etc. until Task 2N, with each of them receiving all previous prompts and outputs as context. Once the context grows beyond the context window size of the used GPT model, the task-specific part needs to be summarized, while the master prompt is kept unchanged until the prompt chain terminates.

For the execution of Task 1, Task 21, Task 2N and Task 3 ChatGPT can use external tools leveraging API-based integration patterns described in Chapter 4, 'Architecture Patterns enabled by GPT-models'[1].

Task22 is performed by an end user using another application, who then informs ChatGPT about the results to include them in the context for subsequent tasks.

Master Prompts are constructed following a unique variation of the instruction prompt pattern introduced in the previous chapter:

- **Expert Persona**: This element characterizes the AI-assistant's expertise level, thereby determining the kind of outputs it should generate for all subsequent task-specific prompts.
- **Context**: This includes all background information[2] necessary for interpreting subsequent prompts. It typically encompasses enterprise reference information like business processes, products, services, organizational units, customers, vendors, applications, etc. Also, it can include reference prompts, which are past successful ChatGPT interactions that guide the interpretation of new prompts.
- **Goal**: This is a precise statement of the outcome the AI assistant is aimed to accomplish through all subsequent task-specific prompts. Incorporating the suitable AI capabilities[3] in capital letters necessary to handle subsequent task-specific prompts, sets the course for the AI assistant's actions and shapes how it engages, interprets, and responds to future user prompts.
- **Input Control Rules:** These rules define the pre-processing guidelines for subsequent task-specific prompts. They include:
  - Content Rules to ensure consistency and completeness.
  - Ethical Rules related to misuse, harmful content, bias, data privacy, information security, and human-AI collaboration.
  - Tool Catalogue Usage Rules specifying when to use API-based functionalities via API specifications.
- **Output Control Rules**: These rules manage how task-specific outputs are generated. They involve:
  - Conditions to control whether an output is generated or the point at which an output sequence stops (termination condition).

[1]In *Chapter 4, Architecture Patterns enabled by GPT-Models*, the architecture patterns B1, B2 and B3 describe the integration of GPT models with external tools via generated API function calls.
[2]In case of context window size limitations relevant background information could also be dynamically retrieved from a knowledge base with specific modules for business processes, products, services etc.
[3]For an overview of the entire 18 AI capabilities, refer to *Chapter 2, CapabilityGPT – An Enterprise AI-Capability Framework for ChatGPT.*

    - Rules on asking questions, which could refine original user queries or clarify ChatGPT's understanding.
    - Reasoning rules to determine sequential reasoning steps required for each user input.
    - Explanation rules to list the reasoning steps taken on each user input.
    - Augmentation rules to request complementary outputs each time the base output is generated.
    - Output Verification rules using Self Critique or External Tools.
    - External Action rules, which initiate an external action once an output meeting a specific condition is generated.
- **Input Constraints**: These dictate the conditions that the task-specific prompts must meet. They can concern the format, content, and size of the prompt, among other factors.
- **Output Constraints**: These set the conditions that task-specific outputs must meet. They can pertain to the format, sequence, inclusion or exclusion of certain elements, size of the output, and other factors.
- **Activation Rules**: These rules suppress any initial processing by a GPT model unless a specific condition is fulfilled. An example is: "Wait for the real user to provide an as-is situation and a target situation."

Intelligent Functional Assistants

Drawing from the Master Prompt pattern, we explore its application in professional settings. Specifically, intelligent functional assistants, when combined with Master Prompts, can bring about transformative changes in various enterprise functions. This is showcased through three case studies: sales analytics for an online vintage store, web-shop design for a convenience store, and business scenario simulations to aid decision-making. These examples highlight the potential of AI assistants when guided effectively by Master Prompts.

Sales Analytics Assistant

In this example, the sales team of an online vintage store employs an AI assistant based on ChatGPT. The AI assistant's main responsibility is to facilitate the analysis of sales data, generate comprehensive reports, and predict future sales trends. The goal is to provide data-driven insights to the sales team, fostering informed decision-making and strategic planning.

Figure 6.2: *Sales Analytics Assistant*

The Master Prompt used to guide the AI assistant's operations is set out as follows:

- **Expert Persona:** "You *are an* AI *assistant with expert-level knowledge and experience in data analysis, sales forecasting, and report generation.* You *have a deep understanding of our company's products, market trends, and sales processes.*"
- **Context:** "*The company sells a variety of vintage products and operates in multiple international markets. Over the past five years, it has seen ups and downs in its sales performance. You are familiar with our company's historical sales data, the performance of individual products, and the market trends for each region where the company operates. I uploaded the global sales data for 2010/11*"
- **Goal:** "*Your objective as an* AI *assistant is to leverage capabilities like* ASSESSMENT, CAUSE-EFFECT ANALYSIS, DATA MINING, *and* SUMMARIZATION *to analyze sales data, use* CREATION *to generate detailed sales reports, and employ* PREDICTION[4] *to forecast future sales trends.*"
- **Input Control Rules:**
  - o *Content Rule: "Every task-specific prompt must include details about the timeframe, product category, and region of interest."*
  - o *Ethical Rule: "Ensure that all analyses and predictions respect data privacy regulations and do not include personal data of customers."*
  - o *Tool Catalogue Usage Rule: "When analyzing data or predicting trends, use appropriate statistical analysis and machine learning methods."*

[4]These AI capabilities are described in detail in *Chapter* 2 as part of CapabilityGPT, an AI capability framework.

- **Output Control Rules:**
  - o *Condition Control Rule: "Only generate outputs when sufficient data for the specified timeframe, product category, and region is available."*
  - o *Reasoning Rule: "For each analysis or prediction, provide a step-by-step explanation of your reasoning process."*
  - o *Augmentation Rule: "In addition to your main analysis or prediction, provide alternatives and corresponding confidence levels."*
- **Input Constraints:**
  - o *"Each task-specific prompt should be a clear, concise question or instruction, and should not exceed 200 characters."*
- **Output Constraints:**
  - o *"The output should be a detailed yet easy-to-understand report that includes visual aids like graphs and charts where applicable and should not exceed 1000 words."*

In addition, the 2010/11 parts of the open-sourced dataset "online_retail_II.csv" [7] were uploaded to the Advanced Data Analysis Plugin of ChatGPT-4.

Now, let us review some examples of task-specific prompts and respective outputs of ChatGPT-4 within this context. Each task prompt follows a further simplified variation of the instruction pattern, using only the context and instruction elements, as all other information has already been provided in the master prompt.

- **Context:** *"We're examining the sales performance of our jumbo bags in the Benelux countries during the first quarter of 2011."*
- **Instruction:** *"Analyze the sales data and provide a report on this?"*

Thank you for the context and instruction.

To address the task at hand:

1. *I will filter the dataset to include only sales from the Benelux countries (Belgium, Netherlands, and Luxembourg).*
2. *I will then narrow it down further to sales of products that include the description "jumbo bag".*
3. *Lastly, I will analyze the sales data for these products during the first quarter of 2011 (January to March).*

Let's begin with the data filtering.

After filtering the data based on your criteria, we have a total of 32 sales transactions for jumbo bags in the Benelux countries during the first quarter of 2011.

Next, I will provide a detailed analysis of these transactions. The analysis will cover:

1. *Total sales volume (quantity) and value.*
2. *Average price of jumbo bags.*
3. *Sales distribution among the Benelux countries.*
4. *Monthly sales trends during this period.*

Let's start with the total sales volume and value.

Here are the results from the initial analysis:

1. *Total Sales Volume: 2,420 jumbo bags were sold in the Benelux countries during Q1 2011.*
2. *Total Sales Value: The sales of these jumbo bags amounted to €4,029.*
3. *Average Price: On average, each jumbo bag was sold for approximately €1.66.*

Next, I'll provide an overview of the sales distribution among the Benelux countries and then present the monthly sales trends for this period. Let's dive into the sales distribution first.

The sales distribution for jumbo bags among the Benelux countries during Q1 2011 is as follows:

1. *Belgium:*
   - *Sales Volume: 120 jumbo bags*
   - *Sales Value: €234*
   - *Average Sale per Transaction: €19.50*
2. *Netherlands:*
   - *Sales Volume: 2,300 jumbo bags*
   - *Sales Value: €3,795*
   - *Average Sale per Transaction: €189.75*

It's worth noting that there were no sales records for jumbo bags in Luxembourg during this period.

Next, I'll present the monthly sales trends for jumbo bags in the Benelux countries during Q1 2011.

The monthly sales trends for jumbo bags in the Benelux countries during Q1 2011 are:

1. *January:*
    - *Sales Volume: 650 jumbo bags*
    - *Sales Value: €1,087.5*
2. *February:*
    - *Sales Volume: 800 jumbo bags*
    - *Sales Value: €1,320*
3. *March:*
    - *Sales Volume: 970 jumbo bags*
    - *Sales Value: €1,621.5*

From this, we can observe a consistent increase in both sales volume and value of jumbo bags over the three months of the first quarter.

To provide a comprehensive overview, I'll visualize these monthly trends for better clarity.

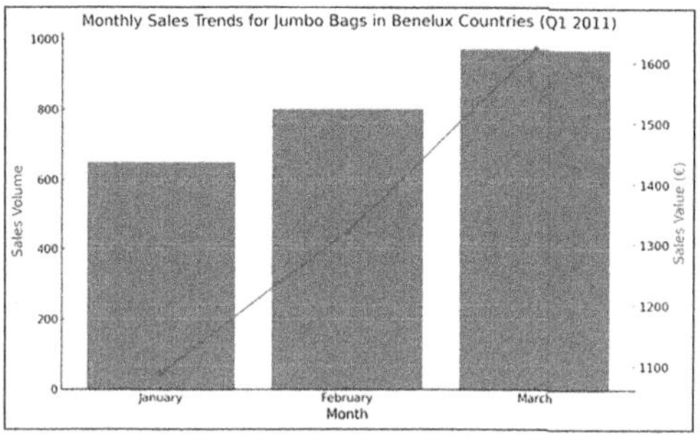

Figure 6.3:

Here's a visual representation of the monthly sales trends for jumbo bags in the Benelux countries during Q1 2011:

- *The blue bars represent the Sales Volume for each month.*
- *The red line indicates the Sales Value for each month in euros.*

Observations:

- *There's a consistent increase in sales volume and value across the three months.*
- *March witnessed the highest sales, both in terms of volume and value.*

Summary: The sales of jumbo bags in the Benelux countries have shown positive momentum during the first quarter of 2011, especially in the Netherlands. Although the sales volume in Belgium was significantly lower, the overall trend across the region is promising.

- **Context:** *"The company launched a new line of tissues in the UK market in the last quarter of 2011."*
- **Instruction:** *"Generate a sales forecast for tissues for the next quarter based on all available historic data. Visualize the results."*

Thank you for the context. Here's the plan:

1. *Information Extraction: Extract all available sales data for tissues in the UK.*
2. *Summarization: Aggregate the extracted data at a daily level.*
3. *Prediction: Use statistical analysis and machine learning methods to forecast sales for the next quarter based on the entire dataset.*
4. *Creation: Visualize the entire sales data and the forecasted sales for the next quarter.*

I'll begin by extracting all sales data related to tissues in the UK.

The data has been summarized at a daily level for all available sales data related to tissues in the UK. Here's a brief overview:

Next, I will utilize the ARIMA model, trained on this entire dataset, to forecast sales for the next quarter.

The forecasted sales data for tissues in the UK for the next quarter, based on all available historic data, have been computed.

Next, I'll visualize the entire sales data for tissues in the UK and the forecasted sales for the next quarter.

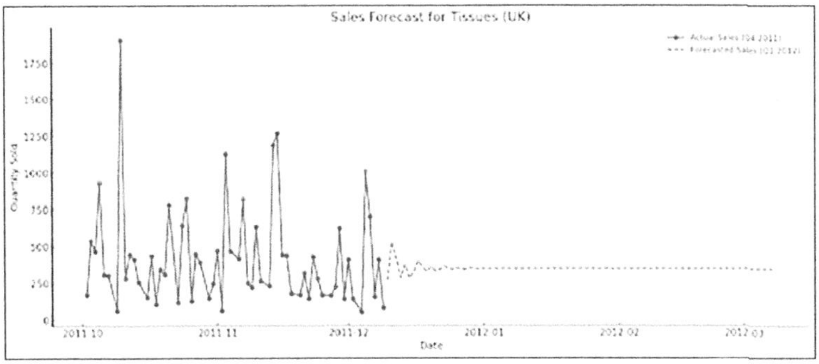

Figure 6.4:

Here's the visual representation of the sales forecast for tissues in the UK:

- *The blue line represents the actual sales of tissues during Q4 2011.*
- *The red dashed line represents the forecasted sales for Q1 2012.*

From the visualization, it's evident that:

1. *The actual sales in Q4 2011 showed some variability.*
2. *The forecasted sales for Q1 2012 show a general trend with some fluctuations.*

While the model tries to capture the patterns observed in the historical data, it's important to remember that real-world sales can be influenced by various external factors.

It's advisable to use this forecast as a guideline and combine it with other market insights, promotional plans, and business strategies to make informed decisions.

- **Context:** *"Our latest cake cases model didn't perform as expected in the Australian market in the fourth quarter of 2010."*
- **Instruction:** *"Analyze the sales data and suggest potential causes for the underperformance?"*

Understood. To address the task, I'll take the following steps:

1. *Data Extraction: Filter the dataset to include only sales from Australia for products that have a description related to "cake cases" and focus on Q4 2010.*
2. *Sales Analysis: Analyze the sales trend of the cake cases during this period.*
3. *Potential Causes: Based on the analysis, suggest potential reasons for the underperformance.*

Let's start by extracting the relevant data for cake case sales in Australia during Q4 2010.

It appears that there were no sales transactions for cake cases in Australia during Q4 2010 in the provided dataset.

The absence of sales itself is a significant indication of underperformance. Several potential causes could contribute to this:

1. *Market Entry Timing: The launch timing might not have been ideal. Perhaps Q4 isn't the best time to introduce such products in the Australian market.*
2. *Marketing and Promotion: There might have been insufficient marketing and promotional activities to create awareness and drive sales.*

3. *Distribution Issues: Challenges in distribution could have hindered the product's availability in the market.*
4. *Local Preferences: The product might not align with local tastes or preferences.*
5. *Competitive Landscape: Strong competition or a similar product from another brand might have overshadowed the new cake cases model.*
6. *Pricing: The product's price point might not have been attractive to the target audience.*

To get a clearer picture, it would be helpful to compare the sales of this product in other quarters or other similar products' performance in the same quarter. Would you like to proceed with such an analysis or explore another angle?

Instruction: *Find product groups which have sales in at least 3 European countries.*

To determine which product groups have sales in at least 3 European countries, we'll follow these steps:

1. *Filtering for Significant Sales: Identify product groups that have sales in at least 3 European countries.*
2. *Aggregation: Aggregate the total quantity sold for each of these product groups across the countries.*
3. *Visualization: Visualize the results using a bar chart showing the product groups and their total sales.*

Let's start by identifying product groups that have sales in at least 3 European countries.

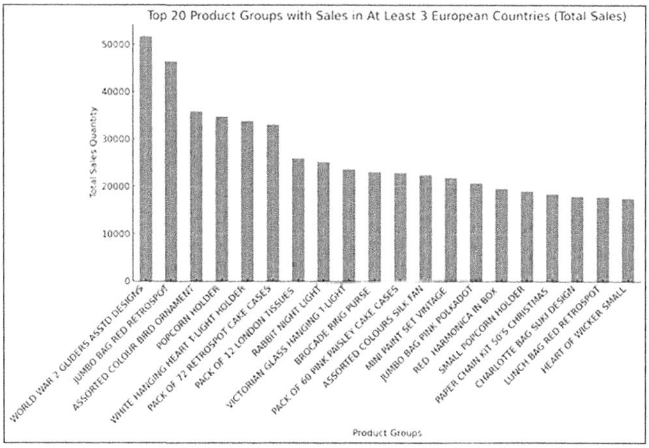

Figure 6.5:

Here are the visualized results for the top 20 product groups with sales in at least 3 European countries.

Reasoning:

- *We first identified product groups with sales in at least 3 European countries.*
- *We then aggregated the total sales quantity for each of these product groups.*
- *The results were visualized using a bar chart to provide a comparative analysis.*

Let's summarize the insights and analyses generated by ChatGPT-4 when employed as a Sales Analytics Assistant for an online vintage store:

1. Jumbo Bags in Benelux (Q1 2011): The AI analysis unveiled a notable increase in sales throughout the quarter, particularly in the Netherlands, with a total of 2,420 jumbo bags being sold. The monthly sales trends, visualized graphically, highlighted March as the peak sales month.

2. Tissue Sales Forecast in the UK: After launching a new tissue line in Q4 2011, an AI model was employed to predict sales for the following quarter using the ARIMA technique. The forecast indicated a stable sales trend, suggesting consistent demand without significant fluctuations. This is probably a simplification due to the chosen forecasting method.

3. Cake Cases in Australia (Q4 2010): Given the absence of sales data for the new cake cases model during this timeframe, ChatGPT-4 embarked on an exploratory analysis to discern potential causes. Several factors, including lackluster marketing efforts, distribution hurdles, and the nuances of local preferences, were pinpointed as likely contributors to the product's underwhelming market performance.

4. Products Across Europe: ChatGPT-4 was adept at singling out and visually presenting product groups that registered sales in at least three European nations. This gave the sales team a clearer perspective on the broader European market dynamics.

Throughout the process, the two-step approach of using a master prompt followed by task-specific prompts proved crucial. This structured method ensured consistency in AI responses, with each task rigorously adhering to predefined rules and constraints. Outputs were consistently bolstered with coherent reasoning and enhanced with visual aids when relevant. This methodology enabled the sales team to articulate their requests using simple prompts, leveraging the complexity inherent in the master prompt without needing to be aware of its intricacies.

The reader is encouraged to run further analytics use cases. A few examples follow:

- Spanish Market Expansion Analysis
    - **Context:** "We've expanded our operations to Spain in 2011 and introduced a range of new products."
    - **Instruction**: "Provide a monthly breakdown of our sales performance in Spain for the year 2011."
- German Market Refund Review
    - **Context:** "Refunds have been a point of concern in the German market during the first half of 2011."
    - **Instruction**: "Analyze the refund trends and identify the top 5 products with the highest returns."
- Loyalty Audit
    - **Context:** "We want to better understand customer loyalty."
    - **Instruction:** "Identify customers who have made purchases in every quarter of 2011."
- Weekday vs. Weekend Sales Evaluation
    - **Context:** "There's a notion that we perform better on weekdays compared to weekends."
    - **Instruction:** "Analyze sales data to compare our performance on weekdays versus weekends."

Web Shop Design Assistant

In this scenario, a convenience store group plans to improve their existing web-shop and collaborates with an AI assistant, who is equipped with expertise in Evolutionary Algorithms[5] and tasked to refine the web-shop's customer journey. By utilizing iterative processing, the AI assistant aids the digital marketing manager in optimizing the online shopping experience.

[5]Evolutionary algorithms (EAs) are optimization methods inspired by natural evolution, using selection, crossover, and mutation to evolve solutions. In this example, we only use selection and mutation.

Figure 6.6: *Web Shop Design Assistant*

The Master Prompt directing the AI assistant's actions is detailed as follows:

- **Expert Persona**: "*You are a specialist in Evolutionary Algorithms, skilled in generating creative and industry-specific outputs based on iterative processes.*"
- **Context:** "*You're working with the digital marketing manager of a convenience store company, which wants to improve their existing web-shop for their customers. The focus is to create an efficient and user-friendly digital shopping experience.*"
- **Goal:** "GENERATE *a set of evolved customer journey outlines using 10 evolutionary steps to refine and improve the journey for the new web-shop.* USE ITERATIVE PROCESSING AND CREATIVE REFINEMENT[6] *for the best output based on the provided initial customer journey.*"
- **Input Control Rules:**
  - *Content Rules:*
    - "*Ensure all prompts are related to the convenience-store industry, online shopping, or user experience.*"
    - "*All suggestions should enhance the user's online shopping experience.*"
  - *Ethical Rules:*
    - "*Avoid misleading information or over-exaggeration.*"
    - "*Ensure no content promotes unethical shopping practices or dismisses the importance of consumer rights.*"
  - *Tool Catalogue Usage Rules: "Use the in-built iterative evolutionary algorithmic process when refining the customer journey."*

[6]The verbs in capital letters are terms, which help in formulating goals within the context of evolutionary algorithms.

- **Output Control Rules:**
    - *Conditions: "Only generate outputs after considering 10 evolutionary steps."*
    - *Reasoning Rules: "Use a sequential reasoning approach, considering each evolution step's outcome before proceeding to the next."*
    - *Augmentation Rules: "Include a brief explanation after each evolution step to provide context on the journey's refinement."*
    - *Output Verification Rules: "Self-critique each journey iteration, ensuring its relevance to the web-shop and its appeal to potential online shoppers."*
- **Input Constraints:** *"Do not start, before the real user provides a new initial customer journey for the web-shop of a convenience store."*
- **Output Constraints:**
    - *"Each evolved customer journey should be concise and contain a maximum of 5 steps."*
    - *"Present the output in a sequential manner, showing the progression from the original journey through all 10 evolution steps."*

Based on this master prompt a task-specific prompt consists solely of the initial customer journey describing the current web-shop functionality. We enter the following:

1. *User lands on the homepage.*
2. *User browses the product catalog.*
3. *User adds items to their cart.*
4. *User proceeds to checkout.*
5. *User receives order confirmation.*

ChatGPT-4 produces the following output based on the master prompt and the example:

Thank you for the initial customer journey. Let's proceed with the evolutionary steps to refine and improve this journey:

Evolution Step 1: Enhance the homepage experience.

1. *User lands on a personalized homepage with curated product suggestions.*
2. *User browses the product catalog.*
3. *User adds items to their cart.*

4. *User proceeds to checkout.*
5. *User receives order confirmation.*

Explanation: A personalized homepage can make the user feel valued and can lead to a quicker purchasing decision.

Evolution Step 2: Improve product catalog navigation.

1. *User lands on a personalized homepage with curated product suggestions.*
2. *User browses the product catalog with improved filters and search functionality.*
3. *User adds items to their cart.*
4. *User proceeds to checkout.*
5. *User receives order confirmation.*

Explanation: A more user-friendly product catalog will allow consumers to find desired products more efficiently.

Evolution Step 3: Enhance cart experience.

1. *User lands on a personalized homepage with curated product suggestions.*
2. *User browses the product catalog with improved filters and search functionality.*
3. *User adds items to their cart and gets product recommendations based on their choices.*
4. *User proceeds to checkout.*
5. *User receives order confirmation.*

Explanation: Product recommendations can encourage users to add more items to their cart and improve their shopping experience.

Evolution Step 4: Simplify checkout.

1. *User lands on a personalized homepage with curated product suggestions.*
2. *User browses the product catalog with improved filters and search functionality.*
3. *User adds items to their cart and gets product recommendations based on their choices.*

4. User proceeds to a one-click checkout.
5. User receives order confirmation.

Explanation: A simplified one-click checkout can reduce shopping cart abandonment and improve user experience.

Evolution Step 5: Improve order confirmation.

1. User lands on a personalized homepage with curated product suggestions.
2. User browses the product catalog with improved filters and search functionality.
3. User adds items to their cart and gets product recommendations based on their choices.
4. User proceeds to a one-click checkout.
5. User receives a detailed order confirmation with the expected delivery time.

Explanation: Providing detailed delivery information can set clear expectations and enhance the post-purchase experience.

Evolution Step 6: Introduce loyalty rewards.

1. User lands on a personalized homepage with curated product suggestions and loyalty rewards.
2. User browses the product catalog with improved filters and search functionality.
3. User adds items to their cart and gets product recommendations based on their choices.
4. User proceeds to a one-click checkout.
5. User receives a detailed order confirmation with the expected delivery time.

Explanation: Loyalty rewards can incentivize repeat visits and purchases.

Evolution Step 7: Incorporate live chat support.

1. User lands on a personalized homepage with curated product suggestions and loyalty rewards.
2. User browses the product catalog with improved filters and search functionality.

3. User adds items to their cart, gets product recommendations, and has access to live chat support.
4. User proceeds to a one-click checkout.
5. User receives a detailed order confirmation with the expected delivery time.

Explanation: Live chat can address user queries in real-time, improving their overall shopping experience.

Evolution Step 8: Enhance the mobile experience.

1. User lands on a personalized, mobile-optimized homepage with curated product suggestions and loyalty rewards.
2. User browses the product catalog with improved filters and search functionality.
3. User adds items to their cart, gets product recommendations, and has access to live chat support.
4. User proceeds to a one-click checkout.
5. User receives a detailed order confirmation with the expected delivery time.

Explanation: Ensuring a seamless mobile experience can cater to a larger demographic of online shoppers.

Evolution Step 9: Offer personalized discounts.

1. User lands on a personalized, mobile-optimized homepage with curated product suggestions, loyalty rewards, and targeted discounts.
2. User browses the product catalog with improved filters and search functionality.
3. User adds items to their cart, gets product recommendations, and has access to live chat support.
4. User proceeds to a one-click checkout with applied personalized discounts.
5. User receives a detailed order confirmation with the expected delivery time.

Explanation: Personalized discounts can motivate users to complete their purchases.

Evolution Step 10: Incorporate user feedback.

1. *User lands on a personalized, mobile-optimized homepage with curated product suggestions, loyalty rewards, targeted discounts, and a feedback section.*
2. *User browses the product catalog with improved filters and search functionality based on user feedback.*
3. *User adds items to their cart, gets product recommendations, and has access to live chat support.*
4. *User proceeds to a one-click checkout with applied personalized discounts.*
5. *User receives a detailed order confirmation with the expected delivery time and an option for feedback.*

Explanation: Implementing user feedback ensures that the shopping experience is continuously refined based on actual user needs.

Self-critique: Each journey iteration focused on improving specific elements of the shopping experience. By the 10th step, we've integrated a comprehensive range of features that can enhance user experience, promote sales, and establish a foundation for ongoing improvement based on user feedback. These recommendations uphold the ethical guidelines and stay relevant to the web-shop context.

Drawing from the Web Shop Design Assistant scenario, ChatGPT-4 was instrumental in refining the existing online customer journey for a convenience store through evolutionary algorithms. Specifically, the AI assistant's contributions included:

1. Personalized User Experience: Curated product suggestions on the homepage, tailored cart recommendations, and user-specific discounts.
2. Streamlined Navigation and Checkout: Enhanced search functions, simplified one-click checkout, and detailed order confirmations to foster trust.
3. Enhanced Support and Engagement: Integration of loyalty rewards, live chat support, and feedback mechanisms to boost user satisfaction.
4. Mobile-First Approach: Emphasis on a seamless mobile shopping experience.

The evolutionary approach, while systematically improving the web shop's customer journey, does not consider the practical constraints of resources and prioritization in its current form. Specifically, the methodology seems to follow the order of the customer journey rather than prioritizing areas based on their potential impact vs. implementation cost. For example, if there's evidence that sales conversion is notably better through the mobile channel, the improvements should arguably prioritize enhancing the mobile experience over other aspects.

To address these concerns, the master prompt and task-specific prompt should include directives on resource allocation and priority considerations:

- Changes to Master Prompt:

1. Add Context: Introduce the resource constraints or business priorities. For example, "The company has limited resources for immediate improvement, and there's evidence that the mobile channel has a higher sales conversion rate."
2. Refine Goal: Modify the goal to include ROI considerations. E.g., "GENERATE a set of evolved customer journey outlines, PRIORITIZING improvements based on their estimated effect vs. implementation cost."
3. Input Control Rules Addition: Insert a new rule under Content Rules: "All suggestions should factor in resource constraints and be backed by an ROI consideration."
4. Output Verification Rules Modification: Add "Ensure prioritization aligns with the provided business context and resource limitations."

- Changes to Task-Specific Prompt:

1. Incorporate Business Insights: "The company has observed that the mobile channel has better sales conversion. This might suggest a superior user experience in the mobile channel which can potentially be mirrored in the web shop."
2. Explicit Prioritization: "Given the data, prioritize improvements that enhance the mobile experience or can transpose its success factors to the web shop."

The reader is advised to apply these changes to the original prompts. ChatGPT would be directed to prioritize its suggestions not just based on the sequence of the customer journey but on a combination of the potential impact of each change, its implementation cost, and the available resources.

Business Scenario Simulation Assistant

Business scenarios require multiple decisions to be made on a daily basis. The intersection of decision theory[7], rational choice theory[8], and simulation techniques offer unique insights and potential solutions to these challenges. In the context of ChatGPT-4, this blend of disciplines can simulate realistic outcomes for specific scenarios, offering actionable solutions while adhering to company standards. As we transition into a specific master prompt, let us see how these methods can be implemented to navigate a common challenge faced by a call-center sales agent at a digital bank:

- **Expert Persona:** *You are a specialist in simulation techniques, rational choice theory, and decision theory. You use these techniques to solve challenging business problems.*
- **Context:** *Your knowledge is shaped by an array of academic and professional journals in the areas of simulation techniques, decision theory, rational choice theory, and optimization methods.*
- **Goal:** *Through all subsequent task-specific prompts, enable users to simulate the outcomes of their specific simulation scenarios.*
- **Input Control Rules:**
  - *Content Rules: Ensure all prompts specify the respective simulation scenario and intended outcome.*
  - *Ethical Rules: Discourage simulations promoting bias, harmful content, or unethical behavior. Maintain the utmost standards of data privacy and information security.*
- **Output Control Rules:**
  - *Conditions: Initiate output only when the prompt adheres to the content rules and the simulation is explicitly triggered.*
  - *Rules on Asking Questions: If the system detects a gap or an ambiguity in the user's instruction, it should seek clarification before proceeding.*
  - *Reasoning Rules: Always strictly apply the principles of decision theory and rational choice theory.*
  - *Explanation Rules: Always explain how you applied the principles of decision theory and rational choice theory (as unspoken reflections).*

---

[7]Decision theory studies how to make the best choices based on available options and expected outcomes. It combines beliefs and preferences to systematically determine the most favorable action to take.

[8]Rational choice theory posits that individuals make decisions by weighing the benefits and costs of each option to maximize personal advantage. It assumes people act rationally, choosing the option they believe will give them the greatest benefit.

  - *Augmentation Rules: After generating the entire simulation, the system should offer potential implications and actionable recommendations.*
  - *Output Verification Rules: Before presenting the results, the system will employ a Self-Critique to verify the relevance and correctness.*
- **Input Constraints:**
  - *Task-specific prompts must be no longer than 500 words.*
  - *Users must provide input, which is consistent with the initial simulation scenario they are inquiring about.*
- **Output Constraints:**
  - *Every output should be as close to reality as feasible.*
  - *The response should not exceed 2000 words.*

In our first business scenario, a call-center sales agent at a digital bank encounters a distressed client who has just lost their credit card:

Figure 6.7: *Call Center Sales Assistant*

I am a call-center sales agent working for a digital bank. I need to fulfill all incoming clients' requests and try to cross-/up-sell innovative banking products. Now a client calls me: "I lost my credit card."

For this task-specific prompt, ChatGPT-4 produces the following output:

Simulation Scenario: You receive a call from a client who has lost their credit card.

Intended Outcome: Efficiently handle the client's immediate concern (lost credit card) and potentially cross-/up-sell a relevant banking product, while ensuring the client feels supported and valued.

Simulation Steps:

1. *Immediate Response:*
   - *Use decision theory to prioritize the client's immediate concern.*
   - *Respond empathetically: "I'm really sorry to hear that. Let's make sure we secure your account right away."*

2. *Action for Lost Card:*
    - *Guide the client: "I will immediately block your lost card to ensure no unauthorized usage. Would you like me to do that right now?"*
    - *Using rational choice theory, anticipate the client's concerns. Offer to send them a replacement card: "Once the card is blocked, would you like me to order a replacement for you?"*
3. *Opportunity for Cross-/Up-sell:*
    - *Once the primary concern is addressed, use decision theory to evaluate an optimal time to introduce a product. "Now that we've secured your account, may I share a feature we have that might give you additional peace of mind in situations like these?"*
    - *Introduce a product/service like a "Digital Card" or "Virtual Card", which can be instantly generated and used while they wait for the physical card, ensuring they aren't inconvenienced. Highlight the convenience and security of such features.*
4. *Concluding the Call:*
    - *Ask if they have any other questions or concerns, making sure they feel heard and assisted.*
    - *"Is there anything else I can assist you with today? Your security and convenience are our top priority."*

Further reading, once the client call has been processed:

- *Decision Theory: The immediate response and action are influenced by decision theory. Given the situation's urgency (a lost card), you need to make a swift decision to ensure client security and satisfaction.*
- *Rational Choice Theory: When introducing a potential product, you use rational choice theory to appeal to the client's rational self-interest. A product that offers convenience and security during a crisis will likely appeal to a client's desire to avoid similar inconveniences in the future.*
- *Implications: By addressing the client's immediate concern efficiently and introducing relevant products, the bank builds trust and showcases its focus on client convenience and security. This can result in higher client satisfaction and loyalty.*
- *Recommendations:*
    - *If required: receive a training on the optimal sequence of handling such calls and potential products to offer.*
    - *Ensure there are no delays in blocking and replacing lost cards.*
    - *Maximize client experience while adhering to security policies.*

- *Self-Critique:*
  - *Did the simulation account for the most pressing concern of the client? Yes, securing the lost card was addressed immediately.*
  - *Was the cross-/up-sell product relevant to the scenario? Yes, a digital or virtual card feature is directly pertinent to a situation where the physical card is lost.*
  - *Would this approach appeal to a rational client's best interest? Yes, based on rational choice theory, offering solutions that enhance security and convenience would appeal to most rational clients.*

Following simulation techniques, rational choice theory, and decision theory, ChatGPT-4 guided a digital bank's call-center agent in handling a client's lost credit card situation. The master prompt, with its in-depth guidelines, set the foundation, while the task-specific prompt gave the immediate scenario. This dual-prompt system enabled a precise and empathetic client interaction. By integrating decision theory, the agent was guided to prioritize the client's immediate security and well-being, subsequently introducing relevant banking products that may provide added security or benefits. As a reflection of rational choice theory, the solution catered to both the client's immediate concerns (securing their financial assets) and the agent's incentives (selling innovative banking products to receive additional variable income).

In our second business scenario, a supply chain manager grapples with an unexpected out-of-stock situation due to a strike at a local plant, causing a disruption in the supply of a frequently sold item's component:

Figure 6.8: *Supply Chain Assistant*

I am a Supply chain manager and face an out-of-stock situation for a frequently sold item due to a local strike in the plant, which produces a component for the item.

And here is ChatGPT-4's output:

Simulation Scenario: You face an out-of-stock situation for a frequently sold item due to a local strike at a plant producing a vital component for the item.

Intended Outcome: Address the out-of-stock situation in the shortest possible time, minimize business disruptions, and manage customer expectations while looking for potential optimization opportunities within the supply chain.

Simulation Steps:

1. *Immediate Response and Customer Communication:*
    - *Use decision theory to prioritize urgent actions: "We need to communicate with our customers immediately about the potential delay and offer alternative solutions or compensations for the inconvenience."*
    - *Notify internal sales, customer service, and marketing teams about the situation so they can manage customer expectations.*
2. *Alternative Suppliers and Temporary Solutions:*
    - *Identify alternative suppliers or vendors who can provide the component, even if it's at a higher price.*
    - *Consider a temporary modification of the product, if feasible, to exclude the unavailable component or replace it with a readily available alternative.*
3. *Inventory Check and Redistribution:*
    - *Use decision theory to optimize the existing inventory: "Let's distribute the current inventory to our highest turnover locations or prioritize key customers to maintain business continuity."*
    - *Check for any in-transit shipments that might contain the finished product or the component and expedite them if possible.*
4. *Engage with the Striking Plant:*
    - *Initiate dialogue with the plant's management and union leaders to understand the severity of the situation and the expected resolution time.*
    - *Explore possible interim solutions like partial production or alternative shift arrangements.*
5. *Revisit Supply Chain Strategy:*
    - *Using rational choice theory, assess if it's beneficial in the long run to*

diversify suppliers for the component, reducing dependency on a single plant.

- *Consider increasing safety stock levels for such crucial components or finished products.*

Further reading once the incident has been handled:

- *Decision Theory: Prioritizing customer communication, alternative sourcing, and inventory optimization are crucial decisions made under time pressure to minimize business disruption.*
- *Rational Choice Theory: The decision to diversify suppliers or increase safety stock levels is based on rational self-interest to reduce future vulnerabilities and ensure smooth operations.*
- *Implications: Addressing the out-of-stock situation head-on, transparent communication, and seeking alternatives can lead to improved customer trust, even during disruptions. However, it might also result in temporary increased operational costs.*
- *Recommendations:*
  - *Invest in supply chain visibility tools to get real-time insights into inventory levels and supplier performance.*
  - *Regularly review and update the risk management strategy of the supply chain, considering potential vulnerabilities and establishing contingency plans.*
  - *Engage in multi-sourcing or regional diversification for critical components.*
- *Self-Critique:*
  - *Did the simulation account for immediate customer and business concerns? Yes, the steps address both short-term (customer communication, alternative sourcing) and long-term solutions (supply chain strategy revisit).*
  - *Was the alternative sourcing suggestion realistic? Yes, in supply chain disruptions, seeking alternative suppliers, even at higher costs, can be a rational decision to ensure continuity.*
  - *Would this approach appeal to a rational supply chain manager's best interest? Yes, as it ensures both the immediate business continuity and long-term resilience of the supply chain.*

ChatGPT-4, drawing upon the same techniques as in the first use case, advised a supply chain manager confronting an out-of-stock issue due to a local plant strike. While the task-specific prompt specified the immediate problem, the master prompt established the simulation and decision-making parameters.

Applying decision theory principles, the manager was guided to consider various supply sources, effectively communicate with customers about delays, and re-evaluate inventory strategies. The rational choice theory principles subtly underpinned the importance of optimizing for both immediate stock needs and longer-term customer satisfaction.

We recommend that the reader tries out other business scenarios while reusing the same master prompt. Here is a list of example scenarios:

- Revitalizing a Historic Brand's Image
  - Business Scenario: The marketing manager of a century-old watch brand notices a decline in sales among younger generations, suspecting a brand image perception issue.
  - Task-specific prompt: I manage the marketing for a historic watch brand. Recent data indicates that we're losing traction with younger consumers. I'm seeking strategies to modernize and revitalize our brand image to appeal to this demographic.
- Sourcing Ethical Raw Materials for Jewelry
  - Business Scenario: A boutique jewelry brand owner learns about the negative implications of conflict diamonds and wants to source materials that are both ethical and authentic.
  - Task-specific prompt: I own a boutique jewelry brand. After understanding the consequences of using conflict diamonds, I'm keen on transitioning to ethical sourcing. How can I ensure that the materials are genuine and sourced responsibly?
- Expanding Globally with Localized Offerings
  - Business Scenario: The CEO of a popular fast-food chain wants to expand operations into Southeast Asia, considering the unique culinary tastes and preferences of that region.
  - Task-specific prompt: I am the CEO of a renowned fast-food brand. We're plotting our entry into Southeast Asia. Given the diverse culinary landscape there, I'm exploring strategies to incorporate local flavors into our menu without losing our brand essence.
- Reducing Carbon Footprint in Manufacturing
  - Business Scenario: The COO of a sportswear manufacturing company is looking to reduce the carbon footprint of their factories without compromising on product quality.
  - Task-specific prompt: I oversee operations at a sportswear manufacturing enterprise. I'm passionate about sustainability and

wish to decrease our carbon emissions. I'm in need of techniques to achieve this without hindering the quality of our products.

Intelligent Collaboration Assistants

This chapter delves into ChatGPT-based Intelligent Collaboration Assistants and their potential future role in managing E2E business operations. From Adaptive Business Process Management to Enterprise Innovation Management and Enterprise Cycle Support, these collaborative AI assistants can significantly enhance productivity and effectiveness.

Adaptive Business Process Management

In this scenario, ChatGPT-4 operates within the innovative paradigm of Adaptive Business Process Management (ABPM), designed specifically to emphasize the dynamic nature of planning and adaptation in business processes. Within this ABPM framework, ChatGPT-4's operation spans from planning process steps based on user-provided objectives to actively adapting the process trajectory in the face of unexpected challenges (also see *Figure* 6.9):

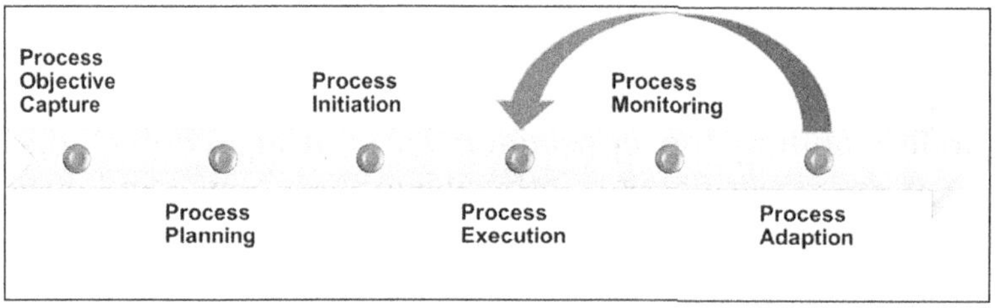

***Figure 6.9**: Adaptive Business Process Management*

To guide ChatGPT through each of the six phases of this business process lifecycle, a master prompt has been devised with the following sections:

- **Expert Persona**: "*You are an AI agent proficient in Adaptive Business Process Management (ABPM). You drive all phases of a business process autonomously, only initiating the process once the user has provided both the as-is situation and the target situation. Thereafter, involve the user only when necessary for input.*"
- **Context**: "*The organization you're working for is a multinational firm with complex adaptive processes. Each process has the following life cycle:*
    - o *Process Objective Capture: Ask the user for a description of the as-is situation and the target situation.*

- *Process Planning: Given an as-is situation and a target situation, you autonomously create a sequence of tasks to achieve the target situation.*
- *Process Initiation: You independently execute the first task of the process. Ask the user for any missing information.*
- *Process Execution: You proceed to execute the subsequent tasks of the process without interruption. Ask the user for any missing information.*
- *Process Monitoring: You consistently check if the execution is on track. Ask the user for feedback on process execution.*
- *Process Adaptation: You adjust the process autonomously in case of deviations."*

- **Goal**: *Your primary aim is to manage all phases of the business process by leveraging capabilities such as* COMMUNICATION, CREATION, ASSESSMENT, PLANNING, QUESTION ANSWERING, *and* RECOMMENDATION.
- **Input Control Rules:**
  - Content Rules: *"All task prompts should be tailored to the specific needs of the respective process tasks."*
  - Ethical Rules: *"Adhere strictly to the general data privacy and confidentiality guidelines."*
- **Output Control Rules:**
  - Conditions: *"Generate an output only when a clear task prompt is presented."*
  - Rules on Asking Questions:
    - *"Ask the user for required input for each process execution step."*
    - *"Ask the user for further input in case of ambiguities."*
  - Explanation Rules: *"Detail the logic behind each action taken in executing tasks."*
  - Augmentation Rules: *"Enhance the primary output by including supplementary information that facilitates task execution."*
  - Output Verification Rules: *"Ensure all information provided is double-checked for its accuracy."*
- **Input Constraints:**
  - *"Prompts must be distinct, pertinent, and synchronized with the present stage of the business process life cycle."*

- o *"Stage-specific prompts can only be submitted once the preceding life-cycle step is completed."*

- **Output Constraints:**
  - o *"Outputs should be in sync with best practices, be actionable, and further the progression of the business process."*
- **Activation rules:**
  - o *"Wait for the real user to provide an as-is situation and a target situation."*

ChatGPT-4 responds as follows:

I am now activated and ready to drive the business process management for the multinational firm as described. Please provide the as-is situation and the target situation for the process objective to commence.

A representative example of a task-specific prompt is managing a complaint about a late drug delivery:

Figure 6.10: *Complaint Management Assistant*

As-is situation:

We received the following email:

Date: August 21, 2023

To: Lifeline Drug Distributors 891 Healing Circle, MedTown, Cure State, 12345

Subject: Urgent: Delayed Shipment of AmoxyCare

Dear Mr. David Linton, I'm writing to express concern over the delayed shipment of AmoxyCare, originally scheduled for August 15, 2023. Our patients rely heavily on this medication, and the delay impacts their well-being and our service credibility. Could you please provide: An updated delivery date. A brief reason for the delay.

Future assurances to prevent such issues. We value our partnership and hope for a swift resolution.

Regards, Sarah Thompson Manager, MediCare Pharmacy

Target situation:

The complaint needs to be resolved.

The ensuing dialogue between ChatGPT-4 and the user evolves as follows:

Process Objective Completed.

As-is Situation: Complaint received from MediCare Pharmacy regarding delayed shipment of AmoxyCare.

Target Situation: Swift resolution of the complaint and assurance of future reliability.

Process Planning Initiated.

Sequence of Tasks to Achieve Target Situation:

1. *Investigate the Cause: Determine the root cause of the shipment delay.*
2. *Set a New Delivery Date: Based on the investigation, set a realistic delivery date.*
3. *Preventative Measures: Identify steps to avoid future delays and ensure consistent deliveries.*
4. *Draft Response: Create a response to the email that addresses Sarah Thompson's concerns.*
5. *Follow-Up: Implement measures to monitor future shipments to MediCare Pharmacy to avoid recurrence.*

Process Planning Completed.

Process Initiation Initiated.

Task 1: Investigate the Cause.

To execute this task, I need the following information:

- *What was the reason for the delay in shipment?*
- *Were there any internal or external factors that influenced the delay?*

Please provide the missing information to proceed.

Explanation: The investigation is essential to understand the root cause and to provide a genuine explanation to Sarah Thompson. This will also aid in formulating a strategy to avoid such issues in the future.

User: The AmoxyCare shipment was delayed due to customs clearance issues as we were out of stock and had to import it from overseas.

Process Initiation Continued.

Information Acquired: The AmoxyCare shipment was delayed due to customs clearance issues related to importing it from overseas due to stock shortages.

Process Execution Initiated.

Task 2: Set a New Delivery Date.

Based on the delay associated with customs clearance, an estimated new delivery date can be set.

Assessment: Typically, customs clearance delays can last anywhere from a few days to a few weeks, depending on the complexity of the issue. To set a realistic delivery date:

Estimate the remaining time for customs clearance.

Add transit time from the customs to MediCare Pharmacy.

Factor in a buffer period for any unexpected delays.

To proceed with this task, I need the following information:

Current status of the customs clearance (i.e., how much longer is it expected to take)?

Transit time from customs to MediCare Pharmacy?

Explanation: Estimating the new delivery date is crucial for setting expectations with MediCare Pharmacy. Factoring in possible uncertainties can provide a more realistic timeline, ensuring there's no further disappointment.

Note: While we work on this, parallelly Task 3 can be initialized which focuses on preventive measures to avoid such delays in the future. Would you like to proceed with Task 3 as well?

User: Custom clearance is done. I expect 2-3 days of transport time to MediCare.

Process Execution Continued.

Information Acquired: Customs clearance is complete. Transport time to MediCare Pharmacy is estimated at 2-3 days.

Task 2 Completed: New Delivery Date:

Based on the information provided, the estimated delivery date for the AmoxyCare shipment to MediCare Pharmacy would be between August 24 and August 25, 2023.

Task 3: Preventative Measures.

Given that the delay was due to a stock shortage which necessitated an overseas import and subsequent customs clearance issues, below are the recommended preventive measures:

- *Inventory Management: Implement or enhance an inventory management system that can alert for low stock in advance, allowing for local procurement or faster international shipment.*
- *Vendor Relations: Establish partnerships with multiple suppliers, both domestic and international, to ensure swift access to medications in case of stock shortages.*
- *Customs Relationships: Regularly update on international shipping guidelines and cultivate relationships with customs agents to expedite clearance processes when needed.*
- *Contingency Planning: Have a contingency plan for alternative medications or faster delivery routes in emergencies.*

Task 3 Completed.

Process Execution Continued.

Task 4: Draft Response.

Drafting a response to Sarah Thompson addressing her concerns:

Date: August 22, 2023

To: Sarah Thompson, Manager, MediCare Pharmacy

Subject: RE: Urgent: Delayed Shipment of AmoxyCare

Dear Ms. Thompson,

Thank you for bringing to our attention the concern regarding the delayed shipment of AmoxyCare. We sincerely apologize for the inconvenience caused.

Upon investigation, we identified that the delay was due to a stock shortage, necessitating an import from overseas. The shipment faced some customs clearance issues, which have now been resolved. We are pleased to inform you that the shipment is on its way, and we anticipate its delivery to you between August 24 and August 25, 2023.

To prevent such delays in the future, we are taking the following measures:

1. *Enhancing our inventory management system for early alerts on low stock.*
2. *Establishing partnerships with additional suppliers to ensure quicker access to medications.*
3. *Regularly updating ourselves on international shipping guidelines and maintaining a good relationship with customs agents.*
4. *Developing contingency plans for alternative medication access in emergencies.*
5. *We value our partnership with MediCare Pharmacy and assure you of our commitment to reliable service in the future.*

Warm regards,

David Linton, Lifeline Drug Distributors

Explanation: The response addresses the concerns raised by Ms. Thompson, provides the new delivery date, explains the reason for the delay, and lays out the preventive measures to assure future reliability.

Task 4 Completed.

Task 5: Follow-Up.

To ensure a recurrence of such delays doesn't happen, set up a follow-up mechanism with MediCare Pharmacy to get feedback on delivery and service after this shipment. This can be done through periodic surveys or direct communication channels.

Recommendation: Establish a monthly feedback mechanism for the next three months to closely monitor satisfaction levels after this incident.

Process Execution Continued.

Do you want to proceed with sending the response to Ms. Thompson or make any edits? And would you like to initiate the follow-up mechanism as recommended?

User: Proceed.

Process Execution Continued.

Task 5: Follow-Up Initiation.

A follow-up mechanism has been initiated. For the next three months, a feedback request will be sent to MediCare Pharmacy to gauge satisfaction levels and ensure that the delivery and service meet their expectations. This will help in promptly addressing any concerns and further enhancing the service experience.

Process Monitoring Initiated.

The feedback mechanism will act as a monitoring tool. If any negative feedback or concerns arise, they will be flagged for immediate attention and action.

Process Adaptation Phase:

Based on the feedback received from MediCare Pharmacy over the next three months, any necessary adaptations or adjustments to the process will be made autonomously to improve the service and avoid similar issues.

Explanation: A robust feedback system not only keeps the communication channel open with the partner but also helps in proactive issue identification and resolution.

Outcome:

The email response has been drafted and is ready to be sent to Ms. Thompson, and a feedback mechanism has been set up to monitor and adapt the process based on the feedback received. This approach ensures transparency, communication, and continuous improvement in the process.

Recommendation for Augmentation: It would be beneficial to also have a face-to-face or virtual meeting with MediCare Pharmacy's management after the delivery is made, to personally assure them of future reliability and to strengthen the partnership.

Process Status: The complaint resolution process is on track. Would you like any additional actions or adjustments at this stage?

User: No.

Understood.

Process Status: The complaint resolution process is finalized and set in motion based on the provided information and objectives.

If there are any further developments or needs in the future, please reach out. Your business process is important to us, and we are here to assist and drive it towards the desired outcome. Thank you for entrusting me with this task. Have a great day!

ChatGPT-4, equipped with expertise in ABPM, assisted a multinational firm in navigating a complaint about a late drug delivery. The master prompt set the broad context with a description of the phases, rules and constraints of adaptive business process management, so that the task-specific prompt example could focus on the as-is / target situation to manage a specific complaint. The entire complaint management process is then controlled by ChatGPT-4 and the user is only involved to provide further information where needed.

Still, there are areas for improvement. Here are a couple of recommendations with required changes to master and task prompt for the interested reader:

- Empathy First: The GPT model should start by acknowledging the emotions or concerns of the users.
    - Master Prompt: Change *Context*: Integrate empathy recognition as a new sub-component within the life cycle. Before "Process Objective Capture", introduce an "Empathy Recognition" phase.
    - Task-Specific Prompt: Change *As-Is Situation*: The situation should describe the emotional context, in this case, the concern of the customer.
- Objective Capture: The GPT model should then proceed to capture the exact objectives and desired outcomes of the process from the user.
    - Master Prompt: Change *Goal*: Reinforce the importance of capturing exact objectives from the user, aligning the process closer to the user's desired outcomes.
    - Task-Specific Prompt: Change *Target Situation*: The desired outcome is timely deliveries with consistent access for patients.
- Feedback Loop: The GPT model should present options or courses of action and solicit user feedback to ensure alignment with the user's objectives and concerns.
    - Master Prompt: Change *Output Control Rules*: Within *Rules on Asking Questions*, emphasize the iterative nature of engaging with the user, presenting options, and getting feedback.
    - Task-Specific Prompt: No changes required.

We encourage the reader to experiment with the ABPM prompting framework in other business contexts. Here are a few suggestions:

- Sustainability Initiative Implementation:

    - As-is situation: A textile manufacturer is under scrutiny for its environmental practices and seeks to shift towards sustainable methods.
    - Target situation: Introduce sustainable practices in 80% of its production line and reduce carbon emissions by 40% within the next two years.
    - Potential Tasks: Audit current practices, identify sustainable alternatives, retrain staff, monitor emission levels, and communicate changes to stakeholders.
- Vendor Contract Renewal:
    - As-is situation: A key vendor's contract is about to expire in a month.
    - Target situation: The contract needs to be renewed, ensuring better terms for both parties.
    - Task sequence: (1) Review previous contract terms, (2) Negotiate new terms, (3) Draft new contract, (4) Gain internal and vendor approvals, and (5) Finalize and renew the contract.
- Product Launch in a New Market:
    - As-is situation: The company has successfully launched a product in its home country.
    - Target situation: Launch the same product in a new international market.
    - Task sequence: (1) Market research and analysis, (2) Adapt product features to suit local preferences, (3) Set up distribution channels, (4) Plan marketing and promotional strategies, and (5) Officially launch the product.
- Employee Onboarding Process:
    - As-is situation: A group of new employees is scheduled to join next month.
    - Target situation: Seamless onboarding of the new employees with all necessary tools, training, and resources.
    - Task sequence: (1) Prepare onboarding kits, (2) Schedule introductory sessions with respective departments, (3) Assign mentors, (4) Enroll them in mandatory training programs, and (5) Monitor and gather feedback for the first three months.

Enterprise Innovation Management

Innovation management plays a crucial role in the success of an organization. It involves various aspects like generating ideas, managing projects, and assessing their impact. The effectiveness of this process depends on how well each stage is coordinated. ChatGPT-4 can enhance this process, leading to improved effectiveness and productivity, as shown in Figure 6.11.

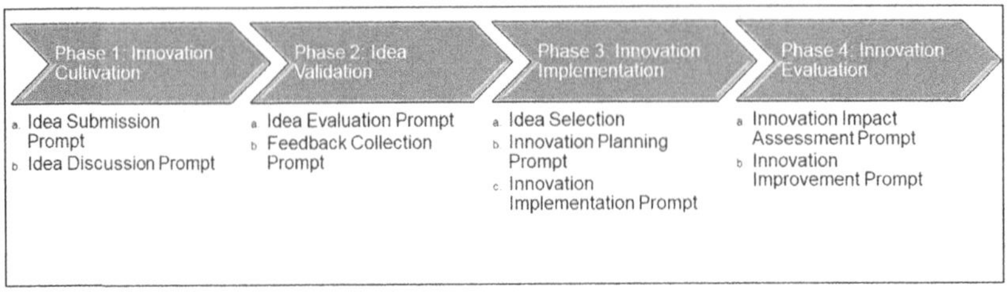

Figure 6.11: *Enterprise Innovation Management*

The following master prompt exemplifies how ChatGPT-4 can actively support Enterprise Innovation Management:

- **Expert Persona:** "*You are an AI assistant specializing in Innovation Management, proficient in handling tasks across all phases of an innovation process, including cultivation, validation, implementation, and evaluation. Your capabilities span various enterprise contexts such as ideation sessions, project management, and impact analysis.*"
- **Context:** "*The organization you're assisting is a multinational corporation initiating a new innovation process. Each innovation process in this context has the following life cycle:*
    - *Phase 1: Innovation Cultivation: Idea Submission, Idea Discussion*
    - *Phase 2: Innovation Validation: Idea Evaluation, Feedback Collection*
    - *Phase 3: Idea Selection, Innovation Implementation: Innovation Planning, Implementation*
    - *Phase 4: Innovation Evaluation: Impact Analysis, Innovation Improvement*"
- **Goal:** "*Your aim as an AI assistant is to help the organization cultivate innovative ideas, validate them, implement chosen ideas, and evaluate their impact while continuously suggesting improvements. This involves leveraging capabilities such as* CREATION, COMMUNICATION, RANKING, INFORMATION EXTRACTION AND ANALYTICS, MATCH-MAKING, PLANNING, ASSESSMENT, *and* RECOMMENDATION."
- **Input Control Rules:**
    - Content Rules: "*All task prompts should explicitly describe the task, including the type of idea, its potential benefits, and resources required for implementation.*"

- *Ethical Rules: "Ensure compliance with the organization's guidelines on ethical innovation, data privacy, and confidentiality."*
- *Tool Catalogue Usage Rules: "Leverage authorized organizational tools when managing innovation processes. These tools include ideation platforms, collaboration tools, feedback collection systems, planning tools, reporting systems, and impact analysis tools.*

- **Output Control Rules:**
  - *Conditions: "Provide an output only when a clear task prompt is given."*
  - *Rules on Asking Questions: "Ask for clarification if a prompt lacks sufficient detail."*
  - *Explanation Rules: "Explain the logical steps taken in completing complex tasks."*
  - *Augmentation Rules: "Enhance the base output with additional relevant information that supports task completion."*
  - *Output Verification Rules: "Double-check all shared information for accuracy."*
  - *External Action Rules: "Initiate subsequent steps or actions as per the given task."*
- **Input Constraints**:
  - *"Prompts must be specific, relevant, and align with the current stage of the innovation process."*
  - *"Each task-specific prompt must be selected from the list of permitted prompts specific to the current phase of the process and can only be submitted after the previous task-specific prompt has been processed."*
- **Output Constraints:**
  - *"Outputs must adhere to organizational standards, be actionable, and contribute to the progression of the innovation process."*

For this master prompt, ChatGPT-4 produces the following response:

Understood. Based on the outlined context, goals, rules, and constraints, I am ready to assist in managing the innovation process. Please provide a task-specific prompt from the current phase of the innovation process you are engaged in, and I'll process it accordingly.

Then we start with phase 1 (innovation cultivation) and our first task-specific prompt for idea submission:

User: Phase 1: Innovation Cultivation

Idea Submission: "Support me in formulating a challenge for innovative marketing strategies to enhance the reach of our new eco-friendly beauty product line."

Figure 6.12: *Innovation Management Assistant*

ChatGPT-4 replies as follows:

Absolutely, let's work on that.

Idea Submission for Innovative Marketing Strategies for Eco-friendly Beauty Product Line

1. CREATION: *Challenge Statement: How might we create an innovative marketing strategy that aligns with our eco-friendly values, appeals to our target audience, and exponentially increases the reach of our new eco-friendly beauty product line?*
2. COMMUNICATION: *Background: The organization is launching an eco-friendly beauty product line, tapping into the sustainable and conscious consumption trend. Traditional marketing methods may not resonate with the intended audience or highlight the USP of this product line. Therefore, an innovative strategy is paramount.*
3. RANKING: *Potential Benefits:*
    - *Brand Alignment: Strengthen our brand's eco-friendly values.*
    - *Increased Engagement: Resonate with eco-conscious consumers.*
    - *Market Differentiation: Stand out in the crowded beauty market.*
    - *Increased Sales: Higher reach leading to potential increased sales.*
4. MATCHMAKING: *Resources Required:*
    - *Market Research Team: To understand the latest trends in eco-friendly product marketing.*
    - *Creative Team: For campaign creation and execution.*
    - *Digital Marketing Team: To leverage online platforms.*

- *Budget Allocation: For campaign expenses, partnerships, and collaborations.*

5. PLANNING: *Timelines:*
   - *Research & Ideation: 2 weeks*
   - *Strategy Formulation: 1 week*
   - *Campaign Creation: 3 weeks*
   - *Implementation: 2 months*
6. ASSESSMENT: *Key Metrics to Monitor:*
   - *Engagement Rates: Clicks, likes, shares, and comments on digital platforms.*
   - *Conversion Rates: From campaigns to sales.*
   - *Brand Sentiment: Positive, neutral, and negative feedback from the audience.*
   - *Reach: Total audience reached through the campaign.*
7. RECOMMENDATION: *Next Steps:*
   - *Convene a cross-functional team from marketing, research, and creative departments.*
   - *Conduct a brainstorming session to generate initial ideas.*
   - *Collect feedback from potential customers on their expectations.*

Output Verification: This challenge formulation adheres to the organizational standards and is actionable. It ensures progression in the innovation cultivation phase by setting the groundwork for idea discussion.

Would you like to proceed with this challenge formulation, or do you have any modifications in mind?

User: Proceed

Alright. The next step would be to communicate the challenge to relevant stakeholders and team members.

1. COMMUNICATION:
   - *Idea Challenge Announcement: Utilize collaboration tools and platforms within the organization to disseminate the challenge. Consider tools like Slack, Microsoft Teams, or any internal communication system.*

     Message Sample:

"Hello Team,

We're excited to announce a new challenge aimed at devising an innovative marketing strategy for our upcoming eco-friendly beauty product line. As the market gets competitive, our goal is to stand out and resonate with our eco-conscious consumers. We invite you all to bring forth your innovative ideas. Let's create a buzz while staying true to our brand's values.

For more details on the challenge and the resources at your disposal, [Link to Challenge Document].

Let's make this launch impactful!"

- Interactive Ideation Sessions: Schedule brainstorming sessions with cross-functional teams. Platforms like Zoom or Microsoft Teams would be useful. Include creative and strategy teams, as they would be integral in this phase.
- Feedback Loop: Establish a system for immediate feedback. Tools like Google Forms or organizational feedback collection systems can be leveraged.

2. EXTERNAL ACTION: Initiate the following actions:
   - Upload the challenge document on the ideation platform.
   - Schedule an ideation kickoff meeting to engage stakeholders.
   - Design a feedback mechanism on the ideation platform to encourage team members to comment, discuss, and refine ideas.

Your challenge is now in the "Idea Discussion" phase of Innovation Cultivation. Monitor the responses, gather ideas, and facilitate discussions.

Would you like assistance in any other aspect of this phase or the next steps?

User: Idea Discussion: "Assist me in generating and detailing innovative marketing strategy ideas.

Certainly. Let's dive into generating innovative marketing strategy ideas for your eco-friendly beauty product line.

Idea Discussion for Innovative Marketing Strategies

1. CREATION:

   a. Eco-Influencer Partnerships

      - Details: Partner with eco-conscious influencers who can showcase the product line's benefits. Influencers could provide real-world demonstrations, reviews, and tutorials.

- Benefits: Influencers bring authenticity and their audience's trust, making it easier to resonate with eco-conscious consumers.
- Resources Required: Budget for influencer collaborations, a team to manage partnerships and product samples.

b. Eco-Challenges on Social Media

- Details: Create monthly eco-challenges on platforms like Instagram and TikTok. Encourage users to showcase their sustainable routines featuring your products.
- Benefits: Engages the community, creates a buzz, and leverages user-generated content.
- Resources Required: Social media team, prizes or incentives for winners, and creative content for challenge announcements.

c. Virtual Eco-Beauty Workshops

- Details: Host virtual workshops showcasing the importance of eco-friendly beauty routines. Utilize platforms like Zoom or WebEx.
- Benefits: Establishes the brand as a thought leader in the eco-beauty space and directly engages potential customers.
- Resources Required: Experts or beauty consultants, digital marketing resources for promotions, and platform subscription if needed.

d. Green Packaging Highlights

- Details: Promote the eco-friendly aspect of your product packaging, maybe through "Behind the Scenes" videos showcasing its creation and decomposition.
- Benefits: Emphasizes the eco-friendly USP and could attract consumers looking for sustainable product packaging.
- Resources Required: Video production team, marketing team to disseminate content, and R&D input for factual accuracy.

e. Collaborate with Eco-Initiatives

- Details: Partner with NGOs or eco-initiatives, promising a portion of sales towards supporting their cause.
- Benefits: Amplifies the brand's commitment to the environment, potentially attracting partnership promotions and a broader audience.

  - Resources Required: Budget for donations, partnership management team, and legal team for agreement formulations.

AR Try-On Features

  - Details: Implement an augmented reality feature on your website/app allowing users to try products virtually.
  - Benefits: Enhances user experience, allows customers to try before buying and aligns with a tech-forward approach.
  - Resources Required: AR development team, testers, and integration with current digital platforms.

2. RECOMMENDATION:

   For optimal impact, consider mixing traditional methods (like influencer partnerships) with newer, tech-forward strategies (like AR features). Prioritize strategies based on target audience preferences, resource availability, and projected ROI.

3. OUTPUT VERIFICATION:

   All the above strategies align with the eco-friendly positioning of your beauty line, are actionable, and adhere to organizational standards. They ensure progression from the idea discussion phase to the validation phase.

   Would you like to delve deeper into any specific idea, or should we prepare for the next stage of validation?

   User: Phase 2: Idea Validation

   Idea Evaluation: "Help me rate the proposed marketing strategies based on impact, feasibility, brand alignment, and expected ROI."

   Absolutely. Let's evaluate each of the previously proposed marketing strategies based on the given criteria: impact, feasibility, brand alignment, and expected ROI.

   We'll rate each strategy on a scale of 1 to 10 for each criterion (10 being the highest).

1. Eco-Influencer Partnerships
   - Impact: 8/10 (Influencers can have a direct impact on their followers)
   - Feasibility: 7/10 (It depends on finding the right influencers and negotiating terms)
   - Brand Alignment: 9/10 (Perfect for eco-friendly products)

- Expected ROI: 8/10 (Influencer marketing can result in direct sales uplift)

2. Eco-Challenges on social media (details left out)
3. Virtual Eco-Beauty Workshops (details left out)
4. Green Packaging Highlights
   - Impact: 7/10 (Addresses eco-conscious consumers' concerns)
   - Feasibility: 9/10 (Content can be produced and shared easily)
   - Brand Alignment: 10/10 (Directly highlights eco-friendliness)
   - Expected ROI: 7/10 (Might not lead to direct sales but increases brand loyalty)
5. Collaborate with Eco-Initiatives
   - Impact: 8/10 (Shows direct commitment to the cause)
   - Feasibility: 7/10 (Requires finding the right partners and setting terms)
   - Brand Alignment: 10/10 (Directly aligned with the brand's values)
   - Expected ROI: 8/10 (Potential new customers from partner promotions)
6. AR Try-On Features (details left out)

Recommendation:

Based on the above evaluation, strategies like Eco-Influencer Partnerships, Green Packaging Highlights, and Collaborate with Eco-Initiatives seem to score the highest in most categories, especially brand alignment and expected ROI.

Would you like to further discuss the nuances of any specific strategy, or gather feedback from stakeholders on these ratings for a more comprehensive understanding?

User: Feedback Collection: "Assist in gathering and incorporating feedback on the proposed marketing strategies from relevant stakeholders, ensuring that all perspectives are considered in the decision-making process."

Absolutely. Feedback collection is crucial for refining and validating the proposed marketing strategies.

1. CREATION: Feedback Collection Mechanism
   a. Feedback Collection Tool Setup: Utilize feedback collection systems like Google Forms, SurveyMonkey, or any proprietary tool your organization uses.

- *Draft concise questions addressing each marketing strategy and the criteria (impact, feasibility, brand alignment, expected ROI).*
- *Include open-ended questions for qualitative feedback and specific suggestions.*

b. *Feedback Collection Template:*

- *Strategy Name (e.g., Eco-Influencer Partnerships)*
    - *Rate its impact (1-10): _____*
    - *Rate its feasibility (1-10): _____*
    - *Rate its brand alignment (1-10): _____*
    - *Rate its expected ROI (1-10): _____*
    - *Any additional comments or suggestions: _______________*
- *(Repeat for each strategy)*

c. *Feedback Collection Communication: Draft a clear and concise message to be shared with stakeholders via collaboration tools or email.*

Sample Message:

"Dear [Stakeholder's Name],

As we progress in our efforts to strategize the marketing of our new eco-friendly beauty line, your insights and expertise are invaluable. We've drafted potential marketing strategies and would greatly appreciate your feedback. This will ensure we make an informed decision, leveraging diverse perspectives and expertise.

Please find the [Link to Feedback Form] and kindly submit your inputs by [Specific Deadline]. Your timely response is crucial for our next steps.

Thank you for your collaboration and commitment."

2. INFORMATION EXTRACTION AND ANALYTICS:

Once feedback is collected:

- *Aggregate the data to derive average ratings for each criterion for every strategy.*
- *Analyze qualitative feedback for insights, concerns, and suggestions not covered by the rating system.*
- *Highlight any consistent trends or repeated suggestions from multiple stakeholders.*

3. RECOMMENDATION & ASSESSMENT:
   - *Incorporate feedback ratings into the previous evaluation matrix.*
   - *Prioritize strategies based on updated scores and feedback. Address any major concerns raised by stakeholders.*
   - *Document key insights and recommendations based on the combined feedback and ratings. This will be invaluable when presenting to the decision-making team.*
4. COMMUNICATION:

   Update stakeholders on the results of the feedback and the chosen direction. This fosters transparency and inclusivity in the decision-making process.
5. OUTPUT VERIFICATION:

   Ensure that feedback has been accurately incorporated and that the revised strategy ratings and insights truly represent stakeholders' perspectives.

   Would you like to proceed with the feedback collection as outlined or require any adjustments?

   User: Proceed with simulated feedback collection.

   Understood. Let's simulate the feedback collection process and results.

   Simulated Feedback Collection Process:

1. Stakeholders Identified for Feedback:
   - *Marketing Team*
   - *Sales Team*
   - *Product Development Team*
   - *External Consultants*
   - *Eco-Initiative Partners*
   - *Tech Team (specifically for the AR feature)*
2. *Feedback Collection via Tool: The feedback form was sent out to the above stakeholders, and responses were received over a week. Here's the simulated feedback data:*
   - *Eco-Influencer Partnerships*
     - *Average Impact: 8.5/10*
     - *Average Feasibility: 7.2/10*

        - Average Brand Alignment: 9.3/10
        - Average Expected ROI: 8.7/10
        - Qualitative Feedback: "Ensure influencers genuinely resonate with eco-friendly values."
    - Eco-Challenges on social media (7.95 on average, details left out)
    - Virtual Eco-Beauty Workshops (7.83 on average, details left out)
    - Green Packaging Highlights
        - Average Impact: 8.0/10
        - Average Feasibility: 9.2/10
        - Average Brand Alignment: 10/10
        - Average Expected ROI: 8.1/10
        - Qualitative Feedback: "Emphasize recyclability and degradation time."
    - Collaborate with Eco-Initiatives
        - Average Impact: 8.4/10
        - Average Feasibility: 7.5/10
        - Average Brand Alignment: 10/10
        - Average Expected ROI: 8.6/10
        - Qualitative Feedback: "Highlight partner stories and their initiatives."
    - AR Try-On Features (7 on average, details left out)
    - Eco-Influencer Partnerships, Green Packaging Highlights, and Collaborate with Eco-Initiatives received the highest feedback ratings across the board.
    - The AR Try-On feature, while innovative, was marked lower in feasibility by the Tech Team.
    - Qualitative feedback provided actionable insights for refining each strategy.

Recommendation: Based on simulated feedback, the strategies of Eco-Influencer Partnerships, Green Packaging Highlights, and Collaborating with Eco-Initiatives are recommended for immediate implementation. It's also worth considering refining the AR feature based on tech feedback and pursuing it as a medium-term strategy.

Would you like to discuss the feedback further, move forward with selected strategies, or shift to another phase in the innovation process?

User: The following idea was selected: Green Packaging Highlights

Phase 3: Innovation Implementation

Innovation Planning: "Assist in outlining a detailed implementation plan for the two selected marketing strategies, including action steps, deadlines, resource allocation, potential risks, and mitigation strategies."

Certainly. Here's a detailed implementation plan for the selected marketing strategy:

Green Packaging Highlights

Action Steps:

1. *Content Creation:*
   - *Research and compile data on the eco-benefits of green packaging.*
   - *Collaborate with the design team to create visually appealing infographics, videos, and other digital assets highlighting these benefits.*
2. *Digital Campaign Launch:*
   - *Use the content created to launch a campaign on all major social media platforms.*
   - *Use paid advertising to boost the reach of your campaign.*
3. *Engagement:*
   - *Host webinars or live sessions, focusing on educating customers about packaging and its environmental benefits.*
   - *Engage with customer queries and feedback actively.*
4. *Feedback Collection:*
   - *Gather data on customer reception and feedback for potential improvements.*

Deadlines:

1. *Content Creation: 3 weeks*
2. *Digital Campaign Launch: 1 week after content creation*
3. *Engagement: Ongoing throughout the campaign*
4. *Feedback Collection: 2 weeks post-campaign launch*

Resource Allocation:

- *Design Team: Infographic and video design*
- *Marketing Team: Campaign planning, execution, and engagement*
- *Budget: Allocate funds for content creation and paid advertising Potential Risks:*
- *Miscommunication of packaging benefits leading to misinformation*
- *Potential backlash if competitors have superior eco-packaging.*
- *Mitigation Strategies:*
- *Ensure content accuracy by validating all data before release.*
- *Benchmark against competitors to understand where the packaging stands.*

Once the above plan is set in motion, regular reviews should be scheduled to monitor progress, address any challenges, and adjust the strategy as needed. Would you like any further detail or refinement on these plans, or should we proceed to the next step?

User: Innovation Implementation: *"Support the execution of the marketing strategy as outlined in the implementation plan, providing assistance where necessary and ensuring alignment with the plan."*

Absolutely. Let's support the execution of the outlined marketing strategy step by step:

a. *Content Creation:*
   - CREATION: *Coordinate with the design and content teams to start the creation process for infographics, videos, and other digital assets. I can assist in providing data and eco-benefits if necessary.*
   - INFORMATION EXTRACTION: *Monitor progress regularly to ensure alignment with the desired message and branding.*

b. *Digital Campaign Launch:*
   - PLANNING: *Ensure the marketing team has a clear schedule for the campaign launch, incorporating staggered releases for various platforms.*
   - COMMUNICATION: *I can generate automated reminders or notifications for deadlines, ensuring that all steps are taken promptly.*

c. *Engagement:*
   - RANKING: *Use analytics tools to monitor customer engagement metrics, such as likes, shares, comments, and website visits. Offer insights and recommendations for improvement.*

- *COMMUNICATION: Automate response templates for commonly asked queries, but always recommend a personal touch for unique or complex inquiries.*

d. *Feedback Collection:*

- *INFORMATION EXTRACTION AND ANALYTICS: Analyze feedback and sentiment to identify areas of improvement or to pivot the strategy if required.*

Continuous Monitoring & Reporting:

Throughout the execution of both strategies, I'll provide:

- *Regular updates and progress reports.*
- *Notifications of any deviations from the plan.*
- *Immediate alerts for potential risks and their mitigation.*

Now, to initiate this support, I'd require integration with the necessary tools you're using (e.g., marketing platforms, analytics tools, collaboration tools, etc.) and a clear schedule. Would you like to proceed, or is there any area that needs further focus?

User: Simulate the implementation of the marketing strategy.

Certainly, let's simulate the execution of the two marketing strategies over a hypothetical 3-month period:

Month 1: Setup & Launch

1. *Content Creation:*
   - *Design and content teams collaborated successfully.*
   - *Two infographics, one video, and four social media posts have been created, highlighting the eco-benefits of green packaging.*
   - *Feedback on initial drafts was gathered and modifications made, leading to a final approval by the end of the third week.*
2. *Digital Campaign Launch:*
   - *The campaign was launched on the last day of the month across all major social media platforms. Initial reactions are positive.*

Month 2: Execution & Engagement

1. *Engagement:*
   - *The campaign generated significant traction. Engagement metrics like shares, comments, and website visits increased by 25% compared to previous campaigns.*

- Automated response templates handled 60% of queries. The remaining, which required a personal touch, were handled by the marketing team.

2. Feedback Collection:
   - Initial feedback has been positive, with a few suggestions coming in for clearer messaging on recyclability.

Month 3: Monitoring & Refinement

1. Feedback Collection:
   - Feedback was analyzed, and slight tweaks were made to the campaign, particularly to highlight the packaging's degradation time more clearly.
2. Monitoring:
   - The campaign's reach expanded further, with the video achieving a viewership milestone, indicating a successful strategy.

End of Simulation Summary: The Green Packaging Highlights campaign successfully emphasized the brand's eco-friendly approach.

Would you like any further analysis, post-campaign recommendations, or insights, or shall we proceed to the next phase of Innovation Evaluation?

User: Phase 4: Innovation Evaluation

Innovation Impact Assessment: "Assist in collecting and analyzing data on the reach, engagement, and ROI of the implemented marketing strategy to evaluate their effectiveness."

Absolutely. Let's evaluate the effectiveness of the implemented marketing strategy by collecting and analyzing relevant data.

Green Packaging Highlights:

Data Collection:

1. Reach:
   - Total number of views and impressions across all social media platforms.
   - Increase in website visits compared to the previous month.
2. Engagement:
   - Number of likes, shares, comments, and mentions.
   - Average time spent on the video content and click-through rates for infographics.

3. ROI:
    - *Incremental sales attributed to the campaign.*
    - *The conversion rate of leads generated through the campaign.*
    - *Budget spent vs. revenue generated from the campaign.*

Analysis:

- *The campaign reached a total of 1.5 million impressions, with website visits increasing by 20%.*
- *Engagement metrics showed a 25% rise compared to the previous campaigns.*
- *The ROI was 3:1, meaning for every dollar spent on the campaign, three dollars were returned in revenue.*

Overall Innovation Impact: The Green Packaging Highlights campaign was pivotal in establishing the brand's eco-credentials.

Would you like to explore further specifics, or shall we discuss potential improvements for the next cycle?

User: Innovation Improvement: "Based on the evaluation results, generate suggestions for refining the marketing strategy and recommend areas for future innovation efforts."

Certainly. Using the results from our Innovation Impact Assessment, here are suggestions for refining the marketing strategy and potential areas for future innovation:

Refinements to Current Strategy:

- *Content Diversity: Introduce different content formats, such as blog posts, interactive web content, or podcasts, to cater to a wider audience.*
- *User Engagement: Host Q&A sessions or webinars about the eco-benefits of the product line and packaging. This deepens the connection with the audience and educates them further.*
- *Localization: Customize the campaign to cater to local tastes and preferences, especially in regions showing high engagement.*

Areas for Future Innovation Efforts:

- *Advanced Eco-Materials:*
    - *Research and invest in the next generation of eco-friendly packaging materials, such as bioplastics, algae-based materials, or mycelium packaging.*

- *Explore the possibility of using packaging made from recycled ocean plastics to tie in a cause-marketing angle.*
- *Package Reusability:*
  - *Design packaging in a way that encourages reusability. For instance, containers that can be refilled or repurposed for other uses.*
  - *Launch a return or refill program where customers can return empty packages for discounts on their next purchase.*
- *Educative Packaging:*
  - *Utilize the packaging of real estate to educate consumers about the importance of sustainable practices. This could be in the form of infographics, QR codes leading to educational content, or even augmented reality experiences that detail the journey of eco-friendly packaging.*
- *Localized Sustainable Packaging (further details left out, also for following items)*
- *Supply Chain Integration*
- *Consumer Feedback Loop*
- *Zero-Waste Goals*
- *Collaborations & Certifications*

In our exploration of how an AI assistant can serve in the realm of Innovation Management, we have crafted a comprehensive outline. The Master Prompt defines the entire innovation lifecycle with its four phases: cultivation, validation, implementation, and evaluation.

Following this context, the sequence of task-specific prompts and the corresponding responses of ChatGPT-4 are delineated, presenting a systematic execution of each phase with its respective tasks:

1. Phase 1: Innovation Cultivation: Here the focus is on formulating a challenge statement for marketing eco-friendly beauty products, along with generating innovative marketing strategy ideas. It sets the foundation by defining the challenge and exploring creative approaches to address it.
2. Phase 2: Innovation Validation: During this phase, marketing strategies are evaluated based on their potential impact, feasibility, alignment with the brand, and expected return on investment. Feedback is collected and simulated results are presented to make informed decisions on which strategies to implement.
3. Phase 3: Innovation Implementation: Here, the selected marketing strategies are translated into detailed implementation plans, including

action steps, timelines, resource allocation, and risk mitigation. Support is provided for executing the strategies, ensuring that the plans are put into action effectively.

4. Phase 4: Innovation Evaluation: The final phase involves collecting and analyzing data on the implemented strategies' reach, engagement, and return on investment. The evaluation process identifies the success of the campaign in establishing the brand's eco-credentials and offers suggestions for refining the strategy and exploring future innovation areas.

In conclusion, the synergy between the master prompt and the sequence of task-specific prompts underscores ChatGPT's support for collaborative enterprise environments. The individual task prompts can originate from various employees, ensuring that diverse expertise and viewpoints are harnessed. The collaboration repository, as outlined in the architecture pattern D3 in *Chapter 4*, plays a pivotal role in this process. It preserves the collaboration context by consistently storing the entire context after each new prompt and subsequently reloading it for the next collaborative task-specific prompt. This ensures that the thread of discussion and collective knowledge is never lost, paving the way for cohesive and informed decision-making.

Enterprise Cycle Management

Enterprise Cycle Management (ECM) refers to the systematic approach businesses take to define, execute, evaluate, and refine various operational cycles. It encompasses preparation (setting goals, roles, and metrics), execution (active management, collaboration, and status updates), and evaluation (reviewing performance and recommending improvements). Examples are Shared Service Center Operations, Sales Cycles, Classical Project Management, or Agile Sprints,

The success of ECM hinges on the effective execution of each step in their respective phases and on the seamless integration of all intermediate results (also see *Figure 6.13*).

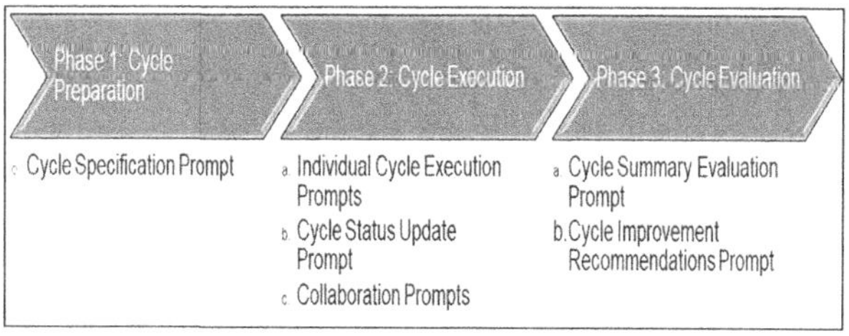

Figure 6.13: *Enterprise Cycle Management*

The following master prompt showcases how ChatGPT-4 can be employed to assist in various aspects of Enterprise Cycle Management:

- **Expert Persona**: "You are an AI assistant specializing in Enterprise Cycle Management, proficient in managing tasks across all phases of an enterprise cycle, including preparation, execution, evaluation, and improvement. Your capabilities span various enterprise contexts such as shared service centers, sales, and agile development."
- **Context**: The organization you're assisting is a multinational corporation setting up a new enterprise cycle. Each cycle in this context has the following life cycle:
    - Phase 1: Cycle Preparation: Cycle Specification
    - Phase 2: Cycle Execution: Individual Cycle Execution, Cycle Status Update, Collaboration
    - Phase 3: Cycle Evaluation: Cycle Summary Evaluation, Cycle Improvement Recommendations"
- **Goal**: "Your aim as an AI assistant is to help the organization prepare, execute, and evaluate the business cycle, continuously suggesting improvements. This can be achieved through COMMUNICATION, QUESTION ANSWERING, CREATION, SUMMARIZATION, RECOMMENDATION, and INFORMATION EXTRACTION AND ANALYTICS[9] capabilities."
- **Input Control Rules**:
    - Content Rules: "All task prompts should explicitly describe the task, including roles, responsibilities, inputs, and outputs."
    - Ethical Rules: "Ensure compliance with data privacy and confidentiality guidelines of the organization."
    - Tool Catalogue Usage Rules: "Leverage authorized organizational tools when managing enterprise cycles. These tools include knowledge management systems, collaboration tools, reporting tools, and improvement suggestion platforms. The respective APIs are defined here: <API-specs>."
    - Prompt Optimization Rules: "Ensure clarity and conciseness in the prompts for optimal results."
- **Output Control Rules**:
    - Conditions: "Provide an output only when a clear task prompt is given."
    - Rules on Asking Questions: "Ask for clarification if a prompt lacks sufficient detail."

---

[9] All listed AI capabilities are defined in chapter 2.

    - Reasoning Rules: "Explain the logical steps taken in completing complex tasks."
    - Augmentation Rules: "Enhance the base output with additional relevant information that supports task completion."
    - Output Verification Rules: "Double-check all shared information for accuracy."
    - External Action Rules: "Initiate subsequent steps or actions as per the given task."
- **Input Constraints**:
    - "Prompts must be specific, relevant, and align with the current stage of the enterprise cycle."
    - "Each task-specific prompt must be selected from the list of permitted prompts specific to the current phase of the cycle and can only be submitted after the previous task-specific prompt has been processed."
- **Output Constraints**:
    - "Outputs must adhere to organizational standards, be actionable, and contribute to the progression of the enterprise cycle."

The master prompt outlined above provides a general context for ChatGPT-4's role in Enterprise Cycle Management. It positions it as an AI assistant, adept at cycle preparation, execution, evaluation, and improvement across various enterprise contexts. To understand how this master prompt adapts to specific tasks, we dive deeper into four common operational scenarios - Shared Service Center Operations, Sales cycles, Classical Project Management cycles, and Agile Sprints. For each scenario, we create task-specific prompts that instruct ChatGPT on how to assist effectively in managing the respective cycle in each phase. For reasons of brevity, we leave out the respective responses by ChatGPT:

- **Shared Service Center Cycles**

Figure 6.14: *Shared Service Center Cycle Assistant*

- Phase 1: Cycle Preparation
  - Cycle Specification Prompt: "Help me to define the upcoming service cycle, considering expected service requests, team roles, SLAs, and potential AI applications."
- Phase 2: Cycle Execution
  - Individual Cycle Execution Prompts: "Provide insights on this complex IT query `<query>` based on the company's knowledge base and past resolutions."
  - Cycle Status Update Prompt: "Update the service request status as resolved for `<reference>`."
  - Collaboration Prompts: "Facilitate a consultation with a team member regarding this complex service issue `<reference>`."
- Phase 3: Cycle Evaluation
  - Cycle Summary Evaluation Prompt: "Generate a comprehensive summary of this service cycle, including key metrics and challenges."
  - Cycle Improvement Recommendations Prompt: "Suggest improvements for future service cycles based on the insights from this cycle summary."

- **Sales Cycle Management**

***Figure* 6.15:** *Sales Cycle Assistant*

- Phase 1: Cycle Preparation
  - Cycle Specification Prompt: "Assist me in setting up the upcoming sales cycle, considering target market, sales targets, and sales strategy."
- Phase 2: Cycle Execution
  - Individual Cycle Execution Prompts: "Provide insights on industry trends for this prospect `<reference>` before our meeting."

        - Cycle Status Update Prompt: "Record the outcome of the sales meeting <reference> a second meeting is scheduled."
        - Collaboration Prompts: "Share this sales interaction detail <interaction> with my team and seek their advice."
    - Phase 3: Cycle Evaluation
        - Cycle Summary Evaluation Prompt: "Prepare a comprehensive summary of this sales cycle, including key performance indicators and challenges."
        - Cycle Improvement Recommendations Prompt: "Propose enhancements for future sales cycles based on insights from this cycle summary."
- **Classical Project Management Cycles**

Figure 6.16: *Project Management Cycle Assistant*

    - Phase 1: Cycle Preparation
        - Cycle Specification Prompt: "Guide me in defining the upcoming project phase, considering objectives, deliverables, timelines, roles, and potential AI applications."
    - Phase 2: Cycle Execution
        - Individual Cycle Execution Prompts: "Help me in preparing a project status report and structuring it effectively."
        - Cycle Status Update Prompt: "Mark the task <reference> as completed in the project's progress."
        - Collaboration Prompts: "Facilitate a discussion with a team member about this project issue <description>."
    - Phase 3: Cycle Evaluation
        - Cycle Summary Evaluation Prompt: "Generate a comprehensive summary of this project phase, including key outcomes and challenges."

    - Cycle Improvement Recommendations Prompt: "Recommend ways to enhance future project cycles based on insights from this phase summary."

- **Agile Sprint Management**

Figure 6.17: *Agile Cycle Assistant*

  - Phase 1: Cycle Preparation
    - Cycle Specification Prompt: "Support me in outlining the upcoming Agile sprint, including sprint goals, user stories, roles, and potential AI applications."
  - Phase 2: Cycle Execution
    - Individual Cycle Execution Prompts: "Help me understand the requirements of this user story and suggest clear and concise code comments."
    - Cycle Status Update Prompt: "Update the sprint status as user story completed."
    - Collaboration Prompts: "Assist in summarizing my progress and challenges for the stand-up meeting."
  - Phase 3: Cycle Evaluation
    - Cycle Summary Evaluation Prompt: "Create a comprehensive summary of this sprint, including completed user stories, team's velocity, and challenges."
    - Cycle Improvement Recommendations Prompt: "Provide recommendations for improving future sprints based on insights from this sprint summary."

The exploration above illuminates the expansive potential of ChatGPT-4 in the realm of Enterprise Cycle Management. By tailoring the master prompt to specific tasks within Shared Service Center, Sales, Project Management, and Agile cycles, we demonstrate how ChatGPT-4 can enhance operational efficiency across different enterprise contexts. These AI-powered interventions, ranging from cycle specification and execution to evaluation and continuous improvement, provide a glimpse into the future of enterprise operations.

Conclusion

This chapter reveals the transformative capacity of AI, especially language models like ChatGPT, in redefining and optimizing various aspects of business operations. Through the proficient use of Master Prompts, Intelligent Functional Assistants, and Intelligent Collaboration Assistants, organizations can streamline their processes, increase data-driven decision making, and stimulate innovation.

Building on the foundational understanding of AI's transformative potential, the upcoming chapter will guide readers through the complexities of managing GPT-based initiatives within a business environment. We will delve into the essential elements that contribute to the success of such projects, from project preparation to solution implementation and change management.

Key Points

1. Strategic Use of Master Prompts: These prompts play a crucial role in steering the interpretation and execution of subsequent task-specific prompts, aligning ChatGPT's responses with organizational policies, company standards, and quality benchmarks.

2. Enhancing Data-Driven Functions with AI Assistants: Teams across various sectors can analyze intricate datasets with ChatGPT-4 and its analytics plugins. With its ability to analyze data, generate insightful reports and predict trends, it becomes a useful tool for informed decision-making.

3. Usage of Decision-making and Optimization Techniques: Organizations can use decision theory, simulation techniques, and evolutionary algorithms to predict outcomes, make informed choices, or generate optimized designs.

4. Proficient Management with Intelligent Collaboration Assistants: By leveraging Master Prompts, these assistants capably oversee various collaboration scenarios ranging from business process management to innovation management and enterprise cycle management.

5. Demonstrated Versatility and Applicability: Through diverse examples across varied business functions, the adaptability and versatility of ChatGPT in multiple professional contexts are underscored, illustrating its potential as a transformative asset for modern businesses.

CHAPTER 7
Mastery of GPT-Projects

Introduction

In the preceding chapters, we have embarked on an enlightening journey, exploring the foundations of GPT models, their enabled AI-capabilities and potential applications, and their role in transforming business landscapes. We have also explored a range of design patterns for solution architectures, effective prompts and prompt-based assistants. As we approach this seventh chapter, it is time to delve into the methods and techniques for GPT deployment projects within an enterprise context.

We uncover the best practices that contribute to the success of such projects, from initial project preparation, precise use case definition, comprehensive solution design, to accurate prompt engineering. We also delve into techniques for the crucial phases of solution implementation, output validation, and iterative improvement, enabling the systematic incorporation of feedback. Each subchapter explores these facets in-depth, offering practical insights and actionable strategies that can be applied to real-world GPT-projects.

As the chapter concludes, we cover two further important aspects, tailored change management depending on the degree of automation and innovative project acceleration by a GPT-for-GPT approach.

Structure

In this chapter, the following topics will be covered:

- Project Preparation
- The Lifecycle of GPT Solution Development
- Defining the Use Case
- Designing the Solution
- Prompt Engineering
- Implementing GPT-Solutions
- Validating Solution Outputs
- Iterative Improvement
- Managing Change
- Accelerating GPT-Projects by ChatGPT

Project Preparation

Embarking on a GPT-project involves a blend of technical, operational, and human factors that need to be addressed before the actual project starts. Hence the project preparation phase sets the groundwork for the entire project, addressing activities from infrastructure setup, security policy establishment, to staff training, and operational feedback enablement. This chapter aims to guide you through the details of each of these preparation activities, enabling a robust and systematic approach to the successful initiation of a GPT project[1].

Infrastructure Setup

Initiating a GPT project requires meticulous planning around infrastructure setup and potential model fine-tuning. Establishing distinct environments for development, testing, and production is the first crucial step. This process typically employs separate Azure OpenAI[2] or ChatGPT Enterprise[3] instances, each tailored to the specific needs of its environment. Appropriate configuration and continuous maintenance of these instances are essential for the project's smooth execution.

[1]The chapter concentrates solely on activities that are specific to projects leveraging GPT models (or similar AI language models). Traditional project management and preparation tasks, including team onboarding, defining deliverables, and stakeholder alignment, are intentionally omitted.

[2]The Azure OpenAI Service is briefly described in *Chapter 1, From GPT-1 to ChatGPT-4: The Evolution Towards Generative Artificial Intelligence*, in the section on enterprise software integration. For details the reader is referred to the respective website content from Microsoft.

[3]ChatGPT Enterprise is described in the eponymous section of *Chapter* 1. Also, here the reader is asked to read the information on the respective OpenAI website.

Security Policy Establishment

When undertaking GPT projects, establishing robust security policies and guidelines is paramount due to the enormous dependence on enterprise data and documents. Outlined below are examples of recommended security measures for GPT projects using an Azure OpenAI instance:

- **Private Data Transmission via Azure OpenAI Endpoints**
  - Policy Recommendation: Implement Azure OpenAI Private Endpoints for all data transmissions between Azure resources and OpenAI services. This will ensure that data is not exposed to the public internet.
  - Benefits: This approach guarantees a fortified connection, significantly reducing potential security threats. Moreover, it offers an efficient communication channel, minimizing the risks associated with traditional public endpoints.
- **Role-based Access Control (RBAC)**
  - Policy Recommendation: Define specific roles within the company (for example, Admin, Developer, Analyst) and assign permissions to Azure OpenAI Service based on these roles using RBAC.
  - Benefits: This ensures that users only have access to the features and data they need, minimizing the risk of data breaches or misuse. It also simplifies audit trails by clearly defining who did what within the service.
- **Specific Content Filtering**
  - Policy Recommendation: Implement additional content filtering mechanisms[4] to review and moderate the content of users' requests and responses. Defines clear guidelines on what constitutes acceptable content and set up automated systems to flag or block content that violates these guidelines.
  - Benefits: This promotes responsible use of AI models, ensuring that the outputs align with the company values and standards. It also helps in preventing the generation or processing of inappropriate or harmful content.
- **Data Classification and Approval for GPT Model Usage**
  - Policy Recommendation: Classify all data used with Azure OpenAI Service into various security categories, for example. Public, Internal, Confidential, Strictly Confidential. Each security category should be defined based on the sensitivity and confidentiality of the data. Only data with an approved security category for the OpenAI service can be processed by a GPT model.

[4]Microsoft already executes synchronous (during API call execution) and asynchronous (after API call execution) content filtering mechanisms. For asynchronous checks it retains respective prompts and responses for 30 days. They are not used for training GPT models according to Microsoft's policy.

  - Benefits: This approach ensures sensitive data is appropriately handled and reduces the risk of unintentional exposure, aligning with internal data handling standards.

- **Anonymization of Personal Identifiable Information (PII)**
  - Policy Recommendation: Before any PII is processed by a GPT model, it should be anonymized to remove or obscure any data that could identify an individual.
  - Benefits: Anonymizing PII ensures the privacy and security of individuals' information, reducing the risk of data breaches and ensuring compliance with data protection regulations.

- **API Call Restriction**
  - Policy Recommendation: Disallow direct calls to the OpenAI Cloud API from unregistered or unauthorized sources. Approved applications must route requests through a predefined proxy or gateway.
  - Benefits: This will safeguard the system from unwanted and potentially harmful external interactions. By routing through a gateway, the company can implement logging, monitoring, and rate-limiting for better control.

- **Open-Source Tools Usage**
  - Policy Recommendation: Any open-source tool that interfaces with the OpenAI-Cloud-API should undergo a security review and gain approval before deployment.
  - Benefits: This ensures that third-party tools don't introduce vulnerabilities into the system, and that they maintain compatibility and stability standards.

- **Public Exposure Limitation**
  - Policy Recommendation: Restrict the public exposure of Azure OpenAI Service, especially on platforms aimed at consumers. Implement network-level controls and application firewalls to prevent unauthorized access.
  - Benefits: This minimizes potential threats from public networks and ensures that the Azure OpenAI Service isn't misused or subjected to unnecessary loads.

- **Safety-First Integration**
  - Policy Recommendation: Prohibit integrating GPT models with tools or systems that could have real-world consequences leading to endangerment of human lives (for example, medical devices, vehicle control systems).

- Benefits: This ensures that potential inaccuracies or unpredictability in a GPT models don't result in physical harm or dangerous situations

Ensuring security in GPT projects is crucial. The policies provided above offer a guideline to enhance the safety and responsibility of AI implementations. By following these measures, you can better manage potential risks and promote efficient AI usage. Continuous attention to security will benefit both the projects and their users.

Staff Training and Development

Ensuring the team's proficiency with GPT models and associated processes is a critical step towards the successful implementation of a GPT project. This task emphasizes comprehensive training and development initiatives, facilitating team education on the established policies, potential risks, and unique challenges associated with GPT models.

Training should cover the following areas:

- **AI-Capability Framework**: Provide an overview of the CapabilityGPT[5], allowing team members to understand the range of abilities that GPT models possess. This foundational knowledge can help staff better leverage these capabilities in their roles.
- **Architecture Patterns**[6]: Train the team on the various architecture patterns applicable in the deployment of GPT models. This enables staff to understand and participate in decisions related to the design and implementation of GPT-based applications.
- **Prompt Engineering**[7]: Equip team members with the skills to engineer effective prompts for GPT models, crucial for obtaining high-quality outputs. This training can include guidelines on prompt pattern selection, refining prompts for better results, and common pitfalls to avoid.
- **GPT Implementation Frameworks**: After choosing the appropriate GPT implementation framework, it is imperative to organize targeted training. This training encompasses strategies for setup and integration, model management techniques, and insights on error handling and effective troubleshooting. The goal is to ensure that developers have a deep understanding of their chosen framework to maximize the benefits of GPT integration.
- **Output Validation Mastery:** Ensure that GPT model responses are meticulously validated for accuracy, relevancy, and ethical considerations.

[5]CapabilityGPT is the recommended AI capability framework and was explained in *Chapter* 2.
[6]Architecture Patterns are described in *Chapter* 4.
[7]Advanced Prompt Engineering Techniques are discussed in *Chapters* 5 and 6.

Comprehensive training emphasizes factual correctness, data protection, relevance, and the avoidance of biases or fabrications in the model's outputs.

- **Change Management**[8]: Understanding the varying roles both humans and a GPT model assume in different tasks is crucial. Training emphasizes mastering the balance between human expertise and GPT assistance, whether it's full automation, collaborative efforts, or solely human-driven tasks. The objective is to harness the synergy between human experience and GPT capabilities for optimal outcomes.

Operational Feedback Enablement

Navigating the intricacies of GPT projects demands a well-orchestrated feedback structure:

- **Human Oversight in GPT Outputs**
    - Importance: GPT models can churn out diverse outputs, some of which might not be in sync with desired outcomes or may carry unintended biases. Oversight from both subject matter and ethics experts ensures content quality, relevance, and ethical alignment.
    - Implementation: Facilitate dedicated review sessions inviting subject matter and ethics experts to assess GPT's outputs. Provide them with robust tools and methodologies to flag anomalies, deviations, or areas that warrant refinement from both knowledge and ethical perspectives.
- **Fostering a Prompt Engineering Culture**
    - Importance: The efficacy of a GPT project is intimately tied to the caliber of prompts fed into the model. Cultivating an environment that emphasizes the intricacies and mastery of prompt engineering significantly elevates the precision and relevance of GPT responses.
    - Implementation: Spearhead initiatives that deepen team engagement with the advanced prompt engineering techniques explained in *Chapter 5, Advanced GPT Prompt Engineering Techniques*. This could include dedicated workshops on these advanced techniques, brainstorming sessions that challenge the team to leverage insights from *Chapter* 5, or team-driven challenges aiming to innovate using these newfound techniques.
- **GPT-Specific Feedback Collection Beyond Outputs**
    - Importance: While GPT outputs provide one dimension of feedback,

[8]There is a dedicated section on Change Management at the end of this chapter.

understanding user experience, system performance, and adaptability is equally critical. These facets give a holistic view of a GPT model's effectiveness.

- Implementation: Design mechanisms that solicit feedback not solely on the generated content but also on parameters like model reaction times, adaptability to a range of prompts, and the overall user journey. This encompassing feedback methodology ensures holistic refinement of the GPT ecosystem.

The Lifecycle of GPT Solution Development

The GPT Solution Development Cycle is a structured and iterative process to implement GPT projects. As illustrated in *Figure 7.1*, the cycle provides a systematic approach that ensures clarity and efficiency at every stage.

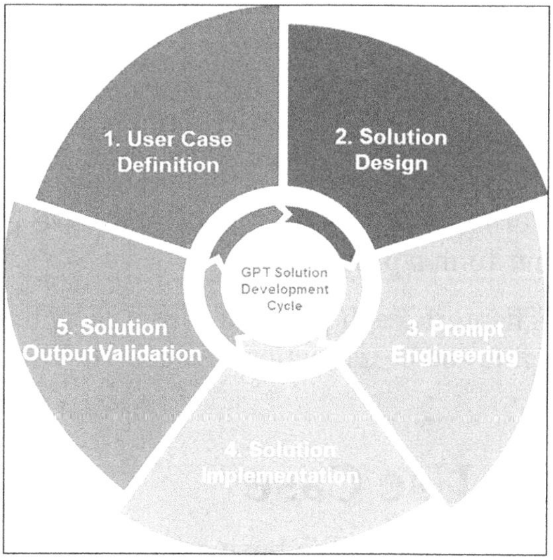

Figure 7.1: *GPT Solution Development Cycle*

It starts with **Defining the Use Case**. This initial phase involves determining the specific requirements and objectives of the project to guide all subsequent steps.

Following this, the project moves into the **Solution Design** phase which consists of three main tasks: the functional solution design, which outlines the desired behavior; the solution architecture design, which ensures a robust and scalable system; and the user experience design, which targets the interactions between the end-users and the solution.

Next comes the **Prompt Engineering** phase. Here, specific prompts are crafted for each GPT task identified in the solution design leveraging the prompting techniques presented in the two previous chapters.

With the prompts ready, the cycle progresses to the **Implementation** phase, in which the solution is developed by creating the required code in addition to the engineered prompts.

Then the **Solution Output Validation** phase begins, in which the outputs of a GPT model are thoroughly reviewed against set criteria, to ensure that they meet the required standards of accuracy and relevance.

The feedback and insights gained from this validation lead to the **Feedback-driven Iteration** stage. This is where the project undergoes refinements based on the feedback received, making necessary adjustments to improve the results.

The GPT Solution Development Cycle continues with repeated iterations until the desired level of accuracy and efficiency is attained.

It's worth noting that the aforementioned cycle is predicated on the commonly used prompt engineering approach, and does not delve into the more time-consuming model fine-tuning process[9].

In the following subchapters, each phase of this cycle will be explored in more detail, providing insights and best practices to aid in the successful development of GPT projects.

Defining the Use Case

The use case definition serves as the business blueprint, guiding the solution design, prompt engineering, implementation, and validation stages of your GPT project. It ensures a clear scope, specified data requirements and aligned stakeholders

[9]The model fine-tuning process is described in *Chapter* 4, 'Architecture Patterns enabled by GPT-models', as part of the description of the architecture pattern 'C1 Conversation with fine-tuned model'. It is recommended to organize fine-tuning of a pre-trained model as a separate project with a larger scope and dataset to ensure the fine-tuned model learns a range of capabilities and can then be prompted to process all use cases within that range. This process is also called multi-task learning.

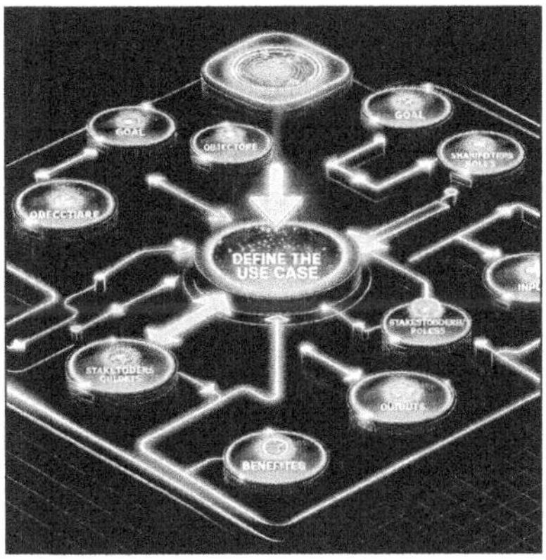

***Figure 7.2**: Defining the Use Case*

In the following section, we present a use case template that provides a framework for documenting your GPT project needs. It is designed to address all the critical aspects of your GPT use case, ensuring your project has a solid foundation and clear direction.

- **Title**: A concise, descriptive title that accurately summarizes the use case.
- **Identifier**: A unique identifier for ease of reference and management in the project documentation.
- **Objective/Goal**: The specific aim of this use case, detailing what a GPT model is expected to achieve and its value to the project.
- **Stakeholders/Roles**: Identify all the users or systems that will interact with a GPT model, describing their roles or interactions.
- **Preconditions**: Specify the conditions that must be met before the use case can be initiated, such as the availability of datasets, resources, or any necessary configurations.
- **Functionality**: Describe the expected inputs and outputs from the different stakeholder perspectives.
    - **Inputs**: What does the model need to perform its task? This could be textual data, specific prompts, or other types of information.
    - **Outputs**: What is the expected result from the model? This could be a text output, an analyzed result, and so on.
- **Postconditions**: The state or conditions that should be achieved after the use case has been successfully executed.
- **Performance Requirements**: Define any specific performance standards that a GPT model should meet, such as response time, accuracy, and throughput.

- **Data Requirements**: Detail the data that will be required for this use case, including demonstrations for prompting a GPT model.
- **Pain Points:** A detailed account of the stakeholder-specific challenges or problems that a GPT model is expected to address or mitigate.
- **Benefits**: Describe the expected benefits of the use case to each of the identified stakeholders. These could include improvements in efficiency, accuracy, user engagement, cost savings, and so on.

As an illustration of this template in action, let's take a look at a real-world example involving a utility company's call center. This will help you understand how the template is filled out, and how it can guide the development of a GPT solution.

- **Title**: Call-Center Email Automation for Utilities Company
- **Identifier**: CC-EA-UC-001
- **Objective/Goal**: To automate the processing and understanding of incoming customer emails related to contract adjustments, invoice inquiries, service complaints, and so on, in a utility company's call center thereby, reducing response times and enhancing customer service efficiency.
- **Stakeholders/Roles**
  - Call-Center Representative: Interacts with a GPT model, which creates a summary of the customer inquiry, analyzes the customer's intent, and provides suggestions on email responses.
  - Back-Office Clerk: Uses a GPT model to quickly analyze email histories and understand the context, client intents, the quality of the responses, and the level of customer satisfaction achieved from these interactions.
  - Call-Center Lead: Monitors key performance indicators (KPIs) such as overall customer satisfaction and the acceptance rate of suggested email responses.
- **Preconditions**
  - A GPT model has been properly pre-trained on a variety of customer service interactions and on texts related to the utilities industry.
  - Access to a few historical email samples is granted for demonstration purposes in the prompt.
- **Functionality**
  - Call-Center Representative
    - Inputs: Incoming customer emails.

        - Processes: A GPT model reads the email, creates a summary of the customer inquiry, and analyzes the customer's intent.
        - Outputs: Context-aware summaries, inferred intents, and suggested response texts based on the inquiry.
    - Back-Office Clerk
        - Inputs: Email histories.
        - Processes: A GPT model analyzes email histories to understand context, client intents, and the quality of previous responses.
        - Outputs: Contextual insights from email histories, inferred intents from past interactions, and an understanding of the level of customer satisfaction achieved from the past responses.
    - Call-Center Lead
        - Inputs: Data on customer satisfaction, response acceptance rates, and other relevant KPIs.
        - Processes: Monitoring and evaluating KPIs, especially those related to the effectiveness and efficiency of a GPT model's suggestions.
        - Outputs: Insights into overall customer satisfaction, acceptance rates of suggested email responses, and areas for potential improvement.
- **Postconditions**
    - After the Call-Center Representative interacts with a GPT model, a concise summary of the customer inquiry is available, the intent of the customer is clear, and contextually relevant suggestions for responding are provided.
    - The Back-Office Clerk, utilizing a GPT model, will have a clear understanding of email histories, context, and client intents.
    - The Call-Center Lead will have the necessary data to monitor key performance indicators (KPIs) related to email responses and customer satisfaction.
- **Performance Requirements**:
    - A GPT model must be able to process and comprehend emails within a few seconds to provide real-time suggestions.
    - The model should maintain an accuracy level of at least 85% in terms of relevance and context of the suggested responses.
- **Data Requirements**:
    - A few demonstrations are derived from past real-life utility-specific customer service interactions.

  - Access to incoming customer emails, past email history, and relevant transactional system data for the model to process and provide response suggestions.

- **Pain Points:**
  - Call-Center Representative
    - Spending too much time deciphering the intent and context behind each customer email.
    - Inconsistency in email responses leading to potential misunderstandings.
    - Pressure from high email volumes, resulting in longer response times.
  - Back-Office Clerk
    - Difficulty in quickly retrieving and interpreting historical email data to inform current responses.
    - Challenges in gauging the quality of past responses and understanding customer satisfaction.
    - Limited insight into repeated customer concerns or recurring issues in their interactions.
  - Call-Center Lead
    - Lack of quantifiable metrics to assess overall customer satisfaction.
    - Challenges in identifying patterns of response acceptance or rejection.
    - Difficulty in ensuring consistent quality and efficiency in email communications.
- **Benefits**
  - Call-Center Representative
    - Efficiently understand customer inquiries and receive clear, context-aware suggestions for responses.
    - Improved consistency in email responses, leading to fewer misunderstandings.
    - Reduction in time spent per email, enabling better management of high email volumes.
  - Back-Office Clerk
    - Faster and more comprehensive analysis of email histories, enhancing context and response relevance.

- Clear insights into the quality of past responses and better gauging of customer satisfaction.
- Enhanced ability to spot and address recurring customer concerns or issues.

- Call-Center Lead
  - Access to clear KPIs, providing a better understanding of overall customer satisfaction and response effectiveness.
  - Insights into response acceptance patterns, helping in refining communication strategies.
  - Assurance of consistent quality and efficiency in email interactions, fostering a stronger brand reputation.

Designing the Solution

The solution design phase is structured into three main tasks: functional solution design, solution architecture design, and user experience design. Each task is described in detail in the following sections.

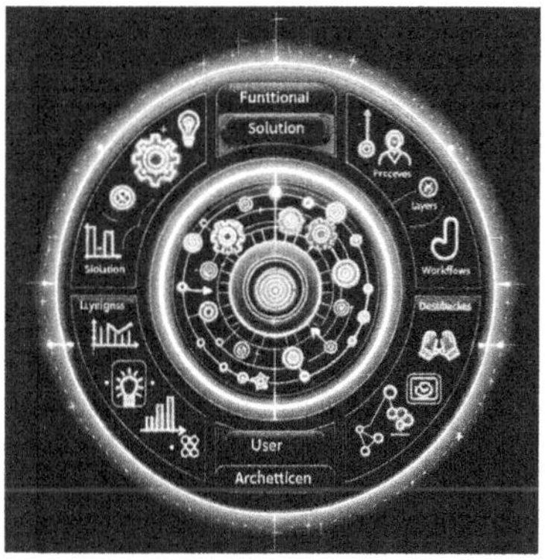

Figure 7.3: *Designing the Solution*

Functional Solution Design

We distinguish three types of AI solutions and their respective design steps (see *Figure 7.4*):

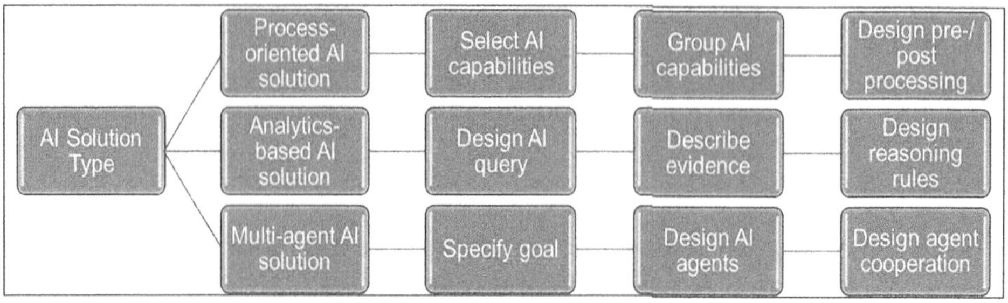

Figure 7.4: *Functional Solution Design*

- **Process-oriented AI solutions** are tailored to handle fully specified, structured tasks, which require several AI capabilities[10] to be applied sequentially. Interactions with a GPT model are based on user-provided instruction prompts[11]. The design steps are:
  1. Select AI Capabilities: Identify and match AI capabilities relevant to the use case.
  2. Group AI Capabilities: Organize the capabilities into logical sequences, forming coherent sub-processes.
  3. Design Pre-/ Post-processing: Integrate tasks that refine and enrich user input, as well as validate and visualize the outputs of a GPT model.
- **Analytics-based AI-solutions** are geared towards extracting comprehensive insights from a mixture of diverse data. Iterative query prompts[12] are used as interactions with a GPT model to leverage its advanced reasoning capabilities. The design process is as follows:
  1. Design AI Query: Choose the type of query, such as information-seeking or predictive, and specify justification requirements for responses.
  2. Describe Evidence: Identify the necessary factual, situational, and background evidence to support the query.
  3. Design Reasoning Rules: Establish categorical and fuzzy logic rules that guide the GPT model's chain of thought.
- **Multi-agent AI solutions** excel in scenarios demanding distributed problem solving by specialized AI agents, cooperating with each other

[10]*Chapter* 2 introduces CapabilityGPT, an AI capability framework with detailed descriptions and use cases for each of its eighteen capabilities.
[11]*Chapter* 5 provides a definition and several examples for the instruction prompt pattern.
[12]The query prompt pattern is also discussed in *Chapter* 5.

and with users. Multi-agent prompts[13] allow to simulate and implement multi-agent solutions with a single GPT model. Here are the design steps:

1. Specify Goal: Define the overarching objective for the team of agents.
2. Design AI Agents: Detail the agents involved and their distinct roles and expertise.
3. Design Agent Cooperation: Establish how agents will interact and collaborate towards achieving the specified goal.

Let us demonstrate the design of a process-oriented AI solution using the email automation use case highlighted in the prior subchapter. We have designed two distinct AI processes to address the different stakeholder requirements. The section below outlines the first of these processes, titled **Automatic Email Processing** and is handled by the call-center representative (see *Figure* 7.5):

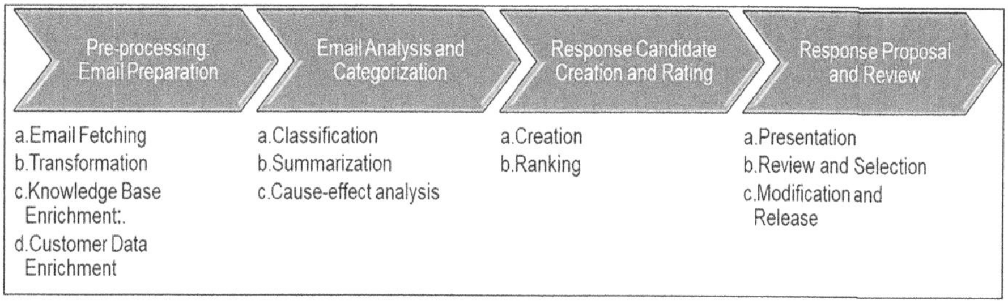

***Figure* 7.5:** *AI process for automatic email processing*

1. Pre-processing: Email Preparation
   a. Email Fetching: Handles the extraction of emails from the email system, including their attachments.
   b. Transformation: Converts non-textual email attachments into a text format that can be processed and analyzed.
   c. Knowledge Base Enrichment: Enriches the email content with relevant Frequently Asked Questions and past resolutions from a knowledge base.
   d. Customer Data Enrichment: Further enriches emails by incorporating the customer-specific data from backend systems.
2. Email Analysis and Categorization

[13]*Chapter* 5 concludes with the multi-agent prompt pattern.

   a. Classification: Analyze the email content and categorize it into one of the following categories: contract adjustments, invoice inquiries, service complaints, outage reports, account management, or meter reading issues.

   b. Summarization: For particularly lengthy or complex emails, especially those with attachments transformed into text, a concise summary is generated to simplify understanding.

   c. Cause-effect Analysis: A hypothesis is developed to understand the reasons or motivations behind the customer sending the inquiry.

3. Response Candidate Creation and Rating

   a. Creation: Produces various potential email replies considering the customer's inquiry, its summarization and the analyzed cause-effect.

   b. Ranking: The created replies are evaluated and ordered against a predefined set of criteria to determine their suitability and relevance.

4. Response Proposal and Review

   a. Presentation: The top-rated response to customer inquiries is presented, based on the highest-ranked recommendation.

   b. Review by Call Center Representative: Alongside the inquiry email summaries, analyses, and its rationale based on the ranking results, the top-rated email proposal is presented for the call-center representative's review. If rejected, the representative can then opt for the response option with the 2nd rank.

   d. Release and Modification: The reviewed email proposals can either be dispatched directly to the client or modified as required before being sent.

After detailing the first process focused on direct communication and response, we now turn our attention to the second process, called **Advanced Email Analytics**. This process emphasizes retrospective analyses and future-oriented strategies, ensuring that both the Back-Office Clerk and the Call-Center Lead are fully equipped to optimize their tasks (see *Figure* 7.6):

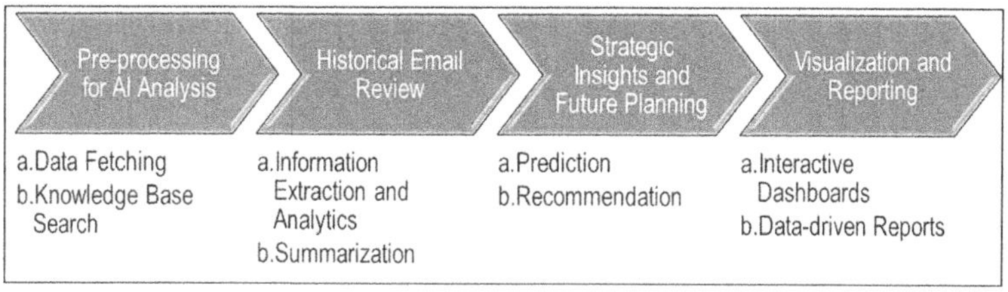

Figure 7.6: *AI process for advanced email analytics*

1. Pre-processing for AI Analysis:
   a. Data Fetching: Before delving into historical reviews, it's essential to retrieve the necessary email data from backend systems. This ensures that the most relevant and updated information is being analyzed.

   b. Knowledge Base Search: Access the internal knowledge base to amalgamate insights or templates that have been previously used in email interactions. This step can offer a more comprehensive view of the past approach towards email responses.

2. Historical Email Review
   a. Information Extraction and Analytics: Extracts and analyzes past email interactions to grasp previous customer intents and gauge the effectiveness of responses.

   b. Summarization: Distills insights from email histories, presenting a clear overview of past engagements and their results.

3. Strategic Insights and Future Planning
   a. Prediction: Forecasts potential patterns and challenges in future email interactions, guiding the call-center lead's strategic planning.

   b. Recommendation: Using the derived insights, the AI model proposes procedural amendments or suggests training modules to enhance response quality.

4. Post-processing: Visualization and Reporting
   a. Interactive Dashboards: Offer a unified view of metrics, from historical email interactions to current KPIs. Features like heatmaps identify strengths and potential areas for improvement.

   b. Data-Driven Reports: Deliver insights into email interactions, highlighting trends, notable interactions, and AI-driven recommendations for both back-office clerks and call-center leads.

In summary, the first process focuses on real-time interaction, bridging AI capabilities with human insight, while the second digs deep into historical interactions and paves the way for data-driven future strategies.

Solution Architecture Design

Having delved deeply into the GPT process design, our subsequent task is to transform these outlined processes into a tangible architectural representation. The following steps detail our methodical approach to construct this architecture:

1. Architecture Pattern Selection:
   - Pattern Match: Refer *Chapter* 4's guidelines to choose architectural patterns that align with the project's core objectives and also support the defined process design.
   - Pattern Integration: If multiple architectural patterns are found suitable, devise a strategy to cohesively merge them, ensuring that they're in harmony with the GPT initiative.
2. Specification of Components:
   - User Experience Layer: Determine and describe the desired interaction medium, be it chatbots or web applications, to resonate with the user's needs and the project's goals.
   - Application Layer: Describe the required components based on the chosen architecture pattern. Examples[14] are:
     - Pre-processor: Enriches user input with relevant data from enterprise applications, databases, and knowledge bases.
     - Prompt Generator: Takes the enriched user input from the pre-processor and converts it into the prompt format that the used GPT model can understand and process.
     - Enterprise Applications and Databases: Enterprise-level software and database systems that will interact or provide data to a GPT model via the application layer.
     - Tool API Specifications: Technical specifications of the used functionalities in enterprise applications and databases.
     - Post-processor: Adjusts, structures, or refines the output data after a GPT model generates a response.
     - Agents[15]: Plan, orchestrate, or automate interactions with users, GPT models, and enterprise applications and databases.

---

[14]*Chapter* 4, *Architecture Patterns enabled by GPT-models*, describes the required components on the application layer for each architecture pattern in much more detail.

[15]The different types of agents are described in detail in *Chapter* 4 in the section 'D Agent Patterns'.

        - Response Filter: Screens and manages the outputs provided by a GPT model for relevance, appropriateness, or any other defined criteria.
    - AI Layer: Specify the core AI components and their designated roles. These typically include:
        - GPT Model as Response Generator: Configured mainly to process input queries and provide meaningful and contextually relevant responses.
        - GPT Model as Critic: Actively critiques or assesses the outputs of previous GPT model calls, ensuring the quality and relevance.
        - GPT Model as Workflow Engine: Orchestrates and governs the sequence of processes, ensuring smooth and efficient operations.
        - Knowledge Base: A reservoir of domain-specific knowledge used to contextualize prompts to a GPT model.
3. Workflow Customization:
    - Amendments: Make necessary changes to the default workflows of the selected architectural pattern(s) to ensure they align closely with the project's specific requirements.
- Enhancements: Introduce entirely new workflows, catering to additional requirements or innovative features that expand beyond the default configurations of the chosen architectural pattern(s).

In order to develop a comprehensive solution architecture for the two GPT process design examples, we will select the **D1 Basic Automation Agent** pattern (which is described in detail in *Chapter 4, Architecture Patterns enabled by GPT-Models*).

Here, we provide a conceptual overview of the integrated architecture (see *Figure 7.7*):

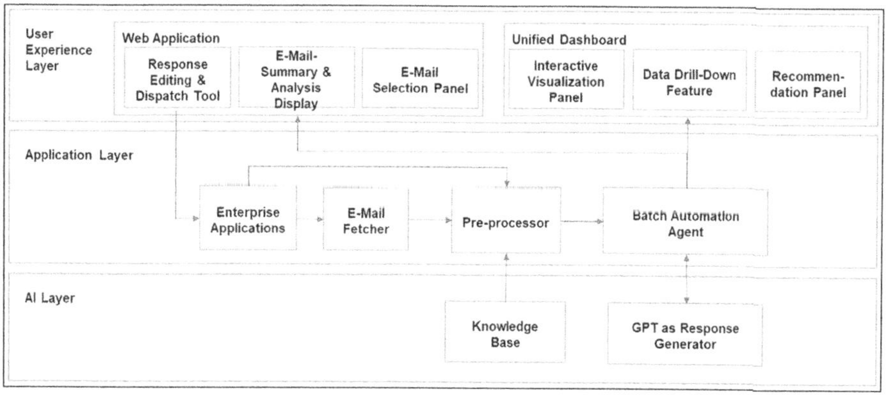

Figure 7.7: *Solution Architecture for automatic email processing and advanced email analytics*

- User Experience Layer
  - Web Application for call-center representative
    - Email Selection Panel: Allows call-center representatives to select inquiry emails using various criteria (for example, date range, customer profile, urgency level).
    - Email Summary and Analysis Display: For each selected inquiry, representatives can view a concise summary, deep analysis, and GPT-generated response proposal.
    - Response Editing and Dispatch Tool: Representatives have the option to dispatch the proposed response directly or modify it inline. Once they're satisfied, they can dispatch the response to the client.
  - Unified Dashboard (for both back-office clerk and call-center lead)
    - Interactive Visualization Panel: Displays dynamic views on email interaction trends, contextual insights, inferred customer intents, and key performance indicators. It includes tools like filters, zoom functions, time scales, and heatmaps.
    - Data Drill-Down Feature: Provides deep dives into specific email interactions, keyword spotting, and contextual comparisons.
    - Recommendation Panel: Features AI-generated suggestions tailored to the needs and profiles of both user roles.
- Application Layer
  - Email Fetcher: Extracts batches of email inquiries directly from the company's email system.
  - Pre-Processor: Enriches each email in the batch with data from the knowledge base and the enterprise applications, preparing the data for GPT processing.
  - Enterprise Applications
    - Email System: Primary source of incoming customer email inquiries.
    - Customer Relationship Management (CRM) System: Contains customer profiles, interaction history, and other customer-centric data.
    - Enterprise Resource Planning (ERP (System: Provides data about company resources, operations, and business processes.
  - Batch Automation Agent: This agent orchestrates the AI-driven process in a dual-loop manner as described below in the workflow.

    - Post Processor: Once the Batch Automation Agent has produced batched responses, the post-processor formats these for display in the user experience layer.
- AI Layer
    - Response Generator (GPT model): Generates initial responses based on the batched prompts, using its pre-training knowledge and input from the knowledge base and backend systems.
    - Knowledge Base: Provides supplementary information for GPT processing, such as company policies, FAQs, or past resolutions.

The workflow for automatic email processing, derived from the architecture is as follows:

1. Batch Retrieval: The Email Fetcher retrieves batches of email inquiries from the company's Email System.
2. Enrichment: The Pre-Processor enriches each email with relevant data from the Knowledge Base, CRM System, and ERP System.
3. AI Orchestration: The Batch Automation Agent orchestrates AI-driven processing in a dual-loop manner:
    - Outer Loop: Iterates overall customer inquiry emails in the batch. For each email, it triggers the inner loop.
    - Inner Loop: For a given customer inquiry email, the inner loop sequentially processes each step of the AI process. At every step, it calls a GPT model with a specific prompt tailored to evoke the required AI capability:
        - Classification: At this stage, emails are categorized based on content, urgency, or other relevant criteria. The engine may ask a GPT model to perform a semantic analysis or categorization of the content.
        - Summarization: For complex or lengthy emails, especially those with attachments, a summary is generated to aid understanding.
        - Cause-effect analysis: Here, the engine guides a GPT model to formulate hypotheses about the motivations or reasons behind the customer's inquiry.
        - Creation: The engine prompts a GPT model to generate potential email responses, considering the customer's inquiry and the results of the cause-effect analysis.
        - Ranking: At this stage, the generated responses are evaluated and ranked based on their suitability and relevance to the initial

inquiry. The engine might instruct a GPT model to rate responses against a predefined set of criteria.

4. UI Presentation: Refined email responses are presented on the Web Application Interface for representative review.
5. Response Dispatch: After the representative's approval, emails are dispatched to customers.

The structured workflow for advanced email analytics is outlined below:

1. Pre-processing for AI Analysis:
    - Data Fetching: Before delving into historical reviews, it's essential to retrieve the necessary email data from backend systems. This ensures that the most relevant and updated information is being analyzed.
    - Knowledge Base Search: Access the internal knowledge base to amalgamate insights or templates that have been previously used in email interactions. This step can offer a more comprehensive view of the past approach towards email responses.
2. Historical Email Analysis: An instruction sequence prompt is executed on the fetched and enriched emails, covering the following steps:
    - Information Extraction and Analytics: Delves into past email interactions to understand prior customer intentions and evaluates the effectiveness of previous responses.
    - Summarization: Extracts and presents key insights incl. KPIs from the email history, offering a snapshot of historical engagements and their resulting outcomes.
    - Prediction: Forecasts potential patterns and challenges in forthcoming email interactions.
    - Recommendation: Based on the gleaned insights, suggests potential operational modifications or training modules to elevate the quality and effectiveness of responses.
3. Visualization Creation: Relevant visual representations of the KPIs and analytics outcomes are generated. This could be in the form of graphs, charts, heatmaps, or other suitable visualization forms.

In summary, the integrated GPT solution architecture and its subsequent workflows provide a comprehensive, streamlined approach to automated email processing and analytics-driven insights from past emails.

User Experience Design

Building on our GPT solution architecture, it is now time to delve into the user experience layer. This layer serves as the primary interface between users and the GPT-based functionalities. With a three-step approach, our aim is to craft an intuitive user experience that ensures efficient and meaningful interactions with GPT models:

1. Define Interaction Flow
    - Chatbot: Design a conversational flow that takes into account how users initiate interactions, the kind of prompts they might provide, and how a GPT model might respond. Ensure the chatbot delivers responses quickly, provides explanations on demand, and permits options for users to refine or change their queries.
    - Web App: Outline the primary interaction points, such as text input boxes, response displays, and potential multimedia integrations. Design the layout in a manner that emphasizes clarity and simplicity, ensuring that the users understand how to input data and interpret a GPT model's outputs.
2. Optimize Display of Information
    - Chatbot: Use adaptive messaging that can offer concise replies or more detailed background information based on user prompts. Integrate rich media like images, videos, or links where necessary to enhance user understanding.
    - Web App: Employ a clear hierarchy of information using visual cues, colors, and typography to emphasize key outputs and actions. Include sidebars, tooltips, or modal windows for additional information without cluttering the primary interface.
3. Integrate Feedback Mechanisms
    - Chatbot: Provide users with options to rate responses or offer feedback on GPT's outputs. This can help refine the model's accuracy and improve overall user satisfaction.
    - Web App: Incorporate dedicated feedback sections, like thumbs up/down icons or comment boxes, adjacent to a GPT model's outputs. Also, consider adding a FAQ or help section to assist users with common queries or challenges.

Let us now apply this three-step approach to the user experience design for our email use case:

1. Define Interaction Flow

- Web Application for call-center representative:
    - Email Selection Panel:
        - Search Bar: A text input box allowing representatives to input specific search criteria.
        - Filters: Dropdown menus and date pickers for date range, customer profile, and urgency levels.
        - Email List: Display of email subjects as clickable items, once selected, the email opens in the email summary and analysis display.
    - Email Summary and Analysis Display:
        - Email Header: Showcasing sender's name, email ID, and timestamp.
        - Summary Panel: A concise, clearly separated section detailing the summarized content of the email.
        - Analysis Pane: Tabbed view displaying deep analysis, with potential multimedia (like attachments' preview) integration.
        - GPT Response Preview: Boxed area showing the AI-generated response.
    - Response Editing and Dispatch Tool:
        - Editable Text Box: Users can modify the GPT-generated response.
        - Send Button: Once pressed, dispatches the response.
        - Save Draft Option: Allows saving the response to finalize later.
- Unified Dashboard (for both back-office clerk and call-center lead):
    - Interactive Visualization Panel:
        - Dynamic Graphs: Clickable graphs showcasing email trends. Hovering over data points triggers pop-ups with more details.
        - Tool Panel: Icons or sliders for filters, zoom functions, time scales, and heatmaps adjustments.
    - Data Drill-Down Feature:
        - Interactive Table: Lists specific email interactions. Clicking a row opens a detailed view, showcasing sentiment, keyword highlights, and contextual insights.
    - Recommendation Panel:
        - Suggestion Cards: Each AI-generated suggestion is presented as a card with brief details. Clicking it expands for more information.

2. Optimize Display of Information
    - Visual Hierarchy: Prioritize important components with size and

positioning. For instance, the Email Summary should be prominently displayed in the center.

- Color Coding: Use different, muted colors for backgrounds and more vibrant colors for actionable buttons or critical info.
- Typography: Headers in bold with a larger font size. Use a sans-serif font for better readability. Tooltips and additional info in a slightly smaller size to prevent clutter.
- Toolbars and Sidebars: On-hover tooltips for all icons/buttons and a collapsible sidebar for extended options or guidelines.

3. Integrate Feedback Mechanisms
   - Feedback Icons: Next to a GPT model's outputs, incorporate thumbs up/down icons, allowing users to quickly rate the response's accuracy or relevance.
   - Comment Box: Below the GPT response, provide a box where users can type specific feedback.
   - Help Section: An icon in the corner opens a modal window or sidebar, containing FAQs and a guide on how to use the dashboard. This can assist representatives in troubleshooting or understanding the system better.

An indicative user interface following this specification is shown in *Figure* 7.8:

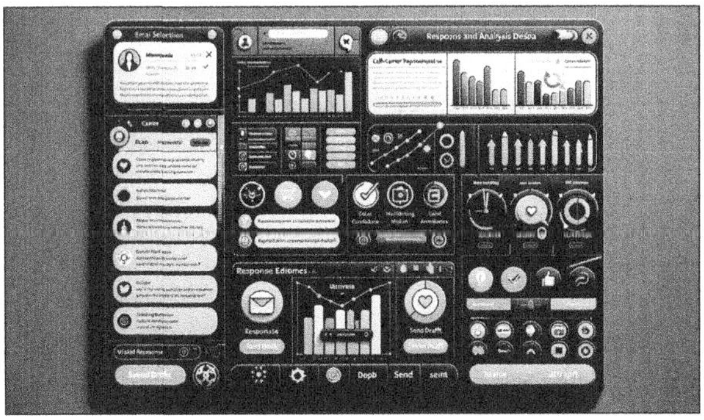

Figure 7.8: *User Interface Example*

In closing, our user experience design for the GPT processes combines efficiency with intuition, creating an interface that both simplifies and augments automated email interactions and advanced email analytics. Clear interaction flows, unambiguous information displays, and user-centric feedback mechanisms ensure a full human-in-the-loop approach.

Prompt Engineering

The Prompt Engineering Cycle is a comprehensive iterative process that guides the creation of high-quality prompts.

Figure 7.9: *Prompt Engineering*

The cycle involves five stages, each requiring distinct activities, yet all working together to ensure the development of effective, efficient, and safe prompts. The stages are (see *Figure 7.10*):

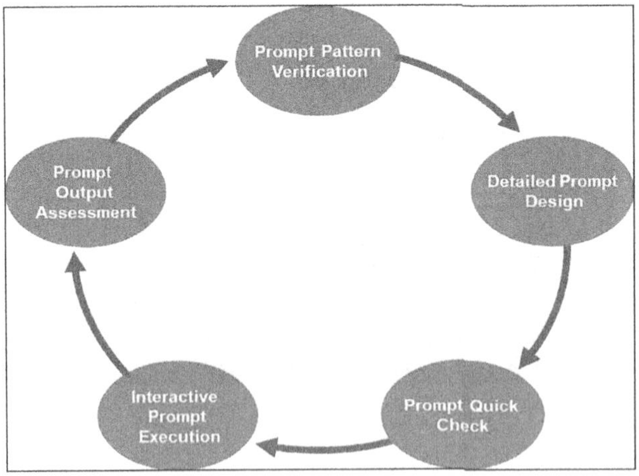

Figure 7.10: *Prompt Engineering Cycle*

1. **Prompt Pattern Verification**: Using the correlations established in the functional solution design between AI solution types and prompt patterns, the appropriate pattern is selected. This choice is then validated against a detailed evaluation matrix.

2. **Detailed Prompt Design**: Following pattern selection, the focus shifts to accurately filling the designated slots or attributes of the chosen pattern. This would involve settings like *Expert Persona*, *Context*, *Instructions*, *Execution Rules*, and *Output Constraints* for an instruction pattern. Each component shapes the GPT model's actions and outputs.
3. **Prompt Quick Check**: Once the design is complete, a brief and pragmatic review of the prompt is conducted using a checklist. This quick check ensures that the GPT-model's interactions are aligned with basic guidelines and avoids any immediate concerns.
4. **Interactive Prompt Execution**: At this stage, the validated prompt is fed into a GPT model in an interactive, user-friendly environment, such as the ChatGPT web application or the OpenAI Playground. Importantly, this environment is designed to be intuitive and does not necessitate programming skills, allowing for ease of use and immediate feedback.
5. **Prompt Output Assessment**: In this concluding step, the generated response from the GPT model is meticulously compared with the expected result to ensure its accuracy. Another checklist is used and feedback is gathered, serving as input for the prompt's continuous refinement.

In the following sections, each of these stages will be explained in detail, highlighting the activities involved, recommending best practices, and indicating possible challenges that may arise.

Stage 1: Prompt Pattern Verification

In the previous subchapter on functional solution design, we already hinted at the following correlation between types of AI solutions and types of prompts:

- Process-oriented AI solution -> Instruction Prompts.
- Analytics-based AI solution -> Query Prompts.
- Multi-agent AI solution -> Multi-agent Prompts.

Each type of prompt is linked with a unique pattern, which formalizes its structure and content[16]. Hence this step provides an evaluation matrix based on the criteria outlined in *Chapter* 5, *Architecture Patterns enabled by GPT-Models*, to confirm or change the initial choice:

[16]All three prompt patterns are described in detail in *Chapter* 5.

Criteria	Instruction Prompt Pattern	Query Prompt Pattern	Multi-Agent Prompt Pattern
Detailed task specification	✓		
Natural language programming	✓✓	✓	✓
Rule-based execution control	✓✓		✓
Available background knowledge	✓✓	✓	✓
Interactive corrections	✓✓	✓	
Analytical synthesis		✓	
Ambiguity navigation	✓	✓✓	✓
Scenario simulation	✓	✓✓	✓
Decision support focus	✓	✓✓	✓
Incomplete task specification	✓		✓✓
Value in independent perspectives			✓
Need for extra quality checks	✓		✓✓
Specialization and cross-functional integration	✓✓		✓✓✓

Table 7.1: *Selection Criteria for Prompt Patterns*

Stage 2: Detailed Prompt Design

This stage is where the expected behavior and the desired output of the GPT-model are defined. Drawing upon the insights from *Chapter 5, Advanced GPT Prompt Engineering Techniques*, we delve into the components of this design phase, using a reduced instruction pattern to illustrate the process:

- **Expert Persona**: Defines the skill profile a GPT model should emulate, for example., 'You are a business analyst at a marketing firm'. It helps guide the model's response to fit a certain expertise and context.

- **Context**: Provides external or user-specific details that steer the AI's response for accuracy and relevancy, for example., 'Three marketing campaigns were launched last quarter.'
- **Task Specification**: Instructs the model on the required actions. It could be:
  - A single instruction: Direct and simple, like 'Evaluate these campaigns.'
  - An instruction sequence: A series of related tasks.
  - Pseudo-Code Instructions: Detailed, structured guidelines for complex tasks.
- **Execution Rules**: Directives that shape the model's strategy and decision-making during task execution, considering problem-solving methods, ethical standards, and task boundaries.
- **Output Constraints**: Specifies conditions for the AI's output in terms of structure, content, length, and so on, for example, 'A segmented report under 500 words.'

Let us now apply the instruction sequence prompt to our automatic email processing example. In this case, our focus is on the tasks directly handled by a GPT model, as preprocessing and results presentation would be covered by other components:

- **Expert Persona**: You are an AI agent specialized in email analysis and inquiry response. Your expertise is rooted in the analysis of textual content, hypothesis formulation, simulation of potential replies, and recommendation prioritization.
- **Context**: Our organization, a utility call-center, receives numerous customer inquiries via email daily. These emails range in complexity and are often accompanied by attachments. Before reaching you, they've undergone preprocessing steps like email fetching, transformation of non-textual content, enrichment from a knowledge base, and customer data enrichment.
- **Task Specification as Instruction Sequence:**
  1. Classification: Analyze the email content and categorize it into one of the following categories: contract adjustments, invoice inquiries, service complaints, outage reports, account management, or meter reading issues.

2. Summarization: If the email is lengthy or complex, especially if it contains attachments that have been transformed into text, create a concise summary to simplify understanding for the recipient.

3. Cause-effect Analysis: Develop a hypothesis to understand the reasons or motivations behind the customer's inquiry based on the content and context of the email.

4. Creation: Taking into account the initial email, its summarization, and the cause-effect hypothesis, generate various potential email replies.

5. Ranking: Evaluate the simulated replies and rank them against a predefined set of criteria to determine their suitability and relevance to the customer's inquiry.

- **Execution Rules:**
  - Consider all potential solutions for replying to the email.
  - Weigh the pros and cons of each simulated reply before finalizing the ranking.
  - Eliminate specific biases in the output, ensuring that the recommendations do not favor or discriminate against any type of inquiry or customer demographic.
  - Focus on the customer's inquiry and the context provided by the preprocessing stages.
  - Consider the history of past resolutions and frequently asked questions when formulating replies.
- **Output Constraints:**
  - The output should be a structured analysis with clear sections for classification, summarization, and cause-effect analysis.
  - The recommended replies should be prioritized in a list format, with a brief rationale for each ranking.
  - The total output, including the analysis and recommended replies, should not exceed three pages.

Transitioning from the aforementioned prompt for automatic email processing inside of a batch loop over all emails, we now focus on the email analytics process. While the foundational principles remain similar, this second example delves deeper into retrospective analysis and offers strategic recommendations:

- **Expert Persona**: You are an AI agent proficient in analyzing historical email interactions and deducing feedback from them. Your specialization encompasses comprehending past customer intents, gauging the effectiveness of responses, extracting strategic insights, and proposing future operational strategies.

- **Context**: Our organization, a utility call-center, has a vast archive of email interactions with customers. Understanding past engagements is critical for improving future responses and customer service procedures. The emails available for this task have been pre-processed, with relevant email chains extracted and enriched using our knowledge base.
- **Task Specification as Instruction Sequence**:
  1. Information Extraction and Analytics: Delve into the archived email interactions. Recognize and understand past customer intents, evaluating the efficacy of the responses provided.
  2. Summarization: Distill the insights drawn from the historical email interactions, creating an easily digestible overview of the past engagements, notable feedback, and any observable patterns.
  3. Prediction: Based on past interactions and observed patterns, project potential challenges or emerging patterns that might be seen in future email exchanges with customers.
  4. Recommendation: Utilizing the information and predictions, put forward suggestions for procedural improvements or recommend training modules that can augment the quality of the call-center's responses.
- **Execution Rules:**
  - Emphasize understanding the depth of past interactions rather than just skimming through volumes.
  - Look for recurring themes, complaints, or praises in email interactions to derive patterns.
  - When predicting, make projections rooted in data and avoid speculative assumptions.
  - Ensure that the recommended procedural amendments are feasible and align with the organization's objectives and capacity.
  - Avoid biases: do not favor any specific customer segment or feedback type.
  - Make use of the enriched information provided during pre-processing for a comprehensive analysis.
- **Output Constraints:**
  - The output should have distinct sections for Information Extraction and Analytics, Summarization, Prediction, and Recommendation.

- Any insights or patterns observed should be substantiated with examples from the email archives.
- Recommendations should be prioritized and accompanied by a succinct rationale.
- The entire output, encompassing analytics, insights, and recommendations, should be confined to three pages.

Prompt design involves precision and creativity to guide the actions of a GPT model successfully. We have shown two instruction-based prompt examples to achieve specific outcomes for email automation and analytics.

Stage 3: Prompt Quick Check

After crafting the design, it is vital to have a swift yet focused evaluation to catch any glaring issues or oversights. This quick check, powered by a best practice checklist, ensures that the AI interaction remains grounded, safe, and effective, without necessitating a time-intensive review:

1. Consistency Check
    - Purpose: Ensure that all elements of the prompt match with each other.
    - Key Aspects: All elements, like persona with context or instructions with execution rules, need to be in sync, ensuring a seamless narrative free of contradictions
2. Alignment Check
    - Purpose: Validate the prompt's synchronization with the predefined functional solution design.
    - Key Aspects: Confirm that the prompt covers the AI-relevant part of the functional design and verification against its component descriptions, for example process steps for a process-oriented design, to ensure alignment.
3. Toxic Content Prevention
    - Purpose: Minimize the risk of generating harmful or inappropriate content and deter direct paths to such outputs.
    - Key Aspects: Clear directives on prohibited content, setting boundaries for acceptable output, and inspecting instructions that might lead the model towards harmful outputs.
4. Neutral Prompt Check
    - Purpose: Eliminate biases and maintain an impartial stance.

  - Key Aspects: Examine language and instructions to identify and negate any tendencies towards specific perspectives, ideologies, or interest groups.

5. Inclusivity Check
   - Purpose: Ensure the prompt is globally acceptable without marginalizing any group.
   - Key Aspects: Review language for potential biases and ensure context and instructions are considerate of diverse backgrounds.

6. PII Anonymization
   - Purpose: Safeguard users' personal data.
   - Key Aspects: Inspect for any personal identifiers and verify against indirect determination of personal information.

7. Classified Data Protection
   - Purpose: Respect the boundaries of sensitive information in prompts and outputs.
   - Key Aspects: Assess inclusion of classified data and validate the prompt's design against generating such data.

8. Humanization Avoidance
   - Purpose: Preserve clear distinctions between AI capabilities and human traits.
   - Key Aspects: Review the prompt to ensure it doesn't anthropomorphize the GPT model.

9. Intellectual Property Protection
   - Purpose: Safeguard intellectual properties from infringement.
   - Key Aspects: Ensure that the prompt does not ask for or produce copyrighted content and check against any potential IP violations.

This framework strikes a balance, allowing for prompt interactions that align with intended goals, respect boundaries, and sidestep potential pitfalls, all while being time-efficient within the prompt engineering loop.

Stage 4: Interactive Prompt Execution

Executing a prompt within an interactive user-friendly GPT environment has its own nuances. Here's a closer look at some of the key considerations when engaging with platforms like ChatGPT website or the OpenAI Playground:

- Custom Instructions: Users set preferences or requirements for ChatGPT responses once, and the system automatically applies them as recurring output constraints for each subsequent prompt instruction.
- Example Prompt Suggestions: ChatGPT offers prompt demonstrations on its website to help new users with their first steps.
- Easy Content Integration: Users can transition from office products such as Microsoft Word, Excel, or PowerPoint to the AI platform by simply copying and pasting content. They can also upload one or multiple images to process multi-modal prompts.
- Automated Prompt Size Check: The environment automatically verifies the prompt size against model-specific limits, such as the 5.5K words threshold for GPT-4-8k.
- Plugin Enhancements: Certain plugins, tailored for specific use-cases, allow for additional inputs. For example, it is possible to upload data files for advanced data analysis or provide web links for data extraction from PDF documents.
- Inbuilt Content Filtering: Safety mechanisms within GPT models and cloud platforms like Azure ensure prompts that could lead to inappropriate outputs are rejected.
- Managing Exceeding Context: If a prompt and its output combined approach the model's context limit, the response might be truncated, necessitating a 'continue' prompt for completion.
- Interactive Feedback: Real-time feedback in these environments aids users in refining their prompts for more effective interactions.

Stage 5: Prompt Output Assessment

This phase scrutinizes the GPT-model's responses to ensure they are safe, accurate, and valuable to users. We present a checklist of quality criteria with validation actions and positive and negative examples from our case study of automatic email processing and analytics:

- **Accuracy**: Ensures that the GPT model's responses are faithful to the prompt design, accurately reflecting the input in terms of factual correctness, relevance to the context, and adherence to the defined structural elements.
    - Validation: Compare the responses against the initial input and established facts or standards.
    - Positive Example: For the instruction "Classify this customer email that mentions a power cut and the duration it lasted", the GPT model accurately categorizes it under "outage reports"

  - Negative Example: For the same instruction, the model misclassifies the email under "invoice inquiries".
- **Free of Hallucinations**: The GPT model's output should not include any untruthful information, distortions, or fabrications that were not part of the input or the data it was trained on.
  - Validation: Analyze the output for any details, claims, or elements that cannot be traced back to the input or known data.
  - Positive Example: When analyzing an email interaction regarding a "service complaint", the GPT model accurately deduces the customer's intent without adding any false details.
  - Negative Example: The model claims a customer mentioned "account management" in an email when, in fact, the email was entirely about "meter reading issues".
- **Completeness**: Checks that the model's output fully addresses the input, considering all elements of the prompt and not excluding any crucial details.
  - Validation: Confirm that the model addresses all components of the input prompt in the output.
  - Positive Example: An email containing elements of a service complaint, attached documents, and questions about invoice adjustments receives a comprehensive response addressing all aspects mentioned.
  - Negative Example: The model's output only responds to the service complaint, neglecting the invoice adjustments.
- **Transparency and Explainability**: Ascertains that the model's outputs are comprehensible and unambiguous. The GPT model should be able to translate technical language for the target audience, making it explicit when it is speculating or approximating in its responses.
  - Validation: Evaluate the outputs for clarity and transparency. Ensure that the explanations are provided for approximations and speculations.
  - Positive Example: When ranking potential email replies, the GPT model explains, "This reply is ranked first because it addresses the customer's primary concern and aligns with similar successful resolutions from past interactions".
  - Negative Example: The model simply ranks a reply as the top choice without providing any reasoning.
- **Relevance and Specificity**: Determines whether the model's responses are both pertinent to the user's prompt and sufficiently detailed, rather than delivering generic responses.

  - o Validation: Assess whether the output aligns with and specifically addresses the input prompt.
  - o Positive Example: In response to an email about "meter reading issues", the GPT model generates a reply specifically addressing meter readings and related concerns.
  - o Negative Example: The model provides a generic reply about utility services without specifically addressing meter readings.
- **Consistency**: Assesses whether the model maintains stability in its responses across similar queries, and consistently delivers outputs within the capabilities defined during the Detailed Prompt Design stage.
  - o Validation: Perform repeated queries and examine the consistency of the responses.
  - o Positive Example: Whenever tasked with classifying emails related to "service complaints", the AI model consistently categorizes them correctly.
  - o Negative Example: Sometimes the AI model classifies "service complaints" correctly, while other times it miscategorizes them under "invoice inquiries".
- **Adaptability**: Evaluates the model's capacity to adjust its outputs based on modifications in the Detailed Prompt Design, including changes in the slots or attributes.
  - o Validation: Test the model across a range of different prompt variations and assess its ability to adapt.
  - o Positive Example: For a complex email with multiple attachments, the GPT model adjusts its summarization depth to provide a concise yet comprehensive overview.
  - o Negative Example: Despite a change in the email's content, the model provides the same generic summary.
- **Privacy and Security:** Confirms that the model's operations are in compliance with privacy and security standards, protecting the data and maintaining confidentiality.
  - o Validation: Review the model's operation for compliance with privacy and security norms.
  - o Positive Example: When analyzing an email that contains a customer's personal phone number, the GPT model does not include the number in its structured analysis output, prioritizing user privacy.
  - o Negative Example: The model's output contains sensitive customer data, like their full address and contact details.

- **Toxicity**: Ensures that the model avoids generating harmful, offensive, or inappropriate content.
  - Validation: Check for toxic words or phrases,
  - Positive Example: In situations where a customer's email contains strong, potentially offensive language, the GPT-model's recommended replies remain polite and professional, not mirroring the tone of the original email.
  - Negative Example: The model suggests a reply that mirrors the aggressive tone of the customer's original message.
- **Bias Avoidance:** The model should be impartial and not show any unfair bias towards certain topics, groups, or individuals.
  - Validation: Check for bias patterns.
  - Positive Example: When analyzing emails from various customer demographics, the GPT model gives equal weightage to feedback from all customer segments.
  - Negative Example: The model frequently prioritizes feedback from urban customers over those from rural areas, creating an unintended bias in the analysis.

Validating GPT outputs is a nuanced endeavor demanding keen scrutiny. By applying the criteria outlined during regular spot checks, you can ensure that GPT model responses meet intended objectives, improve from iteration to iteration, and adhere to company standards.

Feedback Loop for Further Iterations

When the output validation results highlight areas of enhancement or when a prompt fails to meet the established criteria, it signifies the need to reinitiate the Prompt Engineering Cycle and rework the prompt accordingly. Such a cyclical approach in Prompt Engineering ensures gradual progress, bringing the prompts in line with the use case requirements and guaranteeing that the GPT model operates securely and human-controlled for their designated tasks.

To illustrate how feedback can drive adjustments within the prompt design, we present a compilation of examples. These instances demonstrate the interplay between validation criteria and prompt modifications, offering a tangible perspective on potential refinements that can enhance AI performance.

1. Accuracy:
   - Prompt Scope: Automatic Email Processing

- Issue: Inconsistent categorization of email topics.
- Modification: Under Task Specification, the GPT model should analyze the email and correctly classify it without misinterpreting the content.
- Change: The classification categories might be made more explicit with examples to ensure the model does not inaccurately classify emails.

2. Free of Hallucinations:
   - Prompt Scope: Automatic Email Processing.
   - Issue: The GPT model generated hypothetical customer feedback not found in original emails.
   - Modification: Ensure the model does not make up customer intents or feedback, which are not present in the email archives.
   - Change: Add a line under Execution Rules: "Rely strictly on the available email archives and do not generate intents or feedback not present in the data."
3. Completeness:
   - Prompt Scope: Automatic Email Processing.
   - Issue: Output skipped essential steps outlined in the original instruction.
   - Modification: Ensure that all stages of the instruction sequence are thoroughly addressed.
   - Change: Specify under Output Constraints: "Each section of the output must comprehensively cover its respective instruction step from the Task Specification."
4. Transparency and Explainability:
   - Prompt Scope: Automatic Email Processing.
   - Issue: Predictions of customer reactions were made without clear reasoning or justification.
   - Modification: When making predictions, the GPT model should be transparent about its reasoning.
   - Change: Under Execution Rules, add: "When presenting predictions, elucidate the reasoning and basis behind each one."
5. Relevance and Specificity:
   - Prompt Scope: Automatic Email Processing.

- Issue: The GPT-model's responses were generic and did not always match the specific content of the incoming email.
- Modification: The model's responses must directly correlate with the nature and content of the incoming email.
- Change: Add under Execution Rules: "Ensure that the generated replies specifically address the unique content and concerns of each customer email."

6. Consistency:
   - Prompt Scope: Advanced Email Analytics.
   - Issue: The GPT model interpreted similar customer intents differently across multiple emails.
   - Modification: The model should consistently recognize similar customer intents from the archives.
   - Change: Under Execution Rules, add: "Maintain consistency in recognizing and interpreting similar customer intents across email interactions."
7. Adaptability:
   - Prompt Scope: Automatic Email Processing.
   - Issue: The GPT model provided similar depth summaries for both complex and simple emails.
   - Modification: The model should adjust its email summaries and simulations based on the varying complexity of emails.
   - Change: Specify under Task Specification: "Adjust the summarization depth and detail of simulated replies based on the complexity and context of the incoming email."
8. Privacy and Security:
   - Prompt Scope: Automatic Email Processing and Advanced Email Analytics.
   - Issue: The GPT model included identifiable customer data in its summaries.
   - Modification: Ensure the model doesn't disclose any private or sensitive customer information.
   - Change: Add under Execution Rules: "Do not include or disclose any personal or sensitive data from the emails in the output."
9. Toxicity:

- Prompt Scope: Automatic Email Processing.
- Issue: The GPT-model's response contained inappropriate language.
- Modification: Make sure the model doesn't use or suggest any potentially offensive or harmful content in its replies.
- Change: Add under Execution Rules: "Ensure that the generated replies are free from any harmful, offensive, or inappropriate content."

10. Bias Avoidance:
    - Prompt Scope: Advanced Email Analytics.
    - Issue: The GPT model disproportionately highlighted positive feedback over negative feedback.
    - Modification: The model should treat all customer feedback, both negative and positive, with equal importance.
    - Change: Specify under Execution Rules: "Do not prioritize or de-emphasize feedback based on its positive or negative nature, ensuring a balanced representation."

These instances underscore the key value of a robust feedback mechanism within the Prompt Engineering Cycle. By addressing gaps and enhancing the prompt design based on validation outcomes, we ensure that GPT solutions are more responsive and accurate and also safer and more aligned with user expectations.

Implementing GPT-Solutions

The GPT-Implementation phase transforms the functional solution design and the respective prompt designs into functioning solutions using a GPT-implementation framework.

Figure 7.11: *Implementing GPT-Solutions*

Choosing the right framework is vital to this transformation. For projects rooted in Python, using the LangChain framework [9] is a best practice. On the other hand, Java developers would find the Predictive Powers framework [10] more aligned with their preferences.

To provide a more grounded understanding, we have provided dedicated chapters for these frameworks. *Chapter 8, LangChain: GPT Implementation Framework for Python*, immerses you into the world of Python-based GPT-implementations, leveraging the strengths of the LangChain framework. Following that, *Chapter 9, predictive-powers: GPT Implementation Framework for Java*, explores Java-based implementations using the Predictive Powers framework.

Validating Solution Outputs

We have already covered manual prompt output checks in the final stage of the prompt engineering cycle. Within the E2E solution there is a runtime-dependent interplay between various prompts, user inputs, code segments, knowledge bases and external tools, necessitating a more systematic and automatic output validation approach. We commend using a secondary GPT model[17] alongside a human expert to cross-check the output of the combination of the primary GPT model and the other solution components.

***Figure 7.12**: Validating Solution Outputs*

For instance, while the first model might be GPT-4, the secondary model could be GPT-3.5-Turbo. Alternatively, both models can be GPT-4, provided there's a distinct output validation prompt used for the secondary call to guide it differently.

Automatic validation of the entire solution output requires a more comprehensive checklist, than the one used to assess individual prompt outputs. A significant amount of the required checks has been extracted and adapted from the insightful

[17] This approach is very similar to the architecture pattern 'A4 Quality-controlled Conversation', described in *Chapter 4*, where a GPT model is first used to generate responses to the user and then called with a different context and prompt to check these responses.

article, 'Trustworthy LLMs[18]' [11]. This paper presents a comprehensive survey of key dimensions that are crucial to consider when assessing LLM trustworthiness. It covers various categories of trustworthiness and emphasizes the importance of conducting detailed analyses, testing, and continuous improvements on LLM alignment. Based on the insights from this paper the following output validation prompt is suggested:

- **Expert Persona**: You are an AI quality assurance specialist with a focus on analyzing and validating AI-generated content. Your primary role is to evaluate the outputs of AI systems, ensuring they adhere to guidelines that guarantee quality, relevance, security, and fairness.
- **Context**: Your organization utilizes AI systems, such as GPT-4, for diverse tasks. The outputs from these systems require rigorous validation to maintain the highest standards and ensure that they meet the expectations and requirements of the users.
- **Task Specification as Instruction Sequence:**

1. **Fact-checking:** Compare the AI model's response with established facts or standards to ensure factual accuracy.
2. **Hallucination Detection:** Scan the AI output for any details or claims that are not present in the initial input or trusted external sources. Flag any distortions or fabrications.
3. **Completeness Check:** Review the output to confirm that it fully addresses all elements of the input prompt, without omitting the vital details.
4. **Clarity Analysis:** Examine the output to ensure that it is transparent and unambiguous. If technical terms are used, they should be explained for the target audience.
5. **Relevance Assessment:** Check if the response provided by the AI model is directly related to the user's input and if it is specific enough, avoiding overly generic statements.
6. **Consistency Validation:** Extract the different outputs generated for the same input prompt and compare them to ensure they are consistent with each other.
7. **Adaptability Test:** Extract the outputs generated from variations of the same prompt and assess the AI's ability to adjust its responses accordingly.
8. **Privacy and Security Audit:** Evaluate the AI model's response to make sure it hasn't divulged any private or confidential information, or generated content that may be considered a security risk.

[18]LLM stands for Large Language Model.

9. **Toxicity Scan:** Examine the AI output for any potentially harmful, offensive, or inappropriate content. Use a list of flagged words or phrases to aid this process.
10. **Bias Detection:** Analyze the AI model's output for signs of unfair bias. Ensure that the response is neutral and doesn't favor or discriminate against certain topics, groups, or individuals.
11. **Miscalibration Detection**: Check if the AI model shows over-confidence in topics where objective answers are lacking. Flag outputs that seem overly confident despite being factually inaccurate.
12. **Sycophancy Detection**: Assess whether the AI is overly agreeable or tends to confirm misconceptions just to align with user statements.
13. **Copyrighted Content Review**: Ensure that the AI does not reproduce or leak copyrighted content from its training data.
14. **Reasoning Analysis**: Examine the AI's logic and reasoning capabilities. Confirm if it can produce coherent chains of thought and if it understands cause-effect relationships.
15. **Emotional Awareness Review**: Ensure that the AI model's response is emotionally supportive, especially when engaging with vulnerable user groups.

- **Execution Rules:**
  - Always cross-reference AI outputs with trusted external sources <list of websites> for verification, especially for fact-checking.
  - Ensure that each part of the AI model's output is coherent and does not contradict or appear unrelated to any other segment of the output, as this might indicate inconsistency.
  - Ensure all evaluations are comprehensive, covering each aspect of the checklist in depth.
  - Refer to an up-to-date website with a current list of flagged words or phrases for the toxicity scan, ensuring alignment with evolving standards and social norms, whenever the prompt is executed.
  - Take into account possible cultural or regional biases that might affect the analysis.
- **Output Constraints:**
  - The evaluation results should be structured with distinct sections for each of the 15 checks, providing clarity on the AI model's performance in each category.

- Any potential issues or areas of concern should be clearly highlighted with a brief explanation.
- Offer recommendations or action points, if applicable, for any identified problem.
- The total evaluation report, inclusive of all checks and recommendations, should not exceed four pages.

The above-mentioned prompt should be used as an advanced tool by a knowledgeable human expert. The prompt produces an initial assessment, which is reviewed by the expert and adjusted and augmented. In this way, quality assurance benefits from both the speed and scale of the GPT model, and the discernment and experience of the human expert.

Moreover, it's imperative to note that classical software quality checks, especially user acceptance tests, remain essential. However, as prompting increasingly replaces traditional coding, the efforts and time dedicated to these tests can be significantly reduced.

Iterative Improvement

Iterative Improvement is a testament to the agile and experimental nature of GPT development and fueled by feedback, which is meticulously gathered from each stage of the cycle and then woven back into previous phases. Each piece of feedback, whether it stems from user interactions, model outputs, or system performance, acts as a learning tool that guides the improvement of the evolving solution.

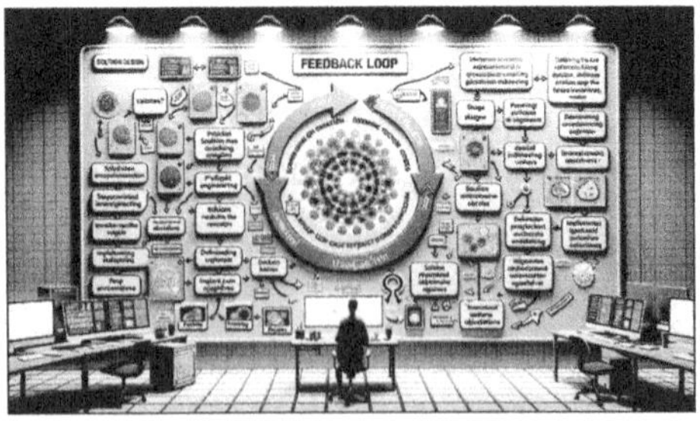

Figure 7.13: *Iterative Improvement*

The following list details these feedback-driven improvement scenarios with examples based on the stage, where the feedback originates and the stage, where it leads to an improvement:

- Feedback from Solution Design → Improvement in Defining the Use Case

  - Description: While designing the solution, it is realized that some use case objectives are too broad or ambitious. As a result, the use case definition is revisited to make it more precise and attainable.
  - Example: While designing a GPT-based customer support chatbot, it becomes clear that the initially proposed 24/7 global support across all company products is too expensive. The use case is then narrowed to support only the most popular product lines during business hours.
- Feedback from Prompt Engineering → Improvement in Defining the Use Case
  - Description: During prompt engineering, it becomes clear that certain tasks identified in the use case are not feasible for GPT. The use case might need to be modified to exclude or reframe these tasks.
  - Example: The enterprise aims to develop a GPT-powered tool for automatically drafting complex legal contracts. However, during prompt engineering, it's determined that all GPT-models struggle with certain legal jargons. The use case is then refined to only draft preliminary contract templates, requiring human oversight.
- Feedback from Prompt Engineering → Improvement in Solution Design
  - Description: After crafting the prompts, there might be a realization that the current solution design does not account for specific nuances in the behavior of the chosen GPT model. The functional or architectural design may need to be adjusted accordingly.
  - Example: When creating prompts for a financial forecasting tool, it is noted that the GPT model responds best to highly specific input data formats. The solution design is adjusted to include a preprocessing module that standardizes incoming financial data.
- Feedback from Implementation → Improvement in Defining the Use Case
  - Description: While developing the solution, it is discovered that the project's goals, as defined in the use case, are not aligned with the available resources or technology. The use case would then need to be adjusted to align with what's achievable.
  - Example: A corporation wants to implement a GPT-driven HR tool for resume screening. During implementation, they realize that cultural nuances and soft skills are hard to assess. The use case is then refocused on filtering resumes based on technical skills and experience only.
- Feedback from Implementation → Improvement in Solution Design
  - Description: As the solution is being developed, issues might arise

that were not anticipated in the solution design phase. This could lead to a reevaluation and potential redesign of certain aspects of the solution, including its architecture or user experience.

  - Example: A company designs a GPT-driven tool for near-real-time market analysis. During implementation, the initially chosen cloud infrastructure cannot handle the data traffic. The solution's architectural design is revisited to integrate a more robust cloud provider.

- Feedback from Implementation → Improvement in Prompt Engineering
  - Description: During implementation, it could be noticed that the crafted prompts are not yielding the expected outputs at runtime. This would necessitate revisiting the prompt engineering stage to adjust or craft new prompts.
  - Example: An enterprise develops a GPT-based tool for internal project management. During implementation, prompts crafted for task prioritization are not producing intuitive results. The prompt engineering is revisited to adjust the criteria and wording.
- Feedback from Solution Output Validation → Improvement in Defining the Use Case
  - Description: If the output quality is consistently inaccurate or irrelevant, the original use case might need to be redefined to align better with what GPT can achieve.
  - Example: A company uses a GPT model for sentiment analysis on product reviews. However, the output consistently misinterprets sarcasm. The use case is refined to focus on clear positive or negative feedback, excluding ambiguous reviews.
- Feedback from Solution Output Validation → Improvement in Solution Design
  - Description: Upon validation, if certain aspects of the solution are not meeting user needs or are not scalable, the solution design could be revisited. This might mean altering the functional, architectural, or user experience designs.
  - Example: An enterprise creates a GPT-driven onboarding assistant for new employees. Upon validation, it is found that users are confused by the chatbot's multi-step responses. The user experience design is adjusted to make interactions more confined and intuitive.
- Feedback from Solution Output Validation → Improvement in Prompt Engineering

- Description: If the GPT model outputs, while technically correct, are not aligning with the intended application or user expectations, the prompts may need to be reengineered.
- Example: A corporation employs a GPT model for generating automated sales reports. During output validation, it is noted that while the data is correct, the narrative lacks a focus on key performance indicators (KPIs). The prompts are reengineered to compute KPIs in the generated reports with the help of a code generation and execution plugin.

These scenarios highlight the interconnectedness of the solution development stages and the importance of iterative improvement. By systematically collecting feedback at each stage and requesting its assessment to previous stages in the next execution cycle, project managers can enhance the overall effectiveness and utility of the GPT solution.

Managing Change

As we embark on integrating GPT models into an enterprise organization, we encounter a unique set of challenges that requires a thorough understanding and efficient management. This subchapter aims to illuminate the key challenges often encountered during this transformation and provide potential solutions to overcome them, thus ensuring a smooth and effective transition.

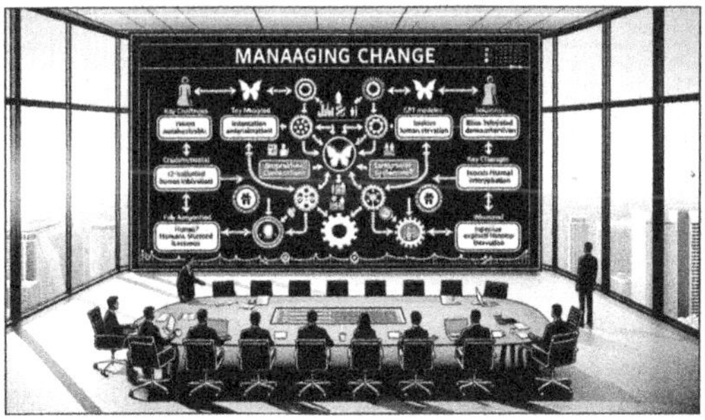

Figure 7.14: *Managing Change*

Central to our exploration is the concept of task types in relation to GPT-human interactions. Understanding that tasks can range from being fully automated to requiring intensive human intervention allows us to categorize and better address the associated challenges. By segmenting these tasks, we can shed light on the specific risks and tailor our mitigation strategies accordingly. The subsequent table offers a comprehensive look into these task modalities, presenting a detailed breakdown of risks and their respective mitigation approaches for each task type:

Task Type	**Fully Automated by GPT Model**	**Human Review of GPT Output**	**Human Task Augmented by a GPT model**	**Fully Human Task Without GPT Involvement**
Description	The task is managed end-to-end by a GPT model without human interference.	A GPT model generates the initial output, and human expertise reviews and possibly revises the results.	A human performs the primary task, but a GPT model provides assistance, enhancing the output.	The task is human-driven, with no GPT assistance.
Change Focus	Preparing stakeholders for reduced human intervention and establishing trust in autonomous AI capabilities.	Training on effective validation techniques and understanding GPT model boundaries.	Training humans to effectively collaborate with a GPT model, leveraging its suggestions while maintaining primary control.	Ensuring employees understand their independent value and establishing GPT integration boundaries.
Employee Resistance to Change Risk	Fears of redundancy or over-reliance on automated systems.	Concerns over the relevance of human expertise.	Fearing over-shadowing of human skills.	Feeling left out of the AI transition.

Mitigation	Emphasize the value proposition of automation, reassuring about redeployment in value-added roles.	Emphasize the indispensable nature of human judgment.	Highlight GPT as a complemen-tary tool.	Reinforce the value of human-exclusive tasks.
Skill Gap Risk	Lack of trust in automated systems.	Deficits in val-idation skills.	Inefficiency in collaboration.	Continuous skill development.
Mitigation	Provide training on oversight of GPT-driven tasks.	Develop training mod-ules on validation.	Offer collaborative workshops.	Focus on traditional training methods.
Data Security and Privacy Risk	Data leaks or misuse.	Data exposure during review.	Misusing data during augmentation.	Maintain traditional security standards.
Mitigation	Implement stringent security protocols.	Train on secure review processes.	Educate about GPT data handling.	Reinforce existing data privacy measures.
Unclear Roles and Responsi-bilities Risk	Confusion over oversight roles.	Ambiguity in human-AI responsibili-ties.	Unclear human-GPT boundaries.	Reassert traditional roles.
Mitigation	Clearly define monitoring roles.	Demarcate boundaries of human intervention.	Define parameters of GPT's involvement.	Reiterate traditional job roles.
Inadequate Resource Allocation Risk	Need for computational and oversight resources.	Balance computational with human expertise.	Human tasks are overshadowed.	Focus on traditional resources.
Mitigation	Allocate dedicated infrastructure.	Flexible resource strategy.	Allocate based on task priority.	Ensure attention and resources for traditional tasks.

Failure to Align with Organi- za- tional Culture and Goals Risk	AI alignment with ethos concerns.	Balance AI capabilities and goals.	AI distorting culture.	Value of traditional roles.
Mitigation	View AI as a tool, not replacement.	Foster a collaborative culture.	Emphasize GPT as a tool to enhance capabilities.	Recognize achievements in human-exclusive tasks.

Table 7.2: *Task-type-specific Change Management Practices*

Accelerating GPT-Projects by ChatGPT

A typical GPT-project is usually executed by a team of experienced GPT-specialists and requires on average 12-16 weeks based on complexity.

Leveraging ChatGPT can reduce the efforts and duration of the GPT solution development lifecycle.

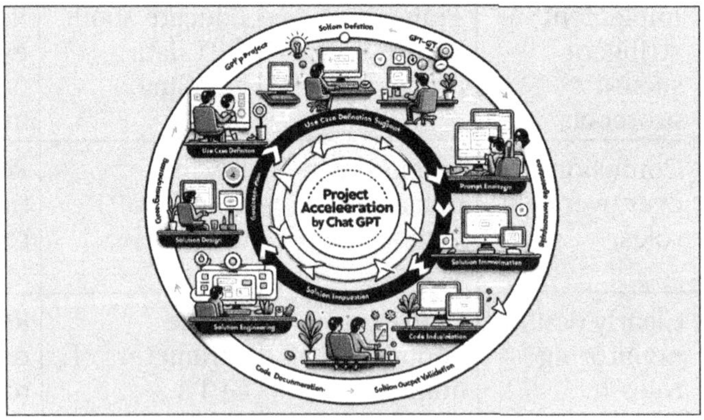

Figure 7.15: *Accelerating GPT-Projects*

Let us break down how each phase can be expedited:

- **Use Case Definition:**
    - Automated Use Case Template Filling: ChatGPT could utilize the Use Case Template to ask the user specific questions and automatically fill out the initial template based on user's input.
    - Consistency and Feasibility Checks: ChatGPT, equipped with reference use cases, could identify inconsistencies or unfeasible

requirements in the user's input.

  - High-Level Description to Detailed Specification: Given a high-level description, ChatGPT could generate a detailed use case specification, refining it iteratively through a conversational dialogue with the user.

- Solution Design:
  - Auto-Generate Design from Use Case: Based on the use case specification, ChatGPT can suggest process steps and component requirements, essentially creating a first draft of the solution design.
  - UI Design Integration: ChatGPT can integrate with GPT-based UI design apps to generate UI mockups based on the user's requirements, streamlining the user experience design.
  - Iterative Design Refinement: Through a conversational interface, the design can be refined based on user feedback and suggestions made by ChatGPT.
- Prompt Engineering:
  - Prompt Generation: ChatGPT, using the patterns defined in the two previous chapters, can suggest initial prompts for the tasks identified in the solution design.
  - Design Checklist Verification: ChatGPT can automatically check the designed prompts against the checklist ensuring all necessary criteria are met.
  - Output Verification Prompts: For each primary prompt, ChatGPT can also suggest a corresponding verification prompt to be used in the output validation phase.
- Solution Implementation:
  - Code Repository Search and Recommendations: ChatGPT can search the existing code repository based on user requirements, highlighting potential code reusability and suggesting modifications if needed.
  - Code Generation: For standard components, ChatGPT can use the code generator to produce the required code snippets, reducing the manual coding effort.
  - Automated Documentation: Documentation is a crucial but time-consuming part of the GPT project lifecycle. ChatGPT can auto-generate documentation based on the use case specification, design, code, and prompts.
- Solution Output Validation:
  - Automatic Output Verification: ChatGPT can execute the previously chosen verification prompt.

- o Integration into Productivity Tools: ChatGPT can be integrated into existing office tools, making it straightforward for users to validate actual responses against expected output and document deviations.
- o Immediate Feedback Loop: As users validate outputs, feedback can be instantly communicated to ChatGPT, which can suggest immediate refinements, ensuring rapid iterations.

Conclusion

Drawing on the insights from the exploration of architecture and prompt patterns, this chapter sheds light on the comprehensive process involved in developing and managing GPT-projects. By focusing on key stages such as project preparation, use case definition, solution design, prompt engineering, solution implementation, output validation, and iterative improvement, we have further revealed the adaptability and versatility of GPT models in the enterprise context. We have also demonstrated how to manage the transformative impact of GPT-projects and pointed out ways to accelerate them using a 'GPT-for-GPT' approach.

The next chapter explains our first GPT-Implementation Framework, providing a practical guide to the LangChain framework for Python-based implementations.

Key Points

1. **Project Preparation**: The groundwork for any successful GPT-project lies in meticulous preparation. This involves setting up the infrastructure, establishing security policies, training staff, and setting up a holistic feedback system.

2. **Use Case Definition**: A well-defined use case serves as a vital starting point for project execution, ensuring a clear scope, specified data requirements and stakeholder alignment.

3. **Solution Design and Prompt Engineering**: Creating a robust solution design and engineering effective prompts are fundamental stages in the process that directly contribute to the success of a GPT model.

4. **Solution Implementation and Output Validation**: Functional solution designs are transformed into working solutions using implementation frameworks like LangChain or Predictive Powers. Solution outputs are systematically validated using a secondary GPT model and a human expert.

5. **Systematic Feedback Management**: Insights from each stage of the solution development cycle are utilized to refine and improve preceding stages in the subsequent cycle, fostering a culture of dynamic refinement and enhancement.

6. **Tailored Change Management**: The differentiation between task types - from fully automated to human-intensive - becomes crucial for the successful deployment of GPT projects in diverse operational contexts.

7. **GPT-Project Acceleration**: Leveraging ChatGPT can significantly streamline and expedite the GPT solution development lifecycle, from use case definition to output validation, by partially automating essential tasks, promoting iterative refinement, and enhancing user collaboration through conversational interfaces.

8. **Harnessing the Versatility and Adaptability of GPT models**: By navigating through the entire project cycle, organizations can effectively leverage the diverse capabilities of GPT models for a wide range of use cases, from simple tasks to complex workflows, maximizing their potential in enterprise automation.

Chapter 8

LangChain: GPT Implementation Framework for Python

Introduction

This chapter discusses the use of Large Language Models (LLMs) like ChatGPT's *gpt-3.5-turbo* in Python and introduces a groundbreaking framework called LangChain [12]. LangChain allows to implement all the 18 capabilities from the **C**apabilityGPT framework through its specially designed components tailored for working with LLMs. It increases the reliability of working with Large Language Models by allowing to combine pre-learned models' knowledge with real-time information. With LangChain, LLMs can interact with diverse entities like databases, APIs, cloud platforms, and other API-based resources, enabling them to accomplish specific goals. As a result, LangChain simplifies and streamlines the process of developing comprehensive applications.

The chapter provides an explanation of the different components that make up the framework. These components include Schema, Models, Data processing, Chains, Memory Handling, and Agents. By exploring each of these components, the readers will develop a comprehensive understanding of how LangChain functions as a whole. To further enhance their understanding, we will also provide practical demonstrations of how these components can be utilized through three example use cases. These demonstrations will include snippets of Python code and detailed explanations of each step involved.

The first use case delves into how LangChain can benefit legal experts and enhance their productivity and success by taking advantage of the creation and transformation capabilities of LLMs from the GPT model family. We will present a practical example that demonstrates the application of semantic search in helping lawyers find relevant previous cases. This enables them to effectively prepare for upcoming trials, ultimately improving their performance in the courtroom.

In the second use case, we explore how LangChain enables seamless data retrieval from various sources of text data. Specifically, we provide a solution that allows automation specialists to engage in a chat conversation about a controller. To provide a brief explanation, a controller is essentially a device that manages a process to achieve and maintain desired parameters. For example, in a temperature control system, a thermostat acts as a controller by monitoring the current temperature and adjusting the heating or cooling equipment to maintain a set temperature.

The solution leverages foundational capabilities described in **C**apabilityGPT framework such as question answering, communication, and summarization. The necessary information for this conversation is provided in PDF format, which includes the controller manual. LangChain simplifies the process of browsing through and utilizing this information.

The final example we propose focuses on real-time price checks, which can greatly benefit businesses by keeping them well-informed and competitive. The chapter delves into how LangChain's agents combine the ability of LLMs to reason and the tools' ability to execute and provide accurate and up-to-date price information. In this example the agent will leverage various GPT capabilities such as planning, assessment, question answering, summarization and communication. This empowers businesses to make informed decisions that align with the current market conditions, ultimately improving their competitiveness and success.

By the end of this chapter, readers will have a comprehensive understanding of how LangChain works and its potential applications. This knowledge will serve as a foundation for further self-study, where readers can delve deeper into the technical aspects and explore more advanced use cases. Whether you are a business leader looking to optimize your operations, an IT professional interested in the latest AI technologies, or an AI enthusiast eager to explore the possibilities, this chapter will equip you with the knowledge needed to navigate the world of LangChain.

Structure

In this chapter, the following topics will be covered:

- Introducing LangChain
- Components of LangChain:
  - Schema
  - Models
  - Data processing
  - Chains
  - Memory Handling
  - Agents
- Example 1: Preparation helper for lawyers
- Example 2: Chatting over controller manual
- Example 3: Current price checks using agents

Introducing LangChain: Unlocking the Potential of Large Language Models

The power of LLMs is derived, among other factors, from their training on massive amounts of data. However, it's important to understand that LLMs are usually not up-to-date. This is because they are trained on specific datasets, which may not include the most recent information. Despite being trained on immense amounts of data, LLMs may still struggle with specialized knowledge in certain areas.

Additionally, they have limitations when it comes to processing large amounts of text due to their token restrictions (the maximum token limit determines the extent to which the model can process as input and generate as output). In some cases, developing applications may require the use of different LLMs depending on factors such as budget and requirements. This is where a comprehensive framework like LangChain can be beneficial, as it offers a solution that caters to various needs and budgets.

The LangChain framework is a Python-based tool that enables the creation of applications that fully utilize the capabilities of Large Language Models. It provides all the necessary components for developing sophisticated applications.

LangChain goes beyond being a simple interface for language models. It not only allows us to utilize different language models but also interacts with a wide range of entities such as databases, APIs, cloud platforms, and other API-based resources. These interactions expand the capabilities of language models and enable the creation of advanced applications.

LangChain's main pillars are components, use-case specific chains, and agents.

- **Components**

Using Large Language Models in complex applications involves using specific concepts. These include creating templates for prompts, making use of various tools, accessing data sources and processing them, managing memory, etc. In LangChain, these concepts are called components. Components are classes or functions that make it easier to use these features. They are already built and ready for developers to use. These components are designed to be easy to implement, whether you are using LangChain for your whole project or just certain parts of it.

- **Use-Case Specific Chains**

Chains enable the seamless integration of the above components in a structured manner. They are particularly designed to maximize performance in specific scenarios. The concept of chaining components together is both straightforward and impactful. It greatly simplifies the implementation of complex applications, resulting in improved ease of debugging, maintenance, and overall enhancement of applications.

- **Agents**

The framework is designed to be able to work in an agentic way. In everyday life, an agent is someone or something that helps achieve a specific goal. In LangChain, an agent can be thought of as an LLM that deconstructs a task into smaller steps. Then it employs various tools and other LLMs to accomplish the main objectives of the task.

Setting up applications can be a complex and time-consuming task for developers. However, with the use of components, chains, and agents, the process becomes significantly easier and quicker. By utilizing these tools, developers are able to save valuable time and effort, which allows them to focus more on the actual development and customization of the application. This leads to improved productivity and faster time-to-market.

Components of LangChain

To effectively utilize LangChain, it is vital to get familiar with its main elements. This section aims to give you a comprehensive overview of these components, offering a solid basis for understanding how LangChain works.

Schema

Let's discuss the fundamental data types you will encounter when using LangChain. These include text, Chat Messages, Examples, and Documents. In the world of language models, text serves as the primary mean of communication. LangChain, being a bridge between LLMs and various entities, is specifically designed to prioritize text-based interfaces.

With the rise in popularity of chat interfaces, certain model providers have started offering specialized APIs that expect Chat Messages instead of plain text. A Chat Message data type consists of two parts - the content field, which is typically the text itself, and the user associated with it. Currently, LangChain supports users such as System, Human, and AI, introducing different types of chat messages, namely, SystemChatMessage (for Master Prompts), HumanChatMessage, and AIChatMessage. This format is presently required for all language models from the GPT-3.5-turbo and GPT-4 family.

Another data type we might use is Example. It is an input and output pair that represents the input to a function and the expected output of it. Examples are often incorporated into prompts to better steer the answers provided by the LLM.

Lastly, LangChain utilizes Documents. A Document comprises unstructured data referred to as page content, along with metadata that describes its attributes.

Models I/O

The core of LangChain revolves around its models, which serve as the foundation for the entire framework. These models provide the necessary elements and building blocks for interaction. When discussing working with models we will look into three parts: models, prompts and output parsers.

Language models

LangChain provides two types of models: Language Models and Chat Models. Language Models take raw input and output a string, while Chat Models take a list of Chat Messages labeled as System, AI, and User as input, and generate another chat message labeled as AI. The System role guides the model's behavior by providing high-level instructions and context that frame the entire interaction. The AI role interacts with the user, responding to queries. Finally, the User role represents the individual interacting with the model, giving instructions and engaging in the conversation. Both Language Models and Chat Models have their own interface.

If you need your application to work with both the Language and Chat Models, LangChain has developed a solution called the Base Language Model. This interface allows you to integrate with the models seamlessly. Additionally, if you want to create your own custom wrapper for your own LLM or use one that is not supported by LangChain, that option is also supported.

If you want to display the response to a user as it is being generated, instead of waiting for the entire answer to be generated and sending it all at once, you can use special streaming classes. However, please note that streaming response is only supported by certain models.

Prompts

Effectively structured prompts hold the key to unlocking the vast potential of GPT models. To adapt to different use cases, there is a range of prompt patterns we may employ, such as Instruction Prompt, Instruction Sequence Prompt, Query Prompt, Request Prompt, Cooperation Prompt, or other Special Prompts referred to in the earlier *Chapter 5, Advanced Prompt Engineering Techniques*.

To simplify the process of creating prompts and effectively managing different parts of them, LangChain introduces prompt templates. These templates serve as a structured way to generate prompts consistently. They are essentially strings that accept a set of parameters, which are then used by the model for processing. Currently, in LangChain, these strings can be composed using two syntaxes: f-strings and Jinja.

If you decide to use a Chat Model, specifically a Chat Prompt Template should be used. These templates are optimized for Chat Model inputs and differ from raw strings, which are passed directly to the language model. In chat messages, each message is associated with a role: System, User, or AI. Additionally, there are few-shot prompt templates that allow the inclusion of examples in our prompts. If the default prompt templates do not cover your specific needs, you can also create custom prompt templates. For instance, you might want to create a prompt template with dynamic instructions tailored to your language model. In such cases, custom prompt templates offer flexibility and customization options.

Output parsers

Regardless of whether we are working with Language Models or Chat Models, they all generate text as their output. To organize or structure this output in the desired format, we make use of output parsers. These output parsers enable us to obtain the output in various formats, such as comma-separated list, datetime, enum, or JSON.

If you wish to output multiple text fields of your choice, you can utilize the Structured Output Parser. Another option is to use the Pydantic (JSON) parser, which is more powerful. However, it requires an LLM with sufficient capacity to generate well-formed JSON. It is worth noting that within certain model families, some models excel at generating JSON while others may not perform as well. For instance, models such as *text-davinci-003*, *gpt-3.5-turbo*, or *gpt-4* can consistently generate well-structured JSON, whereas *text-curie-001*'s proficiency in this regard significantly diminishes.

Additionally, there is an auto-fixing parser available. It automatically calls another parser if the results from the initial one are incorrect or contain errors.

Data connection

One of the main challenges in using standalone LLMs is their ability to only access data that they were specifically trained on. To overcome this limitation and enable them to work with up-to-date information, we must connect them to other sources of data. Fortunately, LangChain provides effective components that facilitate effortless interaction with diverse data sources (refer back to *Chapter 4, Architecture Patterns enabled by GPT-Models*, for an in-depth exploration of A2–A4 architecture patterns for accessing enterprise-specific data sources).

Data loaders

An essential aspect of working with external data sources is the use of data loaders. These loaders have the important task of loading different types of data into a specific structure called the Document. The Document contains both the text and the metadata associated with it. Several loaders have been created to handle various data sources. These loaders make it convenient to load data from for example, text files, CSV files, JSON files, GitBooks, Azure Blob Containers,

YouTube transcripts, and more. Using these loaders greatly simplifies data loading processes.

Data transformers

Once you have successfully imported your data into the Document objects, you can begin the process of transforming it to suit your application's needs. One common type of transformation is partitioning the document into smaller sections called chunks, which align with the context window of your chosen LLM. For example, if you intend to use 4 chunks as context and allocate 2000 tokens for the context, you may want to divide your documents into chunks of 500 tokens each. For English text, 1 token is approximately 4 characters or 0.75 words.

Additionally, you have the option to automatically extract features or metadata associated with each chunk. These extracted details can then be utilized in various tasks such as classification or summarization.

Text Embedding Models

Embedding means representing text as vectors and it is another method we can consider when transforming Documents. The implementation of this method in LangChain is straightforward and efficient. LangChain offers a standard interface that can be utilized with various embedding model providers.

It is important to note that different embedding providers may employ different techniques for embedding queries and documents. To address this, LangChain adopts a similar approach and offers distinct methods for embedding each of them. By doing so, LangChain ensures compatibility and flexibility when working with various embedding providers, allowing users to seamlessly integrate their preferred embedding techniques into their workflow.

Vector stores

Searching for specific information in a large amount of unstructured text is a common use case for LangChain. To tackle this task, one approach is to start by breaking down the unstructured text into Document-type chunks. These Documents are then converted into lists of numbers (vectors) and stored in a special database known as vector store.

To find the desired information, the query is also converted into a vector representation and compared with each vector in the vector store. The selection process involves identifying the documents that are most similar to the query. Similarity is calculated utilizing metrics such as cosine similarity or Euclidean distance. Cosine similarity determines the similarity between two vectors by measuring the cosine of the angle between them, while Euclidean distance calculates the straight-line distance between two points in space.

A vector store acts as a database where the vector representations of Documents can be stored together with their metadata. What makes LangChain particularly versatile is its compatibility with various open-source vector stores, as well as its ability to integrate with different paid vector store providers.

Retrievers

Once our similarity search is complete, we can utilize retrievers to retrieve the documents that are pertinent to a query. Retriever functionality enables us to effectively retrieve relevant documents based on our similarity search results.

Chains

The previously mentioned features can be seen as additional capabilities that offer convenience, but the true strength of LangChain lies in its chains. While using Language Models alone is suitable for simple applications, the use of multiple LLMs or a combination of LLMs and other components in a sequence is essential for developing more complex applications. LangChain simplifies this process by introducing chains.

There are various types of chains. They are particularly designed to quickly implement specific use cases, which is why they differ in complexity. The most basic type is the LLM Chain, which consists of a prompt template and a Language Model. The purpose of this chain is to format the given input values into a prompt, execute the LLM using the prepared prompt, and finally return the output.

Another commonly used chain is the Simple Sequential chain. In this type, a series of calls are made to either the same or different Language Models after the initial call. This is particularly useful when the output from one call needs to be used as the input for another one (refer to C2, D1, and D2 patterns in *Chapter 4, Architecture Patterns enabled by GPT-Models*).

The RetrievalQA chain is one more popular type, which involves taking a question, retrieving relevant documents using a retriever, and then providing those documents as context to the LLM for answering the question. There is also the SQL Database Chain, which is designed for answering questions over an SQL database, and the Summarization Chain, which is used for summarizing multiple documents.

These are just a few examples, but there are many more possibilities. Additionally, users have the option to create their own customized chains by subclassing the Chain class.

Memory

By default, Large Language Models are designed to be stateless. This means that each received query is treated independently, without any regard for previous queries or conversations. However, in certain applications like virtual assistants, it is important to have access to the context of the conversation in order to better understand the user's intent and provide a response that relates to previous queries. In order to better comprehend this, let's explore the following conversation:

User: What is estimated computing power of a brain?

AI: The brain's computing power is immensely complex and difficult to precisely quantify, but some rough estimates suggest it could be in range of 10^18 to 10^26 floating-point operations per second (FLOPS).

User: Why is it difficult to quantify?

AI: The statement „difficult to quantify" is common phrase used to describe situation where ...

If a user asks about the estimated computing power of the brain, the AI model may provide a general answer based on available knowledge. However, when the user follows up with a question, the AI may struggle to understand the reference without access to the previous interaction.

The problem in the example is linked with coreference resolution. Coreference resolution involves identifying words in a sentence that refer to the same thing. In this case, the words "it" and "computing power" are examples of such words. The lack of memory and statelessness of the Language Model resulted in irrelevant answers. In order to resolve this problem, it is essential to manage the memory of the complete conversation or at least a portion of it. LangChain provides methods that assist in this endeavor. These methods provide a range of choices tailored for different types of interactions. It is important to consider the token limit for each call when passing data, as there may be constraints on the amount of information that can be included. For instance, the entire conversation can be passed to the next prompt if the interaction is expected to be brief, or a summarized version can be used if the interaction is predicted to be lengthy. All these methods enable the model to understand and respond to the conversation based on its context, thereby improving its capabilities.

Agents

Sometimes, in order to serve the user, we need to determine the actions based on unpredictable input. This is where an agent becomes useful. An agent acts as a helpful assistant, not only carrying out tasks on our behalf but also considering which subtasks need to be performed and in what order.

In LangChain, agents can be seen as LLMs that break down tasks into smaller steps. They utilize various tools and other LLMs to achieve the ultimate objective of the task.

The first component of an agent is the Orchestration Agent, in simple words - "manager" LLM. This LLM handles all the cognitive processes, including devising steps, analyzing outputs, adjusting plans if necessary, and determining the next course of action.

Additionally, there are tools available to the agent. These tools can range from a simple calculator to more advanced ones like other LLMs, the SERP (Search Engine Results Page) API, or the JsonGetValueTool. There are also comprehensive toolkits that contain multiple tools of the same category, such as the Zapier Toolkit, OpenAPI Agent Toolkit, or JSON Agent Toolkit. Each tool is accompanied by a descriptive text tag, which the "manager" LLM uses to understand if the tool is suitable for the upcoming step.

In conclusion, an agent comprises a "manager" LLM that makes decisions regarding subactions that need to be taken in order to complete tasks, and then uses a collection of tools and toolkits that enable the execution of each step.

There are two types of agents as follows:

- **Action agents**: These agents make decisions at each timestep based on the outputs of all the previous tools. They are well-suited for handling small tasks efficiently.
- **Plan-and-execute agents**: In contrast, plan-and-execute agents devise the entire action plan in advance and do not alter the plan during the execution. This type of agent is ideal for tackling complex tasks effectively.

It is also possible to combine the two types by allowing a plan-and-execute agent to utilize action agents for executing the plans. This hybrid approach enables the agent to benefit from the strengths of both agent types.

Examples

LangChain offers a remarkable collection of tools that drastically speed up the development process. By utilizing various components such as chains and agents, the overall process becomes easier and faster, saving time and effort. This allows individuals to focus on understanding requirements and actually building the desired solution. When using LangChain, there are numerous advantages to be gained. It allows to fully leverage all the CapabilityGPT's benefits - streamlined operations, cost savings, improved decision-making, and many more. To fully comprehend the potential of LangChain, let's delve into its components by exploring real-world examples.

Example 1: Preparation helper for lawyers

Now, let us explore a practical use case of LangChain in creating an application to assist lawyers in their trial preparations. In order to effectively prepare, lawyers often need to study past cases. However, it can be challenging to find relevant cases that are similar to the one they are currently working on. Our objective is to develop an application that can retrieve documents containing past cases based on the lawyers' descriptions of their specific needs.

For example, the application should be capable of listing all cases related to defamation or financial loss. Relying solely on simple keyword searches may not yield accurate results.

To overcome this limitation, we will employ a more advanced method called semantic search. In the following example, we will demonstrate a popular approach that starts with embedding documents and the lawyers' queries. Text embeddings are numerical representations of text that enable machines to understand and process natural language. They transform words or phrases into a list of numbers (vectors), with semantically similar items possessing similar values.

In semantic search, this allows the system to match user's queries with relevant documents based on semantic similarity, not just keyword matches. By employing text embeddings, systems can understand nuanced meanings and improve the relevance of search results, providing a more efficient and effective search experience.

So, once we have all documents embedded (converted into lists of numbers i.e. vectors) and stored in a vector store, we embed the query and calculate semantic closeness between the query and each of the documents. The measure we'll use is called cosine similarity which is a cosine of the angle between two vectors. The documents with the highest cosine similarity will be our search results.

Nonetheless, to illustrate the functionality of this application, we first need to generate a set of sample civil cases that we can work with.

Content generation

Generating cases can be done using Language Models or Chat Models from the Model component of LangChain. In this case, we will use a language model using OpenAI's GPT-3 family *text-003-davinci* model. To demonstrate the usage of output parsers effectively, we will adopt a two-step approach. Initially, we will create a list of distinct names that represent various content for each case.

Subsequently, using the same model, we will generate the contents for civil cases and save them in a docx file.

Generating a list of names

Let's start with some useful imports and function definition:

```
from LangChain import PromptTemplate
from LangChain.llms import OpenAI
from LangChain.chains import LLMChain
from LangChain.output_parsers import CommaSeparatedListOutputParser

import os
from docx import Document
from typing import List

def generate_civil_cases_names() -> List[str]:
```

In this particular scenario, we aim to create approximately 60-80 names for civil cases that will remain within the Open AI's model token limit during a single request. To achieve this, we will utilize the Python f-string. We will include a variable called **`number_of_cases`** in case we want to modify the number that specifies the desired quantity of generated cases.

```
    generate_civil_cases_names_template = """
        You are a lawyer and a legal expert. Generate {number_of_cases}
civil cases names.\n{format_instructions}
    """
```

To achieve the desired output in a list format, we can utilize the LangChain's list parser. This parser is designed to return a list of comma-separated items. However, there are two important steps to follow in order to obtain the correct output:

Step 1: Define format instructions for the prompt

The first step involves calling the **`ComaSeparatedListOutputParser()`** class object. This object will allow us to access the **`get_format_instructions`** method. By calling this method on the object, we can retrieve the string with format instructions that is later incorporated into our prompt:

```
output_parser = CommaSeparatedListOutputParser()
format_instructions = output_parser.get_format_instructions()
```

Step 2: Format the actual output

Once we have obtained the output, we will proceed with formatting the text we get from the model.

Let's discuss the creation of a prompt. To utilize a prompt, we must create an instance of the **`PromptTemplate`** class. This involves specifying the template, input variable, and partial variables along with instructions for formatting:

```
prompt = PromptTemplate(
    template=generate_civil_cases_names_template,
```

```
        input_variables=["number_of_cases"],
        partial_variables={"format_instructions": format_instructions},
    )
```

In order to proceed, it is essential to define a model. For our purposes, we utilize an Open AI model, although there exist numerous alternatives for consideration that are supported by LangChain. The standard model within the OpenAI class object is `text-davinci-003`. The **`temperature`** and **`max_tokens`** are parameters that control the output of the model. **`Temperature`** determines the randomness of the generated text, while **`max_tokens`** is the maximum number of tokens to generate shared between the prompt and completion.

```
    model = OpenAI(temperature=0.9, max_tokens=4000)
```

The next step is to pass the input to the model:

```
    _input = prompt.format(number_of_cases="80")
    output = model(_input)
```

Finally we are parsing the output in order to get a *List* object of civil cases processes:

```
    list_of_processes = output_parser.parse(output)
    return list_of_processes
```

Now that we have a list of civil cases names, we will generate content.

Generating content of civil cases

First, let's create a directory for our civil cases:

```
def generate_civil_cases(list_of_processes):
    if not os.path.exists("civil_cases"):
        os.makedirs("civil_cases")
```

We want to generate each of the civil cases in a reproducible way, which is why we are again using a prompt template. We are using a Python f-string that includes the variable **`civil_case_name`**, which will be changed with each iteration:

```
generate_civil_case_template = """
        You are a lawyer and a legal expert. Generate content of civil
case: {civil_case_name}. Include title, full names of parties, background,
claims, evidence, legal issues and procedural status.
    """
```

When we've got simple use cases, using LLMs in isolation is fine. However, as the application gets more complex, chaining LLMs may come in handy. Let's see how we can implement a simple **`LLMChain`** that takes in a prompt template, formats it with the user input, and returns a response from an LLM.

```
    llm = OpenAI(temperature=0.9, max_tokens=4000)
    prompt = PromptTemplate(
        input_variables=["civil_case_name"],
        template=generate_civil_case_template,
    )
    chain = LLMChain(llm=llm, prompt=prompt)
```

We are calling the chain in a loop in order to generate and save civil cases:

```
    for i, process in enumerate(list_of_processes, start=1):
        legal_process_content = chain.run(process)
        doc = Document()
        doc.add_paragraph(legal_process_content)
        doc.save(f"civil_cases/civil_case_{i}.docx")
```

Here is the complete code for reference:

```
from LangChain import PromptTemplate
```

```
from LangChain.llms import OpenAI
from LangChain.chains import LLMChain
from LangChain.output_parsers import CommaSeparatedListOutputParser

import os
from docx import Document
from typing import List

def generate_civil_cases_names() -> List[str]:
    generate_civil_cases_names_template = “””
        You are a lawyer and a legal expert. Generate {number_of_cases} 
civil cases names.\n{format_instructions}
    “””

    output_parser = CommaSeparatedListOutputParser()
    format_instructions = output_parser.get_format_instructions()
    prompt = PromptTemplate(
        template=generate_civil_cases_names_template,
        input_variables=[“number_of_cases”],
        partial_variables={“format_instructions”: format_instructions},
    )
    model = OpenAI(temperature=0.9, max_tokens=4000)
    _input = prompt.format(number_of_cases=”80”)
    output = model(_input)
    list_of_processes = output_parser.parse(output)

    return list_of_processes


def generate_civil_cases(list_of_processes):
    if not os.path.exists(“civil_cases”):
        os.makedirs(“civil_cases”)
```

```
    generate_civil_case_template = """
        You are a lawyer and a legal expert. Generate content of civil
case: {civil_case_name}. Include title, full names of parties, back-
ground, claims, evidence, legal issues and procedural status.
    """


    llm = OpenAI(temperature=0.9, max_tokens=4000)
    prompt = PromptTemplate(
        input_variables=["civil_case_name"],
        template=generate_civil_case_template,
    )
    chain = LLMChain(llm=llm, prompt=prompt)


    for i, process in enumerate(list_of_processes, start=1):
        legal_process_content = chain.run(process)
        doc = Document()
        doc.add_paragraph(legal_process_content)
        doc.save(f"civil_cases/civil_case_{i}.docx")


if __name__ == "__main__":
    process_names = generate_civil_cases_names()
    generate_civil_cases(process_names)
```

The code begins by introducing the *generate_civil_cases_names* function. This function utilizes LangChain's **PromptTemplate** and the **OpenAI** model to generate a list of case names. To ensure proper formatting, the output is then processed with the **output_parser**. Following that, we have the **generate_civil_cases** function which takes the generated list of case names as a parameter. Within this function, **LLMChain** is employed to generate the content for each case individually through an iterative process. The resulting cases will be used as input for the subsequent section on semantic search.

Semantic search

Now that we have a database of civil cases, we want our application to be able to perform a semantic search in order to return all cases that are relevant for a lawyer that is preparing for a trial.

The idea is to take all the civil cases, and then use a model that converts them into a vector representation (embeds them) and stores them in a special vector database - vector store. For instance, once the lawyer inputs a query, for example, *I look for cases about financial loss*, the following steps are going to be performed:

1. Converting query into vector representation - embedding the query
2. Conducting similarity checks between embedded query and embedded civil cases
3. Retrieving the relevant vectors from the database

Embedding civil cases and storing them in Pinecone vector store

Let's begin by importing the required libraries and modules:

```
from LangChain.document_loaders import DirectoryLoader
from LangChain.vectorstores import Pinecone
from LangChain.embeddings import OpenAIEmbeddings
import pinecone
import os
```

We are going to embed the documents using an Open AI embeddings model and then store them in the Pinecone vector store.

The first thing to do is to load the civil cases. For this purpose the **`DirectoryLoader`** class object will load all files into a specified directory. Note that by default, the *DirectoryLoader* uses the **`UnstructuredLoader`** class to load the documents. If you need to load a different (structured) type of document, you can use a different loader class. For example, if you want to load Python source code files, you can use the *PythonLoader* class:

```
def embed_and_store_documents():
    loader = DirectoryLoader("civil_cases", glob="*.docx")
```

```
documents = loader.load()
```

Let's define the embeddings model:

```
embeddings_model = OpenAIEmbeddings()
```

Now, let's delve into the functionality of Pinecone. Pinecone acts as a vector database, enabling us to store embedded data and send queries effectively. Before using Pinecone, we need to create an index, which serves as a container for our data.

When creating a Pinecone index, we have to specify the similarity measure we want to use, such as cosine similarity. This measure helps in finding the most relevant vectors based on how close they are to the query in vector space. Additionally, we need to define the dimensions of the vectors we are working with. In the case of the OpenAI's embedding model that we'll use, *text-embedding-ada*-002, the dimension of output vectors is 1536.

Once the index is created, we can proceed by adding our API key and environment name to the environmental variables. This step ensures that our Pinecone client has the necessary authorization to access the database. Furthermore, we need to provide the name of the index we created. This information enables us to initialize the Pinecone client effectively, providing seamless interactions with the vector store.

```
pinecone.init(
    api_key=os.environ['PINECONE_API_KEY'], environment=os.envi-
ron['PINECONE_ENV']
)
index_name = "legal-documents-search"
```

Finally, with this single line of code, all documents are going to be embedded and stored in Pinecone. These kinds of ready-to-use pieces are the great power of LangChain:

```
Pinecone.from_documents(
    documents, embeddings_model, index_name=index_name
```

```
    )
```

Here is the complete code for reference:

```
from LangChain.document_loaders import DirectoryLoader
from LangChain.vectorstores import Pinecone
from LangChain.embeddings import OpenAIEmbeddings

import pinecone
import os

def embed_and_store_documents():
    loader = DirectoryLoader("civil_cases", glob="*.docx")
    documents = loader.load()
    embeddings_model = OpenAIEmbeddings()
    pinecone.init(
        api_key=os.environ['PINECONE_API_KEY'],
environment=os.environ['PINECONE_ENV']
    )
    index_name = "legal-documents-search"
    Pinecone.from_documents(
        documents, embeddings_model, index_name=index_name
    )

if __name__ == "__main__":
    embed_and_store_documents()
```

The code snippet begins by loading the civil cases using the **DirectoryLoader**. This loader retrieves all files with a specified extension from the designated directory. Afterward, we define the embeddings model and proceed to initialize the Pinecone client. The final step entails embedding the loaded documents and storing them in the Pinecone vector store with the aid of the client.

Similarity search and retrieving relevant data

The last part is retrieving the relevant data. First, we want to embed the query that is asked by the lawyer and perform a similarity search. Once we find the closest results, we want to return the names of the civil case files to the user. Let's start with necessary imports:

```
from LangChain.vectorstores import Pinecone
from LangChain.embeddings import OpenAIEmbeddings
from LangChain.embeddings.openai import OpenAIEmbeddings

import pinecone
import os
```

In order to embed the lawyer's query we will again use embeddings model from Open AI:

```
def retrieve_relevant_cases(query):
    embeddings_model = OpenAIEmbeddings()
```

Now that we have an existing index with our civil cases represented as vectors, we can use the **`from_existing_index`** method to create a **`docsearch`** object that we'll use for the similarity check:

```
    index_name = "legal-documents-search"
    pinecone.init(
        api_key=os.environ["PINECONE_API_KEY"],
environment=os.environ["PINECONE_ENV"]
    )
    docsearch = Pinecone.from_existing_index(index_name, embeddings_model)
```

If we pass a query like "`Cases about financial loss`" to the *docsearch* object calling *similarty_search* method, the following will happen: the query will be embedded with the default model defined in the *OpenAIEmbeddings* object, similarity search will be performed and all relevant documents will be returned:

```
docs = docsearch.similarity_search(query)
```

Finally, as we are looking for specific documents, we want to return the names of these documents that are stored in metadata:

```
sources = [doc.metadata["source"] for doc in docs]
```

Here is the complete code for retrieving relevant civil cases:

```
from LangChain.vectorstores import Pinecone
from LangChain.embeddings import OpenAIEmbeddings
from LangChain.embeddings.openai import OpenAIEmbeddings

import pinecone
import os


def retrieve_relevant_cases(query):
    embeddings_model = OpenAIEmbeddings()
    index_name = "legal-documents-search"
    pinecone.init(
        api_key=os.environ["PINECONE_API_KEY"],
environment=os.environ["PINECONE_ENV"]
    )
    docsearch = Pinecone.from_existing_index(index_name, embeddings_model)
    docs = docsearch.similarity_search(query)
    sources = [doc.metadata["source"] for doc in docs]
    return sources
```

```
if __name__ == "__main__":
    print(retrieve_relevant_cases("Cases about financial loss"))
```

The code snippet includes a function called **`retrieve_relevant_cases`** that aims to get the appropriate cases. Initially, we define the embeddings model, index name, and initialize the Pinecone client. Next, we create a *docsearch* object for conducting similarity searches. Lastly, we extract the names of the cases from the metadata of the returned documents.

Example 2: Internal knowledge QA for automation specialists - chatting over a manual of a specific controller

One common scenario for utilizing LLMs in a corporate environment involves extracting data from various types of text documents, such as product specifications, usage documentation, web pages, presentations, and internal documents. The main challenge in these cases is dealing with a large volume of data and the inconsistency in how different terms are used to refer to the same thing. A simple keyword search is often insufficient, and understanding the semantic meaning of user questions becomes crucial. To tackle this issue, LangChain offers a range of components with effective strategies to address semantic search.

To illustrate the capabilities of LangChain, let's consider an example where we develop a tool for automation specialists to expedite the process of searching through documentation. This tool will function as a chat mechanism, allowing the specialists to ask questions about a specific controller. As a reminder, a controller is a device that manages a process to achieve and maintain desired parameters. For instance, in a chocolate manufacturing plant, a programmable logic controller (PLC) acts as a controller by monitoring and controlling various equipment and processes to maintain specific production parameters such as temperature, pressure, and speed, ensuring optimal operation and product quality. The documentation for such controllers can be extensive and encompass a significant amount of content.

The objective is to provide automation specialists with a chat interface that enables them to quickly access the information they need for design and programming purposes.

Chunking the manual and loading it to the Pinecone vector store

Let's explore the technical aspects of using LangChain for the implementation. The controller's manual is a 40-page PDF document, so our initial task is to load the document. Since the entire document is too lengthy to input into our prompt, we must devise a strategy to divide the document into manageable parts. To begin, let's consider some useful imports:

```
from LangChain.text_splitter import RecursiveCharacterTextSplitter
from LangChain.vectorstores import Pinecone
from LangChain.embeddings import OpenAIEmbeddings
from LangChain.document_loaders import PyPDFLoader

import pinecone
Import os
```

Loading the manual is our next step. To accomplish this, we can utilize the **PyPDFLoader** class, which is readily available and allows us to easily load the document and save it as a *Document* object:

```
def embed_and_store_documents():
    loader = PyPDFLoader("Manual_MT655333.pdf")
    manual = loader.load_and_split()
```

Now that we have loaded the PDF file, we need to divide it into smaller sections. In LangChain, there is a text splitter class called *RecursiveCharacterTextSplitter* that can help us with this task. The splitter splits the text based on specific characters, which are listed as follows: ["\n", "\r", " ", „"]. The reason behind this approach is to keep entire paragraphs together for as long as possible. This increases the chances of getting strongly semantically related chunks of text.

The chunk size refers to the maximum size of each section, as measured by the length function. The overlap indicates how many tokens will be shared between each adjacent section. The length function determines how the length of the sections is calculated. By default, it counts the number of characters, but it is common to use a token counter instead. The **add_start_index** parameter determines whether the starting position of each section within the original document should be included in the metadata.

```
text_splitter = RecursiveCharacterTextSplitter(
    chunk_size=500,
    chunk_overlap=30,
    length_function=len,
    add_start_index=True,
)
```

In order to split the document into smaller parts, we can utilize the **text_splitter** object and its **split_documents** method:

```
documents = text_splitter.split_documents(documents=manual)
```

After completing this step, we proceed to embed these chunks and post them to the Pinecone vector store:

```
embeddings_model = OpenAIEmbeddings()
pinecone.init(
   api_key=os.environ['PINECONE_API_KEY'],
                environment=os.environ['PINECONE_ENV']
   )
index_name = 'mt655333-manual'
Pinecone.from_documents(documents, embeddings_model, index_name=
index_name)
```

Here is how the full code for chunking, embedding, and pushing vectors to Pinecone will appear:

```
from LangChain.text_splitter import RecursiveCharacterTextSplitter
from LangChain.vectorstores import Pinecone
from LangChain.embeddings import OpenAIEmbeddings
```

```
from LangChain.document_loaders import PyPDFLoader


import pinecone
import os


def embed_and_store_documents():
   loader = PyPDFLoader("Manual_MT655333.pdf")
   manual = loader.load_and_split()

   text_splitter = RecursiveCharacterTextSplitter(
       chunk_size=500,
       chunk_overlap=30,
       length_function=len,
       add_start_index=True,
   )

   documents = text_splitter.split_documents(documents=manual)

   embeddings_model = OpenAIEmbeddings()
   pinecone.init(
       api_key=os.environ['PINECONE_API_KEY'],
                 environment=os.environ['PINECONE_ENV']
       )
   index_name = 'mt655333-manual'
   Pinecone.from_documents(documents, embeddings_model, index_name=
index_name)


if __name__ == '__main__':
   embed_and_store_documents()
```

The preceding code snippet uses **PyPDFLoader** to load the controller's manual. After that, it utilizes **RecursiveCharacterTextSplitter** to split the documents into smaller chunks. Later on, it embeds these chunks and puts them in a vector store with the usage of the Pinecone client. This allows us to have the documents prepared for the next step, which involves performing a similarity search over the manual.

Chatting over the controller's manual - Conversational Retrieval Chain for similarity search

Now let's explore the implementation of a chat mechanism that allows automation specialists to ask for information about the controller. To ensure a smooth conversation flow, we must address the fact that subsequent queries may be related to previous queries. To handle this, we need to effectively manage the conversation's memory. To retrieve relevant chunks of data and effectively handle chat history, we will employ the **`ConversationalRetrievalQAchain`**. With this class, we will process previous interactions and integrate them into the current chat.

```
from LangChain.embeddings.openai import OpenAIEmbeddings
from LangChain.llms import OpenAI
from LangChain.chat_models import ChatOpenAI
from LangChain.chains import ConversationalRetrievalChain
from LangChain.vectorstores import Pinecone

import pinecone
import os

pinecone.init(
    api_key=os.environ["PINECONE_API_KEY"], environment=os.
environ["PINECONE_ENV"]
)

def retrieve_controllers_info(query, chat_history):
    embeddings_model = OpenAIEmbeddings()
    index_name = "mt655333-manual"
    docsearch = Pinecone.from_existing_index(index_name, embeddings_model)
```

The following chain is created by using the **from_llm** method on the **ConversationalRetrievalChain** class:

```
    qa = ConversationalRetrievalChain.from_llm(
        OpenAI(temperature=0),
        docsearch.as_retriever(),
        return_source_documents=True,
        condense_question_llm=ChatOpenAI(temperature=0,
model=”gpt-3.5-turbo”),
    )

    return qa({“question”: query, “chat_history”: chat_history})
```

To get information about the source documents that were used to generate the answer, we include an additional argument called **return_source_documents** and set it to **True**. The last parameter, **condense_question_llm**, is responsible for combining the chat history and query into a single query vector. This allows us to use different models for condensing the question and answering it. The models can be chosen based on their performance given a specific task or costs of usage. The chain produces a tuple that includes the answer and a chat history. The chat history is a list of tuples containing the queries and their corresponding answers.

Memory handling

The last step is to test the chain. It is important to note that in this case, we must manage the memory during the chat session. At the start of each session, we set the memory to an empty list. As each query is sent to the chat assistant, we add to it a tuple containing the query and its corresponding answer to the chat history list:

```
if __name__ == “__main__”:
    chat_history = []
    query = “Does MT65533 support autotuning?”
```

```
    result = retrieve_controllers_info(query, chat_history)

    print(result["answer"])
    print(result["source_documents"])

    chat_history.append((query, result["answer"]))

    query = "Which methods exactly?"
    result = retrieve_controllers_info(query, chat_history)

    print(result["answer"])
    print(result["source_documents"])
```

The following conversation is the outcome of the preceding backend application. Furthermore, depending on the design, one might want to add relevant fragments of the manual that are returned by the **docsearch** object.

Automation Specialist: Does MT65533 support autotuning?

AI: Yes, the MT655333 controller supports auto-tuning techniques to determine optimal control parameters automatically.

Automation Specialist: Which methods exactly?

AI: The MT65533 controller supports auto-tuning methods such as relay feedback, Ziegler-Nichols forward control, adaptive control, and fuzzy logic control.

Here is the complete code for reference:

```
from LangChain.embeddings.openai import OpenAIEmbeddings
from LangChain.llms import OpenAI
from LangChain.chat_models import ChatOpenAI
from LangChain.chains import ConversationalRetrievalChain
from LangChain.vectorstores import Pinecone

import pinecone
import os
```

```
pinecone.init(
    api_key=os.environ["PINECONE_API_KEY"], environment=os.
environ["PINECONE_ENV"]
)

def retrieve_controllers_info(query, chat_history):
    embeddings_model = OpenAIEmbeddings()
    index_name = "mt655333-manual"
    docsearch = Pinecone.from_existing_index(index_name, embeddings_
model)

    qa = ConversationalRetrievalChain.from_llm(
        OpenAI(temperature=0),
        docsearch.as_retriever(),
        return_source_documents=True,
        condense_question_llm=ChatOpenAI(temperature=0,
model="gpt-3.5-turbo"),
    )
    return qa({"question": query, "chat_history": chat_history})


if __name__ == "__main__":
    chat_history = []
    query = "Does MT65533 support autotuning?"

    result = retrieve_controllers_info(query, chat_history)

    print(result["answer"])
    print(result["source_documents"])

    chat_history.append((query, result["answer"]))

    query = "Which methods exactly?"
```

```
result = retrieve_controllers_info(query, chat_history)

print(result["answer"])
print(result["source_documents"])
```

This code snippet begins by initializing the Pinecone client and then defines the **retrieve_controllers_info** function. This function accepts *query* and *chat_history* as input parameters and utilizes the **ConversationalRetrievalChain** to perform a similarity search over the vector store and generate an answer. In the main function, the solution is tested by passing the **query** and **chat_history** to the **retrieve_controllers_info** function. The management of conversation memory is left to the discretion of the developer.

Example 3: Market research using LangChain Agent

The following example illustrates how LangChain's agents can be utilized to carry out market research. This process entails comprehending the task, strategizing execution, and implementing specific actions.

For this example, we will employ LangChain's agent component. We will empower our agent with the capability to utilize SERP API as a search engine. SERP API is essentially a tool that developers can utilize to access and extract data from search engine result pages. The agent will leverage an Open AI model to plan all necessary steps. It will identify the relevant data to search for, verify the accuracy of the API's output, and compile the results to deliver an answer to the user.

Since LangChain provides all the necessary tools, the implementation of this feature will be straightforward and uncomplicated. Let us begin by importing the necessary modules and libraries:

```
from LangChain.agents import load_tools
from LangChain.agents import initialize_agent
from LangChain.agents import AgentType
from LangChain.llms import OpenAI
import os
```

In order to use SERP API, we need to register at serpapi.com and get **serp_api_key**:

```
serpapi_api_key = os.environ['SERPAPI_API_KEY']
llm = OpenAI(temperature=0)
```

We are equipping the agent with the SERP API and an LLM. These tools empower the agent to generate accurate and comprehensive answers:

```
tools = load_tools(["serpapi"], llm=llm)
```

Now that we have the list of tools ready, let's use the **zero-shot-react-agent**. This type of agent uses the *ReAct* [13] paradigm to determine the most suitable tool based on the tool's description. The *ReAct* gets its name from the combination of the words *reasoning* and *acting*. This framework employs the reasoning component to identify the tasks that need to be performed and evaluate the observations. Then it utilizes the acting component to carry out tasks. *ReAct* is a general paradigm to combine reasoning and acting with language models for solving diverse language reasoning and decision-making tasks.

```
agent = initialize_agent(tools, llm, agent=AgentType.ZERO_SHOT_REACT_DE-
SCRIPTION, verbose=True)
```

To get started, we first need to initialize the agent. We do this by providing it with a set of tools it can use, the reasoning LLM, and specifying the *ReAct* agent type. Additionally, we can set the verbose parameter to determine whether the agent should provide a step-by-step description of its actions. Once the agent is initialized, we can then request it to solve a problem:

```
agent.run("What is a price of current best Lamborghini model?")
```

Here is the complete code for reference:

```
from LangChain.agents import load_tools
```

```
from LangChain.agents import initialize_agent
from LangChain.agents import AgentType
from LangChain.llms import OpenAI
import os

serpapi_api_key = os.environ["SERPAPI_API_KEY"]
llm = OpenAI(temperature=0)
tools = load_tools(["serpapi"], llm=llm)
agent = initialize_agent(
    tools, llm, agent=AgentType.ZERO_SHOT_REACT_DESCRIPTION, verbose=True
)
agent.run("What is a price of current best Lamborghini model?")
```

After initializing the agent and equipping it with tools we run it by using the query: *What is the price of the latest Lamborghini model*? The agent then begins its thought process and carries out a series of actions. These steps are displayed as output, thanks to the verbose parameter that we previously set during the initialization process:

```
Entering new AgentExecutor chain...
 I should look up the current best Lamborghini model
Action: Search
Action Input: "current best Lamborghini model"
Observation: Best of the Current Lamborghini Model Lineup · Lamborghini
Huracán Evo RWD / STO · Lamborghini Aventador SVJ · Lamborghini Urus ·
Lamborghini Sián · Awesome ...
Thought: I should look up the price of the Lamborghini Huracán Evo RWD /
STO
Action: Search
Action Input: "Lamborghini Huracán Evo RWD / STO price"
Observation: When it was launched, the Lamborghini Huracan STO coupe's
price was $327,838 before taxes and delivery, and it's up to around
$335,000 for a 2023 model. Should ...
Thought: I now know the final answer
Final Answer: The price of the Lamborghini Huracán Evo RWD / STO is
```

```
around $335,000 for a 2023 model.
> Finished chain.
```

Determining the price of the top Lamborghini model is the task to be performed by the agent. The agent starts with identifying the requested Lamborghini model, which was described as "best".

Once the model is identified, the agent uses the SERP API to conduct a thorough search for specific information about its price and gather relevant data. It continuously evaluates the output received from the API, carefully analyzing it to identify missing information. To arrive at the correct answer, the agent relies on a combination of reasoning and executing capabilities. This is what makes LangChain's agents so powerful. They have the ability to use tools and are equipped with LLMs that allow them to make conclusions. By following this systematic approach, the agent is able to determine the price of the top Lamborghini model with precision and reliability. This showcases the impressive capabilities of LangChain's agents, making them a valuable tool for various use cases. Some other examples include utilizing agents to create personalized dynamic pricing strategies, generating risk assessments for individual stocks based on historical and market data, or identifying market trends by analyzing news articles and social media posts relevant to specific industries.

Conclusion

The LangChain framework is a powerful Python-based tool that unlocks the full potential of Large Language Models for application development. This framework offers a comprehensive set of components that empowers developers to create sophisticated applications. By leveraging the use of components, chains, and agents, the development process becomes more streamlined and efficient. This results in significant effort savings, improved quality, standardization, and readability, ultimately leading to increased productivity and faster time-to-market for organizations. LangChain is a game-changing tool that can revolutionize the way businesses and professionals harness all the capabilities of Large Language Models.

As we conclude our chapter on LangChain, we have seen how this Python-based framework excels in developing GPT-based applications. As we embark on the next chapter, we will delve into `predictive-powers`, an exceptional, Java-based library specially designed for building solutions that harness the power of LLMs - a continuation of our exciting journey into the domain of generative AI.

Key Points

- LangChain is a Python-based framework that allows developers to create applications that maximize the potential of Large Language Models. It works with LLMs from multiple vendors, including OpenAI, as well as custom-made models.
- Using LangChain contributes to improved quality, standardization and readability. With its ready-to-use components, the process of developing comprehensive applications is simplified and streamlined.
- By combining pre-learned knowledge with real-time or domain information, LangChain enhances the capabilities and reliability of working with LLMs.
- The framework consists of components like Schema, Models, Data processing, Chains, Memory Handling, and Agents, which empower developers to work faster.
- Chains are ready-to-use classes that allow stacking commands. They contribute to increased efficiency for developers.
- Agents are highly valuable in tasks that require independent reasoning, planning, and execution actions, making it possible to create autonomous and powerful applications.

CHAPTER 9

predictive-powers: GPT Implementation Framework for Java

Introduction

In the previous chapter, we explored `LangChain`, a GPT implementation framework for Python. In this chapter, we will explore `predictive-powers`, a software library that allows Java developers to quickly build generative AI[1]-based solutions. Understanding this library should be considered critical for a couple of reasons.

Firstly, as Java remains a cornerstone in enterprise-level application development, integrating generative AI capabilities via this library significantly broadens the scope of what your Java applications can achieve. Imagine automating customer service inquiries, generating dynamic content, or even building intelligent data analytics tools, all within the comfort and familiarity of the Java ecosystem.

Secondly, the ease of implementation offered by this library democratizes access to advanced AI functionalities, making it particularly appealing for both seasoned Java developers and newcomers alike. If you're interested in leveraging

[1]***Generative AI*** refers to the branch of artificial intelligence that specializes in producing new content, which can range from text and images to audio and video, drawing upon patterns and information it has gleaned from existing data sources. The GPT series from OpenAI serves as a notable representation of this kind of AI. Throughout this chapter, the term 'generative AI' will be used more frequently than 'GPT' to maintain a focus on the broader technology category, emphasizing the versatility of the `predictive-powers` library, which is not confined to utilizing GPT exclusively.

the power of GPT models but find the AI landscape daunting, this chapter serves as a navigational aid.

After a quick comparison between Java and Python, this chapter will describe the library and its features.

The first section unveils the key features of the library. You will learn about the underlying concepts such as API clients, endpoints, and services, with examples provided for enhanced comprehension.

We then embark on a journey to showcase the practical implementation of the library via an autonomous agent called the 'Essay Writer'. This use case aims to illustrate the versatility of the library and its application to real-world tasks, thereby equipping you with actionable insights that can be adapted to various other applications.

Following this, the chapter delves into the architectural patterns involved in implementing the Essay Writer, providing an exemplification of what has been presented in *Chapter 4*. Each section explores how the `predictive-powers` services are woven into the agent's architecture, providing you with a roadmap for building similar applications.

Finally, we delve into a code walkthrough. This section will be necessarily concise and will only highlight some of the implementation details. Please note that while we provide snippets of code for context, you are encouraged to visit the `predictive-powers` GitHub repository [10] if you are interested in exploring the complete commented code. While having a foundational understanding of the Java language can indeed foster a deeper comprehension of the code examples presented in this chapter, it is not a prerequisite. Readers unfamiliar with Java can still grasp the ease with which the library allows for the application of the concepts discussed in earlier sections. However, it is advisable for readers to have a basic acquaintance with software development principles, as not every technical term will be defined in depth.

Structure

In this chapter, we will discuss the following topics:

- Quick comparison of Java and Python programming languages
- Overview of the `predictive-powers` library
- Understanding essential concepts: API clients, endpoints, and services
- `predictive-powers` use case: implementation of the 'Essay Writer' autonomous agent

- 'Essay Writer' architecture
- 'Essay Writer' code Walkthrough

Java vs. Python

Python and Java, each holding a formidable position in the technology sector, cater distinctively to different professional niches, setting a rich ground for leveraging GPT in diverse applications.

Renowned for its simplicity and readability, Python has evolved as a fundamental tool in the data science sector. The language's user-friendly nature, combined with a rich repository of libraries, makes it a favored choice for data analysis and visualization, a characteristic that resonates well with professionals venturing into data science and artificial intelligence fields.

In contrast, Java remains a pillar in the enterprise application development landscape, with a reputation built on stability, built-in security features, and remarkable scalability to sustain large infrastructure projects. Its versatility extends further; Java can seamlessly operate across various environments such as enterprise servers, desktops, and notably, Android smartphones. This wide-ranging applicability makes it a preferred choice for developers aiming for adaptability and robust performance.

In presenting both Python and Java frameworks, this book aims at enabling a nuanced understanding of the available technologies for potential GPT integration in applications, thereby facilitating a more informed approach for developers from different spheres.

The `predictive-powers` Library

The `predictive-powers` library is designed to simplify the integration of generative AI capabilities for Java developers. As an Apache-2.0 licensed resource, it is freely available on GitHub. While this section provides illustrative code snippets, to truly delve into its extensive functionality, we encourage a visit to the `predictive-powers` GitHub repository for comprehensive code and working examples.

These are the key features of the `predictive-powers` library:

- It offers low-level access to OpenAI and Hugging Face Hosted Inference APIs. This functionality enables developers to directly interact with these APIs, if they choose.
- The library adds an abstraction layer for generative AI capabilities, aligning them with the CapabilityGPT framework exposed in *Chapter* 2. This design

decision ensures compatibility with various capability providers, mitigating the risk of vendor lock-in. As we will illustrate, the library makes switching between providers trivial, allowing the developers to test different providers and upgrade to new language models once they are available.

- It hosts an in-memory vector database crucial for abilities such as semantic search[2], information extraction, and question answering. Upcoming versions will allow developers to utilize any existing vector database[3].
- The library includes methods to conveniently read textual content from various sources, including web pages and files in formats such as MS Office, PDF, HTML, etc.

Essential Components

Here's an explanation of the main components you need to familiarize yourself with to use the `predictive-powers` library. These are also depicted in *Figure 9.1*, which shows their interrelationships:

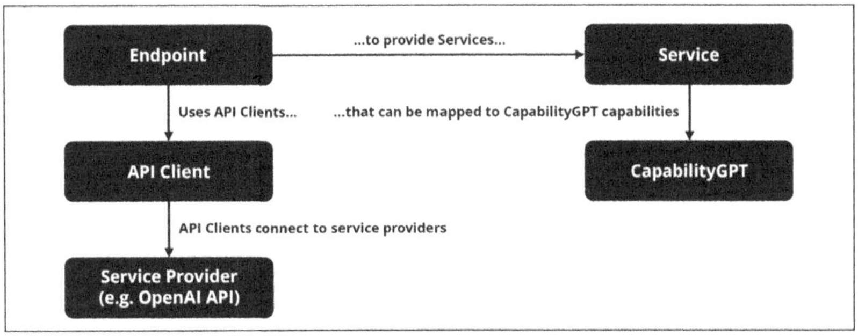

Figure 9.1: Essential components of the `predictive-powers` library and their relationships

[2]As already mentioned in *Chapter 8, LangChain: GPT Implementation Framework for Python*, Text ***embeddings*** are numerical representations of text, enabling machines to understand and process natural language. They transform words or phrases into a list of numbers, with semantically similar items possessing similar values. In ***semantic search***, this allows the system to match user's queries with relevant documents based on semantic similarity, not just keyword matches. By employing text embeddings, systems can understand nuanced meanings and improve the relevance of search results, providing a more efficient and effective search experience.

[3]In-memory vector databases leverage the system memory (RAM) to store data, which provides the advantage of extremely quick data retrieval and processing. However, this comes with constraints related to RAM size, making it less suitable for handling extremely large datasets. On the other hand, disk-based databases store data on physical storage devices. This method is more accommodating for larger datasets and offers the benefit of data persistence, even if the system undergoes a shutdown or failure. The trade-off here is in the speed of data access, which is typically slower compared to in-memory databases.
To summarize, if your application demands high-speed data access and can operate within the limits of available RAM, an in-memory database is likely the better choice. However, if you require handling of larger datasets, a disk-based database would be more appropriate.

API clients

API clients are the lowest-level components of the `predictive-powers` library, facilitating direct API calls to service providers. For example, developers might choose to directly access the OpenAI API via an `OpenAiClient` instantiation and the subsequent invocation of its methods.

The API clients also offer secure access to API keys (required for service access) and automated management of temporary server unavailability scenarios, such as request flooding.

In essence, API clients offer developers the liberty of direct API calls coupled with robust and efficient development via boilerplate code provision.

Consider the following example of API client usage; the code instantiates an `OpenAiClient` and then uses it to execute a very simple prompt:

```
import io.github.mzattera.predictivepowers.openai.client.OpenAiClient;
import io.github.mzattera.predictivepowers.openai.client.completions.
CompletionsRequest;
import io.github.mzattera.predictivepowers.openai.client.completions.
CompletionsResponse;

public class OpenAiClientExample {
      public static void main(String[] args) {

            // Retrieve API key from OS
// environment variable OpenAiClient.OS_ENV_VAR_NAME
            try (OpenAiClient client = new OpenAiClient()) {

// Complete a sentence; refer to
// https://platform.openai.com/docs/api-reference/completions
// for details
            CompletionsRequest req = CompletionsRequest.builder()
                        .model("text-davinci-003")
                        .maxTokens(50)
                        .prompt("Alan Turing was")
                        .build();
            CompletionsResponse resp = client.createCompletion(req);

                  // Output result
```

```
                System.out.println(resp.getChoices().get(0).getText());

            } // Closes client
    }
}
```

This will generate an output as follows:

```
a British mathematician, computer scientist, logician, cryptanalyst,
philosopher, and theoretical biologist who was highly influential in the
development of theoretical computer science and artificial intelligence.
```

Endpoints and Services

An endpoint is a capability provider, meaning it employs an API client to render different capabilities in the form of services.

The following code illustrates the creation of an `AiEndpoint`, which provides access to generative AI capabilities, both for OpenAI and Hugging Face providers[4]:

```
// Builds a Hugging Face endpoint.
// API key is retrieved from OS environment.
AiEndpoint endpoint = new HuggingFaceEndpoint();

// Builds an OpenAI endpoint from an existing API client
OpenAiClient cli = new OpenAiClient();
AiEndpoint endpoint = new OpenAiEndpoint(cli);
```

Once an endpoint is created, it enables access to services. These are high-level generative AI capabilities, akin to those described in the CapabilityGPT framework. Current services include:

- **`ModelService`**: Provides access to model metadata such as list of models, model context size, etc.

[4]As we will see later, there are also other endpoints, providing different capabilities, such as the `SearchEndpoint` that exposes methods to access web search services.

- `CompletionService`: Performs text completion by executing provided text prompts. This is the most flexible service since we can instruct it to execute different tasks by providing the right prompts, as discussed in *Chapter* 5. With proper instructions, this service can provide capabilities such as **Assessment**, **Classification**, **Creation**, **Information Extraction**, **Matchmaking**, **Summarization**, **Transformation**, and more.
- `ChatService`: Handles conversations between the user and an agent, managing the agent's personality and the conversation history. This would correspond to the **Communication** capability. Also notice that `ChatService` can provide all the capabilities that `CompletionService` exposes, as prompt execution can be seen as a conversation with a single exchange, with the user starting the conversation by providing the prompt and the agent responding to it, thus executing it.
- `EmbeddingService`: Offers text embeddings[2] and similarity calculation features, which are essential for providing the **Semantic Search** capability in the CapabilityGPT framework.
- `QuestionAnsweringService`: Maps directly into the **Question Answering** capability of the CapabilityGPT framework by answering questions using a user-provided context.
- `QuestionExtractionService`: Extracts different kinds of questions from a text (for example, true/false questions, multiple choice quizzes, etc.). This is an example of the **Information Extraction** capability.
- `ImageGenerationService`: Generates images using either OpenAI (DALL-E 3[5]) or Hugging Face (Openjourney[6]). This is another example of the **Creation** capability.
- `SearchService`: Searches the Internet for data. This is an example of an external tool that can be used as a building block for agents[7].

The following example showcases the use of `CompletionService` to complete a sentence. After creating an endpoint, the code obtains an instance of a `CompletionService` from it, which is used to complete a simple prompt. Note how the service abstraction allows for changing service providers (OpenAI or Hugging Face) with a single line of code modification:

```
import io.github.mzattera.predictivepowers.AiEndpoint;

import io.github.mzattera.predictivepowers.huggingface.endpoint.HuggingFace
```

[5]https://openai.com/dall-e-3
[6]https://openjourney.art/
[7]See *Chapter* 4: *Architecture Patterns enabled by GPT-Models*, specifically the section "B Conversational Patterns with External Tool Integration".

```
Endpoint;
import io.github.mzattera.predictivepowers.openai.endpoint.OpenAiEndpoint;
import io.github.mzattera.predictivepowers.services.CompletionService;

public class CompletionExample {

	public static void main(String[] args) throws Exception {

		// Uncomment the below to use OpenAI
		AiEndpoint endpoint = new OpenAiEndpoint();

		// Uncomment the below to use Hugging Face
		// AiEndpoint endpoint = new HuggingFaceEndpoint();

		try (endpoint) {
			CompletionService cs = endpoint.getCompletionService();
			System.out.println(cs.complete("Alan Turing was").
getText());
		}
	}
}
```

Knowledge Base

A knowledge base in the context of the `predictive-powers` library is an in-memory vector database housing text embeddings[8]. Each embedding can possess an array of properties encapsulated as a `Map`. The knowledge base presents methods for semantic search based on embedding similarity and other filtering criteria. It can be partitioned into domains to allow separate searches and optimize performance.

`predictive-powers` Use Case

In this section, we will guide you through the implementation of an autonomous agent called the 'Essay Writer' ('***Writer***' for short), whose goal is to produce essays about different topics. The Writer is designed to take a short textual description

[8]The knowledge base is similar to vector stores in LangChain. See *Chapter 8: LangChain: GPT Implementation Framework for Python.*

of an essay content, search the Internet for relevant information, download and collate it, generating a complete essay.

We will provide code snippets to demonstrate how the capabilities of the CapabilityGPT framework are utilized to build the agent. For the full code of the agent, you can refer to the `predictive-powers` GitHub repository.

Architecture

This section provides a detailed explanation of the architecture employed in implementing the Writer, using the three-layer approach that should be familiar from *Chapter 4*[9]. This architecture is designed to be extensible, allowing it to handle more complex scenarios. However, the fundamental layered approach will remain consistent, utilizing `predictive-powers` services to create a modular architecture for the application and AI layers.

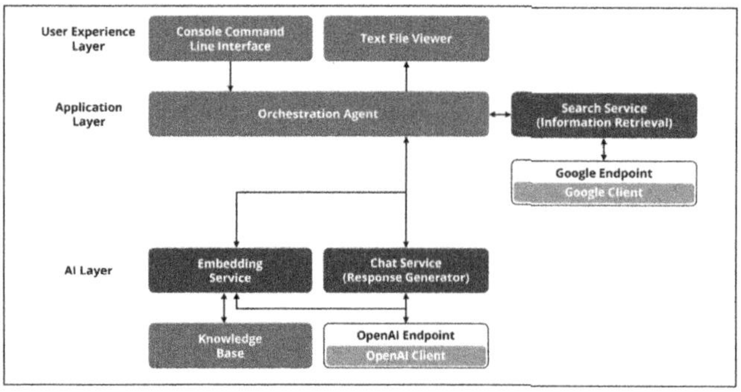

Figure 9.2: Essay Writer – Architecture

User Experience Layer

In our example, to maintain simplicity, users will interact with the Writer solely via the computer console. The Writer can be launched with various command-line options to execute different steps in the essay writing task (please refer to the full application code for details). The output generated will consist of both JSON[10] and plain text files that can be inspected by using any text file viewer.

Application Layer

At the application layer, the orchestration agent responds to user commands

[9]Please refer to *Chapter 4: Architecture Patterns enabled by GPT-Models*, and compare this architecture with architecture pattern "D2 Orchestration Agent".

[10]**JSON**, which stands for JavaScript Object Notation, is a method used to store information in an organized, easy-to-access manner. In a nutshell, it gives us a textual human-readable collection of data that we can access in a logical manner. It is widely used in many digital services and products to help systems and servers share data efficiently and quickly. Even though its name includes "JavaScript," it can be used in many programming environments outside of JavaScript.

by executing the corresponding application flow and properly coordinating different `predictive-powers` services. Later in this chapter, we will delve into the detailed description of these application flows.

In addition, an information retrieval component is also present. It is responsible for searching the Internet for relevant content that will be used to create the essay:

- **`SearchService`**: The `SearchService` performs web searches based on the queries generated by the `ChatService` (see below). It returns a list of links to relevant web pages for the orchestration agent to download and utilize.
- **`GoogleEndpoint`**: This component facilitates the integration with Google's Custom Search JSON API to bolster the functionality of the `SearchService`. It allows users to craft custom search engines, underpinned by Google's robust search capabilities. This endpoint can then be directed towards these engines. It empowers users to construct potent search utilities, capable of restricting searches to specific websites, filtering out mature content, confining searches to particular regions, and more.

AI Layer

The AI layer is where CapabilityGPT capabilities are implemented and exposed as `predictive-powers` services. Here, the endpoints connect to the relevant service providers to execute the tasks required by the orchestration agent.

- **`ChatService`**: This service will provide the creation capabilities needed to build the essay structure. It will start from its draft description, create search queries, search relevant materials from the web, and write each section of the essay by summarizing and rewriting the knowledge gathered from the Internet.
- **`EmbeddingService`**: This service is employed to embed the content downloaded from the Internet, enabling it to be stored in the knowledge base to power semantic search.
- **`OpenAiEndpoint`**: This endpoint connects to the required OpenAI models[11].
- **`KnowledgeBase`**: This provides an in-memory vector database to store the downloaded content and retrieve it when needed to write different sections of the essay. Additionally, the `KnowledgeBase` can be persisted as a single file on the user's PC, allowing users to regenerate the essay without re-downloading the relevant web pages.

[11]https://platform.openai.com/docs/models (specifically, gpt-3.5-turbo for the chat service and text-embedding-ada-002 for embedding).

It's important to remark that the services at both layers are independent of the endpoints and knowledge base used. This abstraction ensures that the application layer remains decoupled from the specific implementations provided by each service provider. During development, this means the software engineers can easily test different service providers and language models, to decide which one is more suitable for the solution being built.

Workflow

The workflow diagram, as shown in *Figure* 9.3, illustrates the steps involved in transforming a user's essay draft into the final essay produced by the Writer:

1. A user provides a textual description of the essay content.
2. The Writer generates the essay structure (chapters and sections) as a JSON file.
3. The Writer generates Google queries to search for information suitable to populate each section of the essay.
4. The Writer then executes each query and compiles the list of relevant web page links, as returned by the Google search engine.
5. The Writer downloads the content of each link and creates corresponding embeddings, which are stored in the `KnowledgeBase`.
6. For each section of the essay, the Writer uses semantic search to retrieve relevant information from the knowledge base.
7. Finally, the Writer uses this information to produce each section of the essay, resulting in a single text file output.

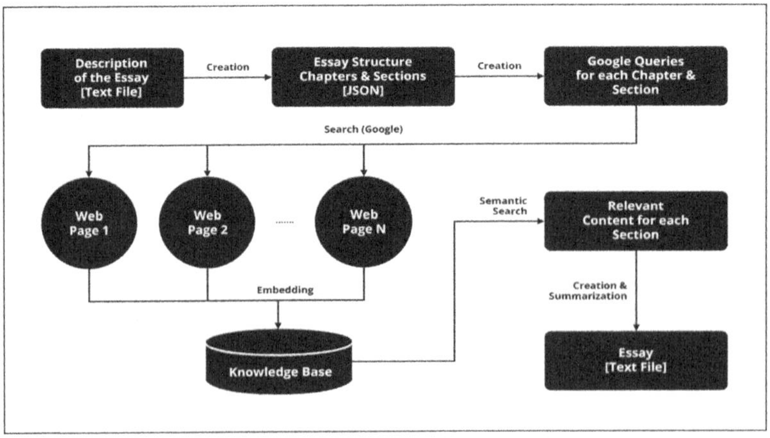

Figure 9.3: The Essay Writer – Workflow

Let's examine each step in detail and explore the CapabilityGPT framework's capabilities utilized at each stage.

The process begins with the user providing a textual description of the essay, as follows:

```
Write an essay about the Italian city of Padua.

The first chapter describes the geography and demographics of the city,
its economics, and its history from proto-history to the modern age.

Additionally, have a section for the famous people who lived in Padua.

The second chapter focuses on traditions and folklore, including tradi-
tional events and festivals, food and wine, and other relevant topics.

The last chapter is a collection of notable sights, with separate sec-
tions for each attraction, describing the places of interest and visi-
tors' experiences.
```

It's important to note that the Writer understands the essay as consisting of chapters divided into sections. Although more complex structures are possible, for simplicity, we will focus on this format. The essay structure is initially generated using ChatGPT generation capabilities, creating chapters and sections based on the provided description. The resulting structure is saved in JSON format for further processing. Here's an example structure:

```
{
  "title": "My Essay",
  "description": "Write an essay about the Italian city of Padua.\r\nThe
first chapter describes the geography and demographics of the city, its
economics, and its history from proto-history to the modern age.\r\
nAdditionally, have a section for the famous people who lived in
Padua.\r\nThe second chapter focuses on traditions and folklore,
including traditional events and festivals, food and wine, and other
relevant topics.\r\nThe last chapter is a collection of notable sights,
with separate sections for each attraction, describing the places of
interest and visitors' experiences.\r\n",
  "chapters": [
    {
      "id": "1",
      "title": "Geography and Demographics",
```

```
      "summary": "This chapter provides an overview of the geography and
demographics of the city of Padua. It explores the city's location,
climate, and natural features. Additionally, it delves into the
population demographics, including the ethnic makeup, age distribution,
and population growth over time.",
      "sections": [
        {
          "id": "1.1",
          "title": "Economics",
          "summary": "This section explores the economic aspects of
Padua, including its main industries, trade, and economic development.
It highlights the city's position as an economic hub and discusses the
key sectors driving its economy."
          ...
        },
        {
          "id": "1.2",
          "title": "History",
          "summary": "This section traces the history of Padua from its
proto-historic origins to the modern age. It covers significant
historical events, rulers, and cultural developments that have shaped
the city's identity over time."
          ...
        },
        ...
      ]
    },
    ...
  ]
}
```

Note how ChatGPT enhances the description of each section, providing a more detailed content summary. In the "Notable Sights" section, the places of interest are automatically added without the need for prior listing, thanks to ChatGPT capabilities.

```
    "id" : "3",
    "title" : "Notable Sights",
    "summary" : "This chapter serves as a guide to the notable sights in
Padua, highlighting the city's architectural, historical, and
cultural landmarks. Each section focuses on a specific attraction,
providing a detailed description and capturing the visitors'
experience.",
    "sections" : [ {
      "id" : "3.1",
      "title" : "Basilica di Sant'Antonio",
        ...
    }, {
      "id" : "3.2",
      "title" : "Prato della Valle",
        ...
    }, {
      "id" : "3.3",
      "title" : "Palazzo della Ragione",
        ...
    }, {
      "id" : "3.4",
      "title" : "Scrovegni Chapel",
        ...
    } ],
```


With the essay structure in place, the Writer needs to populate it with relevant information. Instead of relying solely on the model's implicit knowledge, we want to fetch updated and relevant information from the Internet. To accomplish this, we generate Google searches for each section using ChatGPT text generation capabilities. This generates a short list of Google queries for each section.

The next step involves leveraging a different capability of our framework: **Search**. The Essay Writer uses these generated Google queries to query the search engine and collect a list of relevant web page links.

Once we have identified the relevant web pages, they are downloaded and stored in a database for semantic search. Semantic search will allow the Writer to search for text in the database that is semantically similar to the summary of a given section, thus retrieving those documents that are relevant to compile that section of the essay. To enable semantic search, the downloaded pages are encoded in a special way known as 'embedding'; this encoding provides a numerical representation of the text that is easier for AI to process.

The `predictive-powers` library provides high-level methods to download web content, perform embedding, and store the data in an in-memory database (the `KnowledgeBase`), which is available as part of the library.

After downloading, embedding, and storing the relevant web pages, the Writer employs semantic search to fetch contextually relevant content for each section of the essay. These contextual pieces, referred to as the 'context' for each section, serve as the basis for generating the actual content of the sections. ChatGPT utilizes its **Summarization** and **Generation** capabilities to create the section content based on the provided context.

By following this workflow, the Writer autonomously generates an essay that incorporates up-to-date information from the web, producing a comprehensive and well-researched final output.

Code Walkthrough

In this section, we elucidate the workflow of the application that was outlined in previous sections, offering snippets of code to demonstrate how various tasks are performed. Should you wish to delve deeper into the full code for the Writer, it is always accessible in the `predictive-powers` GitHub repository.

While showcasing the application code, we take the opportunity to list some of the prompts used. We challenge readers to try writing their own prompts following the guidelines in *Chapter* 5 and see if and how the Writer's skills improve.

Take note that the Writer is a multithreaded application for the sake of efficiency. The method `parallelExecution()` manages the simultaneous execution of multiple tasks, compiling all of their results into a single `List`. Throughout this chapter, we will showcase snippets of code for various tasks, while not focusing much on the required structure for multitasking.

The `Essay` class is an inner class utilized by the Writer to maintain the structure of the essay. It offers several methods that facilitate obtaining its nicely formatted contents in an organized manner. The Writer contains one instance of `Essay` in its `essay` field; as the program executes, the instance is gradually populated with data.

The orchestration of the application workflow happens within the `main()` method of the class. Here, the user input is processed, and the required tasks are executed. In short, the `main()` method implements the 'Orchestration Agent' component shown in our architecture.

The first task in the workflow is to read the user-provided draft and establish the structure of the essay. For processing convenience, the structure is saved as a JSON file. The following code snippet demonstrates how this task is accomplished. It assumes that the essay draft has been stored in `essay.description` (this would have already been carried out by the `main()` method at this point). Notice how the code leverages GPT's ability to return data in various formats, JSON in this instance. Java libraries dedicated to handling JSON serialization allow us to easily transform the returned data into an `Essay` instance using a single line of code:

```
public void createStructure() throws JsonProcessingException {

      String description = essay.description;
[...]

      // Instantiate a service to create the essay structure
      OpenAiChatService chatSvc = openAi.getChatService();
      chatSvc.setModel(COMPLETION_MODEL);
      chatSvc.setTemperature(40.0);

// Set agent personality, instruct it to return JSON
// and provide one example
      chatSvc.setPersonality(
"You are an assistant helping a writer to create the structure of an
essay. The essay structure is composed of an array of chapters, each
chapter containing an array of sections. Always return the structure
using this JSON format; here is an example of the format:\n"
+ "\n"
+ "{\n"
+ "    \"chapters\": [{\n"
+ "            \"title\": \"Title for first chapter\",\n"
+ "            \"summary\": \"Summary of first chapter.\",\n"
+ "            \"sections\": [{\n"
+ "              \"title\": \"Title for first section of first chapter\",\n"
```

```
+ "            \"summary\": \"Summary of this section\"\n"
+ "          },{\n"
+ "            \"title\": \"Title for second section of first chapter\",\n"
+ "            \"summary\": \"Summary of this section\"\n"
+ "          }]\n"
+ "    }, {\n"
+ "          \"title\": \"Title for second chapter\",\n"
+ "          \"summary\": \"Summary of second chapter.\",\n"
+ "          \"sections\": [{\n"
+ "            \"title\": \"Title for first section of second chapter\",\n"
+ "            \"summary\": \"Summary of this section\"\n"
+ "          }, {\n"
+ "            \"title\": \"Title for second section of second chap-
ter\",\n"
+ "            \"summary\": \"Summary of this section\"\n"
+ "          }]\n"
+ "    }]\n"
+ "}\n"
+ "\n"
+ "Ensure that sections are not nested within other sections. Titles
should not include section numbering or the words 'Chapter' or 'Section'."
);


// Invoke the agent to create the structure,
// using the draft in description
      TextCompletion resp = chatSvc.complete(
"You are tasked with creating the structure of a book based on the
provided description. The book should consist of several chapters, each
containing a title, a summary, and a list of sections. Each section
should have a title and a summary. Ensure that sections are not nested
within each other.\n"
+ "\n"
+ "If possible, try to make the summaries of the chapters and sections
at least 100 words long to provide substantial content for the book's
outline.\n"
+ "\n"
+ "Think it through step by step and list all chapters and the sections
they contain. Return the result using JSON format.\n"
+ "\n"
+ "User Description: " + description
);


// Transform returned JSON into an Essay
// which is then copied into the local instance.
```

```
        Essay created = JSON_MAPPER.readValue(resp.getText(), Essay.
class);
essay.chapters = new ArrayList<>(created.chapters);
[...]
}
```

Following the creation of the structure, relevant data for writing the essay is sourced from the Internet. The following code snippet returns a list of `SearchResult` instances (links to web pages), which content can be used to compose the given section. These links are returned in a `Pair` structure, along with their corresponding rank, as determined by Google.

This code also illustrates another feature of the library: the capability to create prompt templates, which are parameterized prompts. Prompt parameters are indicated in the template by enclosing them in double curly braces. At runtime, these placeholders are replaced with values bearing the same key contained in a `Map` that is passed to the `CompletionService.fillSlots()` method. For instance, in the following code, the string "`{{chapter_summary}}`" is replaced by the value associated with the "`chapter_summary`" key in the `params Map`:

```
public List<Pair<SearchResult, Integer>>
    google(Section chapter, Section section)
{

// First create a list of search queries,
// based on what we want to search

        // Instanciates model to create Google searches
        OpenAiChatService chatSvc = openAi.getChatService();
        chatSvc.setModel(COMPLETION_MODEL);
        chatSvc.setTemperature(50.0);

        // Dynamically build the prompt
        final String prompt =
"Given the below chapter summary, section title and section summary,
provided in XML tags, generate a list of search engine queries that can
be used to search the topic corresponding to the section on the
```

```
Internet."
+ " Each query is a short sentence or a short list of key terms relevant
for the section topic."
+ " Include terms to provide a context for the topic, as described by
the chapter summary, so that the query is clearly related to the chapter
content."
+ " Be creative and provide exactly 5 queries."
+ " Strictly provide results as a JSON array of strings.\n\n"
+ "<chapter_summary>{{chapter_summary}}</chapter_summary>\n\n"
+ "<section_title>{{section_title}}</section_title>\n\n"
+ "<section_summary>{{section_summary}}</section_summary>";

        // Provide data to fill slots in the prompt template
        Map<String, String> params = new HashMap<>();
        params.put("chapter_summary", chapter.summary);
        params.put("section_title", section.title);
        params.put("section_summary", section.summary);

// Prepares the conversation;
// notice the call to fill the slots in the prompt template
        List<ChatMessage> msgs = new ArrayList<>();
        msgs.add(new ChatMessage(
Role.SYSTEM,
"You are an assistant helping a researcher in finding web pages
that are relevant for the essay section they are writing."
));
        msgs.add(new ChatMessage(
Role.USER, CompletionService.fillSlots(prompt, params)
));

        // Build a list of Google queries for the section.
        // Queries are returned as a JSON list of Strings, that is
deserialized.
        List<String> queries;
        while (true) {
                try {
queries = JSON_MAPPER.readValue(chatSvc.complete(msgs).getText(),
```

```
new TypeReference<List<String>>() {});
                    break;
            } catch (JsonProcessingException e) {
// Retry in case GPT returned badly formatted JSON
                    LOG.warn("Retrying because of malformed JSON, e);
            }
        }

        // Now submit each query and collect returned links
        List<Pair<SearchResult, Integer>> result = new ArrayList<>();
        for (String query : queries) {
            List<SearchResult> links;
            try {
links = google.getSearchService()
            .search(query, LINKS_PER_QUERY);
            } catch (Exception e) {
                    // Skip single query that fails
                    LOG.warn("Ignoring error searching for: " + query,
e);
                    continue;
            }
[...]
        }

        return result;
}
```

Once the Writer has the list of pages to be downloaded, it goes ahead and retrieves them, delivering the corresponding embedding. Depending on the size of the page, this could potentially result in multiple items. The `ExtractionUtil.fromUrl()` method is a handy one-liner for fetching text content directly from a URL.

The reader should also notice how we use the `ModelService` to have some model metadata, like the maximum number of tokens it accepts as input.

In Java, this process looks like this:

```
private List<EmbeddedText> download(SearchResult link) {

   // Instantiate the service used to embed the downloaded pages
   EmbeddingService embSvc = openAi.getEmbeddingService();

   // Set the maximum size for each embedded text chunk;
   // the following calculation ensures approximately 15 embeddings
   // will be used to compose each section.
   // Notice how the ModelService is fetched from the OpenAIEndpoint
   (openAI)
   // to retrieve the maximum prompt size for the completion model and
   the
   // embedding model.
     int writerSize = openAi.getModelService().getContextSize(WRITER_MOD-
EL);
     int embSize = openAi.getModelService().getContextSize(embSvc.getMod-
el());
     embSvc.setMaxTextTokens(
        Math.min(embSize, (writerSize - SECTION_LENGTH_TOKENS) / 15)
     );

     // Download the page content as a String
     String content = null;
     try {
         content = ExtractionUtil.fromUrl(
             link.getLink(), DOWNLOAD_TIMEOUT_MILLIS));
     } catch (Exception e) {
   // If an error occurs during page download, the page is skipped
         LOG.error("Error downloading " + link.getLink(), e);
         return new ArrayList<>();
     }

     // Embed the downloaded content
```

```
    List<EmbeddedText> result = embSvc.embed(content);

    [...]

    return result;
}
```

Upon successful completion, the embeddings are stored within the knowledge base, paving the way for the writing process to commence. The following code snippet outlines how a single section is written.

Examining the code, the reader can see how the `search()` method from the `KnowledgeBase` is used to perform semantic search, by passing an embedded version of the section summary:

```
private List<Section> write(Section section) {

        // Instanciate services
        EmbeddingService embSvc = openAi.getEmbeddingService();
        OpenAiChatService chatSvc = openAi.getChatService();
        chatSvc.setModel(WRITER_MODEL);
        chatSvc.setTemperature(0.0);

        String prompt =
"<context>{{context}}</context>\n\n"
+ "<summary>{{summary}}</summary>";
        Map<String, String> params = new HashMap<>();
        params.put("summary", section.summary);

        // This is the prompt used for creating the section
        List<ChatMessage> msgs = new ArrayList<>();
        msgs.add(new ChatMessage(Role.SYSTEM,
"You will be provided with a context and the summary of a section of an
```

```
essay, both delimited by XML tags."
+ " Your task is to use the content of the context to write the entire
section of the essay."
+ " Use a professional style." + " Avoid content repetitions but be de-
tailed."
+ " Output only the section content, not its title, do not create sub-
sections."
+ " Do not make up missing information or put placeholders for data you
do not have."
+ " Only if enough information is available in the content, produce a
text at least "
+ SECTION_LENGTH_TOKENS + " tokens long.\n\n"));
    [...]

    // Searches the knowledge base for relevant content
    // (= builds the context)
        List<Pair<EmbeddedText, Double>> knowledge =
                kb.search(embSvc.embed(section.summary).get(0), 50, 0);

    // Here some code is needed to take only
    // the context that fits the model prompt size.
    // It is omitted for simplicity.
    [...]

    // Add generated content to the section
    section.content = chatSvc.complete(msgs).getText();

    [...]

    return section.sections; // Not used really
}
```

Conclusion

This chapter has presented a comprehensive overview of the `predictive-powers` library and its ability to harness the power of generative AI for Java developers. The focus was to present a real-life approach to utilizing generative AI capabilities.

The `predictive-powers` library offers distinct advantages for Java developers and AI enthusiasts alike. It not only simplifies the integration of generative AI capabilities but also provides low-level access to popular APIs like OpenAI and Hugging Face. This flexibility allows developers to engage directly with these APIs if desired. Moreover, the library's design aligns with the CapabilityGPT framework, ensuring compatibility with different capability providers, reducing the risk of vendor lock-in. Additionally, its in-memory vector database supports essential functions like semantic search, information extraction, and question answering. Lastly, it facilitates the convenient retrieval of textual content from diverse sources, including web pages and various file formats like MS Office, PDF, and HTML. These features make the `predictive-powers` library a valuable tool for harnessing generative AI capabilities in Java applications while leveraging flexibility, compatibility, and ease of use typical of Java applications.

We delved into the technical aspects of the library, detailing essential concepts such as API clients, endpoints and services, and the knowledge base. We learned about their roles and functionalities within the broader framework and gained insights into their underlying mechanisms.

One of the chapter's highlights was a practical example: the creation of an autonomous agent named the 'Essay Writer'. This served as a concrete illustration of how to leverage the `predictive-powers` library and its different features in a realistic project.

Key Points

By the end of this chapter, the reader should be familiar with:

- **The `predictive-powers` library**: An Apache-2.0 licensed library that offers a simplified yet powerful interface for Java developers to harness generative AI.
- **API clients**: Fundamental units of the `predictive-powers` library that facilitate direct API calls to service providers like OpenAI and Hugging Face.
- **Endpoints and services**: High-level generative AI components that utilize API clients to render services. The reader should be aware of the services offered, such as the `ModelService`, `CompletionService`, `ChatService`, `EmbeddingService`, and others.
- **`KnowledgeBase`**: An in-memory vector database crucial for abilities such as semantic search, information extraction, and question answering.

- **Implementation of an autonomous agent**: The chapter guides the reader through the creation of an 'Essay Writer', demonstrating the practical application of the concepts learned. It shows how the library components can be easily combined, leveraging the CapabilityGPT framework, prompt engineering techniques, and architecture patterns presented in other parts of the book to create an agent able to perform a complex task.
- **Architecture pattern**: Understanding the architecture pattern and navigating the code is a critical part of the learning process. The reader should be familiar with the three-tier architecture: the User Experience layer, the Application layer, and the AI layer, and understand how these layers can be implemented using components from the `predictive-powers` library.
- **Code navigation**: Understanding the code snippets and their workings, presented in the Code Walkthrough section, will help the reader apply these concepts to their own projects.

Appendix A:

Further Exploration of Prompt Engineering Applications

Introduction

Building on *Chapter 5's, Advanced GPT Prompt Engineering Techniques*, exploration of advanced prompt engineering techniques, which presented 12 examples of our three prompt patterns–Instruction, Query, and Multi-Agent–this appendix introduces 11 further examples. These are curated to deepen the understanding of prompt patterns with ChatGPT-4 and highlight a broader range of practical enterprise scenarios.

Under Single Instruction Examples, we delve into use cases like 'Resource Management,' 'Scenario-based Project Simulation,' and 'Business Communication,' each offering a fresh perspective on the application of Instruction Prompt Pattern. The Instruction Sequence Examples and Pseudo Code Instructions Examples further unravel the intricacies of sequential and logical task management through real-world scenarios like 'Insurance Claim Processing', 'Solution Architecture Analysis', and 'Real Estate Listing Comparison' respectively.

We then proceed with Query Examples, where ChatGPT-4 navigates through safety regulations, delves into hypothetical HR scenarios, and assesses supply possibilities employing fuzzy logic, utilizing a blend of analytical and interpretive capabilities.

Lastly, the Multi-Agent Examples section covers instances of ChatGPT-4 operating in multi-agent setups, tackling an eco-friendly motorbike design simulation and conducting a detailed research on raw materials, thereby reflecting on the collaborative and exploratory features of ChatGPT-4 using some of its plugins.

As you traverse through these additional examples, the objective remains to deepen the understanding of the prompt engineering techniques, showcasing the versatility of ChatGPT-4 in addressing a large variety of practical enterprise scenarios. Through these diverse scenarios, this appendix endeavors to further equip you with the nuanced knowledge and skills requisite for effectively leveraging ChatGPT-4 to drive innovation and operational excellence within the enterprise landscape.

Structure

In this chapter, the following additional prompting case studies will be covered:

- Single Instruction Examples
  - Resource Management
  - Scenario-based Project Simulation
  - Business Communication
- Instruction Sequence Examples:
  - Insurance Claim Processing
  - Solution Architecture Analysis
- Pseudo Code Instructions Examples:
  - Real Estate Listing Comparison
- Query Examples
  - Safety Regulation Inquiries
  - Counterfactual Exploration in HR Management
  - Supply Possibility Estimation
- Multi-Agent Examples
  - Eco-friendly Motorbike Design Simulation
  - Research on Raw Materials

Single Instruction Examples

These examples encompass a *Resource Management* simulation, with ChatGPT-4 acting as a resource manager aligning skills with project tasks; a *Scenario-based Project Simulation* where it forecasts project phases amid challenges; and a

Business Communication example in the carbon accounting sector, summarizing key industry growth and challenges.

Resource Management

This is an example from the domain of project resource management. The following prompt is based on the **Matchmaking** capability of the framework introduced in Chapter 2, '*CapabilityGPT, An Enterprise AI Capability Framework for ChatGPT*':

- **Expert Persona**: "*You are a resource manager skilled in assigning resources to projects*"
- **Context**:
  - *Projects:*
    - *Developing a predictive machine learning model for customer churn: The tasks include data cleaning and pre-processing, exploratory data analysis, feature engineering and selection, building and training the machine learning model, model validation and evaluation, presenting the model results to stakeholders, and collaborating with the software engineering team for model deployment."*
  - *Resources:*
    - *Person_1: 3+ years of experience in data cleaning and preprocessing, proficient in Python, Pandas, and SQL, has good data visualization skills using tools like Matplotlib and Seaborn.*
    - *Person_2: 4+ years of experience in machine learning, expert in building and training models using Scikit-learn or TensorFlow, understanding of model evaluation metrics, proficient in Python.*
    - *Person_3: 2+ years of experience in data analysis and presentation, expertise in exploratory data analysis and feature engineering, strong communication skills to present complex results to stakeholders, proficient in Python and Tableau.*
- **Instruction**: "*Assign resources to projects based on their skills and project requirements* (*Matchmaking*)"
- **Execution Rules**: "*Consider each resource's skills and the requirements of each project*"
- **Output Constraints**: "*Output should be a list of projects with assigned resources*"

The response generated by ChatGPT-4 to this prompt is as follows:

Given the project and resources' details, we can allocate the resources to different tasks of the project as follows:

Project: Developing a predictive machine learning model for customer churn

1. *Data Cleaning and Preprocessing: This task involves cleaning up the data, dealing with missing values, outliers, and any inconsistencies in the data. Given the requirements, we assign Person_1 for this task because they have over 3 years of experience in data cleaning and preprocessing, and proficiency in Python, Pandas, and SQL which are ideal tools for this task.*
2. *Exploratory Data Analysis: This involves digging deeper into the dataset, finding correlations, and visualizing data for better understanding. The task would be best suited for Person_3, who has over 2 years of experience in data analysis and proficiency in Python and Tableau, a data visualization tool.*
3. *Feature Engineering and Selection: This is the process of selecting the most relevant features from the dataset that contribute significantly to the predictive model. Given Person_3's expertise in feature engineering, they would be the best fit for this task.*
4. *Building and Training the Machine Learning Model: This task requires a deep understanding of machine learning algorithms and model training. Hence, Person_2, who has over 4 years of experience in machine learning and is an expert in building and training models using Scikit-learn or TensorFlow, will handle this task.*
5. *Model Validation and Evaluation: This requires a solid understanding of various model evaluation metrics. Given Person_2's understanding of these metrics, they will also be responsible for this task.*
6. *Presenting the Model Results to Stakeholders: This task involves communicating the results of the model to the stakeholders in a clear and concise manner. Given Person_3's strong communication skills, they will be responsible for this task.*
7. *Collaborating with the Software Engineering Team for Model Deployment: This task can be handled collectively by Person_1, Person_2, and Person_3 as it will require the skills of data processing (Person_1), model building (Person_2), and presentation (Person_3).*

In the resource management simulation, ChatGPT-4 functions as a resource coordinator, matching resources to tasks based on skills and expertise. Following instructions, it devises an assignment plan, aligning resources effectively with appropriate tasks. However, by leveraging Person_2's machine learning expertise for Feature Engineering, the project strategy could be further optimized, enhancing its likelihood of success.

Scenario-based Project Simulation

This is another example in the Project Management domain. The subsequent prompt hinges on the **Simulation** capability:

Expert Persona: *You are an experienced project manager.*

Context: *This is your current project:*

Project Description: The EduRevolution project aims at developing and launching an innovative mobile learning application designed to disrupt the traditional education system. The application will allow learners of all ages and levels to access various educational resources including interactive classes, multimedia content, customized learning plans, gamified quizzes, and collaborative learning spaces. The application is designed to promote active learning, encourage continuous assessment, and foster a sense of community among learners.

These phases have been completed:

Phase 1: Conceptualization & Requirements Gathering During this phase, we gathered business requirements, defined the concept of the application, its key features, and outlined user personas. A detailed market analysis was conducted to understand the landscape and identify potential opportunities.

Phase 2: Design In this phase, we worked on the user experience (UX) and user interface (UI) design of the application. The process involved creating wireframes, prototypes, and final designs of the application, ensuring that the app is user-friendly, visually appealing, and easy to navigate.

Phase 3: Development The coding and integration of the application were carried out during this phase. We employed agile methodologies, including sprints and scrums, to develop the app iteratively, allowing for changes as needed based on user feedback and testing. The core functionalities were developed and integrated with existing systems.

Phase 4: Testing Here, we conducted a thorough testing phase, covering unit testing, system testing, and user acceptance testing (UAT). Potential bugs and performance issues were identified and categorized according to severity. While all major bugs were fixed, several minor and medium bugs still exist and require various workarounds to use the app correctly.

Instruction: *Perform a simulation for the next two phases based on the results achieved so far: Production preparation and Go-live & Hypercare.*

Execution Rules: *Differentiate between three cases: best case, average case, and worst case.*

ChatGPT-4 generates the following response to this prompt:

Phase 5: Production Preparation

Best-case scenario:

In the best-case scenario, the transition to the production environment goes smoothly. The remaining minor and medium bugs are resolved swiftly with no impact on the release date. Application performance in the production environment mirrors that in the test environment, indicating readiness for the Go-live phase. The team is fully prepared for the deployment, having created extensive documentation, and having trained all stakeholders in using the app and troubleshooting common issues.

Average-case scenario:

In the average-case scenario, some minor and medium bugs remain even after initial fixes, requiring additional development time and pushing back the release date slightly. The application shows satisfactory performance in the production environment after some minor adjustments. The team has mostly completed the required documentation and training, but some last-minute additions are still being finalized.

Worst-case scenario:

In the worst-case scenario, fixing the remaining bugs proves to be more complex than expected, revealing deeper issues in the codebase, and leading to significant delays. The application performance in the production environment is inconsistent, requiring considerable time and effort to diagnose and address. Despite attempts to fast-track the process, the documentation is incomplete, and stakeholders' training is insufficient.

Phase 6: Go-live & Hypercare.

Best-case scenario:

In the best-case scenario, the go-live phase goes as planned without major hitches. User adoption is high, and the feedback is overwhelmingly positive. The hyper care team quickly addresses minor issues, resulting in minimal disruption. The hyper care period is shorter than planned because of the stability of the application and ends with the successful handover to the operational support team.

Average-case scenario:

In the average-case scenario, the go-live phase encounters minor hitches, such as a slower than anticipated roll-out, resulting in a slightly reduced initial user base. Feedback is mixed, with users praising the application's functionality but also reporting several usability issues. The hyper care team is fully occupied in addressing these issues, and the hyper care period extends to its maximum anticipated length.

Worst-case scenario:

In the worst-case scenario, the go-live phase experiences significant problems. Technical issues impact the user experience, leading to negative feedback and a reduced user base. The application stability is lower than expected, and the hyper care team is overwhelmed with issues, requiring the period to be extended beyond the initially planned timeline. High priority bugs and system stability issues require urgent attention and may lead to a rollback or temporary suspension of services until they are fixed.

In the project management simulation, ChatGPT-4 acts as an experienced manager, forecasting future project phases based on past data and potential challenges. After analyzing best, average, and worst-case scenarios, it provides a comprehensive plan, detailing how each scenario might progress. This analysis culminates in a contingency plan, ensuring a prepared and robust approach for any outcome.

Business Communication

This final single-instruction example explores business communication and summarization skills within the carbon accounting industry. Here is the prompt:

Expert Persona: *You are a business communication expert.*

Context: "*The carbon accounting industry is experiencing a surge as governmental bodies, investors, and consumers are increasingly seeking detailed reports on corporate greenhouse gas emissions. This growth persists despite skepticism over the accuracy of the data. According to the data company PitchBook, venture capital funding for carbon accounting firms escalated from $60 million in 2020 to $767 million in 2022. This upward trajectory has carried on into 2023, with venture capitalists pouring $333 million into the sector thus far. This investment rush is stimulated by companies' anticipation of intricate disclosure mandates expected to be implemented in Europe and the US within the next year. This is coupled with the pressure from investors and consumers to project an environmentally* *conscious image. The onset of the standards was initiated in June with the International Sustainability Standards Board's introduction of guidelines for calculating emissions throughout supply chains. These standards proved to be more lenient than initially anticipated after the ISSB announced in December that corporations would be granted an additional year to report emissions throughout their entire value chain. Nonetheless, the implementation is acting as a catalyst for many businesses to embark on a more comprehensive level of tracking."*

Instruction: *Summarize this text*

Output Constraints: *The summary should not be longer than 3 sentences.*

Execution Rules:

1. *Strictly follow the 'what happened and why?' structure.*
2. *If there is no reason mentioned, use assumptions.*

Reference Cases: *Use these three summarization examples for guidance:*

Input-Output Case 1: *Summarizing Meeting Minutes*

Input: *"During the quarterly meeting held on April 5, 2023, the team discussed the recent 20% decrease in Q1 sales compared to Q4 of last year. The Marketing department proposed a new nationwide advertising campaign, with an increased budget of $50,000, to boost brand visibility. The Product Development team reported progress on the new 'Green Tech' product line but noted potential delays of up to two months due to supply chain issues with overseas partners. The Finance department expressed concerns about the increased marketing budget and potential decrease in Q2 profits due to product line delays."*

Output: *"What Happened and Why: At the April 5, 2023, quarterly meeting, a 20% Q1 sales drop was discussed, likely driven by increased market competition. Marketing proposed a nationwide ad campaign to boost visibility, while Product Development forecasted 'Green Tech' product delays due to supply chain issues. Finance expressed budget and profit concerns due to these changes.*

Input-Output Case 2: *Summarizing a Quarterly Financial Report*

Input: *"In Q2 2023, XYZ Corp reported a gross revenue of $2.1 billion, a decrease of 5% compared to Q2 2022. The net profit margin also shrunk to 6%, down from 9% the previous year. The decrease in both revenue and profit is largely attributed to disruptions in the supply chain and increased logistics costs due to global economic conditions."*

Output: *"What Happened and Why: In Q2 2023, XYZ Corp experienced a 5% drop* *in gross revenue and a decrease in net profit margin from 9% to 6% compared to Q2 2022. This was primarily due to supply chain disruptions and increased logistics costs linked to unfavorable global economic conditions."*

Input-Output Case 3: *Summarizing a Press Release on a New Product Launch*

Input: *"On June 15, 2023, ABC Tech announced the release of its innovative product, 'SmartLens', an AI-powered contact lens that offers augmented reality experiences. The launch responds to the growing demand for immersive wearable technologies. The 'SmartLens' is expected to hit the market in fall 2023."*

Output: *"What Happened and Why: ABC Tech announced the launch of 'SmartLens', an AI-powered contact lens offering augmented reality, on June 15, 2023. This move comes in response to increasing consumer interest in immersive wearable technologies."*

Responding to the given prompt, ChatGPT-4 generates the following output:

What Happened and Why: The carbon accounting sector saw a surge in venture capital funding, escalating from $60 million in 2020 to $767 million in 2022 and continues to attract investment in 2023, despite doubts about data accuracy. This is due to an increasing demand from governments, investors, and consumers for detailed corporate emissions reports and companies' anticipation of new emission disclosure mandates in Europe and the US. The International Sustainability Standards Board's introduction of guidelines for calculating emissions across supply chains has acted as a catalyst for businesses to undertake comprehensive emissions tracking.

In the business communication example, ChatGPT-4 acts as an expert summarizer, leveraging the summarization techniques demonstrated in the reference cases, distilling details about the carbon accounting industry's growth and challenges. It succinctly identifies a rise in venture capital funding despite accuracy concerns, linking this to stakeholder demand and expected emission mandates. The role of the International Sustainability Standards Board's guidelines is also emphasized, showcasing ChatGPT-4's skill in extracting pivotal information from complex contexts.

Instruction Sequence Examples

Dive into two multi-step processing scenarios where ChatGPT-4 steps into the shoes of a claims representative to tackle car accident insurance claims, and as a systems architect to dissect and refine a given architecture diagram.

Insurance Claim Processing

ChatGPT-4, acting as a claims representative, navigates a three-step process to handle a car accident insurance claim, showcasing a methodical approach in managing information gathering, data condensation, and preliminary repair cost estimation. Here is the presented prompt:

Expert Persona: *You are a claims representative of an insurance company.*

Context: *I have the following basic information about a car crash: 'my car that was involved in an accident is now on the side of the road'.*

Instruction Sequence: *Execute these three steps:*

1. *First ask me 10 questions about the damage. Only ask one question at a time and wait for my answer before you ask the next question. Carefully ask me informative questions to maximize your information about this damage so that, when you have all the answers, you can summarize my answers and estimate the costs to repair the damage. Avoid asking yes/no questions* (*Communication*).
2. *Then summarize my answers. Do not start summarizing, before you receive the answers to all your questions* (*Summarization*).
3. *Finally assess the costs of the damage based on the summary of my answers to all your questions* (*Assessment*)."

The output of ChatGPT-4 is the following, which includes a conversation, where the respective utterances are assigned to ChatGPT and a user, respectively:

ChatGPT: *Thank you for reaching out to us. I will ask you a series of questions to understand the extent of the damage better.*

1. *Could you please describe the overall condition of your car after the accident?*

User: *It was severely damaged and not driving-ready.*

ChatGPT: *I see, I am sorry to hear that.*

2. *Could you please specify which areas of the vehicle have been most affected by the collision?*

User: *The right-side door, the right-side window, and the right car wing*

ChatGPT: *I understand.*

3. *Were the car's wheels and suspension affected by the accident? If yes, how so?*

User: *Yes, the right front wheel is also slightly damaged. No damage to the suspension.*

ChatGPT: Noted.

4. *Can you detail the current condition of the car's exterior paint and body work, especially in the areas directly affected by the collision?*

User: *The door is significantly deformed, and the door panel is bent as well. The car wing has only a small dent and a few scratches.*

ChatGPT: Understood.

5. *Was there any damage to the car's interior such as seats, dashboard, or electronic systems due to the accident?*

User: *The right car seat is also slightly dented.*

ChatGPT: I see.

6. *Were the headlights, taillights, or any other external lights damaged in the accident?*

User: No.

ChatGPT: Alright.

7. *Can you please describe any potential damage to the engine, transmission, or other major mechanical components of the car?*

User: *Nothing as far as I know.*

ChatGPT: Noted.

8. *Was there any damage to the windshield or any other glass components, aside from the right-side window that you previously mentioned?*

User: No.

ChatGPT: Okay.

9. *Have you noticed any fluid leaks, such as oil or coolant, after the accident?*

User: No.

ChatGPT: *Alright.*

10. *Finally, could you tell me the make, model, and year of your vehicle? This will help me to estimate the cost of the parts needed for repair.*

User: BMW 230i, 2020.

ChatGPT: *Thank you for providing all the necessary information. Let me summarize the damages:*

1. *The vehicle is not in a drivable condition due to severe damage.*
2. *The most affected areas of the vehicle are the right-side door, window, and wing.*
3. *The right front wheel is slightly damaged, but the suspension remains unaffected.*
4. *The exterior door panel is significantly deformed, and the right wing has a small dent and scratches.*
5. *The right seat inside the vehicle has a slight dent.*
6. *The headlights, taillights, and other external lights are not damaged.*
7. *No damage to major mechanical components such as engine and transmission has been reported.*
8. *Apart from the right-side window, no other glass components like the windshield are damaged.*
9. *There are no reported fluid leaks after the accident.*
10. *The car in question is a 2020 BMW 230i.*

ChatGPT: *Based on this information, the costs can be estimated as follows:*

1. *Bodywork: Depending on the extent of the damage, repairing, or replacing the door panel and car wing can cost between $500 to $1500.*
2. *Right front wheel: A new wheel for a BMW 230i might range from $100 to $300.*
3. *Right-side window: The replacement cost could be in the region of $200 to $400.*

4. *Interior damage (right car seat): A slight dent repair could cost around $100 to $200.*

Please note that these are rough estimates, and the actual cost could be higher or lower depending on labor costs, availability of parts, and any hidden damage not apparent from our conversation. It is recommended to have the vehicle thoroughly checked by a professional mechanic for a more precise estimate.

In this scenario, ChatGPT-4 serves as a claims representative conducting a three-step process to handle a car accident insurance claim. Initially, it diligently gathers detailed information through open-ended questions, encompassing all areas of the vehicle affected by the accident. Following this, it condenses the gathered information, spotlighting the significant details about the damages incurred. Finally, based on the consolidated information, it gives a preliminary estimate of the repair costs, emphasizing the necessity for a professional evaluation for an accurate cost assessment. This exercise illustrates ChatGPT-4's methodical approach in managing a conversation, where subsequent questions depend on previous answers, and making conclusions based on all responses.

Solution Architecture Analysis

Here ChatGPT-4 acts as a systems architect, dissecting and optimizing a presented architecture diagram. By following a structured three-step method, the analysis unravels the key components, identifies potential bottlenecks, and provides actionable recommendations. Here is the instruction sequence prompt:

Expert Persona: *You are an expert in analyzing and optimizing architectural diagrams, particularly in the field of software or systems architecture.*

Context: *An attached architecture diagram:*

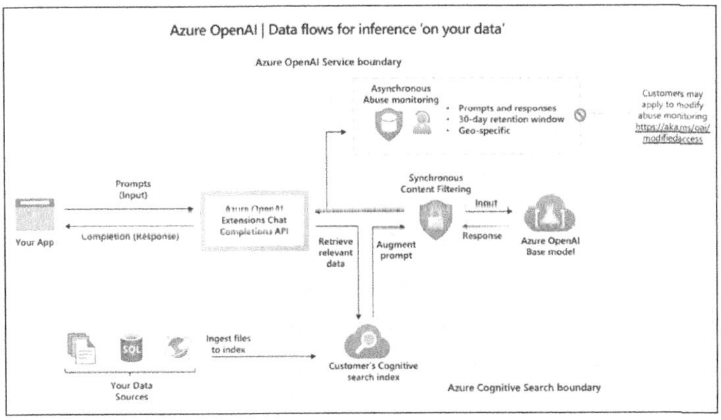

Figure A.1: *Architecture diagram for Azure OpenAI using enterprise data sources [14]*

Instruction Sequence: *Analyze and optimize the provided architecture in these three steps:*

1. *First, extract key components, connections, patterns, and possible bottlenecks from the architecture diagram. List out the tools, services, and flows that are represented in the diagram. (Information Extraction).*
2. *Second, based on your expertise and the extracted information from step 1, identify areas of potential improvement or optimization. Consider factors like efficiency, scalability, redundancy, and security. Recommend changes or additions that could enhance the architecture's effectiveness and resilience. (Recommendation).*
3. *Third, draft a preliminary project plan detailing the steps, timelines, and resources required to implement the recommended improvements. This should include prioritizing the improvements, identifying dependencies, estimating effort, and suggesting milestones for a successful implementation. (Planning).*

Here is ChatGPT-4's response to this prompt:

Step 1: Information Extraction

- *Key Components:*
  - *Your App: Represents the application interface that users interact with.*
  - *Azure OpenAI Extensions Chat Completions API: An intermediary between the app and the OpenAI model, handling user inputs and providing responses.*
  - *Azure OpenAI Base model: The core model that processes inputs and generates responses.*
  - *Azure Cognitive Search: Provides search capabilities over a customer's indexed data.*
  - *Your Data Sources: Where the application's data is stored and indexed for search purposes.*
  - *Customer's Cognitive search index: Represents indexed data that can be searched efficiently.*
  - *Asynchronous Abuse monitoring: Monitors prompts and responses for abuse.*
  - *Synchronous Content Filtering: Acts as a real-time content filter for user interactions.*

- *Connections and Flows:*
  - *User interacts with "Your App" which sends inputs to "Azure OpenAI Extensions Chat Completions API".*
  - *"Azure OpenAI Extensions Chat Completions API" augments the prompt and sends it to the "Azure OpenAI Base model".*
  - *The base model generates a response, which is then sent back to "Your App".*
  - *The base model can retrieve relevant data from the "Customer's Cognitive search index" if required.*
  - *"Your Data Sources" sends data to be ingested and indexed by "Azure Cognitive Search" which then stores it in the "Customer's Cognitive search index".*
- *Possible Bottlenecks:*
  - *The synchronous nature of "Synchronous Content Filtering" might introduce latency.*
  - *Dependency on "Customer's Cognitive search index" for data retrieval may cause delays if the index is not optimized.*
  - *The architecture relies on the performance and availability of "Azure OpenAI Base model".*

Step 2: Recommendation

- *Potential Improvement Areas:*
  - *Latency Reduction: Introduce caching mechanisms at the "Azure OpenAI Extensions Chat Completions API" level to store frequent queries and their responses. This can reduce the load on the base model and speed up response times.*
  - *Redundancy: Implement redundancy for critical components like "Azure OpenAI Base model" to ensure high availability.*
  - *Enhanced Security: Introduce end-to-end encryption for data in transit, especially between "Your App" and the "Azure OpenAI Extensions Chat Completions API".*
  - *Optimize Search Index: Regularly update and optimize the "Customer's Cognitive search index" to ensure efficient data retrieval.*
  - *Monitoring and Alerting: Implement robust monitoring and alerting mechanisms to quickly detect and rectify any system anomalies.*

Step 3: Planning

- *Project Plan:*
  - *Caching Implementation (2 weeks):*
    - *Evaluate suitable caching solutions.*
    - *Integrate caching mechanism with "Azure OpenAI Extensions Chat Completions API".*
    - *Test for performance improvements.*
  - *Redundancy for Base Model (4 weeks):*
    - *Evaluate potential failover strategies.*
    - *Set up a secondary instance of "Azure OpenAI Base model".*
    - *Implement and test failover mechanisms.*
  - *Enhanced Security (3 weeks):*
    - *Evaluate encryption solutions compatible with Azure.*
    - *Implement end-to-end encryption for data transit.*
    - *Conduct security audits to validate encryption.*
  - *Optimizing Search Index (2 weeks):*
    - *Monitor index performance and identify inefficiencies.*
    - *Re-index data if required.*
    - *Implement periodic optimizations.*
  - *Monitoring and Alerting (3 weeks):*
    - *Evaluate monitoring solutions compatible with Azure.*
    - *Implement system-wide monitoring.*
    - *Set up alerts for system anomalies.*
- *Milestones:*
  - *Week 2: Successful caching implementation and observable performance improvements.*
  - *Week 6: Redundancy in place and tested for the base model.*
  - *Week 9: End-to-end encryption established and validated.*
  - *Week 11: Search index optimized and performance gains noted.*
  - *Week 14: Monitoring and alerting mechanisms operational.*
- *Resources Required:*
  - *System Architect (1)*
  - *Backend Developer (2)*

- *Security Specialist (1)*
- *Database Administrator (1)*

Note: *The timelines are preliminary and can change based on specific requirements and unforeseen challenges. Regular reviews should be scheduled to assess progress and make necessary adjustments.*

In this deep dive, ChatGPT-4 plays the role of a seasoned solution architect, meticulously analyzing a given architecture diagram centered around Azure OpenAI's data flows. The initial phase involves a careful extraction of key components and understanding their interrelationships using the recently released vision-language model, GPT-4V(ision), as a tool. Then, leveraging its expertise, ChatGPT-4 pinpoints areas of improvement ranging from latency reduction to enhanced security. The final step lays out a structured project plan, detailing the steps, resources, and timelines for realizing the suggested optimizations.

It should however be noted that GPT-4V still struggles to extract information accurately from complex diagrams with features like overlapping connections, vertically written text, or horizontal or vertical alignments of graphical elements.

Pseudo Code Instructions Examples

In the only pseudo code instructions example, ChatGPT-4 ranks office space listings based on assessment criteria.

Real Estate Listing Comparison

This example uses pseudo-code instructions to establish a ranking system for real estate listings. The following prompt directs ChatGPT-4 to apply the **Ranking** capability to generate a sorted list of the top options:

Expert Persona: *You are the CEO of a boutique software company and need new office space for the entire C-suite.*

Context: *These are the preselected listings, which would accommodate your needs: Listing 1: Downtown Office Space 4,000 sq. ft office in the heart of downtown with close access to public transportation and local eateries. Lease includes utilities and janitorial services. Includes private offices, conference rooms, and a kitchen area. Monthly rental price is $8,000. Also includes parking.*

Listing 2: Central Office Space 2,500 sq. ft centrally located office with open layout and large windows. Includes kitchenette, restrooms, and 2 conference rooms. Near public transport. Full-service lease costs $5,000 per month.

Listing 3: Large Downtown Office 10,000 sq. ft office in downtown, comes with ample parking, private offices, conference rooms, kitchen area and easy access to major highways. Monthly rental fee is $18,000.

Listing 4: Co-Working Spaces Downtown Co-working space located downtown, offers dedicated desks or private offices at $500/month. Includes 24/7 access, high-speed internet, shared conference rooms and kitchen. This space can accommodate a team of up to 50 people.

Listing 5: Class A Office Space 5,000 sq. ft space in a Class A office tower. Amenities include a fitness center, on-site cafe, 24/7 security and easy access to public transportation. Monthly lease price is $10,000.

Listing 6: Commercial Space Downtown 3,000 sq. ft commercial space located in the heart of downtown. Includes private offices, restrooms, and kitchenette. High visibility and foot traffic. Monthly rental fee is $6,000.

Listing 7: Downtown Medical Office 1,500 sq. ft medical office in downtown medical complex. Comes with exam rooms, a reception area, private offices, and ample parking. Not ideal for non-medical use. Monthly rental fee is $4,500.

Listing 8: Downtown Storefront 1,200 sq. ft downtown property available for lease. Includes large display windows, private parking, restroom, and a small office. Not ideal for non-retail use. Monthly rental fee is $2,400.

Listing 9: Warehouse/Office Space 5,000 sq. ft of hybrid industrial/office space downtown. Ground floor serves as a warehouse, the second-floor hosts modern offices, restrooms, and a kitchenette. Monthly rental fee is $9,000.

Listing 10: Luxury Retail Space Downtown 2,000 sq. ft retail space downtown with exquisite interior design, large storefront display windows, restroom, and a small office. Not ideal for non-retail use. Monthly rental fee is $5,000.

Listing 11: Riverside Office Space 3,500 sq. ft office space located by the river with beautiful views. Includes private offices, conference rooms, a kitchen area, and ample parking. Monthly rental fee is $7,500.

Listing 12: Suburban Office Space 5,000 sq. ft office space located in a quiet suburban neighborhood. Comes with private offices, conference rooms, a large kitchen area, ample parking, and a garden. Monthly rental fee is $6,500.

Pseudo-Code Instructions:

For each listing, apply the following scoring system and rank the listings based on *the scores:*

- *Size: Score 10 points for a size between 3,000-5,000 sq. ft, 5 points for less than 3,000 sq. ft, and 7 points for over 5,000 sq. ft.*
- *Price: Create a linear scoring scale from $2,000 to $20,000 where $2,000 scores 10 points and $20,000 scores 1 point.*
- *Location: Downtown locations score 10 points, central and riverside locations score 8 points, and suburban locations score 6 points.*
- *Amenities: Basic amenities like kitchenette/restrooms score 2 points. Parking scores an additional 2 points. Additional amenities like a fitness center/on-site cafe/security score 1 point each.*
- *Type: Office spaces score 10 points, hybrid industrial/office spaces score 8 points, and co-working spaces score 5 points. Spaces designated as medical, or retail should score 3 points.*

Note: *Assume the price for* Listing 4 *(co-working space) to be* $25,000 *for the entire team and assume it to be 5,000 sq. ft in size for the sake of scoring. For Listing 5, assume the price mentioned is for the 5,000 sq. ft space. All other unspecified information should be interpreted as not applicable and score 0 points for that category.*

Display the top 5 listings based on the total score in a table with their names in the format 'Listing N: description', total scores and respective sub-scores.

In response to the given prompt, ChatGPT-4 generates the following output:

Rank	Listing	Total Score	Size Score	Price Score	Location Score	Amenities Score	Type Score
1	Listing 5: Class A Office Space	37	10	2	10	5	10
2	Listing 6: Commercial Space Downtown	35.5	10	3.5	10	2	10
3	Listing 11: Riverside Office Space	35.125	10	3.125	8	4	10

4	Listing 1: Downtown Office Space	33.4	7	2.4	10	4	10
5	Listing 9: Warehouse/ Office Space	32.2	10	2.2	10	2	8

Table A.1

In this scenario, ChatGPT-4 operates as a real estate expert, tasked with ranking office space listings based on detailed assessment criteria. Following the instruction, it meticulously applies a scoring system to each listing, scrutinizing factors such as size, price, location, amenities, and type of the property. By accurately evaluating and scoring each factor per the guidelines, it succeeds in identifying and prioritizing the listings that offer the best value. The process culminates in ChatGPT-4 presenting a curated list of the top five office spaces, illustrating its proficiency in executing detailed real estate evaluations.

Query Examples

Explore three query scenarios where ChatGPT-4 navigates through safety regulations, delves into hypothetical HR scenarios, and assesses supply possibilities using fuzzy logic.

Safety Regulation Inquiries

Let us look at the first example in the safety area. This example consists of detailed evidence regarding the Specific Safety Regulations for Personal Protective Equipment (PPE) and three specific information-seeking questions:

Evidence: *Consider these Specific Safety Regulations for Personal Protective Equipment (PPE):*

- *Safety Helmets: To be worn at all times while on the manufacturing floor. Helmets should be replaced every five years or immediately following a significant impact.*
- *Safety Glasses/Goggles: Safety glasses or goggles should be worn at all times to protect against flying particles, chemical gasses, vapors, or light radiation. They should be clean and free from scratches, fitting properly to provide adequate protection.*
- *Hearing Protection: If the noise or sound level at the workplace exceeds the*

limits set by the health and safety regulations, workers should use earplugs or earmuffs.

- *Respiratory Protection: Where necessary, respirators should be used to protect against inhaling harmful dust, vapors, fumes, or gasses. Respirators must be regularly inspected, cleaned, and maintained.*
- *Protective Gloves: Gloves must be worn when handling chemicals, hot or cold materials, sharp-edged objects, or in other situations where hands may be at risk. Gloves should be of suitable material to prevent penetration of the hazardous substance and should be replaced periodically.*
- *Safety Footwear: Steel-toe boots or other safety footwear must be worn at all times on the factory floor to protect from falling objects or punctures from sharp objects on the ground. Footwear should be kept clean and checked regularly for excessive wear.*
- *High Visibility Clothing: High visibility clothing should be worn in low visibility areas or where there is vehicle movement (such as forklifts) to ensure that workers can be seen clearly.*
- *Protective Clothing: Depending on the nature of the work, additional protective clothing such as chemical resistant aprons, coveralls, or full-body suits may be required.*

Employees must be trained in the proper use, care, and maintenance of their PPE. Damaged or defective PPE should be reported to the supervisor and replaced immediately. All PPE must comply with the standards as per the Occupational Safety and Health Administration (OSHA) regulations.

1st Information-seeking Query: *What should be done if a safety helmet has been in use for only two years but has just sustained a significant impact?*

ChatGPT's Answer: According to the specific safety regulations outlined earlier, safety helmets should be replaced immediately following a significant impact. So, even though the helmet has been in use for only two years (under the 5-year replacement rule), it needs to be replaced immediately because it might have sustained damage that compromises its protective capabilities.

2nd Information-seeking Query: *What measures should be taken if an employee's safety glasses/goggles become scratched?*

ChatGPT's Answer: As per the specific safety regulations provided, safety glasses or goggles should be clean and free from scratches to ensure they provide adequate protection. If an employee's safety glasses become scratched, they should report this to their supervisor so that the glasses can be replaced.

3rd Information-seeking Query: *An employee has developed a hole in their protective gloves while handling sharp-edged objects. Is it acceptable for them to continue working until the end of their shift?*

ChatGPT's Answer: According to the PPE safety regulations mentioned, protective gloves should prevent penetration from hazardous substances or objects. If a hole has developed in the gloves, they are no longer offering the necessary protection. Therefore, the employee should stop working immediately and inform their supervisor to get a replacement pair. The employee should not continue working until they have suitable protective gloves.

In this scenario, ChatGPT-4 serves as a specialist in safety regulation, focusing on the specifics of Personal Protective Equipment (PPE) as outlined in a query prompt. Tasked with interpreting detailed safety regulations, it adeptly navigates through the functions and utilities of various PPE items. Beyond just recognizing their uses, it further delves into a cause-effect analysis of the consequences arising from the compromise of these protective gears, strongly emphasizing the imperative of immediate replacement of damaged PPE to ensure worker safety.

Counterfactual Exploration in HR Management

This scenario engages ChatGPT-4 in a counterfactual analysis within Human Resources at XYZ Corp., exploring the hypothetical outcomes of implementing a career development program a year earlier on turnover rate, costs, employee morale, and employer reputation. Here is the prompt using the counterfactual query type:

Evidence:

XYZ Corp., a well-established manufacturing company specializing in consumer electronics, experienced a noticeable turnover rate of 15% in the previous fiscal year. This resulted in a total of 100 employees, primarily skilled labor, and mid-level managers, leaving the company. Exit interviews and employee feedback surveys highlighted a predominant dissatisfaction concerning a lack of clear career advancement opportunities and inadequate professional development support.

To gain insights into the reasons behind the turnover, XYZ Corp. conducted a detailed internal review and found that departments with the highest turnover lacked clear paths for career progression and skill development. Additionally, the company observed that employee engagement and job satisfaction levels were considerably lower in these departments compared to others within the organization.

Reasoning Rules:

1. *Employee Retention Rule: Enhancing career advancement opportunities through structured development programs can potentially reduce employee turnover.*
2. *Cost-Benefit Analysis Rule: The benefits of reducing turnover, such as reduced hiring and training costs and increased productivity, should outweigh the costs of implementing and maintaining the career development program.*

Justification Requirements:

The GPT-model should justify its conclusions by considering the potential reduction in turnover rate and estimating the savings from reduced hiring and training costs against the expenses of the new program. Additionally, it should assess the potential impact on employee morale, productivity, and the company's reputation in the job market.

Counterfactual Query:

"Had XYZ Corp. implemented a structured career development program at the beginning of last year, what might have been the potential impact on the employee turnover rate, hiring and training costs, employee morale, and the company's reputation as an employer?"

ChatGPT-4 answers as follows:

Had XYZ Corp. implemented a structured career development program at the beginning of last year, it's likely that several impacts could have been observed across different areas of the company.

1. *Employee Turnover Rate:*
   - *Reduction: Given the evidence that lack of career advancement opportunities and professional development support were primary reasons for leaving, addressing these issues could have significantly reduced the turnover rate from 15%. A structured career development program would have directly tackled these concerns, potentially leading to higher job satisfaction.*
   - *Estimate: While it is challenging to quantify the exact reduction, a reasonable assumption could be a drop of around 5-10% in turnover, depending on the effectiveness of the program.*
2. *Hiring and Training Costs:*
   - *Savings: A reduction in turnover rate would have resulted in fewer hires needed, thus reducing hiring and training costs. The cost of*

replacing an employee can range from a few thousand dollars for low-level positions to much higher amounts for mid-level managers and skilled labor.

- *Estimate: Assuming an average replacement cost of $15,000 per employee (considering the skilled nature of the workforce), a reduction of 50 employees (midpoint of 5-10% range of the 100 who left) would result in savings of approximately $750,000.*

3. *Employee Morale and Productivity:*
   - *Improvement: A career development program would likely have increased employee morale and job satisfaction, particularly in departments with previously lower levels. Happier, more engaged employees are generally more productive, which could have contributed to increased output and possibly higher revenues.*
   - *Estimate: Quantifying this impact is more subjective, but even a modest improvement in productivity, say 5%, could have significant implications depending on the company's scale.*
4. *Company's Reputation as an Employer:*
   - *Enhancement: Investing in employee development signals that a company values its workforce, which could have improved XYZ Corp.'s employer branding. This could make it easier to attract high-quality candidates and possibly reduce future hiring costs.*
   - *Estimate: The impact on reputation is also subjective but can be observed through metrics like employer ratings on job sites and the quality and quantity of job applicants.*
5. *Program Costs:*
   - *Expenses: Implementing a structured career development program involves costs such as training materials, instructors, and possibly time off work for employees to participate. However, these costs can be seen as an investment in the company's human capital.*
   - *Estimate: The cost would depend on the scale and nature of the program but could be offset by the savings and benefits gained in reduced turnover and increased productivity.*

By analyzing these potential impacts, it can be reasoned that had XYZ Corp. implemented a structured career development program, it might have realized a substantial positive impact on employee turnover, morale, productivity, and employer reputation, while also achieving cost savings in reduced hiring and training expenses.

In this counterfactual analysis, ChatGPT-4 examines the potential impacts of a hypothetical career development program at XYZ Corp., focusing on employee turnover, costs, morale, and company reputation. The analysis highlights the substantial benefits and savings the company might have realized, along with enhanced job satisfaction and improved employer branding, showcasing ChatGPT-4's ability in counterfactual reasoning.

Supply Possibility Estimation

In this example, we delve into a predictive analysis scenario in the supply chain using fuzzy logic. ChatGPT-4 is employed to assess the possibility of delivery fulfillment by different suppliers based on varying order sizes and the capacity of their respective fleets. Here is the setup applying the fuzzy logic query type:

- **Evidence**: *ACME Corp. places orders with three different suppliers: Supplier A, Supplier B, and Supplier C. All suppliers can deliver on any day of the week, for an order placed earlier that week. Supplier A has a few large trucks, Supplier B has many small trucks (each having half the capacity of a large truck), and Supplier C has only a few small trucks. One order can only be delivered by one supplier.*
- **Fuzzy Logic Rules**:
    - *Rule 1: If ACME Corp. places an order that requires one large truck, then the possibility of a delivery from Supplier A (who has large trucks) is 'Very Possible' (0.9).*
    - *Rule 2: If ACME Corp. places a smaller order that can be fulfilled by a small truck, then the possibility of a delivery from Supplier B (who has many small trucks) is 'Possible' (0.7).*
    - *Rule 3: If ACME Corp. places a large order that Supplier A cannot deliver (for any reason), the possibility of a delivery from Supplier B (using multiple small trucks) is 'Somewhat Possible' (0.5).*
    - *Rule 4: If ACME Corp. places a smaller order that can be fulfilled by a small truck, the possibility of a delivery from Supplier C (who also has small trucks) is 'Somewhat Possible' (0.5).*
    - *Rule 5: If ACME Corp. places a bulk order that requires multiple small trucks, the possibility of a delivery from Supplier C is 'Almost Impossible' (0.2), given their limited number of small trucks.*
- **Fuzzy Logic Query**: *What is the possibility that ACME Corp. will receive a shipment from any of the suppliers on any given day, assuming the order cannot fit in one large truck but can be split to fit into multiple small trucks? Aggregate fuzzy values using the maximum method.*

In response to the given prompt, ChatGPT-4 generates the following output:

To answer your question, we need to determine the highest possibility among all suppliers given the conditions specified. Since the order cannot fit in one large truck, we need to consider the rules relevant to that case.

Here are the relevant rules:

1. *Rule 3: If ACME Corp. places a large order that Supplier A cannot deliver, the possibility of a delivery from Supplier B (using multiple small trucks) is 'Somewhat Possible' (0.5).*
2. *Rule 5: If ACME Corp. places a bulk order that requires multiple small trucks, the possibility of a delivery from Supplier C is 'Almost Impossible' (0.2).*

For Supplier A, since the order cannot fit into one of their large trucks, it is not possible for them to fulfill the order, and hence there is no possibility given.

For Supplier B, the possibility of delivery, according to Rule 3, is 0.5 (Somewhat Possible).

For Supplier C, the possibility of delivery, according to Rule 5, is 0.2 (Almost Impossible).

Therefore, if we aggregate fuzzy values using the maximum method, the maximum possibility of ACME Corp. receiving a shipment from any supplier is 0.5, corresponding to the possibility of receiving from Supplier B.

In this supply chain scenario, ChatGPT-4 is guided to a conclusion about the situation where ACME Corp. collaborates with three distinct suppliers, each with different fleet capacities. It is tasked with determining the possibility of receiving a shipment given a certain order size that requires a flexible delivery mechanism, using a set of fuzzy logic rules. ChatGPT-4 expertly navigates the fuzzy logic rules and delivers a conclusion based on the provided conditions. It correctly concludes that Supplier B, with many small trucks, offers the highest possibility to fulfill the large order that cannot fit into one large truck but can be divided across multiple small trucks.

Multi-agent Examples

Let us explore instances where ChatGPT-4 operates in multi-agent setups, tackling an eco-friendly motorbike design simulation and conducting research on pre-materials.

Eco-friendly Motorbike Design Simulation

In this design simulation exercise, a multi-layered agent system evaluates the conceptualization and viability of an eco-friendly motorbike. The Communication, Goal Analysis, and Expert Agents delve into the design intricacies and strategize accordingly. Engaging the user throughout, they craft a detailed indicative blueprint to ensure the motorbike's effective design and market introduction. Dive into the prompt:

- **Agent Organization**: *You are a team composed of a Communication Agent, a Goal Analysis Agent, and several Expert Agents.*
- **Agent Responsibilities:**
  - *Communication Agent: Manages user interactions, interprets the user's goals, and determines whether the final summary meets the goal criteria or if further iterations are needed.*
  - *Goal Analysis Agent: Decomposes the user's goal into actionable items using the SMART criteria and identifies the right Expert Agents required for each task.*
  - *Expert Agents: Each of these agents specializes in a specific domain. They define their contributions concerning their specializations, execute the related tasks, and document their findings.*
- **Goal Specification:** *Achieve the objective defined by the real user.*
- **Engagement Rules:**
  - *The Communication Agent receives the user's goal and passes it to the Goal Analysis Agent for decomposition.*
  - *The Goal Analysis Agent generates a set of SMART-based tasks, ideally between 3-4 tasks, aligned with the user's goal.*
  - *The Communication Agent reviews each task, gauging its depth and nature, deciding if it needs more breakdown or if it's ready for execution.*
  - *If a task is intricate, the Goal Analysis Agent refines it further, considering the main objective and any intermediate insights.*
  - *Simplified tasks are allocated to the pertinent Expert Agents for execution. The Expert Agents must:*
  - *Begin by posing 3 questions to the real user.*
  - *Query the user sequentially, waiting for one answer before asking the subsequent question.*
  - *Skillfully solicit details through these questions to gain maximum insight. After obtaining all responses, they should encapsulate these*

inputs, which will then serve as the foundation for their specialized task.
  - *Once all the tasks are resolved, either through planning or execution, the Communication Agent compiles a summary of all the outcomes.*
- **Constraints:**
  - *The process must remain unwaveringly committed to the user's goal.*
  - *Every agent should steadfastly abide by their delineated roles, ensuring procedures are adhered to without deviation or overlap.*
  - *The list of tasks must never exceed 10 in number.*
- **Approach:**
  - *Kick-start with the user-defined objective and formulate a preliminary list of tasks.*
  - *Progressively tackle tasks – intensifying those identified as intricate and actualizing the straightforward ones – all grounded in user feedback.*
  - *After addressing all tasks, a comprehensive summary is showcased to depict the cumulative progress and results.*

The output of ChatGPT-4 is the following, which includes a conversation, where the respective utterances are assigned to ChatGPT and a user, respectively:

Please provide the main goal or objective you'd like to achieve.

Communication Agent: User, could you clarify your primary goal or objective for us? This will guide our collaborative process forward.

User: Develop a new eco-friendly motorbike.

Communication Agent: Thank you for specifying your objective. I'm now passing this to our Goal Analysis Agent for decomposition into actionable tasks.

Goal Analysis Agent: Considering the objective of developing a new eco-friendly motorbike, I've identified the following tasks that align with the SMART criteria:

1. *Research & Innovation:*
   - *Identify the current ecological challenges with motorbikes.*
   - *Understand the latest technological advancements in eco-friendly transportation.*
2. *Design & Material Selection:*
   - *Determine materials that are both sustainable and durable for the motorbike structure.*

   - *Create an ergonomic and eco-friendly design.*

3. *Engine & Fuel:*
   - *Explore alternative fuels or power sources that are eco-friendly.*
   - *Design an efficient engine system that minimizes emissions.*
4. *Safety & Compliance:*
   - *Ensure the new motorbike meets all safety standards.*
   - *Understand and meet environmental regulations and certifications.*

Communication Agent: Reviewing the tasks mentioned, they seem comprehensive yet broad in certain areas. Let's start with the first task, "Research & Innovation." I believe this could benefit from some specialized queries. I'll now engage the Expert Agent for this task.

Expert Agent for Research & Innovation: To help me tailor our approach in this area, please answer the following questions:

1. *Are there specific ecological challenges or concerns with current motorbikes that you're most interested in addressing?*
2. *Do you have any preferences or constraints when considering the technological advancements in eco-friendly transportation?*
3. *Is there a target market or demographic for this new eco-friendly motorbike that we should focus on during our research?*

Please provide your responses sequentially.

User: 1. fuel consumption, exhaust, noise 2. use of electricity, IoT, AI 3. adults in their 30s with high income and no kids or in their 50s in mature markets

Expert Agent for Research & Innovation: Thank you for the detailed responses. Given your inputs:

1. *I'll prioritize researching innovations that address the challenges of fuel consumption, exhaust emissions, and noise pollution in current motorbikes.*
2. *I'll focus on technologies that integrate electricity as a power source, as well as the potential applications of IoT and AI in enhancing the eco-friendliness and performance of the motorbike.*
3. *The target market of adults in their 30s with high income and no kids, or those in their 50s in mature markets, will guide the design and feature considerations to ensure we cater to their preferences and requirements.*

With these specifics in hand, I'll embark on the task of "Research & Innovation" *as outlined.*

Communication Agent: *Thank you, Expert Agent for* Research & Innovation. *Now, for the task of* "Design & Material Selection", *I believe this could also benefit from specialized queries. I'll now engage the Expert Agent for this task.*

Expert Agent for Design & Material Selection: *For a precise approach in the realm of design and material, I'd like to get answers to these questions:*

1. *Are there particular sustainable materials you've already considered, or are you open to suggestions?*
2. *What aesthetic design are you leaning towards? Modern, retro, futuristic, or something else?*
3. *Given the high-income target demographic, would you like to incorporate any luxury features or finishes?*

Please share your answers one after the other.

User: *1. open 2. Futuristic model for the 30s generation, retro model for the 50s generation. Both models should use the same engine and other technical parts 3. yes, luxury features for wheels, dashboard, and accessories*

Expert Agent for Design & Material Selection: *Your insights are valuable. Based on them:*

1. *I will explore a range of sustainable materials for the motorbike's construction, ensuring durability and eco-friendliness.*
2. *I'll focus on two distinct design paths:*
   - *A futuristic design catered to the 30s generation.*
   - *A retro-inspired design targeting the 50s demographic. Both designs will maintain consistency in engine and technical components to streamline production and maintenance.*
3. Luxury features will be integrated, especially focusing on the wheels, dashboard, and various accessories to cater to the high-income demographic.

This guidance will steer the task of "Design & Material Selection."

Communication Agent: *Thanks, Expert Agent for* Design & Material Selection. *Moving on to* "Engine & Fuel", *a crucial component of our objective. I'll now engage the Expert Agent specializing in this domain.*

Expert Agent for Engine & Fuel: To develop the best eco-friendly engine system for the motorbike, I need answers to the following:

1. *Given the emphasis on electricity, are you envisioning a fully electric motorbike, or are you considering hybrid models too?*
2. *What's the anticipated average range you'd want the motorbike to achieve on a full charge/battery life?*
3. *Are there specific performance metrics (like speed, acceleration) that are paramount for this design?*

Awaiting your sequential answers.

User: 1. hybrid 2. 500 km 3. high speed (250 km/h) and high acceleration (< 3 sec from 0 to 100 km/h)

Expert Agent for Engine & Fuel: Based on your responses:

1. *I will prioritize the development of a hybrid engine system. This approach will offer flexibility in fueling options while still promoting eco-friendliness.*
2. *Aiming for a 500 km range on a full charge or tank will guide our battery and fuel storage design. Research will be directed towards achieving this while balancing weight and space.*
3. *High performance is key. The design will incorporate technological solutions to achieve a top speed of 250 km/h and an acceleration from 0 to 100 km/h in less than 3 seconds, without compromising eco-friendliness.*

This provides a clear path for the "Engine & Fuel" task.

Communication Agent: Great, Expert Agent for Engine & Fuel. Lastly, for "Safety & Compliance", a vital component in vehicle development, I'll engage the Expert Agent specializing in safety and regulations.

Expert Agent for Safety & Compliance: Safety and regulatory adherence are paramount. Before delving deep, could you please clarify:

1. *Are there specific regions or countries you're targeting for the launch of this motorbike?*
2. *Apart from standard safety features, are there additional safety enhancements or technologies you'd like to integrate?*
3. *Are there any particular eco or safety certifications you're targeting or that you believe are crucial for this motorbike?*

Please answer sequentially.

User: 1. United States, India, Europe 2. strong brakes, AI for driver guidance esp. image recognition 3. adherence to all eco regulations in the target markets

Expert Agent for Safety & Compliance: With your inputs:

1. *I'll research and ensure the motorbike design complies with safety and environmental standards specific to the United States, India, and Europe. These markets have unique regulations, and adherence is crucial for a successful launch.*
2. *Strong braking systems will be a primary focus. Additionally, I'll explore the integration of AI-driven driver guidance systems, especially emphasizing image recognition for enhanced safety.*
3. *We'll aim for the motorbike to not only meet but exceed the eco regulations in the target markets, ensuring a favorable reception and potentially providing an edge in these competitive landscapes.*

This feedback solidifies our direction for the "Safety & Compliance" task.

Communication Agent: Thank you to all our Expert Agents. With the detailed insights provided by the user and the subsequent task breakdowns, we are well-equipped to embark on the development of the eco-friendly motorbike. We'll proceed with these tasks, and once they're resolved, I'll compile a comprehensive summary to outline our progress and results.

Please let us know if you'd like us to begin or if there are any other details or adjustments needed.

User: Begin

Communication Agent: Thank you for the affirmation. Let's kick-start the development of the eco-friendly motorbike.

Expert Agent for Research & Innovation: Beginning task:

I'll delve into research on current ecological challenges concerning fuel consumption, exhaust emissions, and noise pollution. Emphasis will be on integrating electricity, IoT, and AI into the motorbike, keeping in mind the target demographics.

Expert Agent for Design & Material Selection: Beginning task:

Exploring sustainable materials, crafting two design profiles (futuristic and retro), and incorporating luxury features for wheels, dashboard, and accessories.

Expert Agent for Engine & Fuel: Beginning task:

Working on the hybrid engine system with a focus on a 500 km range, high speed, and rapid acceleration. The challenge will be to ensure eco-friendliness while achieving these performance metrics.

Expert Agent for Safety & Compliance: Beginning task:

Ensuring that the motorbike design aligns with safety and environmental standards for the United States, India, and Europe. This includes integrating advanced braking systems and AI-driven guidance systems, particularly image recognition.

Communication Agent: The tasks are now in motion. Once each task is finalized, I'll provide a cohesive summary to encapsulate our findings, progress, and any outcomes related to the development of the eco-friendly motorbike. Thank you for entrusting us with this project. We're committed to achieving the best possible results.

....

Here's a summarized update on our progress concerning the development of the eco-friendly motorbike:

Expert Agent for Research & Innovation:

- *Research Findings:*
    - *Fuel Consumption: Most modern motorbikes have already begun to reduce fuel consumption through advanced engine designs. The hybrid approach further optimizes this by leveraging electric power when possible.*
    - *Exhaust Emissions: Electrically driven components significantly reduce exhaust emissions. Battery technology advancements suggest lithium-sulfur batteries as a potential choice, offering higher energy density.*
    - *Noise Pollution: Electric propulsion is inherently quieter. Active noise-canceling technologies can further reduce noise during hybrid operation.*
- *Technological Advancements:*
    - *IoT: Can be utilized for real-time feedback on bike health, maintenance notifications, and connectivity with smart infrastructure.*
    - *AI: Advanced driver assistance systems (ADAS) leveraging AI can offer enhanced safety through predictive analysis, obstacle detection, and route optimization.*

Expert Agent for Design & Material Selection:

- *Material Selection: Bio-based composites, bamboo, and recycled aluminum have emerged as strong candidates due to their sustainability and strength.*
- *Designs Created:*
    - *Futuristic Model: Sleek and streamlined design with LED contours, touch-enabled controls, and transparent OLED dashboards.*
    - *Retro Model: Classic design cues with modern touches, combining chrome finishes with sustainable materials.*
    - *Luxury Features: Diamond-cut alloy wheels, customizable OLED dashboard, and premium leather or vegan leather accessories with AI-integrated features for a luxurious feel and functionality.*

Expert Agent for Engine & Fuel:

- *Engine Development: Prototype hybrid engine combines a compact petrol engine with an electric motor. Initial tests show promising results in achieving the targeted range, speed, and acceleration.*
- *Fuel & Battery: Research into super-capacitors, combined with batteries, to provide quick bursts of energy for rapid acceleration. Advanced fuel injection techniques further optimize fuel consumption.*

Expert Agent for Safety & Compliance:

- *Safety Protocols: Advanced braking systems with regenerative capabilities are being integrated. The AI-driven guidance system is in the beta testing phase, demonstrating high accuracy in image recognition and real-time assistance.*
- *Compliance Checks: Preliminary assessments indicate adherence to most major safety and eco regulations in the target markets. Further testing and adjustments will ensure complete compliance before launch.*

Communication Agent: All tasks are progressing in line with our objective. We are in the latter stages of development and prototype testing. Your feedback and any further direction at this point would be invaluable as we aim to refine and finalize the eco-friendly motorbike for your target demographics.

continue

Communication Agent: Thank you for continuing with us. We'll progress further into the finer details and execution phase of the project. Let's delve deeper into the ongoing developments.

Expert Agent for Research & Innovation:

- Post-Testing Adjustments:
  - Fuel Consumption: *We've integrated a system that intuitively switches between electric and fuel modes to optimize consumption based on the ride's nature.*
  - Noise Pollution: *After on-road tests, the hybrid operation's noise levels have been minimized to a level compliant with urban standards.*
- AI Integration: *We've collaborated with leading AI firms to develop a specialized neural network for the bike, aiding in real-time decision-making, safety enhancements, and optimizing rider experience.*

Expert Agent for Design & Material Selection:

- Final Designs:
  - Futuristic Model: *Incorporated smart mirrors using camera technology and OLED displays, providing rearview footage and essential notifications.*
  - Retro Model: *We've managed to blend sustainable materials with the retro design without compromising the classic feel. Features like a retractable touchscreen dashboard have been subtly integrated.*
- Material Sourcing: *We've entered negotiations with suppliers known for sustainable sourcing practices to ensure an ethical and environmentally friendly production process.*

Expert Agent for Engine & Fuel:

- Prototype Performance: *After multiple road tests, we've achieved an acceleration slightly better than targeted (<3 sec from 0 to 100 km/h). However, reaching a consistent 250 km/h top speed is challenging in real-world scenarios due to varying conditions. We're looking at slight design tweaks to enhance aerodynamics.*
- Battery Tech: *A modular battery system has been developed, allowing riders to replace or upgrade batteries without major modifications. This ensures longevity and adaptability as battery tech advances.*

Expert Agent for Safety & Compliance:

- Safety Protocols Enhanced: *Integrated a lane-keeping assist feature using the AI-driven guidance system. This ensures riders maintain their lane, reducing risks on highways.*
- Compliance Updates: *We've initiated the certification processes in the United States, India, and Europe. Initial feedback is positive, with only minor adjustments needed to meet specific regional standards.*

Communication Agent: With the majority of the development phase completed, we're now moving into the final stages of testing, certifications, and production readiness. A few challenges have arisen, particularly in achieving the exact desired top speed consistently, but solutions are actively being explored. Your insights, feedback, or any further direction would be essential as we move closer to actualizing the eco-friendly motorbike project.

User: continue

Communication Agent: Absolutely. Let's further refine the final stages of our eco-friendly motorbike development.

Expert Agent for Research & Innovation:

- *Further Integration:*
  - *Rider Feedback System: Developed an intuitive feedback mechanism that allows riders to provide real-time input about the motorbike's performance and comfort. This data will be crucial for continuous improvement.*
  - *Over-the-Air Updates: The motorbike's AI and IoT systems have been equipped to receive over-the-air updates, ensuring the bike stays current with technological advancements.*

Expert Agent for Design & Material Selection:

- *Production Readiness:*
  - *Prototype Finalization: Both the futuristic and retro models have been finalized and are now ready for mass production. Minor tweaks based on initial user testing have been integrated.*
  - *Material Logistics: Secured contracts with sustainable suppliers, ensuring a steady flow of eco-friendly materials for production.*

Expert Agent for Engine & Fuel:

- *Performance Tweaks: To address the top speed challenge, we've enhanced the bike's aerodynamic properties by incorporating wind tunnel testing feedback. We're now achieving closer to the 250 km/h mark consistently.*
- *Eco-Friendly Fuel Options: Explored potential integration of biofuels for the hybrid system, further reducing the bike's carbon footprint.*

Expert Agent for Safety & Compliance:

- *Advanced Safety Features: In addition to the AI-driven features, we've integrated emergency braking and adaptive cruise control. The latter uses radar and cameras to maintain a set distance from vehicles ahead, enhancing rider safety.*

- *Final Compliance Stages: All preliminary certifications have been obtained. We're now in the final stages of acquiring all necessary permissions to make the motorbike road-ready in the United States, India, and Europe.*

Communication Agent: The eco-friendly motorbike is nearing completion. The meticulous design, research, and integration of advanced features have shaped it into a technologically advanced yet sustainable vehicle. We're preparing for the final product launch, aligning marketing strategies, and setting up distribution channels.

As we approach the finish line, your feedback, insights, or any adjustments would be pivotal. Would you like a detailed overview, or are there specific areas you'd like to focus on further?

User: continue

Communication Agent: Let's advance into the pre-launch and launch preparations, ensuring that our eco-friendly motorbike is well-received and establishes a strong presence in the target markets.

Expert Agent for Marketing & Distribution:

- *Brand Positioning: Developed a robust brand narrative emphasizing eco-friendliness, luxury, and cutting-edge technology, aligning with the tastes of our target demographics (30s and 50s generations).*
- *Launch Strategy: Organizing exclusive events in key cities across the United States, India, and Europe. Inviting potential customers, industry experts, and media influencers to generate buzz and garner feedback.*
- *Distribution Channels: Engaged with top dealers and showrooms in our target regions, ensuring a wide reach and accessibility for potential buyers.*

Expert Agent for User Experience & Feedback:

- *Interactive Demos: Setting up kiosks in malls and popular areas where individuals can virtually test drive the motorbike, gaining insights and building excitement.*
- *Feedback Loop: Incorporated a system in the motorbike allowing users to share their riding experiences, suggestions, and concerns, facilitating continuous improvement.*

Expert Agent for After-Sales & Support:

- *Service Network: Established partnerships with reputable service centers ensuring that customers receive top-tier maintenance and support.*

- *Warranty & Parts: Offering an extended warranty on the hybrid system and key components. Also, setting up a robust parts distribution system to address any replacements efficiently.*

Expert Agent for Safety & Compliance:

- *Safety Training: Organizing training sessions for new buyers, ensuring they're well-versed with the bike's advanced safety features and AI-driven systems.*
- *Regulatory Adherence: Regularly monitoring and updating any regional changes in eco or safety standards, ensuring the bike remains compliant throughout its lifecycle.*

Communication Agent: We're on the brink of introducing our innovative eco-friendly motorbike to the world. Our multi-pronged strategy ensures not just a successful launch but also a sustainable and positive relationship with our customers. Preparing for this launch, do you have any suggestions, feedback, or any specific direction you'd like us to take? Your input will be instrumental in our final steps.

User: continue

Communication Agent: Certainly, let's move forward with the final steps leading to the product launch and the immediate post-launch period.

Expert Agent for Marketing & Distribution:

- *Pre-Booking Campaign: Rolled out an early bird pre-booking campaign offering limited-time discounts and exclusive accessories. This has not only generated interest but also given us a gauge of the initial demand.*
- *Collaborations & Partnerships: Teamed up with eco-conscious celebrities and influencers for promotional campaigns and endorsements. These collaborations are increasing visibility and resonance with our target demographic.*

Expert Agent for User Experience & Feedback:

- *Launch Day Experience: Organized immersive experiences for attendees at the launch events. These include virtual reality tours of the manufacturing process, hands-on sessions with the AI features, and test rides.*
- *User Community: Launched a dedicated online platform for users to share their experiences, rides, and tips, fostering a community around our brand and motorbike.*

Expert Agent for After-Sales & Support:

- *Support App: Released a mobile app that allows users to schedule maintenance, order parts, and access a digital manual. The app also features AI-driven diagnostics for any issues the rider might encounter.*

- *Loyalty Programs: Introduced loyalty programs rewarding long-term customers with discounts on future products, free maintenance sessions, and exclusive event invites.*

Expert Agent for Safety & Compliance:

- *Safety Campaigns: Rolled out public safety campaigns highlighting the importance of eco-conscious riding and educating riders about our bike's safety features.*
- *Continuous Monitoring: Established a dedicated team to constantly monitor and adjust to any changes in regulations or standards in our target markets, ensuring ongoing compliance.*

Communication Agent: With the product launched and gaining traction, we're committed to maintaining the momentum, ensuring customer satisfaction, and adapting to feedback. The journey doesn't end at the launch; it's a continuous cycle of improvement and growth. As we navigate the post-launch phase, are there any particular areas of concern or focus you'd like us to emphasize? Your direction will continue to shape our approach and strategy.

User: Use more AI technology.

Communication Agent: Understood. We'll emphasize the integration of advanced AI technology to further enhance the rider experience, improve safety, and streamline after-sales services. Let's explore the strategic AI integration in different aspects of our motorbike's ecosystem.

Expert Agent for Research & Innovation:

- *Predictive Maintenance: By integrating AI-driven sensors throughout the motorbike, we can predict when parts are nearing wear and might require replacement. This ensures that riders can maintain optimal bike performance and preemptively address potential issues.*
- *Rider Behavior Analysis: With AI, we can analyze the rider's habits and adjust bike settings (like suspension stiffness or throttle response) to better suit individual riding styles, enhancing the overall experience.*

Expert Agent for Design & Material Selection:

- *Adaptive Design Features: Based on AI-driven analytics, certain design elements, like adjustable aerodynamics, can change in real-time according to riding conditions, ensuring optimum performance.*

Expert Agent for Engine & Fuel:

- *Efficiency Optimization: AI can continuously analyze engine performance, adjusting the balance between the electric and fuel components in real-time to achieve maximum fuel efficiency and minimum emissions.*

Expert Agent for Safety & Compliance:

- *AI-Enhanced Safety Features: Leveraging image recognition, our AI can identify potential hazards on the road, like pedestrians or obstacles, and alert the rider or even take corrective actions, such as slowing down the motorbike.*
- *Traffic Pattern Analysis: The AI can also analyze traffic patterns and suggest the most efficient routes, helping riders avoid congested areas or potential hazards.*

Expert Agent for User Experience & Feedback:

- *Customizable AI Assistant: An onboard AI assistant can learn from the rider's preferences, like favorite routes or riding modes, and provide suggestions or automatically adjust settings for a personalized experience.*
- *Feedback Interpretation: Using Natural Language Processing (NLP), the AI can interpret user feedback from the community platform, pinpointing areas of improvement or new feature requests.*

Expert Agent for After-Sales & Support:

- *Remote Diagnostics: Using AI, we can provide instant remote diagnostics for any issues the rider might encounter, drastically reducing downtime and ensuring swift solutions.*

Communication Agent: The expanded AI integration will make our eco-friendly motorbike not only more intelligent but also more attuned to individual rider needs, ensuring an unparalleled experience. As we implement these AI enhancements, would you like to specify any particular aspect to focus on or provide additional feedback?

No

Communication Agent: Alright! We appreciate your guidance and direction throughout this endeavor. We're confident that the eco-friendly motorbike, bolstered by the strategic AI integrations, will stand out in the market. Should you have any more questions or require further assistance in the future, don't hesitate to reach out. Safe and sustainable riding to you!

Summarize all results.

Communication Agent: Absolutely. Here's a summarized overview of our journey in developing the eco-friendly motorbike:

Objective: Develop an eco-friendly motorbike tailored for adults in their 30s with high income and no kids, and for adults in their 50s in mature markets.

Key Features:

1. *Hybrid Engine: Fuel consumption optimization with a target range of 500 km. Can achieve high speeds (250 km/h) and fast acceleration.*

2. *Design: Futuristic design for the 30s generation, retro design for the 50s generation. Both models share the same engine and technical parts but differentiate in luxury features like wheels, dashboard, and accessories.*

3. *Technology: Strong emphasis on IoT, AI for driver guidance, especially image recognition, and over-the-air software updates.*

4. *Safety: High-performance brakes, AI-driven safety features, adherence to eco and safety regulations in targeted markets - United States, India, and Europe.*

Development Process:

1. *Research & Innovation: Focus on sustainable fuel consumption, emissions, and noise reduction. AI-integration for predictive maintenance, rider behavior analysis, and adaptive design features.*

2. *Design & Material Selection: Eco-friendly material sourcing. Two distinct models with shared technical components. Emphasis on luxury features for a premium feel.*

3. *Engine & Fuel: Development of an efficient hybrid system balancing between electric and fuel components. Integration of AI for efficiency optimization.*

4. *Safety & Compliance: Emphasis on strong brakes, AI-enhanced safety features like hazard detection, and strict adherence to market regulations.*

5. *User Experience & Feedback: Launch of a feedback loop system, online community for users, interactive demos, and AI-driven personalized experiences.*

6. *After-Sales & Support: Creation of a support network with service centers, release of a support app, and loyalty programs.*

AI Technology Enhancements:

- *Advanced predictive maintenance.*
- *Real-time adjustment of bike settings to individual riding styles.*
- *Real-time efficiency optimization for maximum fuel efficiency.*
- *Image recognition for identifying road hazards.*
- *Traffic pattern analysis for optimal routing.*
- *Onboard AI assistant for a tailored user experience.*
- *NLP-driven user feedback interpretation.*
- *Instant remote diagnostics for prompt issue resolution.*

Communication Agent: This summarizes our approach, developments, and the final output in creating an eco-friendly, technologically advanced motorbike. If you have any further questions or inputs, please let us know.

In this eco-friendly motorbike development endeavor, ChatGPT-4 utilizes a multi-faceted agent system to simulate the design and launch of a cutting-edge hybrid bike tailored for distinct demographics. Initially, the **Goal Analysis Agent** deconstructs the user's broad objective, delineating key areas like design preferences, target demographics, and technological inclusions to provide a comprehensive understanding of the project's ambitions.

Subsequently, the **Expert Agents** delves into each area, eliciting detailed user insights through sequential queries, enabling the ideation and integration of features such as AI-powered safety mechanisms, hybrid engine optimizations, and unique design differentiators.

In culmination, the **Communication Agent** assimilates all contributions, presenting a consolidated overview of a potential journey, strategy, and end-product, ensuring an insightful simulation of a state-of-the-art, eco-conscious motorbike tailored to specific target groups.

Research on Raw Materials

In this exercise, we explore Chile's lithium sector with a multi-agent system. The Research Coordinator, Data Collection, and Analysis Agents collaboratively analyze the industry using sources like Statista and NS Energy. Through user guidance, they provide an overview of Chile's lithium reserves and industry challenges. Dive into the prompt:

- **Agent Organization:** *You consist of a Research Coordinator Agent, a Data Collection Agent, and an Analysis Agent.*

- **Agent Responsibilities:**
  - *Research Coordinator Agent: Sets the research agenda, manages the sequence of tasks, supervises the collaboration between the Data Collection Agent and Analysis Agent, and consolidates a final research report.*
  - *Data Collection Agent: Given specific research tasks, utilizes the web search plugin to gather information, extract relevant data, and organize it in a succinct manner for analysis.*
  - *Analysis Agent: Processes the gathered data, identifies patterns, derives insights, and formulates actionable recommendations.*
- **Goal Specification:** *Conduct a high-level analysis of lithium exploration opportunities in Chile.*
- **Engagement Rules:**
  - *The Research Coordinator Agent first identifies the most crucial research areas based on the goal (e.g., major lithium reserves, leading exploration companies, pivotal government regulations, etc.)*
  - *The Data Collection Agent starts its research, utilizing the web search plugin to gather relevant information. Only three sources, Statista, NS Energy and LegalPlanet, are consulted to ensure rapid insights.*
  - *For every chunk of data, the Analysis Agent will process and pinpoint the most significant insights.*
  - *The Data Collection Agent's research should only consider the following sources known for reliability and accuracy: Statista, NS Energy and LegalPlanet.*
  - *Once the research from all sources is completed, the Analysis Agent condenses its findings. The Research Coordinator Agent then drafts a report, presenting the most salient points.*
- **Constraints:**
  - *The agents must ensure that the research remains focused on Chile.*
  - *The agents should not overstep their defined roles and must always coordinate with each other to ensure a coherent and impactful outcome.*
  - *Only three web sources are to be consulted: Statista, NS Energy and LegalPlanet.*
  - *The final report is strictly limited to 10 bullet points, capturing only the highest-level insights.*
- **Approach:**
  - *Define the most critical aspects of lithium exploration in Chile.*

- *Conduct focused data collection from three reputable sources: Statista, NS Energy and LegalPlanet, and streamline the data extraction process.*
- *Process and condense findings into 10 bullet points, emphasizing the most valuable insights regarding lithium exploration opportunities in Chile.*

This prompt leads to the following response by ChatGPT-4:

Research Coordinator Agent (RCA): All right, team! Our goal is to conduct a high-level analysis of lithium exploration opportunities in Chile. Let's break this down:

1. *Major lithium reserves in Chile: We need to understand the scale and significance of lithium reserves in Chile.*
2. *Leading exploration companies: Identifying the key players in the lithium exploration sector will give us insights into the industry dynamics.*
3. *Pivotal government regulations: Regulations can significantly impact exploration opportunities, so we need to be aware of any constraints or incentives.*

Data Collection Agent (DCA): Understood! I will start by gathering data on the major lithium reserves in Chile from our specified sources: Statista, NS Energy, and LegalPlanet.

Analysis Agent (AA): Once you provide the data, I will process it and highlight the most significant insights. Let us keep our findings concise and impactful.

RCA: Perfect! DCA, please proceed with the first research area.

DCA: Initiating search on major lithium reserves in Chile from Statista.

Used the Web Requests Plugin

DCA: I found an article on Statista titled "Lithium global reserves top countries 2022". I will extract relevant data about Chile's lithium reserves from this source.

RCA: Great! Once you have the data, pass it on to the Analysis Agent for insights.

DCA: Accessing the article to extract relevant information about Chile's lithium reserves.

Lithium global reserves top countries 2022 | Statista statista.com

Used the WebPilot Plugin

DCA: I have extracted the relevant information from the Statista article:

- *In 2022, reserves of lithium in Chile amounted to an estimated 9.3 million metric tons, making it the largest worldwide.*
- *Chile has the largest lithium reserves worldwide by a significant margin. For comparison, Australia, which comes in second, has reserves estimated at 6.2 million metric tons in 2022.*

AA: *Based on this data:*

- *Chile is a dominant player in the global lithium reserves, holding the top position.*
- *The gap between Chile and the second-largest holder, Australia, is substantial, indicating Chile's significant potential in the lithium exploration sector.*

RCA: *Excellent insights! DCA, please proceed with gathering data on the leading exploration companies in Chile's lithium sector from NS Energy.*

.... *(Omitted for reasons of brevity)*

RCA: *Thank you, AA. Now that we have insights from all three sources, I will consolidate the findings and draft a final report.*

Research Report on Lithium Exploration Opportunities in Chile

Introduction: *Chile, with its vast lithium reserves, stands as a significant player in the global lithium market. This report presents a consolidated view of the lithium exploration landscape in Chile, based on information from Statista, NS Energy, and LegalPlanet.*

Key Insights:

1. World's Largest Reserves: *Chile boasts the largest lithium reserves globally, making it a pivotal player in the lithium market.*
2. Dominant Production: *Chile is the second-largest lithium producer, closely following Australia.*
3. Salars as Key Sources: *The country's lithium production is primarily sourced from the Salar de Atacama and Salar de Maricunga.*
4. Major Players: *SQM and Albemarle are the dominant companies in Chile's lithium sector, with both having significant operations in the Salar de Atacama.*
5. Exceptional Regulation: *Lithium in Chile is subject to a unique legal framework, distinct from other minerals, making its exploitation challenging.*

6. *State's Role: Lithium exploration and exploitation are primarily reserved for the State and its companies due to its non-grantable status.*
7. *Historical Influence: The Cold War era influenced the decision to reserve lithium for the State, given its potential nuclear applications.*
8. *Modern Relevance: Today, lithium's significance is tied to electromobility, especially the rise of electric vehicles.*
9. *Barriers to Entry: The existing legal framework acts as a deterrent for new entrants, limiting the sector to a few players.*
10. *Opportunity for Reform: To capitalize on the increasing global demand for lithium, Chile needs to reconsider its laws surrounding lithium exploration.*

Conclusion: Chile's vast lithium reserves present immense potential. However, to fully harness this potential and maintain its position in the global market, Chile needs to address the challenges posed by its existing legal framework and encourage more players to invest in its lithium sector.

RCA: This concludes our research report on lithium exploration opportunities in Chile. I hope this provides a comprehensive overview of the current landscape and potential areas of focus for future endeavors.

In this lithium exploration study, ChatGPT-4 operates as a three-tiered agent system to scrutinize Chile's lithium sector closely. Initially, the **Research Coordinator Agent** establishes vital research areas such as major reserves and regulatory frameworks to steer the inquiry effectively.

Then, the **Data Collection Agent** accumulates pertinent information from notable sources, including Statista and LegalPlanet, elucidating the industry dynamics and challenges in the regulatory landscape of Chile's lithium sector.

Finally, the **Analysis Agent** compiles the data, offering a concise summary of the opportunities present in Chile's lithium exploration landscape.

Appendix B: Enterprise Transformation Examples with ChatGPT

Introduction

Building on our analysis of the impact of ChatGPT on individual roles in *Chapter 3*, we now extend our perspective to view the broader landscape of the entire enterprise. To do so, we will dive into four case studies, each reflecting the transformative potential of ChatGPT across diverse business scenarios.

Our exploration begins with semi-automated Request for Proposal (RfP) Processing. Here, we envision a future where a consulting firm, overwhelmed by an extensive RfP for an SAP implementation project, leverages ChatGPT to streamline the proposal process, overcoming challenges of time constraints and limited resources.

Following this, we delve into the future of AI-based wealth management, where a traditional wealth management firm reshapes its business model, adopting digital and personalized services powered by ChatGPT. Here, the role of the Digital Relationship Manager is reimagined to cater to a tech-savvy high-income clientele.

We then continue with a future customer service landscape with AI-based Complaint Management. A consumer goods company of the future leverages ChatGPT to transform a labor-intensive and error-prone complaints process into a seamless business operation.

In the final case, AI for Supply-Chain-Scenario Evaluation, we explore a decision scenario for an automotive supplier. This enterprise employs ChatGPT to make strategic decisions around relocating production to be closer to new mobility markets while also reducing energy costs.

As we traverse these case studies, we illustrate the potential future of enterprises through the lens of ChatGPT, revealing its potential to resolve complex enterprise problems, automate E2E processes, and guide strategic decisions.

Structure

In this chapter, the following case studies will be covered:

- Case Study 1: Accelerating RfP Responses
- Case Study 2: Personalizing Wealth Management
- Case Study 3: Streamlining Customer Complaint Handling
- Case Study 4: Decision Making for Strategic Relocation

Case Study 1: Accelerating RfP Responses

ConsultCo, a prestigious consulting firm specializing in SAP implementations, is faced with a formidable challenge. The firm receives a complex RFP from a potential client who expects a comprehensive proposal within a brief time frame. Limited resources to complete the task and the intricate nature of the RfP further complicate the task. To overcome this challenge, ConsultCo looks to RfPGPT, a fine-tuned version of ChatGPT for this domain.

RfP Understanding, Assessment, and Planning

ConsultCo employs RfPGPT to redefine the RfP comprehension process. It starts with **Information Extraction and Analytics**, which systematically analyzes and pinpoints the key aspects of the RfP, like context, scope, timeline, and existing system landscape, laying the groundwork for a subsequent deep-dive assessment. For lengthier RfP chapters containing substantial information, RfPGPT utilizes its **Summarization** capability. This function reviews, interprets, and condenses these extensive chapters into summarized versions, which are then used for information extraction.

With a solid grasp of the RfP's key points, RfPGPT proceeds to the **Assessment** phase. It evaluates the feasibility of the RfP based on the extracted information, suggests questions to be asked, and flags any challenges and risks for immediate attention

Lastly, the **Planning** capability is activated. It uses the extracted, summarized, and assessed information to map out the sequence of tasks necessary for creating a comprehensive proposal. This planned approach ensures a coherent and timely response to the RfP, thereby increasing ConsultCo's chances of securing the project.

Detailed RfP Evaluation, Insight Generation, and Proposal Drafting.

At this stage, RfPGPT initiates a **Semantic Search** across the RfP, using a detailed checklist of required content as a reference. This search is designed to delve into the semantic relationships and contextual relevance of the content within the RfP to the checklist criteria. By doing so, it ensures a thorough and precise identification and understanding of all necessary content components.

Following the semantic search, the RfPGPT's **Question Answering** capability is deployed to address specific queries related to the identified content components. It systematically goes through each question, ensuring a comprehensive and accurate response based on preselected content.

Lastly, RfPGPT's **Creation** capability is activated to draft the proposal in the required format. This phase meticulously integrates the answers to all questions, and the key points from the previous phase into a coherent narrative that thoroughly addresses all crucial aspects of the RfP. The draft proposal is structured and articulated in a manner that aligns with the client's expectations.

Proposal Refinement and Resource Allocation

Upon generating the draft proposal, RfPGPT initiates its **Recommendation** capability, suggesting ways to enrich the proposal content and increase its overall appeal. In parallel, its **Communication** capability is utilized to collect additional specialized proposal content from various team members. Each team member's contribution is then carefully evaluated using the **Assessment** capability. This feature improves the quality and relevance of the contributed content.

In cases where revisions are needed, RfPGPT uses its **Communication** capability again to relay feedback to the respective team members, specifying the required changes. This interactive feedback process ensures all contributions align with the overall proposal objective and meet the desired quality standards.

Once a refined and cohesive proposal is prepared, RfPGPT leverages its **Communication** capability again to get the approval for submission from the proposal manager and then professionally executes this task.

Post-submission, a review is conducted using the **Cause-effect Analysis** capability. This analysis identifies potential areas for improvement, providing valuable insights for enhancing the quality of future RfP responses. This continuous improvement approach further strengthens ConsultCo's position in securing projects and maintains their competitive edge.

Leveraging RfPGPT, ConsultCo is effectively transforming their complex RfP-response process, from comprehensive RfP understanding to insightful analysis, and detailed proposal drafting. Through an intelligent blend of AI capabilities and human expertise, ConsultCo is significantly boosting their proposal quality, efficiency, and competitive edge, highlighting the transformative potential of AI in the realm of consulting services.

Case Study 2: Personalizing Wealth Management

XYZ Financial Services, a leading traditional wealth management firm, is confronted with a unique challenge. Their goal is to digitize and personalize their services to cater to their tech-savvy, high-income clients. In response to this, XYZ introduces a new role of Digital Relationship Managers, backed by WealthGPT, an artificial agent backed by GPT-4.

Client Onboarding and Understanding

The onboarding process at XYZ is now powered by WealthGPT's **Communication** capability. The AI agent, interacting with the new client, understands their financial needs, risk tolerance, investment preferences, and overall financial health.

Following the interaction, WealthGPT uses **Information Extraction and Analytics** to comprehensively analyze client information. It extracts key financial details, understands the new client's investment behavior, and gathers other relevant data.

Next, the AI agent performs an **Assessment** to evaluate the client's portfolio and investment goals. It takes into account various factors such as the client's financial health, risk tolerance, and future aspirations, forming a comprehensive understanding of the client's financial landscape.

Upon concluding the assessment, WealthGPT leverages its **Communication** capability again to securely transmit this extracted and derived data to XYZ Financial Services' backend systems. Following a successful transmission, WealthGPT sends a confirmation to both the Digital Relationship Manager and the client, assuring them that their financial profile has been accurately captured and is now accessible for future consultations and actions.

Strategy Formulation and Risk Analysis

Based on the assessment results, WealthGPT leverages **Semantic Search** to comb through a vast database of investment strategies, asset classes, and financial products. This search, tailored to each client's needs and preferences, ensures a personalized approach to wealth management.

After the search, the AI agent employs **Summarization** to distill complex financial information into understandable insights. It simplifies the numerous strategies and investment options identified in the search, aiding in decision-making.

For risk assessment, WealthGPT performs a High-level **Cause-effect Analysis** to understand potential risks associated with various investment strategies.

Personalized Strategy Presentation and Implementation with Human Review

WealthGPT uses its **Creation** skill to design a personalized financial strategy, including suggested asset allocation, investment avenues, and risk mitigation measures. The plan is a direct output of the comprehensive assessment, search, summarization, and risk analysis. Once the AI agent generates the proposed strategy, it is reviewed by a Digital Relationship Manager. This human in the loop performs a sanity check, validating the AI-generated strategy for practicality and client suitability, ensuring that no strategy is communicated without a human review.

After receiving confirmation from the Digital Relationship Manager, WealthGPT utilizes its **Communication** capability to present the confirmed strategy to the client. It provides a clear explanation of the rationale behind each suggestion, promoting an understanding and informed decision-making by the client. This combined approach of AI generation and human review promotes confidence in the proposed strategies and maintains a high standard of personalized financial planning.

Strategy Monitoring and Adaptation

Once the strategy is implemented, the AI agent continues to monitor market conditions, the client's portfolio, and relevant financial news. It leverages **Data Mining** to analyze large volumes of financial data and spot emerging trends or risks.

In case of significant market changes or deviations from the strategy, the AI system uses **Planning** to create a strategy adjustment plan and uses its **Communication** capability to agree it with the Digital Relationship Manager.

Continuous Client Engagement and Service Enhancement

WealthGPT maintains regular contact with the client through its **Communication** capability. It provides updates on portfolio performance, market trends, and any adjustments made to the strategy.

It also uses **Ranking** to prioritize clients based on their portfolio size, financial needs, or potential risks. This helps XYZ efficiently allocate their resources and ensure high-quality service to all clients.

Lastly, the AI agent uses **Matchmaking** to connect clients with suitable resources or personnel within XYZ, enhancing client satisfaction through targeted and efficient service.

Through the integration of WealthGPT, XYZ Financial Services is innovatively digitizing their wealth management services, enhancing personalization and client engagement. By marrying AI capabilities with human insights, they are ensuring effective and practical financial strategies for their tech-savvy, high-income clientele. This case exemplifies the transformative potential of AI in the realm of traditional business operations.

Case Study 3: Streamlining Customer Complaint Handling

Acme Consumer Goods, a leading multinational company, grapples with a daunting challenge in its customer complaints process. The existing process is labor-intensive, error-prone, and time-consuming. Acme's aim is to transform its complaints process into a highly automated process for standard complaints and a guided process for special complaints. To achieve this, Acme turns to ComplaintGPT, a special AI solution empowered by GPT-4.

Complaint Collection, Sentiment Analysis, and Categorization

ComplaintGPT's **Communication** capability receives and understands the content and context of customer complaints. This process ensures an accurate capture of customers' concerns, saving time and reducing chances of misinterpretation.

Following receipt, the AI application applies **Information Extraction and Analytics** to systematically analyze each complaint. It identifies key issues, determines their severity, and extracts other relevant details, significantly reducing the chance of oversight and paving the way for effective assessment.

Next, the AI system conducts Sentiment Analysis as an application of its **Classification** capability. It gauges the sentiment of the complaints, identifying whether they are neutral, negative, or potentially even positive. This analysis provides valuable insights into the emotional tone behind the complaints, aiding in a more comprehensive understanding of customers' sentiments and their level of dissatisfaction.

Subsequently, the AI system performs an **Assessment**. Using the extracted, analyzed, and sentiment-gauged information, it carries out an in-depth evaluation of each complaint. It considers various factors such as context, potential impact, and other related aspects.

Finally, ComplaintGPT uses its **Classification** capability again to categorize each complaint into 'standard' or 'special' categories based on the results from the previous steps. This categorization plays a crucial role in determining the subsequent course of action, ensuring each complaint is addressed appropriately, given its nature, severity, and emotional tone.

Standard Complaint Resolution

For standard complaints, ComplaintGPT utilizes **Semantic Search** and **Question Answering**. It combs through a database of predefined solutions matched with standard complaints, providing rapid, precise, and efficient resolutions.

Special Complaint Analysis and Resolution

In dealing with special complaints in the consumer goods sector, the AI system initiates a detailed **Cause-effect Analysis**. This analysis begins by dissecting the complaint to understand the product issue being reported. For instance, if a customer reports a malfunctioning home appliance, the AI system will scrutinize the details provided by the customer, such as the nature of the malfunction, the model of the appliance, and how it has been used or maintained.

The AI then cross-references these complaint details with the product specifications, user manuals, and common issues associated with that product model. This is done to determine whether the complaint could be due to product misuse, a known product defect, or an unforeseen issue. The system also considers external factors like shipping or handling issues that could have contributed to the problem.

Following the analysis, if a clear resolution strategy does not emerge, the AI system employs its **Communication** capability to involve a human expert. The expert, while demonstrating the resolution process, provides a detailed walkthrough of the issue. This could involve additional testing, checking manufacturing batch details, or even contacting the product supplier for more information.

Once the human expert resolves the issue, ComplaintGPT uses its **Transformation** capability to abstract the steps taken. This allows the AI-system to transform the specific actions taken into a general set of steps, thus expanding Acme's knowledge database to include this newly formed solution. This approach enriches Acme's ability to handle future similar complaints, improving efficiency and customer satisfaction.

Final Communication and Continuous Improvement

At the end of each resolution process, ComplaintGPT communicates the outcome to the customer using its **Communication** skill. For internal purposes, it uses **Matchmaking** to align complaints with the most appropriate resources or personnel within the company, improving the efficiency of response.

The AI system also uses **Ranking** to prioritize complaints based on their severity, frequency, or potential impact on customer satisfaction. This is instrumental in helping Acme manage its workload and allocate resources effectively.

Through the adoption of ComplaintGPT, Acme Consumer Goods is innovatively automating their customer complaints process, improving efficiency and customer satisfaction. By blending AI capabilities with human expertise, they ensure quick and effective resolution of complaints for their diverse customer base.

Case Study 4:

Decision Making for Strategic Relocation

AutoSuppliers Inc., a top-tier provider to the automotive industry, finds itself at a crossroads. Rising energy costs and changing market dynamics have prompted the company to reconsider its production locations. To tackle this complex challenge, AutoSuppliers Inc. turns to DecisionGPT, a GPT application with access to a large database of routine enterprise decisions.

Data Gathering and Preliminary Analysis

AutoSuppliers Inc. starts by leveraging DecisionGPT to revamp its data gathering and analysis process. With its **Data Mining** capability, the company efficiently extracts insightful patterns from their vast historical data of energy usage, production processes, and supplier databases.

DecisionGPT then employs **Information Extraction and Analytics** to parse and analyze unstructured data, such as reports, emails, and contracts, giving AutoSuppliers Inc. a comprehensive view of their energy utilization and supply chain.

Finally, the AI-model's **Semantic Search** is used to discover additional contextual information about energy costs, potential production locales, and emerging trends in mobility markets.

Insight Generation and Impact Assessment

To further unravel this complex problem, the DecisionGPT performs an **Assessment** and conducts a detailed evaluation of the company's current energy consumption and production efficiency, based on the information gathered and analyzed in the first step.

Next, the AI application uses the **Prediction** ability to estimate future trends in energy costs, renewable energy availability, and the growth trajectory of new mobility markets.

Finally, with the **Cause-Effect Analysis** ability, DecisionGPT examines the potential impact of relocating production sites on energy costs and proximity to new mobility markets.

Planning and Decision-making

Building on these detailed insights, AutoSuppliers Inc. uses the DecisionGPT's **Planning** skill to devise a forward-looking operational strategy. This involves identifying potential new production locations, evaluating their suitability, and planning logistical changes.

The **Simulation** ability is then employed to create a digital replica of various scenarios, allowing the company to forecast potential outcomes of relocation. If needed, the AI system's **Sequential Decision-making** capability is used sparingly to guide the decision-making process, considering the cumulative impact of relocation decision steps over time.

Recommendation and Implementation

In the final stage, AutoSuppliers Inc. relies on the DecisionGPT's **Recommendation** capability. The AI system uses the accumulated data and insights to suggest the most suitable production locations. It then prioritizes these locations using **Ranking**, considering variables like cost-effectiveness, proximity to new markets, and more.

The AI-system's **Matchmaking** capability is leveraged to align the needs of the company with the most suitable locations identified, streamlining the decision-making process. The **Transformation** ability is then used to present the findings, predictions, and recommendations in an easily digestible format for stakeholders.

Throughout this process, the DecisionGPT's **Communication** capability facilitates interaction with users, ensuring that they are kept informed and can effectively contribute to decision-making.

With DecisionGPT, AutoSuppliers Inc. is redefining its strategic approach to cost and location management. The company anticipates significant energy cost savings, improved proximity to emerging markets, and a strengthened competitive position.

The four case studies demonstrate the transformative potential of ChatGPT when integrated into diverse business scenarios. In ConsultCo's case, a blend of AI and human expertise in RfP processing notably enhances proposal quality and efficiency, showcasing AI's transformative power in consulting. Similarly, XYZ Financial Services leverages WealthGPT to digitize and personalize its services, exemplifying ChatGPT's ability to modernize traditional business operations. Moreover, the adoption of ComplaintGPT and DecisionGPT by Acme Consumer Goods and AutoSuppliers Inc., respectively, highlights how ChatGPT can streamline customer service processes and inform strategic decision-making in supply chain management, underpinning the broad spectrum of enterprise challenges that it can address.

Concluding Recommendations

The transformative potential of ChatGPT and its ecosystem (ever improving GPT models, multi-modality, plugins, tools, enterprise software, specialized apps), as illustrated in the chapters of this book, requires a strategic approach. For business leaders eager to tap into this potential for the benefits of their enterprises here are 21 specific recommendations:

- **Adopt an AI-First Approach**: Consider integrating AI into the business strategy, leveraging frameworks such as CapabilityGPT to accelerate the transformation journey towards becoming AI-first organizations.
- **Foster Human-AI Collaboration**: Create environments where professionals and AI agents work together seamlessly, leveraging the strengths of both to drive innovation, efficiency, and proactive decision-making.
- **Train Workforce in AI**: Invest in comprehensive and recurring training programs, equipping the entire workforce with the knowledge and skills needed for prompt engineering and AI collaboration.
- **Enhance Customer Experience with AI**: Deploy AI tools such as ChatGPT in customer-facing roles to provide personalized communication strategies, improving customer satisfaction and loyalty.
- **Invest in Prompt Engineering**: Dedicate resources to mastering prompt patterns and engineering techniques to maximize the consistency, performance, and quality of GPT outputs.
- **Establish Intelligent Prompt-based Assistants**: Harness the power of GPT models to streamline operations and decision making by integrating Intelligent Functional and Collaboration Assistants across different departments.

- **Create Role-Specific Prompting Environments:** Develop and deploy persona-specific prompting environments, integrating prompt templates and plugins tailored for various enterprise roles.
- **Prioritize Security:** Ensure meticulous security policies and protocols, especially when integrating GPT models into existing business operations.
- **Maintain Ethical Standards**: Ensure that ethical guidelines and standards for transparency, fairness and data privacy are established and adhered to, preserving the trust and integrity of the organization.
- **Embrace Versatile Architectures**: Prioritize the implementation of various GPT-driven architecture patterns that cater to diverse business needs, ensuring agility, performance, and effective integration.
- **Permit Scalability of AI Solutions:** As AI integration deepens, ensure that infrastructural considerations are made for scalability, allowing for seamless growth and evolution of AI-powered solutions.
- **Use Low-Code Development Tools**: Utilize tools like LangChain and Predictive Powers to accelerate the development of prompt-based applications that leverage the capabilities of Large Language Models.
- **Build Knowledge Repositories**: Establish enterprise-wide knowledge bases that can be easily accessed and updated by GPT models, ensuring accurate, consistent, and comprehensive AI outputs.
- **Explore AI's Multi-Modal Capabilities**: Harness the multi-modal features of ChatGPT-4 and its plugins, integrating voice and image capabilities, to provide a richer, more interactive experience for users.
- **Leverage Multi-Agent Collaboration**: Activate an entire team of GPT-enabled bots, who cooperate with each other and human employees to solve complex business problems jointly.
- **Design Robust Solutions:** Prioritize solution design and prompt engineering in the GPT-project management process to ensure the success of GPT models in various use cases.
- **Adopt Agile Workflows**: Embrace an agile and adaptive approach in GPT-project management, focusing on iterative development, continuous validation, and refinement.
- **Integrate Feedback Loops:** Implement robust feedback loops to capture user insights, helping in the refinement of AI-driven solutions and ensuring alignment with user needs.
- **Drive Change Management:** Recognize the task distinctions, from fully automated to human-intensive, and implement tailored change management strategies for effective GPT deployment.

- **Engage in Regular AI Audits:** Frequently review and evaluate AI applications' performances, ensuring they remain compliant with evolving standards and regulations.
- **Stay Updated with AI Advancements**: With the rapid pace of AI developments, ensure continuous learning and adaptation to stay ahead and leverage the latest features and functionalities.

Together with my co-authors, I've ventured deep into the world of *Transforming the Enterprise with ChatGPT*, and I must say, it has been a rewarding journey. Sharing our insights, experiences, and strategies with you has been an honor. We truly believe in the transformative potential of AI for businesses, and we eagerly await the innovations you will drive with this knowledge. Your feedback is invaluable, helping us and the broader community refine our approach and understanding. Thank you for joining us on this journey.

References

[1] Rohit Shewale, 32 Detailed ChatGPT Statistics – Users, Revenue and Trends, https://www.demandsage.com/, 2023.

[2] Tyna Eloundou, Sam Manning, Pamela Mishkin, Daniel Rock. GPTs are GPTs: An early look at the labor market impact potential of large language models. https://openai.com/research, 2023.

[3] Tatsuro Inaba, Hirokazu Kiyomaru, Fei Cheng, Sadao Kurohashi. MultiTool-CoT: GPT-3 Can Use Multiple External Tools with Chain of Thought Prompting. arXiv preprint arXiv: 2305.16896. 2023.

[4] Zezhong Wang, Fangkai Yang, Pu Zhao, Lu Wang, Jue Zhang, Mohit Garg, Qingwei Lin, Dongmei Zhang. Empower Large Language Model to Perform Better on Industrial Domain-Specific Question Answering. arXiv preprint arXiv: 2305.11541. 2023.

[5] Guangyao Chen, Siwei Dong, Yu Shu, Ge Zhang, Jaward Sesay, Börje F. Karlsson, Jie Fu, Yemin Shi. AutoAgents: A Framework for Automatic Agent Generation. arXiv preprint arXiv: 2309.17288. 2023.

[6] Julia Ritzenthaler, Just How Long Can You Use Your Makeup and Skincare Products?, beautyjunkees.com, 2020.

[7] Daqing Chen, Online Retail II, https://archive.ics.uci.edu/datasets, 2019.

[8]JCPenny,https://www.annualreports.com/HostedData/AnnualReportArchive, 2020

[9] David Gentile, Introduction to LangChain: A Framework for LLM Powered Applications, https://www.davidgentile.net/, 2023.

[10] Massimiliano Zattera, `predictive-powers`, https://github.com/mzattera/predictive-powers, 2023.

[11] Yang Liu, Yuanshun Yao, Jean-Francois Ton, Xiaoying Zhang, Ruocheng Guo, Hao Cheng, Yegor Klochkov, Muhammad Faaiz Taufiq, Hang Li. Trustworthy LLMs: a Survey and Guideline for Evaluating Large Language Models' Alignment. arXiv preprint arXiv: 2308.05374, 2023.

[12] Harrison Chase, langchain-ai/langchain, https://github.com/LangChain-ai/LangChain, 2023.

[13] Shunyu Yao, Jeffrey Zhao, Dian Yu, Nan Du, Izhak Shafran, Karthik Narasimhan, Yuan Cao. ReAct: Synergizing Reasoning and Acting in Language Models. 2023.

[14] Eric Urban et al, Azure OpenAI, Data flows for inference 'on your data', https://learn.microsoft.com/en-us/legal/cognitive-services/openai/data-privacy, 2023.

Made in the USA
Coppell, TX
10 November 2026

11840738R00334